Late Egyptian Grammar

An Introduction

GRIFFITH INSTITUTE PUBLICATIONS

General editor   John Baines

Friedrich Junge

Late Egyptian Grammar

An Introduction

SECOND ENGLISH EDITION

translated from the German by
David Warburton

2005
Griffith Institute, Oxford

ISBN 0 900416 85 8

British Library Cataloguing-in-Publication
A catalogue record for this book is available from the British Library

Printed and bound in Great Britain from originals supplied by the author
at The Alden Press, Oxford

Contents

Preface

Author's preface

This introduction to Late Egyptian grammar is primarily intended to provide an instruction manual for Late Egyptian like those used for introductory courses in Middle Egyptian. There are not many introductions to the language of the New Kingdom (see, however, Neveu, *La langue des Ramsès*), perhaps because Late Egyptian is not taught everywhere, but perhaps also because Late Egyptian is generally assumed to be simpler and better understood than Middle Egyptian. While the latter is not fundamentally disputed, this introduction can serve a useful role easing access to the existing Late Egyptian grammars, and as a guide to the relevant secondary literature. I can unhesitatingly recommend that the interested student turn to the outstanding contributions which have made the understanding of Late Egyptian possible: the present work would be inconceivable without Paul Frandsen's *Outline of the Late Egyptian Verbal System* and Sarah Groll's adaptation of Černý's textual material in Černý/Groll, *A Late Egyptian Grammar*.

This introduction is based on traditional instruction in Late Egyptian insofar as it is assumed that the student already has a grasp of Middle Egyptian. In principle, it should be possible to introduce the student to the Egyptian language directly with Late Egyptian. The peculiarities of Late Egyptian orthography argue against this approach, however, and scholarly tradition has followed another route. Late Egyptian is thus introduced here through the structure of Middle Egyptian, but this introduction also aspires to accompany the student later, serving as a reference work as well, with indexes indicating problems which are frequently encountered, and suggesting solutions. In attempting to produce both a manual and a reference work, it was impossible to avoid compromises.

In the course of the presentation the density increases; this leads to redundancies, repetition, and apparently similar descriptions in different contexts. Unless related to grammatical difficulties, only those words which appear in the examples and exercises are listed in the glossary (§ 9). References to texts and publications are listed in the bibliography (§ 8), but the citation forms are not consistent, as I have attempted a compromise between easy access to recent publications and compatibility with earlier grammars and publications, including the Erman/Grapow *Wörterbuch* (so, here we list *pLansing* instead of *LEM*, but *LRL* instead of *pBibl. Nat. 197*, etc.).

As with the German edition, this version of the text remains tied to the earliest. The new printer driver software was not able to handle my soft fonts (transliteration, Coptic, hieroglyphs). Some of the hieroglyphs are from my own fonts, but most are from the earliest version of GLYPH (for DOS), and those GLYPH hieroglyphs had to be imported into word processing and layout software in mirrored form. Thus in some citations, the signs do not always correspond to the original. In other cases, the positions of signs in relation to one another and the base line vary from the source, as do the sizes of the signs and the space between them; the hieratic dot cannot be correctly drawn, and the group ⸗ does not allow another sign to be placed above it (as is usual in cases like ꜥḏd or r ḏd).

The English edition would never have been appeared without David Warburton: In going to the immense trouble of translating and transforming a grammar that was strongly rooted in German grammatical thinking and writing, he carried the lion's share of the burden. I wish to express to him my heartfelt gratitude. The help of many other colleagues and students was also of vital importance for its completion. To Christian Leitz I owe a considerable number of corrections. Thanks to the hard work of Heike Sternberg-el Hotabi, Roxane Kieselbach, Christian Opitz, and Daniel Werning the indexes were ready in time. In the final stage of the process Robert Simpson went over the English text with a grammarian's eye, made many extremely valuable suggestions and put admirable energy into making the text as flawless as was in his power. Of course I take full responsibility for all remaining mistakes. Finally I would like to thank John Baines for accepting this book among the publications of the Griffith Institute and for accompanying its production process.

In this second, and revised, edition, I owe not a small number of corrections and revisions to David Warburton and, not at least, to Deborah Sweeney and her careful review in *Lingua Aegyptia* 12. I am most grateful to both of them. Less easy was to include the remarks of François Neveu (review in *BIFAO* 59, 2002, 260ff) since we differ grossly in attitude towards theoretical and practical issues of grammar and text understanding. And I should have wished him to read in a closer and less biased way. Nonetheless I tried to include what seemed appropriate to me.

Finally, I thank Robert Simpson who went over the text again, and John Baines who offered the opportunity for a second edition and again took care of its production.

Translator's preface

My interest in translating this grammar was to present a workable grammar of Late Egyptian for those who want to use the texts. I was quite conscious that many students of Egyptian civilization are interested in reading Late Egyptian texts but lack a simple introductory grammar, since many of those available are intended for grammarians or students of linguistics. This book fills that gap and the translation will help those who do not feel fully at home in German, while those interested in linguistics will not be disappointed either (although the German edition will have satisfied many of them).

As a person of habit, and one who regards grammar as a tool to be used in order to understand texts in order to "get to the point", my initial desire was to force Junge's Grammar into the straightjacket of Sir Alan Gardiner's terminology. In fact, however, this is impossible because Junge has a different overall interpretation of the grammar, and thus the English text is virtually identical in terminology to the German text.

Gardiner's *Grammar* was designed as an introduction, and its extraordinary documentation compensates for the seeming lack of a rigorous grammatical system. Junge's book is dominated by a grammatical system, with the exercises and examples designed to enable the student to master the language, but also conveying a particular understanding of that language at the same time. This system stands in stark contrast to what Sir Alan himself admitted to be the seeming "formlessness" of his book. In fact, of course, Gardiner's book is a masterpiece of didactic organization, and an understanding of that work is a precondition for the use of Junge's. Since, however, both Sir Alan and Junge are grammarians at heart, each has his own interpretation of those fundamental features which dominated ancient Egyptian grammar.

Needless to say, this book speaks for itself, but for those who do not keep abreast of linguistic debates, one can point to some of the differences between this text and Gardiner's *Grammar*, so as to avoid confusion at the outset. One of the problems is that even fundamental terms such as "subject" and "predicate" do not carry specific meanings in Egyptology. In modern linguistics, the terms refer to formal grammatical — and not semantic — categories. Sir Alan's *Grammar* and H. J. Polotsky's early work distinguished grammatical, logical and even semantic subjects and predicates. Polotsky later adopted an approach in which subject and predicate were understood primarily as "logical" categories with semantic/pragmatic significance. This appreciation of the subject and predicate as logical rather than strictly grammatical categories is central to understanding the dominant role played by the role of the adverbial sentence in Junge's work.

Whether logical, semantic or grammatical, predicates are traditionally distinguished as being either verbal or non-verbal. Grammatical verbal predicates are easily understood and classified. Non-verbal predicates can be adverbial, adjectival or nominal, and this implies the existence of corresponding categories of sentences. In contrast to the earlier custom, Sir Alan declined to use the term "nominal sentence" for all the "non-verbal" sentence patterns, and classified sentences according to his understanding of their predication as "nominal or pronominal", "adjectival" and "adverbial". While Anglophone grammarians followed Gardiner's lead, in German usage the term "nominal sentence" was retained, although it was specified that these sentences did not necessarily involve nominal (in the sense of substantival) predication. Middle Egyptian is dominated by verbal sentences of different kinds with identical morphology, which are supplemented with adverbial clauses, but these stand alongside sentences belonging to the other categories. Late Egyptian is, however, dominated by adverbial sentences which were traditionally termed pseudo-verbal constructions, and witnessed an increase in other classes of non-verbal expression. Junge has demonstrated that adverbial sentences are a key to Egyptian linguistic evolution, for they form the bridge between Old Egyptian and Coptic. Since these concepts form an integral part of the argument from the linguistic standpoint, this book retains Junge's approach and usage, including the term "nominal sentence", although this does not accord with normal usage in English.

This means that, as presented, Junge's book can be used both as an introduction to the grammar of Late Egyptian, and as a guide to the linguistic evolution of ancient Egyptian. It should not be too difficult to grasp the grammatical intricacies because the presentation is rigorously systematic, and he has provided numerous references to existing grammatical works.

I have always felt that a Late Egyptian grammar and a new hieratic palaeography for Dynasties XIX and XX were absolutely essential tools, and thus when Junge first mentioned that he was writing a Late Egyptian grammar I volunteered unhesitatingly and unthinkingly to translate it. It must be admitted that I already regretted this seconds later, realizing (a) that Junge was far more capable than I of producing an English version, and (b) that in order to translate the work, I would in fact have to understand it myself. My previous efforts at grasping his grammatical treatises had not convinced me that I had really understood them. It was thus with no little trepidation that I began, but the German book was written in a clear style, and Junge reviewed my entire translation.

0. Introduction

0.1 "Late Egyptian"

The modern designations for the various stages of the ancient Egyptian language language
correspond only superficially to the periods of ancient Egyptian history to which they stages and
their
seem to be related. Thus "Old Egyptian" still means the language of the Pyramid Texts terminology
and tomb inscriptions of the Old Kingdom, but "Middle Egyptian" comprises not only
the "Classical" language of all genres of text associated with the Middle Kingdom but
also those of the early part of the New Kingdom (Dynasty XVIII); sometimes it is even
used to characterize the language of religious texts from the New Kingdom to Roman
times. "Late Egyptian" is, however, the term used in English for the language of the
Late New Kingdom, rather than that of the Late Period, while the French *néo-égyptien*
and the German *Neuägyptisch* seem to follow the chronological framework more closely
in refering to the language of the New Kingdom. After Adolf Erman's *Neuägyptische
Grammatik*, "*Neuägyptisch*"/"Late Egyptian" was at first used as a quite general term
for the language of all genres of text from the Ramesside period and Dynasty XXI — the
second half of the New Kingdom. The political and religious convolutions of the short
Amarna period were said to have brought a linguistic form to the fore which had hitherto
been spoken but not yet written; earlier recorded use of this colloquial form was
considered to surface in texts otherwise written in Classical Egyptian, and these are
occasionally termed *Frühneuägyptisch* ("Proto-Late Egyptian") in German.

To characterize this colloquial form more closely, Jaroslav Černý and those scholars "real Late
following his path sought to exclude hieroglyphic texts and literary sources (like the texts Egyptian"
published as *Late Egyptian Stories* — *LES*) from the description of Late Egyptian, striving
to reserve the term exclusively for the language used in documents like those published
as *Late Ramesside Letters* (*LRL*) or as *Ramesside Administrative Documents* (*RAD*). In
accordance with this exemplary approach to the language — in comparison with those
used for other stages of the language — recent Late Egyptian grammars thus deal with
the non-literary texts, the letters, documents, records, etc. written on ostraca and papyri
from late Dynasty XIX to early Dynasty XXI. This Late Egyptian is thus mainly
characterized by the appearance of those linguistic forms which come to dominate the

later stages of the language, while the traces and remnants of the earlier stages are phased out.

This type of Late Egyptian serves as the foundation of the present grammar. Although such restrictions were of great importance in the history of research, they have undesirably narrowed the field of study and increased its distance from the realities of speech and language. Thus an attempt is made here to draw again upon the grammar of those genres of New Kingdom texts that were excluded in the purist approach.

0.2 Texts and character of Late Egyptian

0.2.0 Preliminary remarks

categories of texts; linguistic norms and registers

Were one to apply general conditions to the use of language and linguistic norms in their written form, it could be posited that the use of language depends not only on period, but also on social and textual criteria, i.e., that language use depends upon context. In the three hundred and fifty years between late Dynasty XVIII and early Dynasty XXI, Late Egyptian was bound to change, and it did. The extent to which the changes are preserved in texts depends upon their social functions. Letters and memoranda are subject to different linguistic norms than state documents. It is thus even more important with Late Egyptian than with Middle Egyptian to grasp the linguistic register of any given text. The texts themselves can be ranked in a hierarchy of linguistic norms.

the effects of writing

The very manner in which a text is written conveys a strong message: the types of text recorded in hieroglyphs (stelae and temple inscriptions) are more resistant to linguistic innovation than cursive hieratic texts (papyri and ostraca). Playing with linguistic norms and with the frequency and method of use of more ancient or more colloquial forms is another means of expression used by ancient Egyptian authors; recognizing this sometimes enables one to grasp nuances of form and content. It is thus useful quickly to review the general genres of the Late Egyptian texts with which this grammar is concerned.

Decorum describes the interaction of pictorial and written decoration emphasizing the integration of the socio-cultural norms which it is intended to convey. It is common in private and royal stelae and tomb inscriptions. The concept was introduced by John Baines. Cf. *Fecundity Figures* (Warminster 1985) pp. 277ff.; also idem, in: *Man* N-S 18 (1983): 572ff.; Baines/Eyre, in *GM* 61 (1983): 65ff.

0.2.1 Survey of the textual genres

The texts surveyed here are classified according to their chronological position and speech situation; "speech situation" refers to the circumstances in which the text was used or developed. The texts are therefore generally characterized as representing "daily life", "literature" (*belles lettres*), social or ideological "declarations" (termed "decorum" texts: private or royal stelae, tomb inscriptions, so-called "historical" texts) or "theological" texts. For the publication data of these and other texts, the bibliographic abbreviations at the end of this volume should be consulted (§ 8.1, where the texts cited in abbreviated form will also be found; abbrevations: p = papyrus; o = ostracon; vs. = verso; rt. = recto).

(1) Late Dyn. XVIII

daily life: ostraca (oAmarna)

decorum: Tomb inscriptions (cf. in general Sandman, *Akhenaten*); boundary stelae (cf. § 8.1. The main text of later boundary stelae uses a highly developed form of Middle Egyptian — called Late Middle Egyptian here — while the king's speech employs a language which is clearly coloured by Late Egyptian) [text categories of late Dyn. XVIII]

belles lettres: Astarte (reign of Horemhab)

theological: Great Hymn (cf. § 8.1; highly developed, very subtle Middle Egyptian/Late Middle Egyptian)

(2) Dyn. XIX

daily life: correspondence: pCairo 58053-58060; pLeiden I 360-368; written on ostraca (selection), reign of Ramesses II: oDM 116; 118; 303; 314; 317; 321; 324; 328; 560; 581 (cf. also *KRI* III 534-540; 544); reign of Merenptah: oCairo 25581; 25504; oMichaelides 13 (cf. also *KRI* IV 151-153; 155-158) [correspondence]

administrative documents (reign of Seti II): oCairo 25556; oNash 1 and 2 (*HO* I pl.46,2; 47,1) (cf. also *KRI* IV 302-303; 315-320) [administrative documents]

didactic (school texts): pAnast. II-VI; pKoller; pSallier I and IV vs.; pTurin A and B; pBologna 1094 [didactic texts]

belles lettres: pAnast. I; Doomed Prince (reign of Seti I/ beginning of Ramesses II); Taking of Joppa (same date as Doomed Prince); Harris Love Songs (pHarris 500 rt.; same date as Doomed Prince); pD'Orb (Two Brothers; reign of Seti II)

decorum: (texts in hieroglyphic versions) Qadesh Poem/Qadesh Bulletin (Ramesses II; mainly Late Egyptian syntactical structures, but still with some "Middle Egyptianisms" in morphology and orthography); Hittite Treaty (Year 21 of Ramesses II); Libyan War (Merenptah); Israel Stele (Merenptah)

theological: pLeiden I 350 rt. (Great Hymn to Amun from Year 52 of Ramses II; an example for spread of Late Egyptian orthography within vestigial

Middle Egyptian — specifically: Late Middle Egyptian — linguistic structure)

(3) Dyn. XX

correspondence

daily life: correspondence: pTurin 1896; *LRL* (reign of Ramesses XI); written on ostraca (selection), reign of Ramesses III: oDM 121 (cf. also *KRI* V 565); oBerlin P 10628; 10630 (cf. also *KRI* V 564f); reign of Ramesses IV: oBerlin P 10627; oDM 429 (cf. also *KRI* VI 155f); reign of Ramesses VIII: oDM 115 (cf. also *KRI* VI 448)

administrative documents

administrative documents: pSalt 124 (early Dyn. XX/reign of Ramesses III); Strike Papyrus (Year 29 of Ramesses III); Harim Conspiracy (reign of Ramesses IV); Elephantine scandal (reign of Ramesses V); pNaunakhte (cf. also *KRI* VI 236-243; Year 3/4 of Ramesses V); Tomb Robbery Trials (pAbbott/pLeAm/pBM 10052-10054; cf. also *KRI* VI 468-516; 764- 837; reign of Ramesses IX)

didactic texts

didactic: pLansing — oracles: pBM 10335 (reign of Ramesses IV); on ostraca: oDM 133 (reign of Ramesses VII, cf. also *KRI* VI 425f)

belles lettres: HorSeth (reign of Ramesses V); Beatty Love Songs (pChester Beatty I vs.; reign of Ramesses V); Wenamun (reign of Ramesses XI or better: Dyn. XXI)

decorum: (texts in hieroglyphic versions) War with Sea Peoples (Year 8 of Ramesses III); 2nd Libyan War (Year 11 of Ramesses III)

(4) Dyn. XXI

daily life: correspondence: el Hiba letters

belles lettres: Moscow literary letter; (Wenamun)

decorum : (texts in hieroglyphic versions) Banishment Stela

theological: pNeskhons (reign of Pinodjem)

0.2.2 Linguistic hierarchies and linguistic evolution

Late Egyptian seems to appear quite unexpectedly for the first time in the speeches of the King in the Amarna boundary stelae, in the midst of a text composed in formal Middle Egyptian (cf. Exercise § 2.1.7[1]), apparently illustrating the assumptions of Sethe and Stricker on the history of the language (cf. § 0.2.3): while the written language remained unchanged, spoken forms did change, and it was the King who finally pushed these changes through, in the spirit of the revolutionary realism of the Amarna period. This must however be judged in light of the following considerations:

(1) Colloquial language differs from the language of writing not only in grammar, but also in the content of the messages conveyed: when writing one obeys different linguistic norms. In learning to write, the users of a given language have also learnt involuntarily to observe the unwritten rules governing expression in any given kind of text — they move to another register. The Egyptians of course will have behaved in the same fashion, even if it is true that only a small proportion of the population was actually literate.

colloquial language — written language

Linguistic systems, norms, registers and the ranked hierarchy of norms: Even if a competent speaker is not conscious of the fact, every use of language is rule-governed. The complete set of rules is the system of a language which determines "what can be said". The choice made by the speaker depends upon the context: who is addressed on which occasion and under which circumstances; whether in speech or in writing; whether in a letter or in a story. The decisions will be guided by those linguistic norms relating to the specific circumstances. "Norm is a system of obligatory forms which are socio-culturally determined. It does not correspond to what 'can be said' but to what 'has already been said', and what 'you' normally say in the community" (E. Coseriu, *Synchronie, Diachronie und Geschichte*, Munich, 1974, p. 47). The conventional norm for a given situation can also be called a "Register" — which can be understood metaphorically in the sense of registers which can be linguistically "pulled" (introduced into Egyptology by Orly Goldwasser, in *Fs-Lichtheim*, pp. 200-240; cf. also the literature cited there).
The more oral and written speech acts are made in a specific speech situation, the more style and refined forms of expression increase and the more older and customary forms are accumulated. Thus the speech acts belonging to a socially and culturally important speech situation reflect more developed and elaborate norms or registers than others do. Classifying these speech acts according to the degree of elaboration leads to the establishment of a hierarchy of norms.

(2) The use of language in any kind of text is determined by tradition, and the effect of this increases with the cultural significance of the text. Every language and every linguistic norm or register is, however, also subject to change through that very use which the community makes of language, and thus the norms or registers change for written languages also. The speed with which changes appear in particular types of text depends upon their relative positions in the norm hierarchy: the more developed the norm, the slower it changes.

traditional use of language

(3) Language and writing conventions are two different systems. Writing does not develop at the same pace as the language: changes in the structure and pronunciation of words and forms are not necessarily mirrored in written usage. Conversely, changes in written forms need not reflect changes in other linguistic forms.

language and script

(4) The members of a community using a given language do not usually recognize changes in their language as linguistic innovations, and innovations emerge so slowly that even outside observers — meaning us — can only recognize them when comparing forms in texts that are

language change

separated from each other by long periods of time.

Middle
Egyptian —
Late Egyptian

(5) The differences between Classical Middle Egyptian and Late Egyptian are not so fundamental as is widely assumed: all Late Egyptian forms and expressions were in principle present in Middle Egyptian. The main difference from Middle Egyptian is that Late Egyptian is dominated by forms which were rarely used earlier but were already in existence, and that certain usages characteristic of Middle Egyptian were finally abandoned. In short, the linguistic change can be characterized as a change in the frequency with which forms were used, accompanied by shifts — sometimes major — in their roles within the network of linguistic relations.

writing
conventions
and their
dissolution

Developments in Late Egyptian can be summarized thus: although the abandonment of earlier writing conventions is a specific characteristic of New Kingdom texts, earlier forms do in fact persist in the texts for a long time. The relationship of the conventional writing symbols ("graphemes") to the phonetic segments that differentiate lexically distinct linguistic items ("phonemes") is not so clearly defined as in Middle Egyptian, making it possible that linguistic changes remain unrecognized. Adjustments in written forms then give evolutionary changes the appearance of abruptness.

"Late
Egyptianisms"

Developments in the forms and morphology of Late Egyptian — linguistic predecessors of the royal speeches in the Amarna boundary stelae — can be observed as early as Dyn. XVII or early Dyn. XVIII or even in the late Middle Kingdom, in those texts lacking stylistic pretensions or representing textual genres less burdened with tradition, e.g., letters and administrative records. Late Egyptianisms in such texts or in literary and theological texts of later date do not betray authors who are unconsciously "slipping" into colloquial usages, but are symptoms of linguistic evolution.

hierarchy of
norms and
registers

Temporal linguistic demarcation is thus less real in the period of the New Kingdom than has been generally assumed. Slightly oversimplifying, one can "diagnostically" classify New Kingdom texts according to the proportion of Middle Egyptian linguistic expressions (veiled by their written form). The texts which are culturally most significant — by definition the most conservative — show the highest proportion of Middle Egyptianisms; from the everyday texts through literary to ideological and theological works, the proportion of Middle Egyptian elements increases constantly — or rather these have been maintained longest in the linguistically more protected higher registers of the hierarchy of textual expression. The "Middle Egyptian" of Ramessid theological texts disguised by Late Egyptian writing habits is thus only a manifestation of a perfectly normal use of language. It is only at the end of Dyn. XX that we perceive the re-appearance of a "purer" form of Middle Egyptian displaying all the signs of a language specifically taught in schools, a form which was destined to survive for the rest of ancient Egyptian history as a scholastic language similar to Latin in Europe.

The following concepts are used to distinguish the various linguistic norms and registers in use during the New Kingdom; examples will appear in the exercises.

Designation	Characteristics	Examples
Late Middle Egyptian	Middle Egyptian sentence structure and Middle Egyptian orthography; sparing use of Late Egyptian forms, words and writings	Great Hymn, Amarna; pLeiden I 350 rt.
"Medio"-Late Egyptian	generally Late Egyptian sentence structure with numerous Middle Egyptian syntactical elements and forms; still generally Middle Egyptian orthography	boundary stelae, Amarna; Doomed Prince; Qadesh-Poem/Qadesh-Bulletin; War with Sea Peoples
Late Egyptian	purely Late Egyptian sentence structure with Late Egyptian forms and writings; occasional Middle Egyptianisms in forms and orthography which progressively disappear	oDM; *LEM*; *RAD*; Two Brothers; HorSeth; Wenamun
"Neo"-Middle Egyptian	Egyptian Second Language; based on Middle Egyptian structure and orthography; own linguistic and writing development. Used from the end of the New Kingdom on	not included in the present work

Observation:

Winand, *Études*, §§ 22-29, uses terms analogous to those used here: generally "Late Middle Egyptian" is Winand's "*néo-égyptien partiel*", "Medio-Late Egyptian" his "*néo-égyptien mixte*", "Late Egyptian" "*néo-égyptien complet*".

0.2.3 Bibliography

Kroeber, *Neuägyptizismen*; Sethe, *Geschichte der ägyptischen Sprache*; Stricker, *Indeeling*; Schenkel, *Sprachwissenschaft*, § 1.1 — linguistic evolution

Junge, *Sprachstufen*; Junge, *Sprache*; Winand, *Études*, §§ 2-50 — revised

J. Baines/C. Eyre, Four notes on literacy, in: *GM* 61, 1983, 65ff; J.J. Janssen, Literacy and Letters at Deir el-Medina, in: Demarée/Egberts, *Village Voices*, 81ff — literacy

cf. also *LÄ* IV s.v. Papyrus-Verzeichnis — texts

0.3 Writing materials: papyrus and ostraca

0.3.1 Demand for writing materials

A fundamental feature of Egyptian history seems to have been the progressive extension of writing into virtually every sphere of life. For the formative period of the Old Kingdom, most of the recorded utterances preserved are monumental, such as ideological texts engraved in stone (as decorum texts). It is probable that during this period, the number of literate individuals was very limited, and that while the conventions were being established, there was little divergence in the written forms of the language. By the New Kingdom, however, writing was widely used and subject to the conventions developed during the intervening thousand years. Besides socially significant texts and those that are somehow specific to language activity — *belles lettres* texts — there are now also abundant records of business affairs, everyday life and even personal activities (including expressions of religious sentiment).

The monumental demands the imperishable and thus inscriptions in stone. The momentary is satisfied with the transient, and thus the demand for cheap and easily accessible writing material increased over time. From the very beginning, papyrus ("paper") was such a material, and its importance gradually increased (even being an export product well into classical times).

Not only a great part of the records concerning daily life but also considerable evidence of literary activity comes from the village of Deir el-Medineh. And there the supply of papyrus seems not to have matched the rising demand which was only met by re-using papyrus ("palimpsests"), along with the parallel use of limestone flakes and potsherds, which are termed "ostraca" in Egyptology.

> **Recto/Verso; Palimpsest:** The inscribed horizontal fibres of the inner side of the papyrus are called the Recto (abbreviated "rt.", "rto.", "ro."). The inscribed reverse is the Verso ("vs.", "vso.", "vo."). Frequently the recto is not designated as such.
>
> Certain editors term the side with the beginning of a text the "recto" regardless of the fibers, which has led to the emergence of the term "real" recto, meaning the technical recto. The recto of an ostracon is always the side with the beginning of the text. In German, the recto is occasionally abbreviated Vs., for *Vorderseite*, which can lead to confusion.
>
> Many Ramesside texts are written on papyrus which originally bore another text. The earlier text was "erased" by washing it away, and the second text written on the papyrus when dry. If papyrus was accidentally exposed to water, it could be dried and the text preserved, so that these "erasures" were clearly deliberate. Papyri bearing two texts of this type are termed "palimpsests".

0.3.2 Production and use of papyrus

production of papyrus

In antiquity, the papyrus plant (*ṯwfy*) grew wild in thickets up to 4 m high in the shallows along the Nile banks and in the swamps of the

Delta. To obtain writing material, the triangular stem of the plant was peeled, cut into pieces 42-44 cm long, and split into thin strips. The strips were laid out in parallel — slightly overlapping — rows which were then covered with another set of strips laid perpendicularly over the first set. The strips were glued together by pressure and pounding. When dry, the surfaces were polished with a smooth stone and the edges trimmed. The dimensions differed from one period to another, but in the Ramesside Period, the pages were generally 42 cm high.

Papyrus reached the consumer in rolls which were usually formed in the Ramesside Period by gluing together some 20 sheets ($q^{c}h.t$). The joins only overlapped by one or two centimetres, and the longest known scroll is the 40.5 m long pHarris I. Although some texts were written on complete rolls ($^{c}r.t$), most rolls were cut in half before use,

preparation

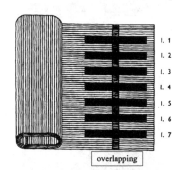

so that they were 20 cm high. Scrolls were kept in covers, and these in wooden boxes ($hr.t-^{c}$). Papyrus is rolled so that the horizontal fibres run inside, along the length of the scroll, while the vertical strips run outside, parallel to the ends of the scroll.

l. 1
l. 2
l. 3
l. 4
l. 5
l. 6
l. 7

For a longer text, the scribe spread the scroll in front of himself (or herself) with the rolled part on the left and an uncovered "page" on the right, and wrote on the horizontal fibres of the inner surface, from right to

technique of writing on papyrus

overlapping

left. This inscribed inner surface is termed the recto. The scroll was rolled up again starting from the end on the scribe's right. In earlier times, it was conventional to inscribe the papyrus in vertical columns, writing from the upper right to the lower left, so that the scroll could be rolled up practically column by column. From Dyn. XII it was usual

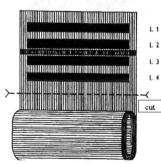

l. 1
l. 2
l. 3
l. 4

cut

to open up an entire page at a time, and to write in horizontal lines from top to bottom.

At first, the outer surface, the verso of the papyrus was not used, and the scroll was re-rolled after completion, so that the beginning of the text was at the beginning of the scroll again. The need for writing materials during the New Kingdom was, however, such that the back was very frequently inscribed as well. The scribe could simply take the inscribed papyrus and start writing

verso

without re-rolling the scroll, so that the first page of the verso text was on the back of

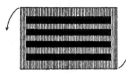

the last page of the recto text. If a papyrus with an uninscribed verso had been re-rolled, the scroll could simply be turned over, and the first page of the verso text would be on the back of the first page of the recto text, but the other way up.

letters and official documents

Some letters and official documents (and one literary text, Wenamun) were prepared differently. The scribe took the scroll and unrolled it away from himself, and wrote in lines parallel to the end of the papyrus until about half of the text was completed, at which point the text was cut off from the rest of 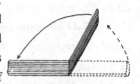 the scroll. He then turned the sheet over and wrote so that the first line of the recto was on the back of the last line of the verso. The recto of such a text is thus written perpendicular to the fibers, and the verso parallel to the fibers. The length of such a text reflects the scribe's decision, and the breadth depends upon whether the papyrus had been halved (21 cm) or quartered (11 cm).

addressing letters

When finished, the scribe would turn back to the recto and fold it several times, beginning with the end of the recto text, which ended up on the inside of the narrow packet, with the uninscribed bottom bit of the verso on the outside. The packet was then folded in half, and the ends tied together. On the upper surface the name of the recipient was written, and on the other side, that of the author.

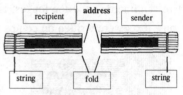

0.3.3 Ostraca

Large smooth limestone flakes were surprisingly among the writing materials favoured by the community at Deir el-Medineh, where these waste products were used for notes, records, sketches, school exercises, and even letters and inventories. These thousands of flakes — called "ostraca" (n-$\underline{d}$-r) — have not only considerably augmented the number of texts preserved from the New Kingdom, and contributed to our understanding of its chronology and administration, but have also thrown much light on obscure aspects of daily life.

oDM 18 (Dyn. XIX)

0.3.4 Bibliography

writing material

R. Drenkhahn, *LÄ* IV s.v. Papyrus, Papyrusherstellung; L. Gestermann, *LÄ* V s.v. Schreibmaterial; W. Helck, *LÄ* IV s.v. Ostraka

technique

Černý, *LRL* (Introduction XVII-XIV); Jaroslav Černý, *Paper and Books in Ancient Egypt*, London 1952; Manfred Weber, *Beiträge zur Kenntnis des Schrift- und Buchwesens der alten Ägypter*, Diss. Köln 1969; R. Parkinson/S. Quirke, *Papyrus*, London 1995

0.4 Conventions of text description

0.4.1 Hieroglyphic transcription

Many New Kingdom texts were written in hieratic — particularly those in "typologically pure" Late Egyptian. In the interest of readability, these are generally published in Egyptological hieroglyphs.

The basic principles of transcription established by Gardiner in 1929 demand that all the cursive hieratic signs be faithfully reproduced in the same relative positions in the hieroglyphic transcription, regardless of how genuine Egyptian hieroglyphs would have been used to write the same words and forms. To understand the difference, one need only turn to the hieroglyphic versions of the Qadesh poems and the transcription of pSallier III. Publications which preceded Gardiner's article (even the second edition of Erman's *Neuägyptische Grammatik*) observed different systems, frequently endeavouring to transcribe hieratic as the editor thought an Egyptian craftsman would render the same text in hieroglyphs.

conventions of transcription

Gardiner's system renders Late Egyptian texts still more alien to the eyes of those accustomed to Middle Egyptian, as Erman warned. There is a whole series of variants and new signs. Many words are abbreviated so much as to be unidentifiable while others are written with many more signs than seemingly necessary; the signs at the ends of some words degenerate into mere strokes, while other words are loaded with determinatives. Many signs come to bear a significance in transcription which they do not have in the cursive hieratic. None of this impinges on the fundamental correctness of the method, but it should be borne in mind when viewing Late Egyptian texts, and above all one

appearance of the texts

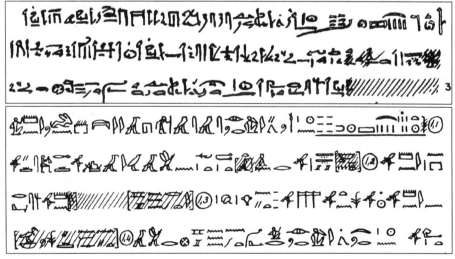

Introductory passage of "Wenamun", hieratic and in hieroglyphic transcription

should not hastily and harshly judge the written forms as corrupt and confused, as was once done.

special signs;
rubra

Hieratic abbreviations and idiosyncratic writings are reproduced in hieroglyphic transcription. The ⟍ is used not only for any number of complicated signs, but also for 𝕬 and frequently even for ⟨, ⟨, and ⌒. Merely in order to fill up an empty space above another sign, a dot was inserted[1], as in 𝕬, which can, however, equally well be intended to be 𝕬 or 𝕬. Formalistic precision and consistency result in transcriptions such as ⏉𝕏𝕬 for the phoneme b, although such writings are intended to distinguish the similar hieratic signs for 𝕤 and 𝕍. The sign ⌣ is reversed in hieratic, but this reversal does not appear in the hieroglyphic transcription used here. Headings, paragraph introductions and numbers written in red ink are usually marked by underlining the hieroglyphic transcription.

line columns

Hieroglyphic texts of the New Kingdom differ from those of the Middle Kingdom, but not particularly dramatically. Some Ramesside inscriptions testify to an increasing tendency to dispense with the traditional square units in favor of rectangles, so that individual lines of text consist of a series of short columns, which are read from top to bottom (cf. the Israel Stele, the Hittite Treaty or the text below). This New Kingdom innovation survived in monumental marginal texts until hieroglyphs themselves ceased to be used in Late Antiquity.

Part of the titulary of Ramses IV; marginal inscription from the southern pylon of the temple of Medinet Habu

0.4.2 Scholarly transliteration

varieties of
transliteration

While the hieroglyphic transcription of hieratic is subject to widely accepted conventions, the same is not true of the transliteration of the hieroglyphic into Roman letters, and it is not even certain that it could be systematized without an effort completely disproportionate to the task. Phonetic changes (cf. § 1.1) and other shifts in the relationship between the graphemes and morphemes/phonemes mean that the scholarly conventions applied to

1   In the examples this dot will frequently not be represented since the set of GLYPH hieroglyphs used here did not have it — or it eluded me.

Middle Egyptian cannot be used blindly. Both Erman and Černý agreed that any proposed system would be arbitrary and both concluded that it was "better" or "safer" not to. Two basic tendencies have crystallized: the moderate historical attitude which maintains the system used for Middle Egyptian, and the moderate "phonematic" one endeavouring to represent the hieroglyphic transcription in the transliteration. The latter method would transcribe  "the one who sends forth" as *r.hꜣb*, the former as *ꞽ.hꜣb*.

methods used here

In this work, I attempt to employ a descriptive phonematic transliteration determined by the constraints that words must be recognizable in the dictionary or *Wörterbuch* and grammatical endings in the grammars. Inconsistency is thus system: it means that the endings of words find little descriptive attention and that idiosyncrasies of writing are not represented if regular. The endings of the infinitives of weak verbs are seldom transcribed except in explanation or to mark specific forms (e.g. *gmy* will be used as the citation form of the verb "to find", *gm* for its infinitive, in the explanatory notes, however, sometimes etymologically *gm.t*; with object suffix *gm=s*, but as representing the written evidence or in explanation as *gm.t=s*, even *gm.tw=s* as respresenting the writing). Syntagmas are usually given in a conventional form, in general in the form used in the secondary literature (i.e., *m-dy.t sdm=f* for the negative causative imperative, even if *dꞽ/dy*, *dy.t* or *dꜣy.t* is transliterated otherwise).

structure sign; asterisk

Grammatical morphemes are separated by dots, suffixes by a double hyphen, and words are separated by a space as in English: e.g., *tꜣy=f ꜣḥ.t* "his field". Single concepts and compound prepositions or adverbs joining two morphemes are joined by a hyphen, e.g., *zꜣ-Rꜥw*; when those elements became inseparable, they are joined by a dot, e.g., *m.dꞽ*. The causative *s* is separated from the morpheme with a colon, e.g., *s:mn*. Group writings (syllabic script) are represented with hyphens (e.g., *ꞽ-r-k*, or *ꞽw-r'-kꜣ*, for "Uruk"). When a transliteration sign is used to represent a phoneme, it is put between slashes (e.g. /*d*/), braces mark morphemes (e.g., {*sdm*}).

Hypothetical, imaginary or artificial forms, and "etymological" or over-literal translations, etc., along with hypothetical transliterations and forms which are not recorded are all indicated with an asterisk (*) and impossible forms with two asterisks.

0.4.3 Notes on translation

In general, in translating Egyptian, Egyptologists are inclined to keep their translations as literal as possible, on the assumption that this somehow reduces the degree of interpretation, while simultaneously demonstrating that one has grasped the grammatical structure of the Egyptian text. As a matter of principle, this system will not be observed in this work.

translation is
interpretation

A "justificatory translation"[2] fails to achieve the object of representing the statements of one language in another. The attempt to replicate the structure of one language in another merely gives the alien structure an inappropriate role, and is more likely to block understanding than to enhance it. All translation is interpretation, and one cannot avoid this by translating literally. The unavoidable discussion of translation difficulties of a grammatical and semantic nature belongs in the notes and not in the text.

free translation

If a free translation is preferred to a literal one, this does not imply that imprecision is permissible. The art of translation is that of giving the precise sense in appropriate phrases in one's own language, regardless of whether one succeeds in every case or not. Success depends upon mastering not only the mechanics of the other language, but also one's own.

In this book many of the translations of the examples will be free, but if necessary the accompanying notes will provide translations bridging the gap between the free translation and the Egyptian structure — to ease understanding, but not as substitute or alternative translations. The basic meaning of the words in question will be found in the Glossary (§ 9). If desirable, the same words will be rendered differently in different contexts. Formulaic expressions such as ⁿh wḏ3 snb will be abbreviated in transliteration and usually left untranslated, except where they should be given a greater weight of meaning.

0.4.4 Bibliography

comparison
hieroglyphic-
hieratic

Qadesh Poem *KRI* II 25ff (§§ 67ff; K stands for the hieroglyphic original at Karnak, L for the one at Luxor; S stands for the hieroglyphic transcription of Papyrus Sallier III; for the hieratic version of pSallier III 1,4-2,9 = *KRI* II §§ 74-107, cf. Möller, *Hieratische Lesestücke* II, p. 25f.)

illustrations

Illustrations of the ways of writing on papyrus from Černý, *LRL* (Introduction XVII-XX)

transcription/
transliteration

Gardiner, The Transcription of New Kingdom Hieratic, in: *JEA* 15, 1929, 48-55; Kammerzell, Zur Umschreibung und Lautung des Ägyptischen, in: Hannig, *Handwörterbuch*, XXIIIff; earlier method: Erman, *Neuägyptische Grammatik*, §§ 39-43

translation

W. von Koppenfels, Intertextualität und Sprachwechsel: Die literarische Übersetzung, in: U. Broich/U. Pfister, *Intertextualität. Formen, Funktionen, anglistische Fallstudien*, Tübingen 1985, 137ff (with further literature)

2   T. E. Peet, *The Present Position of Egyptological Studies. An inaugural lecture delivered before the University of Oxford on 17 January 1934*, Oxford 1934, 16.

0.5 Grammatical terminology

Although it might seem somewhat paradoxical, consistency is not necessarily a virtue in the use of grammatical terminology. An introductory grammar must use familiar terms, but it is impossible to avoid the use of new ones. Scholarly tradition is built up as new insights are gained and thus old and new must be blended together, as linguistic understanding increases and changes our perspectives. Some older terms must be incorporated into this — if occasionally with slightly different meanings — but some have to be replaced, and others must be introduced as linguistic data are described differently. Although potentially confusing for the new student, the terminological debate cannot be resolved today. This grammar attempts to keep links to the older grammars of Middle Egyptian with which the student is familiar but which are bound to an older terminology, while current linguistic debate is largely expressed using terminology which varies from scholar to scholar. It is thus not the moment to develop a new terminology, even if this were to result in consistency.

As a paradigm verb, *sḏm* is written only *sdm* here (*sdm=f*). In order to enable the student to recognize notions when new forms of analysis and description are introduced, a number of synonomous terms are employed (such as subject, actor, agent; or emphatic *sdm=f* and nominal *sdm=f*). At the same time, terms are used in a more general or more analytic way (prospective *sdm=f*, e.g., is also termed subjunctive-prospective *sdm=f* where dependent on verbs, occasionally abbreviated to subjunctive *sdm=f*, etc.). Middle Egyptian "pseudo-verbal constructions" (with Old Perfective/Stative or *ḥr* and infinitive — *zḫȝ.w ḥr sḏm* "the scribe is listening") are grouped together with other prepositional compounds (*zḫȝ.w m pr=f* "the scribe is in his house") as the "Adverbial Sentence" (Gardiner's "sentence with adverbial predicate"), but it should be noted that the term Adverbial Sentence is used as equivalent to "First Present" (the usual term for the Late Egyptian form). References to sections refer only back to the earlier parts of the book (to sections which have already been covered); as long as grammatical terms have not yet been explicitly introduced, the commentary notes to the examples attempt to paraphrase forms which will be assigned terms later on (as in the vague "Late Egyptian future expression" for the *ı͗w=f r sdm*), which is later called the "Third Future". Those dependent clauses which assume an adverbial role with regard to the sentence governing them are termed circumstantial clauses or forms ("Circumstantial Present", e.g., is thus the circumstantial or adverbial form of the Adverbial Sentence alias First Present; note that the "Adverbial Sentence" uses an adverbial as one constituent, while its "adverbial" or "circumstantial form", i.e., the Circumstantial Present, is the form of the Adverbial Sentence used in the role of an adverb!). As a rule, all the terms and concepts are explained in detail in the course of the book.

1. Orthography and writing system

1.1 The written form of linguistic signs in Late Egyptian

1.1.0 "Old" writing and "new" language

The principles of writing the Egyptian language have not changed very much, but not a few signs which appear to be identical to those of Middle Egyptian have acquired new values as a result of sound change. As writing is governed by normative rules only to the extent that more or less individual manners of instruction may allow, sound changes can equally easily remain concealed in familiar forms or appear in new writings. The personal pronoun *sw*, e.g., has been reduced to *s'*, and it can still be encountered as ⳼ or already as ⳼. Thus in the texts both conventional and modernized forms appear side by side. The register hierarchy prevails here, too, so that religious texts and monumental inscriptions bearing the weight of tradition are more inclined to reflect entrenched conventions. In the ways words and phrases are written, hieroglyphic and cursive hieratic texts can thus differ considerably, a difference which is emphasized by the Egyptological hieroglyphic transcription of hieratic.

1.1.1 Sign redundancy

In many cases, Late Egyptian words cannot be read as in Middle Egyptian. This is particularly true for endings:

Thus phonograms like *-w*, *-y*, *-t*, *-tỉ* appear, but seemingly without any identifiable redundant phonograms function as graphemes, meaning that the writings do not fulfil any linguistic role, and can consequently be ignored: ⳼ *ꜥqw* for *ꜥq*, "enter"; ⳼ *ḫprw* for *ḫpr*, "become"; or ⳼ for *ỉy* "come"; ⳼ for *psy* "cook" (which also has a characteristically redundant duplication of *z* and *s*). A typical transfer is to be noticed in ⳼ *qdw* and even ⳼ **qdnw* for *qd* "form; substance", since the final *n* can also be written *nw*: ⳼ **wstn-nw* for *wstn* "stride; go".

marking
grammatical
gender

Another consequence is that the -.*t* ending can no longer serve as an indicator of a grammatical feminine, with ⸢hieroglyphs⸣ *p3 šrỉ* "the boy" (Coptic ⲠϢⲎⲢⲈ) and ⸢hieroglyphs⸣ *t3 šrỉ* "the girl" (ⲦϢⲈⲈⲢⲈ); Coptic reveals that the two were, however, vocalized differently. Grammatically feminine are also, e.g., designations for vessels like ⸢hieroglyphs⸣ *d3d3.w* "jar", or ⸢hieroglyphs⸣ *3ᶜᶜ* "vessel".

complement-
ation

These examples also show that although the biliteral signs are frequently written with complementary uniliteral graphemes, it is not clear that the graphemes correspond to phonemes (that, e.g., the *-3* of *p3* was pronounced — probably it was not: presumably *p3* was already pronounced like the Coptic article Ⲡ-. Incidentally, original hieroglyphic texts spell *p3* without the phonetic complement *-3*, although hieratic texts do write it).

redundant
semograms

The use of determinatives is widespread, but oddly, not those with specific classificatory functions, rather the more general ones, which classify less precisely. Such generic determinatives, which do not clearly determine, like ⸢sign⸣ , ⸢sign⸣ , ⸢sign⸣ or ⸢sign⸣, are combined together as in ⸢hieroglyphs⸣ *nḥm* (infinitive) "take". They will also be found abbreviated to mere strokes: ⸢strokes⸣. While the determinatives seem to lose significance as indicators of meaning, their role as word separators increases. The plural strokes very often serve a similar role, but mostly in conjunction with other determinatives.

> Grapheme, morpheme, phoneme: Concepts for the smallest units of a structural linguistic description. A phoneme is the smallest phonetic element which can differentiate lexically distinct linguistic items (e.g., *bear - wear*). A morpheme is the smallest meaningful element of given words (clear*ly*; *you*; he look*s*). A grapheme is the smallest written element which distinguishes phonemes, morphemes and other units of language or writing (semograms). Phone, morph, and graph apply to the still smaller elements which are not yet distinctive. If several elements can represent one morpheme, phoneme or grapheme, these are termed allomorph, allophone or allograph.

"image"-
writings

Occasionally writings appear to be nearly incomprehensible, and earlier Egyptologists tended to describe these forms as "wild" or "corrupt". Examples include ⸢hieroglyphs⸣ or ⸢hieroglyphs⸣ as playful forms of "20" (the number)[1] which can hardly be transcribed, except perhaps with the Coptic ϪⲞⲨϢⲦ). Or comparably ⸢hieroglyphs⸣ for *mšᶜỉ* "go"; or ⸢hieroglyphs⸣ for ⸢hieroglyphs⸣ *gbgb.t* "stricken".

a new writing
system

These writings are the reflections of a new system of writing, the mechanisms of which will be briefly explored here. Admittedly, the derivation and peculiar character of this system are such that even when its principles have been mastered the search for a given

---

1   Cf. WB V 552,8.

word can prove to be a bit of an ordeal, involving consideration of the various possibilities
and searching in the dictionary until something suitable is found (and generally something
is found!).

1.1.2 Causes: Historical sound change

(1) Note

Before proceeding further, it is advisable to issue a warning that a "sound change" is not
easy to pin down, given the nature of the writing system. The effects of a change can be
recognized, and conjectures about its nature can be made, without it always being possible
to identify with certainty either the original sound or its product, or even the approximate
date of the change. Transliterations are mere approximations, best regarded as purely
conventional names for signs. Generally, for philological purposes or "pragmatic" use
of the texts, this type of uncertain knowledge and approximate representation is not a
cause for concern. For deeper discussions of phonetics and phonology, cf. Schenkel,
Sprachwissenschaft, or Loprieno, *Ancient Egyptian*.

(2) Loss and weakening of elements in syllable-final position

In syllable- and word-final position, /n/, /r/ and /t/ can be dropped or weakened into a
secondary glottal stop (-ꜣ; aleph):
— /n/ can disappear in the suffixes -ṯn, -tn (> -t) or in the forms of the demonstratives /n/
(pn > p).
— A secondary glottal stop derived from /t/ and /r/ can be written as -ỉ (with /r/, rarely /t/; /r/
also -ꜣ), as occasionally already in Middle Egyptian (zwrỉ "drink", for zwr > zwỉ); mostly,
however, it is not written. Examples: ꞏꞏꞏ ỉtrw "river; Nile" becomes
(ỉắt|rˇw > ỉấꜣ|rˇw > Coptic ЄIOOP); ꞏꞏꞏ hrww "day" develops into
ꞏꞏꞏ , ꞏꞏꞏ (hắr|wˇw > hấꜣ|wˇw > hấw > Coptic ϨOOY), but with a plural
ꞏꞏꞏ hrw "days" (*hā|rˇw > Coptic ⲀϨⲢⲈY).
    The loss of the feminine -.t ending in principle already began to take effect during the fem. -.t
Middle Kingdom, as can be established from the appearance of the ancient word
ꞏꞏꞏ bd.t "emmer", which had long been written ꞏꞏꞏ bty (cf. also under [2]),
Coptic ⲂⲰⲦⲈ.
— If a change in the syllabic structure shifts the /t/ or /r/ from the end of one syllable to preservation
the beginning of the next, they are maintained, e.g., in the preposition ꞏꞏꞏ ḥr (ḥˇ' >

Coptic ⲀⲒ), followed by a noun (status nomi-nalis), but with suffix 𓏤𓆑 ḥr=f (ḥ⁻|ráf ; status pronominalis) which can also be rein-forced in appearance by writing 𓏤𓏤. This reappearance of weakened or dropped pho-nemes when the syllabic boundaries shift occurs particularly frequently with the t-infinitives of those verbs followed by an object suffix.

word writings — Such changes are occasionally written by maintaining the earlier word writings ("sche-matograms") and merely adding the new sounds (as in Middle Egyptian zwr >zwỉ; more systematically in the following § 1.1.3[3]):

𓏤𓏤𓏤 for tr >tỉ "time"; or 𓏤𓏤 for ḫpr "become", "be" (ḫā|par > ḫāp⁻', Coptic ⲰⲰⲚⲈ).

> **Syllable structure, syllable-initial/syllable-final position:** Egyptian words can have one or more syllables. Each syllable begins with a consonant — which is thus in "syllable-initial position"; the syllable contains a short or long vowel, and it may or may not end with a consonant. If it ends without a consonant, the syllable is "open" with a long vowel, and another syllable must follow, e.g. the first syllable in nā́ṭar (nṭr) "god". If it ends with a consonant — which thus is in "syllable-final position", the syllable is "closed" and the vowel usually short, e.g. zắḫ-ȝaw (zš) "scribe". The stress falls on either the last syllable (ultima) or the last but one syllable (penultima) of the word — the "tonic syllable"; the stress may be shifted when grammatical endings and suffixes increase the number of syllables. Stressless — "pretonic" or "post-tonic" — syllables can be severely shortened.

(3) Neutralizing phonological contrasts

Occasionally the contrast of phoneme pairs is neutralized:

depalatization — Depalatization of /ḏ/ and /ṯ/. Primarily in syllable-final position, but also in syllable-initial position, /ḏ/ and /ṯ/ become /d/ und /t/, without this necessarily being expressed in writing, i.e., depending upon whether it is being written phonologically or traditionally. In hieratic, the length of the signs above or below often partly determines the length of the signs for t or d — thus it is not always unambiguous whether t or d is to be read.

Examples: 𓏤𓏤 or 𓏤𓏤 for rmṯ >rmt "people" (with further reduction to a secondary glottal stop, cf. Coptic ⲢⲰⲘⲈ); 𓏤𓏤 for snḏ >snd "fear"; 𓏤𓏤 or 𓏤𓏤 for ṯnw > tnw "number"; 𓏤 or 𓏤 for ḏb.t >db.t "brick".

"develarization" — Develarization. That /q/ lost its velar feature becoming /g/ or /k/ (as in Demotic and Coptic) can be seen where the grapheme for /q/ has occasionally replaced the graphemes for /g/ and /k/. Examples: 𓏤𓏤 for 𓏤𓏤 sgnn "unguent" (Coptic ⲤⲞϬⲚ); 𓏤𓏤 for 𓏤𓏤 mkḫȝ "neglect". The absence of a group-writing sign for -ẖ- (cf. § 1.2.1 infra) indicates that the difference between -ḫ- and -ẖ- had already disappeared (as later in Ptolemaic and Coptic).

— Devoicing of the dentals, or else the neutralization of retroflex (emphatic) articulation: cf. Schenkel, *Sprachwissenschaft*, §§ 2.1.2; 2.1.3. /d/ becomes /t/, as in for *ḫd* >*ḫt* "travel north"; this applies occasionally also for /d/ derived from /ḏ/, as in *nḏ* >*nty* "flour" (Coptic ⲚⲞⲈⲒⲦ). Writing variants like for *ḏd=f* "to say it" may also signal such a neutralization (*ḏd=f* >*ḏt=f*), but they could just as easily be forms of the status pronominalis of the infinitive. /d/ > /t/

— In certain environments (e.g., before labials) the articulation of the phonemes *m* and *n* can be neutralized; the graphemes for *m* and *n* may thus serve as allographs for either (the grapheme *m* can be the phoneme *m* or *n*, and likewise the grapheme *n* can be *n* or *m*). nasals

(4) Syllable reduction

— Particularly in compounds, the strong tonic stress of Egyptian may bring about a reduction of unaccented, mostly post-tonic syllables, especially in compounds, as for *ẖr.y-ḥ3b.t* "lector priest". by accent

— Reduction of root consonants by assimilation; assimilation of *s* to *š* and subsequent reduction make *pš* (Coptic ⲠⲰϢ, 2-lit. verb) out of *psš*/ *pšs* "separate" or *šp* out of *šzp* "receive" (Coptic ϢⲰⲠ; the hieroglyphic writing is however inconclusive). by assimilation

1.1.3 Effects: The suspension of definiteness in writing

(1) The relations between phoneme and grapheme

The phonological system of a language and the ways in which linguistic signs are noted in writing are two separate systems of symbols, which influence each other only indirectly. Changes in one system do not necessarily result in simultaneous changes in the other. The writing system is, however, more conservative than the phonetic system: written signs are consciously learnt as conventions and passed on as such, while phonetic changes occur unconsciously. In this fashion, historical sound change thus weakens the specific conventional relationship between the sign and what is signified, between the grapheme and the phoneme.

This phenomenon is familiar in all European languages, and particularly evident in English. The writing system, the language of graphemes, has virtually never been adjusted to account for phonetic change, so that the sign inventory will always reflect an earlier stage of the language, although representing a later one: the languages of the phonemes and graphemes are destined to go separate ways. Despite its different type of writing system, Late Egyptian betrays the same tendency. Historical sound change results in shifts of the following types:

(2) Adjustment of phonograms

Some of the traditional phonograms denote new phoneme values, which increases the number of allographs (graphemes used for several phonemes):

m and *n* — As prepositions before nouns, or in word-initial position, the graphemes for *m* and *n* can be exchanged. As an example: the Middle Egyptian independent pronoun *ntf* is generally written *mntf* in Late Egyptian (but Coptic ⲚⲦⲞϤ!); the same is true of other words (morphemes) beginning with *m* or *n*.

r, ỉw, ỉ — As a preposition preceding nouns and as a word-initial morpheme (a prefix), can frequently be exchanged with or (since *r, ỉw, ỉ* are allographs of one phoneme).

t, d; ṭ, ḍ — , , , can still occasionally have the phonological denotations assigned to them for Middle Egyptian, but are frequently mere allographs for the phoneme /t/. Exactly what is meant in any given unfamiliar word must be established by looking in the dictionary.

(3) Reassignment of schematograms

Traditional schematograms — the conventional grouping of signs that was specific to certain words — may become new phonograms:

effects of schematograms — Schematograms permit a word to be identified even if the written form is incomplete. This is familiar from earlier times, the schematogram — [HQT]^{vessel} — actually denotes *ḥnq.t* "beer", or the schematogram stands for *rmṯ* "men"; "people". In the latter case the sound change in syllable-final position, *rmṯ* > *rā|mˉt* > *rā|mˉ* ' > Coptic ⲢⲰⲘⲈ, means that the schematogram [$RṮ$]$^{man,\ woman}$ shares only the R with the phoneme sequence /r/, /ā/, /m/ that it is supposed to represent.

Even words which were written earlier with individual graphemes each of which corresponded to individual phonemes, i.e., using the "alphabetic" or elementary graphemes, can also become schematograms, such as , which even after the sound change (*ỉẵt|rˉw* > *ỉẵ3|rˉw*) continued as the written form of *ỉ3rw* "river".

complemented schematograms — This means that a schematogram could also be retained despite changes in the phonemic structure of the word — and this now explains examples like the already-mentioned

Middle Egyptian development of 🖼️ *zwr* "drink" to *zwỉ*: as with the multiliteral signs taking "phonetic complements", a multiliteral schematogram can also be complemented by a uniliteral grapheme that marks the phoneme change — hence the writing 🖼️ for *zwỉ*.

— Thus, a new kind of multiliteral sign was   schematogram created out of schematograms. This might be   — phonogram illustrated by the following chain of examples: 🖼️ *šm.t* "go" which develops sound-his-torically to *š'* (**šĭmỉ̃t > šỉỉ̃' > š̆'* > Coptic ϢⲈ), occasionally written 🖼️ (We-namun 1,12), thus 🖼️ comes to serve as a biliteral phonogram *š'* in words like 🖼️ *mšꜥỉ* "march, travel" (*mắšꜥaỉ >* *mắꜥš̆'* > Coptic ⲘⲞⲞϢⲈ).

— These new multiliteral signs are complemented in the traditional fashion (frequently   new with "group signs", cf. infra § 1.2.1): 🖼️, e.g., becomes a new "biliteral" sign for *ḫp*   multiliteral (<*ḫpr*, cf. § 1.1.1) and is complemented with *p* (◻️), 🖼️. Or: 🖼️ is phonemically   signs only *ḥ'* (<*ḥr*), but followed by a suffix it is complemented with a second *r* as 🖼️ (the so-called "status pronominalis" of the preposition): the first *r* was no longer considered to be a "phonetic complement" to the original biliteral sign for *ḥr*. Infinitives reveal the same tendency, e.g., 🖼️ for *ḏȝy* "ferry across", but complemented with -.*t*/ -.*tw* when followed by the object suffix, 🖼️ *ḏȝy.t=f* "to take him across" (status pronominalis).

(4) Hypercorrection and hypercharacterization

In the case of the -.*t* infinitive of *ḏȝy* "ferry across", we observe that what is still   hyper-intrinsically present can be emphasized or even over-characterized against the background   characterization of phonetic loss. Similarly, if it was considered worth emphasizing that an /r/ was retained — in the syllable-initial position, for example — it could be written doubled, as in

⸻ for *rmỉ* "weep". Writings like ⸻ may thus mark /n/ as retained even in syllable-final position; in a writing like ⸻ for *ḥn=ỉ* "hurry" (pD'Orb 3,1) this emphasis of its presence may even show the interference of the forms proper to another linguistic norm, i.e., *sḏm.n=f* forms — the use of which was however no longer quite clearly grasped.

hypercorrection   Examples like these are attempts at analogous adjustment to forms and writings which are erroneously taken to be standards; they arise when scribes realize that changes have taken place, but are uncertain about where and when — they correct even when there is no reason for it. Such over-correction (termed "hypercorrection" in linguistics) also explains how, e.g., the -.*t* ending (- ⸻) preceding object suffixes of the infinitives of the 3ae inf. verbs (like *ḏȝy*) is transformed into a generalized marker of the infinitive for other verbal classes, too, as in

(LRL 20, 4-5)   ⸻ for *ỉw=tn ḥȝp=f r=ỉ* "and keep it secret from me".

Over the course of linguistic history, another movement of hypercorrection created a whole series of object pronouns out of this infinitive marker (cf. infra § 2.2.1).

In the realm of phonemic writings, cases such as ⸻ *sfd* for the grammatically feminine ⸻ *zf.t* "knife" (or *wdf* for *wḏf* "hesitate", etc.) illustrate the attempt to hypercorrectly reverse a mistakenly assumed sound change /d/ > /t/ (or /ḏ/ > /d/). The same may apply to the common spellings of -*tw/tỉ* with ⸻. Since the possible graphemes are all allographs of the phonemes concerned, it is, however, difficult to be certain about the conclusions.

1.1.4 Bibliography

graphophone-   F. Kammerzell, Zur Umschreibung und Lautung des Ägyptischen, in: Hannig, *Hand-*
mics   *wörterbuch*, XXIIIff; F. Kammerzell, Aristoteles, Derrida und ägyptische Phonologie. Zu systematischen Verschiedenheiten von geschriebener und gesprochener Sprache, in: *Sesto Congresso Internazionale di Egittologia, Atti* Vol. II, Turin 1993, 243ff; Junge, *Sprachstufen*

orthography   Erman, *Neuägyptische Grammatik*, §§ 8-28; Černý/Groll, *Late Egyptian Grammar*, §§ 1.1-1.11; Winand, *Études*, §§ 61-72; Loprieno, *Ancient Egyptian*, § 2.4(d)

phonemics   Schenkel, *Sprachwissenschaft*, § 2; Erman, *Neuägyptische Grammatik*, §§ 44-55; Loprieno, *Ancient Egyptian*, § 3.5

Sethe, *Verbum* I, §§ 57-313 (rich, but somewhat superficially organized; cf. §§ 205-207 further linguistic material for the usage of plural strokes)

1.2 Notes on the Late Egyptian writing system

1.2.1 "Group writing" and its signs

(1) The emergence of new graphemes

These sound changes and their reflection in writing are all part of a continual process of transformation. The changes occur so gradually and at such different rates and find expression in such different forms that the transformation takes place beyond the consciousness of a speaker. While some forms and words reveal that older relations of language and writing still dominated, others have suffered drastic shifts. While the traditional writing system was still in use, it was continuously augmented with new allographs and graphemes which emerged from the traditional phonograms and schematograms (cf. supra § 1.1.3) and which consist of particular groups of signs, whole grapheme complexes.

The new graphemes are also used according to the principles of the traditional system, however. Multiliteral signs are also complemented, and words are classified semantically with determinatives (semograms) — only the signs themselves are the product of such transformations. The "devaluation" of the uniliteral complementary graphemes — the elementary or alphabetical graphemes — was countered with signs which re-established a way of denoting a specific phoneme unambiguously.

Essentially, two new classes of signs can thus be identified. On the one hand are those two new classes of signs semograms or determinatives forming a sign group of several signs, used as complex determinatives. On the other is a new set of elementary graphemes which were intended to substitute for the older alphabetic, uniliteral or one-phoneme, graphemes. These new uniliteral signs can be read as the signs of a syllabic writing, but the more neutral term "group writing" is employed in this book.

(2) Determinative complexes and complex determinatives

— Two or more simple determinatives can be combined together, whether logically or combination of semograms not. Examples: combination of ⌣ ("tooth") and 𓀁 ("man with hand at mouth") with ✚𓀁 *wnm* "eat" or 𓀁 *iry=i* "I will do it!", meaning "yes"; but 𓀁 *nḥm* (inf.) "take". The plural strokes are often added without regard for the number of the noun (cf. supra § 1.1.1).

combination
semogram —
phonogram

— Determinatives/semograms and earlier phonograms can be combined (particularly for signs like those for -y or -t). In [hieroglyphs] *šmsy* "follow", the determinative/semogram is combined with a redundant -y-sign, in [hieroglyphs] *hȝy* "go down", the -t is redundant (this applies to forms other than the 3ae inf. infinitives).

transfer of
sign groups

— Association transfers whole groups of signs from one word to another. Examples: [hieroglyphs] *psd* "the back" (< *psḏ*; semogram group from [hieroglyphs] *šᶜd* "cut", via the sign group [hieroglyphs]); [hieroglyphs] *wȝḏ* "vegetables" (semogram group from [hieroglyphs] *smw* "greens"); [hieroglyphs] *dns* "be heavy" (rather than [hieroglyphs], taking elements from [hieroglyphs] *s:mn* "establish").

(3) The elementary graphemes of group writing

The signs listed here are used increasingly as one-phoneme signs, where it seemed useful to specify the phoneme. In Demotic, they are completely established as such. The sound -*l* was now occasionally written (in hieroglyphs with the sign [hieroglyph], and in hieratic with the group [hieroglyphs]), but it did not acquire the character of a phoneme (a segment that can differentiate lexically distinct linguistic items), and thus remained a mere variant of /r/ which can be written with the r/n graphemes.

transliteration	group writing	transliteration	group writing
j / ỉ	[hieroglyphs]	*ḥ*	[hieroglyphs]
y	[hieroglyphs]	*ḫ*	[hieroglyphs]
ᶜ	[hieroglyphs]	*s*	[hieroglyphs]
w	[hieroglyphs]	*š*	[hieroglyphs]
b	[hieroglyphs]	*q / ḳ*	[hieroglyphs]
p	[hieroglyphs]	*k*	[hieroglyphs]
f	[hieroglyphs]	*g*	[hieroglyphs]
m	[hieroglyphs]	*t*	[hieroglyphs]
n	[hieroglyphs]	*ṯ / č*	[hieroglyphs]
r	[hieroglyphs]	*d / ṭ*	[hieroglyphs]
h	[hieroglyphs]	*ḏ / č̣*	[hieroglyphs]

1.2.2 Uses of group writing

(1) Purpose

It must again be emphasized that group writing was intended primarily to enable the specification of phonemes, replacing the earlier "alphabetic"/one-phoneme graphemes, because these were no longer always able to fulfill their roles due to historical sound change. Making the effort to record the specific phonemes which have been heard is particularly desirable when encountering new words in one's own language or words from foreign languages. "Loan words" are thus mostly written in group writing. But even in the writing of familiar words, the new signs were increasingly employed, initially, however, in such a way that only parts of the word were written in group writing.

(2) Examples of "loan words"

> Foreign words were frequently employed in the diplomatically active, militarily expansive and culturally open society of the New Kingdom. Mostly Old Canaanite or Akkadian (Middle Assyrian or Middle Babylonian) in origin, they reflect particular modes of expression (of administrative officials, soldiers, merchants, gardeners), and accompanied imported wares and technologies: particularly luxuries, military goods and administrative technical terms (chariots, weapons, horses, fortifications, corvée labour and obligatory payments); agricultural and manufactured products (plants and animals, vessels). Foreign words are not understood as foreign, and are treated as words of one's own language (as "loan words"). There is no causal relationship between the use of foreign terms and the use of group writing — although frequently assumed in the earlier Egyptological literature.

A few selected examples from the numerous classes of new words which flowed into Egypt from the Near East and the Mediterranean:

— Geographical terms (toponyms): y-r'-dw-n3 / y-r-d-n = yrdn "(river) Jordan"; îw-r'-k3 = îrk/ 'rk "Uruk"; or w3-îw-ry-ya/ w-y-r-ya = wîlya "Ilios (Troy)" (*Wilịya Ϝιλιος, preserving the digamma!);

— Canaanite terms: y-m "(the) sea" (yam > Coptic ЄIOM); m-r-k-b-tỉ.t = mrkbt "chariot" (cf. Arabic markaba; Coptic ВЄРЄ6ⲰⲨⲦ); q-r-ḏ-n "hoe" (from Canaanite גלזן g-l-z-n).

(3) Examples of Egyptian words

Group writings can be employed in the most varied fashion for Egyptian words, without these necessarily being "loan words":

partial group writing — Partial group writings: [hieroglyphs] *b3-ḫn, bḫn* "villa; fortress"; [hieroglyphs] *wr-r-y.t, wrry.t* "chariot"; [hieroglyphs] *k-w.wy, ky.wy* "others" ([hieroglyphs] > Coptic **ⲔⲞⲞⲨⲈ**); [hieroglyphs] *ḥ-w-w, ḥwy* "strike"; [hieroglyphs] *sgnn* "unguent".

complete group writings — Complete group writings: [hieroglyphs] *ỉ-r-m, ỉrm* "(together) with" (for earlier [hieroglyphs] *ḥnᶜ*, of which there is a Late Egyptian variant [hieroglyphs] *r.ḥnᶜ*); [hieroglyphs] *b-n-r, bnr/bl* "outside" (*r-bnr* > Coptic **ⲈⲂⲞⲖ**); [hieroglyphs] *ḥ-r-r.w, ḥrr* "flower". Or [hieroglyphs] *k-ḏ-n, kḏn* "charioteer", which was borrowed by Akkadian as *gu-zi*.

1.2.3 Syllabic writing and vowels

syllabic writing Essentially, the signs used in group writing are intended to indicate consonants, just like the signs of the traditional system of writing. To a limited extent, however, they could also indicate vowels (particularly in names, as in toponyms and personal names, as is known from the Ptolemaic period with the writings of "Ptolemy" and "Cleopatra"). This is the reason for the occasional use of the term "syllabic writing" for group writing, reflecting a lengthy controversy about the degree to which the "syllabic" signs are intended to indicate vowels.

vocalic values In summary one may state: a few signs are used as syllabic signs in the cuneiform sense (such as final [hieroglyph] for *ya/ja*, [hieroglyph] for *ku*, [hieroglyph] for *nu*, [hieroglyph] for *bi*). Most group writing signs are, however, employed to designate syllables according to a variant of the so-called Devan-āgari-principle, by which the basic form of the

> **Methods of syllabic writing.** (1) Devan-āgari-principle (from Sanskrit): The basic form of the sign denotes a specific consonant and the vowel -a, the other vowels (e, i, o, u) and no vowel are indicated by additional signs. (2) Cuniform-principle: Every sign denotes a specific sequence of consonants and one or more vowels.

group writing sign records a specific consonant and the vowel -*a*, or no vowel at all. The other vowels are then indicated by additional signs. These "vowel markers" are (cf. Edel, *Ortsnamen*, and Schenkel, *Syllabische Schrift*) roughly the following:

vocalic value	a	i	u
(1) following consonants (apart from glottal stop/ "aleph")	ø (a)	\\ (i)	[hieroglyph] , ⲉ (u)
(2) following glottal stop/ "aleph"	[hieroglyph] ('a)	[hieroglyph] , [hieroglyph] ('i)	[hieroglyph] ('u)

Examples: [hieroglyph] *nim* "who?" (Coptic **ⲚⲒⲘ**); [hieroglyph] *'u-r-k* "Uruk"; [hieroglyph] *ku-nu-š* "Knossos" (Linear B: *ko-no-so*); [hieroglyph] *w-'i-ri-ya*

"Ilios" (*Wiliya, cf. supra); [hieroglyphs] mu-k-'a-n "Mykene" (*Mukānā > Μυκήνη).

1.2.4 Bibliography

Erman, *Neuägyptische Grammatik*, §§ 17-18; 29-38   group writing

Edel, *Ortsnamen*; W. Helck, *Die Beziehungen Ägyptens zu Vorderasien im 3. und 2.*   syllabic
Jahrtausend v.Chr., *ÄA* 5, Wiesbaden [2]1971, 539ff; Schenkel, *LÄ* V s.v. Schrift;   orthography
Syllabische Schrift; J. Zeidler, A New Approach to the Late Egyptian "Syllabic
Orthography", in: *Sesto Congresso Internazionale di Egittologia, Atti* Vol. II, Turin
1993, 579ff (recent attempt at defining the syllabic writing signs of Egyptian anew; the
number of signs accepted there goes far beyond those accepted by Edel and Schenkel)

J.E. Hoch, *Semitic Words in Egyptian Texts of the New Kingdom and Third Intermediate*   loan words
Period, Princeton 1994; M. Burchardt, *Die altkanaanäischen Fremdworte und Eigen-*
namen im Aegyptischen, Leipzig 1909-1910

1.3 Exercises

1.3.1 Reading

Transliterate and give meanings:

1.3.2 An ostracon (oDM 1262 vs.)

Ostracon oDM 1262 vs. (from Deir el-Medina; transcription by G. Posener) is a short
Ramesside prayer to Thoth in the form of the moon, and can be assigned to the category
of texts characterized as expressing personal piety ("persönliche Frömmigkeit"). Published and commented on by Fischer-Elfert, Lit. Ostraka, p. 68f.

1.3.2 Exercise: oDM 1262 vs.

Purpose: Transliterating a Late Egyptian text; analysing and identifying what distinguishes this from a Middle Egyptian text (e.g., in orthography, vocabulary, forms and syntax).

Translation: (vs. 1; unclear beginning; the servant of the [house....] says ...; vs. 2) "I will raise my voice that Thoth may hear it (vs. 3) in the hour of his eclipse. Turn your face (vs. 4) to the servant of your house. Forget me not! (vs. 5) I am your servant, O Lord of Hermopolis."

Notes:

vs. 4   After -r the suffix of the 1st person singular — 1.p.s. =i —is to be restored;

vs. 5   after the sign for the numeral "8" restore nw (of the town name ḫmnw) and the "village sign" to be restored — of which there is perhaps a trace to be identified in vs. 6.

1.3.3 A Decorum text (MedHab 80)

The preamble of the victory inscription of regnal year 11 of Ramesses III on the west or inner face of the first pylon in the temple at Medinet Habu. This copy reproduces only the first 12 columns on the second Libyan war on the south tower of the pylon (cf. the publication of the Epigraphic Survey, II, pl. 80; cf. *KRI* V: 59f.). The text is largely formulated in the participial style of the "eulogies"; it is akin to that of the autobiographies, particularly those of Dyn. XVIII.

Purpose: Example of a hieroglyphic "Late Middle Egyptian" text of Dyn. XX, with limited interference of Late Egyptian elements in orthography and morphology; group writing.

Notes:

Structure of the   (1) Date in regnal years; (2) heading for the entire text (including the parts which are
text   not presented here): "Beginning of the victory record of Egypt which the king has

text
contin-
ues

1.3.3 Exercise: MedHab 80

made last"; followed by phrases relating to the king's capacities through office; (3) the king's divine father from whose body he was born and who provided him with the necessary power authorizes the king: "The intellect of god who created earth once again in order to strengthen the borders of the 'beloved land' with great victories, selected a lord"; (4) besides Amun, Mont, Seth, Anat and Astarte also take their places beside the king in battle.

col. 1   from Dyn. XIX on the name of the month indicated is *msw.t-Rᶜw* (Coptic ⲘⲈⲤⲞⲠⲎ, based on the names of the festivals of the lunar months applied to the annual calendar);

col. 1-2   *s:mn nḥt.w*: "to make victories endure (by recording them)";

col. 2   *šzp ns.t*: "receive the throne"; *m* (> *n*) *ỉhhy*: as an adverbial to the preceding participle — do something "with exultation, with public approval";

           dỉ.t nrỉ: infinitive as paragraph heading; roughly "There was spreading of fear in every land by the sole lord";

col. 3   *nzw šꜣᶜ ḫpr tꜣ*: "king who started earth's (coming into) existence";

           ỉstw r.f: Late Egyptian graphem variant of the earlier *ỉs ṯ*; *ỉstw r.f* introduces the background of an action (a kind of parenthetical summary: "now this is the way it was"); for the use of the particle, cf. Erman, *Neuägyptische Grammatik*, § 677;

           sentence structure of the adverbial sentence with predicative *sdm.n=f*: NP (*ỉb n ṯr pn*) with participle plus AP (*stp.n=f*, col. 4, as predicative/rhematic circumstantial *sdm.n=f*): "the heart of this god, who ..., selected NN"; *m wḥm-ᶜ*: the "human leg" sign (Gardiner E 56, *rd*) has replaced the "animal-leg" sign (Gardiner F 25, *wḥm*);

col. 4   note that in the writing of *ḥr*, 🔺 and 🔺 are not clearly distinguished (cf. also col. 12); *stp.n=f* is "Middle Egyptian" circumstantial *sdm.n=f* as predicate/rheme of the whole sentence; "make someone king whom he himself has created" (< "to select as ruler someone who is such and such");

col. 7   *sỉꜣ ᶜnḫ my Mḥy* "have knowledge of life like the 'Provider'"; *Mḥy* is an epithet of the god Thoth (etymologically either "Provider" or as the "Filler" who causes the crescent moon to become full again); *ỉp*, here meaning "capable of judgment" or similar;

           zꜣ-Rᶜw is here the epithet of Shu as the following name in the cartouche of Ramesses III is not his "Son of Re" name, but his *nzw-bỉt* name (cf. col. 1); curiously, however, the craftsman began with this impression, too, as the initial "Riᶜa-massesa Hiq-ana" was later corrected to "Was-muᶜa-Riᶜa Mai-Amana";

col. 8   *pry <m> Rᶜw*: "(Egg), which came forth from Re"; the graphic loss of the preposition *m* is not rare in Late Egyptian; the expression paraphrases (1) the following "son of Re" title itself, and (2) the "content" of that name: "Re bore him";

col. 9   *pḥ.ty ꜥꜣ.t s:qꜣ.t* "great 'exalted' might" is a deferred object of the participle of *sr*, parallel to *nḥt.w*; *pḥ.ty* is fem.; the noun *mỉ.t.t* is frequently used for the preposition *mỉ* in Late Egyptian;

col. 10   *r dḫ=w r dr=w*: "in order to subject them and subdue them"; *=w* is the Late Egyptian form of the suffix pronoun 3rd pl. c. *=sn*, here following parallel prepositional infinitives;

col. 11-12 *wḏᶜ-rꜣ* as a writing (circumstantial *sdm=f*) of *wḏᶜ-ry.t* "vindicated at the highest level", thus: "while in the end Amun vindicates him";

col. 12   the preposition *ḥr-tp* here has the meaning of "(from) above down on someone or something", thus: (he does not turn back) "with the sword of Egypt over the Asiatics" "when the sword of Egypt is already hanging above the Asiatics".

2. Morphosyntactic features and peculiarities

2.0 Notes on typological change

2.0.1 The analytic tendency in the development of forms

Many Late Egyptian morphological and syntactical variations can be cursorily described as expressing an "analytic tendency" when compared to Middle Egyptian. While Middle Egyptian constructions and phrases are generally characterized by syntactic density (as in the "participle style"), the speakers of the New Kingdom tend to dissolve this density, expanding the individual parts of the construction. A Middle Egyptian sentence like *gmỉ.n=ỉ zỉ sḏr.w* "and I found the man sleeping", appears as *ỉw=ỉ gm pȝ zỉ ỉw=f sḏr* in Late Egyptian (or, etymologically, *ỉw=ỉ ḥr gm.t pȝ zỉ ỉw=f sḏr.w*).

This tendency to make features explicit is expressed morphologically too. Grammatical or semantic features which were formerly expressed through one or few morphemes are now distributed among a larger number of morphemes. This is accompanied by a tendency for linguistic "items defined" to change places with the "items defining", i.e. to place the defining expressions in the "kernel"-position of a syntagma or a group of expressions. These principles can be illustrated thus:

appearance of more explicit features

Middle Egyptian *sḏm.n=f* is synthetically constructed from the root morpheme {*sḏm*} that carries the lexical meaning "hear", and to which the dependent morpheme {*.n*} is joined, thus giving it the meaning "have heard"; with the "3rd person singular masculine" {*=f*} "suffix pronoun" affixed to the stem, {*sḏm.n*} carries both meaning and conjugation. Its char-

principles of synthetic forms

> **Synthetic and analytic types of language:** A characteristic of many languages — especially those W. von Humboldt termed "inflected" — is that certain linguistic elements (morphemes) can perform more than one function. Thus, in the English "he laughs", the morpheme {laugh} carries the meaning (is the lexeme), but is simultaneously the conjugation base, to which the morpheme {-s} is added, which at once signifies the person ("3rd pers."), number ("sing.") and tense ("present"). German and Latin are languages of the "synthetic" type. Linguistic evolution frequently follows a tendency (as in the case of Latin and the Romance languages) described as "analytic", whereby individual functions are distributed among several individual morphemes, rendering the phrase unambiguous: e.g. Latin *legi > habeo lectum > (j') ai lu* "I have read"; French (like English) is thus of the "analytic type".

acteristic conjugation form (generally: the so-called suffix conjugation) distinguishes it from the other conjugations. In Late Egyptian such a form is "analysed" into the "conjugation base" {*iri*} (with reference to tense, "past"), the "actor"-expression {*=f*} and the "meaning"-expression {*sdm*}: *iri=f sdm*.[1]

transfer of marking and "conversion"

The development of noun phrases is comparable, as may be shown with an example like *prw=n* "our house": the mark of grammatical gender (masc., ending -Ø), of specification (definite/indefinite; known/unknown) and of possession is removed from the form of the meaning-expression ("house"), and transferred

> Phrase; nucleus, satellite: All are concepts for the structural description of dependent parts of sentences, i.e., word groups or "phrases". In word groups like "the great house of the king", only the word "house" can stand alone for the entire group, while all the other words are dependent upon it. "House" is thus termed the kernel or "nucleus" of the phrase, and the dependent words are thus "satellites". As the nucleus of the inter-related group or phrase in the example is a noun, the phrase is termed a "noun phrase". If the nucleus is a verb, the phrase is then called a "verb phrase".

to the so-called "possessive article" — *p3y=n pr*. Dependence and independence of the constituents of the phrase are also settled through the relative positions of the constituents. The secondary position is generally indicative of dependence in Egyptian: While *prw* was the pivot of the Middle Egyptian noun phrase *prw=n*, its kernel or "nucleus", and the dependent suffix *=n* its "satellite", in the noun phrase *p3y=n pr* the article form *p3y=n* is now the nucleus of the phrase, with *pr* its satellite. This move in which the **defining** linguistic elements are transferred from the position of satellite to that of nucleus, and conversely the **defined** elements to that of satellite, has been termed "conversion" and is another feature of the "analytic tendency". The manifestations of the analytic tendency will now be pursued, allowing us a survey of the morphology of Late Egyptian.

2.0.2 Bibliography

analytic tendency

F. Hintze, Die Haupttendenzen der ägyptischen Sprachentwicklung, in: *Zeitschrift für Phonetik und allgemeine Sprachwissenschaft* 1, 1947, 85ff; id., 'Konversion' und 'analytische Tendenz' in der ägyptischen Sprachentwicklung, in: *Phonetik* 4, 1950, 41ff; Loprieno, *Ancient Egyptian*, § 4.6.6

conversion

W. Schenkel, Die Konversion, ein Epiphänomen der kemischen (ägyptisch-koptischen) Sprachgeschichte, in: *MDAIK* 21, 1966, 123ff

---

1   Note that this example illustrates the process, but is historically incorrect: the periphrastic *iri=f sdm* comes into use for most verbs only in Late Demotic; in Late Eyptian *sdm=f* has the function of Middle Egyptian *sdm.n=f*.

2.1 Modifying the noun

2.1.1 Determination and its forms

An apparently easily recognizable feature of Late Egyptian is the use of the articles of articles and the *p3, t3, n3*-series. This is, however, more apparent than real. Although Late Egyptian demonstratives texts constantly employ this article, its appearance need not be assumed to betray typological Late Egyptian, as the following must be taken into account:

1. the article is morphologically derived from the similar forms of the earlier demonstrative pronoun;

2. it is by no means immediately clear at what time, and in which texts, the deictic function was reduced to the article function — meaning that some apparent examples of the article are actually still that of the demonstratives;

3. some uses of the demonstratives already in Middle Egyptian (and Late Middle Egyptian) no longer imply the deictic role of the demonstrative, but rather its use as an article (such as *pn* in the "Eloquent Peasant").

Finally it should be noted that such article functions as "definite"/"indefinite", "aforementioned"/"newly introduced" etc. are implicit in Middle Egyptian nouns; in particular the possessive suffixes attached to nouns carry out some of these functions.

With the exception of the *p3, t3, n3*-series, Middle Egyptian demonstrative pronouns position of follow the noun which they specify: ⌐□ *prw pn* "this house"/"the house". The modifiers specified noun is the nucleus of the phrase, and the specifying pronoun its satellite. In Late Egyptian, however, the structure of these noun phrases follows the model of the *p3*-series, with analytic change and conversion moving the pronouns from the satellite position into the nuclear position, and the semantic elements into the satellite position: *p3y pr* "this house".

Middle Egyptian demonstratives agreed with the modified noun in gender and number; indication of apart from fulfilling the article role, Late Egyptian articles themselves also serve to gender and indicate the gender and number of the specified noun (just like the articles in some number European languages): ⸢𓀀⸣ *p3 Rᶜw* "the sun-god Re" > "Re"; ⸢𓀀⸣ *t3 p.t* "the sky". This again is a consequence of the analytical tendency; it leads in turn to a corresponding tendency for the gender and number morphemes of the nouns (*-t, -w*) to be either dropped entirely or to lose their marker role, so that *-t* and *-w* remain only to indicate the end of the word. Even the gender of those words which were formerly not outwardly recognizable as feminine is thus rendered explicit, such as ⸢𓀀⸣ *t3 d3d3w* "the jar".

Possession, which was signalled by adding suffix pronouns to the noun, and occasion- possessive ally still is, is similarly transferred to the article — *prw=n* "our house", ⌐□ , is article construed as *p3=n prw* > *p3y=n pr*, ⟨hieroglyphs⟩ . This form is termed the possessive article, following the term used for its successor in Coptic.[2]

2.1.2 Determiners: suffix pronouns, demonstratives and articles

Like all languages, Late Egyptian possessed a network of forms specifying the range of reference of the noun. These are:

(1) Suffix pronouns

Suffix pronouns were frequently used in Late Egyptian as possessive pronouns attached to nouns of specific semantic classes (namely nouns denoting inalienable things), and as the objects of infinitives, but also as subjects of certain conjugations. Forms:

1.s.c.	*=j; =i*	⟨glyphs⟩	f. marked only by the graphemes; *=tw* after syllable-final *-t*: *ms.t* "to bear" > *mis⁻'* > MICE, but *ms.t=i* "to bear me" > MACT
2.s.m.	*=k*	⟨glyphs⟩	
f.	*= '; =t*	⟨glyphs⟩	*=t* > secondary glottal stop, graphemically ø
3.s.m.	*=f*	⟨glyphs⟩	*=twf* after syllable-final *-t*
f.	*=s*	⟨glyphs⟩	
1.pl.c.	*=n*	⟨glyphs⟩	*=tn* as a rule after syllable-final *-t*
2.pl.c.	*=tn*	⟨glyphs⟩	*=twtn* after syllable-final *-t*; cf. Coptic -THYTÑ
3.pl.c.	*=sn*	⟨glyphs⟩	*=sn* is in reality only *=s'*
	=w	⟨glyphs⟩	

Observations:

3rd pl. *=sn* remained in use in texts ranking higher in the register hierarchy. Its replacement form *=w* appears initially with prepositions, and next, following *iw* (*iw=w* in place of *iw=sn*).

Since the grapheme for the morpheme of the gender-neutral 1st pers. sing. (*=i*, or more precisely, the glottal stop *= '*) can vary according to the gender of the speaker (⟨glyph⟩ or ⟨glyph⟩), the

---

2   Articles and possessive articles are written with group writing signs; a better transliteration would thus be *p=n*, by analogy with Coptic ΠЄΝ-. The traditional transliteration is, however, retained to ensure compatability.

suffix 𓀀 can on occasion be used as grapheme for the 2nd pers. sing. fem. too, representing its phonemically secondary glottal stop; conversely the grapheme ⌒ of the 2nd pers. sing. fem., equally representing this secondary glottal stop, can be used for the 1st pers. sing. of a female speaker.

It should be noted the Late Egyptian conventional form of reference to a general state of affairs ("something"; so-called neuter) is the 3rd sing. masc., occasionally, but less so, the 3rd sing. fem., as generally in Middle Egyptian; the enclitic pronouns (cf. § 2.2.1) still use mainly *st*.

(2) Articles and demonstratives

Articles and demonstratives and their derivatives form related sets as follows:

	Definite			Indefinite	
	sing. masc.	sing. fem.	pl.	sing.	pl.
Demonstratives	*[hierogl.]* ΠΑΪ/ ΠЄ	*[hierogl.]* ΤΑΪ/ ΤЄ	*[hierogl.]* ΝΑΪ/ ΝЄ		
Articles	*[hierogl.]* Π-	*[hierogl.]* Τ-	*[hierogl.]* Ν-	*[hierogl.]* ΟΥ-	*[hierogl.]* ϨЄΝ-
Possessive articles	*[hierogl.]* ΠЄϤ-	*[hierogl.]* ΤЄϤ-	*[hierogl.]* ΝЄϤ-		
Possessive prefix	*[hierogl.]* ΠΑ-	*[hierogl.]* ΤΑ-	*[hierogl.]* ΝΑ-		

Observations:

In the plural of all forms and in the indefinite article, the marking of the grammatical genders is neutralized.

Demonstratives *p3y, t3y, n3y* have a less common parallel form *p3w* (where the number and gender are not specified) which can be used absolutely (as an independent noun) or in front of relative clauses (of the type "that one who"), cf. Erman, *Neuägyptische Grammatik*, §§ 120-121).

articles The forms shown reflect those of the hieratic texts; hieroglyphic texts write *p3* without the complementary *3* using Gardiner's sign G40. The plural *n3* and the indefinite article *wᶜ* initially follow the earlier construction *n3 n* or *wᶜ n*; the plural indefinite article (*nhy*) is not as common as in Coptic, the usual form of the non-definite noun in plural being the noun without an article, but accompanied by plural marking (in the transcription, occasionally indicated as zero-article, Ø-, following S. Groll).

Possessive   Possession is indicated through the addition of the suffix pronouns (*pꜣy=f,*
articles   *tꜣy=f, nꜣy=f*); in the 1st sing. the suffix can be left unmarked (cf. Coptic ΠΑ-).

Possessive   *p(ꜣ) n, tꜣ n.t, nꜣy.w (n)*: Abbreviated compounds of the article/ demonstrative
prefixes   series *pꜣ, tꜣ, nꜣ* with a "genitive" *-n*, meaning "he of/she of" (*p-n ḫtꜣ* "He
              of Hatti").

The independent pronouns of the nominal sentence (cf. § 4.1.2 infra) like [hieroglyphs], [hieroglyphs],
[hieroglyphs] and special forms for the 2nd sing., [hieroglyphs] *twt*, and the 3rd sing., [hieroglyphs] or [hieroglyphs]
swt have, when following a noun, a function as possessive pronouns, like *pr ỉnk* "my house"
("that house of mine").

2.1.3 Use of the determiners

(1) Determination by articles and demonstratives

As a rule of thumb, it can be stated that for the determination of nouns Late Egyptian
articles and demonstratives conform to their general rules of use in modern French, and are in principle similar to those of German or — less so — English.

demonstratives — Demonstrative pronouns refer to objects of speech in the speech situation ("this table here", "this remark"), recalling them to memory or to clarify their position, by reference to previous or current use ("this type of remark"; "that paragraph").

definite articles — Definite articles identify objects of speech as being familiar in the speech situation, whether because they have just been made familiar (explicitly introduced: "A temple was on the river. The temple is dedicated to Amun") or have already been touched on in the discourse ("the aforementioned"; "the thing named"), or whether because they are common knowledge — epistemologically known or culturally familiar (*pꜣ-Rꜥw* "the sun") — or acquire the character of an identification (designation; proper name).

> Determination in a general sense signifies the means by which the range of meaning of a given noun is limited and defined. Not every object in the object class "tree" is thus intended, but only a smaller set of specifically "defined trees". These can be: specified quantities ("some trees", or "all trees" - the latter signifying the entire class as a set of all of the individual members!), objects within reach ("this tree") or those within the speaker's sphere ("his tree"). They can also be things which have been or are now introduced ("A tree is in front of the door; the tree is a birch"), or the reference can be to one member of the class ("a tree") or to the class itself ("the tree is a plant"/"trees are plants"), or to the indication that the class is organized and subdivided ("the trees"/"trees" — there is no plural of indivisible classes like "gold"). "Designations"/"labels" are nouns whose range of meaning is limited and defined to one object, such as proper names. Such defined nouns belong to the set of the "definite" nouns.

— Indefinite articles modify objects of speech by introducing them into the speech situation as previously unmentioned, or not otherwise familiar.

indefinite articles

The following examples illustrate a few of these usages:

(pAbbott 7,8-9)

ḏd pȝy ḥȝ.ty-ᶜ n Nw.t nhy n mdw n nȝ rwḏ.w rmṯ-ỉz.t n pȝ ḫr (The Vizier speaks to the members of the Great Commission): "The Mayor of Thebes (present) has made accusations concerning the controllers and the workmen of the Tomb Building Administration".

Notes:

demonstrative *pȝy*	literally "this Mayor": he belongs to the investigative and judicial commission and is present, and being pointed out.
nhy n mdw	"some words" > "words";
article *nȝ*	the article in *nȝ rwḏ.w* could point to a an earlier reference to the *rwḏ.w* in the text, or to an earlier mention in the speech: it should, however, be assumed that this actually signals the general familiarity of the controllers to the members of the commission.
co-ordination	the combination of *nȝ rwḏ.w* with *rm ṯ-ỉz.t* shows that with co-ordinated nouns ("and"), only the first noun is complemented with the article (the same applies for *ḥnᶜ* "together with; and" or *ḥr*), or more precisely: that the first article applies to all co-ordinated nouns (cf. also Erman, *Neuägyptische Grammatik*, § 192); occasionally suffixes rather than possessive articles accomplish the determination within such series of co-ordinated nouns;
article *pȝ*	in the phrase *pȝ ḫr* determines generally: "The Tomb" is a familiar institution, more precisely, the department of the "Supreme Authority for Works" in the Vizierate, which is responsible for the construction of the royal tomb — and specifically that of the reigning king. This designatory and/or denominative usage of the article is common with many — culturally familiar — institutions.

(Doomed Prince 4,7-9)

ỉw=f ḥr ṯzy r tȝy=f tp-ḥw.t

ỉw=f ḥr gmḥ wᶜ n ṯzm ỉw=f m-sȝ wᶜ n zỉ ˁȝ ...

ỉw=f ḥr ḏd n pȝy=f sḏm nty r-gs=f ỉḫ pȝ nty ḥr šm.t m-sȝ pȝ zỉ ˁȝ nty m ỉy.t ḥr tȝ mỉ.t

ỉw=f (ḥr) ḏd n=f ṯsm pȝy

(The young prince became older.) "And he went up to his housetop, saw a greyhound pursuing an adult man,[3] ...., and said to his servant beside him, 'What is that going after the adult who is coming on the way?' And he said to him: 'That is a greyhound.'"

Notes:

construction	this passage is part of one of those long chains which are constructed with *ỉw=f ḥr sḏm* in Late Egyptian, which is the "circumstantial" form of the Adverbial Sentence or so-called First Present, but which is also termed the "narrative" or "non-initial main sentence" form;
possessive article *t3y=f tp-ḥw.t*	the "solid house" in the desert, in which the Prince lives and which he may not leave, has been treated in the portion of the text that precedes the part cited here;
indefinite article *wˁ (n)*	an indication of the first appearance of a single member of a structured class of semantic items (people, dogs) in speech, text or discourse;
p3 z.t	note the writing of *zỉ* "man", and how the feminine marking is overruled by the masculine article;
article (or possessive article) before relative clauses	the antecedent or reference noun (likewise the unnamed "one who/which"; Egyptian *p3 nty*) is restricted in its range of meaning by the specifying relative clause, and thus has the definite article, which refers forward to the relative clause. The use of the possessive article would actually suggest a translation like "that one of his servants, who stood beside him";
article *t3 mỉ.t*	the very well known way which leads to the prince's palace in the desert;
demonstrative *p3y*	the demonstrative pronouns (as nuclei of the noun clause) can also serve as nouns (here in the Nominal Sentence).

> **Verse points:** As in the story of the "Doomed Prince" (cf. the cited passage, 4, 7-9), many literary and school-texts have clauses marked with black or (more often) red dots. These have been called "verse points" or "dots", and divide the text into a well-proportioned flow of units of meaning (compare the prose rhythm of Classical texts).

(Wenamun 2,75)

ỉw n3y.w t3 dmỉ.t pr r=ỉ r ḫdb=ỉ

(The wind drove Wenamun's ship onto the shores of Alashia.) "And the townspeople came forth against me, to kill me."

Commentary Note:

> *n3y.w t3 dmỉ.t* "those of the town" (possessive prefix before the definite article); actually *dmỉ(.t)* is grammatically masculine, here perhaps modified to the grammatically feminine gender of topographical names and the names of countries (cf. Gardiner, *Grammar*, § 92).

For further examples cf. § 2.1.4(1).

vocative
— In contrast to modern English, but as in ancient Greek, the definite article can also mark the vocative (like *pn* in Middle Egyptian), designating the listener in the speech situation as familiar, where the person is not addressed with a proper name:

(oDM 1262 vs. 5)
ỉnk p3y=k b3k p3 nb Ḫmnw "I am your servant, O Lord of Hermopolis" (the hieroglyphic text is given supra, § 1.3.2);

(Doomed Prince 5,10-11)
ỉy=k tnw p3 šrỉ nfr "Where do you come from, handsome boy?" (for the hieroglyphic text cf. infra, § 3.3.1[3]).

3   Lit. "being behind an adult".

— Among the determiners is *nb*, "all; every" as it defines the applicability of a noun *nb* "all; every" with reference to "every single" of "all the members" of a given set:

(Doomed Prince 5,5)

ỉw=f ḥr dỉ.t ỉn.tw šrỉ.w nb n wr.w nb n p3 t3 n Ḫ-r (The ruler of Mitanni) "He had all the sons of all the princes of the Land of Syria be brought", in the sense of "every single son of every single prince".

An article and *nb* are mutually exclusive (incompatible); their defining effects can be *article and nb* combined only when defining relative phrases: *p3 nty nb m ỉy.t ḥr t3 mỉ.t* "any one of those who are going down the road" > "all those who are going down the road".

Observation:

The demonstrative series *pn, tn* — it is *hrww pn* "this day" in reference to a previously specified date, but *p3 hrww* "today"; "now" (*p3* with demonstrative function) — continues to be used in some expressions and in texts ranked higher in the hierarchy of registers (state ideological and liturgical texts, cf. § 0.2.1).

(2) Absence of articles; determination through suffix pronouns

When considering the significance of the lack of an article, it is important to assess the linguistic register to which a text belongs. The earlier form of determination — avoiding articles and demonstratives — is encountered in those texts reflecting the norms of the hierarchically higher and more conservative registers. The following considerations apply primarily and typically only to the colloquial and literary registers:

Apart from the lack of an article (Ø-article) which marks non-definite plural nouns (cf. supra § 2.1.2[2]), determination in a narrower sense is either undesirable or unconventional in conjunction with certain (indicated or consciously introduced) semantic qualities of the noun, or it bears a particular connotation.

— In order to classify (assign expressions to semantic classes) the noun is left without an article. Nouns thus appear without articles *nouns without articles: classification*

> **Speaker, listener, speech situation:** A speech situation is an abstraction of the specific location in space and time in which communication takes place. This location can be real, as in a conversation or dialogue, or, as a rule, imaginary, created by discourse through a series of texts of mutual relationship, "co-texts". A speaker — "I" (sometimes the author) — conveys to a listener — "You" (reader) — a piece of linguistically coded information, whereby both speaker and listener may constantly change. The speaker expresses what he wants to talk about (object of speech, "he, she, it"), which can be concrete or abstract, can be in a real or imaginary speaking space or cannot (can be pointed out or not), which is familiar to the speaker and/or the listener or must be introduced, and he conveys a message (a statement) about this object of speech.

   °   in the typically classifying Nominal sentence: *ṯzm pȝy* "that is dog-like" ("that belongs to the class 'greyhound'", cf. supra, § 2.1.3[1]);

   °   when following prepositions: *m ḥȝq* "as booty"; *m sẖr.w n ỉtỉ* "in a fatherly manner" (> "in the ways of fathers"); *ỉw=s n=f r ḥm.t* "She will be wife to him"; frequently in expressions of time: *m rwhȝ* "at nightfall";

   °   and in verb-object compounds: *ḏd smy* "report" (<* "give a report"); *ỉr.t ꜥnḫ n nṯr* "swear by god" (< "make an oath by god"). Examples:

(pTurin 1972,7 = LRL 7,14-15)

ỉw=f dỉ.t n=ỉ ø-ꜥq.w ø-ḥnk.t m pȝy=ỉ sẖr n ḥr-ḥȝ.t "And he gave me bread and beer according to my previous custom";

Note:

     ỉw=f dỉ.t the form of *ỉw=f ḥr dỉ.t* in Late Egyptian proper.

(pBM 10052, 16,13)

NN ỉw=f m ø-hȝy m.dỉ tȝy=f sn.t šrỉ "(NN,) being husband to his younger sister";

(pBM 10054 rt. 1,6)

ỉw=n dỉ.t ø-ḫ.t ỉm=w m ø-grḥ (We took the coffins) "and we set them on fire at night"; *m pȝ grḥ* would mean "tonight".

Observation:

Coptic nouns are also used without articles following these same rules (cf. Till, *Koptische Grammatik*, §§ 103-108), as in ⲀⲨ̇ⲬⲒ ⲘⲘⲞⲤ ⲚⲀⲒ Ⲛ̄Ⲥ2ⲒⲘⲈ "I took her to wife".

designations for inalienable objects

   — A closed set of nouns, defined by the feature of being "designations for inalienable objects" do not take an article. Possession of them is indicated with a suffix pronoun. To this group belong the words for:

   °   parts of the body: *ỉr.t* "eye"; *rȝ* "mouth"; *ỉb / ḥȝ.ty* "heart"; "mind"; *ḥr* "face"; *ḏȝḏȝ* "head"; *ḥꜥ* "body"; *ẖȝ.t* "belly"; etc.;

   °   terms related to persons, such as *rn* "name"; *ḏs* "self"; *ꜥ* "condition", "state"; etc.;

   °   property and income, such as *ȝḥ.t/ỉḥ.t* "things"; *hȝw* "possessions"; *bȝk.w* "payment"; *ḥr.t/dnỉ.t* "portion", "share"; etc.;

   °   certain specific topographic designations, such as *pr* "household"; *s.t* "place"; *nw.t* "city";

   °   kinship terms (*m'w.t* "mother"; *zȝ* "son") followed by a proper name in apposition.

Observation:

The nouns listed above are generally those which were still combined with suffix pronouns later in Coptic (cf. Till, *Koptische Grammatik*, § 188; Lambdin, *Sahidic Coptic*, §§ 28.6; 29.4) and which partly have a separate phonemic structure for these constructions (status pronominalis), as in ⲦⲰⲢⲈ, ⲦⲞⲞⲦ≠ϥ "hand", "his hand"; ⲢⲀⲚ, ⲢⲒⲚ≠ϥ "name", "his name".

Occasionally constructions formed with article + noun + suffix also appear, signalling that the functions are as it were "distributed": *p3 wb3=i* "the (temple) forecourt of mine" (says the god Amenophis; *LRL* 28,6); *p3 pr=f* "the household of his" (oDM 303).

— In the various text registers, theological terms, and those of the cult or state administration (e.g., *ḥḏ.t* "The White Crown"; *t3.ty* "the Vizier"; *pr-ˁ3* "Pharaoh"; etc.) can still be found as used in earlier ages, i.e. without articles but with suffix pronouns, if the notion of possession is possible. The usage with or without article varies depending on whether the speakers in question consider these expressions to be common nouns or proper nouns.   *traditional terms*

2.1.4 Attributive modification: Nominal and adjectival satellites of the noun

The range of meaning of any given noun can be controlled or modified by another noun, an adjective, a nominal or adjectival phrase, or sometimes even by an adverbial phrase (Old Perfective as adverbial attribute).

On the one hand its range of meaning can be limited by relating it to the range of meaning of another noun; this is brought about by noun combinations in which the second noun determines the first. Such combinations can be accomplished through direct juxtaposition of the two nouns, either by "apposition" or a "direct genitive" — more precisely: a construct combination. Apposition names an alternative, while the construct/direct genitive modifies by limiting the range of meaning.   *direct nominal attribute*

The combination of the two nouns can also be established by linking the two with the phrase linker *n*, the so-called indirect genitive. The usage bears in fact some resemblance to that of the Indo-European attributive genitives, but the Egyptian construction was originally adjectival (a *nisbe*-adjective formed from a preposition). The functional contrasts that formerly distinguished the direct and indirect   *indirect nominal attribute; phrase conjunction n*

> **Construct; direct Genitive:** A nucleus-satellite combination of two nouns, where the first is the nucleus (governing noun/regens) and the second, the satellite, grammatically dependent (attribute/governed noun/rectum), specifies its meaning, can be so close that the phonematic form of the nuclear noun is considerably reduced through loss of stress and tone (status constructus), cf. Coptic ⲞⲞⲨ "day" in ⲞⲨ-ⲘⲒⲤⲈ "birthday". This "construct combination" is called direct genitive; it is, however, a misleading term since Egyptian does not have a case system (and the same is thus true of the "indirect genitive"). The Egyptian construct combination is formally and semantically quite similar to English compounds like "sunrise", "earthquake", "Vanity Fair", or "women students"; in contrast to Egyptian, it is, however, the first noun which determines and the second one which is determined and the nucleus of the phrase in English.

genitives (specification versus characterization) disappear in Late Egyptian, however: following the analytic tendency, the indirect modification supplants the direct one.

modification by adjectives and relative clauses

On the other hand, the range of meaning of a noun can also be limited by naming those attributes or qualities that the object denoted by the noun should have to make a statement about it valid. Apart from adjectives and relative clauses, particular forms of the verb fulfil this role: the participles and relative forms. Since such participial phrases are nothing but nouns formed from verbs, this type of modification is nothing but a variation of modification through accompanying nouns (apposition; construct/direct genitive), resulting from the semantic quality of the words employed (i.e. denoting qualities); the adjectival attribute can be used as an independent noun, too.

(1) Apposition

Nominal modifications of nouns are termed apposition when they themselves could formally be used with the same significance in place of the modified noun, being merely alternative indications. The most frequent use is with personal names (e.g., modifying names through titles; titles through names). Appositional nouns immediately follow their governing noun/ their nucleus with an article (either definite or indefinite; indefinite, if the naming of a person accompanies that person's introduction into the speech situation):

(pLee 1,3 = KRI V 362, 2-3)

iw=f di.t n=f w^c zḫȝ n rn.w n (Wsr-mȝ^c.t-R^cw mri-ʾImnw)| ^c.w.s. pȝ nṯr ^cȝ pȝy=f nb ^c. w. s. "And he gave him a letter of safe conduct (< 'letter of names') of Usimaare Miamun, the Great God, his lord" (for other readings cf. Neveu, *BIFAO* 59, 2002, 265f);

(Wenamun 2,68-69)

 *iw=f di.t in.tw n=i Tȝ-n.t-Nw.t w^c ḥs(.t) n Km(.t)* "And he had Tentna, an Egyptian singer, brought to me";

Note:

> *Tȝ-n.t-Nw.t*   the woman's name, Tentna, is an "appellative name", and an example of the use of the possessive prefix sing. fem.: "she of 'the city'" > "the Theban".

A pronoun can be modified only by means of apposition:

(HorSeth 5,13)

iw=i di.t n=k tȝy wḫȝ.t wn.in=f ḥr ḏd n=s iw=s iḫ n=i tȝy=t wḫȝ.t (Isis said:) "'I will give you this cake'; whereupon he said to her, 'What is it to me, your cake?!'"

Notes:

> *ỉw=ỉ dỉ.t*   the Late Egyptian form for expressions concerning the future, the so called Third Future *ỉw=ỉ r dỉ.t*; during the New Kingdom, the preposition *r* was increasingly neglected. In contrast to the form *ỉw=ỉ dỉ.t*, which looks exactly like it, but is from *ỉw=ỉ ḥr dỉ.t* (the Circumstantial Present), the Third Future stands at the very beginning of a paragraph (following "Isis said:");
>
> *ỉw=s ỉḫ*   it is possible that Gardiner was correct in suggesting that an *r* be inserted (*ỉw=s <r>ỉḫ*), but it is more probable that the same tendency eliminating the *r* in the Third Future was responsible for its loss here (transition to Coptic Є-).

In longer assemblages, apposition has a tendency to displace the other satellites of the nominal phrase:

rmṯ-ỉz.t ʾImnw-m-ỉn.t zꜣ Ḥ-y n pꜣ ḫr "workman of the Tomb Building Administration, (*pAbbott 5,4*) Amen-em-ine, son of Hay" (< *"man of the Gang Amen-em-ine, son of Huya, of the 'Tomb'").

(2) The direct nominal attribute (Direct Genitive)

The construct combination, with direct attribution of nouns, is still used, but less significant in comparison with its frequency and productivity in the earlier periods. It is still common in those groups of words which employ suffix pronouns rather than possessive prefixes, and in those still widely used phrases where the "rectum" (the modifying second noun) is without an article, phrases which lead to some Coptic attributive compounds and nominal prefixes (e.g., ϬꞆ-ⲬⲞⲈⲒⲦ "olive leaf", from ϬⲱⲱⲂⲈ "leaf"; ⲘⲚ̄Ⲧ-ⲢⲰⲘⲈ "mankind" < **md.t-rmṯ*): such combinations have the character of compound nouns.

Observation: *ky* "other"

Those constructions with the words for "other" also belong here, with the forms masc. sing. ⸗🪶 *ky*, fem. sing. ⸔ *kt*, pl. ⸔ ⊚⸰🪶⸗ *ktḫ* (in Coptic undifferentiated ⲔⲈ-): *ky/kt* assume the role of the specified noun (regens), followed by the specifying noun as an attribute (rectum), *kt ḥm.t* "another woman" (< **"a womanly other"), *ktḫ sḫr.w* "other plans"; these words are nouns and are used as such by themselves, as *ky* "another" (with usage similar to that of Coptic ⲔⲈ/ ⲔⲈ, ⲔⲈⲦ, fem. ⲔⲈⲦⲈ, pl. ⲔⲞⲞⲨⲈ), or in the introductory phrases of letters, meaning "furthermore" and suchlike. If the regens is defined (*pꜣ ky*), it can signify "the other (man)" or alternatively, "and also the (man)": *pꜣy ky rn* "(he bore) this other name as well" (cf. Erman, *Neuägyptische Grammatik*, § 240; Till, *Koptische Grammatik*, § 230).

— A nominal attribute (rectum) without an article classifies the regens. Under the conditions listed (§ 2.1.3), the regens itself can be defined or not (and the intended nuance can usually be reproduced in the translation). Examples: *ḫrw ỉs-b-r* "whip snap" (< *"sound, typical of whips"); *tꜣ ꜥ.t sbꜣ.w* "the school" (< *"the house of instruction"; "the instruction house"); *tꜣ s.t qrs* "the place of burial", "the burial-place"; *rectum without an article* [hieroglyphs] *st ḥr ìr.t t3y=sn íp.t db.t m mn.t* "They are making up their brick quota daily";

Note:

> *st ḥr ìr.t* the use of an unintroduced dependent pronoun (here of the 3rd pers. plur.) is characteristic of the Late Egyptian Adverbial Sentence (or First Present).

[hieroglyphs]

[hieroglyphs]

[hieroglyphs]

wn.ìn p3 sty n t3 nbd šnty ḥr ḫpr m n3 n ḥbs.w n Pr-ꜥ3

ìw=tw ꜥḥ3 m.dì n3 n rḫ.tyw n Pr-ꜥ3 ꜥ.w.s m ḏd

sty sgnn m n3 n ḥbs.w n Pr-ꜥ3

(A braid of the maiden's hair is swept onto the beach where the king's clothes are washed.) "Thereupon the fragrance of the braid clung to Pharaoh's clothing, and (the Royal) One argued with Pharaoh's washermen, saying 'Unguent fragrance is in the clothes of Pharaoh!'"

Notes:

> *t3 nbd šnty* "the lock of hair", "the braid";
>
> *p3 sty n t3 nbd* vs. "the fragrance of the braid" is presented to the reader as something self-evidently
> *sty sgnn* existent, as natural, but "fragrance of unguent", "unguent fragrance" is something unexpected in washed clothes, and furthermore something that can only be classified most generally.

Constructs of this type are frequent in professional and occupational titles, such as *zḫ3.w pr-ḥḏ* "Secretary of the Treasury"; *p3 wḥꜥ-3pd* "the bird catcher" > "the fowler".

defined rectum — A defined nominal attribute (rectum) is used if it is a specific designation, a "labelling noun", or a proper noun (a name or an identifying term analogous to names, as with cultural or epistemological definiteness). The combination itself then assumes designatory character or marks possession in the sense for which the suffix pronouns were still used in Late Egyptian (cf. supra § 2.1.3[2]): *ḥr ìmnt.t p3-ḫr* "west of 'the Tomb'", *t3 ìn.t p3 ꜥš* "the valley of the fir-tree" (not "the fir-tree valley"!); *t3 ḫ3s.t Gbty* "the Coptos Mountains" ("the desert mountains of Coptos").

[hieroglyphs]

[hieroglyphs]

ìw=w ḥmsì m t3 wsḫ.t Ḥrw ḫnty ꜥb.w ìw=tw dì.t p3 wḫ3 m ḏr.t Ḏḥwty "(Now the letter from Neith the Great, the God's mother, reached the Divine Assembly/the Ennead), when they had seated themselves in the hall 'Horus with the Horned Crown', and the letter was placed in Thoth's hand."

Notes:

tȝ wsḫ.t Ḥrw   understood as apposition, but the name could also be understood as a direct nominal attribute "the hall of 'Horus with the Horned Crown'";

m ḏr.t Ḏḥwty   a labelling rectum (name) following a part of the body.

(3) The indirect nominal attribute (Indirect Genitive)

In some traditional uses and in certain hierarchically higher text registers, the phrase linker *n* can still agree with its governing noun, the regens, but in colloquial and literary registers it tends to become invariable. The forms *nt* (occasionally *nty*) and *nw* are generally mere variants or allographs of *n* (and thus no longer markers of gender and number agreement). In this construction, the regens is generally determined by definite or indefinite articles.

— The defined nominal attribute indicates possession and relationship: *nȝ sty n tȝ nbd šnty* "the fragrance of the braid" and *nȝ n ḥbs.w n Pr-ʕȝ* "the clothes of Pharaoh" ("Pharaoh" is an identifying term, "name"; both references to pD'Orb 10,8-10/*LES*, cited above); *nȝ rwḏ.w rmṯ-ỉz.t n pȝ ḫr* "the controllers and workmen of the Tomb Building Administration" (pAbbott 7,8-9; cited above); *wʕ ḥs.t n Km.t* "a singer of Egypt" (Wenamun 2,68-69; cited above); also in chains of attributes like *šrỉ.w nb n wr.w nb n pȝ tȝ n Ḫ-r* "all the sons of all the princes of the land of Syria" (Doomed Prince 5,5; cited supra p. 55). Toponyms and names of countries (*Km.t*; *Ḫ-r*) function as defined nouns. [defined rectum: possession and relationship]

— The undefined nominal attribute without an article classifies its regens by describing its range of meaning (as in English, "the performance of plays"; "the art of love"). This descriptive specification frequently performs the role of an adjective in denoting quality (as in English, "a man of courage"). The construction is thus used [rectum without an article: classification and qualities]

to indicate material or composition:

(HorSeth 6,1)

ỉw=ỉ dỉ.t n=k pȝ ḫtm n nbw nty m ḏr.t(=ỉ) "I will give you the signet-ring of gold I am wearing" (> "the golden signet-ring");

Notes:

ỉw=ỉ dỉ.t   the Late Egyptian form for expressing the future *ỉw=ỉ (r) dỉ.t* "I shall give";

nty m ḏr.t=ỉ   lit. "which is on my hand";

cf. also, *pȝ ỉmw n psš.t* "the tent of mats"; *wrrỉ.t ʕȝ.t nt ḏʕm* "the great chariot of electrum" (Boundary stele U, line 4, infra, § 2.1.7[1]);

to indicate size and content:

(pD'Orb 8,6)   [hieroglyphs]   *mtw=tw ḥr dỉ.t n=k wꜥ n*

ṯbw n ḥnq.t ḥr ḏr.t=k "..., if a jar of beer is placed in your hands (and it overflows...)";

Notes:

> *mtw=tw ḥr dỉ.t*   for *mtw=tw dỉ.t*, the Late Egyptian form used to continue a future expression, the so-called "conjunctive"; forms with *ḥr* — as here — are not etymologically correct, but occur;
>
> cotext   the phrase is preceded by *ḥr ỉw=k ꜥm r ḏd wn.w nk.t r=ỉ* "And you will know that something has happened to me";

to indicate manner and nature:

(pLansing 6,1-2)   [hieroglyphs]

ỉ.ỉr=f tꜣy=f wnw.t n mtr.t n bꜣk.w n pꜣ ꜥḥwty "He spends his noontime for the rent of the cultivator." (< "his hour of midday");

Notes:

> *ỉ.ỉr=f*   Late Egyptian nominal or emphatic *sdm=f*, "he does, i.e. spends, his noontime";
>
> *bꜣk.w n pꜣ ꜥḥwty*   an example of a regens without an article: the "fee" to be paid to the supervisor, the "fee" that is customarily paid by every tenant-farmer ("the" tenant-farmer as a social group). The preceding *n* is the preposition, and not the phrase linker.

If the undefined rectum is abstract, its qualifying — adjectival — character is particularly clear:

(pLansing 11,3)   [hieroglyphs]   *qd=ỉ n=k bḫn n mꜣw(.t)* "I will build you a new villa";

Notes:

> *qd=ỉ*   prospective *sdm=f*, "I will (I intend to) build";
>
> *ø-bḫn*   the lack of an article can be ascribed to the traditionality of the register (school-texts/exercise letters/letter writer's guide) to which pLansing belongs.

Stories use a phrase *m pꜣy=f sḥr.w nty rꜥw-nb* ("according to his daily habit"), the meaning of which suggests that *nty* is merely a writing of *n* (cf. Erman, *Neuägyptische Grammatik*, § 214).

(4) Adverbial attributes

In contrast to Middle Egyptian, the adverbial modification of the noun (adnominal adverbs) occurs only occasionally, mostly in the higher ranks of the register hierarchy:

(Beatty Love Songs vs. C3,10)   [hieroglyphs]   *gm=ỉ ꜥꜣ=f wn* "I discovered that his door was open." (cf. § 2.2.6[2]);

Notes:

> gm=ỉ   Late Egyptian preterite sḏm=f;
>
> structure   sḏm=f with object; the object being the noun + attributive/adnominal Old Perfective.

Alternative explanations are possible (such as an object clause consisting of noun + Old Perfective); various explanations of this type will be discussed at length below.

(5) Adjectives and relative phrases (participles, relative forms and relative clauses)

Adjectives and relative phrases specify those features and qualities which characterize the nature and condition of the classes of nouns to which they refer. Adjectives and relative phrases can also be used as nouns ("nominalization", "complex nouns"). The grammatical gender of the complex nouns is masculine rather than feminine (p3 d.y n=s "that which was given her", rather than Middle Egyptian rdỉ.t n=s). In contrast to Middle Egyptian, however, adjectives, participles and relative forms are far less common than the relative clauses introduced with nty.

— As in Middle Egyptian, Late Egyptian adjectives are primarily derived from verbs: participles of verbs of quality and state such as nfr "be good", ꜥ3 "be large/great" (>adjectives), or participles from fientic verbs (verbs that express action or process). With few exceptions, they no longer agree with their antecedents: they have become invariable in gender and number (fem. and plural graphemes are occasionally added, but they merely indicate adjectivity). *adjective formation*

The derivation of adjectives from nouns or prepositional phrases with the help of the suffix -.y (nisbe-adjectives) is no longer productive. In Late Egyptian, such derived adjectives are lexicalized, i.e. have become individual words with adjectival meaning — the core of a new substitutional category (part of speech) of "real", non-derived adjectives, e.g., p3 ḏw rs.y-ỉ3b.ty n 3ḫ.t-ꜣ̉Itn "the southeastern mountain of Akhet-Aten" (Boundary Stele U, line 8; cf. infra § 2.1.7[1]). *nisbe-adjectives*

> **Participles, Relative forms:** The semantic and morpho-syntactic relationships between participles and relative forms in Late Egyptian are still best understood in terms of nominalization: they derive from the semantic complex of the verb, insofar as one of the arguments of the verb, the actor (agent/ subject), object, or rection (necessary adverbial complement) becomes the nucleus of a noun phrase, and the other become satellites.

Actor nominalization	Object nominalization without actor	Object nominalization with actor	Rection nominalization
active participle	passive participle	relative form	"indirect" relat. form/ passive participle
p3-dỉ n=s st	p3-d.y n=s	p3-dỉ=f n=s	t3-dỉ=f n=s st/ t3-d.y n=s st
"the one who gave it to her"	"that, which was given her"	"that which he gave her"	"she, to whom he gave it"/ "she, to whom it was given"

adjectives

The participles of adjective-verbs — but also *rḫ* "to know" — are not marked as such graphemically, but have the syllable structure and vocalic pattern of participles. Remnants of gender and number agreement can still be observed with *nfr* "good", "beautiful"; *bin* "evil"; *ꜥꜣ* "large/great" (in compounds still preserved in Coptic, e.g. masc. *nāfīr* > -ⲚⲞⲨϤⲈ; fem. *năfrăt* > -ⲚⲞϤⲢⲈ).

— Forms of participles and relative forms:

prefix *ỉ*.-

From Dyn. XIX on, the prefix *ỉ*.- (𓏶, 𓏶 or ⌒) marks the participles and relative forms of 2-rad. fientic/non-adjectival verbs (as *ḏd* "say") and those 3-rad. (*ḫpr* "become"; *ptr* "see"; *wꜥr* "flee"; *wꜣḥ* "lay down"; etc.) and 3ae inf. (*ỉr* "do"; *dỉ* "give"; *ỉy* "come"; *ỉn* "bring"; *gm* "find"; etc.) which have been reduced to two radicals, as well as some genuine 3-rad. verbs and the 4ae inf. verbs: 𓏶𓂝 *ỉ.ỉr* "acting", "he who acts"; 𓏶𓂧 *ỉ.ḏd* "who says"; 𓏶𓅓𓂋𓃀𓂻 *ỉ.hꜣb=k* "what you sent".

Where articles and demonstratives precede the prefix, it is assimilated and remains unwritten, *pꜣ-ỉ.ḏd* (*p-ỉ.ḏd*) > 𓆇𓂋𓂧 *pỉ.ḏd* "that one who speaks", but 𓆇𓏶𓂧 is also possible. Only rarely does the verb *wn* have the prefix.

passive ending

Primarily passive participles of mainly 3ae inf. transitive verbs (but also occasionally active participles) bear an ending -.*y*: mostly 𓏭, but also in forms like 𓏶𓂝𓏭𓏤 *ỉ.ỉr.y* "done"; 𓂞𓏭𓏛 *d.y* "given".

stem formation

The stem of the participles and relative forms is generally no longer subject to change. Where participles are written in the traditional fashion with reduplication/gemination of root consonants it should be taken into account that this is probably merely graphic variation (but cf. the note).

periphrasis with *ỉrỉ*

Increasingly, participles and relative forms (initially primarily those with more than three radicals) are formed with the participle (*ỉ.ỉr*) or the relative form (*ỉ.ỉr=f*) of *ỉrỉ* followed by the actual verbal expression in the infinitive, as *ỉ.ỉr qnqn* "he who hit". For verbs with three radicals or less, such *ỉ.ỉr*-periphrasis is assigned to the imperfective aspect during the New Kingdom.

categories of meaning: imperfective, perfective

Aspect of participles and relative forms is generally reduced to the categories of either (a) active-imperfective (in forms of *ỉrỉ*-periphrasis) with the meaning of an aorist or an incompleted present action ("doing"), or (b) active/passive-perfective for completed past actions ("done").

Observation:

In traditional expressions (e.g., titles) or in higher textual registers of the norm hierarchy, both the earlier forms and the aspect role of the participles and relative forms were still carefully distinguished. As the *sdm.n=f* form has actually become an allomorph of the perfect active *sdm=f* in Late Egyptian,[4] apparent *sdm.n=f* relative forms appear, as do combinations like 𓏶𓂝𓏛 for *ỉ.ỉr=k* "which you did/have done" (for examples cf. Korostovtsev, *Grammaire*, 292f).

With the help of the relative particle or relative adjective  *nty* (also written *r.nty* on relative clauses occasion) entire sentences can be assigned attributive roles. Like Late Egyptian adjectives and participles, *nty* does not generally agree with the antecedent. In form and usage, *nty* is the predecessor of the Coptic ЄT(Є).

— Examples:

(pD'Orb 11,8)

iw nꜣ rmṯ i̓.šm r ḫꜣs.t ḥr i̓y.t r ḏd-smi̓ n ḥm≈f ꜥ.w.s "(After many days passed), the people who had gone abroad came to report to his Majesty.";

Notes:

construction the basic sentence is the Late Egyptian adverbial sentence with *iw* that in principle marks subordination in Late Egyptian: *iw nꜣ rmṯ ḥr i̓y.t* "... while the people were coming" or the like, but forms a closed complex here with the preceding phrase; the relative phrase consisting of the participle with the verb rection *r* + noun is inserted between the subject of the adverbial sentence and its prepositional infinitive.

(pJudTurin 3,1)

i̓r pꜣw i̓r.y nb mnt.w i̓.i̓r sw "As for all that was done, they were the ones who did it."

Notes:

mnt.w Late Egyptian form of the 3rd pl. independent pronoun "they"; corresponding to the earlier *nt.sn*;

construction the basic sentence is the Cleft Sentence/participial statement of the type with *nt.f* + participle, which is placed at the start of a sentence through the use of *i̓r*.

(HorSeth 11,5)

mi̓ ptr≈t nꜣi̓ i̓.i̓r Stš r≈i̓ (Horus says to his mother Isis,) "Come and see what Seth has done to me!"

Notes:

mi̓ ptr≈t Imperative *mi̓* and optative *sḏm≈f* of *ptr*; alternative translation: "come that you see!".

(Beatty Love Songs vs. C1,9-C2,1)

nfr mꜣw.t m ḥnw≈i̓ m nfi̓ i̓.ḫꜥ mꜣꜣ≈s "Mother ought to be good about my affairs where it must be overlooked." (< *"Good should mother be about my affairs concerning that which to observe is better omitted");

Notes:

construction adjectival sentence (*nfr* + noun phrase) with a following chain of adverbials;

nfi̓ old demonstrative *nꜣ*;

---

4   *sḏm≈f* and *sḏm.n≈f* can function interchangeably as past tense.

ỉ.ḥȝꜥ mȝȝ=s   passive participle (*ỉ.ḥȝꜥ*) whose (retained) object is an infinitive (*mȝȝ*) with its own
direct object (*=s*) as the necessary resumptive pronoun: *"that which seeing it is
(better) omitted". Note the fem. resumptive pronoun of the Middle Egyptian type.

(HorSeth 6,1)   *ỉw=ỉ dỉ.t n=k pȝ ḥtm n nbw nty m ḏr.t(=ỉ)* "I will give you the golden signet-ring I am
wearing" (for the hieroglyphic text and comments cf. § 2.1.4[3]);

Note:

nty m ḏr.t(=ỉ)   a relative clause with an adverbial sentence following *nty*. The subject of the adverbial
sentence is regularly dropped when it is identical with the antecedent of the relative
clause — as it were developed out of *pȝ ḥtm nty (pȝ ḥtm) m ḏr.t(=ỉ)*.

(Doomed   *ỉw=f ḥr ḏd n pȝy=f sḏm nty r-gs=f ỉḫ pȝ nty ḥr šm.t m-sȝ pȝ zỉ nty m ỉy.t ḥr tȝ mỉ.t* "And he
Prince 4,7-9) (the young prince) said to his servant who was beside him, 'What is that which is going
behind the adult who is coming on the way?'" (for the hieroglyphic text and comments
cf. § 2.1.3[1]).

(6) Numbers, number-signs and numeral constructions

With the exception of ⟨glyph⟩ *wꜥ* "one", numbers are written with the respective number-signs
(numerals). In combination with the item numbered, the numbers form the nucleus of the
noun phrase, the modified noun, while the numbered item becomes the modifying noun.
Only *sn.w* ("two") is treated as the satellite of what is numbered, ⟨glyph⟩ || *sn sn.w* "two
brothers". *wꜥ* "one" can be either nucleus or satellite: as an indefinite article it is the
nucleus, and as a number, the satellite (⟨glyph⟩ *m bw wꜥ* "in one place"). In lists
(indicating weights and measures, etc.), all numerals can follow their noun, but only as
a writing procedure.

fractions   Fractions are reduced to the common numerator 1, with $^1/_2$; $^1/_3$ etc. These are
generally written with the ⟨glyph⟩ above the signs, as in ⟨glyph⟩ for $^1/_3$ (*r-ḫmtw*: "part 3" of
three), ⟨glyph⟩ for $^1/_4$ etc. The symbol for $^1/_2$ is ⟨glyph⟩; for $^1/_4$ hieratic (and its transcriptions)
has ×. As in Middle Egyptian the only variation is ⟨glyph⟩ $^2/_3$ (*r.wy* "the two parts" of three):
⟨glyph⟩× "7 + $^2/_3$ + $^1/_4$" = "7 $^{11}/_{12}$". Fractions in administrative texts frequently follow
the corn measure; cf. infra § 7.3.

construction   The constructions with the numbers from "three" to "nine" are formed with the direct
nominal attribute (direct genitive), while above "ten", the indirect nominal attribute
(indirect genitive) prevails. Numbered items are construed in the singular (⟨glyph⟩
pȝy 6 rmṯ "these six persons" < *"this hexad of people"). In Coptic, numbers assume
the gender of the item counted, but in Late Egyptian this is virtually never reflected.

ordinals   Ordinal numbers are formed with the prefix *mḥ-* (participle of *mḥ*, "completing" a
number, e.g., *hrww mḥ 3* "the third day"): ⟨glyph⟩ *ỉnk mḥ-6* "I am the sixth".
"The first" has its own form, ⟨glyph⟩ *ḥȝwty*, also used adjectivally.

2.1.5 Notes on linguistic evolution

The development to Coptic by way of Demotic is characterized by a crystallization of the trends and patterns discussed here. The use of articles in Late Egyptian is very much in line with the later linguistic stages, the absence of articles in Coptic being more strictly regulated (which is, however, also related to the disappearance of the register hierarchy and its writing conventions). article

The most striking feature is the disappearance of the direct nominal attribute (Direct Genitive), of adjectives, participles and relative forms: in Coptic, direct nominal attributes, adjectives and participles can only be analysed historically, in lexicalized phrases which behave as individual words, or in nominal prefixes. Modification by attributes is accomplished exclusively in the form of combinations using the indirect nominal attribute (*X n Y*). The relative forms are completely replaced by the relative clause constructions. dirct nominal
attribute

Demotic assumes a characteristic position between Late Egyptian and Coptic. Direct genitives and adjectives still appear, although less frequently, the simple participles and relative forms drop out of use, and appear only in the form of the periphrases with *ỉ.ỉr* and *wnn*. Demotic

2.1.6 Bibliography

Černý/Groll, *Late Egyptian Grammar*, § 2.4; Erman, *Neuägyptische Grammatik*, §§ 59-86; Korostovtsev, *Grammaire du Néo-Égyptien*, 85-91; E. Edel, Die Herkunft des neuägyptisch-koptischen Personalsuffixes der 3. Person Plural *-w*, in: *ZÄS* 84, 1959, 17ff suffixes

Černý/Groll, *Late Egyptian Grammar*, § 3; Erman, *Neuägyptische Grammatik*, §§ 114-127; 171-174; 183-185; Korostovtsev, *Grammaire*, 50-57; Loprieno, *Ancient Egyptian*; § 4.4.3; development: Kroeber, *Neuägyptizismen*, § 1 article,
demonstratives

Černý/Groll, *Late Egyptian Grammar*, §§ 1.9; 4; Erman, *Neuägyptische Grammatik*, §§ 128-132; 159-186 (*nb* "all; every", Černý/Groll, *Late Egyptian Grammar*, § 5.4; Erman, *Neuägyptische Grammatik*, §§ 220-222) determination

Erman, *Neuägyptische Grammatik*, §§ 159-170; Černý/Groll, *Late Egyptian Grammar*, § 4.4 (+ § 4.2.9) nouns without
articles

Erman, *Neuägyptische Grammatik*, §§ 188-191; 200-204; Černý/Groll, *Late Egyptian Grammar*, § 4.5.1; Till, *Koptische Grammatik*, §§ 110-113 apposition,
"direct
genitive"

Erman, *Neuägyptische Grammatik*, §§ 205-215; Černý/Groll, *Late Egyptian Grammar*, § 4.5.2 "indirect
genitive"

Winand, *Études*, §§ 540-594; Erman, *Neuägyptische Grammatik*, §§ 216-219; 223-243; 366-376; 379-386; Černý/Groll, *Late Egyptian Grammar*, §§ 5.1-5.7; 48; 50; Korostovtsev, *Grammaire*, 99-111; 221-225 adjectives,
participles relative forms   Winand, *Études*, §§ 595-611; Erman, *Neuägyptische Grammatik*, §§ 387-398; Černý/Groll, *Late Egyptian Grammar*, § 51; Korostovtsev, *Grammaire*, 289-300

sdm.n-relative   Winand, *Études*, §§ 612-621

relative clauses   Erman, *Neuägyptische Grammatik*, §§ 836-839; Černý/Groll, *Late Egyptian Grammar*, § 53.4

numerals   Loprieno, in: *LÄ* VI s.v. Zahlwort; Gardiner, *Grammar*, §§ 259-265; Erman, *Neuägyptische Grammatik*, §§ 244-252; Černý/Groll, *Late Egyptian Grammar*, § 6

linguistic evolution   Spiegelberg, *Demotische Grammatik*, §§ 41-48 (article); §§ 58-66 (genitive); §§ 67-81 (adjective); §§ 236-248 (participle); Till, *Koptische Grammatik*, §§ 74-86 (form of nouns); 185-196 (suffix pronouns); 87-108 (use of articles); 201-208 (determiners); 110-122 (attributive modification). Cf. B. Layton, Compound Prepositions in Sahidic Coptic, Appendix 1: Threefold Determination in Coptic, in: *Polotsky-Studies*, 261f; Kroeber, *Neuägyptizismen*, 195ff (§ 41.42 [Die Periphrase alter Partizipien])

2.1.7 Exercises

(1) An Amarna boundary stela (Stela U lines 4-14)

One of the eleven stelae — of which five are well preserved today — delimiting the city of Akhet-Aten. The text is from N. de G. Davies, *The Rock Tombs of El Amarna*, Egypt Exploration Society. *Archaeological Survey* 13-18, Vol.V pl.XXV. The transliteration here begins at Sandman, *Akhenaten*, p. 122, line 6.

Purpose: Example of(a) form, peculiarities and arrangement of New Kingdom hieroglyphs; (b) differences in style and form of expression of a Late Middle Egyptian framing text and a Medio-Late Egyptian speech text; (c) use of articles, possessives and demonstratives; and (d) attributes and relative clauses of the earlier type.

Trans-literation (intended as a reading aid, the indentation indicating the degree of subordination) This text is preceded by: Regnal Year 6, 4th month of the "sowing season", day 13, the transliteration starts at the end of line 4:

(4) ... *ḥrww pn ỉw=tw m Ȝḫ.t-ỉtn* **(5)** *m pȝ ỉmw n psš.t*

                   [ỉr]y n ḥm=f m Ȝḫ.t-ỉtn

                   nty rn=f r Pȝ-ỉtn-ḥrw

ḫꜥy.t ỉn ḥm=f ḥr ssm.t ḥr Ꞌwrrỉ.tꞋ Ꜥȝ.t nt ḏꜤm mỉ ỉtn

                   wbn=f m Ȝḫ.t

                            mḥ.n=f tȝ.wy m mrw.t=f

šzp tp wȝ.t nfr.t r Ȝḫ.t-ỉtn **(6)** *m zp [tpy]*

                   ỉrỉ.n [ḥm=f] r snṯỉ=s m mnw n pȝ ỉtn

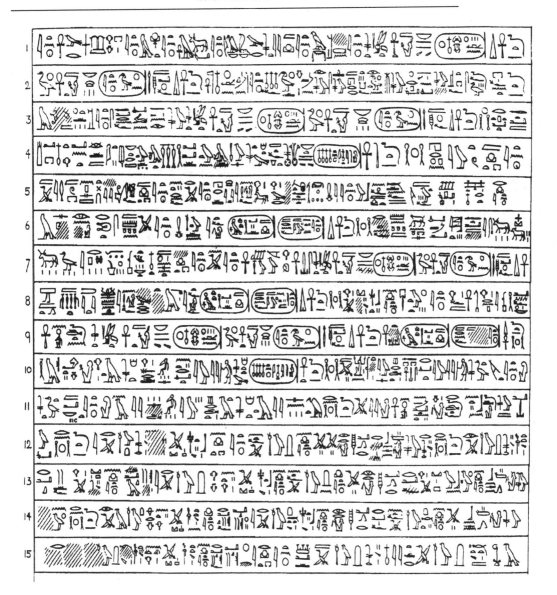

2.1.7 Exercises (1): Boundary Stela U, line 1-15

mỉ wḏ.t.n ỉtỉ=f (ꜥnḫ-Rꜥw-ḥrw-ꜣḫ.ty ḫꜥỉ-m-ꜣḫ.t)|

(m-rn=f-m-Šw nty-m-ỉtn)| dỉ ꜥnḫ ḏ.t nḥḥ

r ỉr.t n=f mnw m-ḫnw=s

dỉ-mꜣꜥ ꜣb.t ꜥꜣ.t m [t ḥnq.t]

ỉwꜣ.w wnḏw.w (7) kꜣ.w ꜣpd.w

ỉrp dqr s:nṯr rnpw.t nb.t nfr.t

m ḥrww n sntỉ ꜣḫ.t-ỉtn n pꜣ ỉtn ꜥnḫ

šzp ḥzw(.t) mrw(.t) ḥr-tp ꜥnḫ wḏꜣ snb nzw-bỉt ꜥnḫ-m-Mꜣꜥ.t nb-tꜣ.wy (Nfr-ḫpr.w-Rꜥw wꜥ n

Rꜥw)| zꜣ-Rꜥw ꜥnḫ-m-Mꜣꜥ.t (ꜣḫ-n-ỉtn)| ꜥꜣ m ꜥḥꜥ.w=f dỉ-ꜥnḫ

(8) šm.t m ḫnty.t

s:mn.t ỉn ḥm=f [ḥr] wrrỉ.t m-bꜣḥ ỉtỉ=f (ꜥnḫ-Rꜥw-ḥrw-ꜣḫ.ty ḫꜥy-m-ꜣḫ.t)| (m-rn=f-m-Šw

nty-m-ỉtn)| dỉ ꜥnḫ ḏ.t nḥḥ ḥr pꜣ ḏw rs.y-ỉꜣb.ty n ꜣḫ.t-ỉtn

stw.t ỉtn ḥr=f m ꜥnḫ wꜣs ḥr rnpỉ ḥꜥ=f rꜥw-nb

(9) ꜥnḫ ḏd.t.n nzw-bỉt ꜥnḫ-m-Mꜣꜥ.t nb-tꜣ.wy (Nfr-ḫpr.w-Rꜥw wꜥ n Rꜥw)| zꜣ-Rꜥw ꜥnḫ-m-Mꜣꜥ.t

nb-ḫꜥ.w (ꜣḫ-n-ỉtn)| ꜥꜣ m ꜥḥꜥ.w=f dỉ-ꜥnḫ ḏ.t

ꜥnḫ ꜛỉtỉ=ỉꜜ (ꜥnḫ-Rꜥw-ḥrw-ꜣḫ.ty ḫꜥy-m-ꜣḫ.t)| (m-rn=f-m-ꜛŠw nty-mꜜ-ỉtn)| dỉ ꜥnḫ ḏ.t nḥḥ

(10) nḏm ḥꜣ.ty=ỉ ḥr tꜣ ḥm.t-nzw ḥr ḥrd.w=s

nty rdỉ.t(w) ꜣwy ḥm.t-nzw wr.t (Nfr-nfr.w-ỉtn nfr.t-ỉy.tỉ)| ꜥnḫ.tỉ ḏ.t nḥḥ

m pꜣy ḥḥ n ꜛrnp.wtꜜ

ỉw=s ḥr ḏr.t Pr-ꜥꜣ ꜥ.w.s

rdỉ.t(w) ꜣwy zꜣ.t-nzw Mr.t-ỉtn

(11) zꜣ.t-nzw Mk.t-ỉtn nꜣy=s ꜛḥrd.wꜜ

ỉw=w ḥr ḏr.t tꜣ ḥm.t-nzw tꜣy=sn mw.t r nḥḥ ḏ.t

pꜣy=ỉ ꜥnḫ n (<m) mꜣꜥ.t

nty ỉb=ỉ r ḏd=f

nty bn ḏd=ỉ sw m ꜥḏꜣ.w (12) r nḥḥ ḏ.t

ỉr pꜣ wḏ rs.y

[nty ḥr] pꜣ ḏw ỉꜣb.ty n ꜣḫ.t-ỉtn

ntf pꜣ wḏ n ꜣḫ.t-ỉtn pꜣy

pꜣy ỉr=ỉ ꜥḥꜥ r tꜣ-ꜥ=f

bn znỉ=ỉ sw r rs.y r nḥḥ ḏ.t

ỉr.w pꜣ wḏ rs.y-ỉmn.ty (13) r-ꜥqꜣ=f

ḥr pꜣ ḏw rs.y n ꜣḫ.t-ỉtn r-ꜥqꜣ

ỉr pꜣ wḏ ḥr-ỉb

nty ḥr pꜣ ḏw ỉꜣb.ty n ꜣḫ.t-ỉtn

ntf pꜣ wḏ n ꜣḫ.t-ỉtn pꜣy

ỉr=ỉ ꜥḥꜥ r tꜣ-ꜥ=f

ḥr pꜣ ḏw wbnw n ꜣḫ.t-ỉtn

bn znî=î sw **(14)** *[r wb]nw r nḥḥ ḏ.t*

îr.w p3 wḏ ḥr-îb

nty ḥr p3 ḏw îmn.ty n 3ḫ.t-îtn

r-ᶜq3=f ᶜq3 ... ...

The text continues.

Notes:

line 4 *hrww pn îw=tw m 3ḫ.t îtn*: construction of the Middle Egyptian type noun + *îw*-sentence, with the noun indicating time used absolutely (cf. Gardiner, *Grammar*, § 88): "On this day (one was ...)"; *hrww pn* refers back to the date specified earlier;

line 5 *nty m=f r P3-îtn-hr.w*: relative clause with Middle Egyptian construction noun + *r* + noun ("whose name shall be 'Aten-is-content'", cf. Gardiner, *Grammar*, § 122);

ḫᶜy.t ḥr ssm.t ḥr wrrî.t: "appearing with horse and chariot" (first *ḥr* is the rection of *ḫᶜî*, the second *ḥr* co-ordinates both nouns);

wbn=f m 3ḫ.t mḥ.n=f t3.wy m mrw.t=f: a characteristic Middle Egyptian expression of the hymns to the Sun-god (sequence *sdm=f - sdm.n=f*; here roughly, "when he, having filled the land with his love, radiates at the horizon");

lines 5-6 the other stelae have: *šzp tp w3.t nfr.t r 3ḫ.t-îtn m zp tpy n gmî.tw=s îrî.n ḥm=f r snṯî=s* "Conceiving it for the first time, His Majesty set out on the fine way to Akhet-Aten, to found it." (<** "Setting out on the fine way to Akhet-Aten at the first time of finding-it-out, which His Majesty did in order to found it"; "which" refers to "Setting out on the way"). Omitting *n gm.tw=s* makes also good sense ("setting out on the way for the first time, which His Majesty did to found");

line 6 *mî wḏ.t.n îtî=f*: "according to what his father NN decreed", Middle Egyptian *sdm.n*-relative form;

the writing *dî (dî m3ᶜ ᶜ3b.t)*: according to its form, it could be a passive *sdm.w* (restricted to legal texts in the later New Kingdom) - "An offering was presented" - parallel to the other introductory sentences, but it could just as easily be an infinitive (in a Late Egyptian phonemic or so to speak, ideographic writing);

line 7 *šzp ḥzw(.t) mrw(.t) ḥr-tp ᶜnḫ wḏ3 snb nzw-bît*: "Receiving favours and love for the benefit of the king's well-being (< Life, Prosperity and Health)" as thanks for the previously mentioned presentation of offerings;

line 8 *stw.t îtn ḥr=f m ᶜnḫ w3s*: "the rays of Aten/the solar disc being upon him with life and power", appositional adverbial sentence following Middle Egyptian syntax; *ḥr mpî ḥᶜ=f*: *ḥr* with infinitive as circumstantial continuation of a phrase falls into disuse in Late Egyptian proper, the construction of *mpî* with object, however, appears only with the Amarna Period;

line 9 *ᶜnḫ ḏd.t.n nzw-bît*: "Oath made by the king": again *sdm.n*-relative form (which is no longer usual in Late Egyptian proper);

line 10 *ndm h3.ty=î ḥr t3 ḥm.t-nzw ḥr ḥrd.w=s*: "and as I am joyful about the queen and her children" (variant of an oath formula). The first *ḥr* is the rection of *ndm*, "to be happy, joyful about something"; the second *ḥr* co-ordinates the nouns *ḥm.t-nzw* and *ḥrd.w* (phrase coordination, cf. § 2.1.3[1] commentary Notes on pAbbott 7,8-9); note the suffix rather than the possessive article with *ḥrd.w* (as in line 11): grammatically coordinated nouns depend upon a common article so that the possessive expression gives way to the suffix construction;

nty rdî.t(w) î3wy ḥm.t-nzw: *nty* is an abbreviated form of *r.nty* "such that"; "because"; "in order to" (Late Egyptian for *r-ntt*), cf. Erman, *Neuägyptische Grammatik*, § 680; Gardiner, *Grammar*, §§ 223; 225: "(I am happy about the queen) for the good ageing of the queen is assured (< given)". The writing *î3wy* as *îwy* in the publication is an exaggerated purist reproduction of the original bird hieroglyph: cf. the parallels;

ỉw=s ḫr-ḏr.t Pr-ˁꜣ: Late Egyptian circumstantial introduced with *ỉw*: "she being in Pharaoh's hand" > "because she was ...";

line 11   *pꜣy=ỉ ˁnḫ m mꜣˁ.t* "(As my father lives and my heart is happy), my oath is truth" (> my oath is true);[5] *ḏd.t=f* as a writing of the status pronominalis of *ḏd* (infinitive with suffix, "to say it"), cf. § 1.1.2(3);

bn *ḏd=ỉ sw*: "I will not say it"; bn *sdm=f* is the negative form of the prospective *sdm=f* in Late Egyptian (cf. Middle Egyptian *nn sdm=f*);

line 12   *ỉr pꜣ wḏ rsy ... ntf pꜣ wḏ n ꜣḫ.t-ỉtn pꜣy*: "Concerning the southern stela ... it is precisely the stela of Akhet-Aten" (> the stela defining the city); construction of sentence: a noun in anticipation by means of *ỉr* + sentence. The sentence itself is a Late Egyptian "three-part" nominal sentence: *ntf, pꜣ-A pꜣy* (*"It, it is the A");

pꜣy ỉrỉ=ỉ ˁḥˁ r rꜣ-ˁ: "the one which I erected being in its due position" (< "which I had made to stand being in its place", i.e., it is the authentic stela); nominalized relative form of *ỉrỉ* with infinitive;

bn *znỉ=ỉ sw*: the negative form of the Late Egyptian prospective *sdm=f*: "I will not step beyond it" (< "I will not pass it");

ỉr.w: passive *sdm*. This form is rare in Late Egyptian proper, being limited to legal texts. Here it indicates a secondary importance of the Southwest Stela with regard to the previously mentioned South Stela on the Eastern Mountain;

line 13   note the two completely different meanings of *ˁqꜣ* in the same sentence: "The such-and-such stela was acurately erected opposite it" (*"was erected opposite it in accuracy");

wbnw: "sunrise" is used here and in the following line to signify the East as it was formerly used in our languages in poetic or antiquated expressions like "to march towards sunrise";

line 14   *r ˁqꜣ=f ˁqꜣ* now: "precisely opposite it"; adverbial to *ỉr.w*, the passive *sdm*.

(2) Literature of Late Dynasty XVIII (Astarte Papyrus lines 3,y-2—4,1)

A badly preserved hieratic text from the reign of Horemhab in the hieroglyphic transcription of A.H. Gardiner, *Late-Egyptian Stories, Bibliotheca Aegyptiaca* I, Brussels 1932, p. 79, lines 10-15: part of a tale of the wishes and demands of the sea and its conflict with the goddess Astarte.

Purpose: Example of a hieratic literary text maintaining the writing style and forms of expression specific to the norms of "Medio"-Late Egyptian",[6] with careful — "Middle Egyptian" — recording of morphemes (fem. -.*t*; preposition *ḥr/r*), regular use of the suffix *=sn*, distinction between subject suffix *=s* and object suffix *=st* in writing (*=st* being an allograph of *=s*).

---

5   Note: in the literature, this is generally understood to be a kind of adjectival construction (cf. § 2.1.4[3]): *pꜣy=ỉ ˁnḫ n mꜣˁ.t* *"my oath of truth" > "my true oath". Opposing this however is the fact that the oath formula would not be complete: **"As my father lives, my true oath, which I will say, which I will not say falsely."

6   Note, too, forms like *ˁḥˁ.n ḏd.n=f* (line 1,x + 12) or the "conjunctive" *ḥnˁ ntk ḏd* (line 2,x +5) in the parts of the text not reproduced here.

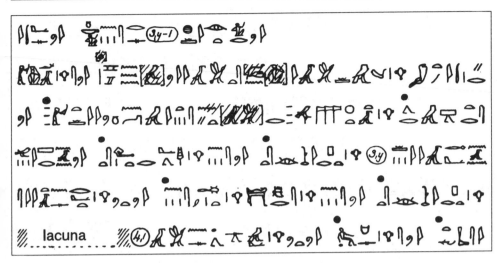

2.1.7 Exercises (2): Astarte Papyrus, line 3,y-2 - 4,1

Notes:

line 3,y-1   The text here begins with the final words of a speech by the sea, where *=sn* refers to the Ennead; the postponed independent pronoun *ink* is in apposition to the suffix *=i*: emphasis by postposition, "I myself", "I however" (cf. Erman, *Neuägyptische Grammatik*, §706; Till, *Koptische Grammatik*, § 388);

iw + noun (or suffix) and adverbial: a type of structure (*iw=f ḥr dỉ.t*) that allows the formation of long chains of clauses, the Late Egyptian circumstantial form of the Adverbial Sentence ("Circumstantial First Present"), also termed "narrative" or "non-initial main sentence";

nty st im nwy.t: *st* is one of the forms of the 3rd pers. pl. dependent pronoun; for the postponed Old Perfective (here *nwy*), cf. Erman, *Neuägyptische Grammatik*, § 706.

(3) Grain collection report (Turin Taxation Papyrus, rt. 4,1-5)

Part of a record in which Tuthmosis, the "Secretary of the Tomb Building Administration" noted grain tax which he collected towards the end of Dynasty XX; the text is published by A.H. Gardiner, *Ramesside Administrative Documents*, Oxford 1948, the part represented here being from p. 40, lines 3-11.

Purpose: Example of a late Ramesside administrative text with characteristic writing conventions, abbreviations, numbers, and units of measure (cf. Appendix § 7.3); apposition and attributes.

Notes:

line 4,1   Regnal Year 12, 4th month of the "Inundation Season" (in the festival and, later, the civil calendars, the month *kỉ-ḥr-kỉ*, Coptic ⲭⲟⲓⲁⲕ), day (*sw*!) 24 of King Ramesses XI; *Pỉ-wr-ꜥ* ("the great chief") and *Ḏḥwty-ms* are proper names; ⌣🖎 is a common abbreviation for 𓏤 𓏏 𓎡 ⌣🖎 *ir.y-ꜥ* "porter" (of the Gang of the Tomb Building Administration in Deir el-Medina); *pỉ ir.y-ꜥ sn.w* "the two porters" (< *"the porter, twofold"). For the grain reference system, cf. the appendix § 7.3.2(3);

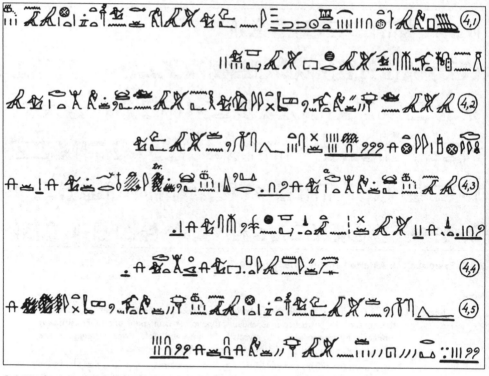

2.1.7 Exercises (3): Turin Taxation Papyrus rt. 4,1 - 4,5

line 4,2   ⟨sign⟩ is here probably ⟨signs⟩   *k-r* "boat" (a cargo vessel of considerable capacity, as can be calculated from this source); *Ḏḥwty-wšby* and *Q3-dr.t* are proper names; (*šzp...m n3 ỉt...*) *m dmỉ ỉwny.t* roughly: "(Receipt of grain) from 'town' Esna (Latopolis)" in contrast to a possible "from 'district' Esna" — i.e. the use of *dmỉ* as a kind of characterization, of labelling;

⟨sign⟩ is the sign for the measuring unit *ḫ3r* "sack" (76.88 litres); ⟨signs⟩ is an abbreviated form for *wp=s*, "to specify it:" (< "to separate it"), to give details (also *wp* alone "specification; detail", cf. line 4,3);

ỉw s:wḏ n NN m X "Arriving and delivering of X at NN";

line 4,3   the "dot" (.) in indications of measure is an abbreviation for the unit of measure of ¹/₄ *ḫ3r*, equal to 1 *ỉp.t* (Coptic ΟΙΠΕ), equal to 4 *ḥq3.t*;

the customary passive in Late Egyptian is formed by adding -.*tw*. A passive *sḏm* (as *dỉ.w* here, *rdỉ.w* in line 4,5) appears virtually only in legal texts and in formulations of accounts like this one; ⟨signs⟩ *dỉw*, "the income", "pay" for employees and workers; *Ỉt-nfr* and *Ḥnsw-ms* are proper names; the sign ⟨sign⟩ is an abbreviation for *dmḏ* "total"; *ḏ3.t* "remainder" is the deficit in an account;

line 4,4   *Ns-Ỉmn-m-ỉpt* (< *Ny-sw Ỉmn.w-m-ỉp.t* "He belongs to Amun-of-Luxor") is a proper name; for the fractions of the Eye of Horus as writings for ¹/₂ and ¹/₄ "oipe" cf. § 7.3.2(3) and Gardiner, *Grammar*, § 266;

line 4,5   read: *rdỉ.w r h3w n NN*.

2.2 Elements of sentence construction

2.2.1 The enclitic (dependent) personal pronouns

Pronouns from the series designated the dependent personal pronouns can be either (a) the object of the Late Egyptian *sdm=f* forms, imperatives, participles and relative forms or (b) the subject of an Adjectival Sentence, but no longer that of an Adverbial Sentence. The older forms are still employed in the higher reaches of the register hierarchy. The forms of Late Egyptian proper and their usage reveal that they have lost their gender differentiation in the singular as well. Assimilated to the suffix pronouns in the course of linguistic evolution, they were eventually completely replaced by them and only traces remain in Coptic. Forms:

1.s.c.	*wi*	𓀀 ; 𓀁	like the suffix, this can occasionally be omitted
2.s.c.	*tw; ti*	𓏏𓂝 ; 𓏏𓅱 ; 𓍿	fem. is only distinguished by the grapheme
3.s.c.	*sw; st*	𓊃𓏲 ; 𓊃𓏏 ; 𓏏𓏤	*sw, st* are only *s'*, and thus each grapheme group can be used interchangeably
1.pl.c.	*n*	𓈖𓏥 ; 𓈖𓏥 ; 𓈖𓏥	
2.pl.c.	*tn*	𓏏𓈖𓏥	
3.pl.c.	*sn; st*	𓊃𓈖𓏥 ; 𓏏𓈖𓏥 ; 𓊃𓏏𓏥	*sn, st* are only *s'*, and thus each grapheme group can be used interchangeably

Observations:

st (sing./pl.) is also used to refer to general situations (neuter).

The transfer of the -.*t*-ending of the 3ae inf. infinitives to all other verb classes (cf. for hypercorrection, § 1.1.3[4], supra), resulted in a general form of status pronominalis of verbs. Through the detachment of the status endings with the object suffix (and their use following *sdm=f* forms) a separate series of direct object pronouns emerged eventually ('Direct Object' Pronouns, cf. Černý/Groll, *Late Egyptian Grammar*, § 2.5), such as 1st pers. sing. ⸢𓏏𓅱𓀀⸣ *tw=i* "me", 2nd pers. sing. ⸢𓏏𓅱𓎡⸣ *tw=k*, 3rd pers. sing. ⸢𓏏𓅱𓆑⸣ *tw=f*, etc. While these object pronouns are certainly used in Demotic, the acceptance of the series is not compelling in Late Egyptian. Cf. Winand, *Études*, §§ 182-186; J. Borghouts, Object Pronouns of the *tw*-Type in Late Egyptian, in: *Orientalia Lovanensia Periodica* 11, 1980, 99ff.

2.2.2 The imperative

(1) Forms

infinitive vs. imperative

A large number of verbs do not differ in the imperative and infinitive, and it is therefore possible that direct command is already often expressed through the infinitive rather than the imperative, as in Coptic. This can be clearly seen only in those cases where the form is followed by a pronoun object:[1] Imperatives take the dependent pronoun (*s:wḏꜣ sw* "Save him!"), while the infinitive takes the suffix (*s:wḏꜣ=f* "Save him!"). On the graphemic level, however, the 1st pers. sing. suffix and the dependent pronoun *wἰ* frequently cannot be distinguished (object just 𓀁). Gender and number of the addressee are generally not distinguished either.

stem extension prefix ἰ.-

The imperatives of the 2-rad. verbs, and those reduced to two radicals (3-rad., rarely 3ae inf.) can receive a stem extension prefix, *ἰ.-*, like the participles: 𓀁 *ἰ.ḏd* "speak!" (>Coptic ⲁϫⲓ-); 𓀁 *ἰ.šm* "go!"; 𓀁 *ἰ.wꜣḥ* "add!" or the like (Coptic ⲁⲩⲱ / ⲟⲩⲟϩ "and"!); and the frequently used 𓀁 *ἰ.ἰr* "do (it)!" (>Coptic ⲁⲣⲓ-). These verbs also exhibit forms without a prefix.

"come" and "give"

The imperatives of *ἰy* "come" and *dἰ* "give" still use the same forms as in Middle Egyptian: — *ἰy*: 𓂿 *mἰ* "come!"; feminine addressees are occasionally distinguished graphically, by forms like 𓂿 *mἰ* (where an internal vowel modification is indicated, cf. Coptic masc. ⲁⲙⲟⲩ, fem. ⲁⲙⲏ). — *dἰ*: 𓂿 oder 𓂿 *ἰmm* (*ἰm/ἰmἰ*) "Give!"

> **Verbal classes and states; classes of meaning.** In Late Egyptian the verb roots are still classified according to their root consonants (2-rad.; 3-rad.; 2ae gem.; 3ae inf.; 4ae inf. — conceptual borrowings from the old Latin-oriented description of Afro-Asiatic and Semitic languages meaning "verba tertiae radicalis infirmae" or "verbs of weak third radical (consonant)", etc.,) although their morphological peculiarities are no longer recorded (infinitive forms, endings) or actually abandoned (syntactic reduplication, "gemination"). Coptic reveals that these verbal classes actually survive, expressed by differences in vocalization. In Coptic, the kind of object construction influences the form (infinitive). The "state"-forms are: (a) without object: "status absolutus" (absolute state), Coptic ⲥⲱⲧⲡ; (b) with nominal object: "status nominalis" (nominal or construct state), ⲥⲉⲧⲡ-; and (c) with pronominal object: "status pronominalis" (pronominal or presuffixal state), ⲥⲟⲧⲡ⸗). Occasionally the Late Egyptian written forms betray the existence of these state-forms, cf. Winand, *Études*, §§ 73-164.
> Verbs can also be classified by meaning, into (a) "fientive" verbs indicating process or activity ("to wash"; "to drop") and (b) "non-fientive" verbs indicating a state ("to be"; "to remain"; or verbs of quality ("to be good"), in Afro-Asiatic languages like Egyptian. The verbs of motion form a sub-class in Egyptian because they have a distinctive morphology.

---

1   If suffix pronouns are not already used as object following imperatives too, as in Coptic.

Observation:

The transliteration *imm* is a convention, and a transliteration *im/imi* would be strictly speaking more appropriate, because in Late Egyptian (and already even in Middle Egyptian) writings, the ⸗ of the earlier 𓇋𓅓𓏭 *imi* has been reinterpreted as an allograph of *m*.

(2) Usage

Imperatives are frequently combined, as with the imperatives of "coming" and "going", e.g., 𓄟𓏏𓄿𓈖𓁹𓏸𓂝𓏫𓇋𓏏𓄿𓄿𓈖 *i.šm i.wn p3 mḫr* "go and open the store room!" (pD'Orb 3,1). The imperative can be strengthened with the particle *my* (originally another imperative), 𓇋𓆓𓂝𓏭𓄿 *i.dd my* "say something!".

combination of imperatives

Imperatives can also be construed as in Middle Egyptian with reflexive pronouns (*i.ir tw* "You act!") or the so -alled ethical dative, 𓄿𓂝𓏤𓈖𓂝𓏫 *ḫ3ᶜ sw n=k* "Leave him on your part!" (> "Leave him alone!"; Wenamun 2,47).

A frequently used expression in address is the combination of an imperative *imm* with a following Late Egyptian subjunctive-prospective *sdm=f*, as in *imm iy=f n=i* "Let him come to me" (*LRL* 19,13-14). The form is the Late Egyptian precursor of the Coptic Causative Imperative (*imm sdm=f* > *imm ir=f-sdm* > ⲘⲀⲢⲈϤⲤⲰⲦⲘ̄); this term will be used here.

Causative Imperative

(3) The negative imperative (Prohibitive)

The prohibitive or negative imperative ("Don't do this or that!") is expressed with the aid of the earlier prohibitive *m* with *di* and *iri*. Already from Dynasty XVIII onward the prohibitive formed with *iri* (*m-ir* > Coptic ⲘⲠⲢ̄-) and following infinitive is the periphrasis of the negative imperative of the relevant verbs (cf. Gardiner, *Grammar*, § 340). Note the analogy of the English prohibitive "Don't (do ...)!".

negation

(pD'Orb 4,1)

𓄿𓂋𓇼𓂝𓈖𓂝 *m-ir dd=f n=i ᶜn* "Don't say that to me again!" (Coptic roughly *ⲘⲠⲢ̄ⳭⲞⲞϤⲚⲀⲒⲞⲚ).

Note:

> *dd=f* written *dd.tw=f*: either a form of the status pronominalis of the infinitive *dd* or — less probably — a marking of the sound change *d* > *d* > *t*.

The negation of the Causative Imperative is the prohibitive *m* with the infinitive *di.t* and the following subjunctive:

Causative Imperative

(HorSeth 2,5)

𓄿𓄿𓈖𓂝𓏭𓈖𓊪𓏏𓄿𓂝𓈖 *m-dy.t iry=n sḫr m ḫm=n* "Let's not make plans when we don't know (anything)!" (< "in our ignorance").

The form *m-ỉr* can make its way into the group with *dỉ.t*, as in *m-ỉr dỉ.t ptr=ỉ sw* "Don't make me look at it!" (Wenamun 2,53). This is the precursor of the Coptic negated Causative Infinitive (*m-ỉr dỉ.t sdm=f > m-ỉr dỉ.t ỉr=f-sdm*[2] > ⲘⲠⲢⲦⲢⲈϤⲤⲰⲦⲘ).

Observation:

The imperative of *ptr* "look!" becomes a substitute for the earlier 𓄿𓏏 *mk*, which, however, continues to appear in the appropriate kinds of texts. Just like *mk*, *ptr* loses its literal meaning, and becomes a particle that somehow "presents" the contents of a statement, something like "You can verify by yourself that it is such-and-such".

2.2.3 Infinitive and Old Perfective

(1) The infinitive

The infinitive is the most commonly used form of the verb. This is a consequence of changes in verbal morphology, where virtually all the earlier forms have been subjected to the analytic tendency, so that the meaning of the verb (its lexical meaning) is introduced via the infinitive (cf. infra § 2.3).

nominal forms of the verb

As in all languages, the use of the infinitive is defined by its dual character: in terms of content it is a verb, but formally it is a noun. Apart from its specific role in verbal forms (where of course it also appears as a noun, particularly after the prepositions *ḥr* and *r*), it can thus be used in virtually the same way as any noun (with determination as grammatically masculine).

status pronominalis

The transitive infinitives of the verbs of the 3ae inf. class reveal usually — but not always — two forms:

1. A form without endings, either with or without an object. (Coptic distinguishes here between the status absolutus ⲘⲒⲤⲈ —

> **Old Perfective; Stative; Qualitative; *Pseudopartizip*:** These terms refer to a form where the fientive ("event representing") verbal content is reduced to a state, condition or quality, e.g., "to come" becomes "to have arrived"; "to do" becomes "to have been done". The form was described as characterizing "the verbal state in which its subject is" by Polotsky (*Grundlagen des koptischen Satzbaus*, p. 173). Its meaning of condition, state or quality is reflected in the term "Stative", which is used for the grammatically analogous form - with much the same endings - in Akkadian, while "Qualitative" is used for the corresponding Coptic forms. The German term *Pseudopartizip* was introduced by Erman for the characteristic Middle Egyptian adnominal usage (on the assumption that it assumed the role of a participle in modifying the noun). Gardiner used the term Old Perfective to designate the same form, and these two terms have usually been maintained in each language. The Late Egyptian Old Perfective is already formally and functionally close to the Coptic Qualitative.

---

2   Occurrences already in Ptolemaic Demotic, then especially in Roman Demotic.

of *msȋ* "to bear" — and the status nominalis ⲘⲈⲤ-);

2. A form with a -.*t* ending preceding the object suffix, the status pronominalis (Coptic ⲘⲀⳡⲦ꞊), written -.*tw꞊/-.tȋ꞊*, e.g., ⟨hiero⟩ *dȋ* "give", ⟨hiero⟩ *dȋ.t꞊ȋ* "give me"; ⟨hiero⟩ *gm* "find", ⟨hiero⟩ *gm.t꞊w* "find them"; ⟨hiero⟩ *mry* "love", ⟨hiero⟩ *mr.t꞊s* "love her".

Observation:

The form of the status pronominalis is of course etymologically that of the *t*-infinitives of the 3ae inf. class, where the word-final -.*t* is lost in the status absolutus (*ms.t>mȋ́|s˘* '), but is recovered when a suffix pronoun is attached since it moves into syllable-initial position (*ms.t꞊f, mȋ́s|t⁀f*). As the *t*-ending can, however, sometimes appear in Late Egyptian with 2-rad. (such as *dd*) or 3-rad. verbs (e.g., ⟨hiero⟩ *hdb.t꞊f* "kill him") as part of a more general tendency of linguistic evolution (being quite common in Demotic), a classification as a particular "state" of the infinitive is appropriate (cf. also § 2.2.1 note.)

— The infinitive can be used as (a) an absolute (cf. Amarna Boundary Stela U, § 2.1.7[1]) *specific usage* or (b) a dependent noun, or (c) the semantic element in verbal, clause and sentence paradigms (cf. the examples in § 2.1.3[1]; and infra). Prepositional uses of the infinitive are also worth particular attention; there is the use

° as adverbial adjunct with the preposition *r*: defining the purpose ("in order to", cf. Wenamun 2,75 in § 2.1.3[1]);

° in (*r-*)*dd* (*"in order to say") introducing direct speech or a (syndetical) clause of *r-dd* content/an object clause (Coptic ⲬⲈ-) following verbs like "report"; "say"; "swear" and the verbs of perception, "see"; "hear"; "recognize"; "know":

⟨hiero⟩ *ȋw꞊w gm r-dd ȋry꞊f st* "And they found that he had done it" (<*"they found the following: He did it"). *(pJudTurin 4,2 = KRI V 352,7-8)*

Notes: structure D. Sweeney, The nominal object clause, in: *Crossroad*, 337ff (cf. p. 223);

   ȋw꞊w gm Late Egyptian circumstantial clause with *ȋw*; historically/etymologically *ȋw꞊w (hr) gm(.t)*;

   ȋry꞊f Late Egyptian preterite *sdm꞊f*.

Observation:

As in Middle Egyptian, infinitives of verbs of motion are generally (with the exceptions of *šm* and *mš͗*) not combined with the preposition *hr*, but rather *m* (cf. the sources listed in Frandsen, *Outline*, § 42 note 2). A series of Coptic qualitatives of verbs of motion are etymologically derived from such constructions (Wente, *Verbs of Motion*, ch.3).

(2) The Old Perfective (Stative)

The use of the Old Perfective endings tends to decline in the course of the linguistic history of the New Kingdom. Although the typical Old Perfective morphemes still appear, particularly in norm-hierarchically higher categories of texts, by the end of Dynasty XX, they were in practice, however, either (a) amalgamated into -.*t* (written -.*tw*; forms with the *t*-ending are occasionally preserved in Coptic), or (b) completely eliminated. All the graphs of the traditional personal morphemes, together with -.*t* and -.*ø*, thus become mere allographs marking the Old Perfective or Stative.

The forms are now as follows:

	Traditional endings		Reduced endings	
1.sing.c.	ⳡⳡⳡ ; ⳡ	-.*kw* ; -.*k*		
2.sing.c.	ⳡⳡ ; 𓏭	-.*tw* ; -.*tï*		
3.sing. masc.	𓀀 ; ⳡ ; 𓏭 ; Ø	-.*w* ; -.*y* ; -.*ø*		
fem.	ⳡⳡ ; 𓏭	-.*tw* ; -.*tï*	ⳡⳡ ; Ø	-.*tw* ; -.*ø*
1.pl.c.	𓏥	-.*n*		
2.pl.c.	𓏥	-.*tn*		
3.pl.c.	𓀀 ; ⳡ ; 𓏥 ; ⸗ ; 𓏭 ; Ø	-.*w* ; -.*y* ; -.*ø*		

Observation:

The 3rd sing. masc. of the Old Perfective of *dï* "give" is frequently written ⳡⳡ (hieratic ⳡ).

An example showing the variants of the Old Perfective endings:

(oPetrie 18 rt. 4-5)

[hieroglyphs] *ïw=ï ïr.t 3bd (n) hrw ïw=ï ḥms.k ïw=ï w*.*ø*

"And I have spent a whole month just sitting around by myself" (< *"sitting being alone").

conditions of usage

— In (a) the Adverbial Sentence and circumstantial clauses derived from it (with *ïw*), and (b) combinations with auxiliary verbs (cf. § 2.2.3[3]) the Old Perfective continues to act as a complementary form of the infinitive. The decline of the Old Perfective endings and the disappearance of the prepositions *r* and *ḥr* preceding the infinitive means that the Old Perfective and the infinitive are graphically identical in many cases. In practice, however, it is easy to distinguish them:

° the infinitive of transitive verbs can have an object, but the Old Perfective of the same verbs does not (passive meaning), with the exception of *rḫ* "know";

° the Old Perfective of many intransitive verbs and verbs of motion expresses past meaning, and a state which has been achieved;

- ° the infinitive with verbs of quality is not frequently used, but appears with a specific meaning: cf. *sw ḥr snb* "he is becoming healthy" as opposed to *sw snb.w* "he is healthy";

- ° the Old Perfective is not used with verbs of eating and drinking, speaking, perception, or those indicating a mental or emotional state.

— Apart from its use in the Adverbial Sentence, the circumstantial clause with *iw* and following auxiliary verbs, the general circumstantial use of the Old Perfective declines considerably in comparison with Middle Egyptian. It is still used relatively frequently to qualify the direct object of a verb of perception (asyndetic clause of content/object clause): *gm=i ʿ3=f wn* "I discovered his door open" (> "I noticed that his door was open"; for the hieroglyphic text and commentary cf. supra, § 2.1.4[4] and infra, § 2.2.6[2]);

specific usage

(Beatty Love Songs vs. C3,10)

or

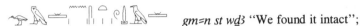 *gm=n st wd3* "We found it intact";

(pAbbott 7,12)

Notes:

    gm=n st   Late Egyptian preterite *sdm=f* 3rd sing.with enclitic pronoun;

    structure   *sdm=f* + object; object = object clause formed of a pronoun + Old Perfective (or direct object pronoun + attributive or adnominal Old Perfective).

iw=f gm=i ḥms.kw wʿ.ø "And he found me alone"

(pD'Orb 5,1)

(< "he found me sitting and being alone"). A comparison with the example from oPetrie 18, 4-5 (above) emphasizes the more traditional usage in the literary register here;

Commentary note:

    iw=f gm=i   circumstantial clause *iw=f (ḥr) gm(.t)* with object suffix *=i*. For *ḥms* as Old Perfective followed by Old Perfective cf. infra, p.85.

Observation:

In sentences with the locational adverbs "here" and "there" the Old Perfective follows, e.g., *tw=tn di ḥms.ti ḥr ir.t iḥ m-rʒ-ʿ* "And what are you up to again here?" (HorSeth 8,3; cf. infra § 2.2.3[3]).

(3) Uses following auxiliary verbs

While the use of the *ḥr* + infinitive construction and the Old Perfective as forms that modify a statement as a whole (sentence adverbs) declined significantly, they were frequently used — the *ḥr* + infinitive construction in particular — in verbal combinations, as the complement of a number of verbs of incomplete predication (linking verbs) indicating the manner in which the verbal process is accomplished. This serves as a means of shading and explicating meaning or of separating the expression of aspect or *Aktionsart* from the verbal meaning and is another characteristic of the analytic tendency.

analytic tendency

auxiliary verbs | Among the verbs appearing in these verbal combinations are *ḫpr* "become", *mḥ* "fill", *wḥm* "repeat", *ßỉ* "carry", and a few verbs of motion such as *šm* "go", *ỉy* "come" with preposition + infinitive (*šm* appears with *ḥr* as well as *r*; cf. the remarks about imperative combinations, supra, § 2.2.2[3]). Although also still in use as verbs of complete predication, such verbs lose their original meaning to a considerable extent when combined with other verbs — they appear in these combinations as verbs that need to be completed by other verbs, appearing virtually only as auxiliaries (cf. Gardiner, § 483), as linking verbs ("fill" > "be occupied with"; "repeat" > "do again"; "carry" > "to set out"). An example of the more traditional usage may show how the development started (cf. Gardiner, *Grammar*, § 163 [11]):

(Astarte 3,y-1) | *ỉw=s ḥr ßỉ=s r šm r ḥr ß psḏ.t* "And she got up to go to the Ennead" (for the text, cf. supra, § 2.1.7[2]).

ʿḥʿ, ḥmsỉ, sḏr | The effect described can be seen with an infinitive or Old Perfective following *ḫpr* "become", but especially following *ʿḥʿ* "stand", *ḥmsỉ* "sit", *sḏr* "lie";[3] their usage displays an organized system:

as infinitives | — Where *ʿḥʿ, ḥmsỉ, sḏr* are themselves infinitives, followed by a *ḥr* + infinitive construction, they describe the **beginning** (inchoative) or the **repetition** of an act ("to set about", "begin", "continue to do something"):

(Doomed Prince 7,14)

wn.ỉn pß šrỉ ḥr ḥms ḥr ỉr.t hrw nfr m pßy=f pr "And then the boy set about celebrating in his house".

As infinitives followed by an Old Perfective, they describe the **beginning of a state** ("become", "to be at"):

(Blinding of Truth 4,5)

ỉw=s ʿḥʿ ỉwr.tỉ pßy grḥ m wʿ ʿdd šrỉ "And that night[4] she became pregnant with a small child".

as Old Perfectives | — Where *ʿḥʿ, ḥmsỉ, sḏr* are themselves Old Perfectives, but followed by *ḥr* + infintive, they describe the coincidence of action and speech, with the **action already occurring** ("to be occupied with", "to be doing", "your word, and I am already at it"):

(HorSeth 8,3)

tw=tn dỉ ḥms.tỉ ḥr ỉr.t ỉḫ m-rß-ʿ "And what are you doing here again?";

---

3   Rarely also *wrš* "spend the day at something"

4   Gardiner's proposed emendation <*m*> *pßy grḥ* is unnecessary (absolute use of a noun expressing time as adverb).

Notes:

  tw=tn dỉ ḥms.tỉ   Late Egyptian Adverbial Sentence (First Present) with subject pronoun 2nd. pers. pl.
           tw=tn;
  m-rȝ-ᶜ   for this adverbial phrase, cf. infra, § 2.2.4(1).

As Old Perfectives followed by Old Perfective constructions, they describe the coincidence of state and speech, with the **state already existing** ("to find something in a certain state", "to already be something"):

(pD'Orb 4,8)

iw=f ḥr gm

tȝy=f ḥm.t sḏr.tỉ mr.tỉ n ᶜḏȝ "And he found his wife pretending to be ill" (< *"he found his wife, being in the state of being ill deceivingly"; another possible interpretation: "he found his wife lying down, being ill deceivingly").

Observation:

Certain modes of expression with meanings close to those of the verbs mentioned can be construed similarly, with a similar meaning, as *nn ỉr=ỉ wnw.t ᶜnḫ.kw* "I will not spend another hour alive" (Doomed Prince 6,16; cf. also pD'Orb 3,7; 5,1; 7,6).

(4) Use after the negative auxiliary verb *tm*

In Late Egyptian, the negatival complement which followed the negative verb *tm*, and which was a verbal noun like the infinitive, is replaced by the infinitive. The negating function of this verbal combination is derived from the "terminating" meaning of *tm* as a verb of complete predication, "cease", "end"; "perish"; "destroy", but also "be complete"; "make complete" ("to be complete" > "to be at an end" > "to be no longer").[5] The function of the combination can be understood at an abstract level of meaning (basic meaning) as "to omit to do something". The construction of this verbal combination is distinct from those functional combinations listed above (§ 2.2.3[3]) in that it is not attached to the infinitive by means of the prepositions *ḥr* or *r*, but rather as an adverbially employed absolute noun.

[margin: the infinitive as Negatival Complement]

As in Middle Egyptian, the construction is used only for the nominal forms of the verb: *tm* takes the form of the infinitive, participle, or nominal/prospective *sḏm=f* form. It may be said that *tm* brings a negative noun or a negative nominal phrase (something like **pȝ tm ỉr.t* "the not-do") into the statement. In the everyday registers of Late Egyptian, it is largely restricted to use as an infinitive and a prospective *sḏm=f* in purpose clauses (or a prospective *sḏm=f* dependent on prepositions or conjunctions) — which can, however, hardly be regarded as a restriction in view of the extended use of the infinitive.

[margin: negating nominal forms of the verb]

---

5   Cf. W. Westendorf, *Grammatik der Medizinischen Texte. Grundriß der Medizin der alten Ägypter* VIII, Berlin 1962, § 360.

negating
infinitives

A widely used form is thus the negation of the infinitive in "pseudo-verbal constructions":

(pD'Orb 5,2)

[hieroglyphs] *ỉ.n=f ḥr ḏd n=ỉ ỉw=ỉ ḥr tm sḏm n=f* "('Come,
and let us lie together a little: loosen your hair!'): so did he speak to me, but I did not
listen to him" (< **"but I was non-listening to him");

Notes:

> *ỉ.n=f ḥr ḏd n=ỉ*   the Late Egyptian form of the "unquote" mark: "'This and that', so he said", with
> the (redundant) qualification, "so he said, speaking to me"; cf. Erman, *Neuägyptische
> Grammatik*, § 714;

> *ỉw=ỉ ḥr tm sḏm*   Late Egyptian circumstantial Adverbial Sentence (or: non-initial main sentence) *ỉw=ỉ
> ḥr sḏm* "while I was listening" (or the like), with negative infinitive *tm sḏm* (infinitive
> of *tm* and infinitive of *sḏm*).

Negation of the infinitive employed as a noun:

(LRL 22,1)

[hieroglyphs]

ỉ³ ỉḫ ỉ³ md.t n p³y tm h³b ỉ.ỉr=k n=ỉ p³ nty <m> ḥ³.ty=k "What is the matter that you did
not entrust me with what is on your mind?" (< **"What is the matter of this not-telling
me about what is on your mind, that you did?");

Notes:

> *ỉḫ*   interrogative pronoun, "What?", as the first noun in a nominal sentence;

> *ỉ³ md.t*   defined second noun in a nominal sentence which is further qualified;

> *p³y tm h³b ỉ.ỉr=k*   determined infinitive of *tm* followed by complementary infinitive *h³b* and relative form
> *n=ỉ   ỉ.ỉr=k* to introduce the actor (the prepositional complement *n=ỉ* and the relative object
> *p³ nty* belong to *h³b*!).

prospective
sḏm=f

Widely and characteristically used is also the prospective *sḏm=f* of *tm* to negate purpose
clauses:

*(pD'Orb 10,
1-2)*

[hieroglyphs]

m-ỉr pr r-bl tm p³ ym ḥr ỉṯ³=t "Don't go out, so that the sea may not seize you";

Notes:

> *tm p³ ym ỉṯ³=t*   prospective *sḏm=f* of *tm* with a nominal actor or subject in a purpose clause;

> *ḥr ỉṯ³=t*   the use of *ḥr* before the infinitive is not etymological. The preposition is used here
> (and elsewhere) as a marker of the infinitive.

2.2.4 Particles, conjunctions, prepositions and adverbs

Only those particles, interjections, conjunctions, prepositions, etc., which appear in
examples and exercises, or are not familiar from Middle Egyptian, will be introduced
here.

(1) Particles and interjections

The term particle here refers to free morphemes which have no influence whatsoever on the grammatical construction of phrases and sentences.

— The interrogative particle *(i)n* with its graphic variants ⁓, ⁓ and ⁓ is placed at the *(i)n* beginning of independent sentences (sentence conjugations), on occasion also at the beginning of those phrases that are not prepositional phrases; example: *(i)n tw=i rḫ.k p3 i.ir=f n=w* "Do I know what he did to them?" (*LRL* 32,11-12). Questions formulated in this manner as well as questions marked only by intonation are questions for corroboration — they require a decision between a "yes" or a "no" answer.

— *is* and *istw* (⁓ or the like) precede independent sentences, in some way interrupting *is; istw* the continuity of a text (a) by providing a "parenthetical" note or (b) by inserting an adversative component, contradicting, restricting or modifying ("but", "yet") a preceding statement. *is* and *istw* frequently introduce an element of doubt into the question: *istw i.ir.tw iri grg r*w-nb di* "But does one commit injustice every day even here?" (Wenamun 2,79). Cf. Erman, *Neuägyptische Grammatik*, §§ 676; 677; 736; 737; Hintze, *Neuägyptische Erzählungen*, 199ff.

— *inn* (⁓ or the like) is used before passages of which the first element is an *inn* independent clause (sentence conjugation), providing the premise (protasis) for the second part of the sentence (apodosis). In translation, it can thus assume the role of (a) "if" in a conditional clause, or (b) "when" in a temporal clause.

— *p3-wn* (⁓ or the like) precedes independent sentences, particularly Adverbial *p3-wn* Sentences (First Present), transforming these into propositions explaining a preceding sentence ("for"); note that *p3-wn* is a particle co-ordinating independent sentences, like "for" in English.

— *r3-*c* as part of a compound preposition with *m* follows the word or clause to which it *r3-*c* refers (Coptic ⲢⲰ), as an adverbial of concession or admission: "still", "yet", "however", "(even) though", "nevertheless", "all the same": *mntk m-r3-*c* mntk b3k n ʾImnw* "And you also, you are a Servant of Amun" (Wenamun 2,32); *ptr tw=i *c*nḫ.kw m-r3-*c** "Look, I'm still alive" (pD'Orb 15,8). Cf. also Erman, *Neuägyptische Grammatik*, § 683.

— *r3-pw* is used alone or in a compound preposition with *m*, as a particle of disjunctive *r3-pw* co-ordination of phrases ("or"), or of clauses ("or", "otherwise", "else"). It can be found alone, between or following the co-ordinated phrases; the compound preposition *m-r3-pw* separates the two (*p3 mzḥ m-r3-pw p3 ḥß̣w* "the crocodile or the snake", pD'Orb 4,4).

hn; h3n3 — *hn; h3n3* (⬚𓅱𓄿 or the like) precedes independent sentences (sentence conjugation-s). Preceding Adverbial Sentences (First Present) without a following sentence, it can express an unreal wish: "If only ...". Where these main-clause constructions are part of a sentence with an independent clause as protasis followed by an apodosis, formed with a *iw*-phrase or *wn* + *iw*-clause of future statement (Third Future), one can speak of a hypothetical conditional sentence: *hn m³w.t rḫ.tỉ ỉb=ỉ ỉw=s ᶜq.tỉ n=s r nw* "If only mother knew my heart, it would have occurred to her before." (Beatty Love Songs vs.C4,3; cf. infra § 2.2.6[2]). The particle can also be joined to the imperative supporter *my* (cf. supra § 2.2.2[2]; *hn-my* > Coptic ⲀⲘⲞⲒ). Cf. Satzinger, *Neuägyptische Studien*, § 1.4.2.2 (109ff).

ḫr — *ḫr* (⊖) is used frequently, sometimes alone, but also in association with other particles. In a variety of ways, it emphasizes contingency or the conditionality of a statement concerning a situation which has been mentioned, or conditions within it, frequently by way of contrast. This leaves considerable room for manoeuvre in translating, possibly (a) by using "but", "also", "and", "then", "therefore", etc; or (b) by syntactic means. This linking particle should not be confused with the preposition *ḫr* "with". Cf. Erman, *Neuägyptische Grammatik*, §§ 666-674, and L. Depuydt, The Contingent Tenses of Egyptian, in: *Orientalia* 58, 1989, 1ff; id., *Conjunction*, 201ff; Neveu, *La particule ḫr*.

k3 — *k3* (⬚𓅱𓆑 or the like) is a also a contingency particle, preceding the independent prospective *sdm=f* (expressing a wish, command, or desired future event), emphasizing its effect of sequentiality or relative future time which can be rendered with "then" in translation. It also appears in "if - then" relationships, as in the classical balanced sentences of the type *mdw=s k3 rwd=ỉ* "Should she speak, I will grow".

gr — *gr* (𓐰, Coptic ⲄⲈ) is an adverbial particle, which means "also", "likewise", "moreover" if placed at the end of the sentence. Followed by an independent pronoun, it emphasizes an earlier pronominal reference, "I too", or similarly, negated, "not me either". Cf. Černý/Groll, *Late Egyptian Grammar*, § 2.1.6; Erman, *Neuägyptische Grammatik*, § 682.

(2) Conjunctions

Conjunction is the term used here for those morphemes which play governing roles in constructions.

ỉn; m — *ỉn; m*: as in Middle Egyptian, the Late Egyptian *ỉn* introduces cleft sentences/parti-cipial statements. Besides *ỉn* there is an *m* that serves in the same role: *ỉn/m X ỉ.ỉr Y* "It is X who did Y". Although there is a phonetic or phonemic relationship between the two, there does appear to be a significant difference in role: *ỉn* introduces nouns which refer to inalienable items (those that do not allow explicit determination), while *m* is applied to divinities, persons, and divine or human qualities. Cf. Groll, *Non-verbal Sentence Patterns*, 58ff.

— *r.nty* (☲), also abbreviated to *nty*, is etymologically derived from Middle Egyptian   *r.nty* *r-nt.t*, "such that", "because", "in order to". In Late Egyptian it introduces direct speech after *ḏd*. In letters and notes, it follows the introductory greeting formulae to introduce the content proper, or mark paragraph divisions in between: *ḥnꜥ ḏd r.nty pꜣy=ỉ pr m šs* "And furthermore: My household is in order" (pBologna 1094, 8,9). Cf. also supra, § 2.1.7(1), commentary notes to line 10, and Erman, *Neuägyptische Grammatik*, § 680.

— *ḏr; m-ḏr* gives subjunctive-prospective *sḏm=f* constructions the role of dependent   *ḏr; m-ḏr* temporal clauses ("as"; "when"; it is the basis of the Coptic Temporal ⲚⲦⲈⲢⲈ-): "Seth became angry *m-ḏr ḏd=sn nꜣ md.t* when they said the words". In style oriented registers, *ḏr* can also appear with an infinitive in this role. As a preposition with a noun, *m-ḏr* indicates a motive or reason ("because of"). Cf. Erman, *Neuägyptische Grammatik*, §§ 631; 664-665.

(3) Prepositions

Prepositions also reveal the effects of the analytic tendency. Outside the Adverbial   the analytic Sentences (First Present), the older simple prepositions (*r, m, ḥr, ḫr*, etc.) are no longer   tendency widely used by themselves. Compound prepositions differentiating the specific roles and nuances of the simple prepositions are favoured instead (e.g., for *m*: *m-ḫnw, m.dỉ, m-ḏr.t*, etc.).

When used with the suffix pronouns, the simple prepositions moreover show special   status forms that already clearly point to the status-pronominalis forms of Demotic and Coptic: pronominalis Status pronominalis 𓄿𓏏 *ỉm=f* for the preposition *m* with the variant 𓄿 (pBM 10052, 5,20) and eventually ___𓄿 (Wenamun 2,77), Demotic *n.ỉm=f*, Coptic ⲘⲘⲞ=ϥ; status pronominalis ☲ *r.r=w* (*LRL* 1,5) for the preposition *r*, Demotic *r.r=w*, Coptic ⲈⲢⲞ=ⲞⲨ; corresponding to the status pronominalis of *r* is the status pronominalis ☲ *ḥr.r=w* (*LRL* 27,12) for the preposition *ḥr*, with variants like 𓊪𓏭𓊪 (*LRL* 9,5). Forms which thus appear to be analogous to *r* are used in Late Egyptian, but are replaced with compounds in Demotic and Coptic.

— *ỉrm; ḥnꜥ/r.ḥnꜥ* are prepositions with the basic meaning of "together with". Apart   *ỉrm; ḥnꜥ/r.ḥnꜥ* from its characteristic occurrence in the norm-hierarchically higher text registers, *ḥnꜥ* tends to be replaced by *ỉrm* (Coptic ⲘⲚ̄-, ⲚⲘ̄ⲘⲀ=) as the language develops; in Late Egyptian the difference of usage between *ỉrm* and *ḥnꜥ* might be described as follows:

ḥnᶜ indicates co-ordination between defined elements ("and") and therefore does not tend to be attached to a suffix pronoun (except in the more "style-conscious" texts): *gm=f sw m.dỉ ḥ.tỉ-s:nṯr NN ḥnᶜ nȝ ỉ₃.w wn ỉrm=f* "He found it in the possession of the incense-burner NN, and of the thieves who were with him" (pBM 10052, 4,17-18). *ỉrm* co-ordinates within phrases, fulfilling the function of "to be together with someone", "to do something together with someone" and is frequently a verbal rection: *ḥmsỉ ỉrm* "to live with someone"; *wnm ỉrm* "to eat with someone". Cf. Erman, *Neuägyptische Grammatik*, §§ 194-196; 620; Černý/Groll, *Late Egyptian Grammar*, §§ 7.1.10; 7.1.11.

Observation:

ḥnᶜ ḏd introduces a different subject in a letter ("and furthermore: ...").

m.dỉ

— *m.dỉ/mdỉ* (Coptic ⲚⲦⲈ-; ⲚⲦⲀ꞊) has many uses, basically revolving around the concept of being "with" someone. Graphemically at first, and then functionally, it coalesced with *m-ᶜ* (to take "away from" someone, etc.). More specifically, *m.dỉ/mdỉ* can have the following meanings (cf. Erman, *Neuägyptische Grammatik*, §§ 622-625; Černý/Groll, *Late Egyptian Grammar*, § 7.3.1):

in the Adverbial Sentence

1. in the sentence-forming (predicative) prepositional-phrase component of the Adverbial Sentence (noun *m.dỉ* noun), "someone or something is with someone or something", as in *ỉw=s m.dỉ NN*, "and she lives with NN" (< "is with him"), or *bn sw m.dỉ=ỉ* "I don't have it" (< "It isn't with me"); also in figurative uses ("to be with someone" in the sense of "to be in relation to someone"): *tw=k m.dỉ=ỉ m ᶜȝ* "As far as I am concerned, you are a donkey" (< *"You are a donkey with me").

as adverbial adjunct

2. as the adverbial adjunct of verbs (verb *m.dỉ* noun), as *ỉw=tw ᶜḥȝ m.dỉ=f* "and one argued with him", especially as a verbal rection that alters meaning: *ỉnỉ m.dỉ* "to aquire, to buy from someone"; *šzp m.dỉ* "to receive from someone, through someone"; *mdw m.dỉ* "to have a claim against someone"; *sdm m.dỉ* "to listen to someone", "to overhear someone".

coordinating phrases

3. in combination with the particle *ḥr* (☉), *m.dỉ* co-ordinates phrases which are separated from each other, "and also", "just as" etc.: *bw rḫ=ỉ s.t nb ... wpw pȝy ḥr nty wn ḥr m.dỉ tȝy ᶜ.t ...* "I know of no place ... except for this tomb, which is open, and also this house ..." (pAbbott 5,7-8); cf. Erman, *Neuägyptische Grammatik*, §§ 196; 672.

(r-)qrỉ/qȝỉ-n

— *(r-)qrỉ-n* or *(r-)qȝỉ-n* (◯▲◭𓏲𓊖; also 𓆑▲◭𓏲𓊖) is a compound preposition formed from the infinitive of the verb *qȝỉ/qrỉ n/r* "to reach someone", meaning "(to be) with/near someone". This preposition can appear either (a) as the rection of verbs or (b) as an adverbial (cf. Erman, *Neuägyptische Grammatik*, § 657): *ỉw=ỉ šm qȝỉ-n=f* "And I went to him" (Wenamun 2,22).

— *(r-)š3ᶜ-m/(r-)š3ᶜ-r* are compound prepositions formed with the infinitive *š3ᶜ* "to   *(r-)š3ᶜ-(m)*
begin", with both spatial and temporal meaning, which also replace several uses of the
simple preposition *r*. *š3ᶜ m/r* refers to a point of departure ("from there, thence", "since
then"), it can be used alone, *š3ᶜ m 3bw* "from Elephantine", or, combined with *r* or *nfry.t
r*, to define both limits: *š3ᶜ m rnp.t 1 r rnp.t 31* "from Regnal Year 1 to Regnal Year 31".
(r-)š3ᶜ indicates some point of termination ("as far as such-and-such"): *r-š3ᶜ nḥḥ* "until
eternity"; *š3ᶜ Nw.t* "as far as 'the Town'".

(4) Adverbs and adverbials

Adverbs — mostly prepositional phrases or prepositional combinations performing
adverbial roles — are essential elements of sentence structure, and thus very common.
They can be joined together in long chains which occasionally have complex structures
themselves. They are generally used at the end of the sentence in Late Egyptian, too,
appearing only exceptionally at the beginning, where they are usually introduced by ⟨⟩
ír.

There are only a few real adverbs: *dî* (⟨⟩) "here" (Coptic ΤΑΙ, ΤΗ), *ím* "there",   adverbs
with its variant writings (⟨⟩, ⟨⟩, also ⟨⟩; Coptic Ⲙ̄ⲘΑΥ), *3s* "quickly", *ᶜq3*
"correctly", *ᶜn* "again", and others derived from the relevant verbs, as well as the
interrogative adverb, *ṯnw* "where?" (Coptic ΤⲰⲚ). *dî*, and also *ím*, generally precede
other adverbs and prepositional phrases.

The most important adverbial phrases are the prepositional phrases: (a) the 'conven-   prepositional
tional' ones formed from simple or compound prepositions with defined nouns; (b) those   phrases
formed from simple prepositions and class-nouns (cf. supra § 2.1.3[2]) which begin to
establish a new set of compound adverbials, *m-mn.t* "daily" (Coptic Ⲙ̄ⲘΗⲚⲈ);
m-p3-hrww "today" (Ⲙ̄ⲠⲞⲞⲨ); *r-bl* "outside" (ⲈⲂⲞⲗ); *m-ḫnw* "within" (Ⲛ̄ⲀⲞⲨⲚ)
or *r-ḫnw* "into, inside" (ⲈⲀⲞⲨⲚ); and many others.

As in Middle Egyptian, many nominal expressions of time are still used absolutely   absolute nouns
(without preposition) to fulfil the role of an adverb, e.g., *rᶜw-nb* "every day": *tw=í ḏd
n n3 nṯr.w rᶜw-nb* "I pray to the gods daily". Used absolutely as adverbials nominal
expressions of location also occasionally appear; such cases are usually attributed to the
loss of prepositions, but this is unnecessary.

2.2.5 Bibliography

Erman, *Neuägyptische Grammatik*, §§ 87-97; Černý/Groll, *Late Egyptian Grammar*, §   enclitic
2.3; Korostovtsev, *Grammaire*, 91ff   pronouns
Winand, *Études*, §§ 255-290; Erman, *Neuägyptische Grammatik*, §§ 347-365;   imperative
Černý/Groll, *Late Egyptian Grammar*, §§ 24; 25; Korostovtsev, *Grammaire*, 232-239

causative imperative	Frandsen, *Outline*, §§ 46-48; Spiegelberg, *Demotische Grammatik*, §§ 187; 219; Černý/Groll, *Late Egyptian Grammar*, §§ 25.2.5; 25.2.6
infinitive	Winand, *Études*, §§ 73-192; Erman, *Neuägyptische Grammatik*, §§ 399-441; Černý/Groll, *Late Egyptian Grammar*, § 11; Korostovtsev, *Grammaire*, 200-220; for the status pronominalis Winand, *Études*, §§ 75-76; Černý/Groll, *Late Egyptian Grammar*, § 2.5; for the Demotic cf. Johnson, *Demotic Verbal System*, 16ff.
Old Perfective/ Stative	Winand, *Études*, §§ 193-254; Erman, *Neuägyptische Grammatik*, §§ 327-346; Černý/Groll, *Late Egyptian Grammar*, § 12; Satzinger, *Neuägyptische Studien*, 133ff; compare Till, *Koptische Grammatik*, § 257;
auxiliary verbs	J.-M. Kruchten, *Études de syntaxe néo-égyptienne. Les verbes ꜥḥꜥ, ḥmsỉ et sḏr en néo-egyptien. Emploi et signification*, Brussels 1982; id., in: *GM 84*, 1985, 33ff; Satzinger, *Neuägyptische Studien*, §§ 2.3.9; 2.7.1.1; 2.7.1.2.2 (ḫpr); Hintze, *Neuägyptische Erzählungen*, 96ff (verbal combinations), Erman, *Neuägyptische Grammatik*, §§ 567-574
tm-negation	Erman, *Neuägyptische Grammatik*, §§ 793-795; Groll, *Negative Verbal System*, §§ 48-57 (167-188)
prepositions	Černý/Groll, *Late Egyptian Grammar*, § 7; Erman, *Neuägyptische Grammatik*, §§ 597-665
adverbials	Černý/Groll, *Late Egyptian Grammar*, § 8; Erman, *Neuägyptische Grammatik*, §§ 588-596

2.2.6 Exercises

(1) Love poetry (pChester Beatty I vs. C1,8 - C2,4)

The second of a cycle of seven interrelated poems. Written in the reign of Ramesses V, they were published by Gardiner, *pChester Beatty I* (pls. XXIIa-XXIIIa). Each of the three stanzas of the piece consists of six verses, divided by verse points. The entire cycle bears a single title, with each individual poem numbered, where the first and last words form a word play with the relevant number, in a kind of "rondeau". A man and a woman speak alternately, with the woman speaking in the two following poems.

> **Purpose:** Example of lyrical language of Dynasty XX, a literary variety of Late Egyptian with interference of more traditional expressions (*nn rḫ≠ỉ*, use of *mk*, demonstrative *nfỉ*); numbers; infinitives and Old Perfectives.

Notes:

> vs. C1,8 ḥw.t "house", but as written here meaning "stanza" or "chapter" (cf. Arabic *bayt*); *sn* "brother" echoes with *snw* "two";
>
> *s:tꜣḥ* "confuse"; "sink". (A hapax legomenon causative of *tꜣḥ* "sink"; "be dipped" > Coptic ⲦⲰϨ "confuse");

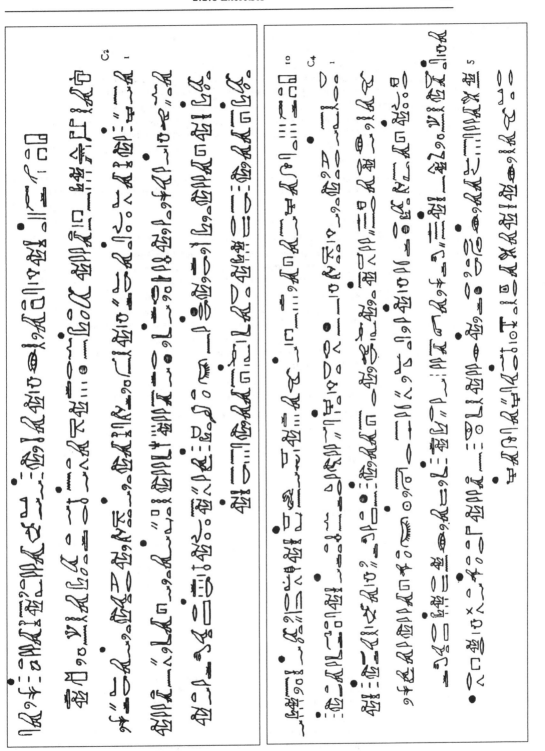

2.2.6 Exercises (1) Beatty Love Songs vs.
C1,8-C2,4

2.2.6 Exercises (2) Beatty Love Songs vs.
C3,10-C4,6

dỉ=f Late Egyptian preterite *sdm=f* (past expression, cf. also *ỉṯỉ* C2,1); *dỉ ṯЗy n=ỉ ẖЗy.t* "cause distress to importune me";

sw m sЗḥ-tЗ Late Egyptian Adverbial Sentence without introductory particle (note the relationship of grammatical number with the preposition *m*: first noun sing. + *m* + second noun pl. means something like "someone is one of those";

vs. C1,9-C2,1   "Mother ought to be good about my affairs where it is to be overlooked" (< *"Fine should mother be in my affairs concerning that which to observe is better omitted"); *ỉ.ḥЗᶜ mЗЗ=s* as passive participle whose object is an infinitive (*mЗЗ*) with its own direct object (*=s*) as the necessary resumptive pronoun: *"that which seeing it is (better) omitted";

vs. C2,1   *sẖЗ.tw=f*: if *ḥdn* is an Old Perfective (as is probable since it is a verb of quality; cf. WB s.v. Belegstellen), then *sẖЗ.tw=f* is a traditional circumstantial *sdm=f* ("when thinking about him");

mrw.t=f status pronominalis;

vs. C2,2   *ỉw.tỉ-ỉb=f* (Coptic ⲀⲦ-ⲎⲎⲦ) "foolish" (< *"one whose mind does not exist");

ỉw swt ỉw=ỉ mỉ qd=f: circumstantial form of the Adverbial Sentence (circumstantial First Present) introduced by the particle *ỉw swt*), subordination unterstood as contrastive: "I, however, I am like him" (< "[he is indeed foolish,] but I too am like him");

bw-rẖ=f: so-called Negative Aorist; Late Egyptian form of Middle Egyptian *n sdm.n=f/n rẖ=f*: to be unable to do something, essentially "not to know" something; *Зby ḥpt=f* "the wish to embrace him" (< *"the wish of embracing him");

mtw=f-ḥЗb: so-called Conjunctive, a form for joining one statement with a previous one (mostly an imperative or a future tense, here a wish): "and that he may appeal to NN" (< "and that he may communicate");

vs. C2,3   *tw=ỉ*: 1st sing. subject pronoun of the Late Egyptian Adverbial Sentence (First Present), replacing the earlier enclitic (dependent) pronoun in this usage;

nbw ḥm.wt: "women's gold" meaning the goddess Hathor, the protectress of lovers;

mЗЗ=ỉ nfr.w=k: prospective *sdm=f* of purpose, "so that ...";

ršw.t for *ršw*; here — as in the following — prospective *sdm=f* of purpose parallel to *mЗЗ=ỉ*.

(2) Another love poem (pChester Beatty I vs. C3,10 - C4,6)

The sixth poem of the same cycle of love poems, published ibid. pls. XXIVa - XXVa.

Purpose: Example of lyrical language of Dynasty XX, a literary variety of Late Egyptian with interference of traditional expressions (such as *nn mỉt.t=f* and participles without *ỉ.* -prefix); numbers; imperative, infinitives, Old Perfectives; preposition *r* + infinitive; particles; interjections; conjunctions.

Notes:

vs. C3,10   *s:wЗ=ỉ n=f*: Late Egyptian preterite *sdm=f* "I passed by on his behalf", with the word play of *s:wЗ* "pass by" with "six" (earlier *srsw/sỉsw*, here fem.), revealing that it has already come close to the Coptic word (ⲤⲞⲞⲨ);

vs. C4,2   *m-ḏr znny=ỉ/ m-ḏr znny.n=ỉ*: conjunction *m-ḏr* + *sdm=f* "when I pass/as I passed". The apparent appearance of a *sdm.n=f* form has two background conditions: (a) the phonemic structure of the word (*znỉ* can be graphemically recorded *znny/znn*, and thus read *znn=ỉ* > *zn.n=ỉ*); (b) since *sdm.n=f* can appear as a variant of the Late Egyptian preterite *sdm=f* in texts of this registers, thus it is also an occasional variant, where the *sdm=f* is the subjunctive-prospective *sdm=f*;

tw=i wˁ.kw r nhm: Late Egyptian Adverbial Sentence (First Present), with the 1st sing. personal pronoun *tw=i*; *wˁi r* + infinitive "to do something alone"; note *ḥntš m* "to delight in something, to enjoy something";

vs. C4,3   *dr mȝȝ=i*: preposition with infinitive + pronoun object (*"since the seeing me"); altogether: "How my heart bursts with joy, my brother, when you become aware of me!" (< "How my heart delights in joy, my brother ...");

iw=s ˁq.ti n=s: the first *=s* (written *st*) summarizes the whole previously described situation; *ˁq n* "enter", "something enters into someone", here as "entering" into someone's consciousness, "become clear, occur to someone";

vs. C4,4   *ḥn=i* is a prospective *sdm=f* introducing a sentence, *znny(=i)* < *sn=i* the same or a prospective *sdm=f* of purpose ("so that"): "then I would hurry so that I might kiss him" or "then I would hurry and kiss him". The following *sdm=f* forms are all independent prospectives, in the sense of hypothetical statements ("should" or similar);

ṯm is a writing variant of *rmi* "weep"; here weep out of embarrassment;

bw rmi=i n rmṯ: in Late Egyptian so-called Negative Aorist *bw sdm=f/bw ir=f-sdm* (cf. infra § 2.3.2[3]: to be unable to do something);

vs. C4,5   *tw=k rḫ=i*: Adverbial Sentence (First Present) with the infinitive of *rḫ* ("know someone", "acknowledge someone", then even "stand with someone");

iry=i; tfi ib=i: preterite *sdm=f* forms ("I had a party arranged and my heart urged that this-and-that should be done");

vs. C4,6   *r rdi.t gmḥ=i*: so called Causative Infinitive ("to let me see" < *"to cause that I see");

nfr-wsi is a possible Late Egyptian writing of *nfr-wi* (cf. Erman, *Neuägyptische Grammatik*, § 684), but here it can still be reduced to the adjectival sentence *nfr-wi si/sw*.

2.3 The construction of verb forms

2.3.0 Periphrasis and its spread

The combination of a auxiliary verb and an infinitive (cf. supra, § 2.2.3[3]) can be so   periphrasis close that the meaning of the former is lost completely, and its function is reduced to that of constructing particular forms of the verb. In a way, such paraphrase with an auxiliary, known as "periphrasis", is already a possible description of the constructions with *tm* (considering *tm* as a pure grammatical function expressing negation rather than as a verb with the meaning "to omit to do something"). In Late Egyptian, *iri* (in the following abbreviated in transliteration to *ir*) becomes increasingly common as a fully grammaticised auxiliary verb of this type.

    Replacing the synthetic constructions of the verbal conjugations by periphrasis is again   analytical a symptom of the analytic tendency in linguistic evolution (cf. § 2.0.1). It is now *iri* that   tendency is conjugated while the verbal content proper is expressed by the infinitive ("isolation of inflexion", *Flexionsisolierung*);[6] it is thus the verb *iri* that retains the traditional conjugation forms, while the specific meaning is conveyed via the infinitive as the object of *iri*. Structurally *iri* takes over the conjugation, becoming the conjugation base;[7] the infinitive has become the meaning expression. Formally it might be represented as follows:

Conjugation modifier	Conjugation base	Actor expression	Meaning expression	
∅	*ir*	*=f*	*sdm*	"He heard/has heard"
bw	*ir*	*=s*	*mdt*	"She does not speak"
r-š3ᶜ	*i.ir.t*	*=k*	*iy*	"until you come"

Such uses of infinitives as that in *iw=f ḥr sdm* can result in an analogical transfer of *ḥr* to forms with *iri*, where the preposition does not properly belong, as if *ḥr* has become a kind of "meaning expression marker", as in ⟦hieroglyphs⟧ *bw ir=k ḥr sdm* for *bw ir=k sdm* "You didn't hear" (pLansing 8,3).

multiliteral
verbs

The *iri*-periphrases began at an early date with the multiliteral verb roots, and in Late Egyptian they prevail initially in negative forms (cf. the prohibitive/negated imperative, § 2.2.2[3]), and only gradually in affirmative forms, so that the entire transformation is really accomplished only in Coptic.

Observation:

In the *iw=f r sdm* construction (Third Future) with nominal actors *iw* is replaced by a form written ⟦hieroglyph⟧ *ir* (Coptic ЄРЄ-). Note that this is a phonemic-graphemic variant which has no connection with the periphrasis (cf. Gardiner, *JEA* 16, 1930, 220ff).

2.3.1 Paraphrased relative phrases

The periphrasis of active (but not passive!) participles occurs in those verbs with more than three root consonants, but can also already be observed in shorter roots. Here during the New Kingdom these remain replacement forms of the imperfective participle. The following examples also represent a particular form of the Late Egyptian participial statement, the Cleft Sentence introduced with *m* (cf. Erman, *Neuägyptische Grammatik*, § 386 and supra, § 2.2.4[2]):

(pD'Orb 4,7)   ⟦hieroglyphs⟧ *m p3y=k sn šri i.ir qnqn(=i)* "It was your younger brother who beat me";

---

6   See Polotsky, *Grundlagen des koptischen Satzbaus*, 171 (§ 5).

7   Cf. Polotsky, *Grundlagen des koptischen Satzbaus*, 175f.

ith n=k nkt "Your outfitting is what brings profit to you" (< "brings things").

The same with the relative form:

[*ih.t n*] *wḏ3 n nzw (Stš.y Mrỉ.n-Pth)* ꜥ.*w.s ỉ.ỉr=tw gm.t=w m.dỉ=f ḥr-s3 zm3-t3* "[the things of] the storehouse of King Seti I, which were found with him after the funeral";

Note:

> *ỉ.ỉr=tw gm.t=w*   =*tw* as impersonal subject of the relative form (or the -.*tw* ending of the passive relative form); the object (=*w*) of the infinitive of *gmỉ* in the status pronominalis is an indirect resumption of the nominal antecedent ([*ỉh.t*]) of the relative form.

2.3.2 The forms of the Late Egyptian *sdm=f*

The *sdm=f* in the narrow sense of the term is a common Late Egyptian form used to make statements about the past. Functionally, it corresponds to Middle Egyptian *(ỉw) sdm.n=f* (cf. infra, § 3.2) and expresses past tense ("I did") as well as perfect tense ("I have done"); it is termed the "preterite" *sdm=f* here.[8] The range of other forms following its construction principle is limited in Late Egyptian: along with the preterite *sdm=f* there is the nominal or emphatic *sdm=f*, and a *sdm=f* form which follows the negation *bw* (< *n*). A *sdm.t=f* form follows the preposition *r* and the same negation *bw*. In Late Egyptian, *ỉrỉ*-periphrasis with the preterite *sdm=f* is limited to verbs with more than three root consonants (*ỉry=f qnqn=ỉ* "he beat me/he has beaten me"), but it has generally taken hold of most of the other *sdm=f* forms. The evolution becomes complete in Demotic and Coptic, with *ỉr=f sdm* > ⲁϥⲥⲱⲧⲙ̄.

(1) The nominal or emphatic *sdm=f*

In texts higher up in the register hierarchy, the nominal *mrr=f* and the nominal *mr.n=f* continue to be used as in Middle Egyptian; in Late Egyptian, therefore, imperfect and prospective forms can likewise be concealed in the invariable *sdm=f*.   *mrr=f/mr.n=f*

Late Egyptian proper, however, uses a *sdm=f* form with the root extension prefix *ỉ.-* instead. Except with *ỉrỉ*, the simple form of this construction is rare, being restricted to   *ỉ.sdm=f/ỉ.ỉr=f sdm*

---

8   Compare, however, Frandsen, *Outline*, and Černý/Groll, *Late Egyptian Grammar*, who use the term "perfect active" *sdm=f*.

a few verbs (*dỉ; ỉw; šm; ỉnỉ; ḏd*). The form generally used is based on a periphrasis with *ỉrỉ*: *ỉ.ỉr=f sdm*, which is closely related in form to the Late Egyptian relative forms.[9]

function
In Late Egyptian, the functions of the traditional forms also coalesce: *ỉ.ỉr=f sdm* is employed for past, present and future. It remains, however, characteristic of this nominal *ỉ.ỉr=f sdm* that the semantic weight of the verbal expression is reduced, but that of the adverbial expression is increased — as in Middle Egyptian (stress, emphasis).

(Wenamun 2,3-5)

ỉw=f wšb ḏd n=ỉ ỉ.ỉr=k ỉy ḥr ỉḫ n sḥn

ỉw=ỉ ḏd n=f ỉ.ỉr=ỉ ỉy m-s3 t3 ṯ.t n p3 wỉ3 ꜥ3 šps n ꜣỉmnw-Rꜥw nzw nṯr.w

ỉ.ỉr p3y=k ỉtỉ

ỉ.ỉr p3 ỉtỉ n p3y=k ỉtỉ

ỉw=k ỉr=f m-r3-ꜥ

"And he responded, asking me, 'Because of what orders did you come?' And I said to him, 'It was because of the wood for the Great and Noble Bark of Amonrasonther that I came! What your father did, and your grandfather did, you too will do!'"

Notes:

hieroglyphic transcription — the sign of the circle (Gardiner N 33) with *ỉy* represents the hieratic "dot" (which can stand various for -*.t*, -*.y* and even the "seated woman" [Gardiner B 2]). Occasionally this transcription of the dot will again be used in the examples to follow;

ỉw=f wšb ḏd n=ỉ — the form of *ỉw=f ḥr wšb ḥr ḏd n=ỉ* common by now;

ỉw=k ỉr=f — future form of the *ỉw*-sentence (Third Future), for *ỉw=k r ỉr=f*;

structure — the main point is expressed with the preposition *ḥr* and the interrogative pronoun *ỉḫ* (i.e., *ỉḫ* with nominal attribute) in the question, the counterpart of which is the prepositional phrase *m-s3 t3 ṯ.t* in the response, which is in exactly the same syntactic role.

(pMayer A rt. 2,19)

ỉ.ỉr.w ḥdb p3y=ỉ ỉtỉ ỉw=ỉ m šrỉ "When my father was killed, I was still a child";

Notes:

ỉ.ỉr.w ḥdb — passive *sdm* in nominal function paraphrased with *ỉr*, or possibly a writing for *ỉ.ỉr=w ḥdb* "When they killed my father";

ỉw=ỉ m šrỉ — circumstantial form of the Adverbial Sentence (Circumstantial First Present);

9 Cf. — as a *locus classicus* — H. J. Polotsky, *Études de syntaxe copte*, Cairo 1944, 69ff.

structure and translation   the main point is the statement of "still being a child", expressed by the circumstantial form. The reduced semantic weight of the verbal expression can be represented in translation with a subordinate clause ("when").

(2) *sdm.t=f* as conjunctional phrase (Terminative)

The form *sdm.t=f* is still comparatively uncommon, as in Middle Egyptian, appearing in the texts higher up in the register hierarchy with the preposition *r* ("until he hears") and sometimes also with other prepositions. Gradually however, this is reduced to a fixed combination (*r-sdm.t=f*), which then adopts the periphrastic form *r-ir.t=f-sdm*.

With the disappearance of the free use of *sdm=f* forms after prepositons, the systematic context (paradigm) is lost, and the *r* reduced to an integral element of the fixed combination, becoming virtually a conjunction. As in other forms (relative phrases, nominal *sdm=f*), the grapheme *r* can also be replaced with the allograph *i.*-: 〰️🦅 *r-ir.t=f-sdm* becomes 🦅 *i.ir.t=f-sdm*.

i.ir.t=f-sdm

(pBM 10052, 15,8-9)

dd t3.ty i.t3y t3y s.t-ḥm.t imm sw m rmt-s3w i.ir.tw=tw gm it3w-rmt r s:ʿḥʿ=s "The Vizier said, 'Seize this woman. Make her a prisoner until a thieving person is found to testify against her.'"

Notes:

dd NN   preterite *sdm=f*;

i.ir.tw=tw gm   for *i.ir.t=tw gm*, the passive form of the periphrasis for *r sdm.t=f*; or use of the impersonal pronoun *=tw* as actor expression of the *i.ir.t=f sdm* form.

In the combination *r-ir.t=f sdm*, it is the conjunction *r* that determines the meaning (function) of the form; therefore its phonemic reduction (Coptic Є-) is countered by using the preposition (*r-*)*š3ʿ*, which is functionally equivalant to *r* in many respects. The conjugation form *š3ʿ-i.ir.t=f-sdm* (further abbreviated *š3ʿ.tw=f-sdm*, in Demotic occasionally *š3ʿ-mtw=f-sdm*) which thus developed is the Late Egyptian precursor of the Coptic Terminative (ϢΑΝΤϤⲤⲰΤⲘ̄); this is also the term used here for the form.

š3ʿ-i.ir.t=f-sdm

(Wenamun 2,36-37)

imm in.tw=f š3ʿ-i.ir.tw=i šm r rsy mtw=i di.t in=tw n=k p3y=k gb nb zp-2 m-r3-ʿ "Let it be brought until I go south and have all your expenses repaid!";

Notes:

in.tw=f and *in=tw*   passive forms of the subjunctive-prospective *sdm=f*;

mtw=i di.t   Conjunctive: a form which continues the imperative, optative and infinitive.

(3) Negations: the Negative Aorist and the "not-yet" form

n sdm.n=f/ n
sdm.t=f

As with the negated imperative (prohibitive, cf. supra, § 2.2.2[3]) the *irĭ*-periphrasis was employed in two forms of the earlier *sdm=f* construction which were used to express a specific kind of negation: in the successors of *n sdm.n=f* ("he was unable to hear") and *n sdm.t=f* ("before he hears/heard"; "he has not yet heard"), the Middle Egyptian negative particle ⌐⌐ is replaced with the Late Egyptian ⅃ℯ, and the *sdm=f* forms by their *irĭ*-periphrasis: *bw ir=f-sdm* "he was unable to hear" and *bw ir.t=f-sdm* "before he hears/heard". It is, however, possible that the *bw* is merely another grapheme for n[10] (the Coptic negative particle is once again N̄-).

bw sdm=f/
bw ir=f-sdm

Like the Middle Egyptian *n sdm.n=f*, the Late Egyptian *bw sdm=f/bw ir=f-sdm* forms negate statements concerning "characterizations, statements of custom, generalizations" (Gardiner, *Grammar*, § 418). They express inability to do something, or deny that a particular situation is ordinary, and are thus designated as the Negative Aorist. The construction appears as *bw sdm=f*, generally in the case of the verb *rḫ* (*bw rḫ=k* > Coptic ⲘⲈϢⲀⲔ), and sometimes also in the text registers towards the top of the hierarchy (in the case of *dĭ* often written as ⅃ℯ⤏); in such texts *bw sdm.n=f* can also be found in this construction, as a direct analogy to the old *n sdm.n=f*. The form *bw ir=f-sdm* is the Late Egyptian precursor of the Coptic ⲘⲈϤⲤⲰⲦⲘ̄. Examples:

(Beatty Love Songs vs. C2,2)

bw rḫ=f n3y=i 3by ḥpt=f "He does not know my wishes to embrace him" (< *"my wishes of embracing him"; for the hieroglyphic text, cf. supra, § 2.2.6[1]);

(Beatty Love Songs vs. C4,4)

bw rm=i n rmṯ "I certainly do not weep because of the people" (within the cotext hypothetical, "I would be certain not to weep"; for the hieroglyphic text, cf. supra, § 2.2.6[2]).

(Wenamun 2,65)

(i)n bw ir=k-ptr n3 gš i.ir-irĭ zp-2 n h3y r Km.t "Can you not see the migrant birds who have already flown down to Egypt twice?"

Notes:

      (i)n for the interrogative particles *n*, *in*, cf. supra, § 2.2.4(1);

      irĭ zp-2 n h3y *"make two times of descending".

preterite bw
sdm=f

It should be noted that along with the Negative Aorist there is another non-periphrastic *bw sdm=f*. Derived from the Middle Egyptian *n sdm=f*, it is common in literary texts and is a way of negating past statements. It can be recognized morphologically in the verb

---

10   The phonemic significance of ⸺ and the relationship between ⸺ *n* and *bw* has given rise to many different interpretations.

ỉy/ỉw "come": for the preterite *bw sdm=f*, it is *bw ỉy=f*; for the Negative Aorist, it is *bw ỉw=f*.

The form *bw sdm.t=f* (thus especially, with verbs of motion), or *bw ỉr.t=f-sdm*, is rare; it describes a situation which should have already arrived, but has not done so at the time of speaking. *bw ỉr.t=f-sdm* is the Late Egyptian precursor of the Coptic ⲘⲠⲀⲦϤ-ⲤⲰⲦⲘ̄. The passive is *bw ỉry.t* + subject. *bw ỉr.t=f-sdm*

bw ỉr.t=k ḏd pȝ rmṯ "You have not yet mentioned the man."   *(LRL 72,13)*

Note: *bw ỉr.t=k ḏd* "not yet" form of *ḏd*, "you have not yet said", here in a writing of *bw ỉr.tw=k* shortened to strokes.

(4) Passive forms

Late Egyptian passives are in a way still construed like the Middle Egyptian forms: morphology

1. there is the passive *sdm* (*sdm.w* passive), which usually shows graphemically the same form as the root itself. *ỉrỉ* ("do", and as periphrasis verb) is generally written *ỉr.w*, but also ; *rdỉ* "give" appears as *dd.tw* or the like, and *gm* "find" very often has . An example of a nominal *sdm=f* in the passive: *ỉ.ỉr.w ḥdb pȝy=ỉ ỉtỉ ỉw=ỉ m šrỉ* "When my father was killed, I was still a child" (cf. supra, § 2.3.2[1], for hieroglyphic text and commentary notes).   *(pMayer A rt. 2,19)*

2. there is the *sdm.tw=f* passive; the stem of the verb receives a -.*t* ending (written -.*tw*, -.*tỉ*), followed by the logical subject, which, if pronominal, takes the form of a suffix pronoun. This is the most common form of the passive construction: *ỉmm ỉn.tw=f ȝˁ-ỉ.ỉr.tw=ỉ šm r rsy mtw=ỉ dỉ.t ỉn=tw n=k pȝy=k gb nb.t zp-2 m-rȝ-ˁ* "Let it be brought until I go south and have all your expenses repaid" (for the hieroglyphic text, cf. supra, § 2.3.2[2]);   *(Wenamun 2,36-37)*

   Note:

   ỉn.tw=f and *ỉn=tw*   -.*t*-passive forms of prospective *sdm=f* as subjunctive following forms of *dỉ* (imperative or infinitive).

3. in some respect and with many peculiarities of its own, there is the Old Perfective of transitive verbs (originally a medial voice), cf. § 2.2.3 (2).

Although closely related to the Middle Egyptian passive, the usage of the various forms has undergone changes. Originating from the passive of Middle Egyptian *(ỉw) sdm.n=f*, the Late Egyptian perfect passive *sdm* is as it were the "natural" passive form of the preterite *sdm=f*, but it is not widely used in everyday registers, its role being virtually restricted to the formulae of legal texts: *ỉn.w NN* "NN was brought (for interrogation)"; *dd.w n=f ˁnḫ n nb* "he was made to swear by the lord". The broader role of the form is taken over by the preterite *sdm.tw/sdm=tw* form: the real Late Egyptian passives are the *sdm.tw* forms.   relative frequence

peculiarities
of the passive
ending -.t

As in many languages, the Egyptian passive originally permitted the actor or subject to remain unidentified, if the speaker so desired. The *sdm.tw* forms, however, can only be admitted as a passive in the strict sense when a suffix appears as the object or "logical subject": (*in.tw=f*). In general, it is in fact more justifiable to take them as active forms with an impersonal actor *=tw* (*sdm=tw p3 zî* "one interrogated the man", rather than *sdm.tw p3 zî* "the man was interrogated"),[11] by analogy with (a) the "Adverbial Sentence" (*tw=tw ḥr sdm* "one hears"); (b) the *iw*-forms (*iw=tw ḥr sdm* "and one hears/while one hears"). This same tendency is paralleled by the use of the active form with the 3rd pers. pl. pronoun *=w*: *sdm=w sw* "They interrogated him/he was interrogated"; in Coptic this replaces the passive completely.

2.3.3 Prepositional formations as conjugation substitutes

prepositions
and verbal
forms

A significant characteristic of Middle Egyptian sentence construction was the possibility of employing nominal verb forms[12], in the same way as nouns and infinitives, as satellites of prepositional nuclei, rendering the verbs dependent on the prepositions: *ḥr m33=f*; *m mrr=f*; *ḥft sdm.n=f*. This type of usage disappears in Late Egyptian, being preserved only

Subject/Agent/Actor; Object; Rection; Semantic complements/ arguments: Important for syntax and translation is the type and number of the possible complements of the verbal meaning, which define the semantic valency of the verb. Verbs without objects (intransitive verbs) have a valency of one: only the subject role is occupied ("X goes"). Verbs which require an object in addition to their subject (transitive verbs), and those which permit an object, have a valency of two ("X presents Y"). Verbs which require yet another complement have a valency of three ("X gives Y Z"; or "X presents Y with Z"). In Egyptian, this third valency role is always a prepositional phrase ("rection" of the verb), defined generally by the preposition *n* or else *m*, *ḥr*, or *r*; modern English usage resembles Egyptian inasmuch as the third valency role is only rarely occupied by an "indirect object", but usually by a prepositional phrase ("to; for"). These verbal rections must be taken into account when translating, because they can alter the meaning: *irî*, e.g., with a valency of one does not mean "make" ("X makes Y"), but "act" ("X acts").
To distinguish it from the (logical) subject of a sentence, the subject of a verb will also be termed the "actor" or "agent" here.

in those prepositional formations characterized by fusion, where verb and preposition are no longer separate paradigmatic entities. These are the combinations of the prepositions

---

11   It is, however, questionable whether the differentiation of the passive ending -.*tw* and an impersonal suffix pronoun *=tw* should consequently be maintained in transliteration.

12   These nominal verb forms are nominal *sdm=f* and *sdm.n=f*, and subjunctive-prospective *sdm=f*.

m-dr, m-ht and *r-tnw* with the subjunctive-prospective *sdm=f* and the combination of *r/r-š3ᶜ* with *sdm.t=f* (cf. § 2.3.2[2] supra).

The functions of the earlier constructions consisting of prepositions with nominal verb forms are partially assumed by constructions in which the infinitive verbal noun is dependent on a preposition. Among these is the "covert" construction of *hnᶜ* with the infinitive — "covert" because the morphology of the construction is no longer clearly recognizable — the so-called Conjunctive (*mtw=f sdm < hnᶜ ntf sdm < hnᶜ sdm ntf*).

preposition with infinitive

There are also two other forms where the subject or actor of verbal forms is introduced by means of (a) the possessive article ("his activity") and (b) relative forms ("the activity which he was engaged in"), i.e.:

m p3y=f sdm/m p3 sdm l.ir=f

1. preposition + possessive article + infinitive: *m p3y=f sdm*, for present and future;
2. preposition + infinitive + relative form of *iri*: *m p3 sdm i.ir=f*, for the past.

As these constructions are not syntactically different from "normal" prepositional phrases, they can be used in the same fashion, as adverbial modifiers of sentences.

(1) Preposition + *p3y=f sdm*

Infinitives with possessive article can appear in any position where a noun could be used. The use after prepositions is just one of several:

iw=i r di.t in=tw

(pCairo 58056 rt. 6-7)

n=k p3 kr m p3y=i spr "I will send you the boat at my arrival";

Notes:

      iw=i r di.t future expression, the so-called Third Future;

      di.t in=tw "cause that one bring", so-called Causative Infinitive.

Translating these constructions poses no unusual difficulties, but where necessary, temporal circumstantial clauses can also be used, e.g., "I will send you the boat when I arrive".

In the form of the Causative Infinitive, this infinitive combination is still common in Coptic: *m-hnw p3 di.t sdm=f > hn p3 di.t ir=f-sdm >* ϨⲘ̄ⲡⲦⲣⲉϥⲤⲰⲦⲘ̄.

(2) Preposition with defined infinitive and relative form

Prepositional phrases with infinitives can relate to the past with respect to the main sentence where the actor or subject is introduced in the relative form of *iri*:

(pBM 10052, 4,7-8)

iw=k in p3y hd im r-bnr (m-)s3 p3 šm i.ir n3 it3w "And you brought this silver out of there after the thieves had gone";

Note:

> ỉm r-bnr   ỉm "there" in the tomb; ỉnỉ X r-bnr/r-bl "to bring out X".

If such a defined infinitive has an object, this follows the relative form — such cases occasionally require some analytical attention: this is why the form has been termed a "split determined infinitive":

(pAnast. VI
33-34)

ỉ.ỉr=w r=k ... ḥr p3 ỉṯ3 ỉ.ỉr=k n3 ḥbs.wt n t3 mr.t m-b3ḥ p3 ỉm.ỉ-r3 pr-ḥḏ "It happened that they acted against you ... because of your seizure of the garments of the weavers in the presence of the Superintendent of the Treasury."

Notes:

ỉ.ỉr=w r=k + adverbial phrase	the function of the Late Egyptian nominal sdm=f (cf. supra § 2.3.2[1]) is represented here by a paraphrase ("it happened that ..."); or else emphatic, "It was because ... that they acted against you";
p3 ỉṯ3 n3 ḥbs.wt	defined infinitive + object "the taking-away of the clothing".

(3) The Conjunctive

By definition the Conjunctive is a form which "conjoins" various expressions. In its Ramesside form its conjugation base is mtw combined with the actor-expression suffix pronoun and the infinitive (mtw=f sdm). In Coptic it is N̄ϤⲤⲰⲦⲘ̄ (but in Boharic, still N̄ⲦⲉϤⲤⲰⲦⲉⲘ as well), with a nominal actor expression N̄Ⲧⲉ-. The prepositions (r, ḥr) occasionally — in specific texts (like pD'Orb) quite frequently — preceding the infinitive are unetymological. They may be understood as markers of the semantic element, adopted from other uses, such as ỉw=f ḥr sdm, where the preposition was frequently omitted, and thus inadvertently reinserted in forms where it did not belong originally (cf. "hypercorrection", supra, § 1.1.3[4]).

Although the Conjunctive can no longer be synchronically so analysed, it is classified as a prepositional formation because it originated in the combination ḥnᶜ + infinitive + independent pronoun (in its use as a possessive pronoun): (ḥnᶜ sdm ntf > ḥnᶜ ntf sdm > mtw=f sdm). The "conjunctive" function was originally derived from the role of the preposition ḥnᶜ, which co-ordinates nouns (a preceding infinitive as a verbal noun with another one). It can appear as an infinitive complement, but more frequently it is the continuation of imperative, optative and Third Future constructions.

(pMayer A rt.
8,18-19)

ỉmm ỉn.tw mtrw mtw=f s:ᶜḥᶜ=ỉ

"Get a witness and let him accuse me!"

Notes:

> ỉn.tw mtrw   passive form of subjunctive-prospective sdm=f, "that a witness be brought";

mtw=f s:ʿḥʿ=i conjunctive of 3rd pers. sing. with infinitive *s:ʿḥʿ* + object suffix, "and (that) he should accuse me".

imm in.tw=f š3ʿ-i.ir.tw=i šm r rsy mtw=i di.t in.tw n=k p3y=k gb nb m-r3-ʿ "Let it be brought until I go south and have all your expenses repaid!" (for the hieroglyphic text, cf. supra, § 2.3.2[2]).   *(Wenamun 2,36-37)*

The unchanged original form *ḥnʿ ntf sdm* will still be encountered in the texts higher up in the register hierarchy (e.g., in the Astarte papyrus). Even in Dynasty XIX, it will still be found in everyday texts:

(oDM 114, 4-5)

m rdi.t t3y.tw n=k ḥnʿ ntk šn.t p3 ḥtr n t3 iz.t nty ḥr pr-ḥd n Pr-ʿ3 ʿ.w.s. "Don't get yourself into trouble: ask about the supplies of the Gang with which Pharaoh's Treasury is charged";

Notes:

m rdi.t t3y.tw n=k   lit. "Do not let someone find fault with you";

ḥnʿʿ   disregard the second *ʿ*;

šn.t   in the original text, this word is written with the hieratic ligature for *šn.t* (cf. Erman, *Neuägyptische Grammatik*, § 19[2]);

t3 iz.t   *t3 iz.t n p3 ḥr*, the "Gang" of the Tomb Building Administration, who lived in Deir el-Medineh;

nty ḥr pr-ḥd   relative clause with *nty*, relating to the *ḥtr* "income, which is at the Treasury".

2.3.4 Bibliography

Erman, *Neuägyptische Grammatik*, §§ 552; 554; Černý/Groll, *Late Egyptian Grammar*, § 48.3.6 (participle); Korostovtsev, *Grammaire*, 298f (relative form)   relative phrases

form: Erman, *Neuägyptische Grammatik*, §§ 302-304; Cassonnet, *Les Temps Seconds*, 135ff (§ 11); function: Frandsen, *Outline*, §§ 85-92 ("that-form", 153ff); Winand, *Études*, §§ 405-457; Černý/Groll, *Late Egyptian Grammar*, §§ 26; 27; Cassonnet, *Les Temps Seconds*   nominal *sdm=f*

Erman, *Neuägyptische Grammatik*, §§ 442-445; Černý/Groll, *Late Egyptian Grammar*, §§ 33; 34; Korostovtsev, *Grammaire*, 303f; Frandsen, *Outline*, §§ 56-59; Winand, *Études*, §§ 464-470   Terminative

Frandsen, *Outline*, §§ 21-24; Černý/Groll, *Late Egyptian Grammar*, §§ 20.5.4-20.5.10; 20.7; cf. also Erman, *Neuägyptische Grammatik*, §§ 768-772; Winand, *Études*, §§ 378-385   Negative Aorist

Winand, *Études*, §§ 326-334   *bw sdm=f*, preterite

bw ìr.t=f-sdm	Černý/Groll, *Late Egyptian Grammar*, § 20.8; Frandsen, *Outline*, §§ 25-28; Winand, *Études*, §§ 459-463
passive *sdm*	Winand, *Études*, §§ 471-475; 476-486; Frandsen, *Outline*, §§ 17-20: Černý/Groll, *Late Egyptian Grammar*, § 16; Erman, *Neuägyptische Grammatik*, §§ 318-326;
.tw-passive	Winand, *Études*, §§ 471-475; 487-539; Erman, *Neuägyptische Grammatik*, §§ 270-272; Loprieno, *Ancient Egyptian*, § 4.6.6.3; (ending *.tw*:) Westendorf, *Der Gebrauch des Passivs in der klassischen Literatur der Ägypter*, Berlin 1953, §§ 3.1 (79ff); 3.6 (107ff)
defined infinitive after prepositions	Frandsen, *Outline*, §§ 60-63; Erman, *Neuägyptische Grammatik*, §§ 409-413; Groll, *Negative Verbal System*, §§ 55-56 (S.178ff); cf. also Černý/Groll, *Late Egyptian Grammar*, § 51.9; Till, *Koptische Grammatik*, § 351
Conjunctive	Kroeber, *Neuägyptizismen*, § 3.4 (history); Winand, *Études*, §§ 709-741; Erman, *Neuägyptische Grammatik*, §§ 575-587; Frandsen, *Outline*, §§ 64-84; Černý/Groll, *Late Egyptian Grammar*, §§ 42-43

3. Sentence conjugations and simple sentences

3.0 The transformation of Middle Egyptian sentence structure into a paradigm

3.0.1 The construction of sentences

Compared with Late Egyptian, Middle Egyptian appears to have a far greater variety of possible sentence structures. Middle Egyptian is dominated by a wide variety of adverbial phrases which are used in correspondingly diverse ways. Adverbial phrases in adverbial clauses play a direct role in the structure of a large number of sentence ("adverbial sentences"), as immediate constituents of the sentence itself, but as adverbial adjuncts or sentence adverbials they are also a means of modifying and enhancing any kind of sentence. Adverbial phrases can be formed of (a) adverbs, (b) prepositional combinations with nouns or infinitives, (c) Old Perfectives, and (d) also forms of *sdm=f* and *sdm.n=f*. Although they need not, sentences constructed from adverbial phrases can begin with *iw*, *ꜥḥꜥ.n* or *wn.in*.[1] Such adverbial sentences also display a broad range of verb forms (*mrr=f; mri=f; mr.n=f*), while graphemically identical *sdm=f* forms can themselves be prospective, subjunctive, nominal or adverbial.

principles of sentence construction in Middle Egyptian

The situation is quite different in Late Egyptian. Adverbial phrases are used as modifiers almost exclusively — but still very frequently — in the form of combinations of prepositions with nouns. A wider set of adverbials — adverbs, prepositions combined with nouns and infinitives, Old Perfectives/Statives — are now basically restricted to the Adverbial Sentences (First Present). The other sentence constructions of the Middle Egyptian type have become morphologically invariable, having developed into morphological units with clearly identifiable forms.

principles of sentence construction in Late Egyptian

Along with the standard initial Adverbial Sentence, these are:

— the *iw*-sentence with *r* + infinitive (Third Future),

— the nominal *sdm=f* sentence,

---

1   *mk* — or later *ptr* — does not have any influence on the construction of the sentence, for the clause itself is still grammatically initial, even when introduced by this particle.

— the preterite *sdm=f* sentence,

— the adhortative sentence with imperative or prospective *sdm=f*,

— the various types of nominal sentences (adjectival sentence, Cleft Sentence/Participial statement; the sentence with *p3y*; the "pure" nominal sentence).

clause
conjugations

Just as the constructions of the independent sentences were thus morphosyntactically fixed, so were a number of constructions which mark logical subordination: The former variety of adverbial phrase constructions was limited through the appearance of fixed constructions formed from conjunctions and specific forms of the verb (the infinitive, subjunctive *sdm=f*, *sdm.t=f*). Only by their etymology can these be recognized as forms of Middle Egyptian prepositional combinations: the "Temporal" (*m-dr sdm=f*) — and a few other similar constructions with conjunctions —, the "Terminative" (*r-ir.t=f-sdm/š3ᶜ-i.ir.t=f-sdm*), and the "Conjunctive" (*mtw=f-sdm*, from earlier *hnᶜ-sdm*, *hnᶜ-ntf-sdm*).

subordination

Aside from the clause conjugations thus constituted, quite different forms of modifying expressions appear in place of the adverbial phrases used as modifiers: it is now independent sentences themselves that serve as modifiers by being subordinated using conjunctions, which are termed "converters" in Egyptology. Converters are grammatical morphemes which "convert" grammatical independence into grammatical subordination. The most important converter in Late Egyptian is *iw*, which converts sentence conjugations into subordinate clauses, into any kind of adverbial or circumstantial clauses, and occasionally even into noun clauses and so-called content clauses.

> Sentence Conjugation, Clause Conjugation are concepts for describing the status of Late Egyptian, Demotic and Coptic verbal formations. "Conjugation" refers to grammatical constructions formed out of (a) a verb form, (b) its actor expression ("subject"), (c) an object, if called for, and (d) any further necessary adjuncts. Such conjugations can be either (a) independent or (b) subordinate and dependent on an independent construction. In the first case they are the minimal form of an independent or main sentence ("sentence conjugation"), in the second case they perform the function of parts of speech in their superordinate sentence conjugation or independent sentence, as subject, object, or adverbial clause ("clause conjugations"). These notions were adopted from H. J. Polotsky, *The Coptic Conjugation System*, and transfered to Late Egyptian grammar by Frandsen, *Outline*, and to Demotic by Johnson, *Demotic Verbal System*.

3.0.2 General parameters of the development

This brief survey permits us to point out the parallels and contrasts between the sentence structures of Middle and Late Egyptian and the difficulty of observing a historical connection between the two. This is primarily related to the complete change in the grammatical character of *iw*. In Middle Egyptian *iw* was employed primarily to begin independent sentences, while in Late Egyptian, it has become a characteristic feature of subordination.

It is the examination of the fundamental structure of sentence formation that allows *structural relations* the understanding of the origins of Late Egyptian in Middle Egyptian. The following table illustrates Middle Egyptian sentence structure as a kind of "free" combination of specific phrases, so that the forms of one column can be joined with those of the other, e.g.: noun + adverb; *ỉw* + noun + Old Perfective; nominal *sḏm=f* + *r* + infinitive; etc.:

Particle/Modifier	Noun phrase	Adverbial phrase
ꜥḥꜥ.n/etc. *ỉw* ∅ (*mk*)	nominal *sḏm=f/sḏm.n=f* noun	*sḏm=f/sḏm.n=f* adverb prep. + noun Old Perfective prep. *ḥr/m* + infinitive prep. *r* + infinitive

It is thus evident that the structural boundary is between the nominal and the adverbial *boundary shift* phrases of such structures in Middle Egyptian. Late Egyptian sentence structure can be derived from them by (a) limiting the range of phrases available, and (b) shifting the structural boundary ("rebracketing"). This shifting eventually established the structural boundary between the modifier and the clauses which follow it. This meant in principle that the sentence structure [*ỉw* + noun] and [preposition + noun] is rebracketed to become [*ỉw*] and [noun + preposition + noun].

The manner in which the Late Egyptian forms were derived from the Middle Egyptian *derivation pattern* forms can best be presented as follows. In a Middle Egyptian Adverbial Sentence like *zỉ ỉm* ("the man is there"), the relationship between the noun *zỉ* and the adverb *ỉm* was the

Modifier	Sentence	
	nominal *sḏm=f*	adverb prep. + noun Old Perfective prep. *ḥr/m* + inf.
ỉw	*sḏm.n=f*	
ỉw	noun	adverb prep. + noun Old Perfective prep. *ḥr/m* + inf.
ỉw	noun	prep. *r* + inf.

same as the relationship of *ỉw zỉ* and *ỉm* in the *ỉw*-sentence, *ỉw zỉ ỉm* ("There is the man there"). In Late Egyptian, the internal relationship of a *ỉw*-sentence of the *ỉw zỉ ỉm* type appears different to the speaker: Apparently it is the — now morphologized — sentence type *zỉ ỉm* (First Present/Adverbial Sentence) itself that follows *ỉw*; it would thus appear that the Adverbial Sentence itself has been "subordinated" to *ỉw*. The clause following *ỉw* can thus be understood as a dependent form of an independent sentence, being made dependent by *ỉw*.

Middle Egyptian > Late Egyptian

zỉ   *ỉm*   >   *zỉ ỉm*

ỉw zỉ   *ỉm*   > *ỉw   zỉ ỉm*

The Late Egyptian sentence conjugation forms are thus derived from the Middle Egyptian *ỉw*-sentence, and this origin likewise clarifies the functional shift of *ỉw*, which has become the marker indicating the dependency of the following clause.

Converter	Sentence		Designation
	nominal *sdm=f*	+ adverb	emphatic sentence/
		+ prep. + noun	(2nd tense)
ỉw	*sdm=f* (<*sdm.n=f*)		preterite *sdm=f*
ỉw	noun	+ adverb	Adverbial Sentence/First Present
		+ prep. + noun	
		+ Old Perfective	
		+ prep. *ḥr/m* + inf.	
ỉw	noun	+ prep. *r* + inf.	Third Future

Observation:

The adverbial phrases (Old Perfective; *ḥr/m* + infinitive) which then drop out of the "emphatic sentence" are replaced with sentence forms converted by *ỉw*.

Third Future

Only in the form of the Third Future does *ỉw* retain its previous role, because this form represented a choice (between two alternatives) made by the speaker, for he could have selected (a) the Third Future or (b) the "future Adverbial Sentence" formed *mk sw r sdm*, with its Late Middle Egyptian *tw=ỉ r sdm* variant.

3.0.3 Bibliography

Kroeber, *Neuägyptizismen*, § 3, in particular §§ 32.2; 3.3; Junge, Über die Entwicklung des ägyptischen Konjugationssystems, in: *SAK* 9, 1981, 201ff (with supplements in *GM* 60, 1982, 93ff); id., *Sprachstufen*; Loprieno, *Ancient Egyptian*, §§ 7.9.1; 7.9.2

3.1 The Adverbial Sentence or the First Present

3.1.1 The forms of the independent Adverbial Sentence

(1) The sentence and its designation

The Adverbial Sentence, otherwise termed the First Present, is a bimembral sentence formed with two phrases: a nominal phrase followed by an adverbial phrase. The noun phrase has the function of the subject, while the predicate (the adverbial phrase) can be (a) an adverb, (b) a preposition combined with nouns (nominal phrases), (c) the prepositions *ḥr* or *m* with the infinitive of a verb or (d) an Old Perfective (Stative).

Actor expression	Predicate expression
	ḥr sdm / m ḥd
*(p3) z*ỉ	*pr.w*
sw	*dy*
	m nw.t

Erman and those who followed him distinguished the use of the "pseudo-verbal forms", preposition + infinitive and Old Perfective following a nominal phrase, from the use of the adverbial sentence with other adverbial phrases. Only the first of these versions of the adverbial sentence was considered a conjugation form and termed the "First Present" (*Präsens I*).

First Present

This term was historically opposed to a "Second Present" which identified those forms using the auxiliary verb *ỉw*. The Late Egyptian "Second Present" proved to be a misnomer however, as a number of completely different forms making use of *ỉw* were incorrectly combined together under this term. It has now been recognized that these are (a) the converted First Present or Circumstantial Present — § 3.1.3 —, (b) a special use of the circumstantial, which came to be known as the "non-initial main sentence" (NIMS), and (c) the Third Future. The connection thus made with the Coptic Second Present is moreover been erroneous, because the Coptic Second Present is the "Second Tense", the nominal/emphatic form, of the present, which in Late Egyptian did not exist in this form.

history of the term

(2) The pronoun set of the Adverbial Sentence

The introductory nominal phrase is replaced by a pronoun formed with the morpheme *tw* and a suffix pronoun, and no longer by an enclitic pronoun as in Middle Egyptian. With the exception of the 3rd pers. sing. and pl. pronouns, which do not have the *tw*-morpheme, this series is historically the precursor of the Coptic First Present pronouns: *tw=ỉ ḥr sdm > tw=ỉ sdm* becomes Coptic ϯϹⲰⲦⲘ̄ "I hear".

1st.sing.c.	*tw=i*	ⳓ ; ⳓ ; ⳓ	†-
2nd.sing.masc.	*tw=k*	ⳓ	K-
fem.	*tw(=t)*	ⳓ	TE-
3rd.sing.masc.	*sw*	ⳓ	ϥ-
fem.	*st*	ⳓ ; ⳓ ; ⳓ	C-
1st.pl.c.	*tw=n*	ⳓ ; ⳓ ; ⳓ	TÑ-
2nd.pl.c.	*tw=tn*	ⳓ	TETÑ-
3rd.pl.c.	*st*	ⳓ ; ⳓ ; ⳓ	CE-
"one"	*tw=tw*	ⳓ ; \\\\	

Observation:

Comparing these (proclitic) pronouns with the suffix pronouns (§ 2.1.2[1]) may show how their morphophonemic similarity led as the language developed to the interferences that the corresponding set of Coptic pronouns displays (cf. esp. the 3rd. masc. sing. ϥ-).

(3) Notes on the use of the preposition *ḥr*

omission

While the preposition *m* continues to be written before verbs of motion, the *ḥr* preceding the infinitive is increasingly omitted in writing. During Dynasty XIX, the *ḥr* was still written frequently — but selectively — in literary texts (e.g., "Two Brothers", "Doomed Prince") and other registers, but virtually disappears during Dynasty XX (cf. the table in Winand, *Études*, 521, and the detailed references, ibid., pp. 413ff).

versus
convention

It is worth noting that morphophonemically the preposition continued to be used longer in the introductory phrases of letters and with nominal subjects while falling away more rapidly after the proclitic pronouns of the First Present: *p3 zẖ3.w ḥr nḏ-ḥr.t n t3 z.t-ḥm.t* "The scribe inquires about the condition of the woman" as opposed to *sw nḏ-ḥr.t n t3 z.t-ḥm.t* "He asks ...". The same is true of some verbs — such as *ḏd* "speak" — where the preposition can still be written, when it has otherwise disappeared completely.

interference

The morphophonemic loss is accompanied by the tendency to "hypercorrection". The preposition occasionally appears as a kind of marker of the lexical element even before forms where it did not belong, as in *tw=i ḥr ḥms.kw* "I sat" (similarly with the Conjunctive, cf. § 2.3.3[3]).

(4) Methods of negation

The First Present or Adverbial Sentence is usually negated with the negative morpheme *bn* (etymologically related to ⌢ *nn*, Coptic **N̄**-):

st *iw n=tn bn st di m.di=n* "They have come to you; they are not here with us".

negation with *bn*

(pLeiden I 365,7)

Observation:

In contrast to the other conjugations, the structure of the affirmative forms is preserved in negative, so that the form belongs to the group of isomorphic negations (cf. S. Groll, *Negative Verbal system*; for the negating particle, cf. J. Osing, *Enchoria* 10, 1980, 93ff).

Another negation, with *bn* followed by *iwn3/in* (Coptic **N̄ ... AN**), appears occasionally, "discontinuous", like French *ne...pas*; the form later provides the negation morpheme proper of Demotic and particularly of Coptic First Present. It apparently occurs at first when the predication expression is a preposition + noun combination:

negation with *bn ... iwn3*

bn sw m šs iwn3 p3 pš

(pMayer B 1)

i.ir=k n=i "It is quite unsuitable, this portion which you have left me";

Notes:

  p3 pš   postpositive apposition to *sw* ("Epexegis" or explication);
  i.ir=k n=i   "(the portion) which you have made for me".

To negate (a) currently continuous, (b) repetitive acts, or (c) sentences using verbs of speech or perception, a parallel negation form is used, the Negative Aorist (§ 2.3.2.[3]):

Negative Aorist

(oBerlin P. 10627,8-9)

tw=k ˁš3 m dri r iqr bw ir=k di.t nkt n wˁ "You enjoy great abundance, yet you never give anything to anyone".

Notes:

  tw=k ˁš3 m dri   Adverbial Sentence (First Present) with Old Perfective, "you are abundant in valuables";
  bw ir=k di.t   Negative Aorist.

3.1.2 Usage

The Adverbial Sentence (First Present) is syntactically an independent form allowing simple statements in a real or fictitious speech situation. The time is either left unstated or assumed to be the present or a relative present (i.e., the same time as the surrounding cotext). The situation is presented either as (a) continual or (b) an actually occuring event (*ḥr/m* + infinitive), or else (c) a state which has been achieved (Old Perfective). The Old Perfective with transitive verbs (passive voice, cf. § 2.2.3[2]) can also characterize an act as past. Examples:

utterance form of presentation

— The expression of the predicate is the Old Perfective of verbs of motion: past movement which ends up in a present or past state:

(HorSeth 7,2-3)

wn.ỉn Stš ḥr ḏd n=f t3 rmṯ bỉn ỉy.tỉ r=ỉ ꜥn "Then Seth said to him, 'The evil person came against me again.'"

Notes:

> *wn.ỉn*   a narrative form common in literary texts (and particularly so in Horus and Seth), and frequently alternating with *ꜥḥꜥ.n*. The story of Wenamun indicates that its use had declined by the end of the New Kingdom;
>
> *t3 rmṯ bỉn*   nominal subject of the Adverbial Sentence at the absolute beginning of a sentence (following the introductory *ḏd*).

— The expression of the predicate is the Old Perfective of other intransitive verbs: present (or past) state:

(LRL 1,5-6)

y3 tw=ỉ ꜥnḫ.k m p3 hrww dw3w ḥr ꜥ.wy p3 nṯr "Yes, I am alive today, but tomorrow is in the hands of god."

Notes:

> structure   two independent statements, the first with a pronominal subject, and the second with a nominal subject (*dw3.w*);
>
> predicate   Old Perfective in the first statement, and prepositional phrase in the second.

(HorSeth 8,3)   *tw=tn dỉ ḥms.tỉ ḥr ỉr.t ỉḫ m-r3-ꜥ* "What are you up to again?", adverb and Old Perfective (cf. supra § 2.2.3[3]) for the hieroglyphic text).

— The expression of the predicate is constructed with an infinitive: present, continuing or repeated actions or situations:

(pAnast. III vs. 3,2)   *st ḥr ỉr.t n3y=sn ỉp.t db.t m mn.t* "They make their lot of bricks daily". *ḥr* + infinitive, continuing activity (cf. supra 2.1.4[2] for the hieroglyphic text).

When the expression of the predicate is the infinitive of an adjectival verb, this indicates the beginning of a state of affairs or that a new situation has now emerged: *ỉw=f ḥr gnn* "he became weak" (pD'Orb 7,9-8,1).

Observation:

There are some rare First Present statements with *r* + infinitive, but restricted to constructions with *ỉb=ỉ*, such as *ỉb=ỉ r ptr=tn*, "I long to see you" (< *"My mind is intent on seeing-you"; *LRL* 1,8-9).

— The expression of the predicate is a preposition with nouns: without a specific temporal context, or relatively simultaneous (cf. also the example *LRL* 1, 5-6 supra):

(Beatty Love Songs vs. C2,1-2)   *mk sw m ỉw.ty-ỉb=f* "He is foolish" (cf. supra, § 2.2.6.[1] for hieroglyphic text).

3.1.3 The Circumstantial First Present

(1) Form

The Adverbial Sentence (First Present) can be subordinated to an independent sentence by introducing it with the morpheme *iw*. This means that, introduced by the "converter" *iw*, an Adverbial Sentence can assume an adverbial — or even nominal — role in a principal sentence: it has the function of an adverbial clause. Such a clause is termed a Circumstantial First Present. *(margin: conversion by iw)*

If the subject of such an affirmative subordinate clause is not nominal, the First Present pronoun series is substituted by *iw* + suffix. The Late Egyptian Circumstantial First Present thus resembles the independent Middle Egyptian *iw*-sentence: in both form and function, *iw=f ḥr sdm >iw=f sdm* is the precursor of the Coptic Circumstantial First Present ЄЧСⲰⲦⳘ. *(margin: form of pronoun)*

The substitution of the pronominal form (*iw=f ḥr sdm* rather than *iw sw ḥr sdm) is however relevant only for the affirmative forms: if the statement is negated with *bn*, the pronouns of the First Present are employed: *iw bn sw ḥr sdm*. The adjoining table compares: "the man hears" and "I hear", with their negations. *(margin: negation)*

	affirmative	negative
independent	*pȝ rmṯ sdm* *tw=i sdm*	*bn pȝ rmṯ sdm* *bn tw=i sdm*
dependent	*iw pȝ rmṯ sdm* *iw=i sdm*	*iw bn pȝ rmṯ sdm* *iw bn tw=i sdm* *iw=i tm sdm*

Observation:

Under certain conditions, the infinitive in the *iw=f (ḥr) sdm* construction can be replaced with a negative infinitive (cf. supra § 2.2.3[4]), i.e., the infinitive of the negating verb *tm* followed by the infinitive of the verb bearing the specific meaning (*iw=f (ḥr) tm sdm*, cf. supra § 2.2.3[4]). This type of negation and the employment of the circumstantial clause in narrative contributed to the designation of the form as non-initial main sentence.

It occasionally happens that the circumstantial sentence is negated with *iwnȝ/ in*, in a form such as *iw bn nȝ nty wȝḥ im=w iwnȝ* "while those who were left are not among them" (*LRL* 9,14). Cf. also Černý/Groll, *Late Egyptian Grammar* § 20.6.2 (313f).

(2) Usage

With the exception of the locational and temporal adverbials, the Circumstantial First Present basically replaced the use of adverbial phrases as sentence extensions, whether prepositional phrases with nouns or infinitives respectively, or Old Perfectives. A Middle Egyptian sentence like *iw ḥd.n ḥm=f ḥr ḥȝq dmi.w* "His Majesty went north, conquering cities" becomes something like *ḥd ḥm=f iw=f ḥr ḥȝq dmi.w* in Late Egyptian. Charac- *(margin: substitutional form of adverbial phrases)* teristic of Middle Egyptian sentences were long chains of adverbial phrases; in Late Egyptian, Demotic and Coptic, long chains of circumstantial clauses are the rule instead.

The Circumstantial First Present is used frequently in all kinds of texts. In order to judge the scope of its use, it is necessary to realize that

sentence extension — it is the basic form of adverbial extension of sentences, and can form long chains in this role;

relative present — it is functionally a form indicating relative simultaneity (relative present), so that it is able to continue the tense implied by the main sentence under many conditions;

non-specific subordination — it is not a specific form of subordination and can thus be used even when other languages express subordination using conjunctions ("when"; "while"; "because"; "as"; "so that"; etc.); it is very much akin in usage to the English abridged adverbial clauses with participles, gerunds or infinitives ("Being sick, having finished, he did this and that", "He hurt himself playing this and that", etc.). While not unknown, conjunctional subordination is less common in Egyptian;

coordination by "and" — it is a form that allows the formulation of "logically looser" relations, which in other languages are expressed, e.g., by coordinating conjunctions like "and". This usage of the Circumstantial First Present has been categorized as an extra form termed "narrative", or "non-initial main sentence" or "non-initial main clause" (cf. infra § 5.2).

With an infinitive as expression of the predicate:

(pLansing 2,3-4)

kri šri ꜥ.wsi ib=k bw sdm=k iw=i mdw "How arrogant you are my boy! You don't listen when I speak!";

Notes:

> ꜥ.wsi ib=k   literally: "How great your heart is!" (< ꜥ.wi-sw/si ib=k);
>
> structure   a Circumstantial First Present subordinated to a Negative Aorist (bw sdm=k).

(Wenamun 2,66)

ptr st iw=w nꜥy r qbḥ.w "Look at them going to the marshes!" (preceding: "Have you not seen the birds who have already flown down to Egypt twice?"; cf., supra § 2.3.2[3], for the hieroglyphic text).

With Old Perfective (or adverbial) as expression of the predicate:

(LRL 23,11-12)

ḫr tw=n di ḥms.ti m B-Ḥw.t iw=k rḫ.tw pꜣy=n sḫr ḥms nty twt=n im=f "We are now living here in 'the mansion', and you know the way of life we have to put up with."

Notes:

> ḥms.ti   ḥmsi used here as a verb of complete predication, and not as an auxiliary verb;

t3-Ḥw.t "the mansion" — the mortuary temple of Ramesses III at Medinet Habu, where the administration of 'The Tomb' (*n p3 ḫr*) took up residence at the end of Dynasty XX;

p3y=n sḫr ḥms "our way of living";

nty tw=n ìm=f relative clause with *nty*, *"(the way of living) which we are in". This case reveals that the First Present is also used when a relative clause has its own actor expression after *nty*.

(LRL 23,13-14)

st ḥms m Nw.t ìw=ì dy ḥms.tw w^c.k ìrm zḫ3.w-mš^c Pn-t3-Ḥw.t-nḫt "They live in the 'City', while I live here alone with the secretary of the army Pentahunakht";

Notes:

st ḥms "they" are the *msw-ḫr*, the youths, sons, apprentices, etc. of the *ḫr*, the Tomb Building Administration; *ḥmsì* here is the verb of complete predication;

Nw.t the "City" par excellence: Thebes;

ìrm in the original text the preposition is written twice, a "dittograph" at a line-break;

Pn-t3-Ḥw.t-nḫt *P3-n t3-Ḥw.t nḫt.w*, proper name (of the sentence type: "He of the 'Mansion' is mighty": "He of the 'Mansion'" being Amun-Re of Medinet Habu).

— Negation of the circumstantial clause with *bn*:

negation

(Doomed Prince 7,8)

ìw=s ḥr ḫpr ḥr z3w p3y=s h3y r ìqr zp-2 ìw bn sw ḥr dì.t pr=f r bnr w^c "And she began to protect her husband zealously, and did not let him go out alone." (Some signs are restored);

Notes:

ìw=s ḥr ḫpr ḥr z3w example of the "narrative" use of the circumstantial (non initial main sentence/clause) in a chain of such; a direct form of address preceded this line; *ḫpr* is function verb (cf. supra § 2.2.3[3]);

ḥr dì.t pr=f infinitive with subjunctive *sdm=f* ("allowing that he goes out"); precursor of the Coptic Causative Infinitive (*dì.t sdm=f > dì.t-ìr=f-sdm >* ⲦⲢⲈϤⲤⲰⲦⲘ̄).

A negation with the infinitive of *tm* has roughly the same effect:

(pJud.Turin 4,12)

ìn.tw=f ḥr p3 sdm ì.ìr=f n3 mdt m.dì p3y ^c3 n ^c.t wn=f r-q3ì-n=f ìw=f h3p=w ìw=f tm dd smì=w "He was brought because he had heard about the affairs from this chamberlain in whose company he was, had concealed it, and failed to report it."

Notes:

ḥr p3 sdm ì.ìr=f "conjugated" infinitive (cf. supra, § 2.3.3[2]) following preposition *ḥr*;

$wn=f$ relative form of the verb wn ($< i.wn=f$) with indirect resumption; wn turns sentences into the past in Late Eyptian;

$iw=f$ tm dd $sml=w$ Circumstantial First Present functioning as a non initial main sentence of the type $iw=f$ (hr) tm sdm ($>$ "he did not report it"), parallel to $iw=f$ (hr) $h3p=w$.

adnominal use

— Not infrequently the Circumstantial First Present is used to qualify an unspecified noun (this usage is rather unfortunately termed a "virtual relative clause"):

(Wenamun 2, 77)

n mn w^c $n.im=tn$ $iw=f$ sdm mdt $Km.t$ "Isn't there anyone of you who understands Egyptian?";

Notes:

⌒ grapheme for the interrogative particle $(i)n$ (cf. supra § 2.2.4[1]);

mn expresses negated existence: "there aren't" (Coptic ⲘⲚ-), etymologically derived from nn wn (nn $sdm=f$ of wn). The affirmative equivalent is wn;

$n.im=tn$ an early precursor of the Demotic and Coptic status pronominalis of im ($n.im=tn >$ ⲘⲘⲰⲦⲚ).

Observation:

In fact, these usages betray the Late Egyptian transformation of the former manner of specifying nouns. In texts of earlier date (or in texts of the New Kingdom higher up in the register hierarchy), this was accomplished via adverbial phrases: the adnominal use of (a) adverbs, (b) the Old Perfective, or (c) prepositional phrases as adverbial attributes. For Late Egyptian examples of this use of the Old Perfective, cf. supra, § 2.2.3[2]).

Tense, Aspect, Mood are notions relating to the temporal position, duration and nature of processes and actions. "Tense" can designate (a) the "absolute" point in time which the speaker wishes to assign to the action related, i.e. in the present, the past, the future, or (b) the form of the verb used: present, preterite, perfect, future form. If the temporal position of an action or process is assigned in relation to the temporal position of another one, tense is relative, i.e. simultaneous, preceding or following, relative present, past or future. "Aspect" describes the relationship of the related actor to the temporal duration of a process or act. If an action is presented as completed at the time stated, this act is described as "perfective"; if the action is still continuing, it is described as "imperfective". "Mood" refers to the degree of reality which the speaker is willing to assign to his statements, the degree to which it can be expected, or desired, or merely recognized as possible ("prospective"). These forms possess reciprocal affinities. A completed act can only be perceived as such if it lies in the past with respect to either the actor or the speaker. A continuing process ("she is running") is present for the actor, but can be past for the speaker ("she was running"). An expected situation must lie in the future for the expectant ("she will be running"), but the speaker can also refer to this in the past ("she will have run"). Middle Egyptian is generally assumed to have had an aspect system, while Late Egyptian is assumed to have had a tense system.

3.1.4 Bibliography

Adverbial sentence/First Present

Winand, *Études*, §§ 622-680 (401ff); Frandsen, *Outline*, §§ 34-42; Černý/Groll, *Late Egyptian Grammar* § 19; Loprieno, *Ancient Egyptian*, § 6.6.1; Erman, *Neuägyptische Grammatik* §§ 464-485; W. Schenkel, Infinitiv und Qualitativ des Koptischen als Verbaladverbien oder Die Jernstedtsche Regel ..., in: *Enchoria* 8 (part 2), 1978, 13ff

Winand, *Études*, §§ 635-640; 649-656   notation of
                                                                         ḥr/m

Černý/Groll, *Late Egyptian Grammar* § 20; Groll, *Negative Verbal System*, Sections   negation
25-34; 41-46; 4-18; Spiegelberg, *Demotische Grammatik*, § 473

Frandsen, *Outline*, § 104; Černý/Groll, *Late Egyptian Grammar* §§ 19.13.1-19.13.6;   Circumstantial
63; Erman, *Neuägyptische Grammatik* §§ 495-497; Junge, *ỉw=f ḥr (tm) sḏm*   First Present

3.1.5 Exercises

(1) Praise of the city of Ramesses (pAnast. II 1,1-2,5)

Dating to the reign of Merenptah, this ode to the city of Ramesses, the Delta Residence, is part of a collection of "examination papers" in Papyrus Anastasi II, published in Gardiner, *Late-Egyptian Miscellanies*, pp. 12-13. pAnast. II gives mostly "eulogies" of this type, besides a series of prayers (cf. [2]; for a general characterization of these texts, cf. Erman, *Schülerhandschriften*).

Purpose: Example of Dynasty XIX higher education in style, text forms and literary registers; use of Adverbial Sentence (First Present), Negative Aorist and Circumstantial First Present.

Notes:

1,1   *pȝ nb n Km.t*: example of determination in a case of culturally specified knowledge, cf. § 2.1.3(1);

qd n=f ḥm=f: preterite *sḏm=f* form, frequently used to specify the absolute tense of the text by way of introduction; also used to state the speech act type "narration": "His Majesty built for himself";

1,2   *ḏȝhy*: the name of the Phoenician and Palestinian coastal region (cf. Gardiner, *Ancient Egyptian Onomastica* I, London 1947, 141*, 145*f) — here specifically the Gaza strip with its hinterland (which later became the Land of the Philistines > Palestine); cf., however, C. Vandersleyen, *Les guerres d'Amosis*, Brussels 1971, pp. 90ff (the whole area of Palestine, Syria, Northern Mesopotamia);

mḥ: circumstantial Old Perfective, dependent on preceding *sw* "being filled with". This is an older construction: "more" Late Egyptian would be *sw r-ỉwd* toponym *r* toponym *ỉw=f mḥ m NP*);

ỉwnw-šmꜥỉ (ỉnw-šmꜥỉ) "Upper Egyptian Heliopolis" as a designation for Thebes (occasionally also for the toponym "Hermonthis"/Armant);

1,3   *ḥw.t-kȝ-Ptḥ* "Mansion of the *ka* of Ptah", as a designation for Memphis;

wbn pȝ šw — ḥtp=f: nouns, "The rise of the Light is there — his setting is here". Or *sḏm=f* forms in a balanced sentence of Middle Egyptian type: "As he rises there, he sets here";

m ḫnw=f: "in it"; or even "in its interior" (in the older sense, dissolving the compound preposition);

ḫꜥ bw-nb nȝy=sn dmỉ: preterite *sḏm=f*, "All of them have left their home-villages";

1,4-1,5   for the topography of the city of Ramesses, cf. Bietak, in: *LÄ* V 138. One should however note that in the text the city is bordered by temple districts in the "West" and "South", but not explicitly in the "East" and "North". The text states that they have been transformed "into" goddesses or that goddesses have come into being in

3.1.5 Exercises (1) pAnast. II 1,1-2,5

them, so that the city is limited by the goddesses themselves, rather than their temples (so that temples need not necessarily be sought in these directions, *contra* Bietak);

p3 bḫn, sw mỉ 3ḫ.t: Adverbial Sentence with noun in anticipation (theme shifting);

1,6 used after cartouches, the names of rulers or palaces, the *ʿnḫ wḏ3 snb* can be abbreviated so that only the sign for *s(nb)* is recognizable in the hieratic, as here;

1,6-2,1 these designations refer (1) to Ramesses II by courtly laudatory epithets: the founder of the city is said to fulfil various symbolic city offices by personifying various divine qualities (as "Ramesses the God", "Month in the Two Lands", "Re among the rulers", "Prosperity of Egypt" < as the one "who refreshes its heart"); and (2) to the monumental statues of the king in front of the temple of the city of Ramesses, which were themselves worshipped. For the king, cf. Habachi, *Features of Deification, Abhandlungen des Deutschen Archäologischen Instituts Kairo* 5, Glückstadt 1969, 27ff;

2,1-2,2 *Ḥt3*: "Hatti" (the Hittite Kingdom); *Qdỉ*: designation for "Kizzuwadna", according to W. Helck, Cilicia (southeastern region of Asia Minor at the Mediterranean Coast, bordering on Syria); note the distinction between the "*wr ʿ3* of Hatti" and the "*wr* of Qedi";

2,2 *ḥn=n - ḏd=n - ỉry=n*: a chain of prospective *sdm=f* forms as independent sentences: "we want, should, desire, want to (do something)";

2,2-2,3 *ỉry=n s:wnwn* (with the preposition *n*: "pay respect to Usi-ma-Re"): periphrasis with 4-rad verb;

dỉ=f t3w: preterite *sdm=f*, "he gave the breath of life";

n mrr=f: an earlier type of form, whether (a) relative form "(to give something) to him whom he loves/chose"; or (b) a nominal *sdm=f* "as he wished" (*n < m*);

ḫpr m mrw.t=f: "be submitted to his will/wish" (Old Perfective);

2,4 structure with independent sentence forming Negative Aorist followed by First Present Circumstantial clause: "it cannot happen, because of such and such". The meaning of the clause can be rendered, "if such and such does not happen, it is in his power" (the reference of the pronoun thus changes from "Hatti" to the fact in general);

2,5 the arm (Gardiner D 41) at the end of the text is a hieratic convention indicating the end of a *ḥw.t*, a stanza (cf. supra § 2.2.6). It may be either a sign transformed from the lower part of ⍓ , with which stanzas are occasionally marked off, or it could be an abbreviation for *grḥ* "end", cf. Grapow, *Sprachliche und schriftliche Formung ägyptischer Texte, Leipziger Ägyptologische Studien* 7, 1936, p. 53.

(2) A profession of faith (pAnast. II 6,5-7)

A short prayer of praise to Amun from the reign of Merenptah, from the same collection of examination texts in Papyrus Anastasi II (published in Gardiner, *Late-Egyptian Miscellanies*, p. 16). Passages of the text are identical to those of pBologna 1094, 2, 3-7, and comparison of the two texts gives a good idea of the various alternatives in orthography and means of expression. Verse points and a break divide the prayer into two stanzas of five verses each.

Purpose: Example of Dynasty XIX higher education in style, text forms and literary registers; usage of negated Adverbial Sentence (First Present).

Notes:

6,5 structure: negated Adverbial Sentence preceded by a noun (*'Imnw-Rʿw*) with numerous appositions;

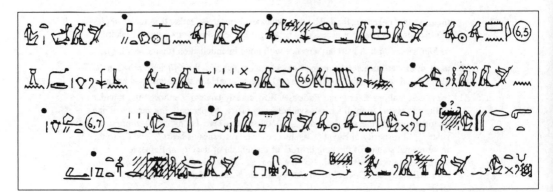

3.1.5 Exercises (2) pAnast. II 6,5-7

6,6 *ḏd ỉnỉ mtr.t*: direct address introduced with *ḏd*, "he did not say: 'Bring evidence!'" (meaning that Amun does not require witnesses); pBologna 1094, 2,5, has *ḏd n ỉnỉ mtr.t* "He does not speak to him who brings testimony", which calls for a nuance of "false testimony";

wpỉ Imnw-Rꜥw pꜣ tꜣ: probably "to divide the land" (from other components of the creation), despite phonetic similarity of the verb *wpỉ* here and in l. 6, 7 where it has the figurative meaning of "judging the guilty"; Caminos, *LEM*, 10 translates both with "judge";

6,6-7 *md.t=f r ḥꜣ.ty*: "his words are for the heart", Adverbial Sentence with preposition *r*: someone or something is directed at something. The parallel pBologna 1094, 2,6, has the preposition *n*: "his words 'belong' to the heart". Caminos (*LEM*, 10) reads *mdw=f* "he speaks", but this does not yield the correct meaning with the rection *r* (*mdw r* means "to speak against" someone!);

6,7 *dỉ=f r ḫꜥw*: possibly the earlier passive *sḏm*, "he (the guilty one) has been rendered". pBologna 1094, 2,6, has *dỉ=f sw r ḫꜥw* "He (Amun) gave him" (preterite *sḏm=f*); *ḫꜥw* is a hapax legomenon: a place to which those condemned by god are sent, "purgatory" or the "lake of fire", etc.;

pꜣ mꜣꜥ r ỉmnt.t: the object position of *dỉ* is occupied twice: "the guilty is given this way, the justified that way".

3.2 The Third Future

3.2.1 Form

(1) Structural features

basic form The Third Future is a trimembral sentence: (1) the first position is occupied by *ỉw*, (2) the second with a noun phrase, and (3) the third with a predicate expression generally formed with the preposition *r* + infinitive: *ỉw=f r sḏm*. In most registers of Late Egyptian proper the preposition *r* is however generally not written, although phonetically it continued to exist (cf. infra § 3.2.3). This means that the Third Future cannot always be morphologically distinguished from the other sentences which are introduced with *ỉw*, since the preposition *ḥr* was likewise graphemically neglected in First Present Cirumstantial, the non-initial main sentence and the one called the "old" *iw*-sentence here. It is therefore necessary to pay attention to other syntactical and morphological details in order to recognize the form; these are:

— The Third Future is the only one of the Late Egyptian conjugation forms beginning with *iw* that can begin an independent sentence. The Third Future *iw=f (r) sdm* will thus be found at the absolute beginning of a sentence, following speech-introducing *dd* and after those conjunctions and converters which indicate the independence of the construction following them, the "direct/indirect indicators of initiality" (S. Groll): *r-dd*; *nty*, but also the circumstantial *iw*! The circumstantial clause *iw=f (hr) sdm*, however, is preceded by an independent sentence or is a member of a chain of dependent clauses.

iw introducing sentence

— Nominal subjects can frequently be preceded by the conjugation base *ir* rather than *iw*: *ir=f (r) sdm* rather than *iw=f (r) sdm*, but this is to be regarded as merely a graphonemic variant, as can be seen in the following example (following *r-dd*):

interchanging with *ir*

hr bw rh=i r-dd ir p3y=i ꜥdd ph r=k "But I don't know whether my boy will turn to you" (< *"I don't know whether 'my boy will turn to you' is correct");

(pBologna 1086, 6-7)

Note:

ir p3y=i ꜥdd ph stands for **iw p3y=i ꜥdd r ph*.

In certain sentence combinations, however, the Third Future can also follow another sentence and thereby assume a position which could be filled by other sentences introduced by *iw*. Confusion could arise in those cases where use of the non-initial main sentence *iw=f (hr) sdm* could be suspected, but this is of course not true of Old Perfectives or adverbial phrases with predicates using the prepositions *m, n, hr*. Such compound sentences, however, in which the Third Future competes in analysis with other *iw*-sentences in second position, are forms which were originally Middle Egyptian and have become fossilized during linguistic evolution. The independent Middle Egyptian *iw*-sentence was thus preserved too; these compound sentences are: (a) those with anticipation by means of *ir*, (b) conditional sentences with *inn*, and (c) oath formulas.

competition with other forms of *iw*-sentences

(2) Negation and adverbial subordination

As in the case of the Adverbial Sentence, the negative form is "isomorphic" with the affirmative one, being formed by simply placing a 𓂧 *bn* at the start of the sentence. During Dynasty XIX and in the register-hierarchically higher categories of texts, this can still also be written as 𓈖 *nn* — compare e.g.

negation morpheme *bn*

(pD'Orb. 4,1-2)

[hieroglyphs]

m-ỉr ḏd=f n=ỉ ꜥn

ḥr nn ỉw=ỉ r ḏd=f n wꜥ

ḥr bn ỉw=ỉ r dỉ.t pr=f m r3=ỉ n rmṯ nb

"Don't repeat that to me again! But I won't tell anyone else either: I won't let the word get out to anyone at all.";

Notes:

> *ḏd=f*   writing of the status pronominalis with an object suffix. The use of the 3rd. sing.
> masc. for a reference to a general thing/a whole situation (neutral) is common in Late
> Egyptian (cf. supra, § 2.1.2[1]. For the possibility of a "direct object pronoun", cf.
> supra § 2.2.1 Observation);

> *r dỉ.t pr=f m r3=ỉ*   literally: "will not let it go forth from my mouth to anyone".
> *n rmṯ nb*

circumstantial form

    Adverbial subordination makes it particularly clear that the *ỉw* in the Third Future belongs to the morphology of the form itself. By means of the converter *ỉw*, the form in its turn is transformed into the status of a (relatively future) circumstantial clause: *ỉw ỉw=f r sdm*. It is negated correspondingly: *ỉw bn ỉw=f r sdm*. This form is attested from the end of Dynasty XX:

(LRL 10, 5-6)

[hieroglyphs]

[mtw=k] 3ty n=s ỉw ỉw=k gm=s r ỉr.t n3y=k ỉpw.ty ỉm=s "and you will be careful with it (the boat), for you will find it useful for carrying out your tasks";

Notes:

> *mtw=k 3ty n=s*   Conjunctive as the continuation form of introductory imperatives, Third Futures, etc.;
> *ỉw ỉw=k gm=s*   Circumstantial Third Future;
> *gmỉ*   here specifically "to find something useful or suitable for something".

3.2.2 Usage

(1) As an independent sentence form

force of the expression

The Third Future is the conventional form for statements related to the future, for announcements and predictions: "This will happen". It is particularly common when the emphasis is on a particular situation logically proceeding from another. The 1st pers. can indicate a firm intention (analogous to English future tense, when "will" is used for the 1st pers.), while the 2nd pers. can express a command (as in English, when "shall" is used with the 2nd pers.). If the speaker desires to express a wish, he will generally employ an independent prospective *sdm=f* instead of the Third Future.

The syntactic independence of the Third Future sentence is clearest where it follows   sentence
expressions which indicate the actual beginning of a sentence, the "direct/indirect   character
indicators of initiality" such as *ḏd* or *nty*:

(LRL 20, 12)

𓀁𓂝𓈖𓀁𓏤𓂋𓏏𓀀𓈖𓏏𓈖𓏤𓂋𓏏𓐍   *iw=f ḏd iw=i ir.t=s r t3y=s s.t mtr.t*

"And he said, 'I shall do it at its appropriate place'".

Frequently the form is used in answering wishes and commands:

(LRL 15, 4-5)

𓀀𓂝𓂋𓏏𓊪𓈖𓏏𓎟𓀀𓂝   *iw=i ir.t p3 nty nb iw=k ḏd=f* "I am going to do

everything that you will say";

Notes:

> relative clause   *nty nb iw=k ḏd=f* is an example of *nty* as a "direct indicator of initiality", followed
> by sentence conjugations (*nty* + Third Future). It should be noted that the sentence
> structure requires an indirect resumptive pronoun (object *=f*).

Negated and with nominal subject/actor:

(pBM 10052,
6, 9-10)

𓈖𓂋𓏤𓀀𓂋𓊪𓏏𓈖𓀀𓅓𓂧𓀀   *bn ir p3y=i sn di.t mdw.tw m.di=i*

"My brother won't let anyone argue with me";

Note:

> *mdw m.di* "to discuss something with someone" has a broader meaning: "to argue with" or "to
> fall into a dispute or conflict with" or even to "be aggressive towards someone".

(2) In clause compounds, parallel to the "old" *iw*-sentence

Given its role of declaring logical results, promises or intentions, this form is quite suited   conditional
to appear as an apodosis in those compound constructions where one situation is affected   sentences
by another, as e.g. after the particle *inn* (cf. supra § 2.2.4[1]):

(pMayer B 4-5)

𓀀𓈖𓂋𓏤𓈖𓏤𓅆𓂝𓀀𓈖𓏏𓅓   *inn bn iw=k di.t n=i im=w iw=i šm* "If

you aren't going to give me any of it, I'll go";

Notes:

> *in*   writing variant of *inn*;
> reference   they are talking about stolen silver (*=w*);
> Protasis   The protasis is also formulated as a Third Future (negated); the whole situation implied
> by the sentence compound is thus put into the future.

In such combinations, as in the oath formulas (cf. infra Appendix § 7.1.3), forms also   *iw*-sentence
occur which have predicate expressions using (a) the Old Perfective or (b) preposition
+ noun combinations. Like the Third Future, they also generally have a future component
(consequence, promise or declared intention).

(pAdoption rt. 23-24)

ĭnn ĭw=s ms bn šrĭ bn šrĭ(.t) ĭw=w m rmṯ-nmḥ.w n pȝ ȝ n Pr-ˤȝ "Whether she gives birth to a son or a daughter, they will be free citizens of the land of Pharaoh"

Notes:

> *bn … bn* allographs for the interrogative pronoun *n … n (nȝ … nȝ)* meaning "either … or", "be it this or that";
>
> *ĭw=w m*   *ĭw*-sentence expressing future time, though with prepositional phrase, "they will be
> *rmṯ-nmḥ.w* citizens".

(pBM 10053 vs. 2,18)

mȝˤ.t pȝ ḏd=ĭ nb mtw=ĭ pnˤ ȝ=ĭ ˤn m dwȝ.w sȝ dwȝ.w ĭw=ĭ dĭ.k tȝ ĭwˤ Kš "(He swore an oath by the lord as follows:) Everything which I have said is true, and if I reverse my statement at any time in the future, I shall be stationed in the garrison of Cush".

Notes:

> *mȝˤ.t pȝ ḏd=ĭ nb* the Late Egyptian Pseudo-Cleft Sentence, with a noun and a specified relative form *(ĭ.)ḏd=ĭ* ("which I have said"): "Truth is what I have said";
>
> *mtw=ĭ pnˤ* the apparent initiality of the conjunctive is deceptive, but typical of the abbreviated forms of oaths: "(As Amun and the Ruler ruler endure), and I do this and that, such and such will occur" (cf. infra Appendix § 7.1.3[2]);
>
> *tȝ ĭwˤ* *<tȝ ĭwˤy.t*; probably an idiomatic expression, *rdĭ Y ĭwˤy.t* "to put Y in the garrison" (to perform military service). It is however also possible to transliterate *rdĭ Y <m> tȝ ĭwˤy.t*.

These *ĭw*-sentence forms no longer have a systemic position in Late Egyptian. As derivatives of the Middle Egyptian *ĭw*-sentence, they have been retained as elements of established formulas.

3.2.3 Notes on linguistic evolution

(1) The "Future" forms of the Middle Egyptian Adverbial Sentence

The Middle Egyptian Adverbial Sentence permits two types of future statement:

future form of the Adverbial Sentence

1. The Adverbial Sentence without introductory morpheme with a nominal or pronominal subject and a predicate expression using the preposition *r* + infinitive or noun. These will be termed the future form of the Adverbial Sentence, and it would be tempting to speak of a First Future: *ĭb n ḥm=k r qbb* "Your Majesty's mood will be brightened up" (< "refreshed"; pWestcar 5,4); *mk wĭ r nḥm ˤȝ=k šḥ.ty* "I am going to take your donkey away, peasant" (Eloquent Peasant B 1,42);

2. The *ỉw*-sentence with preposition *r* + infinitive or noun could be termed the future future form of form of the *ỉw*-sentence, and is the precursor of the Third Future: *ỉw=f r ỉṯỉ.t tȝ.w rs.yw* the *ỉw*-sentence "He will conquer the lands of the south" (Sin B 71-72).

Both forms of expression formulate a distinction in speech act. The future form of the difference Adverbial Sentence refers to an obvious situation or a necessary consequence ("as everyone knows, you will be brightened up"). The future form of the *ỉw*-sentence draws upon the reliability or trustworthiness of the speaker ("Trust me that he is going to conquer the southern lands"), which is ultimately the only serious attitude possible concerning statements about the future.

(2) Selection by linguistic evolution

From the Late Middle Kingdom and the New Kingdom, there are a couple of rare constructions using the Late Egyptian First Present pronouns. These reveal that the future form of the Adverbial Sentence is in a way adjusted to changes in the course of linguistic evolution.

tw=ỉ r tḫn ḥnᶜ=f sḏ ḫȝ.t=f *(CarnarvTabl*
ỉb=ỉ r nḥm km.t ḥ(wỉ.t) ᶜȝm.w *4-5)*

"I will meet with him (the Asiatic), and shatter his body. My will shall save Egypt and subdue the Asiatics".

The disappearance of the opposition separating adverbial sentences with and without *ỉw* led to a loss of this type of distinction in speech acts. Linguistic evolution eliminated the future form of the Adverbial Sentence, with its role being taken over by the future form of the *ỉw*-sentence. As a sentence conjugation with introductory *ỉw*, its future meaning may possibly have also put analogy pressure on the last traces of the old *ỉw*-sentence (*ỉw* + adverbial phrases, cf. supra, § 3.2.2[2]).

Observation:

In idiomatic expressions such as *ỉb=ỉ r* + infinitive, "I will do such and such" ("My will/my mood is directed towards such and such"), the future form of the Adverbial Sentence was preserved for a certain period (cf. also § 3.1.2).

In Demotic and Coptic, a new analytic form within the syntactical framework of the First Future as Adverbial Sentence (First Present) emerged for statements concerning the future. Its Late a new form Egyptian precursors were — not yet paradigmatized — constructions with the preposition *m* + the infinitive of the verb of motion *nᶜy* — *tw=ỉ m nᶜy r ỉr=f* "I am on the way to do it" > "I am going to do it" (cf. French *en train de faire*). By way of the Demotic "Progressive" this construction became the Coptic First Future ϥΝΑϹⲰΤⲘ̄, the functional — and to a certain extent even morphological — heir of the former future form of the Adverbial Sentence.

history of the form

    The Third Future sentence conjugation is preserved in Demotic as *iw=f (r) sdm*, which is the linguistic precursor of the Coptic Third Future ЄЧЄСШТ̄М. The negative *bn iw=f sdm* is likewise present in Demotic, with a less common parallel, *bn=f sdm*, both corresponding to the Coptic Negative Third Future Ñ̄NЄЧСШТ̄М. The alternative conjugation bases (a) *iw-* before pronominal subjects and (b) *ir-* before nominal subjects are also preserved in Demotic and Coptic (Є- und ЄРЄ-). The graphic reappearance of the preposition *r* before infinitives from Dynasty XXV[2] on is paralleled in some Demotic texts (the Setna-Khamwas story, the Myth of the Eye of the Sun), suggesting that phonetically it remained in existence. The "old" *iw*-sentence disappears completely, however.

terminology

    The term "Third Future" is taken from Coptic grammar. There, the following terms are in use: (a) the future form of the Adverbial Sentence = First Future, (b) the converted nominal form or Second Tense of the First Future = Second Future; and (c) the "real" future tense = Third Future. The term Third Future is maintained here although this is the only form for future statements in Late Egyptian.

3.2.4 Bibliography

language history

Gardiner, *Grammar*, §§ 122; 332; 333; Kroeber, *Neuägyptizismen*, §§ 32.2; 33.2; Junge, *iw=f hr (tm) sdm*, 124ff; Johnson, *Demotic Verbal System*, 94ff (progressive); 153ff; Loprieno, *Ancient Egyptian*, § 6.6.2

morphology

Winand, *Études*, §§ 756ff

usage

Frandsen, *Outline*, §§ 29-33; Korostovtsev, *Grammaire*, 378ff; Černý/Groll, *Late Egyptian Grammar*, § 17; Satzinger, *Neuägyptische Studien*, § 2.4.1

forms of the *iw*-sentence

Frandsen, *Outline*, § 115, 3.(2e), 231f; § 81 a-f; Satzinger, *Neuägyptische Studien*, §§ 2.4.1.2 - 2.4.1.3

negation

Černý/Groll, *Late Egyptian Grammar*, § 18; Groll, *Negative Verbal System*, 122ff.

circumstantial form

E. Wente, *iwiw.f sdm* in Late Egyptian, in: *JNES* 20, 1961, 120ff; Frandsen, *Outline*, § 103

First Future

Černý/Groll, *Late Egyptian Grammar*, § 23

2   S. Winand, *Études*, 521.

3.3 The nominal *sdm=f* or the emphatic sentence

3.3.1 Forms and functions

(1) Verbal forms as the subject of the sentence

The role of the subject in the bimembral Adverbial Sentence can be assumed by certain conjugated verbal nouns in Late Egyptian (cf. supra § 2.3.[1]), as in Middle Egyptian, Demotic and Coptic. Semantically, the significance of the verbal message can thus take second place to the predicate expression of the Adverbial Sentence. Although the adverbial adjunct seems to specify the verb on the sentence surface, it is in fact the emphasized predicate of the complex sentence.

i.ir=k iy ḥr iḫ n sḥn ...   *(Wenamun 2,3-4)*

i.ir=i iy m-s3 t3 ṯ.t n p3 wḏ

"Because of what orders have you come here?"

"It was because of the wood for the Bark that I have come" (for the hieroglyphic text, cf. supra, § 2.3.2[1]).

Note:

> structure *i.ir=k iy* is the form of the verb *iy* as a nominal subject in an Adverbial Sentence; *ḥr iḫ* and *m-s3 t3 ṯ.t* are adverbial phrases functioning as predicates.

These forms of the verb have gained some importance in the history of Egyptology as emphatic forms. They are frequently designated the Second Tenses, following the terminology of traditional Coptic grammars. In Coptic all simple tenses of the sentence conjugations can be converted into a second, nominal, tense through the addition of the morpheme Є- or ЄРЄ-. Outside the paradigms of late Demotic and Coptic, there is, however, no "first tense", so that this form is termed the nominal *sdm=f* here (called the "that-form" by Frandsen).   *Second Tenses*

Adverbial phrases play the role of predicate. There are, however, far fewer Late Egyptian adverbial phrases than in Middle Egyptian. Remaining are only (a) adverbs, (b) phrases with preposition + noun or nominal phrase, and (c) phrases with the preposition *r* + infinitive, with the meaning "in order to". Prepositional infinitives, Old Perfectives and other such forms were no longer used directly, but rather as corresponding circumstantial clauses or conjunctional clause conjugations (cf. supra §§ 2.3.2[2] and 2.3.3[3]).   *Late Egyptian adverbial phrases*

The nominal *sdm=f* has the form *i.ir=f-sdm* in the textual registers and categories of Late Egyptian proper, or the form *i.sdm=f/r.sdm=f* with the verbs *iri* "to make"; *rdi* "give"; *dd* "say"; *ini* "bring"; *šm* "go"; *iy* "come" (and a few others). The periphrastic *i.ir=f-sdm* form covers the functions of a past, a present, and, increasingly, a future tense;   *i.sdm=f/i.ir=f-sdm* it still has a simple passive *sdm.tw=f*, too. The meaning of the simple form is, however, one of a prospective or future tense:

(LRL 19,7-8)

i̓.i̓w=i̓ i̓w t3y=f md.t m gs m d̠r.t=i̓ "When I (shall) get back, his affairs will be halfway in my hand"

Notes:

    i̓.i̓w=i̓   form of the prospective nominal *sdm=f*;

i̓w t3y=f md.t+AP   Circumstantial First Present;

    structure   *"it is his affairs being in my hand that I shall come back".

Schematically the usage of forms is represented in the following table:

Subject expression	Predicate expression
i̓.sdm=f/ *i̓.i̓r=f sdm*	prep. + noun/noun phrase prep. *r* + infinitive *i̓w* + sentence conjugation clause conjugation

(2) Negation and adverbial subordination

negation by *bn* ... *i̓n*

A sentence with a nominal *sdm=f* — being a complex variation of the Adverbial Sentence — is negated with the discontinuous morpheme *bn* ... *i̓wn3/i̓n* as is the Adverbial Sentence occasionally (§ 3.1.1[4]):

(RAD 55, 11)

y3 bn i̓.i̓r=n zš n ḥqr=n i̓wn3 "Surely it is not because we were hungry that we went on strike";

Note:

    zš/zni̓   abbreviated from *zni̓/zš t3 5 i̓nb.t/n3 i̓nb.t* "to pass the (five) control points" (of the *md3y*-police on the way from Deir el-Medineh) > "to stop work", "to strike".

negation by *tm*

Using the nominal *sdm=f* of the negative verb *tm*, a negative statement can be made the subject, just like any other verbal noun (infinitives, participles, relatives). The affirmation of the statement remains, so that the statement somehow makes an affirmation about a negative content:

(HorSeth 15,12-13)

i̓.i̓rw=k tm di̓.t wd̠ᶜ.tw=tn ḥr i̓ḫ i̓w=k nḥm n=k t3 i̓3w.t n Ḥrw "Why did you prevent judging you by taking up the office of Horus?"

Notes:

> *tm dỉ.t wḏᶜ.tw=tn*   a kind of semantic nullification of "causing": *"a non-compulsion that you be judged". In English this can be matched with the appropriate verb, e.g., "prevent";
>
> construction: infinitive of *tm* preceding the infinitive of *dỉ* (Middle Egyptian: negative complement), followed by subjunctive-prospective *sdm=f* of *wḏᶜ*;
>
> structure   despite the subject with "negative content" (*ỉ.ỉr=k tm dỉ.t wḏᶜ.tw=tn*), the predication remains affirmative (*ḥr ỉḫ*): a negative "why do you prevent?" would correspond to the syntactically identical positive "why do you cause?".

Like all other sentence conjugations, and simple sentences, the complex Adverbial Sentence with a nominal *sdm=f* can be converted into a circumstantial with *ỉw*:

subordination by *ỉw*

(pMayer A 6,18-19)

ḏd=f nhy n ḫt ḏᶜb pȝ ḥtp.w-nṯr nȝ nty wȝḥ m pȝ wḏȝ

ỉw ỉ.ỉr=ỉ wȝḥ=w ỉm n-ȝby zȝw tȝy ḫt

"He said, 'It was some firewood and charcoal meant for the divine offerings which lay in the storeroom, and it was in order to preserve this seal that I put them there'."

Notes:

> main sentence   Late Egyptian Pseudo-Cleft Sentence: noun (*ḫt ḏᶜb*) + defined relative phrase (*nȝ nty wȝḥ*) "This is what is such and such". Note the determination structure: *nhy n ḫt ... nȝ nty wȝḥ*;
>
> *pȝ ḥtp.w-nṯr*   writing for *pȝ n ḥtp.w-nṯr* "which belongs to the divine offerings" (< *"that of the divine offerings", cf. § 2.1.2[2]), in apposition here;
>
> *nty wȝḥ*   relative clause with Old Perfective; its actor expression is identical with the antecedent of *nty*;
>
> *n-ȝby zȝw*   compound preposition (like *n-mrw.t-n*) with infinitive (*"because of the desire to keep").

(3) Notes on linguistic evolution

Being remnants of the Middle Egyptian conjugated verbal nouns, the nominal *sdm.n=f* and nominal *sdm=f* (*mrr=f* and prospective) will still be found in the higher layers of texts in the register hierarchy (Late Middle Egyptian, Medio-Late Egyptian). Verbs of motion in particular[3] clearly display the morphosyntactical changes of the (nominal) *sdm.n=f* to the Late Egyptian *sdm=f* — Middle Egyptian nominal *sdm.n=f* constructions with verbs of motion employ a *sdm=f* in Medio-Late Egyptian:

nominal *sdm.n=f/sdm=f*

(Doomed Prince 5,10-11)

ỉy=k tnw pȝ šrỉ nfr "Where did you come from, handsome boy?".

---

3   As well as the verbs *sḏr* and *wrš*

semantic
differentiation

Use of the Late Egyptian *i.ir=f-sdm* for both past/perfective and present/imperfective neutralized the Middle Egyptian distinctions of tense, aspect and mood. In some verbs, the prospective/future component is clearly indicated as *i.sdm=f*. It is only with the appearance of the nominalization converter *i.ir* (from the *i.ir=f-sdm* conjugation) that lines are clearly demarcated: in Demotic there are not only *i.ir=f-sdm* forms, but also *i.ir* converted forms of the Third Future and the Aorist. In Coptic this is extended to the entire conjugation system (Є-/ЄТЄ-/ⲚⲦ- + sentence conjugation).

reduction of
use

In Middle Egyptian, the syntactical structures of *sdm=f* nominal forms varied widely, although not always according to clearly describable patterns: (a) as conjugated verbal nouns following prepositions and with prepositional nisbe forms (indirect genitive), (b) as the object of certain verbs, (c) in balanced sentences, and (d) as the nominal phrase acting as a subject in an Adverbial Sentence. These structures still appear in the registers of the literary and liturgical texts, as well as in decorum texts. In Late Egyptian proper, however, the use of the nominal form of the verb has been reduced that it is used almost exclusively as the noun phrase serving as subject in complex Adverbial Sentences. Cf. Frandsen, *Outline*, § 90.

3.3.2 Usage

questions for
specification

In terms of their structure and meaning, these sentences play an important role in questions for specification and their replies (cf. supra § 2.3.2[1] & 3.3.1: Wenamun 2,3-4 & HorSeth 15, 12-13). In Egyptian, questions for specification generally construct the interrogative expression adverbially (an "empty" set), and the answer follows in exactly the same syntactical position ("filled" set). An example of a question for specification:

(oDM 580 rt. 4-5)

 *i.ir=k it3 3h.t=i hr ih* "Why did you take my property?".

emphasis

Using this type of sentence allows the speaker to play with emphasis and the relative significance of information. The emphatic sentence is however also well suited for repartee, dialogues, and argument:

(pNaunakhte I 4,2-3)

bn iw=w r ʿq r pš.t m p3y=i r-3 i.ir=w ʿq r p3 r.wy n p3y=w iti "They (the children) won't get a share of my third; but rather they are admitted to the two-thirds of their father."

Notes:

ʿq r pš.t   "to enter into the division";

r-3   way of writing fractions, here "¹/₃";

r.wy   writing for "two parts" (of three): "²/₃"; cf. Gardiner, *Grammar*, § 265.

A predicate expression using a circumstantial clause indicates the degree to which a *circumstantial clause as predicate*
Late Egyptian nominal *sdm=f* sentence assumes the character of a complex sentence. The
form itself appears as a kind of minimal sentence, as if it serves as the main sentence to
the dependent circumstantial clause. This segmentation does not, however, play a role in
linguistic evolution, as the form loses its conjugated character, becoming a mere
converter.

(LRL 21,8-10)

i̯.ir=i̯ h3b n=tw t3 š͑.t i̯.h3b=i̯ n=tw ḥr n3 ni̯wy i̯w bw i̯r.t t3y=tn h3b i̯y n=i̯ "It turned out that
I had sent the letter which I sent to you about the spears before your message reached
me."

Notes:

    h3b n=tw   variation of *n=tn* "to you";

  i̯w bw i̯r.t NP i̯y circumstantial form of the "not yet/before" form; (cf. §§ 2.3.2[3]; 5.1.1[2]);

    t3y=tn h3b   for *p3y=tn h3b* "your epistle".

This type of sentence can, however, be a part of a compound sentence, as in *in balanced sentence structures*
inn-sentences (conditional sentences) or oaths, where, to be sure, the construction reflects
the construction of the Middle Egyptian balanced sentences in Late Egyptian:[4]

(RAD 72,11-73,1)

w3ḥ ꜣImnw w3ḥ p3 ḥq3 mtw=tw gm 3ḥ.t ḫ3-(n-)t3 i̯w sk3=i̯ sw m i̯w n Nby.t r.šdi̯=tw n3 i̯t
m.di̯=i̯ "As long as Amun and the Ruler endure and leasehold shares of Crown Land
which I have tilled on the 'island' of Ombo should be found, then the corn should be
exacted from me.";

Notes:

w3ḥ ꜣImnw w3ḥ p3   introductory line of an oath: *sdm=f* forms derived from the Middle Egyptian balanced
       ḥq3   sentence variations, which have become fixed and standard expressions in Late
           Egyptian (cf. Oath Formulas, infra Appendix § 7.1);

           writing of *ḥq3* with cartouche: note the *s* at the end, which closes the hieratic
           abbreviation of *͑nḫ wd3 snb*;

  mtw=tw gm   Conjunctive as a form which continues the oath introduction;

     3ḥ.t   cultivated field, here specifically "leasehold field";

    ḫ3-t3   registered land at the king's disposal, which he can lease out, whether it belongs to
           the Crown or to other institutions (cf. Gardiner, *The Wilbour Papyrus* II, 166);

---

4   For the construction of these compound sentences cf. Junge, *"Emphasis" and Sentential Meaning in*
    Middle Egyptian, Wiesbaden 1989, 89f(2).

   ỉw "island", corresponding to the Arabic *jazira*: land with an elevation lying between the extremes of high and low water, so that only a high inundation would cover it;

   Nby.t name of the city called Kom Ombo today;

   r.šdỉ=tw form of the passive nominal *sdm=f*;

   structure the formula of the oath precedes the independent emphatic sentence as a verbally constructed noun phrase.

noun phrase in anticipation

As a noun phrase, the nominal *sdm=f* itself can precede another sentence. This may be considered another realization of the balanced sentence in Late Egyptian:

(pD'Orb 3,1)

pȝ-wn ỉ.ỉr pȝy=ỉ sn <ʿȝ> s:ỉn n=ỉ m-dy.t wdf=w "(Get up and pray give me seed corn so that I can go to the field), since my big brother is waiting for me, don't delay things.";

Notes:

   pȝ-wn conjunctional particle preceding sentence conjugations, "for", "because";

   <ʿȝ> emendation because the written *šrỉ* is excluded, as the younger brother is speaking;

   m-dy.t negated Causative Imperative (cf. supra § 2.2.2[3]);

   wdf=w subjunctive-prospective *sdm=f* "that they delay, be slow" > "that one delays, is slow" (cf. for passive supra § 2.3.2[4]);

   structure *pȝ-wn* introduces a sentence consisting of a negated Causative Imperative which is preceded by a noun phrase in anticipation; this noun phrase on its part is a nominal *sdm=f*.

3.3.3 Bibliography

form and usage Winand, *Études*, §§ 405-457; 487-494; Frandsen, *Outline*, §§ 85-92; Černý/Groll, *Late Egyptian Grammar*, § 26; Groll, *Negative Verbal System*, 172; Cassonnet, *Les Temps Seconds*

methods of negation Frandsen, *Outline*, § 91; Černý/Groll, *Late Egyptian Grammar*, § 27; Groll, *Negative Verbal System*, 141ff; 150ff (§§ 41; 45); Cassonnet, *Les Temps Seconds*, 113ff (§ 10)

subordination Frandsen, *Outline*, § 110; Cassonnet, *Les Temps Seconds*, 73ff (§§ 6; 7)

language history Winand, *Études*, § 185; 405-419; Wente, *A Late Egyptian Emphatic Tense*, in: *JNES* 28, 1969, 5ff; Johnson, *Demotic Verbal System*, 119ff; 125f

3.3.4 Exercise: From a tale of Dynasty XX (HorSeth 5,6-6,2)

Passage from a literary narrative dating to the reign of Ramesses V, published by A. H. Gardiner, *The Library of A. Chester Beatty. Description of a Hieratic Papyrus with a Mythological Story, Love Songs, and other Miscellaneous Texts* (London, 1931), and idem, *Late-Egyptian Stories, Bibliotheca Aegyptiaca* I (Brussels, 1932). The passage cited here is from *LES* 43-44. The "Contendings of Horus and Seth" is a story about gods similar to the mythical comedies of Aristophanes.

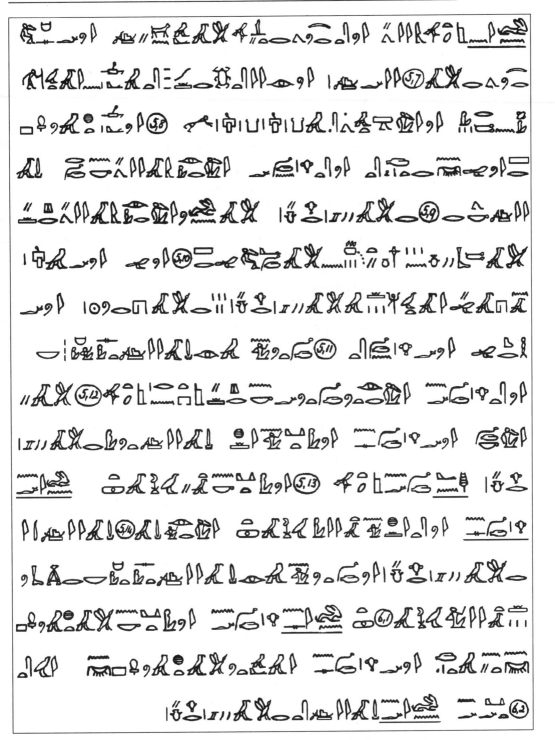

3.3.4 Exercise: HorSeth 5,6-6,2

Purpose: Example of a literary text of Dynasty XX; use of Circumstantial First Present, emphatic forms and Third Future.

Notes:

5,6   *wn.ỉn* (with *ḥr* + infinitive) is a traditional form of narrative texts; similar *ꜥḥꜥ.n* in line 5,12;

ꜥn.ty, the "clawed one" is a reading making sense in the course of the tale, as his toe-nails are removed as a punishment later. The alternative reading is *Nm.ty*. Either reading applies to a cult manifestation of the Hawk god of the 12th Upper Egyptian nome, with its capital at Per-Anti/Nemti - the "House of Anti/Nemti House". The tombs at Deir el-Gebrawi belong to the Overseers of the priests of Anti/Nemti;

spr r: "arrive at", "turn to"; for the use of *ḥmsỉ* as an auxiliary verb "to be doing something", cf. supra § 2.2.3(3);

5,7   "boat": probably to be read *ỉmw*;

ỉw ỉry=s: circumstantial of preterite *sdm=f* (here as characteristically relative past);

wꜥ n ỉꜣw.t n rmṯ: "an old human lady"; note the traditional construction with *wꜥ* and *n*;

m ksks: "bent, crooked" (Lichtheim, *Literature*, derives it from *ksỉ* "to bend");

5,8   *r-ḏr.t=s*: "(jewelry, bonds are) on her hand";

r ḏd ḏꜣy=k: prospective *sdm=f* after *ḏd*; there are two alternative interpretations: either *ḏd* with direct address, literally "(I came to you) to ask, 'Could you ferry me to the middle-island?'" or understand *r-ḏd* as the conjunction (Coptic ϪⲈ) "so that you could ferry me"; cf. infra § 3.4.2(1);

5,8-9   the preposition *r* is written twice (dittography at the line break);

5,9   \\⌶| an abbreviated writing of ⌐◌ *ỉw* "island"; *ỉw ḥr.ỉ-ỉb* "island in the middle", "middle-island", perhaps even then a designation for a strip of land in the Delta surrounded by branches of the river and canals, as it meant later;

pꜣ-wn: conjunction "for" + sentence conjugation (cf. Erman, *Neuägyptische Grammatik*, § 679);

ṯb < ṯꜣb: vessel in the form of a situla;

5,10   *5 r pꜣ hrw*: absolute use of a noun indicating time (cf. Gardiner, *Grammar*, 88): "since five days" (or, "five days until today" < *"five up to today");

5,11   *ḏd.tw n=ỉ*: passive of preterite *sdm=f*;

5,12   *ḏꜣy.tw='*: passive prospective *sdm=f* as a purpose clause, "that", "in order to" (circumstantial form of the Late Egyptian independent prospective *sdm=f*, cf. infra § 3.4.2[2]);

5,13   *ỉw=s (r) ỉḫ n=ỉ tꜣy=t wḥꜣ.t*: "What is it to me, your cake?!"; use of a *ỉw*-sentence or Third Future variation (*r* + noun), where the preposition is not graphically noted, as in the normal writing of the Third Future (cf. for the apposition, supra § 2.1.4[1]);

5,13-14   *ḏꜣ* in *ḏꜣy.tỉ* is written twice, being repeated because of next line; the *.tỉ*-ending can be the infinitive ending, but it could also be a writing for the infinitive with object suffix *ḏꜣy.t=' (< =t)* "ferry you (f.) over";

5,14   *ỉw ḏd.tw n=ỉ m-ỉr ḏꜣy Y*: circumstantial of preterite *sdm=f* with following content clause (direct address); a translation using indirect speech is probably preferable in these cases: "... although I have been told not to ferry over Y";

read *tꜣy=' wḥꜣ.t (< tꜣy=t wḥꜣ.t)*: the 1st pers. sing. pronoun referring to a woman, written 𓏭 is here the 2nd pers. sing.: the same grapheme and the same phoneme, but different morphemes.

3.4. Request sentences: Imperative and Prospective

3.4.0 Areas of meaning and means of expression

(1) Request, wish and command: anticipated and expected actions

As in other languages, Egyptian had several means of expressing that the speaker wants   *Prospective*
something. There are suitably phrased declarative sentences, but in particular there are
specific types of sentences formed with (a) the imperative (cf. supra § 2.2.2) or the
infinitive; (b) the Third Future (cf. supra § 3.2.2); or (c) a modal form of the *sdm=f*.
This latter *sdm=f* form is the so called prospective *sdm=f*, which can be an independent
sentence, but can also be subordinate. When referring to this form here apart from its
role and syntactic position (independent, subordinate), it will be termed "Prospective".

Expressing a wish, a request or a command is by definition restricted to direct forms   *wish or*
of speech. Generally, the imperative is thought to be the form used to express a command,   *command*
while the other forms are taken to express varying degrees of desire, extending to gentle
compulsion. This is however not the entire story, for the power of the wish is actually
expressed by means of particles, adverbs or tone, rather than through specific grammatical
forms. Stylistically and historically imperatives and imperative infinitives, the prospective
sdm=f and the future forms are complementary, but in use they tend to merge into each
other in various ways.

ḥn=tn s:mtr=s (or *s:mtr st*) "Hurry and question them";   *(pJud. Turin 2,5)*

Notes: *ḥn=tn* prospective *sdm=f* 2nd pl. (*ḥn* is quite often used to introduce requests — as in English,
            to "hurry up" and do this or that);
        s:mtr imperative or imperative infinitive.

Characteristic of the imperative is direct address to listeners in a speech situation: the   *imperative*
form implies the presence of the "2nd pers." (sing. or pl.). The independent Prospective   *and optative*
as a form of the *sdm=f* conjugation (prospective *sdm=f*), however, can include both the
1st and 3rd persons as well; in function it can be compared to the English, German and
French Subjunctive, the Greek Optative or the Jussive/Cohortative of the Afro-Asiatic
languages (for Arabic, it is termed the Apocopat). This function will here be called the
Optative also with reference to Egyptian.

In forcefully expressed wishes ("should", "want"), especially those obliging oneself   *volitional*
or another (in the 2nd pers. — but also those expressed in the 3rd pers.), the Prospective   *future*
can assume the role of an instruction or utterance of future intent: "I want to" or "I will"
may change to "I am going to" or "I shall". In such cases, the prospective *sdm=f* can
be distinguished from the Third Future as a subjective or volitional future — a future
depending on the speaker's will (cf. Winand, *Études*, § 349).

future of
possibility

Concerning future situations which the speaker considers to be conceivable or desirable, doubts as well as probability can be expressed in Late Egyptian by using the Prospective in the 3rd pers.: "He probably will...", "He could...".

Potential

To make the distinction clearer, the independent prospective *sdm=f* expressing statements about the future — the future of volition or possibility — will be called the Potential here, reflecting one use of the Optative in Greek.

(2) The subordinate imperative

The languages into which we translate Egyptian do not allow the use of the imperative in subordinate clauses, because our grammar does not permit the logical association of a super-ordinated situation while addressing the listener directly. In the prohibitive (negated imperative), Egyptian does allow this, however. This is made possible by the specific features of the circumstantial converter *iw*, since it (a) expresses subordination only in a general way and does not require expression of logical relationship, and (b) includes simultaneously English co-ordination ("and"; "or"; "but").

(LRL 62,10)

imm šdi.tw=w iw m-ir sdm md.t "Let them (the bread rations) be saved, and don't pay attention to (other) instructions."

Notes:

imm šdi.tw=w   imperative of *di* followed by subjunctive-prospective *sdm=f* as an object clause;

iw m-ir sdm   subordinated prohibitive (negated imperative): "and don't listen to talk".

conjunctive

The function of any conceivable subordinated non-negated imperative is fulfilled by the Conjunctive. This follows an introductory imperative, and links wishes and requests into long chains: "Do this and that, and then you should do something else".

(3) The variants of the Late Egyptian *sdm=f*

Late Egyptian has two forms of independent *sdm=f* sentence: the prospective *sdm=f* and the preterite *sdm=f*. In principle — and aside from established combinations and grammatical constructions (*bw sdm=f/sdm.t=f; r sdm.t=f*; nominal *sdm=f*) — every use of the *sdm=f* form can be reduced to the Optative/Potential or the Preterite, and thus be clearly restricted to (a) wishes or future-oriented utterances and (b) past propositions.

register
dependency

The correct appreciation of the *sdm=f* forms depends however — even more than for other forms — on being conscious of the registers of texts and their position in the hierarchy of norms. Those texts (a) bearing considerable socio-ideological weight (royal or political texts), (b) used in an educational context, or (c) of religious import (such as hymns and liturgies) all tend to maintain the Middle Egyptian usage of the *sdm=f*. During the long history of the New Kingdom, however, the usage of texts of lower register categories and of literature tended to seep into the higher categories. We can thus find that (*iw*) *sdm.n=f* and *sdm=f* (preterite) appear in one and the same text. Even syntactic markers which seem mutually exclusive will be encountered side by side, e.g., the Middle Egyptian *iw*, which marked independence, and the Late Egyptian circumstantial converter *iw*, or the circumstantial converter *iw* and circumstantial *sdm=f*. While this is to be considered interference of earlier usage in the case of preterite *sdm=f* (§ 3.5), it is however still part of the Late Egyptian system with regard to the prospective *sdm=f*.

3.4.1 Forms and functions of the prospective *sdm=f*

Prospective/Subjunctive: Following J. P. Allen, a "prospective *sdm=f*" is distinguished from a "subjunctive *sdm=f*" for Old Egyptian (Old Kingdom Egyptian). "Prospective *sdm=f*" shows a *-w* ending for some classes of verb and is used as a nominal/emphatic and future form, "subjunctive *sdm=f*" has a *-t* ending on some irregular verbs and is used to express wishes, to form object-clauses following other verbs, and to form final clauses (for an overview cf. W. Schenkel, *Tübinger Einführung in die klassisch-ägyptische Sprache und Schrift*, Tübingen 1994, pp. 168-174). Even in Middle Egyptian the morphological and functional distinctions are difficult to grasp and in Late Egyptian all that can be said is that the nominal *i.sdm=f* form could be the functional successor of the earlier Prospective (cf. Winand, *Études*, § 343). The notion "prospective *sdm=f*" (or "Prospective") is thus meant to refer firstly to a form with a prospective meaning, expressing future statements, wishes and intentions; secondly to the form representing an independent sentence conjugation performing the functions of the "Prospective". Where the form is dependent on prepositions or verbs, it is termed "subjunctive-prospective *sdm=f*" (or "Subjunctive"), while the form as a circumstantial clause expressing intent or purpose is termed "final-prospective *sdm=f*".

In contrast to the preterite *sdm=f*, the prospective *sdm=f* can be used for any verb with a suitable meaning. It is not possible to form sentences using the periphrastic construction to indicate the optative-future notion: only in Demotic does the *ir=f sdm* periphrasis appear in dependent, subjunctive-prospective *sdm=f*. The conjugation base (*sdm=*) of strong verbs is immutable, while the 3ae inf. verbs frequently display a stem with -𓏏𓏏: 𓂋𓏤𓀜 *iry=f* "he may/should/will act". The same applies to those verbs whose second root consonant is *-w*, *-ʒ* or *-ʿ*. *iw* and *iy* "come" use both 𓇌𓂻, 𓅓𓂻 *iw=f* and 𓅓𓏏𓂻 *iw.t=f* "he may/should/will come". The passive — better: the form in which the actor remains unidentified — uses the infix or suffix *-.tw*: *sdm.tw=f* "he ought to be heard", *sdm=tw* "one should listen" (cf. § 2.3.2[4]).

The prospective *sdm=f* still displays the syntactical features of Middle Egyptian *sdm=f* usage more distinctly than any other *sdm=f* forms of Late Egyptian. The same form appears independently as a sentence — as the Optative/Potential — and dependently, as a subordinate clause. In subordinate clauses the form can be (a) nominal, serving as an object

sentence forming and dependent

clause, the subjunctive following *rdỉ*, and after certain prepositions (conjunctions), such as *m-ḏr*, *m-ḫt*; or it can be (b) adverbial, serving as a circumstantial clause of purpose — without being marked with the *ỉw*-converter: asyndetical subordination in contrast to the prevailing syndetical. If placed alongside the prospective emphatic *sdm=f* (*ỉ.sdm=f*; § 3.3.1[1]), it resembles a closed paradigm of the Middle Egyptian kind.

negation by bn   The same syntactical status can be read in the form of the negations. Optatives are negated with ⃒ *bn*, the successor of the Middle Egyptian ⎵ with *sdm=f*, which still appears in the higher textual registers. The subordinate prospective *sdm=f* takes the *tm*-negation: *tm=f sdm* "that he may not listen" ("lest he listen").

(RAD 75,6)

       bn dỉ=ỉ ꜥq=f "I will not let him enter".

Notes:

      bn dỉ=ỉ   negated sentence forming prospective *sdm=f* "I do not want to give" (with verbal object clause > "to cause"): negated Optative, Vetitive;

      ꜥq=f   subordinate prospective *sdm=f* in an object clause following *dỉ* "give" (> "cause").

The forms can be summarized as in the following table:

		Form	**Function**	**Meaning paraphrase**
Indepen-dent	complementary to	Imperative/Third Future		
		sdm=f	Optative	"he may/shall/should listen"
	negated	*bn sdm=f*		"he may/must not listen"
	with bound morpheme	*ỉḫ-sdm=k*		"would you please listen"
		ḥr-sdm=f	"contingency"-form	"he will inevitably listen"/"usually he will listen"
Dependent (nominal)	on verbs (as object)	*dỉ sdm=f*	Subjunctive	"cause that he listen"
	on prepositions	*ḏr/m-ḏr sdm=f*	Temporal	"when he listened"
	(conjunctions)	*m-ḫt sdm=f*		"after he has listened"
		r-tnw sdm=f		"whenever he listens"
(adverbial)		*sdm=f*	Finalis	"so that he may listen"
	negated	*tm=f sdm*	Circumstantial	"so that he may not listen"
	complementary to	*r* + infinitive		"in order to listen"

combination with ỉḫ and ḥr   As the table shows, the sentence forming (independent) prospective *sdm=f* enters established combinations with the particle *ỉḫ*, and less commonly with *ḥr* and *kȝ*. All three of these particles are closely related to their Middle Egyptian precursors, and the *ḥr* in particular should not be confused with the widely used Late Egyptian proclitic particle *ḥr*: *iḫ-sdm=k* is a form of polite request generally used with the 2nd pers. (but occasionally also with nominal actors). *ḥr-sdm=f* indicates that something follows from previous conditions, that it has a dependent existence, so to speak, or is "contigent" (being the successor of the Middle Egyptian *sdm.ḥr=f*); it is limited to the higher categories of texts, particularly literary pieces. The same applies to *kȝ-sdm=f*. The latter two forms disappear in the course of the New Kingdom and (*iḫ-sdm=f*) the Third Intermediate Period.

3.4.2 Use of the prospective *sdm=f*

(1) Requests, wishes, and desired or planned actions

The use of the Prospective as an Optative or a volitional future is familiar in Late Egyptian, especially in combination with *iḫ*. In comparison with Middle Egyptian, however, usage has declined:

— In wishes and self-obligations

nfr snb=k "May your health be good" (a common phrase in letters, and hardly limited to the passage cited);

in wishes

(LRL 28,7)

(HorSeth 10,12-11,1)

i.šm sdm.tw pȝ dd=i n=tn wnm=tn swi=tn ḥtp.w n=n rwi=tn mi.nȝ ṯṯṯt rꜥw-nb zp-2 zp-2 (The All-Lord speaks:) "Come and listen to what I have to say to you: 'You may eat and drink, but leave us in peace; pray put an end now to this endless strife'";

Notes:

    sdm.tw   interpreted as imperative, but it would also be possible to read a prospective *sdm=f* as purpose clause, "(Come), that one may hear what is said to you";

    ḥtp.w n=n   imperative: "Be so friendly to us...";

iḫ di=k ḥr=k r ir zḫȝ.w "Please turn your attention to becoming a scribe!"

(pAnast. III 5,5-6)

and especially in formal expressions

wȝḥ ʾImnw wȝḥ pȝ ḥqȝ *bn thi=i* "As long as Amun and the Ruler endure, I will not fail";

(HO pl. 71,1 vs.3)

Notes:

w3ḥ 'Imnw w3ḥ p3   prospective sdm=f in the introductory line of the oath (cf. infra, § 7.1), more literally,
ḥq3   "as truly that they will endure";

bn thì=ì   negated Optative (Vetitive).

in predictions

*(Doomed
Prince 4,3-4)*

— As a Potential Prospective in predictions

ìw=sn ḥr ḏd mwt=f n p3 mzḥ m-r3-pw p3 ḥf3w mìt.t p3 ìw (At birth, the Hathors have come)
"and they said: 'He may well die by the crocodile, the snake, or the hound.'"

Notes:

mwt=f   prospective sdm=f at the very beginning of the sentence ("direct indicator of initiality"
ḏd) as a form expressing that something is likely to happen;

p3 mzḥ   the determination by the definite article (p3 ḥf3w, p3 ìw) specifies explicitly that the
entire class is meant in each case. Neither "crocodiles" in general nor specifically "a
crocodile" are a threat: he is menaced by the entire class of "crocodilish" beings (the
threat to him is the whole category of "crocodilicity" — following Jan Assmann);

m-r3-pw   adverb with the function of disjunctive co-ordination (cf. supra § 2.2.4[1]: "or";

mìt.t   adverbially employed noun: "the same", as a co-ordinating conjunction, as "and
likewise". One could translate literally: "by the crocodile or the snake and likewise
the hound".

One can compare

*(HorSeth 5,8-
9)*

ì.ìr=ì ìy n=k r ḏd ḏ3y=k r {r} p3 ìw ḥr.y-ìb "I have come to you so that you may cross over
to the Isle in the Middle" (for the hieroglyphic text, cf. supra, exercise § 3.3.4):

Notes:

ì.ìr=ì ìy   nominal sdm=f of ìy with the adverbial predicate r ḏd ḏ3y=k;

r ḏd ḏ3y=k   while the conjunctional role of r-ḏd (ⲬⲈ) is already superficially decisive, the
connection to the role of speech introducing ḏd is still perceptible: "in order to say:
'Would you cross over!'" In the course of reinterpretation (by the speaker or in the
course of linguistic evolution) the syntactical independence of the Optative ḏ3y=k
following ḏd (the independent prospective sdm=f) is not changed.

Observation:

The phrases r ḏd ḏ3y=k and ìw=sn ḥr ḏd mwt=f illuminate the interaction of direct speech and
formulations with content clauses. The transformation of ḏd as a form that introduces direct
speech into a conjunction (r-ḏd, Coptic ⲬⲈ) reflects an analogically comparable process in
European languages: the punctuation-mark (or speech pause) that marks the following direct
speech as syntactically independent (i.e., ":") can be transformed into a content clause introduced
by the conjunction "that" (indirect speech). This means in practice that rather than translating,
"and they said, 'he will probably die (young)'", one could just as well translate "and they said,
that he would probably die (young)".

(2) Nominal and adverbial subordination

The prospective *sdm=f* is most commonly used as a Subjunctive. If a noun is the subject in the Adverbial Sentence, it is substituted by the nominal/emphatic *sdm=f* form (supra § 3.3.1[1]); any other noun can be replaced by a noun clause in the form of the prospective *sdm=f*. In Late Egyptian this applies primarily to the objects of transitive verbs, such as *dỉ* "give; cause". For historical reasons, the *sdm=f* can be considered to be "subjunctive" also in certain prepositional combinations (*m-dr/m-ht/r-tnw sdm=f*). These combinations were however already fixed conjunctional clauses so that the prospective *sdm=f* was no longer used freely after any given preposition.

Subjunctive

— Subjunctive as the object of verbs

as an object

(LRL 23,14-15)

ỉḥ dỉ=k twtỉ.tw n3 rmt n p3 ḥr nty ỉm m Nw.t mtw=k dỉ.t ỉn.tw=w n=ỉ r t3y rỉ.t "Please have the men of 'the Tomb' who are there in the City assembled, and have them brought to me on this side";

Notes:

twtỉ.tw passive Subjunctive (subjunctive-prospective *sdm=f*), dependent on the 2nd sing. masc. Optative of *dỉ* (or *twtỉ=tw*). This is the grammatical interpretation suggested by the writing, but it would also be possible to read *twtỉ n3 rmt* "that the men assemble",

Nw.t "the" City = Thebes (on the East Bank: the writer of the letter was at the temenos of Medinet Habu);

mtw=k dỉ.t Conjunctive: continuation form for the co-ordination of imperatives, Optatives, etc. ("hypotactical co-ordination");

ỉn.tw=w passive Subjunctive (of *ỉnỉ* "bring"), dependent on infinitive of *dỉ*.

— As component of the Temporal conjunctional clause

as Temporal

(pAbbott 5,1)

ỉw=tw dỉ.t n=f ỉr.t=f m-dr pḥ=f st (A commission has bound a man's eyes and taken him to the plundered tombs) "And his sight was given to him after he had reached them";

Note:

m-dr pḥ=f Temporal ("when/after something was done"); subjunctive-prospective *sdm=f* of *pḥ* as morphological component of what was formerly a prepositional phrase.

An independent prospective *sdm=f* — the Potential/Optative — is not subordinated as a circumstantial clause with the converter *ỉw*: it is the prospective *sdm=f* itself that is subordinated, as a "final" *sdm=f* in a circumstantial clause that specifies result or purpose ("in order to", "so that"). This differs significantly from the other sentence conjugations.

final circumstantial

(Beatty Love Songs vs. C2,3)

mỉ n=ỉ m33=ỉ nfr.w=k "Come to me, so that I may see your beauty" (for the hieroglyphic text, cf. supra Exercise § 2.2.6[1]);

(HorSeth 14,9)

ỉḫ ḥȝb=k n=n pȝ nty ỉw=n r ỉr=f n Ḥrw ḥnᶜ Stš tm=n ỉr sḫr m ḫm=n "Please send us word about what we should do for Horus and Seth, so that we don't make uninformed plans";

Notes:

ỉḫ ḥȝb=k	sentence conjugation/main sentence with prospective *sḏm=f* in combination with *ỉḫ* as a polite request;
pȝ nty + sentence	nominalized relative clause with its own actor expression/subject, which is not the same as the antecedent of the relative converter (Third Future sentence conjugation), and resumptive pronoun;
tm=n ỉr sḫr	negated final circumstantial (prospective *sḏm=f* of *tm*) to the superordinated sentence conjugation.

r + infinitive   The final-prospective *sḏm=f* form with its own actor expression is an alternative to sentence extension using adverbials formed with the preposition *r* + infinitive (they both share "paradigmatic substitution" features). But it should be noted that although the use of preposition + infinitive forms was less common than in Middle Egyptian, in Late Egyptian their use was still not reduced to the *r* + infinitive ("in order to") as in Coptic (Є- + Infinitive). This prospective *sḏm=f* form in use as a purpose clause is the only form in the texts of Late Egyptian proper in which the features of Middle Egyptian circumstantial *sḏm=f* are still alive and common (cf. supra § 3.4.0[3]).

3.4.3 Causative constructions

(1) The Causative Imperative and its negation

The Subjunctive was also widely used as the object of *ỉmm*, the imperative of *dỉ* "give", "cause". This construction was used in all periods, and was standardized in the paradigm of the Coptic "causative imperative" (*ỉmm ỉr=f-sḏm* > ⲘⲀⲢⲉϤⲤⲰⲦⲘ̄). The implicit 2nd pers. direct address of the imperative was sometimes extended to undefined parties, especially when the Subjunctive was used with the passive -.*tw*/=*tw* forms:[1]

---

1   This was why the form was termed Optative in Till, *Koptische Grammatik*, and elsewhere.

[hieroglyphic text]   *(HorSeth 10,11-12)*

wn.ỉn tꜣ psḏ.t ḥr ḏd ỉmm ꜥš=tw n Ḥrw ḥnꜥ Stš wpỉ.tw=w wn.ỉn=tw ỉnỉ.t=w m-bꜣḥ tꜣ psḏ.t

"And then the Ennead announced: 'Let Horus and Seth be summoned, that they may be judged!' And thus they were brought into the presence of the Ennead."

Notes:

  ỉmm ꜥš=tw no one is specifically addressed with this imperative which is meant as a general instruction;

  wpỉ.tw=w passive, final-prospective *sḏm=f*, "that they be judged";

  wn.ỉn=tw (ḥr) note the identical writings of the passive (*wn.ỉn=tw*) and the status pronominalis of the
  ỉn.t=f infinitive (*ỉnỉ.t=f*).

The Subjunctive following *ỉmm* generally applies to all persons, except for the 2nd, indirect speech
where the simple imperative is employed. If the 2nd pers. is used, as in the introductory
paragraphs of letters, with *ỉmm ꜥnḫ=k* etc., it is a form characterizing "indirect speech":

[hieroglyphic text]   *(LRL 21,7-8)*

r.nty tw=ỉ ḏd n Ḫnmw St.t ꜥnq.t ỉmm ꜥnḫ=tn ỉmm snb=tn "The following: I pray to
Khnum, Satis and Anukis that you be well and healthy" (** "I pray to Khnum, Satis and
Anukis: 'cause — you gods — that you — recipients of the letter — live'", etc.).

Note:

  r.nty (Middle Egyptian *r-nt.t*) conjunction preceding sentence conjugation, introducing the
  actual content in letters and messages, or preceding justifications, explanations, etc.
  This can be translated as a colon ":", or "furthermore", "the following", etc.

Observation:

In such constructions (generally: "I say to god So-and-So *ỉmm n=k ꜥnḫ*, that he give you life",
etc.) it is impossible to translate getting all of the various persons addressed literally "right".
One has to decide to translate either "I pray — concerning you — to god NN, 'give **him** life/cause
that **he** lives'", or "I pray — concerning you — to god NN, that **he** may give life to you/that **he**
may cause that you live".

The negative counterpart of the Causative Imperative is *m-dy.t sḏm=f* ("don't let him negation
listen"; "prevent him from listening"). It is formed with the Prohibitive *m* and a form
of *dỉ*, which is probably best considered to be the infinitive, although it assumes a graphic
appearance which varies considerably from the conventional forms of the infinitive ([hieroglyphs]
; [hieroglyphs]; [hieroglyphs] etc.; cf. Winand, *Études*, §§ 192; 154-155)

[hieroglyphic text]   *(oDM 613,3)*
m-dy.t ꜥḥꜥ=f m pꜣy=f spr r=tn

"Don't let him wait around when he reaches you";

Notes:

  m-dy.t ꜥḥꜥ=f Prohibitive (negated imperative) of *dỉ* with subjunctive *ꜥḥꜥ=f*;

m p3y=f spr   preposition with defined infinitive (*"at his reaching you"; cf. supra § 2.3.3[2]);

r=tn   the doubling of *r* in *r.r=tn* is a writing of the status pronominalis (Coptic ЄΡⲰ=ⲦⲚ).

The Prohibitive form *m-ỉr* also appears with *dỉ*. In its periphrastic form (*m-ỉr dỉ.t ỉr=f sdm* "Don't let him hear!"), the construction is a precursor of the Coptic Vetitive ⲘⲠⲢ̄ⲦⲢⲈϤⲤⲰⲦⲘ̄.

(Wenamun 2,53)

m-ỉr dỉ.t ptr=ỉ sw "Don't make me look at it".

The negated Causative Imperative can also be used with the circumstantial converter *ỉw* (cf. also § 3.4.0[2]). In such cases the form is in a way a paradigmatic substitute for the subordinated negative Third Future.

(LRL 19,11-12)

mtw=k dỉ.t ỉw=f n=ỉ 3s ỉw m dỉ ꜥḥꜥ=f "And have him come to me quickly, without permitting him to stay" (< "and don't let him stay");

Notes:

> *mtw=k dỉ.t*   Conjunctive, here as a member in a chain of conjunctives, which continue an introductory imperative;
>
> *dỉ.t ỉw=f*   Causative Infinitive followed by Subjunctive;
>
> *ỉw m dỉ ꜥḥꜥ=f*   subordinated, negated Causative Imperative (Causative Prohibitive).

(2) Finalis and Causative Infinitive

Finalis

As with the prospective *sdm=f* in general, the prospective *sdm=f* of *dỉ* as a causative followed by a Subjunctive can also be used as a circumstantial clause. In the form of the 1st pers. sing. prospective *sdm=f* (*dỉ=ỉ sdm=f*) in the clause of purpose, it was very long lived (*dỉ=ỉ ỉr=f sdm* > ⲦⲀⲢⲈϤⲤⲰⲦⲘ̄). As the causative-final circumstantial of the 1st pers. following an imperative sentence (i.e., addressed to the 2nd pers.), the emphasis that the speaker is causing something to be accomplished (standardized in Coptic) makes the normal expression of purpose or intention retreat slightly, leaving a shade of promise or prospect:[2] "Seek and ye will find".

2   One could occasionally even say the speaker promises a "reward" for an act requested; combined with its syntactical function of continuative > conjunctive, the form has thus a function that justifies terming it a causative-promissive Conjunctive in Coptic; cf. Polotsky, *Grundlagen des Koptischen Satzbaus* I, 163f (§ 38).

ỉmm ḫꜥ.tw=f r bl ỉrm=ỉ dỉ=ỉ ptr=k ḏr.t=ỉ ỉw=f tꜣy.t=f ḏr.t=f m-bꜣḥ tꜣ psḏ.t "Have him sent out together with me, and I will let you see my hand grasp his in front of the Ennead."

Notes:

> *ỉmm ḫꜥ.tw=f* Causative Imperative with passive prospective *sḏm=f* (*"Cause that he be sent forth");
>
> *dỉ=ỉ ptr=k* Finalis or "promissive conjunctive": prospective *sḏm=f* of *dỉ* as final circumstantial clause. Thus one could of course also translate: "Send him out so that I may let you see my hand doing such-and-such";
>
> *ḏr.t=f* apposition to *=f*; explicatory addition: "how it grasps it, his hand".

As a causative-final circumstantial, the Finalis is in a relation of paradigmatic substitution to the Causative Infinitive, the construction of the preposition *r* + infinitive of *dỉ* "cause" followed by a Subjunctive: (*r dỉ.t sḏm=f*; *r dỉ.t ỉr=f sḏm* > ⲉⲦⲢⲉϥ- ⲤⲰⲦⲘ̄). This corresponds to the relationship between the final-prospective *sḏm=f* and the preposition *r* + infinitive. Like all infinitives the Causative Infinitive is also negated with *tm*: (*r tm dỉ.t sḏm=f*). *causative infinitive*

ḥr ỉw=ỉ hꜣb ḥr=w m-bꜣḥ Pr-ꜥꜣ pꜣy=ỉ nb r rdỉ.t wḏỉ.tw rmṯ Pr-ꜥꜣ r ỉr hꜣw=tn "And I will send to my Lord Pharaoh about it, in order to have one of Pharaoh's men sent to deal with you directly."

Notes:

> *ḥr=w* note the writing of the status pronominalis of the 3rd. pl.;
>
> *r rdỉ.t wḏỉ.tw* Causative Infinitive with passive subjunctive *sḏm=f* (*wḏỉ.tw*; the person not mentioned in the passive form is, as often, Pharaoh — thus the semogram).

3.4.4 Notes on linguistic evolution

The Late Egyptian causative constructions have been given particular attention in this section because they are forms which are preserved in Coptic — by way of Demotic — in two different fashions: *causatives in Coptic*

1. lexicalized, as a class of verbs, the so-called causative verbs such as ⲦⲀⲚϨⲞ=ϥ "to keep him alive" corresponding to ⲰⲚϨ "live" (from *dỉ.t ꜥnḫ=f* "cause that he lives"); *lexicalized*

2. as a grammatical sub-system where the use of the subjunctive-prospective *sḏm=f* and its relationship to the verb *dỉ* "cause" is completely preserved or even reorganized. This took place via forms of *dỉ* in the three morphological patterns of infinitive, *as a sub-system*

imperative and circumstantial, which were essential components of the Egyptian-Coptic sentence structure. As infinitives, the causative constructions can either (a) appear as constituent phrases of the sentence conjugation or (b) extend the sentence. In either case they are, however, no longer so much causatives as conjugated infinitives. As imperatives, they express commands and wishes, with a continuative form of its own, the promissory conjunctive.

development   The development of these causative constructions from Late Egyptian to Coptic via Demotic can be summarized thus:

	Late Egyptian	(Roman) Demotic	Coptic	
Caus. Infinitive in				
Sentence conjugations				
e.g. Preterite	*dỉ=ỉ sdm=f*	*dỉ=ỉ ỉr=f-sdm/ỉr=ỉ-dỉ ỉr=f-sdm*	λ=1-	T- PЄⲈ=ϥ-CⲰⲦⲘ̄
e.g. Present	*tw=ỉ dỉ.t sdm=f*	*tw=ỉ dỉ sdm=f/tw=ỉ dỉ ỉr=f-sdm*	ϯ-	T- PЄⲈ=ϥ-CⲰⲦⲘ̄
Circumstantials	*... r dỉ.t sdm=f*	*... r dỉ sdm=f/r dỉ ỉr=f-sdm*	ⲉ-	T- PЄⲈ=ϥ-CⲰⲦⲘ̄
Neg. Imperative	*m-dy.t sdm=f/ ....m-ỉr dỉ.t sdm=f*	*m-ỉr dỉ sdm=f*	Ⲙ̄ⲠⲢ̄-	T- PЄⲈ=ϥ-CⲰⲦⲘ̄
Caus. Imperative	*ỉmm sdm=f*	*my ỉr=f-sdm*	Ⲙλ-	PЄⲈ=ϥ-CⲰⲦⲘ̄
Finalis	*... dỉ=ỉ sdm=f*	*... dỉ=ỉ ỉr=f-sdm*	...Tλ-	PЄⲈ=ϥ-CⲰⲦⲘ̄

Late Egyptian causatives   Exploring the role of the Late Egyptian causatives is thus motivated by the linguistic evolution, rather than by Late Egyptian syntax. While in Coptic this whole subset of constructions was completely limited to use with *dỉ*, i.e. to causatives, in Late Egyptian the constructions with the verb *dỉ* and subjunctive-prospective *sdm=f* are still part of a larger framework of similar constructions belonging to the framework of conjugation building and subordination — they are not yet a subsystem of their own.

trends of development   It is only after the end of the language history and in overview that some specific phenomena of the linguistic system can be recognized as tendencies of development. Accompanying the emergence of the causative system are

— the disappearance of fixed combinations of the prospective *sdm=f* with particles (*ỉḫ*, etc.) towards the end of the New Kingdom;

— the gradual disappearance of the independent prospective *sdm=f* as an Optative and a Volitive Future. This started in the hierarchically lower registers but then appeared also in formal usage during Dynasty XXI;

— the shift of the optative functions of the independent prospective *sdm=f* to (a) the imperative constructions (both are already used in parallel in Demotic) and (b) the Third Future.

The Late Egyptian sentential system for the expression of intention or possibility was thus not merely complex in itself, but this complexity is also clearly maintained in the subsequent development of the language. The independent forms, imperative and imperative infinitive, *bw ỉr.t≠f sdm*, the prospective *sdm≠f* and the future forms are complementary, and allow the expression of fine nuances in moving from one to the other. This is supplemented by the extreme variety of continuative forms: infinitive + *r*; Conjunctive, Finalis or promissive conjunctive; *bw ỉr.t≠f sdm*; Prohibitive; Third Future with the circumstantial converter *ỉw*; and the *šꜥ-ỉ.ỉr.t≠f sdm*. The expression of commands, wishes, requests and declarations of intent could be expressed through a very elaborate system, a modal system (cf. infra § 5.4.3.[2]) which proved stable until the very end of the Egyptian language.

modal system (margin)

3.4.5 Bibliography

Erman, *Neuägyptische Grammatik*, §§ 347-365; Korostovtsev, *Grammaire*, 232ff; Frandsen, *Outline*, §§ 43-54 — *imperative*

Frandsen, *Outline*, §§ 108-109 — *imp., subordinated*

Vernus, *Future*, Ch.1 — *Third Future vs. Prospective*

Frandsen, *Outline*, § 16; Winand, *Études*, §§ 340-404 — *prosp. forms*

Winand, *Études*, §§ 433-437; Cassonnet, *Les Temps Seconds*, 135ff (§ 11.1) — *ỉ.sdm≠f (emphatic)*

Winand, *Études*, §§ 361-377; Černý/Groll, *Late Egyptian Grammar*, § 30; Neveu, *La particule ḫr*, 219ff (§ 15) — *ỉḫ/kꜣ/ḫr sdm≠f*

Černý/Groll, *Late Egyptian Grammar*, § 22 — *bn sdm≠f*

Frandsen, *Outline*, § 14; Černý/Groll, *Late Egyptian Grammar*, § 21; Erman, *Neuägyptische Grammatik*, §§ 297-298; Hintze, *Neuägyptische Erzählungen*, 191-193 — *Optative/Potential*

Winand, *Études*, §§ 387-397; Frandsen, *Outline*, § 15(1); Erman, *Neuägyptische Grammatik*, §§ 287-290; Hintze, *Neuägyptische Erzählungen*, 193-196 — *Subjunctive*

Frandsen, *Outline*, § 15(2); Černý/Groll, *Late Egyptian Grammar*, §§ 45-47; Erman, *Neuägyptische Grammatik*, §§ 294-296; Polotsky, *Études de syntaxe copte*, Cairo 1944, 1ff (Finalis) — *final clause*

Frandsen, *Outline*, §§ 46-48; Erman, *Neuägyptische Grammatik*, §§ 291-292; Hintze, *Neuägyptische Erzählungen*, 185-187 — *Causative Imperative*

Polotsky, *Grundlagen des Koptischen Satzbaus* I, 141ff; Depuydt, *Conjunction*, 75ff — *Coptic causatives*

Frandsen, *Outline*, § 46; Winand, *Études*, §§ 349ff; 364ff; Johnson, *Demotic Verbal System*, 27ff; 153ff; 218ff; 272ff; 277ff; 279ff; Loprieno, *Ancient Egyptian*, § 4.6.2 (mood) — *linguistic evolution*

3.4.6 Exercise: A small piece with blessings (pAnast. III 4,4-11)

A short text from the reign of Merenptah with blessings dedicated by a scribe to his teacher, Amenemope, a "Fan Bearer on the Right of the King", "First Charioteer" and "Royal Envoy to Syria". It is one of a number of texts preserved on Papyrus Anastasi III, today pBM 10246, published in Gardiner, *Late-Egyptian Miscellanies*, pp. 24-25. pAnast. III has a number of other texts well suited for practice in the linguistic norms of the various forms of expression appropriate for each register. These include another hymn praising the delta residence (cf. supra, § 3.1.5[1]), some impressions concerning the life of the soldier, and a hymn to Thoth.

3.4.6 Exercise: pAnast. III 4,4 - 11

Purpose: Example of Dynasty XIX elevated education: style, textual forms and (Medio-Late Egyptian) textual norms; use of the Prospective and expressions of wish.

Notes:

4,4 *m-pw*: in principle this is a *pw*-sentence with the interrogative pronoun *m* "who is it?", but as elsewhere in Late Egyptian, it occasionally appears as a form of address: "Whoever it is" > "Dear Sir", or similar;

wnn=k mn.tỉ: "Live on!" (< "Be, in carrying on"), cf. also Gardiner, *Grammar*, § 326;

kꝫ ḥnᶜ=k rᶜw-nb a Middle Egyptian type of construction, i.e., an Adverbial Sentence used in apposition to pronominal *=k*: "(Live you on,) bread being with you daily", "you being supplied with bread daily";

wnf.tw/ꝫḫꝫḫ.ø/ḥzỉ.tw: Old Perfectives used in parallel to *mn.tỉ*, in the manner of Middle Egyptian construction;

4,6 *nn ḫᶜm tw ḏꝫy.t*: traditional form of the negated Prospective, "evil shall not come near you";

rnp.t sḫꝫ=tw m nfr.w=k: "the year in which your good will be recalled" (< *"the year concerning which: one will think of your good *in it*"), indirect, impersonal relative form without resumptive pronoun in the case of indications of time. Just as nominal indications of time are expressed directly, as absolute nouns used adverbially (e.g. *tr n rwhꝫ* "in the evening", cf. Gardiner, *Grammar*, § 88), they do not require resumption as antecedents of relative clauses; *sḫꝫ* here takes the preposition *m* (prepositional object), rather than a direct object, to indicate what is recalled;

sn.nw=k "Your equal" (< "Your second");

4,7 *nꝫy=k ꝫbd.w m wḏꝫ*: Adverbial clause used to refer to the pronominal *=k* of *qb=k* as in line 4,4; *wḏꝫ* means "prosperity" although written as "store room" — a common way of writing in the Miscellanies;

4,8 *ḥtp m-ᶜ*: unusual compound preposition, meaning "to be satisfied through someone" (or "to be satisfied with someone", for *ḥtp m*);

wḏ n=k ỉmnt.t: "the West is promised to you", passive *sḏm.w*;

bw ỉꝫw{t}=k: "you do not age", negative Aorist in non-periphrastic form (cf. supra § 2.3.2[3]);

4,9 one hundred and ten years with a body in good health — as becomes a highly honoured person (< "according to what ought to be done to somebody highly honoured");

4,10 the following *sḏm=f* forms with the twin reeds are forms of the final-prospective *sḏm=f*;

4,11 read: *ỉn kꝫ n wᶜ ỉqr*; note that the divine name Thoth is separated with its own verse points.

3.5 The Preterite

3.5.1 The preterite *sdm=f* and its features

(1) The form and its variants in the passive

preterite sdm=f   The Late Egyptian form for recording past events was the preterite *sdm=f*,[3] which must be distinguished from the prospective *sdm=f*, although the two are not always differentiated morphologically (for *iw/iy* "come", the form of the preterite *sdm=f* is ![glyph]).

(LRL 57,7 and passim)

sdm=i md.t nb i.h3b=k n=i hr=w "I have taken note of everything you sent to me about it". (A common phrase in letters);

Notes:

> *sdm=i*   active preterite *sdm=f*;
>
> *i.h3b=k*   relative form with its own actor expression and indirect resumption (*hr=w*);
>
> *hr=w*   note the writing of the status pronominalis of the preposition *hr*.

with transitive verbs   While the Late Egyptian prospective *sdm=f* is the direct successor of the Middle Egyptian prospective *sdm=f*, the Late Egyptian preterite *sdm=f* takes over the function of the Middle Egyptian *iw sdm.n=f*. Both forms are used exclusively with transitive verbs. Intransitive verbs, especially verbs of motion, use the First Present with the Old Perfective. Periphrasis with *iri* is still used only for verbs with more than four radicals. The notion "Preterite" is intended to serve as a neutral designation for statements about the past. In translation, it can usually be rendered as present perfect tense ("I have heard"), or as past tense ("I heard").

postposed speech marking   Morphologically, the *sdm.n=f* is preserved in Late Egyptian in ![glyph] *i.n=f* "said he" (shortened from *i.n=f hr dd*), which follows a quotation from direct speech, even where this has already been mentioned before the quotation (cf. Erman, *Neuägyptische Grammatik*, § 714).

forms of the passive   Along with the usual -*.tw* passive forms of the *sdm=f* (*sdm.tw=f*) — which are really active forms with an unnamed actor — the Middle Egyptian *sdm.w*-passive still appears not only in the more conservative text registers, but also in "real" Late Egyptian legal texts; the verb *di* assumes its reduplicating form in these:

---

3   Cf. for the terminology of the preterite Hintze, *Neuägyptische Erzählungen*, 60; 236 (*punktuelles Präteritum*); Satzinger, *Neuägyptische Studien*, §§ 2.1; 2.3.1.2 ("Präteritum; Perfekt"); in English or French literature usually "perfect active *sdm.f*"/"*sdm.f* perfective".

[hieroglyphs] *dd n=f ꜥnḫ n nb ꜥnḫ wḏꜣ snb* "An oath by the Lord was administered to him" ("he was compelled to swear by the Lord").

(pBM 10052, 4,22 and passim)

(2) Negation and adverbial subordination

The negative counterpart of the affirmative preterite *sdm=f* is the analytical *bw.pw=f-sdm* form "he did not hear". The conjugation base *bw.pw=* can be written in many ways (generally, [hieroglyph] or, [hieroglyph], but also [hieroglyph] followed by later abbreviations such as [hieroglyph], and then in Demotic [hieroglyph]). In contrast to the preterite *sdm=f*, the morpheme which bears meaning (meaning expression) can also be an intransitive verb.

negation

Alongside the *bw.pw=f-sdm*, *bw sdm=f*, the successor of the Middle Egyptian *n sdm=f*, is still used as a form of negation for the preterite *sdm=f* (cf. infra § 3.5.1[3]).

bw sdm=f

Still another form, the rare *bw sdm.t=f/bw ỉr.t=f-sdm* form and its passive *bw ỉry.t* + noun phrase (cf. supra § 2.3.2[3]) can be considered negative forms of the preterite *sdm=f*, or of the First Present + Old Perfective. This is used to indicate that an act has not been carried out in the past, but is still expected, i.e. a "not yet" form. It is thus a form of the perfect or preterite (being the negative counterpart to the perfect *wꜣḥ=f sdm* in Demotic), but the statement formulated with this negation remains in the balance in the moment of utterance, being neither past nor future: something has not yet been done, but one expects that it will be done, yet this remains uncertain:

bw ỉr.t=f-sdm

[hieroglyphs] *pꜣ-wn bw ỉr.t pꜣ ꜥdd gm.t=f*

(oDM 123 rt.2)

"for the boy hasn't found it yet";

Note:

> *pn* writing of *pꜣ* (both *pn* and *pꜣ* are only *p* by now).

Like all sentence conjugations, the preterite *sdm=f* and the *bw.pw=f-sdm/bw ỉr.t=f-sdm* can also be subordinated to another sentence using the *ỉw* converter, as a rule, but not necessarily, conveying relative past tense (pluperfect).

adverbial subordination

[hieroglyphs]

(pAbbott 5,5-6)

bw.pw=tw gm.t=f ỉw rḫ=f s.t nb ỉm "He wasn't convicted of having known any place there";

Notes:

> *ỉw rḫ=f* adverbially subordinated, or circumstantial, preterite *sdm=f*;
>
> *gm.t=f ỉw rḫ=f* a typical construction with the verb *gmỉ*: *gmỉ* followed by object and adnominal (appositional) circumstantial clause. This is very often better translated using an object (that-) clause rather than some form analogical to the circumstantial construction the Egyptian language uses (thus "One hasn't found that he knew any place there" instead of *"One hasn't found him having/to have known any place there").

(3) Notes on linguistic evolution

sdm=f and
sdm.n=f

The precursor of the Late Egyptian preterite *sdm=f* was the Middle Egyptian *ỉw sdm.n=f*. To be more precise, the Late Egyptian *sdm=f* is the successor of the *sdm.n=f*, which evolved as an independent preterite form in the system of sentence conjugations, when *ỉw* became the circumstantial converter by boundary shifting ("rebracketing") in sentential structure and change of function (cf. supra § 3.0.2). As an occasional alternative (allomorph) of the preterite *sdm=f* to which it gave birth, this *sdm.n=f* was used until well into Dynasty XIX in both colloquial and administrative texts — compare the following occurance from the reign of Ramesses II with the letter quoted above (*LRL* 57,7):

(pAnast. IX, 1-2)

sdm.n=ỉ n3 md.t ꜥḥ3 h3b=k

ḥr=w "I have taken notice of the disputed matter, concerning which you sent a letter".

ꜥḥꜥ.n sdm.n=f

In association with *ꜥḥꜥ.n*, the *sdm.n=f* was still used in the relevant textual categories (stories and legal texts) during Dynasty XXI, although far less widely than the *sdm=f* (the combination *ꜥḥꜥ.n sdm=f* is at first used only with nominal actor expressions).

dependency
on registers

The hierarchically higher text registers are naturally subject to interference from the use of the Middle Egyptian *sdm=f* forms. It must be assumed that not only the *sdm.n=f* and the preterite *sdm=f* were in use, but also the nominal and prospective forms of *sdm=f*, along with the *sdm=f*-balanced sentences.[4] In the Neo-Middle Egyptian categories of text, this parallel usage prevailed (as preterite forms, both the *sdm.n=f* and the preterite *sdm=f* remained allomorphs into the Roman era). They even brought back to life those forms which had been reduced or lost in the other textual categories, and these included the *sdm.w* passive, the *ꜥḥꜥ.n sdm.n=f/sdm=f*, and finally the *sdm.ỉn=f*, which in Late Egyptian proper was used only in association with *ḏd* "say".

bw sdm=f/
bw.pw=f sdm

It is easier to follow the evolutionary development of the negations. The clearly recognizable graphophonemic successor of the Middle Egyptian preterite negation *n sdm=f* is the *bw sdm=f*, a form which must be distinguished from the negative Aorist (supra § 2.3.2[3]) *bw rḫ=f/bw ỉr=f-sdm. bw sdm=f* appears in literary texts until the end of the New Kingdom, when it is completely replaced by *bw.pw=f-sdm*. The precursor of *bw.pw=f-sdm*, the earlier *n p3w=f sdm* "he did not hear",[5] was clearly a marginal form. Just why such a marginal form moved as *bw.pw=f-sdm* into the core of the system is explained by the analytic tendency, which makes the relationship between form and function less ambiguous.

4   Apparent present usage, cf., e.g., Korostovtsev, *Grammaire*, p. 246.

5   Cf. Gardiner, *Grammar*, § 484.

Like the prospective forms, the preterite *sdm=f* resisted periphrasing with *iri*. Aside
from verbs with four and five radicals, the *ir=f sdm* form did not appear until Late Demotic
texts of the Roman period (to be precise, mostly in the London-Leiden Magical Papyrus),
whence it reached Coptic as ⲀϤⲤⲰⲦⳘ. The Late Egyptian negation *bw.pw=f-
sdm* > Demotic *bn.p=f-sdm* is the precursor of the Coptic Negative Perfect ⳘⲡⲉϤ-
ⲤⲰⲦⳘ, and the *bw ir.t=f-sdm* of the Coptic ⳘⲡⲀⲦϤⲤⲰⲦⳘ.

development to Coptic

3.5.2 Usage

The preterite *sdm=f* and its negations describe acts and events which took place in the
past with regard to the speaker. It can thus either represent the speech attitude of the
narration ("I heard") or the present perfect (a past event whose effects last into the
present: "I have heard"). In its circumstantial form (*iw sdm=f*) it frequently expresses
the relative past time of an event. With some verbs (*mri* "love"; *msdi* "hate"; *ini*
"bring"; *rh* "know", etc.) the present perfect meaning has a clearly present effect (e.g.,
"to have fetched something" = "to bring it").[6]

Characteristic of the use of the preterite *sdm=f* is that it expresses the beginning of a
chain of events, defining the absolute time. This is then continued with the First Present
Circumstantial *iw=f hr sdm* — in this usage termed the "narrative" or "non-initial main
sentence" (NIMS).

— In independent statements, also in long chains of the same forms (co-ordination); the
independence is easily recognized within content clauses, in the introduction of direct
speech or after *r-dd* (cf. also § 5.3.1(2) infra). Introduced direct speech:

independent statements

dd=f bw.pw=i šm "He said, 'I didn't go'".

(pBM 10052, 10,4)

Content clause introduced with *r-dd*:

(LRL 23,9-11)

sdm={t}n i.dd tw=k iy.ti
    ph=k r Nw.t p3 dmi
    šzp tw ʾImnw m šzp nfr
    iry=f n=k nfr nb

"We have learnt that you have come, and that you reached the City, your (< the) home
town; that Amun received you with favour, and that he treated you well";

---

6   Cf. Frandsen, *Outline*, 198; Johnson, *Demotic Verbal System*, 71 n.70.

Notes:

i.dd   graphic variation of r-dd (Coptic ϪⲈ), here indicating a content clause formed by a First Present ("You have come");

Nw.t p3 dml   it would also be possible to translate "No, the city" (Nw.t as "name" for Thebes);

šzp m šzp nfr   "to receive with a good reception", the so-called complementary infinitive (cf. Gardiner, Grammar, § 298 Obs.).

tense defining   — Tense defining in the introductory passages of longer paragraphs, frequently followed by First Present Circumstantial clauses as narrative "non-initial main sentences":

(pAdoption rt. 16-17)

r.nty in=n ḥm.t Dl-n=l-Ḥw.t-lr.y r swn.t lw=s ms p3y ḥmt.w ḥrd.w "The following: we have paid for the servant Dinaihayera by indemnification, and she bore these three children".

Notes:

r.nty   < r-nt.t; the typical introductory particle in letters and records; "direct indicator of initiality";

inl r swn.t   "to purchase something for its price". House personnel may not really have been "bought", so that it is not a purchase in the strict sense, so much as an indemnity settlement between the previous employer and the future employer;

Dl-n=l-Ḥw.t-lr.y   proper name in sentence form: "Hat(hor) gave me a companion"; dl is also a preterite sdm=f; Ḥw.t is an abbreviation for Ḥw.t-Ḥrw "Hathor".

(pJud.Turin 6,2)

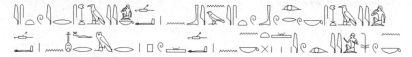   ir.w n=f t3y sb3y.t iw=tw w3ḥ=f

"This punishment was stipulated for him, and he was left to himself" (and he committed suicide).

subordinated   — Subordinated, the preterite sdm=f frequently expresses relative past tense:

(pD'Orb 8,2)

istw ir sḫ3y=k wᶜ n bin

istw bw ir=k sḫ3y wᶜ n nfr m-r3-pw wᶜ nk.t iw iry=l sw n=k

"If you recall an evil deed, can't you recall anything good — or anything else — that I have done for you?";

Notes:

istw   particle marking a tone question, introducing doubt, cf. supra § 2.2.4(1);

ir sḫ3y=k   ir as particle of topicalization ("as for") followed by a sdm=f; because ir-constructions cling to linguistic surroundings where older forms continue to be used, a Middle Egyptian form of sdm=f here follows ir (cf. also Satzinger, Neuägyptische Studien, 46ff);

bw ir=k sḫ3y   negative Aorist;

ı̓w ı̓ry=ı̓   circumstantial preterite *sdm=f* adnominally related to the indefinite determined noun
nk.t.

3.5.3 Bibliography

Winand, *Études*, §§ 317-324; Frandsen, *Outline*, §§ 1-6; Černý/Groll, *Late Egyptian*   active
Grammar, § 14
Winand, *Études*, §§ 471-486; 522-533; Frandsen, *Outline*, §§ 17-20; Černý/Groll, *Late*   passive
Egyptian Grammar, § 16
Winand, *Études*, §§ 335-339 (*bwpw=f-sdm*); 326-334 (*bw sdm=f*); 459-463 (*bw ı̓r.t=f*   negation
sdm); Frandsen, *Outline*, §§ 7-11; ; 25-28; Groll, *Negative Verbal System*, 2ff; 79ff;
Černý/Groll, *Late Egyptian Grammar*, §§ 15; 20.8-20.9; Erman, *Neuägyptische Gram-*
matik, §§ 445; 776-781
Frandsen, *Outline*, §§ 101-102; 106   converted
Winand, *Études*, §§ 292-312   *sdm.n=f*

3.5.4 Exercise: A legal document (pBoulaq 10 rt. 1-15)

The recto of Papyrus Boulaq 10 (= pCairo 58092) dates from early in the reign of
Ramesses III (Regnal Year 8). Published by J. J. Janssen & P. W. Pestman, Burial and
Inheritance in the Community of Workmen at Thebes, in: *Journal of the Economic and
Social History of the Orient* (*JESHO*) 11, 1968, 137ff, with this text p. 144; cf. also *KRI*
V: 449-450. A court record with the plaintiff *Ḥꜣy* son of *Ḥwy* (cf. vso. 1) contesting
claims concerning his father *Ḥwy*, his grandfather *Ḥwy-nfr* and his grandmother *Tꜣ-gmy.t*.
The dispute is among the brothers and sisters of his father, and it centres around
inheritance rights, which are related to burial expenses.

Purpose: Example of a Dynasty XX private legal document, use of affirmative
and negative preterite *sdm=f*; *sdm.n=f*.

Notes:

line 1 *r-rdı̓.t-rḫ.tw*: "to let it be known" (causative infinitive) is a nominalization which is
best rendered with "list", "register", "record", etc. (cf. Erman, *Neuägyptische
Grammatik*, § 425);

line 2 *rdy.n=f*: *n*-relative form (cf. Winand, *Études*, § 616), related to the contents of the list
(*ꜣḫ.t/ı̓ḫ.t* frequently masc.): "(the items....) which he gave" (cf. line 4);

ꜥnḫ n nw.t (< *ꜥnḫ.t n.t nw.t*): "Citizeness". The title is used for married women above
the social level of service personnel;

Tꜣ-[gmy.t]: name (to be restored *pace* line 6) of the grandmother of the plaintiff:
proper name of the appellative type, "The 'Finder'" as a designation of the "Black
Ibis";

s.t-qrs: probably the use of *s.t* for forming abstract nouns, "funeral", rather than for
forming localities, "burial-place" — but both certainly make sense;

line 3 *Pꜣ-[tꜣw-m.]dı̓-'Imnw*: proper name of the sentence type: "The Breath of Life belongs
to Amun";

[Hieroglyphic text, lines 1–15, pBoulaq 10 rt.]

3.5.4 Exercise: pBoulaq 10 rt. 1 - 15

          ir.w n dbn 40 "amounted to 40 deben" (passive *sdm.w*);

line 4 *wḥm zp*: "to repeat the matter" (infinitive + object), going over it again: "(1 Funeral, after he had given her coffin to *P3-[t3w-m.]di-'Imnw* — it amounted to 40 deben all together.) To repeat the matter: what he gave to her was 1 coffin to bury her";

line 5 *Ḥwy-nfr*: name of the grandfather of the speaker (the plaintiff);

          ḥr: here, and in the following, a kind of opposition to the preceding propositions is expressed (with the following statement "contingent" because it depends upon the previous one). *ḥr ptr* serves to state that something contrasting is well known in the speech situation: "it is, however, the case that" (*ptr = mk*);

          pnꜥ X: "to dispute, contest X";

line 7   written *st* in *ḥr iw mbw.pw=s qrs* is possibly (1) the suffix of the 3rd pl.: "they, the children of Tegamya, did not", (2) the 3rd sing. fem. suffix "she, Tegamya, did not". Against (1) is the fact that the 3rd pl. suffix is otherwise written *=w*, as is usual in this type of text register;

      ḥr mbw.pw n3y=s ḥrd.w qrs=(s): note that this second *bw.pw=f sdm* is not introduced by *iw*, and is therefore sentence initial — forming an independent sentence;

line 8   *qrs=(s)*: "bury her, Tegamya";

      gr mnt.s (< in group writing, *m-nty-st*): the particle *gr* placed after the phrase + the independent pronoun 2nd sing. fem. (earlier *nt.s*) is used to emphasize the preceding pronominal reference: "she too", negated, "she didn't either" (cf. Černý/Groll, *Late Egyptian Grammar*, § 2.1.6; Erman, *Neuägyptische Grammatik*, § 682);

      p3 nty st ḥr wḥ3=f: First Present nominalized relative clause with its own subject and resumptive pronoun. *3ḥ.t=s p3 nty st ḥr wḥ3=f* is a Late Egyptian nominal sentence, type Pseudo-Cleft Sentence: noun phrase + nominalized relative clause: "her property is what they claim";

line 10   *m-dr qrs=f*: Temporal: "when he buried";

line 10-11   *i.di.tw 3ḥ.t n qrs*: passive nominal *sdm=f* of *di*, with prospective, anticipatory function: "the goods should be given to the one who buries" (cf. Frandsen, *Outline*, § 87 Ex. 11);

line 11   *ḥr*: probably the postposed speech marker here, "so-and-so says"; the preposition *ḥr* "by", "through" should not however be excluded;

      p3y=i nb nfr: apposition to previously mentioned "Pharaoh";

line 12   *imm iry=w p3 nfr*: probably impersonal, "They may do the appropriate" (cf. § 3.4.3[1]);

line 13   *ḥr ptr di.tw t3 s.t*: the verb *di* was added in above the line later;

      T3y-nḥsy and *Z3-w3dy.t* are proper names of the appellative type: "The Nubian Woman" and "Son of Uto". The precedent mentioned is in oPetrie 16, rt. 6-vso.6 (*HO* pl.21,1);

      m-dr: here preposition before noun, "because of something", cf. Erman, *Neuägyptische Grammatik*, § 664;

line 14   for the writing of *n=s* cf. § 2.1.2(1);

line 15   "King Amenhotep": the blessed King Amenhotep I, who was, together with his mother Ahmes-Nefertari, worshipped by the residents of the Theban West Bank as a kind of "saint", an intermediary with God;

      m A r.di.t st n=f: a type of the Late Egyptian Cleft Sentence: *m* + noun phrase + participle (*r.di.t* for *i.di.t*): "A is the one who gave it to him". For the use of the dative *n=f* following the object, cf. Erman, *Neuägyptische Grammatik*, § 693.

3.6 The preterite converter *wn*

3.6.1 Converting tense in the sentence conjugations

The circumstantial converter *iw* converts independent sentences — both sentence conjugations and nominal sentences (cf. infra Chapter 4) — syntactically to adverb clauses. A ⤚ *wn* preceding a sentence transforms it semantically. It is transformed to refer to a time anterior to that of the surrounding utterances, its cotext, and occasionally

the preterite
habitual

to point out the customariness of activities ("such-and-such is generally done", "we used to do such-and-such").

effects   This means that, with the tense converter

— the preterite *sdm=f* becomes an independent past perfect statement (often of custom, habitual): "(he did this, after) someone had done such-and-such".

— the Third Future indicates future perfect tense: "someone will have done such-and-such (by evening)".

— the First Present as the form of a proposition which is presented as evident, as an act proceeding in the very moment of speaking ("is doing") or as a description of a state is transferred into the past: "someone was doing such-and-such".

— an "emphatic sentence" (sentence with nominal *sdm=f*) can likewise be transferred to past time.

(pBM 10403, 3, 28)

b.py=i ptr hn wn ptr=i wn iw=i dd.t=f n=k "I did not look. Had I looked, I would have told you";

Notes:

> *hn*   particle which is apt to mark a following sentence as a conditional sentence (cf. supra § 2.2.4[1]);
>
> *wn ptr=i*   tense converted preterite *sdm=f*, "I had seen", adjusted to suit the conditional construction;
>
> *wn iw=i dd.t=f*   tense converted Third Future, "I will have said it", adjusted to suit the conditional sentence construction.

wn=f with
First Present
       The Egyptological term converter refers to a morpheme which bears a specific syntacto-semantic meaning, but does not alter the syntactic structure — with the exception of the First Present. Converting First Present, *wn* assumes the guise of that verbal form in which it was used in earlier periods: the *sdm=f* (for an example of the subjunctive form of *wn*, cf. infra § 5.3.2[2]).

(Wenamun 2,78-79)

iw=i dd n=f i.dd n t3y=i hnw.t
wn=i sdm š3ᶜ Nw.t r p3 nty ᵓImnw im r-dd
i.ir.tw grg n dmi nb i.ir.tw m3ᶜ.t n p3 t3 n ᵓa-r-s

"And I said to him: 'Tell my Lady:
"I have heard as far away as No, where Amun is: Even if evil is done in every city, justice is done in the Land of Cyprus''''";

Notes:

   p3 nty 'Imnw ìm   nominalized relative clause of First Present (*'Imnw ìm*): "the (place) where Amun is";

   ì.ìr.tw ... ì.ìr.tw   two nominal *sdm=f* forms in mutual relationship, the Late Egyptian variant of the balanced sentence;

   n p3 t3   *n* for *m* before a noun.

The change in the status of the converter to the *sdm=f* form of *wn* is also reflected in the syntax of the negations. While the negated Third Future is converted in the usual fashion (*wn bn ìw=f r sdm*), the negating morpheme appears with the First Present before the whole expression: negation

bn wn=f ìrm=ì ìwn3 "He was not with me";   *(pMayer A rt. 3,25)*

In terms of both matter and syntax, the Late Egyptian sentence-conjugation tense conversion based on *wn* (Demotic *wn-n3w*) is the precursor of the Coptic imperfect converter using ⲚⲈ-, ⲚⲈⲢⲈ- (with First Present, ⲚⲈⳊⲤⲰⲦⲘ̄). Coptic does not permit the conversion of the Third Future. linguistic evolution

3.6.2 *wn* in relative constructions

Just as the First Present tense conversion still employs the *sdm=f* form of *wn*, using participles and relative forms of *wn*, the First Present can be transformed into a relative clause with relative past meaning (constructions both with and without the *ì*-prefix).

wn=k m n3 šm ì.wn=k ìm=w "You were   *(pBM 10052, 1,6)* thus pursuing those things with which you were occupied";

Notes:

   wn=k m n3 šm   tense converted First Present;

   ì.wn=k ìm=w   relative form of *wn* with resumptive pronoun.

  (pTurin 1977 rt.5-6)

ìmm dì.tw p3 htr wn hr pr n=s n t3y=ì sn.t wn dy m h3r.t hr mn n rnp.t r t3y

"Let the income which used to go to her be given to my sister who has been a widow here for years, up to now."

Notes:

   wn hr pr n=s   participle of *wn* followed by preposition *hr* + infinitive;

   wn dy m h3r.t   participle of *wn* followed by an adverb and a prepositional phrase.

The distinction between the other preterite participles and relative forms and the *wn* relative phrases with the First Present is that the latter expresses a customary activity in the past.

As the ancient Egyptian participles and relative phrases are not preserved in Coptic, *wn*-relative phrases disappeared as well. Coptic Relative constructions are formed with the NϵE- (ϵ-NϵE-) converter, i.e., they are tense-converted sentence conjugations converted to relative phrases.

3.6.3 Bibliography

Frandsen, *Outline*, §§ 96-97

Polotsky, *Coptic Conjugation System*, §§ 10 (with Obs.1+2); 16-18; 28; 35

4. The Nominal Sentence

4.1. Structure and morphology

4.1.1 Defining the nature and role of the Nominal Sentence

Late Egyptian sentence-forming and independent conjugations exist alongside another type of sentence, the Nominal Sentence. By nature, the Nominal Sentence is a sentence formed by two noun phrases (in the following: first term and second term) which are directly linked without the help of a verb.

In Late Egyptian the simplest form of Nominal Sentence — noun + noun — is used far more frequently than in Middle Egyptian, where this type of sentence was virtually never encountered except in religious texts. While being more common, in Late Egyptian it is likewise more frequent in texts of the higher levels of the register hierarchy.

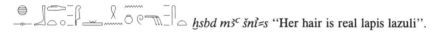 ḥsbd m3ᶜ šnỉ⸗s "Her hair is real lapis lazuli". *(Beatty Love Songs vs C 1,4)*

This quotation illustrates the basic principles of the Nominal Sentence, where at least one of the two terms must be a specified or modified noun. If a pronoun fills one of the positions, it must be an independent pronoun (cf. infra § 4.1.2). The kind of modification determines the classification of the Nominal Sentences: classification of Nominal Sentences

— Adjectival Sentence: the first term is a participle, adjective or adjectival construction; Adj. Sentence

— p3y-Sentence: the second term is a demonstrative from the p3y, t3y, n3y series; p3y-Sentence

— Cleft Sentence: the second term is an undefined relative phrase. Where the relative phrase is defined by a definite article or a demonstrative, the sentence can be distinguished from the narrowly defined Cleft Sentence and termed a Pseudo-Cleft Sentence; Cleft Sentence

— Nominal Sentence proper: subsumed under this title are all the remaining forms of sentence consisting of two noun phrases. At least one of the two parts is specified, either (a) with a definite article, or (b) as an independent pronoun, (c) a proper name, or (d) an identifying (e.g relative) phrase. Nominal Sentence proper

sentence meaning

This classification of Nominal Sentences remains, however, a superficial one, being less analytical than descriptive. Altogether, the sentence is morphologically defined as being constructed with two noun phrases; the meaning of the sentence ultimately depends on the degree and type of definition of the two noun phrases. If only one element is defined or specified, a classification or characterization takes place: "this object is 'tree'/belongs to the category of 'tree'". If both elements are definite or specified, the sentence expresses identification: "This is my tree".

use of article

Understanding the meaning of the sentence depends on whether the nouns forming the sentence are associated with articles or not. In analysing a

Identification, Classification, Characterization are concepts for the description of the semantic relations between the two noun phrases (terms) joined in a nominal sentence. "Identification" generally signifies that the first and second terms are identical ("A is B"). This usually implies that both are individual objects — specified, named or characterized (e.g. by relative clauses). Pronouns, demonstratives and relative phrases carry out this specification. "Classification" means that what is signified by one term can be placed into the semantic class signified or exemplified by the other term ("B is an A"). A particular object is classified: "this object is a tree"; "the tree is a plant". Since a class is defined by its characteristics ("the tree is a botanic object/an object with the quality of being a plant"), an assignment of this type characterizes the assigned object. Cf. Junge, "Nominalsatz und Cleft Sentence im Ägyptischen," in: *Polotsky-Studies*, pp. 443ff; idem, *Syntax*, §§ 5.1.3; 5.1.4; 5.2.2.

Nominal Sentence, it is thus important to note the register of the text in question: the article system commonly used in Late Egyptian (and discussed in the previous chapters) is used widely only in the lowest text registers.

subordination

Like the sentence conjugations, all forms of the independent Nominal Sentence can be converted into syntactically adverbial subordinate clauses with *ỉw*.

4.1.2 The pronouns of the Nominal Sentence

(1) The forms of the independent pronouns

While the dependent pronouns (§ 2.2.1) can fulfil a pronominal function as the second noun phrase of the Nominal Sentence, the position of the first noun phrase is filled by a special form of personal pronoun, traditionally termed the independent pronoun. Among all other Egyptian pronouns, it is the only strong form, i.e. one which can stand alone without being "attached" to any other morpheme. Graphically these pronouns differ only marginally from those of Middle Egyptian, the primary change being the addition of the grapheme *m* to the 2nd and 3rd persons.

1.s.c.	*ink*	𓀁 ; 𓀁	ⲀⲚⲞⲔ ; ⲀⲚⲄ
2.s.m.	*mnt.k*	𓂝 ; 𓂝	ⲚⲦⲞⲔ ; ⲚⲦⲔ̄
f.	*mnt.t*	𓂝 ; 𓂝	ⲚⲦⲞ ; ⲚⲦⲉ
3.s.m.	*mnt.f*	𓂝	ⲚⲦⲟ̄ⳋ
f.	*mnt.s*	𓂝 ; 𓂝	ⲚⲦⲞⲤ
1.pl.c.	*inn*	𓂝	ⲀⲚⲞⲚ ; ⲀⲚⲚ̄
2.pl.c.	*mnt.tn*	𓂝	ⲚⲦⲱⲦⲚ̄ ; ⲚⲦⲉⲦⲚ̄
3.pl.c.	*mnt.w*	𓂝	ⲚⲦⲞⲞⲨ

Observation:

Compare this table with that of Černý/Groll, *Late Egyptian Grammar*, § 2.1. It should be observed that the Coptic unaccented variants in the table above do not correspond to the variants of the hieroglyphic writings!

(2) Specific usage

Their prosodical independence allows these pronouns to be isolated, assuming positions *isolation* both before and after the main sentence — pronominal extraposition:

𓂝 ... *mnt.k iḥ pꜣ in=k n=i gr ink* "And you: *(Wenamun 2,8)* what then did you bring me?!'';

Notes:

mnt.k independent pronoun preceding a Nominal Sentence;

iḥ pꜣ in=k Pseudo-Cleft Sentence with interrogative pronoun as the first term, and a defined relative sentence as the second: "what is it that you have brought?";

gr ink postposed particle *gr* followed by 1st pers. sing. independent pronoun emphasizes the preceding pronominal reference, "me too"; cf. supra § 3.5.4, note to line 8.

They can indicate or emphasize possession (for example, *wꜥ pr ink* "a house of mine"), *indicating* either (1) through appositional modification of unspecified nouns or those which cannot *possession* otherwise be specified or (2) as first term of a Nominal Sentence proper. A special series of possessive pronouns performs this function for the 2nd and 3rd persons sing. — 𓃀 *twt* and 𓂧 , 𓂧 *swt* respectively[1] — as late as Dynasty XXI, when they were replaced by *mnt.k* and *mnt.f*: *pꜣy šri twt* "this son of yours"; *pꜣ swt nb* "all of his".

---

1 Despite their appearance, these are still the Old Egyptian independent pronouns *twt* and *swt* in Late Egyptian guise.

4.1.3 Types of Nominal Sentences

The following sections are mainly concerned with classifying Nominal Sentences by specific elements (such as the *pꜣy*-Sentence) or construction methods (such as Cleft Sentence); the synopsis in the following table is meant to show how determination and specificity of the first and second noun phrases affect the proposition — the statement made by the respective Nominal Sentence.

First Term	Second Term		
Specified Noun/ Independent Pronoun	Specified Noun/ relative phrase		
nỉm	*pꜣ zỉ*	"Who is the man?"	Nom. Sentence proper
	pꜣ nty ỉm	"Who is that one?"	(Pseudo-Cleft Sentence)
	nỉm	"Who is he?"	Nominal Sentence proper
mnt.f	*pꜣy=k ỉtỉ*	"He is your father"	
	mnt.k	"He is you"	
	pꜣ nty ỉm	"He is that one"	(Pseudo-Cleft Sentence)
pꜣy=k ỉtỉ	*pꜣ nty ỉm*	"Your father is that one"	
	pꜣy	"It is your father"	*pꜣy*-Sentence
Unspecified Noun, Adjective/Participle			
zỉ	*pꜣy*	"It is a man"	*pꜣy*-Sentence
	pꜣ nty ỉm	"That one is 'male'"	(Pseudo-Cleft Sentence)
nfr	*pꜣy=k ỉtỉ*	"Your father is perfect"	Adjectival Sentence
	sw	"He is perfect"	
Independent Pronoun/Specified Noun			
mnt.f	*sw*	"He is his"	adjectival Nom. Sentence proper
	pꜣy=k ỉtỉ	"Your father is his"	
	Unspecified Noun, Adj./Part.		
mnt.k	*zỉ*	"You are 'male'"	Nominal Sentence proper
	nfr	"You are perfect"	
ỉn/m pꜣy=k ỉtỉ	*ỉr sw*	"It is your father who did it"	Cleft Sentence
mnt.f		"It is he who did it"	

Observation:

Specified nouns are those designating specific objects (in a variety of ways, meaning that this includes not only defined nouns, but also designations, characterizations, proper names, pronouns, etc.). The continuing scholarly debate about the meaning and nature of Nominal Sentences centres around the question of whether it is possible to harmonize the use of forms and meaning (cf., e.g., Neveu, *La langue des Ramsès*, §§ 39-42). This pragmatic survey suffices for an understanding of the texts, but the nuances of meaning conveyed in any specific text would need to be reflected by adjusting the translation to fit the way information is presented in the Egyptian sentence (this is partially attempted in the following treatment of the types of sentences).

4.2 The simple Nominal Sentence

4.2.1 The Nominal Sentence proper

The sentence with two nouns, which is in a way the basic form of the Nominal Sentence — *ḥsbd m3ᶜ šnῑ=s* "her hair is real lapis lazuli" (cf. supra § 4.1.1) — is uncommon and basically restricted to texts higher up in the register hierarchy. The type appears mostly with specific substitutes of the noun phrases, which can be summarized as follows:

— The first term is an interrogative pronoun and the second a defined noun or a designation (such as, e.g., *rn* "name" or proper name);   *interrogative pronoun + noun*

ỉḫ p3 sḫr n šm ỉ.ỉr=k "What was the thing you were up to?";   *(pBM 10052, 4,6)*

Notes:

> *ỉḫ*   first term (interrogative pronoun "what?");
>
> *p3 sḫr*   second term (defined noun with nominal modification *n šm*);
>
> *šm ỉ.ỉr=k*   construction of infinitive and agent, the infinitive undefined and general ("going about that you have done") > "Your movements", cf. supra § 2.3.3(2).

— The first term is an independent pronoun and the second is (1) a noun without article or a nominalized adjective (classification in both cases: for the use of an adjective, cf. the Adjectival Sentence in the following section), or (2) an interrogative pronoun or a defined noun (identification);   *personal pronoun + noun*

mnt.k šrỉ nỉm "Whose son are you?" ("Of whom are you the son?");   *(Blinding of Truth 5,3)*

y3 mnt.k nfr ḥr mnt.k p3y=ỉ itỉ "Truely, you are perfect, and you are a father to me";   *(LRL 48,15-16)*

Notes:

> *mnt.k nfr*   Nominal Sentence with adjectival second term (*"You are a good [one]");
>
> *mnt.k pꜣy=ỉ ỉtỉ*   Nominal Sentence with defined noun in second position ("You are my father");
>
> *pꜣy=ỉ ỉtỉ*   literally "my father"; here, however, not a physical father but a symbolical one ("You are like a father to me").

ỉnk mnt.f

Where two things are identified using pronouns, the second term is an independent pronoun too, e.g. *ỉnk mnt.f* "I am he" (cf. pAnast. IV 5,1); if the second term is an enclitic (dependent) pronoun, the sentence is adjectival: *ỉnk sw* "It is mine".

noun + noun

— Both first and second terms are explicitly determined (identification): in Late Egyptian, too, this is the basic structure of the balanced sentence, of the type "If he wants, he does", "that he wants is that he acts" (cf. Wenamun 2,78-79, supra § 3.6.1). Where this construction involves not only nouns and nominal *sdm=f* forms, but also relative phrases, it turns into a Pseudo-Cleft Sentence (infra § 4.3.3):

(pBM 10052, 5,8-9)

bpy=ỉ ptr nty nb gr pꜣ ptr=ỉ pꜣ dd=ỉ "I did not see anything more. What I have told you is what I saw." (Hieroglyphic text, infra, Exercise § 4.5);

Notes:

> *nty nb*   "anything" literally *"everything which";
>
> *gr*   postposed adverbial particle, cf. supra § 3.5.4 note to line 8 and § 2.2.4(1);
>
> *pꜣ ptr=ỉ pꜣ dd=ỉ*   two directly related nominalized relative forms ("that which I saw", "that which I said") form a sentence.

one-membral
Nominal
Sentence

Where the speech situation or the context permits, one of the sentence forming phrases may be omitted due to hurried speech or recording. S. Groll classifies such cases as single-part Nominal Sentences ("one-membral nominal pattern"), but it would be more appropriate to refer to a "correspondence ellipse",[2] where the cotext allows the missing element to be supplied with ease. Characteristically, these constructions are of the type *ỉr* + term$_1$, term$_2$:

(LRL 36, 12)

ḫr ỉr Pr-ꜥꜣ ḥr.y nỉm m-rꜣ-ꜥ "And as for Pharaoh — whose master still?"

Notes:

> *ḫr ỉr*   particle of anticipation preceding noun phrase, clause or sentence; an independent sentence should follow (*ỉr* + noun, sentence);
>
> *ḥr.y nỉm*   *"superior of whom"; ellipse for, say, *ḥr.y nỉm pꜣy* *"the chief of whom is he?";
>
> *m-rꜣ-ꜥ*   particle, cf. supra § 2.2.4(1).

The introductory lines of stories are comparable:

---

2   Following Hintze, *Neuägyptische Erzählungen*, 149ff.

[hieroglyphic text]

(pD'Orb 1,1)

ìr mnt.f ḫr=tw sn.w 2 n wꜥ mw.t n wꜥ ìtì ꜣInpw rn pꜣ ꜥꜣ ìw Bꜣtꜣ rn pꜣ šrì "Once, it is said, there were two brothers of a mother and a father; Anubis was the name of the elder and Bata the name of the younger";

Notes:

ìr mnt.f … sn.w 2	literally "As far as it is concerned, [there were] two brothers …";
ḫr=tw	parenthetic speech marker;
ꜣInpw rn pꜣ ꜥꜣ	Sentence with designation (proper name) in first position and *rn=f* (*rn* + noun phrase) in the second;
ìw Bꜣtꜣ	the same type of Nominal Sentence, subordinated with *ìw*.

The Nominal Sentence proper is negated — like the First Present/Adverbial Sentence — with the discontinuous negation *bn … ìwnꜣ*:   *negation*

[hieroglyphic text]

(oBerlin
P.10627, 6-8)

bn mnt.k rmṯ ìwnꜣ ì.yꜣ bw ìr=k dì.t ìwr tꜣy=k ḥm.t mì-qd pꜣy=k ìr.y "You are not a man; hey, you can't even get your wife pregnant like your fellow";

Notes:

bn mnt.k rmṯ ìwnꜣ	negated Nominal Sentence "You are not man";
bw ìr=k dì.t	negative Aorist (cf. supra § 2.3.2[3]) followed by subjunctive *sdm=f*;
pꜣy=k ìr.y	literally *"Your companion".

4.2.2 The Adjectival Sentence

(1) The characterizing Nominal Sentence

Those variations of the Nominal Sentence where (a) the first term is a participle, adjective   *nfr sw* or adjectival construction (*ns-sw A* "he belongs to A"), and (b) the second is generally a determined noun (if pronominal, a dependent pronoun), a noun without article, or a determined relative phrase, are termed Adjectival Sentences. The second term is classified or characterized by the first term (predicative adjective).

 *nfr pꜣ sm.w n s.t ḥmn.t* "The fod-

(pD'Orb 1,10)

der plants of such-and-such a place are excellent";

Notes:

nfr pꜣ sm.w	Adjectival Sentence;
n s.t ḥmn.t	for *m s.t ḥmn.t*.

ns-
"belonging to"

The Middle Egyptian adjectival construction *n.y-sw* A *"it belongs to A" is preserved in a form where *n.y-sw/sỉ/st* is condensed to *ns-* "he/she/it belongs to". The sentence can be composed without overt pronoun — *Ns-H̱nsw* "He/she/it belongs to Khons" — but also with one — *Ns-sw-B3-nb-ḏd.t* "He belongs to the Ram of Mendes" ("Smendes"). Such forms are common in proper names.

particle -.*wsy*

The Middle Egyptian exclamatory particle -.*wy* continues to appear in Adjectival Sentences in literary texts, and closely related genres, such as the miscellanies, but it appears in the form of the enclitic particle -*wsy*. This is a combination of -.*wy* and the following dependent pronoun in an Adjectival Sentence, -.*wy-sw/sỉ* (as in *nfr.wy-sw* "How perfect he is!").

(pAnast.I 28, 2-3)

ḥḏỉ.wsy pr nb ḥr ns=k wỉ3wỉ3.wsy ṯz.w=k "How slanderous is everything which passes your tongue! How ineffectual are your utterances!"

Notes:

ḥḏỉ.wsy pr nb   participle with exclamatory particle and nominalized participle as the second term; in principle it could be analysed as *ḥḏỉ.wy-sw* with an appositional *pr nb* "How slanderous is it, everything which comes out!";

wỉ3wỉ3.wsy ṯz.w=k   the same grammatical form with a noun as the second term.

bn "without"

The Middle Egyptian type of adjectival negation, *nn* + noun (generally an infinitive), was actually used only adverbially, as in *nn 3bw* "without stopping" or the like. In Late Egyptian this appears as *bn* + noun, but is generally explicitly subordinated with *ỉw*, as in *ỉw bn mš⁶* "without army".

nfr + relative phrase

Throughout the history of the language, the Adjectival Sentence persists in a form with nominalized relative phrase as the second term (as a type of Pseudo-Cleft Sentence, cf. infra). In Coptic, this form is reduced to relative clauses with *nty*, but in Late Egyptian (and Demotic) the nominalized relative phrase is still represented by relative forms also. The first term can be an adjective, but also — as in Coptic — an unspecified noun; in Late Egyptian this is characterized by the lack of an article.

(pBM 10052, 14,7)

ꜥḏ3 p3y ḏd=f nb "Everything which he has said is wrong."

Notes:

ꜥḏ3   first term, the noun "untruth", "wrong" without an article;

p3y ḏd=f   demonstrative *p3y* + relative form;

translation more literally "Untruth is everything which he has said". In contrast to Coptic, where the noun is to be translated as an adjective, the Late Egyptian qualitative noun can usually be translated as such.

mnt.f sw

Possession can be expressed with the aid of the independent personal pronoun or the possessive pronoun (§ 4.1.2[2]) in first position — *mnt.f tw, swt tw* "You belong to him"

(< "You are his"). Formally this clause bears an apparent resemblance to the Nominal Sentence type *mnt.k p3y=ỉ ỉtỉ* "You are my father", but it does not identify so much as characterize. As a result of the sentence construction itself, the personal pronoun becomes a possessive pronoun, by being as it were awarded to an object as a property:

(Wenamun 2, 23-24)

mn ỉmw nb ḥr-tp ỉrw ỉw bn ns-st ʾImnw

mnt.f p3 ym ḥr mnt.f p3 l-b-l-n nty tw=k ḏd ỉnk sw

"There are not any boats on the river which do not belong to Amun: the sea belongs to him, as does Lebanon of which you say, 'It belongs to me'";

Notes:

mn + noun	negated "quality of existence": "there is none", "it does not exist";
ỉw bn ns-st ʾImnw	subordinated negated Adjectival Sentence with *ns-*;
mnt.f p3 ym	classifying/characterizing Nominal Sentence with possessive independent pronoun = Adjectival Sentence;
ỉnk sw	the same, a variation of *nfr sw* with a possessive pronoun.

The Adjectival Sentence is negated with *bn*, occasionally with *bn … ỉwn3*, particularly in the case of one-member Nominal Sentences, or correspondence ellipses: *negation and subordination*

bn nfr ỉwn3 p3y gb3 m-b3ḥ t3 psḏ.t "This lapse is not good at all, in front of the Ennead." *(HorSeth 4,9-10)*

Nominal Sentences with adjectival second terms show similar traits:

ḥr ỉnk p3y=tn nfr bn

(LRL 2,1)

ỉnk p3y=tn bỉn ỉwn3 "Your appreciation is mine; your disapproval assuredly not!";

Note:

p3y=tn nfr literally "your good", as *p3y=tn bỉn* "your evil".

Both the affirmative and the negative Adjectival Sentence can be adverbially subordinated with *ỉw*. The passage from Wenamun (2, 23-24) quoted above illustrates both negation and subordination: *mn ỉmw nb ḥr-tp ỉrw ỉw bn ns-st ʾImnw* "There is no boat on the river which does not belong to Amun".

With the exception of bound expressions, the Adjectival Sentence is generally in linguistic retreat during the New Kingdom. The simplest form (*nfr sw*/noun) continues *linguistic evolution* to appear in selfconsciously traditional texts, but it is generally being replaced by other forms of the Nominal Sentence: *mnt.f nfr* and the Cleft Sentence, each having a qualitative noun in the first or second position. This still appears in Early Demotic, but usually in Demotic it is replaced with *sḏm=f* forms and nominal verbs (adjective verbs with the *n3*-prefix — cf. Spiegelberg, *Demotische Grammatik*, §§ 445; 117).

(2) Existence as quality: the Existential Sentence

To emphasize existence, Late Egyptian uses a form of 𓃿 *wn*, followed by an undefined
noun and an adverbial (that cannot, however, be an Old Perfective or *ḥr* + infinitive):

(pD'Orb 3, 5-6) 𓃿 ... *wn pḥ.ty ꜥꜣ ỉm=k* "There is great strength in you";

Notes:

      wn ... ỉm=k   "There is/there is in you";

         pḥ.ty   unspecified noun without an article.

In terms of linguistic evolution this is a *sdm=f* of *wn* (or still more precisely of Middle
Egyptian *ỉw wn* + noun phrase). In the Late Egyptian system *wn* + adverbial phrase can
best be grasped as an adjective in the position of the first term, related to an undefined
second term; a pronoun — or a suffix pronoun — would be excluded because of the
degree of specification implied. This type of sentence tends to become complementary
to the First Present/Adverbial Sentence, as occurs in Coptic. The First Present construction requires a specified subject: *pꜣ zḫꜣ.w m nw.t* "The scribe is in the city". Where the
subject is unspecified or undefined, the speaker falls back on the existential sentence: *wn
zḫꜣ.w m nw.t* "There is a scribe in the city".

In contrast to the negated First Present, the negative counterpart to *wn* is used instead
of the *nn/bn* + noun constructions: 𓂋 ... *mn*, the adjective describing non-existence.
The word emerged out of *nn* + prospective *wn=f*. The latter form itself will still be found
in texts like pLansing 10,8 *nn wn wꜥ* "There is not one".

(Wenamun 2, 23-24) *mn ỉmw nb ḥr-tp ỉrw ỉw bn ns-st ꜣImnw* "There are not any boats on the river which do
not belong to Amun" (hieroglyphic text, supra § 4.2.2[1]).

(LRL 28,11) 𓂋 ... *mn btꜣ r=s* "She suffers no harm" (< *"There is no harm
against her").

The existential adjective form *wn* + the preposition *m.dỉ* (and its negative counterpart
mn m.dỉ) forms the precursor of the Coptic ⲞⲨⲚ̄ⲦⲈ-/ⲞⲨⲚ̄ⲦⲀ꞊ or ⲘⲚ̄ⲦⲈ-
/ⲘⲚ̄ⲦⲀ꞊ respectively. The preposition can already follow *wn/mn* directly, but it need
not.

(LRL 19,15) 𓃿 ... *wn ḥmtỉ ỉm m.dỉ=k* "You have copper there" (< "There is
copper there with you").

mn m.dỉ=w btꜣ "They have not suffered" (*"There
are no damages with them"; cf. the passage from *LRL* 28, 11, supra).

(LRL 3,6)

4.2.3 The *pꜣy*-Sentence

In Middle Egyptian, Late Middle Egyptian and even Medio-Late Egyptian, the second
term of a Nominal Sentence can be the demonstrative *pw*; in Late Egyptian proper, this
role is accomplished by one of the demonstrative pronoun series *pꜣy, tꜣy, nꜣy* (Coptic ⲡⲉ,
ⲧⲉ, ⲛⲉ). In contrast to Middle Egyptian, but as in Old Egyptian, the pronominal second
term agrees in gender and number with the first term. In all stages of the language, this
form of sentence is more dependent on the context than any other sentential form, because
the pronominal second term always requires either an earlier reference or a reference
specifically designated in the speech situation.

In contrast to the Middle Egyptian *pw*-Sentence, the Late Egyptian bimembral
pꜣy-Sentence cannot be enlarged to a trimembral one; there can be no further appositional
specification of *pꜣy*: *dmỉ pw* "This is a home", for example, cannot be transformed into
an independent sentence of the type *dmỉ pw ỉmnt.t* "This, the West, is a home" > "The
West is a home". The *pꜣy*-Sentence is thus always completely dependent upon context or
cotext already mentioned.

Observation:

Where the appositional third term of a Middle Egyptian trimembral *pw*-Sentence is a relative
phrase, in terms of specification, sentential structure and phrase construction the Late Egyptian
Pseudo-Cleft Sentence can be regarded as its successor form. Following the logic of the analytic
tendency, the appositional relationship between *pw* and the following noun phrase is paradigmatized as the basic relationship of the article to the following noun phrase (nucleus — satellite,
cf. supra § 2.1.1): (Noun phrase 1) + *pw*, (Noun phrase 2) is re-interpreted as (Noun phrase 1)
+ *pꜣ* (Noun phrase 2).

The functional properties follow from the structure of the sentence. On the one hand,
the demonstrative second term becomes a highly specified subject which is completely
identified — either from an earlier reference, or in the course of the discourse. On the
other hand, because it cannot be enlarged with a third element, its dependence on the
context is absolute. It thus possesses no meaning beyond reference, and its meaning is
restricted to its reference to something already mentioned, without any lexical meaning
of its own. This type of sentence is thus frequent in answers to real or rhetorical questions,
making it particularly suitable as a form of clarification, explanation or exposition.

Just how the explanation or exposition is accomplished depends upon the specificity
of the first term (noun, infinitive, relative phrase, independent pronoun). Without any
article the intent is explanatory classification. With a definite article it is explanatory

[margin notes]
bimembral sentence

sentence meaning

first term

identification. The indefinite article cannot be used. Because it is explanatory, the explanatory identification should rather be understood as classification by example.

— Explanatory classification:

(Doomed Prince 4,8-9)

ỉḫ pȝ nty ḥr šm.t m-sȝ pȝ zỉ ꜥȝ nty m ỉy.t ḥr tȝ mỉ.t

jw=f [ḥr] ḏd n=f ṯsm pȝy

[The young prince has become older and gone up to the roof of his house, whence he has seen a greyhound pursuing an adult man, and said to the servant beside him,] "'What is that going after the adult who is coming on the way?' And he said to him: 'That is a greyhound.'" (For the cotext, cf. supra § 2.1.3[1]).

Note:

> *ṯsm pȝy*   *pȝy*-Sentence with first term unspecified, without article; one could translate, "That is of the class 'greyhound'".

— Explanatory identification:

(Blinding of Truth 5,7-8)

tw=k ptr pȝy kȝmn nty ḥms r-gs pȝ sbȝ

pȝy=k ỉtỉ pȝy

"You see that blind beggar sitting beside the door. He is your father."

Notes:

> *tw=k ptr*   First Present expression (as in the translation), or as a tonal question (question for corroboration): "Do you see that blind beggar?";
>
> *nty ḥms*   relative phrase without its own agent (agent = antecedent);
>
> *pȝy=k ỉtỉ pȝy*   *pȝy*-Sentence with a first term specified with the possessive article.

This kind of identification carries the nuance of charaterization in the sense of providing an example. This is also true when the first term is a proper noun or a personal pronoun:

(LRL 67,16-68,2)

(ỉ)n pȝ ꜥm ỉ.ỉr=k pȝy m tȝy 20 n rnp.t ỉ.ỉr=ỉ m pȝy=k pr

ỉnk pȝy

pȝ zbṯ ỉ.ỉr=ỉ ỉrm=k pȝy

(The letter writer is irritated because of a joke and strives to justify himself with an anecdote: You are just like a woman who was blind in one eye and lived for twenty years in a man's house, and when he found another woman, he said to the first woman: "I am leaving you because you are blind in one eye". She responds:) "This is what you have learnt after these twenty years that I have spent in your house?" (And the letter writer continues:) "This is the way it is with me. That is the joke I have made with you!"

Notes:

(i)n   interrogative marker starting sentential questions (questions for corroboration; cf. supra § 2.2.4[1]);

p3 ꜥm i.ir=k p3y   *p3y*-Sentence with a determined infinitive (agent introduced by relative form, cf. supra § 2.3.3[2]) as first term: "This is the discovery which you have made"; but also "This is the kind of discovery that you have made";

ink p3y   *p3y*-Sentence with independent pronoun as first term: not identification but rather a kind of classification/characterization by example: "It is like me", "It is like mine";

p3 zbt p3y   *p3y*-Sentence with a determined infinitive as before; it is likewise less identification than characterization by example: "Of this kind is my joke".

It does not appear to be possible to negate the *p3y*-Sentence as such. It is possible that negated phrases such as *bn* + noun + *iwn3* are a kind of substitute construction: *bn t3y=i ḥm.t iwn3* "(she is) not my wife".

4.2.4 Bibliography

Černý/Groll, *Late Egyptian Grammar*, §§ 57.2-57.3; 59.3-59.5; Groll, *Non-Verbal Sentence Patterns*, 12ff (one-member Nominal Sentence)   — Nominal Sentence proper

Erman, *Neuägyptische Grammatik*, §§ 459-461; Groll, *Non-Verbal Sentence Patterns*, 5ff; Černý/Groll, *Late Egyptian Grammar*, §§ 57.4-57.7; Loprieno, *Ancient Egyptian*, § 5.8   — *p3y*-Sentence

Erman, *Neuägyptische Grammatik*, §§ 237; 456-458; 684; Černý/Groll, *Late Egyptian Grammar*, § 59; 60 (negated); Groll, *Non-Verbal Sentence Patterns*, 34ff   — Adjectival Sentence

Frandsen, *Outline*, § 95; Černý/Groll, *Late Egyptian Grammar*, § 28; Erman, *Neuägyptische Grammatik*, §§ 506; 624; 782-785; Loprieno, *Ancient Egyptian*, § 5.10   — Existential Sentence

Černý/Groll, *Late Egyptian Grammar*, §§ 58; 60; Groll, *Non-Verbal Sentence Patterns*, 94ff; Loprieno, *Ancient Egyptian*, § 5.11   — negation of Nominal Sentences

4.3 The forms of the Cleft Sentence

4.3.1 Participles, relative forms and relative clauses with *nty* as parts of a sentence

By far the most common type of Nominal Sentence in Late Egyptian is the form where the second term is a nominalized relative phrase: nominalized participles, relative forms or relative clauses.

(oDM 126,3)   *iḥ n3 nty tw=tn ḥr ḏd.t=w* "What is it that you are talking about?";

Notes:

> *iḥ*   interrogative pronoun as first term;
>
> *n3 nty tw=tn ḥr*   determined nominalized relative clause in the plural as second term: First Present
> *ḏd.t=w*   following *nty*; reference ("those things" which are spoken about) and subject of the relative clause ("you") differ, thus requiring the resumptive pronoun *=w* (**"those things which: you are talking about them").

relative clauses   Relative phrases are termed relative clauses when they are independent sentences transformed into adjectival modifications of nouns (the reference terms/antecedents of the relative phrase) with the relative morpheme *nty*. If the form of such a sentence is the affirmative First Present — as in oDM 126,3 cited supra — the relationship between the modified noun/antecedent and the internal structure of the relative clause is the same as that of participles and relative forms to their antecedents, as follows:

reference term and agent   Where the agent (actor expression) of the relative phrase and its reference term (antecedent) are the same, they do not need to be represented in the relative phrase: The sentence *st ḥr sdm* "she listens" becomes the relative clause *t3 nty ḥr sdm* "she who listens"; the sentence *sdm=s* "she listened" becomes the participle *t3 (i.)sdm* "she who listened".

> **Cleft Sentence** is a term specifying a sentence construction in which one part with a particular weight in the statement is separated or "cleft" off and placed at the beginning of the sentence, where it is then framed by introductory formulas and relative phrases: *"It was John who saw him"*. In Egyptian, "participial statements" (Gardiner, *Grammar*, §§ 227.3; 373) are equivalent to this type of sentence: the separated element is introduced with *in* (in Late Egyptian also *m*) and followed up with undefined participles and *sdm=f* forms (the participles are immutable and do not agree in gender and number with the cleft-off sentential element). Where this element is unintroduced, but accompanied by defined participles, relative forms or relative clauses which agree with it, then the construction is often termed a "Pseudo-Cleft Sentence"; *"John was the one who saw him"*. The form is the precursor of the Cleft Sentence in Coptic. The notion itself was introduced into Egyptology by Polotsky, *Nominalsatz und Cleft Sentence im Koptischen.*

Where the agent of the relative phrase and the antecedent differ, the relative clause requires its own agent, and resumption of the antecedent is necessary (except for the direct object after relative forms): The sentence *st ḥr sdm=f* "she hears him" becomes the relative clause *p3 nty st ḥr sdm=f* "he whom she hears"; the sentence *sdm=s sw* "she heard him" becomes the relative form *p3 (i.)sdm=s* "he whom she heard" (but *p3 i.ir=s sdm=f* with periphrasis!). Where resumption is necessary, the sentence *st ḥr sdm n=f* "she listens to him" becomes the relative clause *p3 nty st ḥr sdm n=f* "he to whom she listens"; or the sentence *sdm=s n=f* "she listened to him" becomes the relative form *p3 (i.)sdm=s n=f* "he to whom she listened".

Conversion into relative clauses with *nty* can take place with the sentence conjugations (a) First Present/Adverbial Sentence, (b) Third Future, (c) sentence with nominal *sdm=f*, and (d) Adjectival Sentence. Only the preterite *sdm=f* cannot be converted thus: the preterite relative phrases are the participle and the relative form. sentence forms and verbal forms

In every case — including Preterite and First Present when the agent and the reference noun are identical — the negative forms of the sentence conjugations are turned into a relative clause using *nty*, whether as *p3 nty bn sw ḥr sdm* "he who does not hear" or as *p3 nty bwpw=f sdm* "he who did not hear". forms of negation

Now, there is no significant structural difference between the Cleft Sentence in question and the ordinary Nominal Sentence (§ 4.2), as can be concluded from this table: terminology

	First Term	Second Term		
(oDM 126,3)	*iḥ*	*n3 nty tw=tn ḥr dd.t=w*	"What is it that you are talking about"	
(pBM 10052,14,7)	*ꜥd3*	*p3y dd=f nb*	"Everything which he has said is wrong"	Adjectival Sentence
(pBM 10052,4,6)	*iḥ*	*p3 shr n šm i.ir=k*	"What was the thing you were up to?"	Nominal Sentence proper

The type of sentence which takes a relative phrase in second position is nevertheless distinguished from the others as a Cleft Sentence. The reasoning behind this is partly that translations usually take a form that is so termed: "It is this that he does" or "It is he who did it". It is also partly that the Late Egyptian Cleft Sentence can function as the precursor of the sentence that is called Cleft Sentence in Coptic, such as Π-ΝΟΥΤΕ Π-ΕΤ-ⲤΟΟΥⲚ "It is God who knows" (< *p3 ntr p3 nty s:wn*).

The sentences can be classified according to the type of the first term and the explicit determination and the form of the relative phrase of the second term as: subtypes

1. The "earlier form", the Cleft Sentence proper: the first term is introduced with *in* or *m* and the relative phrase is an active participle (without article) or the prospective nominal *sdm=f* (§ 4.3.2); Cleft Sentence

Pseudo-Cleft Sentence

2. The Pseudo-Cleft Sentence: the second term is a relative phrase with a definite article or a demonstrative (§ 4.3.3).

4.3.2 The Cleft Sentence proper

One of the forms of the Cleft Sentence used in Late Egyptian corresponds to the "participial statement" (Gardiner, *Grammar* §§ 227,3; 373): [*in* + noun phrase/*ntf*] + [participle/prospective *sdm=f*]. This was still used in literary and religious texts, but a Late Egyptian version was more common, introduced with *m* rather than *in*, with Late Egyptian participles or prospective emphatic *sdm=f*:

Traditional Form		"Late Egyptianized" Form		
in NP	*sdm*	*m* NP	*i.sdm*	past
ntf	*sdm*	*mnt.f*	*i.ir sdm*	present
	sdm=f		*i.ir=f sdm*	future

Observation:

The first term is frequently the interrogative pronoun *nim*, which is an amalgamation of the particle *in* which introduces Cleft Sentences with the interrogative pronoun *m* "who?", "what?".

sentence meaning

    The first term of the Cleft Sentence generally belongs to an identifiable group of nouns, which can be characterized as follows: (a) proper names and pronouns representing names; (b) inalienable objects (social designations like "name" or "title", kinship terms like "mother", or parts of the body like "arm"); (c) semantic classes with a single member (like "sun"); (d) general class designations, abstractions, and terms for materials. Objects and actions expressed by the relative phrases in second position are identified with the first term by isolating them from other categories.

— Examples of the traditional form:

(HorSeth 6,14-7,1)   *in šs3.w-ḥr=k wpi tw.k ḏs=k* "It is your own cleverness that has judged you";

Notes:

    in šs3.w-ḥr=k wpi   participial statement/Cleft Sentence;

                 tw.k   2nd sing. masc. of a developing new object pronoun: the final -.*t* of the 3ae inf. verbs followed by a pronoun becomes independent and is transferred also to other verbs. The form is not status pronominalis with an object suffix because the participle requires a dependent pronoun as object (cf. next example, and supra §§ 2.2.1; 2.2.3[1]).

— Late Egyptianized form with personal pronoun as the first term:

(HorSeth 7,11-12)   *ḥr mk ptr mnt.k i.wpi tw ḏs=k* "So it is indeed you yourself who have judged yourself!"

Notes:

    mnt.k î.wpî tw   Cleft Sentence with independent pronoun and participle with prefix;

        translation   more literally: *"You yourself are indeed the one who has judged yourself".

Or with *m* + noun in first position:

m pȝy=n nb r.rdî.t   *(LRL 45, 10-11)*

îw=n r pȝ nty tw=tn îm "It was our Lord who sent us to where you are";

Notes:

    m NP *r.rdî.t îw=n*   Cleft Sentence "It was A who caused that we come ...";

        r.rdî.t   graphic variant of the participle *î.dî* "who caused";

    r pȝ nty tw=tn îm   First Present nominalized relative clause as indication of location following preposition *r* (*"to that [place] which: you are at it").

The earlier type of Cleft Sentence — in either its traditional or its Late Egyptian guise — is negated with *bn*. And, like all forms of the simple sentence, this form can also be subordinated with *îw*:   *negation and subordination*

ḫr îw m nzw (ʾImnw-ḥtp)ʾ r.dî.t st n=f m tȝ qnb.t (and someone gave him her share before the judges) "because it was King Amenophis who gave it to him in court" (for the hieroglyphic text, cf. supra § 3.5.4).   *(pBoulaq 10 rt.15)*

4.3.3 The sentence with noun plus defined relative phrase: the Pseudo-Cleft Sentence

The most common Nominal Sentence is the one in which the second term is a relative phrase defined by a definite article or a demonstrative which agrees with the first term. The relative phrase can consist of active or passive participles, relative forms or relative clauses formed with *nty*, in which case the relative clause itself can be converted from any of the available sentence forms: First Present, Third Future, Emphatic, Adjectival or even Existential Sentences (for the negations, cf. supra § 4.3.1). In terms of structure and content this type of sentence resembles the Pseudo-Cleft Sentences of the European languages.

The first term can consist of specified or unspecified noun phrases — proper names, personal or interrogative pronouns, defined nouns and participles, but also adjectives, infinitives without article and nouns without article or with the indefinite article. The specificity of the first term is decisive for the meaning of the sentence: a noun determined in a specific way identifies while an undefined noun classifies or characterizes. The indefinite article can specify one individual as the representative of its class: *first term and sentence meaning*

(RAD 73,1-2)

wꜥ ꜣḥ.t n nhy nmḥ.w fꜣỉ nbw r pr-ḥḏ n Pr-ꜥꜣ pꜣ skꜣ nꜣ nmḥ.w "A holding of some private people who pay directly to Pharaoh's treasury is what those private people have tilled";

Notes:

wꜥ ꜣḥ.t ... pꜣ skꜣ Pseudo-Cleft Sentence. The first term is undefined, the second a relative form: what was ploughed was a member of the class of "fields which were ploughed by a specific class of peasants";

nmḥ.w "freeholders" who are obliged to pay "taxes" only to Pharaoh (and not to the temples);

fꜣỉ participle.

Actions can also be organized or classified by an infinitive:

(pBM 10052, 10,8-9)

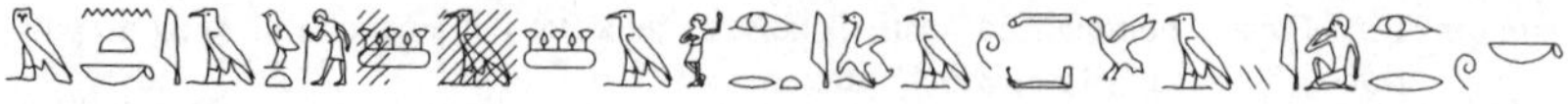

mnt.k ỉꜣw šꜣšꜣ
ỉr.t ỉṯꜣ pꜣy ỉ.ỉr=k

(The father has been silenced with hush money from thieves; he is admonished by his wife, the mother of the speaker:) "You are a foolish old man: what you have done is to act like a thief!";

Notes:

mnt.k ỉꜣw šꜣšꜣ characterizing Nominal Sentence with pronoun as the first term and noun without article as the second;

ỉr.t ỉṯꜣ first term of the Pseudo-Cleft Sentence in the form of an infinitive with object: "become a thief", "act as a thief".

A classifying first term without article, the second being a relative phrase introduced with a demonstrative:

(pD'Orb 15,4)

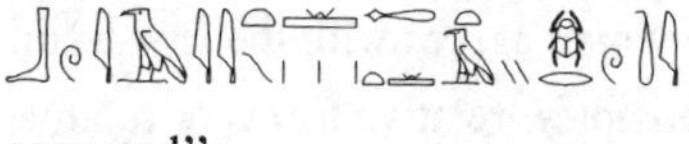 *bỉꜣy.t ꜥꜣ.t tꜣy ḫpr.t* "A great miracle is what has occurred";

Notes:

bỉꜣy.t group-writing variant of *bỉꜣỉ.t* "miracle", cf. pD'Orb 14,8;

tꜣy note that the determination of the relative phrase agrees with the first term;

ḫpr.t earlier form of the participle.

Identification, the second term being a relative clause where the antecedent and the agent of the relative clause are identical:

(pMayer A rt. 2,15)

 *ỉnn nwỉ=tw nbw mnt.w nꜣ nty rḫ*

"If gold was collected, they are the ones who know (it)!"

Notes:

ỉnn nwỉ=tw Protasis in the form of a Preterite introduced with *ỉnn*;

mnt.w nꜣ nty rḫ first term a pronoun, second a relative clause with First Present (Old Perfective) where antecedent and agent of the transformed sentence are identical (*st rḫ* "they know").

Antecedent and agent of a relative clause not the same, with First Present:

ỉḫ m sm.w pꜣ nty (HorSeth 11,9-10)

Stš ḥr wnmỉ=f dỉ m.dỉ=k "Which greens is it that Seth eats here with you?"

Note:

Stš ḥr wnm=f First Present with object pronoun as resumption of antecedent of relative clause.

or Third Future:

ỉḫ pꜣ nty ỉw=n r ỉr=f n pꜣ rmṯ 2 nty 80 n rnp.t r tꜣy ỉw=sn m tꜣ qnb.t "What are we going to do for the two fellows who have been in the court for 80 years?" (HorSeth 2,13)

Notes:

ỉw=n r ỉr=f Third Future in relative clause with resumptive object pronoun;

80 n rnp.t r tꜣy First Present in relative clause, "eighty years it is until this [year]";

ỉw=sn m tꜣ qnb.t Circumstantial First Present related to preceding First Present clause: it is only in this circumstantial clause that the reference to the antecedent occurs (=w);

construction literally "Eighty years it is until this (year) that they are at court". This is a typical form of grammatical organization of a sentence where the circumstantial is used.

The Pseudo Cleft Sentence of this type is negated in two ways: (1) *bn* NP *ỉwnꜣ pꜣ ỉ.sdm=f* is the form used with classifying or characterizing function; (2) *bn* NP *ỉ.sdm=f ỉwnꜣ*. Like all independent sentences, these can also be subordinated with *ỉw*. negation and subordination

4.3.4 Bibliography

Černý/Groll, *Late Egyptian Grammar* § 53; Frandsen, *Outline*, § 117 relative clause

Satzinger, Nominalsatz und Cleft Sentence im Neuägyptischen, in: *Polotsky-Studies*, 480ff; Groll, *Non-Verbal Sentence Patterns*, 47ff; Černý/Groll, *Late Egyptian Grammar* § 57.12; E. Doret, Cleft-sentence, substitutions et contraintes sémantiques en égyptien de la première phase, in: *Lingua Aegyptia* 1, 1991, 57ff; F. Neveu, Vraie et Pseudo Cleft Sentence en Néo-Égyptien, in: *Lingua Aegyptia* 4, 1994, 191ff; Loprieno, *Ancient Egyptian*, § 5.9; Cassonnet, *Les Temps Seconds*, 261ff (§ 19) Cleft Sentence

4.4 Notes on linguistic evolution

4.4.1 Tendencies

While it could be constructed grammatically, the "pure" Nominal Sentence was virtually never used in Middle Egyptian, except in balanced sentences. Most of the Nominal Sentence formations which appear in Late Egyptian can be found in Coptic as well: ⲀⲚⲞⲔ ⲞⲨⲰⲰⲤ "I am a shepherd", ⲀⲚⲄ ⲞⲨⲀⲄⲀⲐⲞⲤ "I am good" (< "a good one"). There is one significant contrast: the use of the articles increases, with the indefinite article being used more widely.

Middle Egyptian Nominal Sentences
  The real Middle Egyptian Nominal Sentence types are thus (a) the fixed participial statements or Cleft Sentences and (b) the *pw*-constructions. The latter form appears as both the bimembral type, which strongly depends upon a preceding context (*dmỉ pw*), and the context-independent trimembral type (*dmỉ pw, ỉmn.t*). Middle Egyptian noun phrases are also very often nominalized relative phrases (participles: *mrr.w nṯr pw, sḏm* *"it is what God loves, he who hears" > "the one who listens is the one God loves"; and relative clauses: *ỉšš.t pw, nty ỉm* "What is it that is there?"). These forms evolved roughly as follows:

Cleft Sentence
  The Middle Egyptian type of Cleft Sentence remains essentially the same in Late Egyptian, carrying out the same function, although morphologically adapted. Since the connection with the Old Egyptian Nominal Sentence such as *ỉn Ḥrw z3 ḥz3.t* ("Horus is the son of the wild cow") had been lost, this type of sentence was actually already alien to the Middle Egyptian sentence structure. Although there was a limited degree of overlap with the *pw*-sentences, the Cleft Sentence itself still had a specific role in "identification by isolation". In Late Egyptian, the form, having become still more alien to the system, gradually loses its functions to the new type of Cleft Sentence, the Pseudo-Cleft Sentence. The form disappears after the end of the New Kingdom.

pw-sentences
  The position of the *pw*-sentences is different. Morphologically adapted, the bimembral *pw*-sentence survives into Demotic and Coptic — ⲞⲨⲰⲰⲤ ⲠⲈ "he is a herdsman". The trimembral *pw*-sentence, however, underwent an adjustment characteristic of the analytic tendency. The appositional semantic specification which was given to the second term *pw* by the third was re-interpreted as a nucleus-satellite group, and thus as a variation of the type of specification where the definite article becomes the nucleus of its appositional satellite. Instead of the form [noun phrase]1 *pw*, [noun phrase]2, we have [noun phrase]1 [*p3* [noun phrase]2] which is the new type of Cleft Sentence, which is used as such in Demotic and Coptic, *nm p3 nty ỉw=f sdm*, ⲚⲓⲘ ⲠⲈⲦⲈⲨⲈⳞⲤⲰⲦⲘ̄ "who is it who will listen?"

In Late Demotic (Roman Demotic) and Coptic a new trimembral Nominal Sentence the late
appears as a striking late parallel to Middle Egyptian. The second term is again *pȝy* (ⲠⲈ) trimembral Nominal
which is again further specified with an appositional and by now defined third term: the Sentence
Cleft Sentence ⲞⲨⲘⲈ ⲦⲈ†ⲬⲰ ⲘⲘⲞⲤ "It is truth that I am speaking" had another
counterpart in the trimembral Nominal Sentence: ⲞⲨⲘⲈ ⲠⲈ ⲠⲈ†ⲬⲰ ⲘⲘⲞϤ
"What I say is true".

4.4.2 Bibliography

Polotsky, *Nominalsatz und Cleft Sentence*; T. Ritter, On Cleft Sentences in Late Egyptian, in: *Lingua Aegyptia* 4, 1994, 245ff; Simpson, *Demotic Grammar*, p.167ff (11.3).

4.5 Exercise

An interrogation protocol (pBM 10052 5,2-23)

Page 5 of papyrus no. 10052 in the British Museum, published by T. Eric Peet, *The Great Tomb-Robberies of the Twentieth Egyptian Dynasty* (Oxford 1930), pls. 28-29; cf. *KRI* VI: 779,2-781,7. The papyrus belongs to the records of the investigation of the tomb robberies, recording the interrogations in Year 1 of the "Repeating of Births" era — *wḥm-msw.t* — which corresponds to Regnal Year 19 of Ramesses XI.

Purpose: Example of a Late Ramesside administrative text with judicial phraseology; use of pass. *sḏm.w*, preterite converter *wn*, types of nominal sentences.

Notes:

line 2 *(r) mḥ hrw 2*: "the second day" (< "to fill two days");

ṯȝ.ty: during this period of the reign of Ramesses XI the Vizier was *Nb-mȝꜥ.t-Rꜥw-nḫt* (clause-type name: "Ramesses VI is mighty" — "Amenophis III is mighty" is also possible, but unlikely);

line 3 *nȝ srỉw n tȝ s.t s:mtỉ*: the council of the investigatory body is composed principally of the Vizier, the chiefs of the treasury and grain silo administration and two "butlers" of Pharaoh — who are essentially the highest officers of the secular executive. The two scribes of the Tomb Building Administration were also members (cf. lines 14 & 17);

dy m ḥr=w: "who were authorized" (passive participle with resumption: the members of the council *"of whom could be said: put under their authority");

line 4 *psỉ-s:nṯr ... n pr-'Imnw*: "Incense-burner of the Estate of Amun" (title or designation for a kind of ministrant who prepared the incense burners, etc.);

Ns-ỉmnw: proper name (cf. supra § 4.2.[1]);

ḏd.tw n=f: (an older) relative form which has become fixed — A "to whom it is said: B";

dd.tw n=f ʿnḫ n nb ʿnḫ wḏȝ snb: "He was made to swear an Oath of the Lord" (< *"An oath was imposed on him");

line 5   *mtw=ỉ ḏd*: Conjunctive as introduction of shortened oath (cf. infra § 7.1.3[2]); "[As long as Amun and the Ruler endure] and I say such-and-such" > "if I say such and such";

ỉw=f ḫšb ḏd: *ỉw*-clause with future senses with parallel Old Perfectives (cf. supra § 3.2.2[2]), "He will be mutilated and handed over". The change of person from *mtw=ỉ ḏd* to *ỉw=f ḫšb* is typical for the rendering of indirect speech: it can be translated in two different ways: "he swears, saying, should I lie, I should be mutilated", or "he swears, saying, if he should lie, he should be mutilated";

Kš: *ỉw=f ḏd Kš* "He will be taken to Upper Nubia" (more elaborately: "be stationed in Upper Nubia", cf. supra § 3.2.2[2]); the location noun is used absolutely as an adverb, thus more precisely: "he will be placed 'Cushwards'";

ḏd n=f: passive *sḏm.w* "it was said to him";

line 7   *ỉrỉ hȝw=f*: "to take possession of it";

line 8   *pš A n B*: "to divide A among B";

m pȝ 5 rmṯ: adverbial apposition to suffix *=n*, "for the five (of us) men", "we, who were five men";

m b-ḏ-n: characteristically without article (cf. supra § 2.1.3[2]): *"He was interrogated by club";

bpy=ỉ ptr nty nb gr: cf. supra § 4.2.1;

line 9   *wȝḥ*: here specifically, "to leave something alone", "to leave off doing something";

ḏd n=f ṯȝ.ty: originally *ḏd.w n=f* "it was said to him" (cf. line 5); on the papyrus, *ṯȝ.ty* was later added above the line, to specify the speaker (cf. line 11); it has simply been taken into the line here to save space;

line 10   the answer of the suspect is not specifically separated from the question of the Vizier (quick dialogue: "Which vessels?" — "These and those");

rr n nbw: golden "bands" attached to furniture and equipment (Coptic ⲗⲏⲗ);

line 11   *ỉ.ḏd=ỉ ʿq*: "(the treasure) the very same I just mentioned" (< "which I named/mentioned correctly");

line 12   *Mr-wr*: "Miwer", name of a large settlement at the entrance to the Fayyum, south of *Il-Lāhūn* (today called *Kōm Madinet Ghurāb* - "Gurob"), where there was an also economically significant portion of the Memphite Court, the "Harem Palace" (cf. B. Kemp, ZÄS 105 [1978] 122ff.);

ḏd m zp-2 (rnrn, rn.w): "to go through a list of names";

line 13   *swḥ.t*: designation of the mummy case (a figurative "egg"), usually of cartonnage (here *n ḥḏ* "of silver" or rather probably covered with silver); *ỉnỉ* is passive *sḏm.w*;

restore: *ỉw=n dỉ.t=s[t n] mstỉ*;

line 14   *zhȝ.w n pȝ ḫr*: the chiefs of the Gang of the Royal Tomb Building Administration included both foremen and the Secretary of the Tomb Building Administration, as well as a second secretary. From the reign of Ramesses XI until Dynasty XXI, this is the famous Thutmose (whom we met above in the Turin Taxation Papyrus, supra § 2.1.7[3], line 4,1, with Nes-Amenope, line 4,4, who was temporarily his assistant as second secretary); cf. infra § 7.4 and Černý, *Community*, 339ff;

line 15   *r mḥ s.t sn.wt*: "comes to two spots!" (< "to complete two spots");

line 16-17   *nȝ ḏnn pȝ mnn* (in group writing *ḏȝ-nȝ-zp2-zp2* > *ḏ-n-nn* > ⲭⲗⲗ, and *mʿ-nỉ-nỉ* as nominal derivative of the verb *mʿn/mʿnn/mnn* "to be wound up", "twisted"): "the rods and the wrist-twisters" as instruments of torture;

line 18   *d.y n=w*: passive participle with resumptive pronoun; that the verb *dỉ* is used without an object, intransitively, here and elsewhere (*dd=tw* and lines 19 & 20), with the prepositional rection *n* is semantically significant: it is not something specific that is "given", but something general: someone is "given a share", is "rewarded" or "bribed" (with the preposition *m*: "with");

t3-zp2-šrì > *T-t-šrì*: proper name ("Tetisheri");

ḥr.y-(ìr.y-)ᶜ3: "Chief Door Keeper", "Chief Porter"; the abbreviated writing ᶜ3 for *ìr.y-ᶜ3* "Porter" is common, cf. supra § 2.1.7(3);

line 19   *m-ḏr sḏm(=w) sw*: "when they learnt it"; Temporal (cf. infra § 5.4.2[1]) with 3rd pers. pl. suffix restored. At the end of the line, the scribe has lost track of his subject (*ìrm=f* and *ìrm=n*); cf. Frandsen, *Outline*, § 102 Ex.10 with notes 6 & 7;

line 20   *f3ì šrì*: "small weight";

construction: *ìw [wᶜ NP p3 dì=n n=w ìm=f]*, subordinated Pseudo-Cleft Sentence;

m.ìm=f: status pronominalis of *m* (as such and as *n.ìm=f* precursor of Demotic *n.ìm=f* and Coptic ⲘⲘⲞϤ);

bn p3 ìnr ᶜ3 ì.pš=n m.ìm=f ìwn3: "(a small weight was the one used before), not the large stone with which we divided it up!" — negated one-member Nominal Sentence, since an otherwise possible Pseudo-Cleft Sentence requires a defined relative form as the second term;

line 21   *t3 s.t ì.ḏd=k ìn(=ì)/ìn n3 ṯbw ... ìm*: "the place from which you said that I took the vessels" (< *"the place, concerning which is true: You said that I took the vessels from it") or without the restored 1st pers. sing.: "the place from which you mentioned the taking of the vessels". This is a good example of the possibility of complex deep packing of indirect references to antecedents: the resumptive pronoun appears only as an adverb of the object clause (*ìn=ì*) of the relative form of *ḏd*;

line 21-22   construction: *ìr* + noun phrase, preceding a *p3y*-Sentence;

ktì s.t mḥ snw.t: "another, second place";

line 22   *r-wì3.tw*: "aside from", here, "distinct from" (adverb or compound preposition of uncertain etymology; cf. Černý/Groll, *Late Egyptian Grammar*, p. 124 with note);

ᶜḏ3: absolute noun, here "Wrong!", "Untrue!";

ì.ìr n3 ṯbw r p3y ḥḏ: almost "it is precisely that treasure to which the vessels belong" (*"to which the vessels are"). This is one of the earliest examples of the use of the nominal converter *ì.ìr* (cf. infra § 5.5.1) before the Adverbial Sentence/First Present (with preposition *r* before noun), and here already in the "autofocal" variant (the adverbial of the Adverbial Sentence is itself the adverbial predicate of the Emphatic Sentence), as in Demotic (cf. Johnson, *Demotic Verbal System*, 104 [Ex.167A-B; D]; 109). In Late Egyptian, the Nominal *sḏm=f* (cf. supra § 3.3) is commonly used as a substitute for the nominalized First Present;

(line 24)   this is not reproduced here, but — as in line 8 — a closing statement is made: "he did not assent to anything more than what he had already said".

5. Clause conjugations and forms of complex sentences

5.0 The syntax of subordination in Late Egyptian

In principle, the Middle Egyptian system of subordination is still present and recognizable in Late Egyptian — the adverbial subordination accomplished through prepositional phrases and certain forms of *sdm=f*; the nominal subordination through subjunctive and nominal *sdm=f*; the attributive subordination through participles, relative forms and relative clauses with *nty*. In spite of the clear link to the Middle Egyptian precursors, the methods and morphology of subordination are, however, among the significant differences separating Middle and Late Egyptian: the preference for (a) unambiguous rather than ambiguous forms, (b) consistent and uniform methods of construction, and (c) clear-cut semantic fields — i.e. the preference for analytic rather than synthetic expression. Linguistic evolution thus reveals shifts in the specific processes and in the web of their interrelated usage. The decisive differences can be summarized as follows: *effects of the analytic tendency*

(1) The normal simple Middle Egyptian sentence gives the impression that its form is determined primarily by the possibilities of combining together various nominal, adverbial and verbal phrases. Its meaning appears to be derived from the various meanings of its component elements. This wealth of phrases and clauses also provided precisely those small elements with which the simple sentence could be extended (cf. supra § 3.0.1). In Late Egyptian however, it is the "minimal sentences" themselves which are the smallest possible units to be combined, taking over a large part of the role of the repertoire of phrases previously available: minimal sentences as the smallest self contained minimal constructions of a language — in Late Egyptian either sentence conjugations or simple Nominal Sentences. The composition of the Late Egyptian minimal sentence is basically firmly fixed and its declarative power clearly defined: *Late Egyptian minimal sentences*

— The First Present with infinitive or prepositional phrase is a sentence form indicating the present or relative present time, while combined with the Old Perfective it can also refer to past time (cf. supra § 3.1.2);

— the Third Future with preposition *r* and infinitive indicates future time, announcements and predictions (cf. supra § 3.2.2);

— preterite *sdm=f* describes past events;

— prospective *sdm=f* formulates wishes;

— the Nominal Sentence either characterizes or specifies, depending on the construction.

bound sentence structures

The forms of the sentences have become morphologically fixed, and they make up a paradigm (cf. supra § 3.0.1). In the course of linguistic evolution, via Demotic into Coptic, the forms will become still more fixed. The "old" *iw*-sentence disappears, or rather shifts into the First Present and Third Future (so that the Old Perfectives and prepositional phrases are no longer employed with the Third Future). This is accompanied by (a) the lexicalization of the Old Perfective, which becomes a mere word-form parallel to the infinitive, (b) the emergence of the Aorist and the First Future, and (c) the disappearance of the Prospective. On the other hand, the repertoire of phrases has been greatly reduced, so that — apart from the exceptions which follow — the possibilities extending a minimal sentence are reduced to adverbs and prepositional phrases.

> Parataxis, Hypotaxis/ Subordination are concepts used to describe sentence extensions and complexes. Several independent sentences or sentence conjugations are linked together to build a compound sentence. The individual sentences can be joined to one another by coordination or "parataxis". Where the sentence-parts are linked in such a way that at least one of them is not independent, the sentence is complex. Such sentences have at least one independent main sentence and at least one dependent clause. These dependent clauses are related to their main clauses by subordination or "hypotaxis". Subordinate clauses can be classified (a) according to their form — as conjunctional clauses or relative clauses, (b) according to their role in the main sentence — as subject clauses, object clauses, or circumstantial clauses, or (c) semantically according to the value of the relationship between main sentence and dependent clause — as causal, conditional, purpose or result clauses.

hypotaxis by conversion

(2) Following the loss of various elements of the repertoire of phrases, these minimal sentences assume the role of the smallest element of sentence enlargement, by subordination. With the exception of the Prospective, they are all subordinated by morphemes: *iw* subordinates the sentence conjugations and nominal sentences adverbially; *nty* subordinates them as relatives. Because these morphemes basically transform or "convert" minimal sentence forms into clause conjugations, i.e. circumstantial and relative or attributive clauses, they are called "converters". The nominal converter *r-dd* potentially belongs to the same group (cf. infra § 5.3.2[2]), but *r-dd* is not usually called a converter because it is actually an adverb belonging to the subordinating sentence, and not to the transformed clause like the other converters.

iw, nty, i.ir

Late Egyptian subordination with *iw* is thus organized as in Coptic. The role of *nty* as a converter had, however, not yet reached its final role. Relative clauses with *nty* and participles and relative forms still have the same relationship as in Middle Egyptian, so that designating *nty* as a converter can only be justified by a comparison to the *iw*-system and from a historical linguistic point of view. The participles and relative forms were destined to be eliminated in the course of linguistic evolution, so that the relative converter ultimately preceded all forms. It is however only with the appearance of the "nominal converter" *ỉ.ỉr* (infra § 5.5.1.) in Demotic that the converter system reached the form which ultimately prevailed in Coptic.

(3) The reduction of the repertoire of phrases left (a) the subjunctive-prospective *sdm=f* in the role of an object clause (supra § 3.4.2[2]), (b) the adverbial *sdm=f* in the form of the Finalis, and (c) a few combinations of prepositions with subjunctive and nominal *sdm=f* or *sdm.t=f*. These combinations must be regarded as bound (infra § 5.4), since (with the exception of the use of the Prospective ,§§ 3.4.1; 3.4.2) neither these *sdm=f* forms, nor any of the prepositions in question, could be replaced with other forms of their respective paradigm. Although they are, viewed narrowly, the last remnants of a diachronically older system of syntax, they did survive into Coptic.

conjunctional conjugations

The Conjunctive, one of the most important Late Egyptian subordinating conjugations, was likewise originally a fixed prepositional combination based on the preposition *ḥn^c* with the infinitive (cf. supra §§ 2.3.3[3]; 5.4.3), and is hence ultimately a non-finite form, which is slowly transformed into a conjugation (*ḥn^c nt.f sdm* > *mtw=f-sdm*).

Conjunctive

5.1. The system of syntactic conversion

5.1.1 The circumstantial converter *ỉw*

(1) The constructions and their functions

With few exceptions, the sentence constructions and nominal sentences — and their negated forms — can all be subordinated to another clause as adverbials by means of the *ỉw*-converter. This can produce (a) an adverbial at sentence level (sentence adverb, adverbial adjunct of a sentence), (b) an adnominal adverbial, i.e. a qualification of a noun — commonly termed a "virtual" relative clause — or (c) the essential component of an emphatic sentence (any sentence where the subject is a nominal *sdm=f*).

The sentence-forms which *ỉw* converts are the following:

			Converted Sentence Conjugations/ Nominal Sentences	
First Present	affirmative	ỉw	noun/pronoun =f	ḥr sdm sdm.w m pr
	negated (Aorist)	ỉw	bn sw ḥr sdm/sdm.w/m pr bw-ỉr=f sdm	
Preterite active passive	affirmative	ỉw	sdm=f sdm.w noun	
	negated	ỉw	bwpw=f sdm	
"not yet"		ỉw	bw ỉr.t=f sdm	
Third Future	affirmative	ỉw	ỉw=f r sdm ỉr noun r sdm	
	negated	ỉw	bn ỉw=f r sdm	
Emphatic Sentence		ỉw	ỉ.ỉr=f sdm m pr	
Nominal Sentence		ỉw	m nzw ỉ.dỉ.t st n=f mn m.dỉ=f šrỉ	
Negated Imperative		ỉw	m-ỉr sdm m-dyt sdm=f	
Vetitive (cf. pD'Orb 7,4)		ỉw	nn sdm=k	
Tense Conversion		ỉw	wn + sentence	

translating the forms

     The interplay between the function and tense of the main, subordinating, sentence and the function and tense of the subordinated ỉw-clause, produce a wide range of possible forms of expression. Pragmatically, when translating the clauses subordinated with the ỉw-morpheme, one should not forget that it is an all-purpose subordinating particle, which has its clearest equivalent in the gerund and participle constructions of English, Italian, Latin or Greek:

(LRL 45,10-11)

tw=n ỉy.tỉ

m pȝy=n nb r.rdỉ.t ỉw=n r pȝ nty tw=tn ỉm ỉw dỉ=f ỉn=n wꜥ šꜥ.t

"We have returned. It is our lord who has caused us to come to the place where you are, he having caused us to bring a letter" (Translation by Frandsen, *Outline*, 194 Ex.1; cf. also Wente, *Late Ramesside Letters,* p.60); similarly *ptr st ỉw=w nꜥy r qbḥw* "Look at them, *(Wenamun 2,66)* (they) going to the cool waters" (Translation by Frandsen, *Outline*, p.208 Ex.3; cf. Lichtheim, *Literature*, 229: "Look at them travelling to the cool water!").

As an all-purpose subordinating particle, however, it also embraces the functions of many of the conjunctions of the standard European languages. Hence it is sometimes advisable to use a combination of both styles in translation, as in the following passage:

(LRL 20,3-6)

ḥr mdw=ỉ m.dỉ Ḥr-n-ꜢImnw-pnꜥ=f ḥr n pꜢ shn n pꜢy=k ḥr.y

ỉmm mdw=f m.dỉ=k gr mnt.f

ỉw=tn hꜢp.t=f r=ỉ

ỉw m-ỉr mdw m-bꜢḥ ky

ỉw ỉ.ỉr=k ršw n pꜢy=k tm mdw ỉrm wꜥ ỉ.ỉr.t(=ỉ) ỉy

"Now, I have talked to Harnamanapnaf about the orders of your superior. Make him talk to you himself, (but) keeping it secret concerning me without talking in anybody else's presence, since you'll be happy if you haven't spoken with anyone until I come back!";

Notes:

hꜢp.tw=f	hypercorrected form of status pronominalis with 3-rad. verbs;
m-ỉr mdw	negated imperative (Prohibitive);
ỉ.ỉr=k rš	nominal *sdm=f* followed by adverbial complement;
n pꜢy=k tm mdw	negated conjugated infinitive after preposition *n*: "because of your not-talking";
ỉ.ỉr.t(=ỉ) ỉy	*r-sdm.t=f* as adverbial complement to conjugated infinitive.

As the examples may have shown, the English *ing*-ending performs about the same function in English as the Egyptian circumstantial converter since it signals subordination or co-ordination without indicating further logical relations. But whenever suitable or advisable, those conjunctions that express logical relations, such as "when", "while", "as", "after", "although", "since", "because", "but", etc., can of course also be used in translation even when Egyptian does not express those relations specifically. And — finally — there is the conjunction "and" which belongs to the group of translational devices that may be used to express the meaning of *ỉw*: although it is not subordinating but co-ordinating, it shares with *ỉw* and the gerund-constructions the faculty of combining propositions while leaving their logical connections unexpressed.

(2) Usage

Subordination in the form of a *iw*-clause is common, being more widely used than any other. The reasons for its wide spread use are:

1. It replaces a number of the Middle Egyptian non-locational adverbial adjuncts;

2. Its construction with sentence conjugations and simple sentences offers a wide range of variants;

3. In the form of the Present Circumstantial, its co-ordinating function ("and") makes it the most important form for continuing narration and reporting, hence called the "narrative" or "non-initial main sentence" (cf. infra § 5.2).

According to what was stated above, it must be assumed that all logical-semantic relations are implicit in every kind of clause, but the particular characteristics of a form lend themselves to the expression of specific relations:

present circumstantial — The Present Circumstantial is logically and semantically open ("and"), but it tends to imply the expression of (a) simultaneity (relative present; "while", "as", "when"), (b) concomitant circumstances or means ("inasmuch as/by doing"), or (c) comparison ("as", "as when", "as if"). When negated, it expresses the absence of a circumstance (which can frequently be translated in abbreviated form as "without doing").

(RAD 57,2-3)

iw=w ꜥš n pꜣ ḥꜣty-ꜥ n Nw.t

iw=f m znny "They called to the Mayor of the City as he passed by";

Note:

> *iw=f m znny*   Present Circumstantial with preposition *m* before verbs of motion.

(Doomed Prince 7,8)

iw=s ḥr ḫpr ḥr sꜣw pꜣy=s hꜣy r iqr zp-2 iw bn sw ḥr di.t pr=f r bnr wꜥ "And she began to protect her husband assiduously, without letting him go out alone" (or "... and did not let him go out alone").

subordinated preterite — The subordinated Preterite (a) can indicate that two separate events took place at the same time in the past (simultaneity in the past; "I met him when he was going home"), and (b) can even provide the reason ("as", "because"), but it (c) is primarily used to describe the relative past of an event with regard to the main clause ("after", "since"). Depending upon the nuances of meaning, some verbs of sentiment (*mri* "love"; *msḏi* "hate") or perception (*rḫ* "know"; *gmi* "find"; "establish"; *ꜥm* "recognize"; *ptr* "see") require a translation implying relative simultaneity. So do *ini* "bring", *ṯꜣi* "take" in connection with motion ("come after having gotten something" > "come having got something"; cf. Frandsen, *Outline*, 198f, and Johnson, *Demotic Verbal System*, 71 n.70).

(pD'Orb 9,4-5)

ỉn.ỉw=k dy wˁ.tỉ ỉw ḫ3ˁ=k nw.t=k r-ḥ3.t t3 ḥm.t n ỉnpw p3y=k sn ˁ3 "Are you here alone having abandoned your city because of the wife of Anubis, your older brother?"

Note:

> *ỉn.ỉw=k*   possibly form of First Present following *ỉn* (cf. D. Silverman, *Interrogative Constructions with jn and jn-jw in Old and Middle Egyptian*, Malibu 1980, 112ff).

(LRL 1,9-10)

t3 ỉḫ tw=ỉ dỉ.t ỉn.tw n=tn p3y ḥmn n šˁ.t ỉw bwpwy=tn dỉ.t ỉn.tw wˁ "So, why am I sending you all these letters without your sending (/although you have not sent) a single one?!"

Notes:

> *t3 ỉḫ*   interrogative pronoun *ỉḫ* with interjection *t3*, in this combination before nouns and First Present in the sense of an indignant (rhetorical) question: "What is this all about?!" (cf. Erman, *Neuägyptische Grammatik*, §§ 687; 740);
>
> construction   First Present with negated relative past Preterite.

m p3y=n nb r.rdỉ.t ỉw=n r p3 ntỉ tw=tn ỉm ỉw dỉ=f ỉn=n wˁ šˁ.t "It is our lord who made us come to you, by making us bring a letter" (for the hieroglyphic text, cf. supra § 5.1.1[1]).

(LRL 45,10-11)

— When subordinated, the "not yet" clauses indicate relative future in a peculiar way: the independent sentence *bw ỉr.t=f sdm* means that an action has not been accomplished prior to being mentioned (i.e., in the past), but that its execution can still be expected for the future at the time of being mentioned, even though its actual execution must remain in doubt ("he has not yet come", cf. supra § 3.5.1[2]). When the "not yet" clause is grammatically subordinated to a main sentence, however, it is anchored in the time of the superordinate main sentence, and what had still not occurred at the time of the main sentence has since occured and is confirmed as fact for some point thereafter ("I went when he had not yet come"). In translating, the conjunction "before" can be employed, since it subordinates the clause and affirms it, but simultaneously shifts the main sentence into the relative past with regard to the dependent clause ("I went before he came"):

subordinated
bw ỉr.t=f sdm

(pJud.Turin 5,4)

ỉw=w mwt n=w dz=w ỉw bw ỉry.t t3y r=w "And they killed themselves before anyone acted against them" ("before they could be executed"); cf. also following example, *LRL* 21,8-10);

Notes:

iw bw iry.t t3y   subordinated passive of *bw ir.t=f sdm*;

statement   here (in recording the verdicts and sentencing in the files of the Harem conspiracy against Ramesses III), the subsequent expression cannot be a fact but the suicide is considered to anticipate a punishment, which would most certainly have been carried out.

subordinated vetitive

— Exceptionally, a negated Vetitive (negated Prospective/Optative/Potential) can be used as a circumstantial, corresponding to the negated imperatives (supra § 3.4.0[2]), if the effect of a negated final circumstantial (*tm=f sdm* "that not") is desired:

(pD'Orb 7,4)

ih p3y=k iy.t m-s3=i r hdb(=i) m grg iw nn sdm=k r3=i hr md.t "What is it, your coming after me to kill me unjustly, without listening to my part of the story?" (< "while you won't hear my mouth speaking");

Note:

nn sdm=k   negation of the independent prospective *sdm=f* in more traditional genres of text, rather than *bn sdm=f*.

circumstantial clause as predicate

— It is worth noting that it is far from uncommon to find circumstantial clauses used as the "predicate" of a nominal *sdm=f*. This example again reveals the subordinated *bw ir.t=f sdm*:

(LRL 21,8-10)   *i.ir=i h3b n=tw t3 š^c.t i.h3b=i n=tw hr n3 niwy iw bw ir.t t3y=tn h3b iy n=i* "I sent the letter about the spears to you (at a time) when your letter had not yet reached me." (For the hieroglyphic text, cf. supra § 3.3.2.)

virtual relative clause

— A circumstantial clause used adnominally is traditionally described as a "virtual relative clause". A noun which is not specified by a definite article — use of the indefinite article is possible — can be provided with additional characteristics by a circumstantial; usually it is not necessary, however, to translate the circumstantial as a relative clause:

(Wenamun 2,62-63)

iw=i nw r 11 n br iw=w n iw n p3 ym "And I saw 11 ships (which were) coming from the sea" (or else "11 ships, as they were coming from the sea");

Note:

iw=w n iw   First Present, for *m iw.t* (preposition *m* with infinitive for verbs of motion).

The following example shows that an adnominal circumstantial clause — like any other circumstantial — can be used to extend the sentence as an adverbial, without having to follow its antecedent noun directly:

(Wenamun 1,10)

ỉw wꜥ rmṯ n tꜣy=ỉ br wꜥr ỉw tꜣy=f nbw [ṯbw 5] "And a man of my boat who had taken [five vessels of] gold fled" (or else "And a man of my boat fled, after taking [five vessels of] gold").

The antecedent is specified (and thus analogous to something grammatical defined) if it is a pronoun, to which the adnominal circumstantial clause can be related in the same way as apposition (cf. supra § 2.1.4[1]):

(LRL 27,10)

 *mtw ꜣImnw ns.t tꜣ.wy ỉn.t=k*

ỉw=k wdꜣ.tw "And may Amun of the Throne of the Two Lands bring you back safely".

— Characteristic of circumstantial clauses is also their ability to create complex sentences:

(HorSeth 6,6-7)

wn.ỉn Stš ḥr dwn=f

   ỉw=f ḥms ḥr wnm ꜥqw r.ḥnꜥ tꜣ psḏ ꜥ.t

      ỉw=f šm r ỉr.t n-ḥꜣ.ty=s

         ỉw bw.pwy.t wꜥ ptr=s ḥrw=f

"And then Seth — who had been in the middle of eating food together with the Great Ennead — got up and went to meet her, whom none had noticed except him.";

Notes:

ỉw=f ḥms	circumstantial clause which goes beyond the preceding pronoun *=f* to the noun *Stš* itself, "Seth was involved in eating" (*ḥms* as auxiliary verb, cf. supra § 2.2.3[3]);
ỉw=f šm	circumstantial clause related to *ḥr dwn=f*: "Seth got *himself* up, he going";
ỉw with negated Preterite	circumstantial clause of relative past time, dependent on the preceding Present Circumstantial!

5.1.2 The relative converter *nty* and attribute conversion

(1) The system of attribute or relative phrases

Like those of many other languages, Egyptian relative phrases offer a highly developed method of systematically (a) qualifying nouns not only in terms of properties but also by providing more detailed information on the syntactic role of properties; and (b) creating nouns expressing properties, as nominalized relative phrases. Beyond that, relative phrases are so common in the texts of all periods and registers that they can themselves

be termed a stylistic typological feature of the
Egyptian language. As a means of expression,
they are at once flexible and compact:

° They supplement the designations of properties by adjectives or adjective verbs, in bring-
ing fientic verbs or complex expressions into
attributive or appositional function — "(the
man,) who guards the children";

° they can themselves also form complex nouns
(nominalized relative phrases) — "he who
guards the children";

° they are transformed (converted) or embedded forms of sentences — "the man
guards the children" — so that they represent
every kind of utterance in a single function,
that of attribute.

> Relative form, relative phrase, relative clause are concepts for elements of sentences enabling the attributive modification of a noun in the form of complex constructions. "Relative form" is the traditional designation for that form of the verb which approaches participles in function but has its own subject or agent (for "the woman whom he sees" a relative form is used, for "the woman who sees" a participle). "Relative phrase" designates all kinds of attributive qualifications. This includes adjectives and participles, relative forms, and expressions transformed by a relative pronoun or a relative particle, usually *nty*. Those relative phrases introduced by *nty* form a subgroup of relative phrases, which are here termed "relative clauses".

participles, relative forms and relative clauses

Participles, relative forms and relative clauses with *nty* are mutually complementary, both morphologically and functionally. Participles and relative forms correspond to *sdm=f* forms. Relative clauses with *nty* correspond to the adverbial and nominal clauses. In Middle Egyptian three basic participial forms (simple, reduplicating/geminating and *sdm.ty=fy*) — each with two active/passive variants — and three relative forms (simple, reduplicating, *sdm.n=f*) served to cover the fields of tense and aspect. In Late Egyptian, active and passive participles and the relative forms were each in principle reduced to one basic form, which was primarily intended to formulate qualities developed in the past (participle and relative form thus correspond attributively to the preterite *sdm=f*). The participle in the *iri*-periphrasis occasionally has a general or customary meaning (custom, aorist: "everything, which she says" or "always says" or "used to say"). Present and future qualities are assumed by the *nty*-relative clauses with the First Present and Third Future.

word order

In principle, all of the relative phrases mentioned directly follow the noun to which they refer — the "antecedent", or "reference noun", of the relative clause. There can be variations, particularly where the length of the relative phrase would severely affect the construction of the sentence. On the other hand, relative clauses can themselves break up syntactic dependencies (as in the infinitive construction of § 2.3.3[2] supra and § 5.4.2[3] infra):

(LRL 10, 13-14)

mtw=k tm dỉ.t ḫꜥ nꜣ ꜥdd šrỉ nty m tꜣ ꜥ.t-sbꜣ dr.t=w m zḫꜣ "And you should not permit the children who are in the school to leave off writing."

Notes:

> *mtw=k tm dỉ.t*   Conjunctive with negated infinitive (negated Conjunctive);
>
> *ḫꜥ A dr.t=f m B*   "A takes his hands away from B"; in the example, the relatively long relative clause specifying the agent A separates the object (*dr.t=w*) from its verb.

The evolutionary trend to reduced linguistic forms is also operative in the negations: **negation** participles and relative forms are no longer negated with the corresponding forms of the negative verb *tm*. Instead, negation takes place using relative clauses with *nty* and negated clause forms.

Observation:

As with the other syntagmas, forms similar to those of the Middle Egyptian relative phrases (imperfective participles and relative forms, *sdm.ty=fy* and -.*n*-relative forms) were maintained in bound expressions and in the hierarchically higher textual registers. In the course of the New Kingdom, while the use of the newer forms increased, the use of the earlier ones declined, or they lost their former function: reduplicating and simple forms, and later even the -.*n*- forms, became simple variants of the relative function.

(2) Antecedents and relative phrases

The noun that is qualified by a relative phrase is called its antecedent. Relative phrases and antecedents are grammatically related to one another in a clearly defined way: the antecedent is always also a nominal element of the relative phrase:

- as agent/subject of the relative phrase: "the man, who guards the children";
- as object: "the children, whom the man guards";
- as part of the adverbial complement: "the house in which the man guards the children"; or with other qualifications. Which element of the relative phrase is represented defines the form and construction of the relative phrase:

Where the antecedent is identical with the agent or subject of the relative phrase, the **antecedent is** form assumes the guise (a) of an active participle or (b), in case of a converted First **agent** Present, that of a relative clause with *nty*, where the antecedent is not again mentioned (cf. supra § 4.3.1). This is of course only possible in the 3rd pers. (with interlocutive objects of speech):

pꜣ rmṯ ỉ.dỉ tꜣ šꜥ.t n sn.t=f "the man who gave the letter to his sister";

pꜣ rmṯ nty ḥr dỉ.t tꜣ šꜥ.t n sn.t=f "the man who is giving the letter to his sister". This is actually *pꜣ rmṯ ntỉ [ø]pꜣ rmṯ ḥr dỉ.t tꜣ šꜥ.t n sn.t=f.*

Relative phrases can, however, have their own agents even if they are identical to the antecedents, if inclusion of them is required by the construction itself. This applies to *nty*-conversions which have their own conjugation bases (Third Future, Emphatic construction) and all negated sentential forms; in principle, this is also a form of resumption:

p3 rmṯ nty iw=f r di.t t3 šꜥ.t n sn.t=f "the man who is going to give his sister the letter";

p3 rmṯ nty bn sw ḥr di.t t3 šꜥ.t n sn.t=f "the man who is not about to give his sister the letter".

antecedent is object
    Where the antecedent is identical to the object of the relative phrase, in the case of preterital attribution this assumes the form of the passive participle or the relative form. The passive participle syntactically corresponds to a relative form without agent. A resumptive pronoun is generally not necessary with participles and relative forms; the relative clause with *nty* has its own nominal agent and refers back to the antecedent:

t3 šꜥ.t i.dy n sn.t=f "the letter which was given to his sister"; (passive participle). It is also possible to introduce the agent with *in*: *t3 šꜥ.t i.dy n sn.t=f in p3 rmṯ* "the letter which was given to his sister by the man";

t3 šꜥ.t i.di p3 rmṯ n sn.t=f "the letter which the man gave to his sister";

t3 šꜥ.t nty p3 rmṯ ḥr di.t=s n sn.t=f "the letter which the man is giving to his sister". Here, the resumptive pronoun serves as the object of the verb, in contrast to the passive participle or relative form where the antecedent itself serves as the object.

with *iri*-periphrasis
    The *iri*-periphrases of participles and relative forms (cf. supra § 2.3.1) also require resumption. It is, however, not the antecedent but the infinitive of the lexical element which is the direct object of the form (*i.ir/i.ir=f*), while the antecedent takes its place only in the relative clause as the object of the infinitive (*sdm*, cf. the following paragraph).

iḫ.t i.ir=tw gm.t=w m.di=f "the things which were found at his place" (literally "with him"; cf. the passage in P. Salt 124 rto. 1,6 and the hieroglyphic text, supra § 2.3.1): the resumptive pronoun is the object suffix *=w* of the infinitive of *gmi*.

antecedent is another member of the clause
    Where (a) the verb of the relative phrase is intransitive, or where (b) the antecedent of a transitive verb is identical with another element of the relative phrase, then this also assumes the form of the passive participle, relative form, or relative clause with *nty*, with its own agent; the resumption is, however, now grammatically mandatory:

sn.t=f i.dy n=s t3 šꜥ.t "his sister, to whom the letter was given";

sn.t=f i.di n=s p3 rmṯ t3 šꜥ.t "his sister, to whom the man gave the letter";

sn.t=f nty p3 rmṯ ḥr di.t n=s t3 šꜥ.t "his sister, to whom the man is giving the letter".

Such resumption relationships can lead to very complex relations, a series of clauses forming a series of frames:

ß s.t i̯.dd=k i̯n(=i̯) nȝ t̠bw … i̯m: "the place from which you said I had brought the vases". *(pBM 10052, 5,21)* The resumptive pronoun only appears as the adverb *(i̯m)* of the content or object clause *(i̯n=i̯)* of the relative form *dd* (cf. supra § 4.5 line 21 for the hieroglyphic text).

Such complicated constructions are often difficult to grasp. Tricks can be used to try to understand them by separating the parts (as here, **"the place, of which it is true: you said, 'I took the vessels out of it'"*), but these constructs of convenience should then be transformed into translations!

Observation:

The regular use of resumptive pronouns does not apply when the antecedent is an expression of time. Since the nominal expression of time is used absolutely as an adverbial (*i̯y=f tr n rwhȝ* "he came in the evening"), the resumption is somehow an "absolutely set zero-position" (*tr n rwhȝ i̯.i̯r=f i̯y ø* "the evening, at which time he came").

Generally, the meaning of a noun is clarified and limited by relative phrases ("only those of whom the following can be said"; "all those of whom it can be said"; cf. infra § 5.1.2[4]); to such a high degree that this specification is grammaticalised in the form of definition or else the noun itself has the character of a designation. For this reason, antecedents are mostly either proper names (designations) or determiners (articles, demonstratives), or nouns qualified by articles (including *nb*, "each", "every"), demonstratives, possessive articles, or pronominal suffixes. Note that personal pronouns themselves, however, cannot be used as antecedents (in nominal sentences the independent pronouns are not the antecedents of the relative phrases!). *[determination of the antecedent]*

Relative phrases follow the same pattern as the adjectives and hence no longer agree in number and gender with their antecedents.

Nominalized relative phrases — complex nouns — differ from attributive or appositional relative phrases in that an article or demonstrative takes the place of the antecedent. While Middle Egyptian nominalized constructions were grammatically feminine — *dd.t.n=f* — they are of masculine gender in Late Egyptian: *pȝ i̯.dd=f* "what he said". *[nominalized relative phrases]*

(3) The attribute conversion of the sentence conjugations

Many of the simple sentence conjugations can be transformed into attributes with the converter ⸗ *nty* (which is also occasionally written *r.nty*). Like Late Egyptian attributes in general, *nty* does not agree with its antecedents, remaining the same for all genders and numbers. In morphology and usage, it is the precursor of Coptic ⲉⲧ(ⲉ).

The *sdm=f* sentence forms are, however, excluded from being converted with *nty*. In earlier usage both the Preterite and the Prospective were represented by participles and *[prospective and preterite]* relative forms. In Late Egyptian this is still true of the preterite *sdm=f*. Prospective forms in attributive function still appear in the earlier type of Cleft Sentence (cf. supra § 4.3.2), and in late Dynasty XVIII they appear as negated Prospectives after *nty* —

(Boundary Stela U, Z.11-12)

p3y=i ʿnḫ n (<m) m3ʿ.t nty ib=i r ḏd=f nty bn ḏd=i sw m ʿd3 r nḥḥ ḏ.t "(As truly as my father lives ...) is this my oath true, which I wish to swear and which I will not swear wrongfully for everlasting eternity" (cf. the hieroglyphic text, supra § 2.1.7);

Notes:

p3y=i ʿnḫ m m3ʿ.t   literally "my oath is truth" (cf. commentary supra § 2.1.7, line 11);

nty ib=i r ḏd=f   relative clause with form originally that of the future of the Adverbial Sentence (*"my heart is directed towards 'saying it'"). In Late Egyptian, however, this has reached the status of a bound expression (and can no longer be analysed in terms of Late Egyptian syntax);

nty bn ḏd=i sw   negated Optative/Potential "I will not say" (cf. supra § 3.4.1) in a *nty* relative clause;

construction   observing the semantic connections, the relative clause does not immediately follow its antecedent (cf. supra § 5.1.1[1]).

During the history of the language the prospective forms were ultimately filtered out of usage but the *nty*-conversion became attached to the Preterite at the expense of the participles and relative forms. The origins of this shift can already be followed during the New Kingdom.

(LRL 14,8-9)

nty hn=k n=f 3.t=k "(... Amun of the Throne of the Two Lands ...) against whom you have leaned your back".

Nominalized relative forms with *nty* (relative clauses) have the definite article. While *nb* ("each", "every", "all") usually follows the antecedent — *p3 rmṯ nb nty sḏm* "every man who hears", the nominalized form has the *nb* after *nty*: *p3 nty nb sḏm* "anyone who hears"; an alternative writing as appears from around the end of Dynasty XX.

The sentence conversions can be systematically summarized as follows:

			Antecedent and Agent	
			identical	different
First Present	affirmative	*nty*	*ḥr sḏm*	*sw ḥr sḏm*
			sḏm.w	*sw sḏm.w*
			m pr	*sw m pr*
	negated (Aorist)	*nty*	*bn sw ḥr sḏm.w/sḏm/m pr*	
			bw-ỉr⸗f sḏm	
Preterite	affirmative		participle	relative form
			ỉ.ỉr sḏm/(ỉ.)wn m pr	*ỉ.ỉr⸗f sḏm/(ỉ.)wn⸗f m pr*
	negated	*nty*	*bwpw⸗f sḏm*	
Third Future	affirmative	*nty*	*ỉw⸗f r sḏm/ỉr noun r sḏm*	
	negated	*nty*	*bn ỉw⸗f r sḏm*	
Emphatic Sentence		*nty*	*ỉ.ỉr⸗f sḏm m pr*	
Nominal Sentence (Adjectival Sentence)		*nty*	*nfr pȝ sḏm*	

(4) Usage

In the general conditions of communication between speaker and listener, the context of the speech situation, relative phrases fulfil two purposes which should be kept apart:

1. descriptive relative clauses: These permit the speaker to recall an object which is generally familiar — either because it is a matter of common knowledge or because it was discussed earlier — and describe it in passing: "those tools I mentioned, which were stolen". Such a characterization is not necessarily essential in order to be understood, and could thus be omitted: "the tools mentioned must be returned"; for the listener, however, it eases identification of the thing meant: "the tools mentioned — which were stolen — must be returned". *types of specification*

2. restrictive relative clauses: These permit the speaker to introduce something at the very moment of talking, and name it explicitly: "those tools which were stolen". Such relative phrases specify in the same fashion as the determiners: "these tools". They establish familiarity in the very speech situation where the objects are mentioned. Such specified relative phrases cannot be omitted without completely changing the statement, or rendering it incomprehensible: "those tools which were stolen must be returned". Nominalized relative phrases — complex nouns — and relative phrases with *nb* can only be used to specify.

definiteness/ specification

Both these functionally different types of relative clauses enable things talked about be regarded as familiar, either because they are already co- or contextually known or because they are introduced explicitly. They are always either (a) marked with the definite article or *nb*; or (b) proper names or an article or demonstrative itself. Under certain circumstances, class designations ("thieves", "gold") can be understood as playing the role of proper names, and then they do not require the definite article.

frequency of use

According to the relative frequency of the various convertible sentence forms, besides the preterite conversions (participle and relative form) the relative clauses most commonly used are First Present conversions, and forms with the Third Future are not uncommon. The use of all other forms is marginal.

First Present

— Present specification through the converted First Present adverbial sentence, where antecedent and agent differ:

(pSalt 124 vs. 1,2-3)

iw=f itȝ tȝ s.t-sḏr nty ḥr=f

iw=f ḥr in nȝ iḫ.t nty tw=tw ḥr dî.t=w n rmt̠ iw=f mwt

"And he (Paneb) stole the bier which was under it, taking the things which are given to a man when he is dead"; the resumptive pronoun is object of the verbal form of the relative clause;

Notes:

tȝ s.t-sḏr nty ḥr=f relative First Present with the agent and antecedent identical: "the bier which was under it (the coffin of the workman Nakhtmin)";

nȝ iḫ.t nty tw=tw relative First Present where the agent (unnamed, *=tw* "one") and antecedent (*iḫ.t*)
ḥr dî.t=w differ. The resumptive pronoun (*=w*) is the object of the verb *dî.t* of the relative clause;

rmt̠ iw=f mwt adnominal circumstantial clause (so-called virtual relative clause) with undefined antecedent which is a class designation, "man, when he is dead", "men, when they are dead", "the deceased" in general (cf. Coptic ⲣⲉϥⲙⲟⲟⲩⲧ).

(LRL 9,4-5 and passim)

tw=i ḏd n ꞽImnw-Rꜥw Ḥrw-ȝḫ.ty ... nt̠r nb nt̠r.t nb nty tw=i znꞽ ḥr=w "I implore Amun-Re-Harakhte ... and every god and every goddess whom I pass"; resumption in the adverbial phrase (*ḥr=w*);

Notes:

tw=i ḏd n GN First Present "I say to god A": a common formula in letters;
ḥr-ḥr=w status pronominalis writing of the preposition *ḥr*.

negation

Relative First Present, negated:

(HorSeth 3,2-3)

m-ỉr ỉr.t n3 zp.w ꜥ3y n grg nty bn st r s.t=w "Don't commit the great injustice, which is inappropriate";

Notes:

> *m-ỉr ỉr.t*   Prohibitive of *ỉrỉ* "do";
>
> *n3 zp.w ꜥ3y n grg*   lit. "these great deeds of injustice";
>
> *nty bn st r s.t=w*   the negated relative clause has its own agent even when it is identical to the antecedent. Here, it is the converted negated Adverbial Sentence, *"they (the deeds) are not at their (proper) place".

The following examples have already been quoted elsewhere:

ỉw=ỉ dỉ.t n=k p3 ḫtm n nbw nty m ḏr.t(=ỉ) "I give you the seal of gold which I wear" (for *(HorSeth 6,1)* the commentary and hieroglyphic text, cf. supra § 2.1.4[3]); the antecedent and the agent are identical, with the relative phrase (relative First Present/Adverbial Sentence) separated from antecedent;

ḥr tw=n dỉ ḥms.tỉ m t3-Ḥw.t ỉw=k rḫ.tw p3y=n sḫr ḥms nty tw(t)=n ỉm=f "We are now *(LRL 23,11-12)* living here in 'the mansion', and you know what it's like" (for the commentary and hieroglyphic text, cf. supra § 3.1.3[2]); antecedent and agent differ, the resumption is accomplished through the adverbial phrase of the relative First Present;

ỉḫ p3 nty ḥr šm.t m-s3 p3 zỉ nty m ỉy.t ḥr t3 mỉ.t ỉw=f ḏd n=f ṯsm p3y "'What is that going *(Doomed Prince 4,8-9)* after the adult who is coming on the way?' And he said to him: 'That is a greyhound'" (for the commentary and hieroglyphic text, cf. supra §§ 2.1.3[1]; 4.2.3); nominalized relative clause (First Present with *ḥr* + infinitive) opposed to an attributive relative clause (First Present with *m* + infinitive), where the antecedent and agent are identical in each case;

tw=k ptr p3y k3mn nty ḥms r-gs p3 sb3 p3y=k ỉtỉ p3y "You see that blind beggar sitting beside *(Blinding of Truth 5,7-8)* the door — he is your father." (for the commentary and hieroglyphic text, cf. supra § 4.2.3); relative First Present with Old Perfective, antecedent and agent are identical.

— Preterital specification with participles and relative forms: preterite

(pLeAm 4,9)

dmḏ ỉṯ3.w wn m p3 mr n p3w nṯr

s:wḏ n p3w ḥm-nṯr tpy n ꜣImnw m hrww pn

zỉ-3

"Total: Thieves who were in the tomb of that god, and who have been turned over to that High Priest of Amun this day, 3 men"; antecedent and agent are identical:

co-ordinated active participles (*wn*; *s:wḏ*) characterize a antecedent of the class designation type.

(pBM 10068 rt. 4,22)

nbw ḥḏ ỉ.dỉ nꜣ ỉtꜣw n nꜣ rmṯ n Nw.t ỉmnt.t Nw.t

šdỉ ỉn tꜣ.ty pꜣ ḥm-nṯr tpy n ꜣImnw

"Gold and silver, which the thieves had given to the people of the City and the 'Western City', which was recovered by the Vizier and the High Priest of Amun"; antecedent and agent differ, relative form and passive participle (*ỉ.dỉ nꜣ ỉtꜣw; šdỉ*) are co-ordinated, and characterize an antecedent of the class designation type (the text continues, detailing the quantities of gold and the people with whom it was found);

Note:

    šdỉ ỉn tꜣ.ty   the customary introduction of an agent with the passive participle (and other passive forms).

But

(pBM 10054 rt. 2,8-9)

ỉw=n ỉn pꜣ ḥḏ pꜣ nbw ỉ.wn=n gm.tw=f m nꜣ (m)ꜥḥꜥ "And we took the silver and the gold which we usually found in the tombs"; the relative form of *wn* (*ỉ.wn=n*) with resumptive pronoun specifies the antecedents here ("that silver that we found");

Note:

    ỉ.wn=n gm.tw=f   relative form of *wn* with First Present (*ỉ.wn=n ḥr gm.t=f*), cf. supra § 3.6.2. With relative forms, the resumption is necessary even when the antecedent is not itself the object of the form (which is impossible with intransitive *wn*), but rather the object of its further subordinated verb. This applies also for the object of the infinitive with the First Present (*ḥr gm.t=f*).

(pJud. Turin 5,8)

ỉnỉ.tw=f ḥr nꜣ btꜣ.w n nꜣ ḥm.t pr-ḫnr wn=f m-ḫnw=w ỉ.sdm=f ỉw=f tm ḏd smỉ=w "He was brought because of the crimes of the women of the harem in whose midst he was, and which he overheard, but did not report"; relative form of *wn* with resumption; relative form of *sdm* separated from its antecedent (*nꜣ btꜣ.w*), without resumptive pronoun;

Notes:

    ỉ.sdm=f   relative form without reference, because the antecedent is the object of the relative form itself;

    ỉw=f tm ḏd smỉ=w   Present Circumstantial (in this use also called non-initial main sentence), permitting two grammatical interpretations: (1), subordinated to the relative form (as part of the relative clause): "the crimes which he heard, but did not report"; or (2) adnominal, parallel to the relative form: "the crimes, which he heard, which he did not, however, report";

tm ḏd　possible negation of infinitive with *ỉw=f ḥr ḏd* (cf. infra § 5.2).

　If the relative Preterite is negated, the relative clause with *nty* with a negated Preterite　negation replaces participles and relative forms:

(pNaunakhte 2,7)

ỉr pꜣ nty bw.pw=f dỉ.t n=ỉ bn ỉw=ỉ r dỉ.t n=f m ꜣḥ.t=ỉ "As for him who did not support me, I shall not make provision for him from my property"; nominalized relative *bw.pw=f sḏm*; as expected, the agent of the relative clause appears despite the identity of antecedent and agent;

Notes:

bw.pw=f dỉ.t n=ỉ　intransitive *dỉ.t* "make a gift to someone". The testatrix Naunakhte is referring to her children, who are to be considered in her will only if they carried out their filial obligations;

bn ỉw=ỉ r dỉ.t n=f　negated Third Future: *"I shall not give to him".

The following examples have already been quoted elsewhere:

sḏm=ỉ md.t nb ỉ.hꜣb=k n=ỉ ḥr=w "I have taken notice of everything you sent to me about　*(LRL 57,7)* it" (for the commentary and hieroglyphic text, cf. supra § 3.5.1[1]); the antecedent (with *nb*) and the agent differ, and the antecedent is not the object of the relative form (*ỉ.hꜣb=k*), hence the presence of the resumptive pronoun in the adverbial phrase (*ḥr=w*).

[*ỉḫ.t n*] *wḏꜣ n nzw (Stš.y Mr.n-Ptḥ) ꜥ.w.s ỉ.ỉr=tw gm.t=w m.dỉ=f ḥr-sꜣ zmꜣ-tꜣ* "[the things]　*(pSalt 124 rt. 1,6)* from the storehouse of King Seti I, which were found in his possession after the burial" (for the commentary and hieroglyphic text, cf. supra § 2.3.1); the restored antecedent and the agent differ and the relative form (*ỉ.ỉr=tw gm.t=w*) is morphologically an *ỉrỉ* pariphrasis, with the semantic element (infinitive of *gmỉ*) as the object of *ỉrỉ*: the resumption is hence accomplished via the object suffix of the infinitive.

— Future qualification by converted Third Future (the agent is must be given, even when　Third Future identical with the antecedent):

(LRL 32,9-10)

rḫ pꜣ ỉmw pꜣ rmṯ r.nty ỉw=k dỉ.t n=f tꜣy šꜥ.t mtw=k ỉr.t rn=f ḥr=s "Find out where the boat and the man to whom you should give the letter are, and put his name on it"; the antecedent (*pꜣ rmṯ*) is the "indirect object" of the verbal form, and thus the reference is made with the preposition *n=*;

Notes:

r.nty   variant writing of the relative converter *nty*;

r.nty iw=k dỉ.t   relative Third Future;

mtw=k ỉr.t   Conjunctive as the continuation of the introductory imperative.

The following examples have already been quoted elsewhere:

(LRL 15, 4-5)   iw=ỉ ỉr.t p3 nty nb iw=k ḏd=f "I am going to do everything that you (will) say" (for the commentary and hieroglyphic text, cf. supra § 3.2.2[1]); nominalized relative clause with Third Future, antecedent identical with the object of the infinitive, resumption via object suffix;

likewise:

(HorSeth 14,9)   ỉh h3b=k n=n p3 nty iw=n r ỉr=f n Ḥrw ḥnᶜ Stš tm=n ỉrỉ shr m ḥm=n "Please send us word about what we should do for Horus and Seth, so that we don't make uninformed plans". (for the commentary and hieroglyphic text, cf. supra § 3.4.2[2]).

forms of nominal sentences
— Specification through conversion of nominal sentence forms is rare (adjectival sentences and emphatic sentences have been cited, cf. Černý/Groll, *Late Egyptian Grammar*, §§ 53.14-53.17, p. 507f.). The following example is that of a converted Existential Sentence (cf. supra § 4.2.2[2]):

(pBM 10054 rt. 2,10-11)   mtw=n in n3 wt nty wn nbw ỉm=w

"And we took the inner coffins on which there was gold";

Notes:

mtw=n in   Conjunctive, which occasionally continues past actions;

nty wn nbw ỉm=w   relative Existential Sentence (Adjectival Sentence).

5.1.3. Bibliography

conversion   Loprieno, *Ancient Egyptian*, § 7.9.5

circumstantial clause with *iw*   Erman, *Neuägyptische Grammatik*, §§ 519-533; Frandsen, *Outline*, §§ 100-113; Černý /Groll, *Late Egyptian Grammar*, § 63; Groll, jw sdm.f in Late Egyptian, in: *JNES* 28, 1969, 184ff; Loprieno, *Ancient Egyptian*, § 6.6.3; Cassonnet, *Les Temps Seconds*, § 6

virtual relative clause   Erman, *Neuägyptische Grammatik*, §§ 830; 832-834; Černý/Groll, *Late Egyptian Grammar*, § 54

relative phrases   Winand, *Études*, §§ 540-621; Černý/Groll, *Late Egyptian Grammar*, §§ 48-53; Erman, *Neuägyptische Grammatik*, §§ 366-398; 821-847

relative clause with *nty*   Frandsen, *Outline*, § 117; Černý/Groll, *Late Egyptian Grammar*, § 53; Erman, *Neuä-gyptische Grammatik*, §§ 836-847

nty+1st Pres.   Frandsen, *Outline*, §§ 36 (2)b; 37 (2)a; 38 (2)a; 41 (2)b

nty +3rd Fut.   Frandsen, *Outline*, § 32 (2)

nty +Emph. S.   Cassonnet, *Les Temps Seconds*, 91ff (§ 7)

5.2 Non-initial main sentence and "old" ꜣIw-sentence

5.2.1 Usage

The Present Circumstantial consisting of *ḥr* + infinitive is apt to express a "natural course of events"[1] quite easily, thanks to its temporal (relative present) and logical-semantic openness ("and"). This use might be illustrated by a sequence of the following kind: "She got up, took her coat, went downstairs, opened the door and went downtown". The *iw=f ḥr sḏm* form is thus a kind of basic form for continuing narrative, hence the most commonly used form of narrative texts and passages. It is the nature of such texts (reports and narratives, etc.) that they are mostly related in the past tense; the style of several literary stories, such as Wenamun, the Two Brothers, and Horus and Seth, is dominated by this form.

Such passages are introduced by an independent verbal form, which is preterital or otherwise congruent with a cotextual preterite. The construction then continues with a long chain of *iw*-clauses:

(Doomed Prince 5,7-10)

wn.in=sn ḥr it̠.t pꜣ ẖrd r pꜣy=sn pr

iw=sn ḥr wꜥb=f

iw=sn ḥr dỉ.t wnm n pꜣy=f ḥtr

iw=sn ḥr ỉr.t ỉḫ.t nb n pꜣ ẖrd

iw=sn ḥr sgn=f

iw=sn ḥr wt rd.wy=f

iw=sn ḥr dỉ.t ꜥqw n pꜣy=f šmsw

iw=sn ḥr ḏd n=f m sḫr.w n s:ḏd

"Then they took the boy to their house, washed him, fed his team, and did everything for the boy, anointed him, took care of his feet, gave food to his retainers, and conversed with him, saying...";

Notes:

       situation   the "Doomed Price" is received by the Syrian princes who are competing for the hand of the daughter of the King of Mitanni;

---

1   cf. Frandsen, *Outline*, § 82[2], quoting Jespersen, *The Philosophy of Grammar*.

wt   here actually "to bandage" or "wrap" the feet hurt by the journey.

ỉr.w n=f tꜣy sbꜣy.t ỉw=tw wꜣḥ=f ỉw=f mwt n=f ḏs=f "This sentence was carried out, and he
was left alone, and he died by his own hand."

Notes:

        ỉr.w   preterite passive *sḏm.w*;

ỉw=f mwt n=f ḏs=f   literally: "and he took his life himself".

5.2.2. Formal criteria

designation of
function

This continuative or sequential function has led to designations such as "*séquentiel*"
(Winand), "*Narrativ*" (Satzinger) or "non-initial main sentence" (NIMS) or non-initial
main clause.[2] The term non-initial main sentence emphasizes its property of appearing
to be an independent sentence in the textual flow while never being used initially. The
effect of continuity and co-ordination ("and") while presenting the "natural course of
events" results from the structure where each individual clause is only related to the verb
of the base sentence, but not to its other members: an ad-verbal clause in the strictest
sense of the word.

formal criteria

Now, by its very nature a dependent — circumstantial — clause cannot be initial; it
is, however, less natural for our languages, the languages of translation, to make use of
circumstantial clauses to build long chains of co-ordinated utterances, as is done with the
Late Egyptian Present Circumstantial. The mere length of the chains is also occasionally
a hindrance to keeping track of the chain-building itself for the analysing observer —
hence apparent "main sentences". As it is, this use of the circumstantial clause with its
specific function has been regarded as a specific form. It is argued that, along with the
functional properties of a "continuous narrative" in relative past time, but also occasionally in the future, these clauses supposedly also have the morphological properties of
being formed with (a) a specific *ỉw* which is neither the converter, nor the *ỉw* of the Third
Future, and (b) *ḥr* + infinitive only, and not Old Perfective or adverbials. It is likewise
alleged that the Present Circumstantial is negated *ỉw bn sw ḥr sḏm*, while the NIMS is
negated with *ỉw=f ḥr tm sḏm*.

in bound
combinations

A final characteristic claimed for the NIMS is its use in certain grammatical contexts,
(a) following nouns with or without *ỉr*, (b) following adverbs preceded by *(ḥr) ỉr* or *ḥr*

---

2   Černý/Groll, *Late Egyptian Grammar*, § 38: "*iw.f (ḥr) stp.f* of the Past".

m.dî, or (c) in association with *(ḥr) wnn=f ḥr sdm*. An example of such a syntactically closed complex:

(LRL 39, 10-12)

wnn tȝy=î šꜥ.t spr r=k îw=k tm rwî=k hȝb n=î ꜥ=k m.dî pȝ nty-nb nty îw=f îy m ḫt "When my letter reaches you, you should not refrain from sending word to me about yourself by anyone who is coming north."

Notes:

construction	*wnn=f ḥr sdm — îw=f ḥr (tm) sdm*; within the frame-work of Late Egyptian this is a vestige of Middle Egyptian syntax: a balanced or emphatic sentence of the [*wnn=f ḥr sdm*]NP [*mdw=f*]AP type. *wnn=f* is a nominal *sdm=f* followed by an adverbial or nominal *sdm=f* which is remodelled into a Present Circumstantial (cf. the systematic treatment of these sentences infra § 6.2.2). The results are sentence complexes of the "if/whenever — then" type;
tm rwî=k (ḥr) hȝb n=î	negative verb *tm* followed by infinitive *rwî* and reflexive object suffix (*=k*), to which the infinitive (*ḥr*) *hȝb* is related: "to restrain someone from doing something";
pȝ nty-nb nty	the most probable explanation (following Wente's comment on this passage, *Late Ramesside Letters*) is the lexicalization of *nty-nb* as a term for "everyone", and thus, "everyone who";
nty îw=f îy	relative Third Future.

Both the usage and the forms can, however, be recognized primarily as those of the Present Circumstantial, whether in the sense of "continuous sequence" (supra §§ 5.1.2; 3.1.2 note), or in certain bound expressions, or constructions which can be recognized as vestiges of Middle Egyptian syntax. And, secondarily, many uses of the Late Egyptian Present Circumstantial betray a relation to the "old" *îw*-sentence (cf. here infra § 5.2.3). The *tm* negation is furthermore not a useful feature for the identification of a sentence, because it is a form of negation which works within the nominal phrase and not at sentence level: *tm* negates not only the infinitive, but every kind of verbal noun (participles and nominal *sdm=f*). *îw=f ḥr tm sdm* is thus an affirmative construction (with negative infinitive) and not complementary to the negative construction *îw bn sw ḥr sdm*.

identity with circumstantial First Present

Observation:

Although the explanation here is different, it must be stated that important analytic achievements have been gained in the debate about the role and form of the NIMS in Late Egyptian Grammar, especially by P. J. Frandsen and S. I. Groll. Lately, partly corresponding to and partly diverging from the explanation given here, G. S. Greig has raised a new argument on the basis of the differences of the negative constructions (cf. *Fs-Lichtheim*, pp. 264ff).

5.2.3 The descendants of the "old" *ỉw*-sentence

(1) Definitions and usage

Generally, it can be said that the NIMS is the Present Circumstantial, used apparently independently or under circumstances where two dependent forms support one another mutually (closed complex type). Aside from the Third Future and *ỉw=f ḥr tm sḏm* there are, however, other forms of *ỉw*-sentence which follow initial expressions with or without *ỉr*. Within the framework of Late Egyptian, they can only be understood as Present Circumstantials (NIMS), but in fact they are in a regular substitutional — paradigmatic — relationship to proper independent main sentences:

(Doomed Prince 5,5-6)

ỉr pȝ nty ỉw=f r pḥ pȝ sšd n tȝy=ỉ šrỉ.t ỉw=s n=f r ḥm.t "The one who reaches my daughter's window shall have her as wife."

Notes:

> *nty ỉw=f r pḥ* relative Third Future "who shall reach the window";
>
> *ỉw=s n=f* "She 'is' to him, belongs to him"; independent *ỉw*-sentence with *n* prepositional phrase (rather than *ḥr* + infinitive in the NIMS role): formally it is a Present Circumstantial, but functionally it is sententially independent.

the Middle Egyptian independent *ỉw*-sentence

Following an *ỉr*-anticipation there should be either an independent sentence (sentence conjugation) or *ỉw=f ḥr sḏm* in the NIMS-role. Formally this is a Present Circumstantial in future time ("shall receive her as wife") and used in a fashion which can be ascribed to the NIMS role. Since this form is in substitutional relation to the sentence conjugations, the construction of this group may best be sought in Middle Egyptian syntax: *ỉr* + noun phrase + *ỉw*-sentence. Hence in such constructions the Middle Egyptian independent *ỉw*-sentence has survived at least into Late Egyptian (cf. supra § 3.2.2[2]), and in them *ỉw=f ḥr sḏm* is therefore merely a sub-variety of that type of sentence. It is characteristic for remnants of this type that they are maintained in particular sentence structures (cf. infra § 6), such as:

(pAdoption rt. 23-24)

ỉnn ỉw=s ms bn šrỉ bn šrỉ(.t) ỉw=w m rmṯ-nmḥ.w n pȝ tȝ n Pr-ʿȝ "If she gives birth — whether to a son or a daughter — they will be free citizens of the land of Pharaoh" (for the hieroglyphic text and comments, supra § 3.2.2[2]);

Notes:

> *ỉnn ỉw=s ms* Third Future with conditional particle *ỉnn*;
>
> *ỉw=w m* independent *ỉw*-sentence.
>
> *rmṯ-nmḥ.w*

Although this vestigial type of sentence cannot be assigned to the clause conjugations, it is similar to the Present Circumstantial — as NIMS — in not filling an initial position. Instead, it is used either to continue the narrative or as an integral component of

combinations. The "old" *iw*-sentence and the Present Circumstantial as NIMS are thus
not fundamentally different, and can be distinguished only in the context of their usage
(cf. infra § 6).

(2) Notes on linguistic evolution

Within the Late Egyptian languistic system, the old *iw*-sentence bears a formal resemblance to both (a) the subordinated Present Circumstantial and (b) the independent Third
Future sentence conjugation. Functionally, in terms of the force of its statements and the
type of its context, it is similar primarily to the First Present sentence conjugation, along
with the Present Circumstantial functioning as NIMS, and occasionally the Third Future.
It is along these lines that it decomposes linguistically: where formally and functionally
neither the Circumstantial nor the Third Future take its place, it merges into the First
Present. This coalescence of the two sentence types can still be grasped in the pronominal
forms of Demotic and Coptic. For the insufficiently differentiated forms of the 3rd pers.
sing. (*sw*; *st*), the pronominal forms *iw=f* and *iw=s* come into use in weakened forms (*iw*
as sign for an initial vowel or a syllabic pronunciation) — and later on also *iw=k* in the
2nd pers. sing. for *tw=k*. It can be summarized thus:

	Late Egyptian		**Demotic**	**Coptic**
	iw-Sentence	First Present	First Present	First Present
1.s.c.	*iw=i*	tw=i	tw=i	†-
2.s.m.	*iw=k*	tw=k	*ti=k* / *iw=k*	ⲕ-
f.		tw(=t)	tw(=t)	ⲧⲉ-
3.s.m.	*iw=f*	sw	*iw=f*	ϥ-
f.	*jw=s*	st	*jw=s*	ⲥ-

Observation:

Cf. Johnson, *Demotic Verbal System*, pp. 32ff. In the plural, the transition from the Late Egyptian
present tense forms to the Demotic and Coptic is quite regular (cf. supra, § 3.1.1[2]).

5.2.4 Bibliography

Frandsen, *Outline*, §§ 49-55; Satzinger, *Neuägyptische Studien*, § 2.7; Černý/Groll, *Late* non-initial
Egyptian Grammar, §§ 37-41; Winand, *Études*, §§ 681-709; Groll, A Short Grammar main sentence
of the Spermeru Dialect, in: *Fs-Westendorf*, Bd.1: Sprache, Göttingen 1984, 58f (*iw=f*
ḥr tm sdm as negation of circumstantial); Junge, *iw=f ḥr (tm) sdm*

ỉw-Sentence   Winand, *Études*, §§ 794-500; Frandsen, *Outline*, § 115 (3. Conclusion [2e]); Eyre, *GM* 18, 1975, 11ff; Satzinger, *Neuägyptische Studien*, §§ 2.4.1.2; 2.4.1.3

5.3 Nominal and adverbial conjugations

5.3.1. Conjunctions and synthetic forms of subordination

(1) Definitions: clause conjugations as nouns

The analytic conversion of sentence conjugations has a significant role in the syntax of subordination — hypotaxis. In certain contexts, however, synthetic forms of subordination were still used, particularly in the form of those conjugations (a) which replace nouns in a superordinate sentence, (b) which express the intention, purpose or goal of an action. Subject nouns can be replaced with a nominal or emphatic *sdm=f* (*ỉ.sdm=f/ ỉ.ỉr=f sdm*; §§ 2.3.2; 3.3), object nouns with a subjunctive-prospective *sdm=f* (§ 3.4.2[2]). Intention or goal is expressed with a final prospective *sdm=f* (§ 3.4.2[2]). The use of the prospective *sdm=f* as an object noun is in the lower registers of the textual hierarchy already restricted to th object of the verb *dỉ* "cause".

verbal form and noun clause   Even if the borderline between (a) the nominal forms of verbs and (b) the genuine clausal constructions created from them cannot be adequately described or defined,[3] certain indications of the transformation of nominal forms into noun clauses can be recognized. The indicators can be (a) the parallels between clause conjugations and sentence conjugations (Prospective), (b) the sententiality of nominal *sdm=f* and necessary adverbials in the subject noun clause and (c) the interchangeability of the dependent (subjunctive-prospective) *sdm=f* with object noun clauses of other kinds such as *ỉw*-clauses and those naming the content of the verb *dd* "speak", "talk": grammatically every form of direct speech is the object of the verb introducing it. Such speech constructions develop into indirect speech and conjunctional noun clause constructions.

conjunctions of noun clauses: *r-dd*; *r.nty*; *ḥnᶜ dd*   With the "nominal converter" *r-dd*, it can be clearly recognized how a conjunction or converter produces noun clauses out of introductions to speech, because the conjunctional function ("that"; ":") and the actual meaning (*r* + infinitive, "in order to say:" or "the following") were used side by side. The conjunction ⨪ *r.nty* (< Middle Egyptian *r-ntt/ḥr ntt*) belongs to this category (Erman, *Neuägypytische Grammatik*, § 680), but it no longer forms noun clauses, being employed to introduce new subjects or paragraphs

---

3   since the nominal forms of verbs are already complexes with verbal nuclei and semantically complementary agents, objects and rection or necessary adverbial qualifiers.

in a text (generally in letters). *ḥnᶜ ḏd* performs a similar role, although the phrase has a different origin (being preposition + infinitive) and grammatically the form is to be taken as the continuation of a real (as when following *tw=ỉ ḏd* "I say to/ask of") or fictive speech or letter introduction.

The realm of the subordinate clauses functioning as adverbials in superordinate clauses was in principle already covered by the circumstantial conversion of the sentence conjugations (*ỉw*-conversion). Other constructions are, however, also formed out of prepositions with nominal conjugations and generally become bound conjugational syntagmas (cf. infra § 5.4). By analogy with the circumstantial clauses and the conjunctional conjugations, the final-prospective *sḏm=f* can also be considered a final circumstantial clause ("so that"), even if the form itself is a synthetic remnant of earlier stages of the language. In the form of its combination with *dỉ* (*dỉ=s sḏm=f* "that she permits him to hear", Finalis) the circumstantial clause of purpose — the final clause — remains part of the linguistic system.

circumstantial clause of purpose

(2) Forms and Usage

For the most part, the forms and their usage have already been presented, and the discussion here is intended to recapitulate the system of set out clause conjugations. The pattern can be as follows (see the table on the following page):

Noun Clauses		Form		Meaning Paraphrase
as subject to adverbials		*ỉ.ỉr=f sdm* + AP	nominal *sdm=f*	"that he listens is AP"
	negated	*ỉ.ỉr=f tm sdm* + AP		"that he doesn't listen is AP"
	in the Cleft Sentence	*mnt.f* + *ỉ.ỉr=f sdm*	prospective nom. *sdm=f*	"It is he who will listen"
as object of verbs		*dỉ sdm=f*	Subjunctive	"cause that he listens"
		gmỉ ỉw=f sdm	*ỉw* + sentence conjugation	"note that he listens"
		sdm r-ḏd sw sdm	"obj.-converter" + sent. conjug.	"perceive that he listens"
circumstantial *sdm=f*		*sdm=f*	final clause	"so that he listens"
		dỉ=ỉ sdm=f	Finalis	"so that I cause that he listens"
	negated	*tm=f sdm/* *tm=f dỉ.t sdm=s*		"so that he does not listen"/"so that he does not allow that she listens"
complementary to		*r* + infinitive	adverbials	"in order to listen"
		r-ḏd + sentence		speech introduction

In Late Egyptian synthetically constructed noun clauses are in decline. The subjunctive *sdm=f* object clause after *dỉ* was still widely used, but uncommon after other verbs — as was the case with its use within noun clauses after prepositions (with the exception of the bound groups, cf. infra § 5.4). The nominal *sdm=f* as the subject of a bimembral sentence (adverbial sentence; emphatic sentence) was still widely used, but no longer appears in the lower stages of the register hierarchy as object, after prepositions or in the balanced sentences of the earlier type.

preposition
with *sdm=f*

(LRL 27,5-6)

Some expressions (apparently preposition + *sdm=f*) could conceal earlier usage, but they can also be analysed otherwise, as in some letter formulae:

tw=ỉ ḏd n ʾImnw-Rʿw Ḥrw-ȝḫ.ty m wbn=f m ḥtp=f ... "I ask of Amun-Re-Harakhte at his rising and setting ... (that he give Life, Prosperity and Health)";

Note:

> *m wbn=f* either — as understood here — preposition + noun (*nomen actionis*, cf. also WB s.v. *ḥtp*) with a suffix pronoun (for the Late Egyptian method of construction, cf. the example pBologna 1086 1,2-3 in § 5.4.2[3]), or preposition + nominal *sdm=f* (cf. Frandsen, *Outline*, 166).

In other cases, such an expression can also appear in more conventional Late Egyptian forms, as a "conjugated" infinitive (cf. infra § 5.4.2[3]), or as a circumstantial:

tw=ỉ ḏd n ꜢImnw-Rꜥw Ḥrw-Ꜣḫ.ty ỉw=f wbn ḥtp m-mn.t "I ask Amun-Re-Harakhte, when he raises and sets daily" (the same ibid., 4-5). *(LRL 39,15-16)*

5.3.2 Noun clauses and content clauses

(1) Subject noun clauses

Aside from the customary use in emphatic sentences, a nominal *sdm=f* can also occasionally be encountered in a subject-noun function in constructions with *ḫpr* "happen" (similar constructions with *ḫpr* will be found in Middle Egyptian, cf. Gardiner, *Grammar*, §§ 188,1; 486 Obs.1; Westendorf, *ZÄS* 79, 66 n.1.: *nominal sdm=f as subject clause*

| *mtw ḫpr ỉ.ỉr=ỉ šm ỉm r šd ḫt* *(pMayer A vs. 6,13)*

"And it happened that I went there to get wood";

Note:

> *mtw ḫpr* unusual form of an impersonal conjunctive (rather than the expected *mtw* + noun + *ḫpr*). This can probably best be understood in terms of the construction with *ỉ.ỉr=ỉ šm*, which could hardly follow *mtw* without making the whole form unclear. Similar deferment is found with *=tw* constructions. But cf. for the construction Cassonnet, *Les Temps Seconds*, 105ff (§ 9, specifically § 9.1.2), and Mark Collier, A note on the syntax of *ḫpr* and omitted impersonal subjects in Late Egyptian, in: *Wepwawet* 2, 1986, 15ff.

A characteristic modification occurs in the structure of the bimembral sentence (Adverbial Sentence/First Present) where the position is filled by nominal *sdm=f — ỉ.ỉr=f sdm* + adverbial phrase, since the clause conjugations now also belong to the sentence-forming ("stressed") adverbial phrases. In opposition to these, which are themselves transformed sentences and primarily forms of sentence extension, the character of the nominal *sdm=f* in subject-noun position is shifted to a kind of sententiality in itself. Compare the constructions with nominal *sdm=f* followed by an adverbial phrase in a question for specification: *in the bimembral sentence*

[*ỉ.ỉr=k ỉtꜢ Ꜣḫ.t=ỉ*]NP [*ḥr ỉḫ*]AP "Why did you take my property?" (for the hieroglyphic text, cf. supra § 3.3.2), *(oDM 580 rt. 4-5)*

with the sentence structure of:

[*ỉ.ỉw=ỉ*]NP [*ỉw tꜢy=f md.t m gs m ḏr.t=ỉ*]AP "As soon as I get back, his affairs will be halfway in my hand" (alternatively, "When I come, his affairs will be halfway mine", for the hieroglyphic text, cf. supra § 3.3.1[1]). The adverbial centre of the expression in the form of a circumstantial clause operates far more independently than the simple adverbial, and thus tinges the noun clause too with an appearance of independency. *(LRL 19,7-8)*

beginning conversion

This seeming sententiality of the noun clause can lead to a reanalysis of the verbal periphrasis *i̯.ir* + noun phrase + infinitive as the nominal converter *i̯.ir*, which then can be recognized by the absence of the infinitive:

(pBM 10052, 5,22)

ḏḏ=f ꜥḏꜣ i̯.ir nꜣ ṯbw r pꜣy ḥḏ ꜥꜣ i̯.ḏḏ(=i) n=tn ꜥn "He said, 'Wrong! It is that those vessels belong to that great treasure which I have already mentioned to you'" (for the hieroglyphic text, cf. supra, § 4.6);

Notes:

nꜣ ṯbw r pꜣy ḥḏ ꜥꜣ Adverbial Sentence (with preposition *r* before the noun), *"the vessels are to that great treasure";

i̯.ir nominal converter before an Adverbial Sentence (rather than the expected *i̯.ir nꜣ ṯbw* infinitive *r pꜣy ḥḏ*).

> Noun clause, content clause are terms describing specific forms of subordination. "Noun clause" refers to a subordinate clause that replaces a nominal element of a sentence (where the translation is typically with a "that" clause). Noun clauses commonly represent the subject or object noun in a larger sentence. Subject clauses: "*Whether he will come* is uncertain"; "*That you will write to me* is cheering". Object clauses: "I do not know *whether she is coming*"; "He knows *that you are ill*"; "She said, *'I was ill'*". The semantic relationship between the main sentence and such subordinate clauses can be described as "content relationship". Such "content clauses" convey the object or content of a superordinate expression of assertion, perception, feeling, thinking or wanting.

Observation:

This is one of the earliest examples of the use of the nominal converter *i̯.ir* before the First Present/Adverbial Sentence (with preposition *r* before noun), in this case in the autofocal variant (the adverbial of the Adverbial Sentence is itself the adverbial predicate of the emphatic sentence), as in Demotic (cf. Johnson, *Demotic Verbal System*, p. 104 [Exx. 167 A-B; D]; 109) and Coptic (cf. Polotsky, *Coptic Conjugation System*, § 30).

in the Cleft Sentence

In the Late Egyptian Cleft Sentence of the earlier type (cf. supra § 4.3.2) the nominal *sḏm=f* of the prospective mood can be used as a complementary form of the participle in expressions concerning the future:

(LRL 13, 6-7)

m ꜣImnw Pꜣ-Rꜥw Ptḥ i̯.ir=w ptr ꜥ=k "It is Amun, Pre and Ptah who will check into your state".

(2) Object-noun clauses

subjunctive *sḏm=f* as object clause

The object-noun clause makes the semantic relations between the superordinate proposition and the subordinate clause particularly clear. In the earlier phases of the language, a noun clause serving as an object after a series of verbs was formed with a different kind of nominal *sḏm=f*: the dependent, subjunctive-prospective *sḏm=f*. Except in the more traditionally minded registers, this object clause construction is used only with the verb *di̯* in Late Egyptian, but in this construction it occurs at least as frequently if not more so. The object clauses of the following example from the introductory formulae of letters display both (a) forms of the intransitive and adjective verbs and (b) the use of the prospective *sdm=f* of *wnn*:

(LRL 39,15-40,2 and passim)

tw=i dd n ʾImnw Pʒ-Rʿw Ḥrw-ʒḫ.ty ... imm ʿnḫ=k imm snb=k imm wnn=k m ḥs.t nṯr.w rmṯ rʿw-nb zp-2 "I ask Amun and Preharakhte [...] every day that 'they' let you live and be healthy, and that 'they' keep you in the favour of gods and men'';

Notes:

structure	cf. sub § 5.3.2(3): the content of the request following *tw=i dd n* god may be phrased in translation as indirect speech: either "I ask them: Let 'him' live'' or "I ask them that 'they' let you live'';
wn(n)=k	subjunctive-prospective *sdm=f* (like *ʿnḫ=k*, *snb=k*) of *wnn* in an object clause following the imperative of *di*.

Although the governing verb *di* is widely employed either as an imperative *imm* or as an infinitive *di.t* followed by object clauses, it can appear in any other form of the verb:

Preterite *sdm=f*:

(Wenamun 2,26-27)

ḥr ptr di=k iry pʒy nṯr ʿʒ pʒy hrw 29 iw=f mni tʒy=k mr "But you have had this great god spend these 29 days moored in your harbor.''

Notes:

iry pʒy nṯr ... hrw 29	subjunctive-prospective *sdm=f* in an object clause following preterite *di=k*, *"that this god (should) do 29 days'';
iw=f mni	Present Circumstantial as an adverbial to the prospective *sdm=f* von *iri* (and thus being part of the object noun clause!): "to cause the god to spend 29 days being moored'';
tʒy=k mr	absolute noun as a locative adverb (an unusual but possible use), to be understood as "in your harbor''.

Relative form:

 *iḫ nʒ mšʿ swgʒ i.di=w iry=k*

(Wenamun 2,22)

"What is all this silly wandering which they have made you do?''

Notes:

iḫ nʒ mšʿ	Nominal Sentence proper with the interrogative pronoun *iḫ* as the first noun (< "What are/signify these travels?''), cf. § 4.2.1;
i.di=w iry=k	relative form 3rd pers. pl. with subjunctive *sdm=f* as an object noun clause.

Participle:

(LRL 45, 10-11) *m pȝy=n nb r.rdỉ.t ỉw=n r pȝ nty tw=tn ỉm* "It was our Lord who sent us to where you are" (for the hieroglyphic text and commentary cf. supra § 4.3.2).

other forms of the object clause   With some of the verbs of perception (such as *gmỉ* "find", "perceive"; *rḫ* "know"; *ʿm* "learn"; *sdm* "hear"; and to a lesser degree, *ptr* "see"),[4] other types of subordinate clause constructions appear. In origin and structure these subordinate clauses need not necessarily be conceived as object clause constructions, or only partially so. They are more probably to be analysed as adverbial qualifications which have the effect of object clauses — produce content relations. This can be illustrated thus:

Verb	Object	Converter	Object Specification	Meaning Paraphrase
gmỉ	*sw*	*ỉw*	sentence: *=f ḥr sdm/bn sw ḥr sdm*	"find him listening"; "ascertain that he listens/had listened"
	Ø		*sdm=f/bw.pw=f sdm*	
gmỉ e.g. *tw=ỉ gm*		*r-ḏd* *r-ḏd*	sentence: *sw sdm*	"I am ascertaining that he listens"

Observation:

In the table, "sentence" signifies that in principle all sentence conjugations and forms of the independent sentence can appear: after *ỉw* these are generally First Present and Preterite. *r-ḏd* serves as a converter (or a conjunction of subordinate clause construction) and is simultaneously still a form introducing speech ("in order to say"). *ptr* "to see" is not structurally compatible with *r-ḏd*, but still uses the construction with qualified object, as does *dỉ* (cf., e.g., pD'Orb 10,6).

Occasionally a kind of object clause construction can be used with *dỉ* "give" that is in principle a construction with a specified object (as e.g. *dỉ sw ḥr šm*, *"render him going" > "cause him to go"). This was relatively common in Middle Egyptian, but gradually dropped out of use in Late Egyptian:

(pSalt 124 rt. 2,15-16) [hieroglyphs] *mtw=tw dỉ.t rmṯ ḥr rs Nfr-ḥtp* "(...) And that people were made to watch Neferhotep" (< *"And that one has rendered people watching Neferhotep").

Examples of the more common constructions:

(pAbbott 7,13-14) [hieroglyphs] *gmy nȝ rmṯ ỉw bw.pw=w rḫ s.t nb* "The people were found not to know any 'place'";

---

4   cf. D. Sweeney, in: *Crossroad*, 337ff.

Notes:

    gmy   passive preterite *sdm=f*;

  ỉw bw.pw=w rḫ   circumstantial of negated Preterite as an adnominal qualification of the object *nȝ rmṯ*.

(LRL 7,11-12)

ỉȝ ỉ.ỉr=ỉ gm ỉw dỉ=f ỉw w^c tzm r tȝy=ỉ ỉw=w gm=ỉ (m) tȝ mtn Ḏbȝ "But I only discovered that he had sent a boat to get me when they found me in the middle of Edfu";

Notes

    ỉ.ỉr=ỉ gm   nominal *sdm=f* of *gmỉ* without object;

     ỉw dỉ=f   Preterite Circumstantial (as a substitute object noun) followed by Subjunctive (*ỉw w^c tzm ...*);

  ỉw=w gm=ỉ   Present Circumstantial of *gmỉ* with object;

    (m) tȝ mt   adverbial expression of place, "in the middle": the hieratic sign is read, with Wente (*LRL*, p. 25 n. b) *contra* Černý (*LRL*, note on passage), as *tȝ* rather than *m*, with *m* restored. The restoration is, however, not necessarily required, as in Late Egyptian locative adverbials (like those of time) are occasionally used absolutely.

    Such constructions with content clauses are opposed to conjunctional clauses which can also be interpreted as being "converted":

    ỉw=w gm r-ḏd ỉry=f st "And they found out that he did it";

(pJud. Turin 4,2)

Notes:

    ỉw=w gm   Present Circumstantial clause (NIMS) without object;

      r-ḏd   "converter" of the content clause ("that"; ":");

    ỉry=f st   the independent Preterite sentence conjugation (after the "direct indicator of initiality" *r-ḏd*), *"they found: He did it".

sdm(=ỉ) r-ḏd nȝ rmṯ ḥn r ỉr.t hȝw m pȝy pr n stȝ "I noted that the people proceeded to take possession of this funerary equipment";

(pMayer A rt. 1,14-15)

Notes:

    sdm=ỉ r-ḏd   "I heard: (The people ...)";

    nȝ rmṯ ḥn   First Present with Old Perfective.

ḥr bw rḫ=ỉ r-ḏd ỉr pȝy=ỉ ^cḏd pḥ r=k "But I did not know that my boy would get to you";

(pBologna 1086, 6-7)

Notes:

    bw rḫ=ỉ   negative Aorist;

  ỉr pȝy=ỉ ^cḏd pḥ   Third Future with nominal agent.

direct speech   *r-ḏd* can also be used in its literal sense (being the preposition *r* with the infinitive of *ḏd* "speak", "talk", "say") to introduce direct address. In contrast to the object clauses, (a) an imperative or vocative can appear in direct speech, (b) the conjunctional syntagmas (§ 5.4) can also be used at the beginning of direct speech, and (c) the pronouns are related to the context of speech (not the report or the narrative outside the speech itself).

(3) Indirect speech

Both direct speech and noun clauses (particularly content clauses) share the characteristic of not belonging immediately to the discourse to which they are attached; they either add a note or cite another speech situation. They also share the characteristic of being embedded at the level of the main text, and belong therefore to another text level. They differ in that noun clauses are dependent upon the main text both grammatically and semantically (being adjusted to a speech situation: "He realised that he was late"), but direct speech is marked by a break in dependency (with pragmatic signals like a pause, break or punctuation: "He realised: 'I am late'") — the principle being that a verb initiating speech is not followed by the expected object clause, but rather by a clearly marked independent sentence. Late Egyptian indirect speech is roughly between the two: grammatically independent, but influenced by the speech situation of the main text, while diverging from the speech situation of the speech quoted.

single actor adjustment   Characteristic of indirect speech is the "single actor adjustment". While in noun clauses all roles and all actors related to an action or a process match the actors of the main text, in indirect speech only a single actor is matched. In particularly clear cases it is for example stated (cf. supra *LRL* 39, 15ff. sub § 5.3.2[2]), "Concerning you, I say to god so-and-so, *imm n=k ꜥnḫ*, that he give you life" < *"Give (you, god) you (correspondent) life": The quoted speech situation of the request-address to the god is changed by the speech situation of the letter into an address to the correspondent. The translation cannot immediately reproduce this, but can represent it in two different ways: translating, (a) "I say — about you — to god so-and-so, 'give *him* life'/'let *him* live'" or (b) "I say — about you — to god so-and-so 'that *he* give you life'/'that *he* let you live'". Compare the observations to §§ 3.4.2(1) & 3.4.3(1).

     The oaths are equally clear: e.g. (for the hieroglyphic text, cf. 7.1.3[1])

(oGardiner 104,1-4)   *ḏd.t.n in-mw P3-ꜥ-m-t3-in.t wꜣḥ ꜣImnw wꜣḥ p3 ḥqꜣ mtw=i mdw m pꜣy ꜥꜣ.t iw=f ḥr 100 n sḫ.t*

"What the water-carrier Pa'amtone said: 'As Amun and the Ruler endure, and I should bring up the affair of this donkey, *I* will be subject to 100 blows'".

Or: "What the water-carrier Pa'amtone said was that as Amun and the Ruler endure, and *he* would bring up the affair of this donkey, he will be subject to 100 blows".

Where all the actors are referred to in the 3rd pers., the adjustment will not be noticed, and the translator can reproduce the text using either direct or indirect speech — *ỉw=sn ḥr ḏd mwt=f* "And they said: 'he will (probably) die'" or "And they said that he would die" (cf. also § 3.4.3[1] Observation).

5.3.3 The final circumstantial clause

The prospective *sḏm=f* was another synthetic form of clause conjugation which had become alien to the Late Egyptian linguistic system, but nevertheless remained very stable throughout the evolution of the language (cf. §§ 5.3.1[1]; 3.4.4; 3.4.2[2]). Viewed systematically, it is the circumstantial of the sentence conjugation "independent prospective *sḏm=f*" — Optative/Potential — as the *ỉw*-conversions are the circumstantials of the other sentence conjugations. The main clause can have any form, but it is frequently an Imperative or Optative Sentence:

(Wenamun 1,21)

ỉ.ỉr nhy hrww dỉ q3ỉ-n=ỉ wḫ3=ỉ sw "Spend a few days here with me, so that I can seek him";

Notes:

    ỉ.ỉr nhy hrww   independent, superordinate Imperative Sentence;

        q3ỉ-n=   compound preposition (cf. supra § 2.2.4[3]), "with someone";

        wḫ3=ỉ sw   final circumstantial clause.

   *ỉmm ꜥš.tw n Ḥrw ḥnꜥ Stš* *(HorSeth 10,11)*

wpỉ.tw=w "Let Horus and Seth be summoned that they may be judged";

Notes:

    ỉmm ꜥš.tw   independent, superordinate Imperative Sentence;

    wpỉ.tw=w   final circumstantial with passive prospective *sḏm=f*.

Functionally this form with its own agent is complementary to the constructions with the preposition *r* + infinitive. Where the agent of the intentional or purposeful action is identical with that of the main sentence, the infinitive phrase appears; where these are different, the final *sḏm=f*: *complementary to r + infinitive*

(LRL 70,1-2)

ỉmm ḥn=w r ỉn n3 ỉt tm n3 rmṯ ḥqr "Let them hurry off to get the grain so that the people don't starve";

Notes:

    ḥn=w r ỉn   "may they go to get": indication of purpose with identical agents (rather than the technically equally possible **ḥn=w ỉn=w n3 ỉt* "may they go so that they fetch grain");

tm n3 rmṯ ḥqr   negated final circumstantial clause (prospective *sdm=f* of *tm*) with nominal agent (*n3 rmṯ*): indication of purpose with different agents.

Traces of the earlier linguistic system can also be recognized in these interactions. The transformation of the syntax of subordination rendered the identification of the agents redundant in the rest of the system (cf. infra § 5.5), but morphologically it was necessary to name the actors, although semantically superfluous.

The following examples have already been cited earlier (cf. supra § 3.4.2[2]):

(Beatty Love Songs vs. C2,3)   *mï n=ï m33=ï nfr.w=k* "Come to me so that I may behold your beauty" (for the hieroglyphic text, cf. supra § 2.2.6 exercise [1]);

(HorSeth 14,9)   *ïḫ h3b=k n=n p3 nty ïw=n r ïr=f n Ḥrw ḥn^c Stš tm=n ïrï sḫr m ḥm=n* "Please send us word about what we should do for Horus and Seth, so that we don't make uninformed plans" (for the hieroglyphic text, cf. supra § 3.4.2[2]).

Finalis   In the form of the prospective *sdm=f* of *dï* followed by a Subjunctive, the circumstantial clause of purpose still has a long history to come — as the "Finalis" or "causative-promissory conjunctive" (*dï=ï ïr=f sdm* > ⲦⲀⲢⲈϥⲤⲰⲦⲘ̄); cf. supra §§ 3.4.3[2]; 3.4.4. Example:

(HorSeth 1,9-10)   *ïmm h3^c.tw=f r bl ïrm=ï dï=ï ptr=k dr.t=ï ïw=f t3y.t=f dr.t=f m-b3ḥ t3 psḏ.t* "Have the two of us sent out, and I will let you see my hand grasp his in front of the Ennead" (for the hieroglyphic text, cf. § 3.4.3[2]);

Notes:

ïmm h3^c.tw=f   imperative main sentence (Causative Imperative, "cause that one sends");

dï=ï ptr=k   Finalis/promissory conjunctive: prospective *sdm=f* of *dï* in the circumstantial clause of purpose.

causative infinitive   Like the final circumstantial clause with the preposition *r* + infinitive, the causative final circumstantial clause is complementary (a) to the Causative Infinitive, (b) to the construction with preposition *r*, and (c) to the infinitive of *dï* "cause" followed by a Subjunctive (*r dï.t sdm=f*); cf. supra § 3.4.3(2).

5.3.4 Bibliography

Frandsen, *Outline*, §§ 15-16; Černý/Groll, *Late Egyptian Grammar* §§ 45-47; Winand, *Études*, §§ 392-399; 403-404 — subjunctive

D. Sweeney, The nominal object clause of verbs of perception in non-literary Late Egyptian, in: *Crossroad*, 337ff; A. Shisha-Halevy, Quelques thématisations marginales du verbe en néo-égyptien, in: *Orientalia Lovaniensia Periodica* 9, 1978, 56f; Groll, *Negative Verbal System*, 245ff — noun clause

Carsten Peust, *Indirekte Rede im Neuägyptischen*, GOF IV 33, Wiesbaden 1996 — indirect speech

Frandsen, *Outline*, §§ 15(2); 16 with n. 7; Erman, *Neuägyptische Grammatik*, §§ 294-296; Černý/Groll, *Late Egyptian Grammar*, § 45.4; Groll, *Negative Verbal System*, 241ff; Johnson, *Demotic Verbal System*, 277ff — final clause

5.4. The conjunctional clauses

5.4.1 Forms of explicit subordination

As has been repeatedly mentioned, sentence conjugations and nominal sentences (and the associated negative forms) can be subordinated as adverbial clauses using *ỉw*. These subordinate clauses have an adverbial function as adverbial adjuncts of a superordinate clause, or as sentence extensions or basic elements of an Emphatic Sentence. *ỉw* is, however, exclusively a morpheme of subordination as such (cf. supra §§ 5.1.1[1]; 3.1.3[2]), and thus so to speak the "zero level" of hypotactic constructions. It subordinates adverbially, but leaves the logical relationships between the main and subordinate clauses implicit, and thus does not explicitly identify the subordinate clauses as causal ("as", "because"), temporal ("when", "after"), concessive ("although", "despite"), or modal ("(just) as", "how") relationships — notwithstanding that the internal conditions of our languages may necessitate us now and then to insert those conjunctions in our translations. *[implicit hypotaxis]*

Like other languages exploiting implicit hypotaxis (participles, gerunds), Late Egyptian also offers the possibility of rendering the logical relationship between main and subordinate clauses explicit. This is accomplished using particular prepositional combinations; almost free combinations of the Middle Egyptian style are still common in the hierarchically higher registers of text while in literary texts and documents from daily life these prepositional combinations are sometimes still productive, but have become mostly morphologically bound forms and are sometimes recognizable only etymologically. One example of the older types of prepositional combination: *[explicit hypotaxis] (pD'Orb 14,3)* [hieroglyphs] *iw ḥȝ.ty=f ꜥḥꜥ r s.t=f*

iw=f ḥr ḫpr mỉ wnn=f "And his heart rested at its place, and he became as he had been";

Notes:

> *ꜥḥꜥ r s.t=f* "to stand at its correct place", Old Perfective;
>
> *ḫpr mỉ wnn=f* traditional construction: prepositional rection of *ḫpr* with nominal form of verb *wnn*, "to be as before".

preposition with verbal form   The majority of such combinations can be traced back to the possibilities available in Middle Egyptian where, besides from nouns and infinitives even nominal verb forms (cf. § 5.3.1) could also depend on prepositions (as in *ḥr mȝȝ=f; m mrr=f; ḫft sḏm.n=f*). As such constructions were no longer usual (cf. supra § 2.3.3), the prepositional combinations which do appear must be understood in the context of the Late Egyptian system as bound combinations. In principle the fixed combinations formed with the earlier prepositions and nominal verbal forms acquired the status of conjunctional conjugations: these are the combinations of the preposition *m-ḏr* with the subjunctive-prospective *sdm=f* — termed Temporal — and the preposition *r/r-šȝꜥ* with *sdm.t=f* — termed Terminative (cf. supra § 2.3.32[2]).

Combinations with the prepositions *mỉ, m-ḫt* und *r-ṯnw/r-tnw* still occasionally appear with *sdm=f*. Where they do appear it is generally with verbs which, like *wbn* and *ḫꜥ*, have religious connotations; hence they are clearly dropping out of use. The combination with *ḫft* appears only in the epistolary expression *ḫft spr tȝy=ỉ šꜥ.t r=k*, "when my letter reaches you":

(pKoller 3,5) [hieroglyphs]

ḫft spr tȝy=ỉ šꜥ.t r=k iw=k ḥr dỉ.t grg pȝ inw m iḫ.t=f nb "When my letter reaches you, you should take care of the tribute in every detail." (*LEM* 118,17 - 119,1);

Notes:

> *iw=k ḥr dỉ.t* "old" *iw* clause or NIMS;
>
> *m iḫ.t=f nb* the tribute "in all its things, details".

preposition with infinitive   Functionally, the other possible Middle Egyptian construction are replaced with combinations of preposition + infinitive, and are thus adjusted to the features of the Late Egyptian language. In the broadest sense these include infinitive combinations like *r-ḏd*, *ḥnꜥ ḏd* + clause (cf. supra § 5.3.1[1]). In the narrow sense include combinations with "conjugated" infinitives — whether only etymologically recognizable like the Conjunctive (< *ḥnꜥ sdm ntf*), or still productive like the combinations of infinitive with possessive pronoun (*pȝy=f sdm*) or infinitive with article and relative form (*pȝ sdm ỉ.ỉr=f*).

anticipation   Reinforced with the particle *ỉr*, conjunctional clauses can now also occasionally precede the superordinate sentence; they can also form the initial phrase of clause complexes which do not include independent elements, consisting rather of a series of mutually supportive phrases (as in Middle Egyptian in general, cf. supra § 5.1 and infra § 6). Sentences beginning with adverbials became normal in Coptic, but not with any of the earlier circumstantial forms, whether in the form of adverbs or of prepositional combinations or circumstantial clauses; and in Late Egyptian too the position following the main clause is still the more common.

Conjunctional clauses are primarily forms indicating temporal subordination; they can be summarized as follows (cf. supra § 3.4.1):

	Form	**Function**	**Meaning paraphrase**
Preposition + infinitive	*m pꜣy=f sdm*		*"on his hearing" > "when/while he hears"
negated	*m pꜣy=f tm sdm*		"when he does not hear"
(preterital)	*m pꜣ sdm ỉ.ỉr=f*		*"on the hearing which he did" > "when/because he heard"
negated	*m pꜣ tm sdm ỉ.ỉr=f*		"when he did not hear"
Conjunctional combination with infinitive	*mtw=f sdm* (<*ḥnꜥ ntf sdm*)	Conjunctive	"and he will hear"
negated	*mtw=f tm sdm*		"and he will not hear"
Conjunctional combination with sdm=f	*ḏr/m-ḏr sdm=f*	Temporal	"when he (had) heard"
	m-ḫt sdm=f		"after he (had) heard"
	r-tnw sdm=f		"whenever he hears"
	(*ḫft spr=f*)		"when he arrived"
Conjunctional combination with *sdm.t=f*	*ỉ.ỉr.t=f sdm/ šꜣꜥ-ỉ.ỉrt=f sdm*	Terminative	"until he hears"

Observation:

m-ḏr compound preposition (earlier form *ḏr* "as", "since", "because"), with the usual writing , as well as the following alternatives , , , and even occasionally ;

r-tnw compound preposition formed with the preposition *r* and the nominal *tnw/ṯnw* "every one" (+ noun or *sdm=f*; *ṯnw rnp.t* "every year") meaning "every time that", "as often as (he hears)";

ỉ.ỉr.t=f sdm < *r* + *sdm.t=f/ỉr.t=f sdm*.

Examples of the rarer conjunctional clauses:

(pLansing 13a, 8-10)

mnt.k ꜥn ḏr.t ḥr s:ḥtpy r-ḥꜣ.t nb nṯr.w r-tnw ḫꜥ=f "You are someone who handles the censer gracefully before the lord of the gods whenever he appears."

Notes:

    structure   Nominal Sentence proper (cf. § 4.2.1) extended with conjunctional conjugation;

    ꜥn ḏr.t   participle of an adjective-verb (*ꜥn*) with a qualifying noun, "someone who is fine-handed" > "someone with graceful movements";

    ḥr   to be "under" something = to carry or hold it;

    r-tnw ḫꜥ=f   conjunctional conjugation as sentence adverbial.

(Graffito KRI III 437,3-5)

iy in zḫꜣ.w Ptḥ-m-wiꜣ ḥnꜥ ity=f zḫꜣ.w Yw-p r mꜣꜣ šw.t mr.w m-ḫt iw.t=sn "(Year 50, 1. pr.t day 6,) Visit of Secretary Ptahemwiya and his father Secretary Yupa in order to view the pyramid fields, after thcy came" (Reign of Ramesses II);

Notes:

    iy in zḫꜣ.w   infinitive of *iy* "come" with agent, *"Coming by the scribe";

    m-ḫt iw.t=sn   preposition with subjunctive *sḏm=f*: conjunctional conjugation as sentence adverbial.

5.4.2 Temporal circumstantial clauses and the conjugated infinitive

(1) The circumstantial clause of anteriority: the Temporal

function and meaning

The conjugation form *m-ḏr sḏm=f* is the most common of the conjunctional conjugations (the various written forms in which it appears are given in the table and observation, supra § 5.4.1). The form implies an unspecified past time relative to the temporal position of the main sentence to which it is subordinated. According to the context, this can be translated with conjunctions like "after", "when", "as", "since", etc. This can occasionally also be done quite specifically, espressing an act as past if it began before the time of the main clause but is still continuing ("he went while I was still eating"). The form continued to play this role and is preserved in Coptic: (*m-ḏr sḏm=f* > Demotic *n-tꜣy sḏm=f/n-drt ir=f sdm* > ⲚⲦⲈⲢⲈϤⲤⲰⲦⲘ).

(Wenamun 2, 76)

iw=i gm.t=s m-ḏr pr=s n pꜣy=s wꜥ pr
    iw=s n ꜥq m pꜣy=s ky

"I found her as she was leaving one of her residences and entering the other."

Notes:

=s	the city-princess Hatiba of Alasia;
m-ḏr pr=s	Temporal;
n pȝy=s wᶜ pr	preposition *n* < *m*; *wᶜ* is the nucleus of the nominal phrase, *pr* the satellite: *"from her one house", i.e. "the (first) one of her (two) houses";
ỉw=s n ᶜq	Present Circumstantial (preposition *n* < *m* with verbs of motion), as the continuation of the Temporal.

 *wr r pȝ hrw m-ḏr*
(Wenamun 1, 50-51)

ỉw=k n pȝ nty ʾImnw ỉm "How long has it been until today since you came from where Amun is?";

Notes:

occurrence	Wenamun 1,50-51 = 1,x+15-x+16;
wr r pȝ hrw	Adverbial Sentence with NP (nominal interrogative pronoun *wr* "how much?") and preposition *r* + NP;
ỉw=k n NP	*ỉw=k m (>n)* place "come from a place".

The nuance of *m-ḏr* as "since", as in this sentence, can occasionally be strengthened "since" with a preceding *(r-)ȝᶜ*, *ȝᶜ-m-ḏr sḏm=f* "since he heard".

The Temporal can stand at the beginning of a sentence if this is not a "closed complex" sentence initial (cf. infra § 6). In contrast to other conjunctional sentences, it does however require the support of the particle 𓇋 *ỉr*:

(pD'Orb 5,1)

ỉr m-ḏr (>n-ḏr.ty) ỉw.t=f r ỉtȝ n=k pr.t ỉw=f gm=ỉ ḥms.kw wᶜ "When he came to get the seed corn for you, he found me sitting alone";

Notes:

ỉr m-ḏr ỉw.t=f	Temporal introducing a sentence; the grapheme *n-ḏr.ty* for *m-ḏr* already adumbrates the Demotic/Coptic writing ⲚⲦ-; the decision to make any particular transliteration is purely pragmatic and the conventional transliteration simplifies its recognition here;
ỉw=f gm=ỉ	Present Circumstantial as NIMS (cf. supra § 5.2);
wᶜ	"seated woman" is used as a semogram of the 1st pers. sing. fem. (here moreover symbolically for the ending of the Old Perfective 1st pers.);
structure	none of the elements is an independent sentence (sentence conjugation or Nominal Sentence), so that the sentence is constructed out of a series of mutually supportive phrases (Temporal & Circumstantial). Such forms will be treated below (cf. infra § 6).

The following examples have already been cited elsewhere (particularly in the earlier exercises):

(Beatty Love Songs vs. C4,2) gmḥ=f r=ỉ m-ḏr znny=ỉ "He looked at me as I passed" (for the hieroglyphic text, cf. supra § 2.2.6 Exercise [2]);

(pAbbott 5,1) ỉw.tw dỉ.t n=f ỉr.t=f m-ḏr pḥ=f st (A commission has bound a man's eyes and taken him to the plundered tombs) "And his sight was given to him after he had reached them" (cf. hieroglyphic text supra § 3.4.2[2]);

(pBoulaq 10 rt. 9-10) ḥr ỉw mbw.pw=w qrs ỉrm pȝy=ỉ ỉty m-ḏr/m.dỉ qrs=f pȝy=f ỉt ḥnꜥ tȝy=f mȝw.t "... although they did not do the burying together with my father when he buried his father and mother" (for the hieroglyphic text, cf. supra § 3.5.4 Exercise);

(pBM 10052, 5,18-19) dd.tw n zḫȝ.w T-t-šrỉ ḥr.y-(ỉr.y-)ꜥȝ P3-kȝ.w-m-pȝ-wbȝ ỉw ỉ.ỉr=n dỉ.t n=w m-ḏr sdm(=w) sw ỉw bpy=w šm r tȝy s.t ỉrm=n "We included the scribe Tetisheri and the Porter Pkaumap-waba, and we included them again when they heard about it, although they did not come with us to that place" (for the hieroglyphic text, cf. supra § 4.5 Exercise).

(2) The circumstantial clause of posteriority: the Terminative

In order to limit the temporal range of validity of the statements made by main clauses, Late Egyptian uses the conjunctional conjugation ỉ.ỉr.t=f-sdm (<r-ỉr.t=f-sdm) with its variant šꜥ-ỉ.ỉr.t=f-sdm, from Dynasty XX (further abbreviated to Demotic šꜥ.tw=f-sdm, Coptic ϢⲀ(Ⲛ)ⲦϤⲤⲰⲦⲘ̅; cf. supra § 2.3.2[2]); it limits the validity "until" a point in time following the time of the main clause. This form of the circumstantial thus combines relative future time with a condition or demand:

(pTurin 1977 rt. 7-8)

ỉmm sw n=s ỉ.ỉr.tw=ỉ ỉy mtw=ỉ ptr pȝ šȝw nb ỉr.t=f mtw=ỉ ỉr.t=f n=s "Give it to her until I come and see what must be done, and do it for her";

Notes:

ỉmm sw n=s   pronominal reference: sw "it" refers to the income of the deceased mother; n=s "her" means the sister of the recipient of the letter;

ỉ.ỉr.tw=ỉ ỉy   Terminative indicating the temporal limits of the validity of the preceding instruction;

mtw=ỉ ptr NP   Conjunctive (like mtw=ỉ ỉr.t=f) as continuation-form of the Terminative;

pȝ šȝw nb ỉr.t=f   nominalized participle of the function verb šȝ + infinitive ("to specify or instruct what is to be done"), "everything that has to be decided to do" (=f is the resumptive pronoun refering to the antecedent, cf. supra § 5.1.2.[2]).

sentence initial   Like the Temporal, the Terminative can also occasionally be the initial phrase in a complex sentence.

(Wenamun 2,66)

šꜥ.tw ỉḫ ỉy ỉw=ỉ dy ḫꜥ.tw "How long am I supposed to stay here, being left behind?" (*"Until what comes am I left here?");

Notes:

context   the preceding sentence is given supra § 3.1.3(2), "Look at them (the birds) going to the marshes!";

š3ʿ.tw ỉḥ ỉy   abbreviated form of *š3ʿ-ỉ.ỉr.t=f-sdm* placed first with the nominal interrogative pronoun *ỉḥ* as agent;

ỉw=ỉ dy ḫ3ʿ.tw   Present Circumstantial with adverb and Old Perfective; for the form of the Old Perfective (*ḫ3ʿ.tw*), cf. supra § 2.2.3(2);

structure   none of the elements is an independent sentence (sentence conjugation or nominal sentence); the sentence is thus constructed with mutually supportive phrases (Terminative + Circumstantial): such constructions are treated at length infra, § 6.

The following examples have already been quoted elsewhere:

ḏd t3.ty ỉ.t3y t3y s.t-ḥm.t ỉmm sw m rmt-s3w ỉ.ỉr.tw=tw gm ỉt3w-rmt r s:ʿḥ ʿ=s "The Vizier said, 'Seize this woman. Put her under guard until a thieving person is found to raise a claim against her.'"; *(pBM 10052, 15,8-9)*

ỉmm ỉn.tw=f š3ʿ-ỉ.ỉr.tw=ỉ šm r rsy mtw=ỉ dỉ.t ỉn.tw n=k p3y=k gb nb.t m-r3-ʿ "Deliver it until I go South and send all your expenses back" (for the hieroglyphic texts of both examples, cf. supra § 2.3.2[2]). *(Wenamun 2,36-37)*

(3) Infinitive constructions as conjugations

Middle Egyptian sentences could be extended with constructions using prepositions and nominal verb forms. In Late Egyptian this role was taken over by syntagmas where the infinitive, as a defined and "conjugated" verbal noun, was dependent on the prepositions. Aside from fulfilling a nominal position after a preposition, infinitives could in principle appear in several different nominal positions in the sentence (e.g., as object, in nominal sentences, as apposition, etc.), and the same is true of this defined and conjugated infinitive. It has the form of *preposition + p3y=f sdm/p3 sdm ỉ.ỉr=f*

— an infinitive qualified with the possessive article: *m p3y=f sdm*, used as a present or future tense (cf. supra § 2.3.3[1]); negated *m p3y=f tm sdm*;

— an infinitive qualified with a relative form of *ỉrỉ*: *m p3 sdm ỉ.ỉr=f*, used as a past tense (cf. supra § 2.3.3[2]); negated *m p3 tm sdm ỉ.ỉr=f*. A pronominal object is used as the suffix of the infinitive (*p3 sdm=s ỉ.ỉr=f* *"the hearing of her that he did"), a nominal object follows the relative form (*p3 sdm ỉ.ỉr=f sn.t* *"the sister-hearing that he did").

The prepositions with which the conjugated prepositional phrases are formed determine the logical relationship to the sentences which they extend: the relations are thus as multi-faceted as the prepositions. These references can be more or less faithfully reproduced in translation with the corresponding verbal nouns (*m-s3 p3y=f šm* "after his going"), but it is frequently more appropriate to translate using a subordinate clause, usually temporal or causal: *the logic of subordination*

Temporal connotation:

(pBologna
1086, 2-3)

[hieroglyphic text]

tw=ỉ ḥr ḏd n pȝ Rꜥw Ḥrw-ȝḫ.ty m pȝy=f wbn m pȝy=f ḥtp ... "I ask Pre-harakhte at his rising and his setting ..., (that he give health, life and prosperity)" (or alternatively, "when he rises and when he sets");

(pKairo 58056
rt. 6-7)

ỉw=ỉ r dỉ.t ỉn.tw n=k pȝ kr m pȝy=ỉ spr "I will send you the boat on my arrival" (or, "I will send you the boat when I arrive"; for the hieroglyphic text, cf. supra § 2.3.3[1]);

(pBM 10052,
4,7-8)

ỉw=k ỉn pȝy ḥḏ ỉm r-bnr (m-)sȝ pȝ šm ỉ.ỉr nȝ ỉȝw "And you brought this silver out of there after the thieves had gone" (for the hieroglyphic text, cf. supra § 2.3.3[2]).

As a causative:

(LRL 18, 4-5)

[hieroglyphic text]

m dy.t ḥȝ.ty=tn m-sȝ=ỉ n-ȝbw pȝy ỉy ỉ.ỉr nȝ ꜥḏd ỉ.wn ỉrm=ỉ "Don't worry about me just because the children who were with me came back" (or "just because of this return by the little ones who were with me");

(LRL 20, 5-6)

ỉw m-ỉr mdw m-bȝḥ ky ỉw ỉ.ỉr=k ršw n pȝy=k tm mdw ỉrm wꜥ ỉ.ỉr.t(=ỉ) ỉy "... without talking in anybody else's presence, for you'll be happy, if you haven't spoken with anyone until I come back!" (*"for you'll be happy about your not talking"; for the hieroglyphic text, cf. supra § 5.1.1[1]).

(pAnast. VI 33-
34)

ỉ.ỉr=w r=k ... ḥr pȝ ỉṯȝ ỉ.ỉr=k nȝ ḥbs.wt n tȝ mr.t m-bȝḥ ỉmy-rȝ pr-ḥḏ "It happened that they acted against you ... because of your seizure of the garments of the weavers in the presence of the Superintendent of the Treasury" (for the hieroglyphic text, cf. supra § 2.3.3[2]).

An example of a concessive reference, where the subordinated clause concedes something, or specifies insufficient counter-justification:

(pAnast. V
21,6-7)

[hieroglyphic text]

ḥr bw ꜥḥꜥ=f r dỉ.t ỉn.tw n=f sm m pȝ ḥsp
m-sȝ pȝ tm dỉ.t ỉ.ỉr=f ꜥm=ỉ m ꜥm n rwhȝ ỉ.ỉr=f ỉy n=ỉ

"He could not even wait to have the greens sent to him from the garden although he didn't let me know which evening he would be coming to me";

Notes:

       bw ꜥḥꜥ=f Negative Aorist;

ꜥm=ỉ m ꜥm	construction with the complementary infinitive (cf. Erman, *Neuägyptische Gramamtik*, § 421); ꜥm=ỉ is the object noun clause of dj.t;
n r-w	< m rwhꜣ (r-w-h);
rwhꜣ ỉ.ỉr=f ỉy n=ỉ	relative phrase (relative form) without the otherwise necessary resumption, since the reference noun is a temporal expression ("absolute" or "zero-reference"), cf. supra § 5.1.2(2) Observation.

5.4.3 The Conjunctive

(1) Construction and usage

Structurally, the Conjunctive is an analytic form of conjugation, formed with the conjugation base *mtw* followed by an agent/subject and a meaning expression in the form of an infinitive (cf. supra § 2.3.3[3]). As with other conjugations of this type, the infinitive can be preceded by the prepositions *ḥr* or *r*, which is systematically inconsistent — the prepositions have become mere markers of the meaning expression. Although the morphological origin of the conjugation as a bound prepositional syntagma can no longer be recognized, the Conjunctive is here classified along with the Temporal and the Terminative as a conjunctional sentence.

Along with the sentences converted with *ỉw* — particularly the Present Circumstantial as NIMS (cf. supra § 5.2) — the Conjunctive *mtw=f sdm* is the most important form of subordination in Late Egyptian (and Demotic and Coptic). Together, the *ỉw*-conversions and the Conjunctive were used to express nuances in a subtle interactive fashion. The conditions governing the use of the Conjunctive can be defined as follows:

1. Basically, it co-ordinates verbal nouns (*ḥnꜥ* as a nominal coordinator); by means of grammatical joining, verbal nouns/infinitives acquire the same functional role as the preceding verbal nouns/infinitives. Thus, according to the principle, from *ỉw=f r sdm ỉw=f r md.t* "He shall hear; he shall speak" comes **ỉw=f r sdm ḥnꜥ md.t ntf > ỉw=f r sdm mtw=f md.t* "He shall listen and speak" — *infinitive coordination*

(Wenamun 2, 54-55)

ỉstw bw ỉr=k rš mtw=k dỉ.t ỉry.tw n=k wꜥ wḏy mtw=k ḏd ḥr=f hꜣb n=ỉ ꜣImnw-Rꜥw ... ꜣImnw-tꜣ-mỉ.t "Can't you rejoice, and make yourself a stele and say on it, 'Amun-Re ... sent me Amun-of-the-Route'?";

Notes:

bw ỉr=k rš	Negative Aorist, "You are not capable of rejoicing";
mtw=k dỉ.t ỉry.tw	Conjunctive as substitute for **bw ỉr=k dỉ.t ỉry.tw* "You aren't capable of having something done";

'Imnw-t3-mi.t "Amun of the Route", a form of Amun as patron of travellers.

verbal form coordination

2. Like the Present Circumstantial as a co-ordinating clause (in "and"-function — NIMS, cf. supra § 5.2), the Conjunctive expresses a natural course of events by coordinating its meaning-expression infinitive with the meaning expression of the reference sentence. If not used in their co-ordinating role, *iw*-conversions can, however, affect other members of sentences, while the Conjunctive can affect only the verbal content of the main clause. Unlike the *iw*-conversions, the Conjunctive co-ordinates actions which are semantically related (such as "eat and drink"). As a sentence extension it is strictly ad-verbal, and never ad-nominal: it can express only processes or actions.

(LRL 47,3-5)

(r-dd) hn=<t>n ir n=i w^c shn

        iw bwpwy=tn šm n=f ^cn

mtw=tn wh3=f i.ir.t=i spr r=tn

"Hurry up, and carry out a task for me, which you have not yet done, and keep at it until I reach you!";

Notes:

iw bwpwy=tn šm *n=f ^cn*	Negative Preterite Circumstantial in adnominal use, "(a task), for which you have never gone";
mtw=tn wh3=f	Conjunctive as the continuation of an initial prospective *hn=tn* "You should hurry", with imperative *ir*.

imperative-prospective co-ordination

3. Generally, the main clause which the Conjunctive continues is a sentence built by an Imperative, Prospective or Third Future, or another type of sentence concerning the future. Although this function is characteristic of the Conjunctive, it is not immediately derived from the origin of the form, but conditioned by the framework of the system within which the Conjunctive fulfils its role — what might be termed the "mood" system of Late Egyptian.

(LRL 32,9-10) *rh p3 imw p3 rmt r.nty iw=k di.t n=f t3y š^c.t mtw=k ir.t rn=f hr=s* "Discover the boat and the man to whom you should give the letter, and put his name on it" (For the hieroglyphic text, cf. supra § 5.1.2[4]).

(2) The Conjunctive as a "mood"

The Conjunctive and the Present Circumstantial — particularly in its function as non-initial main sentence (NIMS) — are complementary in three ways: (a) in terms of the types of sentence which they extend; (b) in terms of the forms with which they share the function of sentence extension; and (c) finally in that they are both the least specific forms within their respective arrays of forms, that they form the "zero"-level of the array. These connections can be summarized as follows:

The Present Circumstantial is primarily used to extend those sentence-forms which describe, state and declare — sentences which make statements about reality: First Present, Preterite, Emphatic Sentence, Nominal Sentence. It works together with the various *iw*-conversions, and the analytic forms, the *m-dr sdm=f* Temporal and the conjugated infinitives (supra § 5.4.2[3]). It is the form most commonly used and least specific in meaning in this category of sentence extension. The category is that of the forms of the "indicative mood" — those which permit the formulation of statements about reality. The other forms make various kinds of logical relationships explicit; the Present Circumstantial (NIMS) leaves them implicit.

indicative mood

The Conjunctive form *mtw=f sdm* is primarily used to extend those sentences which request and predict, express desires or intentions — sentences which makes utterances about considered or reflected, unreal or as yet unreal situations: Imperative, Causative Imperative, Prospective, Third Future, Negative Aorist, and the "not yet" form. It also includes sentences and constructions discussing the future, without being request or future forms in the strict sense. The Conjunctive functions together with the relevant *iw*-conversions (*iw* + Third Future or negative Imperative), final *sdm=f*/Finalis or *r* + infinitive. It is the most commonly used form and the least meaningful in this category of sentence extension. The category here is that of the forms of the "subjunctive mood" — those which are used to reproduce opinions or demands: where wish, possibility, uncertainty, and the unreal are expressed. While other forms make various logical relationships explicit, the Conjunctive conveys them implicitly. This can be summarized as in the table on p. 234.

subjunctive mood

For the complementarity of explicit and implicit forms and the modal component of the Conjunctive, compare:

imm in.tw mtrw mtw=f s:ˁhˁ=i "Bring a witness, and let him accuse me!" (for the hieroglyphic text, cf. supra § 2.3.3[3]) with

(pMayer A vs. 8,18-19)

imm in.tw rmt r s:ˁhˁ=i "Bring someone to accuse me!"

(pMayer A vs. 8,24 and pas-sim)

Sentence forms		Sentence extension forms	
		explicit	implicit
First Present	affirmative	$iw=f$ (hr) $sdm/sdm.w/m$ pr	$iw=f$ (hr) sdm
	negated	iw bn sw (hr) $sdm/sdm/m$ pr	iw bn sw (hr) $sdm/iw=f$ (hr) tm sdm
Preterite	affirmative	iw $sdm=f$	
	negated	iw $bwpw=f$ sdm	**(indicative mood)**
Emphatic Sentence		iw $i.ir=f$ sdm m pr	
Nominal Sentence		iw + Nominal Sentence	
Imperative			$mtw=f$ sdm
	Prohibitive	iw $m-ir$ sdm	$mtw=f$ tm sdm
		iw $m-dyt$ $sdm=f$	
Prospective			**(subjunctive mood)**
		$final$ $sdm=f$/Finalis	
		r + infinitive	
Third Future			$mtw=f$ sdm
	affirmative	iw $iw=f$ (r) sdm	
	negated	iw bn $iw=f$ (r) sdm	
Neg. Aorist			$mtw=f$ $sdm/iw=f$ sdm
		iw $bw-ir=f$ sdm	
"not yet"			
		iw bw $ir.t=f$ sdm	
sentence		$š^c$-$i.irt=f$ sdm	$mtw=f$ sdm

Observations:

For the absence of the explicit (syndetic) subordination of the Imperative by means of iw, cf. supra § 3.4.0(2).

The Conjunctive form also appears quite frequently also as the secondary co-ordinating form in chains of clauses extending sentences, in other words where, within the chain, the primary extension-form is explicit. The same applies to sentences which are extended with the Terminative ("sentence" in the table signifies all sentence conjugations and sentence forms which are possible in this context). As a rule this involves an extension using the Conjunctive of conditional sentences and "closed" syntactic complexes with future meaning (cf. infra § 6.2).

(3) Usage

Continuation with the Conjunctive is very common after

— Imperatives and Causative Imperatives

— sentence building Prospectives (independent prospective $sdm=f$)

— The Third Future and other forms of future expression.

Beyond these usages, the following co-ordination syntagmas can also be formed:

— Continuation of the initial phrase of an oath (prospective *sdm=f* and similar conditional in oaths constructions (e.g., *ỉr*-phrases):

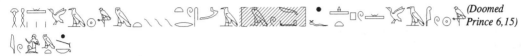

(Doomed Prince 6,15)

wȝḥ pȝ Rᶜw mtw=tw smȝ=f

ḥtp pȝ šw ỉw=ỉ mwt.kw

"As Pre endures, if he should be executed, I will be dead when the sun sets" (< **"As Pre endures, and he is executed, (the following is true): when the sun sets, I am dead");

Notes:

    mtw=tw smȝ=f actually *mtw=tw{tw r} smȝ=f*;

    ḥtp pȝ šw drawn from Middle Egyptian, a slightly Late Egyptianized extraposition (topicalization) formed from a noun phrase followed by an earlier independent *ỉw*-sentence (cf. infra § 6). The preceding, topicalized noun phrase consists of the nominal *sdm=f* of *ḥtp*.

From this derived an apparently independent use of the Conjunctive — by the abbreviation of the initial formula of the oath (without *wȝḥ pȝ Rᶜw*, etc; cf. infra § 7.1.3[2]).

(pBerlin P. 10496 vs. 11-12)

ỉw tȝ qnb.t ḥr dỉ.t ỉry=f ᶜnḫ n nb ᶜ.w.s. r-ḏd

mtw=j ᶜq r pȝy m-ḫ-y jw=f ḥr 100 n sḫ.t 5 wbnw

"And the tribunal made him swear an oath of the Lord as follows: 'If I enter this burial chamber, [I] will be subject to 100 blows and 5 lacerations!'";

Notes:

    mtw=ỉ ᶜq after the initial *r-ḏd*, "independent", but only apparently, since resulting from abbreviation;

    ỉw=f ḥr 100 n sḫ.t old *ỉw*-sentence or Present Circumstantial (in NIMS-function) with the preposition *ḥr* "he will be under 100 blows" (cf. supra §§ 3.2.2[2] and 5.2.3, and Frandsen, *Outline*, § 115,3[2e]);

    pronoun change for the change of the personal pronoun as a structural element of indirect speech, cf.
    =ỉ/=f supra § 5.3.2(3).

— Continuation of the Negative Aorist:

following
Neg. Aorist

(Wenamun 2, 54-55)

 *ı̓st bw ı̓r=k rš*

mtw=k dı̓.t ı̓ry=tw n=k w^c wḏ "Can't you rejoice, and make yourself a stele?" (cf. supra, sub [1]);

Note:

  ı̓st indication of tonal questions.

following prosp. *sdm=f*

— Continuation of final-prospective *sdm=f*:

(LRL 70,1-3)

ı̓mm ḥn=w r ı̓n nꜣ ı̓t tm nꜣ rmt ḥqr

mtw=w ws(f) m pꜣ sḥn n Pr-ꜥꜣ ꜥ.w.s

"Have them go to fetch grain so that the people do not become hungry and neglect Pharaoh's affairs";

Notes:

  tm nꜣ rmt ḥqr negated final *sdm=f*;
  m pꜣ sḥn n Pr-ꜥꜣ "(to be occupied) on Pharaoh's business".

following the Terminative

— The continuation of the Terminative ("until") reveals the characteristic "prospective" function expressing anticipatory thought (naming a situation which at the moment of speaking exists only in thought):

(Wenamun 2,36-37)

ı̓mm ı̓n.tw=f šꜥ-ı̓.ı̓r.tw=ı̓ šm r rsy mtw=ı̓ dı̓.t ı̓n.tw n=k pꜣy=k gb nb.t m-rꜣ-ꜥ "Deliver it until I go South and have all your expenses paid" (for the hieroglyphic text, cf. supra § 2.3.2[2]);

(pTurin 1977, 7-8)

ı̓mm sw n=s ı̓.ı̓r.tw=ı̓ ı̓y mtw=ı̓ ptr pꜣ šw nb ı̓r.t=f mtw=ı̓ ı̓r.t=f n=s "Give it to her until I come and see what must be done, and do it for her" (for the hieroglyphic text, cf. supra § 5.4.2[2]).

In texts with a high proportion of instructions — generally letters from superiors — the Conjunctive can be employed at completely different levels of text structure: continuing immediately preceding statements, but also those which lie further back. Compare as an example pLeiden I 370:

(LRL 9,4) ... *tw=ı̓ ḏd n ꜣImnw-Rꜥw-Ḥrw-ꜣḫ.ty* ... "... I ask Amun-Re-Harakhte ..."
(LRL 9,6) ... *ḫ[nꜥ ḏd] r.nty sdm=ı̓ mdw.t nb* ... "... And (I) say furthermore: I have taken notice of everything ..."
(LRL 9,16) ... *wn(n) pꜣ mw mḥ ı̓w=k šzp n-ḫꜣ.t n tꜣy ꜥqꜣy* ... "... If the inundation rises, you should requisition that barge, ..." ... *(LRL* 10,1) ... *mtw=k dı̓.t sw n nꜣ wḥꜥ* ... "... and give it to the fishermen ..."

(*LRL* 10,9) ... *mtw=k ptr nꜣ ꜥḏd šrî* ... "... and you should look to the children";

Note:

> *mtw=k ptr*   the last conjunctive listed is not in a chain with the others, but goes back to the text organizing infinitive *ḥnꜥ ḏd r.nty*.

Observation:

Those uses of the Conjunctive which have been described as "independent" should be mentioned here (cf. Frandsen, *Outline*, § 83; M. Lichtheim, Notes on the Late-Egyptian Conjunctive, in: *Studies in Egyptology and Linguistics in Honour of H. J. Polotsky, The Israel Exploration Society*, Jerusalem 1964, 4ff): the Conjunctive in these cases is independent only of the immediately preceding forms, and actually dependent on forms appearing earlier in the text.

While the modal component of the Conjunctive remains implicit in the texts cited, *modal nuance* being already present in the forms which the conjunctive continues, it becomes clear in contexts which do not belong to the genuine context of the Conjunctive:

— Continuation of forms of essentially tenseless character, e.g., special infinitive constructions:

(pSalt 124 rt.2, 13)

sḫꜣ r pꜣy=f în tꜣ mḏꜣ.t ꜥꜣ.t n pꜣ rꜣ-ꜥ-bꜣk mtw=f zꜣw=s m tꜣy=f mꜥḥꜥ.t "Accusation concerning his having taken the great spike of the 'Worksite' and (allegedly) broken it in his tomb";

Notes:

> *construction*   for constructions of this type cf. Wente, in: *Polotsky-Studies*, 535ff.;

> *sḫꜣ r*   "Accusation concerning something"; for the hieroglyphic version of the hieratic ligature and reading, cf. Černý, in: *Studies presented to F.Ll. Griffith*, London 1932, 49f n.1;

> *r pꜣy=f în*   conjugated infinitive (with object *tꜣ mḏꜣ.t*) after preposition *r*, *"concerning his taking (the spike)"; *rꜣ-ꜥ-bꜣk* literally "work-in-progress", used to refer to the royal tomb currently under construction, and hence "worksite";

> *mtw=f zꜣw=s*   Conjunctive in "subjunctive" mode, "and that he supposedly broke it".

— Continuation of narrative or reporting statements, particularly where these can be described as habitual, customary, or common. The situation expressed by the Conjunctive is "foreseen" but has not yet become "real" at the time of the utterance. As elsewhere, the Conjunctive interacts with the Present Circumstantial:

(pD'Orb 1,4-7)

ḫr ỉr m-ḫt hrww qnw s3 nn

 ỉw p3y=f sn šrỉ m-s3 n3y=f ỉ3w.t m p3y=f sḫr.w nty rꜥw-nb

 mtw=f wḥꜥ r p3y=f pr r-tnw rwh3

      ỉw=f 3tp m sm.w nb n sḫ.t ...

    mtw=f w3ḥ=w m-b3ḥ p3y=f sn ꜥ3

      ỉw=f ḥms ḥnꜥ t3y=f ḥm.t

  mtw=f zwr

  mtw=f wnm

"Now, when many days had passed, his younger brother kept his cattle, according to his daily custom, and he would return home every evening, loaded with all the plants of the field ..., would lay them before his elder brother, when he was sitting with his wife, would drink and would eat";

Notes:

ḫr ỉr m-ḫt hrww qnw s3 nn	a variation of the "day formulae" which often — written in red, as rubrics — combine the marking of text divisions with narrative "quick-motion" effects. Where adverbials are anticipated (m-ḫt + noun) as here, the grammatically necessary ỉr can often be left untranslated: "after many days after this";
s3	customary abbreviation of the compound preposition ḥr-s3;
ỉw NP m-s3 NP	independent ỉw-sentence as apodosis when an ỉr-clause precedes (NIMS; as grammatical structure a remnant of Middle Egyptian grammar);
nty rꜥw-nb	strange, but fairly common attributive construction of rꜥw-nb — nty being a variant of the phrase conjunction n/n.t;
ỉw=f 3tp/ỉw=f ḥms	Present Circumstantial (with Old Perfective) as adnominal characterization, contrasting with "subjunctive" narrative expressed by the Conjunctive.

5.4.4 Bibliography

conjunctional clauses

Frandsen, *Outline*, § 15(3); 56-59; Černý/Groll, *Late Egyptian Grammar*, §§ 31-36; Winand, *Études*, §§ 392-397; 464-470; Erman, *Neuägyptische Grammatik*, §§ 443; 808-810; Johnson, *Demotic Verbal System*, 226ff; 230ff; Loprieno, *Ancient Egyptian*, §§ 7.9.3; 7.9.4; P. Collombert, in: *LingAeg* 12,2004, 21-44

preposition + infinitive

Frandsen, *Outline*, §§ 60-63; 90 C; Černý/Groll, *Late Egyptian Grammar*, § 51.9; Groll, *Negative Verbal System*, 178-188

Frandsen, *Outline*, §§ 64-84; Černý/Groll, *Late Egyptian Grammar*, §§ 42-43; E. Wente, Conjunctive
The Late Egyptian Conjunctive as a Past Continuative, in: *JNES* 21, 1962, 304ff; Winand,
Études, §§ 709-743; Depuydt, *Conjunction*, 1ff (with bibliography pp. 115ff); Erman,
Neuägyptische Grammatik, §§ 575-587; Kroeber, *Neuägyptizismen*, § 3.4; M. Lichtheim,
Notes on the Late Egyptian Conjunctive, in: *Studies in Egyptology and Linguistics in
Honour of H. J. Polotsky, The Israel Exploration Society*, Jerusalem 1964, 1ff; S.
Sauneron, Quelques emplois particuliers du conjonctif, in: *BIFAO* 61, 1962, 59ff

Hintze, *Neuägyptische Erzählungen*, 264ff in literature

Frandsen, *Outline*, § 81 in oaths

Frandsen, *Outline*, § 82; E. Wente, The Late Egyptian Conjunctive as a Past Continua- modal
tive, in: *JNES* 21, 1962, 304ff; J. Borghouts, A New Approach to the Late Egyptian components of
the
Conjunctive, in: *ZÄS* 106, 1979, 14ff; Winand, *Études*, §§ 685-688 (442ff); Groll, Conjunctive
Negative Verbal Systems, § 52 (173ff); Winand, À la croisée du temps, de l'aspect et du
mode. Le conjonctive en néo-égyptien, in: *LingAeg* 9, 2001, 293-329

5.5 Notes on linguistic evolution

5.5.1 Features of an intermediate position

The clause conjugations clearly demonstrate that Late Egyptian is a link between Middle
Egyptian and Demotic/Coptic in terms of linguistic evolution. Chronologically, this
statement may appear to be self-evident. Hitherto, however, this has not been widely
grasped empirically because linguistically compatible typological systems for both Middle
Egyptian and Demotic/Coptic had to be developed, before the evolution could be
recognized: Late Egyptian usage combines the systematic methods determining
Demotic/Coptic forms of expression with methods governing Middle Egyptian linguistic
forms (cf. supra § 5.0).

On the one hand there is the conversion system — the analytic transformation of simple conversion
sentence forms into clauses — which is characteristic of the later linguistic phases, but system
not yet completely established in Late Egyptian. Subordination of clauses with *ỉw*/Ⲉ- (cf.
supra § 5.1.1) is already highly developped but also marks an absolute reversal of the
functional role of *ỉw*, yet the independent *ỉw*-sentences of Middle Egyptian remain in use
in certain fixed combinations. A position mid-way between Middle Egyptian and the later
linguistic phases is even clearer in the conversion of relative phrases (cf. supra § 5.1.2).
Although in Middle Egyptian *nty* was already a means of transforming clauses into relative
phrases, this usage increases in Late Egyptian. At the same time, however, it was still
competing with participles and relative forms, which ultimately disappear completely in
Coptic (although occasionally still recognizable in lexicalized form).

nominalization
converter

The central nominalization of the verbal sentence, the nominal *sdm=f*, is also related to Middle Egyptian. In this case one can recognize how the "nominalization-converter" *i.ir* crystallized out of the Late Egyptian conjugation *i.ir=f-sdm* (cf. supra § 5.3.2[1]). In the patterns of emphatic clauses of the type [*i.ir=f sdm*]NP [*iw=f md.t*]AP, *i.ir=f sdm* appears (a) analogous to the construction "sentence + [*iw* [*=f md.t*]First Present]AP" as a sentence conjugation and (b) analogous to *iw* [*=f md.t*]First Present as a converted sentence of a type *i.ir* [*=f sdm*]First Present. The differentiation continues in Demotic — where the *i.ir=f-sdm* appears along with forms of the Third Future and Aorist converted with *i.ir* — and in Coptic, the use of this converter is expanded to cover the entire conjugation system (Є-/ЄТЄ-/ṄТ- + sentence conjugations).

noun clauses
and
conjunctions

On the other hand, the use of the synthetic forms of nominal and adverbial clauses declines. To a certain degree Middle Egyptian was typologically determined by the possibility of substituting nominal and adverbial phrases with forms of *sdm=f*. In Late Egyptian, this possibility was severely limited, being reduced to certain specific constructions, or firmly anchored in bound forms (cf. supra §§ 5.3.; 5.4). The combinations of prepositions with the subjunctive *sdm=f* become conjunctional clauses, constructed in an analogous way to the sentence conjugations with conjugation bases, actor and meaning expressions (cf. supra § 2.3.0). Noun clauses are already analytically marked as such (*r-dd* > ХЄ) or, in the form of the subjunctive *sdm=f* have become so specific and so limited to certain usages, that the development has already begun by which in Coptic, they either disappear completely or were reduced to the Т-causatives in lexicalizations. The circumstantial forms of the *sdm=f* are reduced to those with final function, and appear in Coptic merely in the form of the Finalis (promissory conjunctive, future conjunctive of result).

5.5.2 Development of the forms

systematic
balance

It is thus clear that Late Egyptian occupies a middle position, but it is only as an outside observer that one can follow the lines back to Middle Egyptian and on to Coptic. Within the system, of course, assuming for a moment the ability to adopt the position of one speaking the language, Late Egyptian is internally consistent and completely balanced. Normative limitation of certain older uses on the one hand and the extension of other usages (such as the converter or the continuative functions, NIMS and Conjunctive) on the other are merely the results of the speaker's choice and preference for specific syntactic possibilities.

sentence
orientation

It is thus easier to grasp the sentence orientation of the Late Egyptian system — as opposed to the phrase orientation of Middle Egyptian (cf. supra §§ 3.0, 5.0) — which is perhaps its most striking characteristic: the necessity of maintaining the elements of the

sentence completely, even where they are actually redundant in particular contexts. A
Middle Egyptian chain of forms like:

mṯn b3=ỉ ḥr thỉ.t=ỉ ...   (Leb 11-13)

    ḥr sṯ3=ỉ r mwt ...

    ḥr ḫ3ᶜ(=ỉ) ḥr ḫt ...

"Look, my Ba is injuring me ... pulling me to death ... throwing me into the fire" —

would look something like this in Late Egyptian:

*ptr b3=ỉ ḥr thỉ.t=ỉ ...

    ỉw=f ḥr sṯ3=ỉ r mwt ...

    ỉw=f ḥr ḫ3ᶜ(=ỉ) ḥr ḫt ...

    The obligatory designation of person in the Late Egyptian subordinate clause is one of
the characteristic peculiarities of the later stages of the evolution of Egyptian: the
explanation must be sought in the structure of the syntax of minimal sentences.

    The linguistic evolution of the most significant forms discussed here can be summarized
as in this table:

	Late Egyptian	**Demotic**	**Coptic**
Adverbial converter	*ỉw* + sentence	*ỉw* + sentence	Є + sentence
e.g.	*ỉw=f (ḥr) sdm*	*ỉw=f sdm*	ЄЧСШТМ̄
negated	*ỉw bn sw (ḥr) sdm*	*ỉw bn ỉw=f sdm*	ЄНЧСШТМ̄ ⲀⲚ
Relative converter	*nty* + sentence	*nty* + sentence	ЄⲦ(Є)-/ЄⲚⲦ-+sent.
e.g.	*nty tw=ỉ (ḥr) sdm*	*nty ỉw=ỉ sdm*	Є†СШТМ̄
	nty (ḥr) sdm	*nty sdm*	ЄⲦСШТМ̄
negated	*nty bn tw=ỉ (ḥr) sdm*	*nty bn tw=ỉ sdm*	ЄⲦЄ Ⲛ̄†СШТМ̄
Conjunctional clauses			
Temporal ("when")	*m-ḏr sdm=f*	*n-ḏr.t sdm=f/n-t3y sdm=f/ n-ḏr.t ỉr=f sdm*	Ⲛ̄ⲦЄⲢЄЧСШТМ̄
Terminative ("until")	*r-ỉr.t=f sdm/š3ᶜ-ỉ.ỉr.t=f sdm*	*šᶜ(m)tw=f sdm*	ШⲀ(Ⲛ)ⲦЧСШТМ̄
Conjunctive		*mtw=f sdm*	ⲚЧСШТМ̄
Final clause		final-prospective *sdm=f*	
e.g.	*dỉ=ỉ sdm=f*	*dỉ=ỉ sdm=f/dỉ=ỉ ỉr=f sdm*	ⲦⲀⲢЄЧСШТМ̄
Conjugated infinitive	prep. + *p3y=f sdm*	prep. + *p3y=f sdm*	
	p3 sdm ỉ.ỉr=f	*p3 sdm ỉ.ỉr=f/ p3 dỉ.t ỉr=f sdm*	2Ⲙ̄-ⲠⲦⲢЄЧСШТМ̄

5.6 Exercises

5.6.1 Model letter for a woman (pBologna 1094, 9,7-10,9)

A model letter from a letter-writer's guide written during the reign of Merenptah,
preserved on a papyrus in the museum of Bologna. The transcription is that published by
Gardiner, *Late Egyptian Miscellanies* (*LEM*), pp. 9-10. A woman requests one of her
servants to relieve another one — whom she has sacked — of his duties, his "oath of
office".

Purpose: Example of the epistolary style and conventions of Dynasty XIX (cf.
infra § 7.2); the use of clause conjugations (Conjunctive, NIMS,
conjunctional clauses, noun clauses; *ḥnᶜ ḏd*; *r-ḏd*)

Notes:

9,7   *Sȝ-kt > Sk*, Sake: an appelative name ("ass-foal"); the title *šms.w* is given to a higher
level of servants ("retainers") who have voluntarily entered the service of still higher
members of the social hierarchy (including Pharaoh); specifically it refers to messengers;

9,7-8   *m ᶜnḫ wḏȝ snb; m ḥz.t* god NN: typical initial formulae of epistolary style — the
recipient of the letter should be "in life, prosperity, health, and the grace of
Amonrasonther". Grammatically, these phrases are vestiges of the principle governing the construction of Middle Egyptian requests and wishes: a marked absence of the
NP (for the addressee) in the adverbial clause (cf. Junge, *Syntax*, § 8.4.1);

9,8-9   *tw=ì ḏd n* god NN *ìmm snb=k*: the characteristic formula of greeting in epistolary
style; the expression can be translated in two ways: either as "I ask god NN that [he]
(the god) let you (the addressee) be well" or as "I ask god NN, 'Let [him] be well'".
In either case, the pronominal references must be adjusted to the context. The Egyptian
form can not be "translated" literally without punctuation: this is characteristic of
indirect speech;

9,9   *ptr(=ì) tw snb.tì*: "that I see you healthy";

     mtw=ì mḥ: Conjunctive as form of continuation, related to the preceding subjunctive
sḏm=f (cf. supra § 5.4.3[3]);

     ḥnᶜ ḏd: introductory formula for the actual content of the letter: can be translated "to
the effect that", "now", etc., but need not necessarily be translated. Grammatically,
this prepositional combination can be related to a preceding verb whether real or
fictive: "I have done — or said — this-and-that, *ḥnᶜ ḏd* and say now:") — here related
to the First Present in line 9,8 ("I said to God: 'Do this-and-that', and say now ...").
To a certain extent, *ḥnᶜ ḏd* is a formal predecessor of the Conjunctive which continued
to be used;

9,9-10   *ì.ìr=t ḫȝᶜ pȝ rmṯ r-bl*: nominal *sḏm=f*, "that you have sent the man away";

9,10   *r-nfr-n=ì*: "for my benefit";

     ìs/ìst: particle, introducing parenthetical remarks and particularly common before
tonal questions (formal statements transformed into questions by tone: "You have shut
the door?"), here roughly (*ìstw bw ìr.t=k* X) "Have you still not done X?";

10,1   *bn* as negation of Nominal Sentence; here a rhetorical tonal question: "Am I not a
woman?";

10,1-2   structure: *ìr* + NP (protasis), Negative Aorist (apodosis) in tonal question;

10,3   construction: the initial conjunctional clause (*ḫft spr* NP) is continued with a First
Present Circumstantial functioning as NIMS, in a syntactically closed combination of

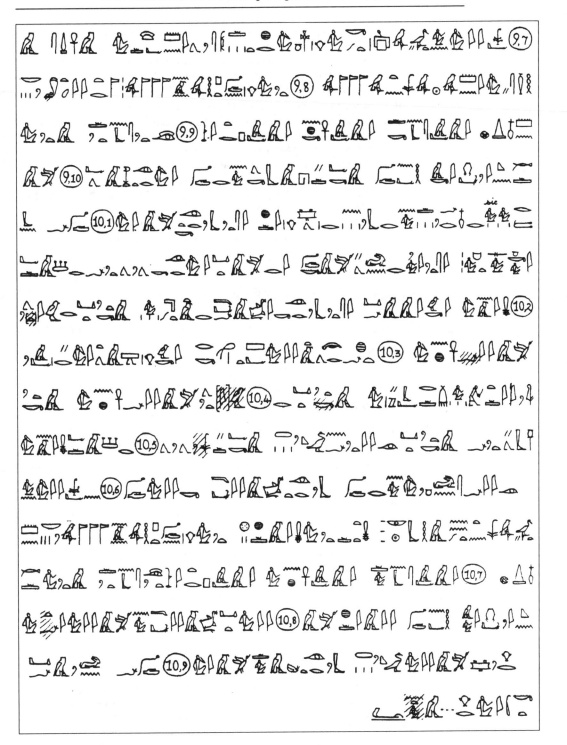

5.6.1 Exercise: pBologna 1094, 9,7-10,9

two non-independent clauses — cf. infra § 6. The Middle Egyptian *iw*-sentence stands at the origin of this form;

ʿpr-bʿy: abbreviated form of the sentence name (Adjectival Sentence) *ʿpr-bʿl* ("Baʿal is well provided" (< *"An equipped one is Baᶜal"));

10,4   *mk sw iw.w*: here actually "he has in fact come";

10,5   *bw-ir=t t3y(=i)*: roughly "You can't strip me altogether, can you!";

(10,1-5)   situation: together with a witness, Amankhau should (1) take a servant to court, whom Sake has sacked, to "liberate" him officially, and (2) provide him with a "pension" because he came to her and complained about her being too hard on him;

10,6   *Nn-nzw m ḥ3b*: sentence name ("Herakleopolis Magna is in festival");

suffixes, 1st sing. and 2nd sing. fem.: here, the 1st sing. (*=i* > *='*) and the 2nd sing. fem. (*=t* > *='*) are also not graphically distinguished, as both have been reduced to a secondary aleph (glottal stop);

10,8   *di.t t3y n=f NN*: "to cause NN to criticize him", "to let NN find fault with him";

ḥri p3y=i ʿqw: "so that my income is endangered" (< "is distant");

10,9   *wn m.di=f k.t ḥrw[=t] mnt.t*.

5.6.2 An Original Letter (pTurin 1975 = *LRL* 37, 4-14)

A short business letter from the office of General Piankhi to the Secretary of the Tomb Building Administration, Thutmose, called *Tjaroy*. It is from the last years of the "Renaissance era" of Ramesses XI, and thus the end of Dynasty XX and the New Kingdom. It was transcribed and published by J. Černý, in his collection of *Late Ramesside Letters* (*LRL*), p. 37.

Purpose: Example of the epistolary style and conventions of Dynasty XX (cf. also infra § 7.2); use of clause conjugations (relative phrases, final clauses, Conjunctive, closed complexes and *iw*-clauses; *ḥnʿ ḏd*; *r-ḏd*)

Notes:

rt. 1 (= *LRL* 37,4)   Typical epistolary form, naming both the writer and the recipient of the letter (*A n B*, "A to B"); both names are also inscribed on the outside of the folded letter (and thus will be found at the bottom of the verso of the opened letter — here, vso. 4, *LRL* 37, 14; cf. supra, § 0.3.2.;

p3 im.y-r3 mšʿ n Pr-ʿ3 ʿnḥ wḏ3 snb: "The" general of Pharaoh in Upper Egypt at this time was Herihor's successor Piankhi, the High Priest of Amun and Viceroy of Nubia during regnal years 25-29 of Ramesses XI (corresponding to years 7-11 of the *Wḥm-msw.t*, "Renaissance" era). He was the supreme commander in the campaign which lasted until year 10 of the *Wḥm-msw.t* era, against the rebel Panehsy, the Viceroy of Nubia who had been relieved. The high position of the writer of the letter is expressed by the fact that he goes straight to the point without any of the usual blessings and obliging phrases. This type of hasty writing and expression (vs. 1, *p3* rather than *p3y*; vs. 2 semogram reversals and abbreviations; vs. 3 abbreviations) is characteristic of other letters from his office too;

T-r-i-ya (imprecise for *T-r-ya*): nickname of the "Scribe of the Necropolis" Thutmose. A large proportion of the Late Ramesside Letters were written either to or by him (for biographical information, cf. Černý, *Community*, pp. 339ff);

rt. 3-4   construction: the First Present *sw m šs* is the main sentence, which is preceded by a noun with extensions (*p3 h3b*) — thus: "as far as the message is concerned" — which is repeated afterwards, more simply;

address:

5.6.2 Exercise: *LRL* 37, 4-14

rt. 3 *wḏꜥ=f*: final clause;

rt. 4 (= 37,6-8) *i̓.n=k*: "thus you said", speech marker placed after the quote (cf. supra § 3.5.1[1]);

rt. 5 *Pn-tꜣ-ḥw.t-nḫt.w*: proper name; Pentahutnakht is *zḫꜣ.w mšꜥ* "Secretary to the Army" or more precisely, *zḫꜣ.w mšꜥ n tꜣ ḥw.t nzw Wsr-mꜣꜥ.t-Rꜥw Mri̓-'Imnw m pr 'Imnw* "Secretary to the Division of the Mansion of King Wasmuaria-Maiamana in the Estate of Amun" (today the temple of Medinet Habu);

pꜣy zḫꜣ.w: apposition to preceding proper name;

vs. 1 (= 37,9) *pꜣ ꜣḫ-mnw*: probably for *pꜣy ꜣḫ-mnw* — the article would be most unusual preceding a proper name. The "affair" of Akhmenu: General Piankhi is referring to provisions for the Libyan mercenaries (Meshwesh) of the Egyptian army, who must have had a camp on the Theban West bank (cf. *LRL* 35, 2-8);

nty i̓w=f ḏd n=k i̓.i̓r sw: relative Third Future with a deeply embedded resumption, back to *tꜣ mdw* "the affair", "which he will ask you to carry out" (or, reflecting direct speech: "of which he will say to you, 'Do it'"); the agreement should be noted: *sw* (which can be either masc. or fem.) refers to the fem. *tꜣ mdw*, which is in turn referred to later in the "reference-neuter" with the suffix *=f*;

the Conjunctives continue the *ỉw*-clause of the parenthetic clause of rt. 4-5;

vs. 2   *ḏd*: abbreviation of *r-ḏd*;

ỉmm dỉ.tw ḥn.t n pȝy ḥmtỉ.y(?)/ bḏ.tỉ(?) ḥrw.y: note the absence of the article with *ḥn.t* (an idiomatic expression *rdỉ ḥn.t* "to issue an order"); the reading for "coppersmith"/"metal-worker" is unclear, the semogram of the title follows the name here. The coppersmith Hori was involved in the production of copper knives, spear-heads and vessels during the period of the correspondence between Thutmose and Piankhi (cf. *LRL* 20,10ff; 21,11-12; 51,4ff; 72,10ff);

vs. 3   the hieratic dot following *hȝb* is the 1st. pers. sing. suffix: read *hȝb=ỉ <n> zḥȝ.w NN (r) dỉ.t dỉ=f n=f*; intransitive *dỉ* with preposition *n* here, something like: "to provide him" (with a task).

5.6.3 A criminal charge (pSalt 124, rt. 2,5-18)

Part of a list of complaints against the Foreman of the Gang of the Tomb Building Administration, Paneb, preserved in pSalt 124 (now pBM 10055). These accusations were made at the end of Dynasty XIX, during the reign of Siptah, and recorded by Amunnakht, the brother of the former Foreman Neferhotep. J. Černý was the first to edit and publish the text (*JEA* 15, 1929, 243ff), and the passage reproduced here is from the recto of the papyrus.

Purpose: Example of an administrative text of late Dynasty XIX; prepositional combinations, circumstantial and relative conversions, Conjunctive.

Notes:

use of Conjunctive   note that the Conjunctive is used to continue both (a) immediately preceding statements and (b) the series of complaints in general: "Charge that he did this *and* (Conjunctive) that, *and that* (Conjunctive) he also did such and such";

2,5   *sḥȝ r*: "accusation concerning"; for the hieroglyphic transliteration of the hieratic ligature (-*r* rather than -*t*) and the reading, cf. J. Černý, in: *Studies presented to F. Ll. Griffith* (London, 1932), p. 49f n. 1 ("reminder concerning"); *sḥȝ r pȝy=f dỉ.t NN r* + infinitive "accusation that he caused NN to do this-and-that";

ḥr-ḏȝḏȝ-n: compound preposition (> ⲉ̣ⲣ̣ⲁⲛ-, ⲉ̣ⲣ̣ⲁ̄ⲱ̄⹀), here probably "at," "by";

Stš.y Mr.n Ptḥ: King Seti II (personal, or Son-of-Re, name);

2,5-6   *ỉw=w ḥr ỉṯȝ*: Present Circumstantial as qualification of an undetermined antecedent (*ỉnr*): he caused the people to break stones, taking (them) away > he caused the people to break stones which they took away;

2,7   read: *znỉ ḥr wꜥr.t*: "to pass by the Necropolis" (*wꜥr.t* is a part of the Necropolis: here, the site of the tomb under construction);

2,8   *mtw=w sḏm ḫrw=w*: "and they (the ones passing by) heard their noise" (the noise of the masons);

2,9   *nȝ ḥnr n Pr-ꜥȝ*: the copper pickaxes belonging to the state which were normally issued to the team specifically for the work;

2,10-12   a list (*r-dỉ.t-rḫ.tw*) of the stone-masons (the six names in line 11 have been omitted from the exercise): *ꜥȝ-pḥ.ty* (appellative name "Great of standing" > "whose standing is high"); *Ks* I und *Ks* II (son of Ramose); *Ḥrw-m-wỉȝ*; *Qn-ḥr-ḥpš=f*; and in line 12: *Ḫnsw; Nḫt-Mnw; Pȝ-ym* (!); *Wnn-nfr*; *ꜥȝ-nḫt=w*;

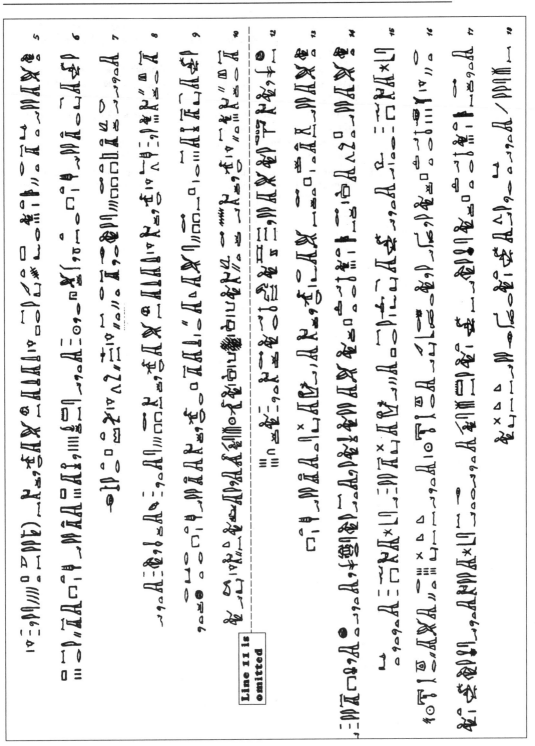

5.6.3 Exercise: pSalt 124, 2,5-18

2,14   Neferhotep (the "younger"), Paneb's predecessor, Foreman of the "left side" of the Gang from regnal year 66 of Ramesses II to year 1 of Seti II (cf. Černý, *Community*, p. 125);

       ỉw mnt.f s:ḫpr sw: converted Cleft Sentence "although it was he who raised him";

2,15-16 for the construction *dỉ rmṯ ḥr rs NN*, "have the men watch NN protectively", cf. supra § 5.3.2(2);

2,16   note the alternation between determination and lack of it with *grḥ* "night" (*m grḥ* "at night"; *m pȝy grḥ* "this night");

2,17   Amenmose was Vizier from the end of the reign of Merneptah to the beginning of the reign of Seti II;

2,18   *msy*: with semogram Gardiner Z6 as a not very respectful abbreviation for King Amenmesse (*'Imnw-msȝ-sw*), Merneptah's successor (for the writing, cf. Osing in: SAK 7 [1979], 270f.).

6. Complex sentences and simple clause groupings

6.0 Outline of the subject

Although text syntax is dominated by the complex sentences formed with minimal sentences (sentence conjugations and Nominal Sentences) and subordinate clauses, there are other types of pattern. These can be reduced to two formal types: (1) those where a dependent phrase precedes an independent main sentence (anticipation), and (2) those where two sentences and/or clauses are bound together.

Sentence structures which begin with a dependent phrase identifying the topic of the discourse ("topicalization") are generally opened with the help of the particle *ir*. The main independent sentence follows the anticipated phrase with *ir*. This can be a sentence conjugation, a Nominal Sentence, or a complex sentence.

anticipation

> Sentence, clause, phrase are terms describing larger units of meaning which have specific syntactic forms. A sentence is an independent proposition, a sequence of words capable of standing alone to make an assertion, ask a question, or give a command. A clause — as understood here — is a group of words that contains all structural elements of a sentence but does not constitute an independent proposition (a sentence), and thus is usually a subordinate clause, with an adjectival, adverbial, or nominal function in another (superordinate) clause or sentence. A phrase is a group of words forming an immediate syntactic constituent of a clause.
> As understood here, complex sentences contain one independent proposition (sentence) and one or more subordinate clauses; clause combinations are specifically bound combinations of clauses and phrases; and clause groupings are groups of several clauses which belong together.

The other type is that of the clause combination or clause grouping, and can be further classified into (a) loosely bound sentences, with two independent clauses semantically bound together, grammatically tied with a particle (such as *inn* or *hn*); and (b) closely bound "closed complexes" in which neither of the parts could stand independently.

clause binding

This division is not, however, unproblematic. Particularly in those sentences opening with an adverbial or a clause, the second position is usually occupied by a formally dependent but semantically independent clause of the *iw≠f ḥr sdm* type (or *iw≠f* + Old Perfective or *iw≠f* + preposition + NP, as the case may be), i.e., those sentences which have been termed "non-initial main sentences" and have been taken to

iw-clause in second position

differ from the Circumstantial Present. Structurally, these sentence structures are formed just like other sentence forms with a preceding element: within the paradigm, *iw=f ḥr sdm* can be replaced by sentence conjugations and Nominal Sentences. On the other hand, some of these sentences must be counted as "closed complexes" — neither the *ir*-phrase nor the *iw*-clause can stand alone.

status in the system

This situation reveals that structurally the form category being discussed here is no longer really part of Late Egyptian syntax: preserved in such covert and grammaticized constructions is the Middle Egyptian independent *iw*-sentence (cf. supra § 5.2.3). Combinations with the "old" *iw*-sentence are thus classified as sentence forms with anticipation. Accordingly, "closed complexes" are understood here, in contrast to other grammatical studies, as signifying only those combinations of the *wnn=f ḥr sdm* — *iw=f ḥr sdm* type (cf. infra § 6.2.2[1]), although they are linguistic remnants of the same kind. Hence all these constructions survived into the following stages only in the form of transformations, although widely used in Late Egyptian.

textual organization

Only superficially do these sentence constructions transgress the limits of sentential structure, whether complex or simple. Insofar as they are merely grammaticized forms of expression they do not really play a part in those higher rules and principles governing the manner in which a speaker forms a sentence using complex sentences and clause combinations. Despite their importance, these higher rules of linguistic usage do not play a part in the presentation which follows.

6.1 *ir* and the anticipation of phrases and clauses

6.1.1 Anticipation and its forms

(1) Providing a framework and establishing the topic: Topicalization

An expression can precede a sentence. The formal conditions are that (a) the sentence be independent (either a sentence conjugation or a Nominal Sentence, but under certain circumstances either a NIMS or an "old" *iw*-sentence); (b) the anticipatory expression is either a definite noun or relative phrase (with or without *ir*), or an expression introduced with *ir*. Nouns — whether following *ir* or unmarked — can be taken up in the sentence itself as pronouns:

(pAnast. V 10,6-7)

p3 šri tw=tw s:ḫpr=f r nḥm=f m qni mw.t=f "The youth, he is raised only to be torn from the embrace of his mother";

Notes:

tw=tw s:ḫpr=f First Present;

p3 šrỉ noun phrase preceding the sentence conjugation.

On a general level it can be stated that the expression placed at the start of the sentence [functions of anticipation] defines the tenor of the following sentence, naming the conditions which restrict the validity of that sentence. The manner in which this is accomplished depends upon whether the initial phrase is a nominal phrase or an adverbial clause.

Anticipatory nouns indicate the topic of discussion, identifying it as something already [nouns in anticipation] familiar to the listener or introducing it into the discourse as something about which the following sentence will make a statement ("As far as this-and-that is concerned: it is such-and-such"). Where these nouns are qualified with a prepositional infinitive, the Old Perfective or other adverbial phrases, they are formally identical with the First Present and will be reinterpreted as such by "rebracketing" even in pronominal form. In effect then, these constructions move into the role of initial adverbials ("As far as this-and-that is concerned under these circumstances: it was such-and-such").

Initial adverbials indicate the conditions limiting the validity of the following sentence. [adverbials in anticipation] On the one hand, they define temporal scope ("As far as the circumstance is concerned, that you came yesterday: it was such-and-such"). On the other hand, they can give a possible reason for the validity of a statement ("As far as the circumstance is concerned, that you have done wrong: it is such-and-such" > "If you have done wrong, it was such-and-such").

In a comprehensive sense, anticipation either (a) singles out a certain specific item [topicalization] from a chain of related things or events, identifying or marking a possible topic of discourse; or (b) establishes the temporal relationships of a chain of related situations. Anticipation is a morphological means of textual organization. Such a means of introducing topics in a text is called "topicalization" here.

(2) Forms and combinations

The basic rule governing the topicalization structure is that (a) nouns or noun phrases used in anticipation can be introduced with the particle *ỉr*, but need not; while (b) adverbials — prepositional combinations or circumstantial clauses — must be introduced by the particle *ỉr*, or sometimes by *ḫr*. The particles *ỉr* and *ḫr* can also be used together. Describing the grouping as a sentence, the initial expression can be called the "first member" or "protasis", and the following independent sentence the "second member" or "apodosis". The sentence types *ỉw=f ḫr sdm* (NIMS), *ỉw=f* + Old Perfective or *ỉw=f m* NP etc. used in the apodosis will be classified as *ỉw*-sentences. They can have past, present or future meaning; where the statement concerns the future, the form cannot be distinguished from the Third Future. Along with Late Egyptian independent sentences in the apodosis, earlier types of sentence were also used in the higher registers of the textual hierarchy.

Anticipation without *ir* is relatively rare, being encountered mostly in the higher registers. Anticipation with *ir* can be viewed in tabular form like this (OP = Old Perfective)

	First member/protasis		Second member/apodosis	
Topicalization of nouns	(*ḥr*) *ir* noun		preterite *sḏm=f*	establishing topics
	noun	+ qualification	First Present	
		(relative/adverbial phrase)	Third Future	
with extension	(*ḥr*) *ir* noun	+ inf./OP/adverb = "First Present"	*iw*-sentence (NIMS)/ (*iw=f ḥr tm sḏm*)	
	(*sw*	*ḥr sḏm*)		organization of time
Topicalization of adverbials	(*ḥr*) *ir* Ø	*ḥr-sȝ/ḥr/m* + noun	*iw*-sentence (NIMS)	
		m-ḫt + noun + OP	*wn.in=f ḥr sḏm*	
		m-ḏr sḏm=f	(*sḏm pw iri.n=f/ʿḥʿ.n sḏm=f*)	
of circumstantial clauses	(*ḥr*) *ir* Ø	*iw=f ḥr sḏm*	Third Future	possible reasons (conditions)
		(*iw=f ḥr tm sḏm*)	Imperative/Prosp.	
		sḏm=f (including *wnn*)	First Present/*bw sḏm=f*	
			iw-sentence (NIMS)	
			Nominal Sentence/ Emphatic Sentence	
			clause complexes	

Observations:

Groupings   In principle, any form of sentence in the apodosis can follow any form in the protasis. The grouping here is supposed to reflect the usual combinations.

Noun   Noun + qualification signifies that in principle complex noun phrases can be topicalized. "Noun" is used as a notion in the table in order to be systematically clear.

Topicalization of adverbials   What can be described as the use of an anticipatory, topicalized noun accompanied by an infinitive, Old Perfective, or adverb cannot be distinguished from the First Present in Late Egyptian in terms of linguistic evolution. *ir* + First Present must thus be understood as a temporal expression. The term "Ø-noun" (zero-noun) refers to a reference noun whose syntactic slot is present but which is not realized as a word (as in the nominalized relative phrases), and which on the other hand demonstrates the parallelism of the constructions.

m-ḫt + noun +   Adverbials of this construction are limited to literary works, like the older
Old Perfective   forms of the apodosis (*wn.ỉn=f ḥr sdm*; *sdm pw ỉrỉ.n=f/ʿḥʿ.n sdm=f*).

Circumstantial   Semantically, the topicalization of circumstantial clauses results in the so-
clauses   called conditional clauses with *ỉr*. By analogy with the Circumstantial Present
after *ỉr*, the *sdm=f* can be recognized as a Middle Egyptian circumstantial
form, preserved here as a linguistic remnant.

clause   In principle, the apodosis can accommodate all possible independent construc-
complexes   tions, and therefore not merely simple sentence forms, but also complexes
and combinations of the most different types.

6.1.2 The topicalized noun phrase

(1) Functions

With or without an initial *ỉr*, the noun phrase in anticipation indicates the matter under discussion. Either a topic can be marked expressly, or a change of the current topic signalled. Where the new topic is adverbially specified (sentential appearance as First Present), the effect is similar to that of a temporal expression.

Anticipation is thus used to identify the subject of discourse when th topic is shifted   topic shifting

— where a topic is introduced anew, is recovered after having been discussed earlier ("Concerning that-and-that which we already discussed, such-and-such is the case");

— or to introduce a topic explicitly which was already implicit in the speech situation ("Concerning what you have thought all along, such-and-such is the case");

— where a specific item needs to be discussed again or given special treatment, having been introduced earlier along with a number of other things ("Regarding A, B and C, as far as B is concerned, one can say such-and-such");

— or where the situation demands clarification of various possible topics ("Regarding A, B, and C, as far as C is concerned, one can say such-and-such, but concerning B one can say so-and-so"). This is quite common in contexts like letters, in which mention is made of the topics of letters received previously.

On the other hand, such specifications can also be understood in a figurative sense: introduction
the topic is identified at the moment where it is first explicitly mentioned — as with the   of topics
specifying relative phrases (cf. supra § 5.1.2[4]), and often by means of them. In the organization of texts it can thus sometimes even be used to identify new subject matter.

It is clear that in every case, the object of discourse is either known in principle or   determination
rendered explicit in the course of the dialogue before actually being discussed. It is thus grammatically marked as definite or defined.

(2) The employment of topicalization

The initial expression, the protasis, can be either a simple noun, or one specified in detail. If it is an independent personal pronoun the effect is more formal (on the lines of, "But me, I do such-and-such"). The nucleus of the protasis is generally — but not necessarily — resumed in the independent reference sentence, the apodosis.

meaning shifts   Topicalization is a process which in origin is more a decision made by the speaker than a grammatical construction (which it then secondarily becomes). There are thus cases where it must be noted that the content of the apodosis does not follow from the content of the protasis but rather that the content of the protasis merely allows the apodosis to be uttered. For the understanding of such constructions it is often advantageous — or even necessary — to introduce the level of the speaker using a paraphrase (thus: "Concerning that-and-that, there is reason to say: such-and-such"), but this must not be confused with a translation (i.e., the paraphrase is to be rewritten to a translation):

(pBM 10052, 4,24)

ir p3 m3ᶜ nty iw=i ḏd.t=f bn ḏd=i rmṯ nb i.ptr=i irm Bw-ḫ3ᶜ=f "Since what I say is true — should I not name all those whom I have seen with Bukhaf?" (<* "Concerning the truth which I will state — there is reason to say: Shall I not name all people whom I saw ...");

Notes:

        structure *ir*-phrase as protasis of a tonal question;

   nty iw=i ḏd.t=f relative Third Future as qualification of the definite noun;

      bn ḏd=i negated prospective *sdm=f*.

    The following examples will illustrate some conventional uses of topicalization:

recovering topics   — The following example may show how a topic is recovered. In letters, the sender mentions things which the recipient mentioned in his own letter:

(LRL 15,7-9)

ḥr ir p3y=k ḏd m-ir nni m h3b n=i ᶜ=n

        ir wn-iḫ ḫpr r=n iw=k ᶜḥᶜ.tw

"As for your writing that [we] shouldn't neglect writing to [you] about our condition — what could possibly happen to us while you are there?";

Notes:

        structure *ir*-protasis with Third Future apodosis (without explicit resumption); NP of *ir* is the nominalized infinitive of *ḏd* "say" + the "object" of the verb — the statement as a quote;

indirect speech	a rendering of the literal: "Concerning your statement: 'Don't neglect to write to me about "our" condition'";
ꜥ=n	adjustment of pronoun to the surrounding text in indirect speech, cf. § 5.3.2(3);
wn-ỉḥ	nominal *sdm=f* of *wn*, with the interrogative pronoun *ỉḥ* as agent ("that what is?"), as nominal subject of the Third Future: *"What existing will happen to us?";
ỉr NP *ḫpr*	Third Future form with nominal subject; cf. for the grammatical analysis also Wente, *LRL*, p. 36, n. m;
r-r'=nn	status pronominalis writing of *r=n*; cf. Coptic ЄⲢⲞ=Ⲛ.

— In order to make it absolutely clear what is being discussed:

clarifying
topics

(pNaunakhte
2,6-7)

ỉr pꜣ wꜣḥ nb ḏr.t=f ḥr ḏr.t=ỉ ỉm=w

ỉw=ỉ r dỉ.t n=f ꜣḫ.t=ỉ

ỉr pꜣ nty bw.pw=f dỉ.t n=ỉ

bn ỉw=ỉ r dỉ.t n=f m ꜣḫ.t=ỉ

(A testatrix says of her children:) "To every one of them who cared for me, I will give my property; but for those who did not provide for me, I will not make provision from my property" (cf. also supra § 5.1.2[4]);

Notes:

structure	repeated *ỉr* protasis with Third Future apodosis (with resumption), affirmative the first time, negative the second time;
pꜣ wꜣḥ ḏr.t=f ḥr ḏr.t=ỉ	nominalized participle, "he who put his hand on mine";
pꜣ nty bw.pw=f dỉ.t n=ỉ	nominalized relative phrase with negative preterite of intransitive *dỉ.t* "to make a gift to someone".

Sentential combinations can become very complex, especially where the anticipated noun phrase is extended and the apodosis is itself already a complex sentence — as may be illustrated by the conjunctional sentence of the letter formula in the next example:

complex
sentence as
apodosis

(HorSeth 8,3-
5)

ỉr pꜣ ꜥḏd 2

ỉw=tn dỉ.t s:km=w ꜥḥꜥy=w m tꜣ qnb.t

ḫft spr pꜣy=ỉ wḫꜣ r-r'=tn

ỉw=tn dỉ.t ḥḏ.t ḥr tp n Ḥrw zꜣ ꜣIs.t

mtw=tn tnhꜣ.t=f (< dhn) r tꜣ s.t n ỉtỉ=f Wsỉr

(Re wrote to the Council of Gods:) "Concerning those two boys whom you are forcing to spend their lives at court: as soon as my decision arrives, you should put the white crown on the head of Horus Son of Isis, and assign him the throne of his father Osiris"; Notes:

structure	*ir*-protasis with a qualified noun, apodosis a complex sentence with initial conjunctional clause (*ḫft spr NP*) followed by NIMS (*iw=tn di̯.t*): "then, when this has happened, you should do this-and-that", with the NIMS continued with the Conjunctive (*mtw=tn*);
p3 ꜥdd 2	note the singular determination with numbers (cf. supra § 2.1.4[6]);
iw=tn di̯.t s:km=w	adverbial phrase (circumstantial clause) in the adnominal qualification of the "boys" (example of the use of defined nouns too with the so-called virtual relative clauses);
ḫft spr p3y=i wḫ3	protasis of the complex sentence relating to the *ir*-phrase; for this conjunctional syntagma, cf. supra § 5.4.1;
iw=tn di̯.t ḥḏ.t ḥr tp	*iw*-sentence (NIMS) as apodosis of the complex sentence: "you should put the crown on the head"; the mood of result follows from the type of protasis (Third Future is not attested in constructions with *ḫft spr*);
mtw=tn dhn=f	Conjunctive continuing the apodosis.

ellipses   In just this type of role it can also happen that an apodosis in the form of a Nominal Sentence is reduced to a single noun because the required information is "included in the package" (correspondence ellipse):

(LRL 36, 12)   *ḥr ir Pr-ꜥ3 ḥr.y nim m-r3-ꜥ* "And as for Pharaoh — whose master still?" (for the hieroglyphic text and commentary, cf. supra § 4.2.1).

introducing topics   — Introducing a new topic — to a certain degree, the figurative use of topicalization — with the *iw*-sentence (*iw* + First Present or NIMS, as the case may be) as the apodosis:

(VerwPrinz 5,5-6)

ir p3 nty iw=f r pḥ p3 sšd n t3y=i šri.t iw=s n=f r ḥm.t "The one who shall reach my daughter's window shall have her as wife";
Notes:

nty iw=f r pḥ	relative Third Future;
iw=s n=f	"She is to him", "belongs to him", *iw*-sentence (NIMS, Circumstantial Present); structurally it acquires future meaning, but in itself remains a relative present.

Occasionally, the introduction of a new topic makes the protasis so detailed that it outweighs the actual sentence — the apodosis — in both length and content:

(LRL 47,7-9)

ir p3y zḫ3.w i̯.wn di̯ ḥ3.t={t}n
    iw mnt.f p3 nty di̯

     ỉw=f rḫ wꜥ ḥy

      ỉw=f m rmṯ ꜥꜣ

       ỉw mtr st pꜣy=f ỉtỉ

 sw ỉrm=k

(The chief workmen of the Tomb Building Administration writes to the General Piankhi, the son of Herihor, in Nubia:) " As for the scribe who was here before us, and who was the one who was appointed, and who knew an inspector who was an influential man, and whose father testified to it — he is with you."

Notes:

  ḥꜣ.t=tn a frequently used abbreviation for the compound preposition *r-ḥꜣ.t*, here used in status pronominalis (and thus *=tn* rather than *=n*, cf. table supra § 2.1.2[1]);

 ỉw mnt.f pꜣ nty dỉ converted Pseudo-Cleft Sentence continuing the relative phrase *ỉ.wn*; *pꜣ nty dỉ* relative clause with Old Perfective, "he who was placed (appointed)";

  ỉw=f m rmṯ ꜥꜣ Circumstantial Present as attributive qualification of *wꜥ ḥy*;

   sw ỉrm=k First Present as apodosis of the anticipated *ỉr*-phrase.

(3) Sententially extended noun phrases

An anticipatory noun can also be specified in a vestigial Middle Egyptian fashion with *ỉr + anticipated temporal clause* adnominal adverbials, i.e., Old Perfective, *ḥr/m* + infinitive, or other prepositions (usually *m*) + nouns (cf. supra § 2.2.3[2]). The circumstances governing whatever is designated by the noun thus assume central importance: from *ỉr z.t ỉy.tỉ* *"Concerning the woman who came" or *"Concerning the woman when she came" we have *"Concerning when the woman came". The result is that semantically the anticipated noun with adverbial specification becomes an anticipated temporal clause. The protasis defines the temporal position of the apodosis:

(RAD 73,7)

ḥr ỉr šmw ḫpr.w ỉw=w ỉn n=ỉ 40 n ḫꜣr n ỉt-m-ỉt ỉm=f "And when harvest time came round, they brought me 40 sacks of barley from there" (*"Concerning the time of the harvest, when it happened, (there is reason to say:) they brought me 40 sacks of barley");

Notes:

  šmw ḫpr.w noun with Old Perfective;

  ỉw=w ỉn *ỉw*-sentence (NIMS).

Or:

(pD'Orb 5,7-8)

ḥr ỉr pꜣ šw ḥr ḥtp

  ỉw=f ꜣtp=f <m> sm nb n sḫ.t m pꜣy=f šḫr nty-rꜥw-nb

       ỉw=f ḥr ỉy.t

"And as the sun was setting, he loaded himself with all the greens of the field as he always did, and came";

Notes:

      p3 šw ḥr ḥtp   noun with prepositional infinitive;

      ỉw=f 3tp=f   *ỉw*-sentence (NIMS);

      sḫr nty-rꜥw-nb   for *sḫr n-rꜥw-nb*, cf. supra § 2.1.4(3) end.

    This type of construction does not only have the effect of a sentence used in anticipation, but was also reinterpreted within the Late Egyptian system by rebracketing (*ỉr* [noun] + [adverbial] > *ỉr* [noun + adverbial]) as the sentence form First Present, as the pronominal forms clearly show:

(pMayer A vs. 6,21-23)

ḥr ỉr tw=ỉ m ỉy r-ḫrỉ ỉw=ỉ gm wꜥb T3-šrỉ zḫ3.w P3-b3kỉ ỉw=w ꜥḥꜥ pḫpḫ m p3y wḏ3 "When I came down, I found the consecration priest Tasheri and the scribe Pabaka occupied in walking around in this storehouse";

Notes:

      tw=ỉ m ỉy   First Present with verbs of motion (with a grapheme *m-n* for *m*);

      ỉw=ỉ gm NN ỉw=w   for the construction of object or content clauses after *gmỉ*, cf. supra § 5.3.2;
          ꜥḥꜥ

      ỉw=w (ḥr) ꜥḥꜥ (ḥr)   for this construction, with the auxiliary verb *ꜥḥꜥ*, cf supra § 2.2.3(3).
      pḫpḫ

(pD'Orb 16,7-8)

ḥr ỉr ḥr-s3 ỉw=tw ḥr dỉ.t m3ꜥ.t=f

ḥr ỉr sw ḥr rmn n3 n rmṯ ỉw=f ḥr ktkt m nḥb.t=f

"Now after he was slaughtered for sacrifice, but while he was on the men's shoulders, he shook his neck" (and two drops of blood fell to the earth; referring to the younger of the Two Brothers, Bata, as a bull, being carried off after slaughter);

Notes:

      ḥr ỉr ḥr-s3   protasis to the following *ỉw*-sentence, being a prepositional phrase used in anticipation, cf. infra § 6.1.3(1);

      dỉ.t m3ꜥ.t=f   status pronominalis of the compound infinitive *dỉ.t m3ꜥ* "to sacrifice, to slaughter ritually";

      sw ḥr rmn   First Present/Adverbial Sentence.

6.1.3 Topicalized adverbials

(1) Prepositional expressions organizing time relations

The anticipatory noun phrase sententially extended by adverbial phrases, that is, the First *ir* + adverbial Present form after *(ḥr) ir* in the first member, can also be reduced in another fashion: phrase the reference noun of the adverbial phrase is itself represented by "zero" (that is, it exists as a syntactic slot but not semantically; cf. the table supra § 6.1.1[2], and the structure of the nominalization in relative phrases). With the aid of *ir*, both adverbials and certain clause conjugations can thus precede the sentences to which they are semantically tied. Being syntactically necessary, the initial *ir* makes anticipation of the adverbial phrase possible, but it is nearly impossible to recreate this in translation. The second member, the independent follow-up clause, is frequently formed from a *iw*-sentence, the construction itself thus being a closed complex within the structure of Late Egyptian syntax.

The framework defined by the protasis thus sets the circumstances that limit the validity *as temporal* of the apodosis. In general, these are expressions which make a statement about the time *framework* related, or can be understood as such.

— The apodosis is a *iw*-sentence or a form of narrative; the protasis is an adverb or a *protasis is* prepositional phrase: *prepositional phrase*

(oNash 1, 4-5)

ḥr ir ḥr-sꜣ hrww qnw iw ꜥnḫ-n-nw.t Nbw-m-nḥm ḥr iy r ḏd n=i bꜣ.w nṯr ḫpr "And a couple of days later citizeness Nabamanhama came to tell me that the might of the god had become manifest" (as she had seen so-and-so as she was stealing the chisel);

Notes:

ḥr ir ḥr-sꜣ hrww qnw	prepositional phrase as protasis "after many days" (*"Concerning this: after many days");
iw NN ḥr iy	*iw*-sentence (NIMS) as second member;
Nbw-m-nḥm	sentence-name ("The gold is in the lotus bud"; gold = Hathor);
r ḏd	speech introduction; the content of the speech is given as indirect speech (more literally, *"in order to say to me: 'a proof of god's power has happened; I saw so-and-so as she ...'").

For the use of corresponding prepositional adverbs (here, *ḥr-sꜣ.y* — etymologically *or adverb* transliterated), the passage pD'Orb 16,7(-8) can be cited: *ḥr ir ḥr-sꜣ iw=tw ḥr di.t mꜣꜥ.t=f* "Afterwards, however, he was sacrificed".

A characteristic fixed use of such constructions will be found in literary works, in the *day formulae* so-called day formulae:

(pD'Orb 1,4-7) *ḥr ỉr m-ḫt hrww qnw s3 nn*

ỉw p3y=f sn šrỉ m-s3 n3y=f ỉ3w.t m p3y=f sḫr.w nty rꜥw-nb

mtw=f wḥꜥ r p3y=f pr r-tnw rwḥ3 ỉw=f 3tp m sm.w nb n sḫ.t ...

mtw=f w3ḥ=w m-b3ḥ p3y=f sn ꜥ3 ỉw=f ḥms ḥnꜥ t3y=f ḥm.t

"When now many days had passed after this, his younger brother kept his cattle, according to his daily custom, and he would return every evening, loaded with all the plants ...., and he would lay them before his elder brother, as he was sitting with this wife" (for the hieroglyphic text and commentary, cf. supra § 5.4.3[3]).

organizing the   Such day formulae can assume complex forms, and are generally used more as a means
narrated time   of organizing a text temporally than to be taken literally (quite often "many days" refers only to brief intervals). It is generally advisable to render these with "some time later" or "after a while", etc. The following example reveals such a complex protasis (extension of the adverbial temporal expression using circumstantial clauses), with an apodosis characteristic of the co-ordinating forms in narration (*wn.ỉn=f ḥr sdm*, constructions with *ꜥḥꜥ.n* or the earlier Nominal Sentence form *sdm pw ỉrỉ.n=f*)

(pD'Orb 2,7-9)

ḥr ỉr m-[ḫt hrww] qn.w ḥr-s3 nn ỉw=sn m sḫ.t ỉw=sn ꜥḥꜥ n pr.t

wn.ỉn=f ḥr h3b p3y=f sn šrỉ ...

"Quite a bit later, when they were in the fields, and they were short of seed-corn, he sent his younger brother off";

Notes:

> *hrww qn.w ḥr-s3*   good example of the qualification of a noun (*hrww*) by a prepositional attribute (*ḥr-s3*
> *nn*   *nn*). Note that this can no longer be read — as in Middle Egyptian texts — *ỉr m-ḫt hrww qn.w sw3.w ḥr-s3 nn* ("after many days after this had passed"), although one occasionally encounters this in the translations (cf. also Hintze, *Neuägyptische Erzählungen*, 16ff). What appears to be *sw3* is a semogram for *qn*;
>
> *ỉw=sn ...*   double extension of the preceding adverbial phrase by a circumstantial clause;
>
> *wn.ỉn=f ḥr h3b*   classic form of narration organization.

adjusting the   It is common for the point of these arrangement formulae to be lost in overly literal
translation   translations: *ḥr ỉr m-ḫt t3 ḥḏ 2.nw hrww ḫpr* should be rendered as "after the world brightened and the next day came" (or even "after dawn the next day") and not "after the world brightened and the second day happened".

— The apodosis is a *ỉw*-sentence, and the protasis an anticipated conjunctional phrase (such as the Temporal):

*(pBM 10052,
13, 24-25)*

ḏd=s ỉr m-ḏr ỉry.tw pȝ ḥrwy n pȝ ḥm-nṯr tpy ỉw pȝ rmṯ ỉṯȝ ḫt n pȝy=ỉ ỉtỉ "She said, 'While the uprising of the High Priest was going on, the man stole some of my father's property'";

Notes:

m-ḏr ỉry.tw	Temporal with passive subjunctive *sdm=f*, "when (the rebellion) was made";
pȝ ḥrwy n pȝ	the rebellion of Amenhotep the High (or First) Priest of Amun in the Thebaid (in about
ḥm-nṯr tpy	regnal year 11 of Ramesses XI), which was defeated by Panehsi, the Viceroy of Nubia, in the service of the king, before he too fell into disgrace and was driven back to Nubia by Herihor and his son Piankhi;
ỉw pȝ rmṯ ỉṯȝ	*ỉw*-sentence (NIMS).

ỉr m-ḏr ỉw.t=f r ỉṯȝ n=k pr.t ỉw=f gm=ỉ ḥms.kw w^c "When he came to get seed corn for   *(pD'Orb 5,1)*
you, he found me sitting alone" (for the hieroglyphic text and commentary, cf. supra §
5.4.2[1]).

(2) Conditions and possible reasons

The effect of topicalization as an indication of the circumstances which govern the
follow-up clause reaches its fullest extent where the anticipatory first member consists
of *ỉr* + Circumstantial Present or *ỉr* + *sdm=f* (metaphorically to be described as the
adverbial qualification of a "zero-noun", cf. supra § 6.1.3[1]). This no longer usually
convey the temporal circumstances of an action, but identifies the conditions relevant to
the follow-up clause: the protasis names a possible basis for the validity of the apodosis.
In translation, this is generally best done using clauses of condition or concession to
reproduce the topicalized Egyptian phrase, using conjunctions like "if"; "if not";
"unless"; "provided that"; "in so far as"; "supposing" etc., or "though"; "while";
"when"; sometimes, however, it will be more advisable to use appropriate abridgements
(of the type "Born in better times, he would have done well"; "Strictly speaking, that is
not true" etc.), or two sentences linked by "and" (such as "Give him an inch and he'll
take a mile").

Two points must be borne in mind, however. (a) Even where the protasis defines the
conditions of use or validity pertaining to the expression in the apodosis, the correspondence to the temporal relationships can remain fluid; thus an absolute participle or other
nominative absolute in English may sometimes serve better than a "if"-clause ("Conditions being favorable, he might succeed" — either temporally, "when conditions are
favorable", or conditionally "if conditions are favorable"). (b) The restrictions imposed
by the protasis can be either factual or hypothetical, and the validity of the limits may
only be clear from the context, being otherwise unstated. Compare the use of "if" in an

English sentence like "If she comes, we can go", which can be either a factual restriction ("Whenever/once she comes, we can go") or a hypothetical restriction ("If she were to come, we could go"). In English such distinctions can be made clear (but need not be); in Egyptian they remain unsignalled — except that they do become clear in the case of clausal extensions: a hypothetical condition is continued with the Conjunctive, and a factual one with a Circumstantial Present (cf. supra § 5.4.3[2]).

(3) Forms of conditionality

ir +
circumstantial
clause

A construction frequently used in the colloquial registers has a protasis *ir* + Circumstantial Present (*ir iw=f ḥr sdm*), and an apodosis formed with a sentence conjugation expressing anticipated or expected actions. Often this is the Third Future, which is precisely the form used to emphasize that one event or action follows logically from another (cf. supra § 3.2.2[1]), although it cannot always be formally distinguished from the "old" *iw*-sentence in these clause groupings:

*(pBM 10052,
3,16-17)*

ir iw=k ḫd <b>.tw iw=k ḫʒꜥ.tw r mw iw nim wḫʒ=k "Supposing you are killed and thrown into the water, who will look for you then?" (*"Concerning what happens if you are killed: who will look for you"?)

Notes:

> *iw=k ḫdb.tw*   Circumstantial Present after *ir* as protasis, here with Old Perfective; *iw=k ḫʒꜥ.tw* is parallel;
>
> *iw NP wḫʒ=k*   Third Future with the interrogative pronoun *nim* as agent.

Other possibilities include the Imperative and the Prospective (Potential/Optative, cf. supra § 3.4.2):

*(pBM 10052,
8,21-23)*

ir iw ky iy mtw=f s:ꜥḥꜥ=k iry=i

dd=f ir iw ky iy mtw=f s:ꜥḥꜥ(=i) iw=k ir.t n=i sbʒy.t nb.t bin

(The vizier said to the delinquent:) "'If someone else came and accused you, then I would act.' He said, '(Yes,) if someone else came and accused me, then you should enforce every severe punishment against me!'"

Notes:

> *mtw=f s:ꜥḥꜥ=k*   Conjunctive as a continuation form of a hypothetical protasis;
>
> *iry=i*   Prospective (independent prospective *sdm=f*) in the sense of a self-imposed commitment, cf. supra § 3.4.0(1);
>
> *dd=f*   the delinquent responds;
>
> *iw=k ir.t*   Third Future.

In expressions and textual registers heavily influenced by tradition — but also *ìr + sdm=f* elsewhere — *ìr* is frequently followed by a *sdm=f* form which is thus employed as a parallel to the Circumstantial Present. This form could thus be identified as a circumstantial *sdm=f*, but has generally been termed a nominal *sdm=f* (cf., e.g., Satzinger, *Neuägyptische Studien*, § 1.3.2.1). Like the "old" *ìw*-sentence, its use in these constructions should be understood as a remnant of Middle Egyptian ways of expression.

ḫr ìr dì=k ʿnḫ=f ìw=ì r mwt n=ì "If you let *(pD'Orb 5,3)* him live, I will kill myself"; or "You will let him live and I shall kill myself".

ìr wnn ìb=k ìry zḫ3.w "If you are intelligent, become a scribe!" *(pLansing 7,5)*

Notes: *wnn ìb=k* *"If your heart/mind exists"; in these constructions *wnn* can also be written *wn*;

   ìrì zḫ3.w *ìrì* with title or profession as object: "to perform an office", more literally: "Perform the office of scribe!" or "Act as a scribe!" ("Do a scribe!").

Thus, forms of prediction or anticipated action are common among the sentence forms forms of the of the apodosis (as in the examples), but there are also "present" — better: not temporally apodosis fixed — forms of expression, particularly characterizations and statements of general validity: forms of the present, *ìw*-sentence, Nominal Sentence forms, etc. For example, First Present:

ìr pry=f m *(pLansing 10,6)*

ḥry-t3 sw g3b.w m mšʿ "If he survives, he suffers from marching" (< *"Concerning the case in which he emerges as a survivor, he is weakened"), describing the soldier's fate;

Negative Aorist:

(LRL 1,11-2,1)

ìr ìry=ì ḥḥ n bt3

   bw ìr=ì wʿ nfr dì.t s:mḫ=w

"If I had done a million evil deeds, could I not do one good one so as to let them be forgotten?";

Notes:

   mood of the a clear example of a hypothetical protasis as expressed in translation;
   translation

   dì.t for *r dì.t*, an abbreviated writing which is not restricted to the Third Future, but also occasionally appears with *r* + infinitive.

ìstw ìr sḫ3y=k wʿ n bìn *(pD'Orb 8,2)*

ìstw bw ìr=k sḫ3y wʿ n nfr m-r3-pw wʿ nkt.t ìw ìry=ì sw n=k

"If you recall an evil deed, can't you recall anything good or anything else that I have done for you?" (for the hieroglyphic text and commentary, cf. supra ·§ 3.5.2).

An Emphatic Sentence as apodosis:

(pAnast. I 10,5-6)

ỉr nfỉ=k r gs=f ỉw=f m znny

                   ỉ.ỉr=f hȝy wȝw mỉ gȝb ḏbȝw

"If you exhale beside him when he passes by, he will fall far off like a leaf" (the speaker is referring to a lightweight colleague);

Notes:

    ỉw=f m znny   Circumstantial Present (with *m* with verbs of motion) as continuation of a protasis stated as factual;

    ỉ.ỉr=f hȝy   nominal *sdm=f*; "it is like a leaf that …".

complex structures

    In the appropriate types of text, these constructions can assume a high degree of linguistic complexity. In the following example, the protasis is so extended that it outweighs the apodosis, but without infringing on the structure:

(pD'Orb 8,4-6)

ḥr ỉr šꜥd.tw pȝ ꜥš

        mtw=f hȝy.t r ỉwtn

        mtw=k ỉy.t r wḫȝ=f

ỉr ỉry=k 7 rnp.wt n wḫȝ=f

        m-dy.t fy hȝ.tỉ=k

ḥr ỉr ỉw=k gm=f

        mtw=k ḥr dỉ.t=f r wꜥ n gȝy n mw qbḥ

        kȝ ꜥnḫ=ỉ ꜥn-wšb=ỉ n pȝ thw=ỉ

"And if the cedar is felled, and falls to the ground, and you come to seek it (the heart) — even if you spend seven years looking for it, do not give up! And if you find it, and put it in a bowl of cool water, then I shall come to life so that I may take revenge on the evildoer.";

Notes:

    šꜥd.tw pȝ ꜥš   example of a passive *sdm=f* in the protasis;

mtw=f ḥ3y.t	Conjunctive as continuation of a hypothetically couched thought (note that, although these later will happen as described — one could translate "when" rather than "if" — they are nevertheless conjectures at this point in the text);
ỉr ỉry=k	the protasis gets, so to speak, a new start, before the apodosis comes (*7 rnp.wt* is written in red);
rnp.wt n wḫ3=f	literally "years of seeking it";
m-dy.t fy (< *ỉt*)	Negated Causative Imperative (cf. supra § 3.4.3[1]) as apodosis;
ỉr ỉw=k gm=f	another *ỉr*-sentence, this time with Circumstantial Present as protasis;
dỉ r	usually *dỉ r* means "to apply something to something"; sometimes, however, a meaning "to put something into something" (a pot, bowl) is possible (cf. von Deines/Westendorf, *Wörterbuch der Medizinischen Texte* I, Berlin 1960, p. 548 IIIb);
k3 ꜥnḫ=ỉ	contingent form with the prospective *sdm=f* ("in that case I shall live") rare in Late Egyptian, cf. supra § 3.4.1 and Winand, *Études*, § 371;
ꜥn-wšb=ỉ n X	< *ꜥn-wbšbt=ỉ*; final-prospective *sdm=f*, "so that I may return an answer to X";
p3 thw	(< *p3 th3.tw*) "the trespasser/transgressor".

This type of protasis is a conditional construction with two grammatically different forms of expression (*ỉr ỉw=f sdm* and *ỉr sdm=f*), but differences in the function can hardly be distinguished: *ỉr ỉw=f sdm* can be understood as a Late-Egyptianized form of *ỉr sdm=f*. {notes on linguistic evolution}

6.1.4 Bibliography

Satzinger, *Neuägyptische Studien*, chap. 1; Erman, *Neuägyptische Grammatik*, §§ 703-705; Junge, *ỉw=f ḥr (tm) sdm*, 124ff; Černý/Groll, *Late Egyptian Grammar* §§ 9.3; 62.4; 62.7; construction with *ḥr jr*: Neveu, *La particule ḫr*, 97ff (§ 7) {*ỉr*-anticipation}

Satzinger, *Neuägyptische Studien*, 6-19 {*ỉr* + NP}

Satzinger, *Neuägyptische Studien*, 36-46 (§ 1.3.1); Frandsen, *Outline*, §§ 36(2)d; 38(2)b; 40(2)c; 41(2)d {*ỉr* + First Present}

Satzinger, *Neuägyptische Studien*, 20-35 (§ 1.2); Frandsen, *Outline*, §§ 52; 53(d); 54; Hintze, *Neuägyptische Erzählungen*, 7-31 (*ḥr ỉr m-ḫt*) {*ỉr* + AP}

Frandsen, *Outline*, §§ 14(7); 54; Satzinger, *Neuägyptische Studien*, § 1.3.2 {*ỉr*-conditional}

6.2 Bound expressions

6.2.1 Clause combinations with conditional force

(1) Form and semantic structure; consequence relations

Topicalization constructions with an independent sentence (apodosis) preceded by an initial dependent clause (protasis) provide one means of expressing conditionality. There are also constructions where the protasis is also formally an independent sentence, which generally has an initial particle (such as *ỉnn* or *hn*). Comparable to the topicalization

construction treated above, here
again the initial expression conveys
the presuppositons and circumstances which determine the validity
of what the apodosis expresses. As
both are syntactically independent
sentences, however, their linkage remains on the semantic level which
determines the mutual dependence of
presupposition and validity. The kind
of relationship can be best understood in terms of the particles in
question, i.e.,

— *inn* (⟨hieroglyphs⟩ etc.), which is best
understood as a variant of the pro-
clitic interrogative particle *(î)n* (⟨hieroglyphs⟩,
⟨hieroglyphs⟩ and ⟨hieroglyphs⟩),[1] and which helps to build
up sentential questions for corrobor-
ation (cf. supra § 2.2.4[1]);

— Wish particles such as *hn/h3n3*
(⟨hieroglyphs⟩ etc.) or *h3/h-n-r/hl*
(⟨hieroglyphs⟩ etc.) "would that".

Query-Response-Relations: The Egyptian conditional combinations with the initial particles *inn, hn,*
etc. are grammaticizations of logical and linguistic
relations joining "semantic presuppositions" of
questions and requests to the answers which they
evoke. These relations can be generally characterized as: "An answer A to question Q is a
sentence satisfying the conditions set by Q". (R.
Conrad, *Studien zur Syntax und Semantik von
Frage und Antwort,* Studia Grammatica 19, Berlin
1978, p. 27, with references). Such a definition
also applies to conditional clauses: "An apodosis
A to protasis P is a clause satisfying the conditions
set by P." Thus a question with an anticipated
response ("Are you coming tomorrow? Then we
will go to dinner") can also be formulated as a
conditional sentence ("If you come tomorrow, then
we will go to dinner"). This response anticipating
"Yes" might be paraphrased as: "Are you coming
tomorrow? (If yes,) then we will go to dinner". For
a discussion of such problems for Egyptian, cf. D.
P. Silverman, *Interrogative Constructions with JN
and JN-JW in Old and Middle Egyptian,* Bibliotheca
Aegyptia 1, Malibu 1980, pp. 105ff; Frandsen,
Outline, pp. 150ff(2).

semantic
binding

    Clauses with these particles can also stand alone, as sentential questions for corrobor-
ation or as request sentences. Such sentences, however, always imply the possibility of
a response or a consequence. Where these are anticipated, the interrogative sentence or
wish on the one side is of course intimately related to the response or consequence sentence
on the other — they are "semantically bound".

    In this fashion, the use of *inn* in the following example joins a First Present sentence
with a *iw*-sentence, where the statement of the First Present is formulated as a question,
which — if affirmed — has the results stated in the *iw*-sentence:

(LRL 68,2)

⟨hieroglyphs⟩ *hr inn tw=k dd ῾r n3 iw=i m*

nmh.w "If you tell me to go away, then I will be an orphan!" < *"And do you say, 'Get
out of here'? (If so, then:) I am an orphan";

---

1   Cf. J. Osing, Die neuägyptische Partikel *jn* "wenn; ob", in: *SAK* 1, 1974, 267-273.

Notes:

> $tw=k \, \underline{d}d$ "interrogative" First Present;
>> $n\underline{3}$ a rare use of the demonstrative as adverb, "here", "from here";
> $\dot{i}w=\dot{i} \, m \, nm\underline{h}.w$ $\dot{i}w$-clause.

Where the particle $\underline{h}\underline{3}/\underline{h}nr$ is used, the sentences are joined by the expression of a wish the result of which — should it be fulfilled — is expressed in the second sentence:

(Doomed
Prince 6,2-3)

$\underline{h}nr \, [bn] \, tw=\dot{i} \, \underline{h}r \, \check{s}n\dot{i}.t \, rd.wy=\dot{i} \, \dot{i}w=\dot{i} \, \underline{h}r \, \check{s}m.t \, r \, pwy.t \, m.d\dot{i}=tn$ "If my feet didn't hurt, I would join you in jumping". < *"Would that my feet did not hurt so much! (If this were not the case:) Then I would go to jump with you."

(2) Combinations with initial particles ($\dot{i}nn$; hn)

Consequence relations and the semantic binding of clauses are not restricted to sentences with initial particles, such as $\dot{i}nn$ or hn. They are, however, clearly marked as such in this form. Altogether, these combinations are not very common. Sentences with $\dot{i}nn$ will be encountered only in texts from daily life. These clause combinations can be presented thus in tabular form:

First member/protasis	Second member/apodosis	
$\dot{i}nn$ First Present	First Present	
$wn \, m.d\dot{i}=f$	$\dot{i}w$-clause	
Emphatic Sentence		
$\dot{i}nn$ pret. $sdm=f$	Third Future	
$bw.pw=f \, sdm$	(Causative) Imperative	
	Cleft Sentence	
$\dot{i}nn$ Third Future	Prospective	
hn pret. $sdm=f$/$bw \, sdm=f$		"counter to
Nominal Sentence	wn + Third Future	reality"
First Present	$\dot{i}w$-clause	form
$wn \, m.d\dot{i}=f$		

Observation:

The analysis as an $\dot{i}w$-clause is certain in the apodosis of the $\dot{i}nn$-combinations, where it is formed with an Old Perfective or prepositional phrases. Where the form is $\dot{i}w=f \, () \, sdm$, it can be understood within the Late Egyptian linguistic system as either a Third Future or a vestigial *ỉw*-sentence with future meaning (cf. supra §§ 3.2.2; 5.2.3). In translation this does not create any difficulties, however.

ỉnn

The following examples with *ỉnn* illustrate the relationship of clause types in protasis and apodosis:

— First Present in the protasis and Imperative in the apodosis:

(oKairo 25672, 1-2)

 *ỉnn n3 ḫtm.w wḏ3 wḫ3 sn* "If the seals are intact, take care of them".

— Third Future in the protasis and Third Future or *ỉw*-sentence in the apodosis:

(pMayer B 4-5)

ỉr n3 ḥḏ ỉ.gm=k

> *ỉnn bn ỉw=k dỉ.t n=ỉ ỉm=w ỉw=ỉ šm r ḏd.t=f n{3} p3 ḫ3.ty-ᶜ n ỉmn.t n3 3ṯw*

"About those pieces of silver which you found — if you don't give me some of them, I will go and tell it to the Governor of the West and the Inspectors!";

Notes:

structure	topicalization sentence with complex apodosis consisting of an *ỉnn*-combinations;
n3 ḥḏ	the plural determination of the material "silver" causes the mass object to be a subdivided quantity, and thus "pieces of silver";
bn ỉw=k dỉ.t	negated Third Future in the *ỉnn*-protasis;
ỉw=ỉ šm	Third Future or *ỉw*-sentence;
ḏd.t=f	hypercorrect status pronominalis of *ḏd*.

With *ỉw*-sentence in the apodosis (*ỉw=w m rmṯ-nmḥ.w*):

(pAdoption rt. 23-24)

ỉnn ỉw=s ms bn šrỉ bn šrỉ(.t) ỉw=w m rmṯ-nmḥ.w n p3 t3 n Pr-ᶜ3 "If she gives birth — be it a son or a daughter, they will be free citizens of the land of Pharaoh" (for the hieroglyphic text and commentary, cf. supra § 3.2.2[2]).

— Preterite *sḏm=f* in the protasis, Third Future in the apodosis:

(LRL 9,11-12)

ỉnn qn=f f3y n3 ỉt ỉw=k šzp=w ỉw=w s:pḫr ỉw=w mḥ mtw=k s:ᶜq=w r t3y=w šnw.t "If he has finished conveying the grain, you should receive it, completely registered, and put it into its granary";

Notes:

ỉnn qn=f	protasis with preterite *sḏm=f*;
ỉw=k šzp=w	apodosis, Third Future;

<table>
<tr><td>ỉw=w s:pḫr ỉw=w mḥ</td><td>extension of the apodosis with two Circumstantial Present clauses with Old Perfective, "it being completely recorded" < *"it being recorded, it being complete"; good example of the typical chains of circumstantials;</td></tr>
<tr><td>mtw=k s:ʿq=w</td><td>Conjunctive as continuation of the statement in the apodosis, "and you should enter it into the granary".</td></tr>
</table>

According to the type of their composition, clause combinations with initial *hn* express desired or supposed presuppositions and conditions for desired or supposed situations, in other words they express wishes and their imagined or perceived consequences. Almost all the sentence forms are represented in the *hn*-protasis. It is typical of the apodosis that apart from *ỉw*-clauses the commonest form used is the Third Future with the preterite converter, *wn ỉw=f r sdm*, literally "he was going to hear", but in translation a conditional perfect tense ("he would have heard") usually conveys the required nuance of conjecture and uncertainty.

hn and similar particles

— Protasis with preterite *sdm=f*, apodosis in the form of Third Future with preterite converter:

(pBM 10052, 4,11-12)

ḏd=f bw.pw=ỉ ptr rmṯ nb
  hn ptr=ỉ wn ỉw=ỉ ḏd.t=f

"He said, 'I did not see anyone; if I had, I would have said so'" (< "I did not see any person. If I had seen, I would have said it!"

Notes:

  ptr=ỉ preterite *sdm=f*;
wn ỉw=ỉ ḏd.t=f preterite-converted Third Future.

The protasis can also show preterite conversion: compare

bpy=ỉ ptr hn wn ptr=ỉ wn ỉw=ỉ ḏd.t=f n=k "I did not look. Had I looked, I would have told you so" (for the hieroglyphic text and comments, cf. supra § 3.6.1).

(pBM 10403, 3,29)

— Protasis with (negated) preterite *sdm=f*, apodosis in the form of a *ỉw*-clause:

(HorSeth 15,2-3)

hn bw ḫpr=k
hn bw msỉ=k
    ỉw ỉt bty ḫpr m-rȝ-ʿ

(Re is speaking to Osiris:) "If you had not come to exist, and you had not been born, emmer and barley would exist all the same";

Notes:

  bw ḫpr=k *bw sdm=f* as a more traditional variant of the negative Preterite, cf. supra § 3.5.1(3);
  bw msỉ=k like *bw ḫpr=k*, but a negation of the passive *sdm.w* with suffix;
  ỉw NP ḫpr *ỉw*-clause (NIMS);

m-rȝ-ʿ   adverbial expression of concession, cf. § 2.2.4(1).

— Protasis with First Present, apodosis in the form of a *ỉw*-clause:

(Beatty Love Songs vs. C 4,3)

hn mw.t rḫ.tỉ ỉb=ỉ ỉw=s ʿq.tỉ n=s r nw "If only mother knew my heart, it would have occurred to her before" (for the hieroglyphic text, cf. *supra* § 2.2.6[2]);

Notes:

    mw.t rḫ.tỉ ỉb=ỉ   First Present with Old Perfective (*rḫ* with object);

    ỉw=s ʿq.tỉ n=s   *ỉw*-clause with Old Perfective "then it would have entered her" (the knowledge that the speaker loves so-and-so).

6.2.2 Closed complexes

(1) The balanced sentence with *wnn*

In the linguistic framework of Late Egyptian syntax, constructions like those mentioned above with initial adverbials or clauses, with a sentence of the *ỉw=f ḥr sdm* (or *ỉw=f* + Old Pefective or *ỉw=f* + preposition + NP) type in the second position, basically belong to the category of closed complexes — neither the *ỉr*-phrase nor the *ỉw*-sentence without the *ỉr*-phrase can stand alone. The justification for the division preferred here is that this *ỉw=f ḥr sdm* (cf. *supra* § 6.0) is mutually interchangeable with the sentence conjugations and Nominal Sentences: the *ỉw*-sentence is in a paradigmatic or substitution relationship to the sentence conjugations and thus belongs to the independent sentence paradigm in these combinations. It must thus be understood as the linguistic remnant of the Middle Egyptian independent *ỉw*-sentence. Closed complexes in the narrow sense can thus only be those where the form of the second term (apodosis) cannot be substituted with an independent sentence.

the pure
balanced
sentence

    Closely bound expressions of this kind are, however, usually linguistic remnants of Middle Egyptian sentence constructions just as much as the *ỉr*-sentences[2]. In them, fossilized and occasionally adapted to Late Egyptian morphology, survives the earlier balanced sentence (*Wechselsatz*), whether of the Emphatic-Sentence type, with a nominal *sdm=f* followed by an adverbial *sdm=f*, or of the type *mrr=f ỉrr=f* "If he wishes, he acts". Such real balanced sentences with a nominal *sdm=f*, both in protasis and apodosis, certainly still appear in Late Egyptian form, as in:[3]

2   Cf. Junge, *ỉw=f ḥr (tm) sdm*, 122ff; id., *"Emphasis" and Sentential Meaning in Middle Egyptian*, *GOF* IV 20, Wiesbaden 1989, 88ff (§ 6.2.3).

3   For further examples cf. Johnson, *Demotic Verbal System*, 248 n. 57.

ỉ.ỉr.tw grg n dmỉ nb ỉ.ỉr.tw m3ᶜ.t n p3 t3 n ᵓI-r-s "(As far away as No, the city of Amun, I have heard:) 'Evil is done in every city, but justice is done in the Land of Cyprus'" (for the hieroglyphic text and commentary, cf. supra § 3.6.1). *(Wenamun 2,78-79)*

It is, however, generally the type with a nominal *sdm=f* in the protasis and an adverbial *sdm=f* in the apodosis that is transformed and widely used. They appear with forms of *sdm=f* in the protasis position, primarily *wnn=f*, and a *ỉw*-clause in the apodosis position. As a result of linguistic evolution, the form in the apodosis become the Circumstantial Present: from **wnn=s ḥr mdw.t sdm=f* "Whenever she speaks he hears" emerges *wnn=s ḥr mdw.t ỉw=f ḥr sdm*. In such combinations, the Circumstantial Present can thus become an element of the Late Egyptian balanced sentence, one that nevertheless displays a semantic independence vis-à-vis the initial clause. *wnn-sentence*

In accordance with their character, these balanced sentence constructions convey the mutual dependence of two statements — "if this, then that". In practice, the effects resemble those of consequence relations (cf. supra, § 6.2.1[1]): the mutual dependence may be represented by any logical dependence relationship, especially a temporal one ("when(ever) this, then that") or a conditional one ("if this, then that"). As a rule, the meaning typically oscillates between temporal and conditional circumstances. In the case of related or reported circumstances, the closed complex has an initial particle *ḥr*. Where the circumstances are predicted or expected, the initial *ḥr* can appear, but it need not. *structure of the utterance*

In the construction of the protasis, a change by rebracketing can be observed. The original nominal *sdm=f* was transformed into a structure of the type with a particle or even converter before an independent sentence, which may itself then in turn admit a circumstantial clause (*wnn ỉw=f ḥr sdm*; the reference situation is not clear). The transformation takes place as with topicalization (cf. supra § 6.1.2[3]) — the *sdm=f* form of *wnn* with adverbial specification becomes a sentence: [[*wnn NP*]NP [*ḥr sdm*]AP]protasis becomes [*wnn* [*NP ḥr sdm*]clause]protasis. The end result is that the sentence is adapted to the structures of the consequence relationships with semantic binding. *forms*

The forms of the closed complexes can be presented thus in tabular form:

First member/protasis		Second member/ apodosis	continuation
sdm=f			Conjunctive (imagined situation)
(*ḥr*) *wnn*	=*f ḥr sdm*	*ỉw*-clause	
	sw ḥr sdm (First Present)	*ỉw=f ḥr sdm*	Circumstantial Present (real situation)
wnn	*ỉw=f ḥr sdm*		

Observation:

Occasionally, imperatives assume the role of the apodosis. In these cases, a balanced sentence relationship is reinterpreted as an consequence relationship: "If this, then that" becomes "If this, then do that!".

(2) Usage

The temporal dependency relationships are illustrated in the following examples:

— Expected situation, temporal-conditional statement; in a very common expression with many variations in letters:

(LRL 12,7-8)

wnn t3y=ỉ šˁ.t spr=k ỉw=k dd n ꞌImnw ỉn wỉ ỉw=ỉ ˁnḫ.k "When my letter reaches you, pray to Amun that he bring me back alive";

Notes:

     t3y=ỉ šˁ.t   the hieratic form of this expression is frequently very abbreviated. The possessive article can be written more or less completely, as in the same letter later (*LRL* 12,13), or as here reduced to strokes and dots;

     ỉn wỉ   Imperative with object pronoun: to be read either thus, or (with imperative infinitive and object suffix) *ỉn=ỉ* "Bring me!". This is a typical device for fitting in pronouns with indirect speech (translations can thus be either "pray to Amun: 'Bring him back alive'" or "pray to Amun that he bring me back alive").

Similarly:

(LRL 39,10-12)

wnn t3y=ỉ šˁ.t spr r=k ỉw=k tm rwỉ=k h3b n=ỉ ˁ=k m.dỉ p3 nty-nb nty ỉw=f ỉy m ḫt "When my letter reaches you, you should not refrain from sending word to me about you by anyone who is coming north" (for the hieroglyphic text and comments, cf supra § 5.2.2).

— As a three-part construction of a temporal-conditional form of statement, conceived as expected (hence the continuation of the apodosis with the Conjunctive):

(pD'Orb 6,9-7,1)

wnn p3 ỉtn ḥr wbn ỉw=ỉ ḥr wpỉ.t ḥnˁ=k m-b3ḥ=f mtw=f ḥr dỉ.t p3 ˁd3 n p3 m3ˁ.tỉ "At the rising of the sundisk, I will litigate with you in its presence, and it will hand over the wrong-doer to the just one".

— With initial *ḥr* in a predicted or expected dependence relationship:

(LRL 21,11-12)

ḥr wnn zḫ3.w P3-n-t3-ḥw.t-nḫt ỉy n=tw r-dd ỉmm sw Ḥrw.y dd b3k=f ỉw=tn tm dỉ.t=f n=f

"When the Scribe Panthunakhte comes to you saying that you should deliver him, Hori, who was put to work, you shall not give him to him" (cf. Neveu, *La particule ḫr*, 70 [3 4.2 ex. 176], but compare Wente, *Letters*, 196, for another rendering);

Notes:

> n=tw   for n=tn;
>
> r-ḏd ỉmm sw   "in order to say, 'Give him, Hori'". Even where there is no need to translate a text
> Ḥrw.y   as indirect speech, it can be rendered thus;
>
> dd b3k=f   passive participle with object clause: "who was caused that he work" (< *"He, concerning whom it may be said: it was caused, that he work").

— Transformation of the *sdm=f* of *wnn* with following adverbial to a sentence conjugation with initial converter *wnn*:

ḫr wnn tw=tw ḥr ỉn.t=w n=k ỉw=k   *(pBerlin P. 11239, 6-7)*

ḫr mḥ ỉm=sn "When they were brought to you, you took possession of them" (the reference is to pieces of copper);

Notes:

> wnn   written wn, which must be understood as merely a graphic variant of wnn in these combinations;
>
> tw=tw ḥr ỉn.t=w   First Present with unspecified agent.

Similarly (*wnn* + First Present and nominal agent with Old Perfective; the form of expression reveals the special "if — then" dependence relationship of the balanced sentence):

wnn wᶜ ᶜnḫ ỉw 1000 ḥr mwt "While one stays alive,   *(pTurin A vs.3,10)*

thousands die";

Notes:

> context   those who go to the audience can be compared to the waves of surf striking the coast: one remains, the others perish;
>
> wnn wᶜ ᶜnḫ   NP with Old Perfective after wnn: either nominal agent of wnn (wnn=f) or First Present with converter wnn; after ᶜnḫ there is a group (seated man with plural strokes) which has been crossed out in red, but this is not reproduced here.

In association with the *wnn*-constructions — in the corresponding textual categories — variations of the earlier type of balanced sentence with the *sdm=f* of other verbs can appear in the protasis:

(pSallier I 7,1)

pr p3 rmṯ n mw.t=f ỉw=f m pd n ḥry=f
wnn p3 šrỉ n šms n wᶜw ỉw p3 mnḫ r mg3

"When the man comes forth from his mother, he runs to his superior; when the boy serves a soldier, the stripling will be a warrior";

Notes:

*pr p3 rm*t   (nominal) *sdm=f* of *pr*ỉ "to come forth" as protasis to an *ỉw*-clause as apodosis (Circumstantial Present as form of a Late Egyptian balanced sentence);

n mw.t=f   < *m mw.t=f* (*pr*ỉ *m mw.t=f*), the parallel passage in pAnast. II 7, 3 has *pr*ỉ *m* ḥ3.t n mw.t=f "come out of the body of his mother";

m pd   preposition *m* with infinitive of a verb of motion;

n šms   < *m šms*, preposition *m* with infinitive of a verb of motion; the parallel passage in pAnast. II 7, 3-4 employs the verb *šms*ỉ "follow" in the Old Perfective;

ỉw p3 mnḥ r mg3   *ỉw*-sentence of the type *ỉw* NP *r* NP: "someone becomes something".

(3) Balanced sentences in the oath formulae

Despite its widespread use in Late Egyptian, the syntax of the *wnn=f ḥr sdm* — *ỉw=f ḥr sdm* balanced sentence construction is a remnant of Middle Egyptian. The balanced sentence forms of the oaths must be understood in the same fashion (cf. the appendix § 7.1). With an initial prospective *sdm=f* of the verb *w3ḥ* and a *ỉw*-sentence, which is paradigmatically interchangeable with an independent sentence, it is structurally derived from the Middle Egyptian topicalization construction and not from the balanced sentence. It is therefore syntactically related to the passage from pSallier I 7,1 cited above. Following the initial *sdm=f* is a Conjunctive, which is the actual content of the oath:

(oGardiner 104,2-4)

w3ḥ ꞌImnw w3ḥ p3 ḥq3

   mtw=ỉ mdw m p3y ꞓ3.t

   ỉw=f ḥr 100 n sḥ.t

"As long as Amun and the Ruler shall endure, and I talk about this donkey, [I] shall be subject to 100 lashes."

Notes:

mdw m p3y ꞓ3.t   in the sense of: to contest the affair of the donkey;

ỉw=f ḥr 100   < *ỉw=ỉ*; pronominal adjustment as characteristic of indirect speech; *ỉw*-clause of the type *ỉw* NP *ḥr* NP.

The following example with an Emphatic Sentence (apodosis) and an oath formula in anticipation (Protasis) illustrates that there are also authentic topicalization constructions in Late Egyptian which are constructional parallels to the foregoing example:

(RAD 72,1-
73,1)

w3ḥ ꞌImnw w3ḥ p3 ḥq3

mtw=tw gm 3ḥ.t ḥ3-(n-)t3 ỉw sk3=ỉ sw m ỉw Nby.t

r.šdỉ=tw n3 ỉt m.dỉ=ỉ

"As long as Amun and the Ruler endure, should fields of Crown Land which I have tilled on the island of Ombo be found, then the corn should be exacted from me." (For the hieroglyphic text and comments, cf. supra § 3.3.2).

A new kind of balanced sentence could be said to have evolved out of this formula by omitting the *sdm=f* phrase of the protasis (which happens quite often). Thus the oath is formed with an initial Conjunctive and a following *iw*-clause or Circumstantial Present (NIMS; cf supra § 5.4.3[3]). The form of such constructions corresponds in a way to that of the closed complexes like those discussed above: a dependent form (Conjunctive) as protasis and a dependent form as apodosis (or, in the case of the "old" *iw*-sentence, a form which was no longer used independently, because it was preserved only in such contexts) semantically bound together in an "if — then" relationship. *(margin: initial Conjunctive)*

(oKairo 25553, rt.5)

mtw=i tm db3 n3 ʿqw iw=w r=i m q3b (Someone was caused to swear an oath of the lord with the words) "If I do not pay for the loaves, they will be charged double to me";

Note:

> *iw=w r=i m q3b* *iw*-clause or Circumstantial Present as apodosis, literally, *"they are against me doubly".

Understanding the evolution of this construction, however, saves the necessity of considering them as sentence types by themselves. The following examples have already been mentioned elsewhere:

iw t3 qnb.t ḥr di.t iry=f ʿnḫ n nb ʿ.w.s. r-dd mtw=i ʿq r p3y m-ḫ-y iw=f ḥr 100 n sḫ.t 5 wbnw "And the court made him swear an oath of the Lord to the effect that, 'If I enter this burial chamber, [I] should be subject to 100 lashes and five lacerations!'" (For the hieroglyphic text and comments, cf. supra § 5.4.3[3]). *(pBerlin P. 10496 vs.11-12)*

m3ʿ.t p3 dd=i nb mtw=i pnʿ r3=i ʿn m dw3.w s3 dw3.w iw=i di.k t3 iwʿy.t Kš "(He swore an oath of the lord as follows:) 'Everything which I have said is true, and if I reverse my statement at any time in the future, may I be stationed in the garrison of Cush'" (For the hieroglyphic text and comments, cf. supra § 3.2.2[2]). *(pBM 10053 vs. 2,18)*

6.2.3 Bibliography

Frandsen, *Outline*, § 115A; Černý/Groll, *Late Egyptian Grammar*, §§ 62.5; 62.8; Satzinger, *Neuägyptische Studien*, § 1.4.2.1; J.Černý, *inn* in Late Egyptian, in: *JEA* 27, 1941, 106-112; Cassonnet, *Les Temps Seconds*, 100ff (§ 8.2) *(margin: inn)*

Frandsen, *Outline*, § 115B; Satzinger, *Neuägyptische Studien*, §§ 1.4.2.2; 1.4.2.3; Černý/Groll, *Late Egyptian Grammar*, §§ 62.6; 62.9; W.Till, Der Irrealis im Neuägyptischen, in: *ZÄS* 69, 1933, 112-117 *(margin: hn, ḥnr)* wnn-construct. Satzinger, *Neuägyptische Studien*, § 1.4.1.1; Frandsen, *Outline*, §§ 98; 116; Černý/Groll, *Late Egyptian Grammar*, §§ 55; 56; K.Baer, Temporal *wnn* in Late Egyptian, in: *JEA* 51, 1965, 137ff; Depuydt, *Conjunction*, 192ff

6.3 Forms of co-ordination in narrative

6.3.1 The classic forms of textual organization

Mainly in literature — and rarely in other textual genres — the sequence of events is formulated using constructions with *wn.ỉn* and *ꜥḥꜥ.n*. These are linguistic forms of Middle Egyptian which have been preserved in the literary registers. In the framework of Late Egyptian grammar, they can be understood as a morphological sub-type of the auxiliary verb constructions (cf. supra § 2.2.3[3]).

forms and
variations

Of the formal variants of the Middle Egyptian *wn.ỉn* constructions (cf. Gardiner, *Grammar*, §§ 469-473), only *wn.ỉn=f ḥr sḏm* remained, being more widely used than the *ꜥḥꜥ.n* construction.

The Middle Egyptian *ꜥḥꜥ.n* construction betrays both tradition and adaption in equal measure. On the one hand, *sḏm.n=f* in association with *ꜥḥꜥ.n* remains in use in the relevant textual categories — narratives and legal texts — until Dynasty XXI (cf. supra § 3.5.1[3]). On the other hand, the Middle Egyptian *ꜥḥꜥ.n sḏm.n=f* is re-formed, in accordance with the development of the language, into the Late Egyptian *ꜥḥꜥ.n sḏm=f* (notably with nominal agents at first). The form *ꜥḥꜥ.n* is also occasionally adapted into *ꜥḥꜥ* in the same way (e.g. pD'Orb 4,10; 6,5; 18,6; HorSeth 1,5). A final characteristic is that the variant *ꜥḥꜥ.n=f* + Old Perfective has largely disappeared, but the *ꜥḥꜥ.n=f ḥr sḏm* form occurs more frequently in Late Egyptian than it did in Middle Egyptian texts.

function

Functionally, the differences between the *wn.ỉn* and *ꜥḥꜥ.n* constructions dwindle. Their use is related to the Circumstantial Present in the NIMS-role. They serve above all to express the natural course of events (cf. supra § 5.2.1), they have an "and" function like the Circumstantial Present, and can serve together with the Circumstantial Present as elements in narrative chains. They are, however, independent sentence forms, in contrast to the Circumstantial Present clause. Like the "old" *ỉw*-sentence, they can be used as the main clause (apodosis) in topicalization or consequence constructions. They can also, however, introduce a paragraph or a smaller textual unit. Together with the Circumstantial Present in the NIMS-role, they can form long chains, but at the same time they organize these chains. They link earlier statements with later ones, as does the NIMS, but they accomplish this in a marked form, so to speak (and this marking is frequently highlighted in writing by the use of red ink). In translation, this nuance can be expressed with conjunctions like "and then", "then", "thereupon" etc., but need not, if their use would appear clumsy (note that it is hardly necessary to use the same translation device all the time merely because the Egyptian uses the same form: languages differ in style).

(HorSeth 4,1-4)

ḥr ỉr sȝ ȝḏ.t ꜥȝ.t wn.ỉn Ḥw.t-Ḥrw nb nḥ.t rsỉ ḥr ỉy

    ỉw⸗s ḥr ꜥḥꜥ m-bȝḥ ỉtỉ⸗s nb-r-ḏr

    ỉw⸗s kfỉ kȝ.t⸗s r-ḥr⸗f

ꜥḥꜥ.n pȝ nṯr ꜥȝ zbỉ ỉm⸗s

    wn.ỉn⸗f ḥr dwn⸗f

      ỉw⸗f ḥms r.ḥnꜥ tȝ psḏ.t ꜥȝ.t

      ỉw⸗f ḥr ḏd n Ḥrw ḥnꜥ Stš ỉ.ḏd r⸗tn

    wn.ỉn Stš ꜥȝ pḥ.ty zȝ Nw.t ḥr ḏd

"*Now after some time, there* came Hathor, Lady of the Southern Sycamore; she took her stand before her father, the Lord of All, and exposed herself in front of him. *And* the Great God laughed at her. *But then* he got up, sat with the Great Council of Gods, and said to Horus and Seth: 'Speak for yourselves!' *Thereupon* Seth, Great of Strength, the Son of Nut, said …'" (italics here indicate red ink in the original);

Notes:

wn.ỉn Ḥw.t-Ḥrw	as apodosis of an *ỉr*-sentence construction organizing the narrative. The apodosis continues the main line, being twice complemented with a Circumstantial Present in the NIMS-role;
ꜥḥꜥ.n pȝ nṯr ...wn.ỉn⸗f	the preceding activity has a result (*ꜥḥꜥ.n*), which in turn has a consequence which is marked as such (*wn.ỉn*). This sets them off from the unmarked consequences, which are expressed by two Circumstantial Clauses continuing the content of the *wn.ỉn* construction;
r-rȝ⸗tn	status pronominalis writing of *r⸗tn* (> ⲈⲢⲰ⸗ⲦⲚ);
wn.ỉn Stš	continuation of the main line of the narrative.

Such relations between the *wn.ỉn* and *ꜥḥꜥ.n* constructions are common. The following example is the continuation of the text from the exercise of § 3.3.4 supra (and the relationship of the forms there should be recalled). The preceding passage is "(6,2; *ḥr ỉr sw m nꜥy*) And as she walked along under the trees, (*wn.ỉn⸗s nw*) she looked around, (*ỉw⸗s*) seeing (6,3) the Council of Gods (*ỉw⸗sn*) eating bread in the presence of the

ꜥḥꜥ.n - wn.ỉn

Lord-of-All in his hall. (*ꜥḥꜥ.n Stš nw*) Then Seth looked up (6,4; *iw=f ptr=s iw=s di iy.ti*) and saw her coming":

(HorSeth 6, 5-7)

wn.in=s ḥr šnti m ḥkꜣ=s

        iw=s ir ḫpr.w=s m wꜥ šri nfr.t n ḥꜥ=s

        iw nn wn mi-qd=s m pꜣ tꜣ r-ḏr=f

ꜥḥꜥ.n=f mr.ti=s r ḏww ꜥꜣ n wr

    wn.in Stš ḥr dwn=f

        iw=f ḥms ḥr wnm ꜥq.w r.ḥnꜥ tꜣ psḏ.t ꜥꜣ.t

        iw=f šm.t r ir.t n-ḥꜣ.ty=s

        iw bw.pwy.t wꜥiw ptr=s ḥrw=f

"*And she* did her magic and turned herself into a girl, with a body so beautiful that the like of her had never been in the entire land. *Thereupon he* desired her very badly indeed. And so Seth got up — as he had been sitting eating food with the Great Council of Gods —, and went to meet her, whom no one apart from him had seen."

Notes:

nn wn	*nn* with the participle *wn*, "the one who is such-and-such does not exist"; the strengthening of the negation with *m pꜣ tꜣ* will become very common in the Demotic Setna-Khamemwese story;
iw=f ḥms	circumstantial complementing the *wn.in*-construction, by providing the necessary background: it thus does not lie on the same logical level as the following circumstantial (*iw=f šm.t*);
ir.t n-ḥꜣ.t	< *ir.t m-ḥꜣ.t* "to meet someone";
iw bw.pwy.t	note the form of the expression *iw bw.pwy.t wꜥyw ptr=s ḥrw=f* *"not one having seen her except him".

Occasionally, the *wn.in* constructions can be used to formulate the text linking parts of a dialogue (just like the circumstantial clause in NIMS-function):

(HorSeth 10,11-12)

wn.in tꜣ psḏ.t ḥr ḏd imm ꜥš.tw n Ḥrw ḥnꜥ Stš wpi.tw=w wn.in=tw ini.t=w m-bꜣḥ tꜣ psḏ.t "And then the Council of Gods announced: 'Let Horus and Seth be summoned, so that they may be judged!' Thereupon they were brought before the Council of Gods". (For the hieroglyphic text and comments, cf. supra § 3.4.3[1]).

The *sdm.ỉn=f* — which should be considered as the systematic origin of the *wn.ỉn* form *ḏd.ỉn=f* — still appears, but quite rarely, in the literary genres, after the verb *ḏd* "say", and occasionally in other registers (particularly where the person speaking is of unusual importance socially).

6.3.2 Bibliography

Černý/Groll, *Late Egyptian Grammar*, § 44.2; Hintze, *Neuägyptische Erzählungen*, *ꜥḥꜥ.n/wn.ỉn* 31-36; Satzinger, *Neuägyptische Studien*, § 2.7; Erman, *Neuägyptische Grammatik*, § 513

Černý/Groll, *Late Egyptian Grammar*, § 44.3; Hintze, *Neuägyptische Erzählungen*, 61 *ḏd.ỉn*
Hintze, *Neuägyptische Erzählungen*, 36-38 *ỉy.t pw ỉr.n=f*

6.4 Notes on linguistic evolution

6.4.1 The evolution of the forms

The constructions studied in this chapter could all be described as morphological units, but they also exceed the limits of the sentence as a Late Egyptian morphological unit. Late Egyptian sentence types are components of these constructions, but the principles of their construction cannot be understood solely in terms of Late Egyptian syntax. These principles — particularly those of the balanced sentences — can be more easily understood in terms of the Middle Egyptian system (cf. supra § 3.0). These constructions preserve forms which have otherwise largely fallen out of use, particularly the independent *ỉw*-sentence. It is, however, worth noting that the basic changes reflecting the Late Egyptian system also affect these relic forms syntactically and morphologically.

One area affected by this is topicalization. An earlier *ỉr* + *sdm=f* does occasionally Late appear in the protasis, but it is generally replaced by an updated form, *ỉr* + Circumstantial Egyptianizing Present (cf. supra § 6.1.3[3]). What had been the qualification of an initial topicalized older noun + infinitive, Old Perfective or Adverb (adnominal adverbial) in terms of linguistic constructions evolution, can no longer be distinguished from the First Present in Late Egyptian. *ỉr* + First Present thus appears as a new form of temporal expression (cf. supra § 6.1.2[3]).

Another area affected by this is the balanced sentence. There are examples which can balanced be understood as the precise reproduction of this type (cf. supra § 3.3.2). In terms of sentence linguistic history, the *wnn*-construction reflects the multi-faceted nature of the *ỉw*-sentence even more than the other combinations of which it forms the second member. This multi-faceted nature comes to the fore (1) in those combinations where it is the remnant of the independent Middle Egyptian *ỉw*-sentence, and (2) because in the framework of

Late Egyptian, the *ỉw*-clause as Circumstantial Present is the most common form of subordinated clause — where it is the heir of the Middle Egyptian circumstantials (particularly the *sdm=f*). It is thus possible to claim two Middle Egyptian sentence constructions as the precursors of the *wnn*-construction:[4]

1. The anticipation with a noun in the form of a nominal *sdm=f* of *wnn* preceding an independent *ỉw*-clause — [*wnn=f ḥr mdw.t*]noun [*ỉw=s ḥr sdm*]clause —; the sententiality of the initial expression (including those where an initial noun is specified in detail) reveals its proximity to the balanced sentence.

2. The Emphatic Sentence formed of the nominal *sdm=f* of *wnn* + an adverbial predicate (whether prepositional infinitive or circumstantial *sdm=f*) — [[*wnn=f ḥr mdw.t*]noun [*ḥr sdm*]adverbial phrase]sentence or [[*wnn=f ḥr mdw.t*]noun [*sdm=f*]adverbial phrase]sentence — the second type being simultaneously a variation of the balanced sentence. In the course of Late Egyptianization both variants coalesce into [*wnn=f ḥr mdw.t*]noun [*ỉw=s ḥr sdm*]adverbial phrase]sentence.

system alienation and disappearance

Despite their superficial adaption ("Late Egyptianization"), these constructions were not really integrated into the Late Egyptian system. Since they did not undergo the decisive changes, and thus remained alien to the system, they eventually disappeared. They were linguistic remnants and thus lost in the course of the evolution of the Late Egyptian-Demotic system: traces remain where the adaption was complete, but they disappear where they could not be integrated.

lines of disappearance

In Demotic and Coptic, the *ỉr* and balanced sentence constructions are no longer present, as the system ultimately reduced the independent *ỉw*-sentence into the Third Future and the Circumstantial Present (and in some respects First Present, cf. supra § 5.2.3[2]). Topicalization allows some of the lines of the disappearance to be followed:

dropping of *ỉr*

Dropping the *ỉr* in the protasis left no other marking for the topicalization constructions except the absolute initial position: the use of a noun or adverbial in anticipation of an independent sentence. Anticipatory use of a noun is only superficially distinguished from the constructions with initial use of nouns in Middle Egyptian by the different nature of the sentence forms which they precede. Where the protasis is a First Present or extended noun which has been reinterpreted into First Present, there develops a clause grouping of the First Present and other sentence types which cannot be distinguished from other conventional chains of sentences.

anticipation of adverbials

The initial adverbials which thus became possible led to new forms of construction without precursors in Middle Egyptian. Temporal expressions need no longer follow the

---

4   Compare F. Junge, *"Emphasis" and Sentential Meaning in Middle Egyptian*, GOF IV 20, Wiesbaden 1989, § 6.2.3.

sentence, but can precede it. *ir iw=f (ḥr) sdm* becomes the Demotic Conditional *iw=f sdm* (and thus, with progressive analytical marking, the Coptic Conditional).

The evolution can be presented thus in tabular form:

Late Egyptian		Demotic		Coptic	
protasis	apodosis	protasis	apodosis	protasis	apodosis
ir + noun (+attribute)	sentence	noun	sentence	noun	sentence
ir + First Present	sentence	(First Present	sentence)	(First Present	sentence)
ir + *sdm=f*					
ir + adverbial	sentence	adverbial of time	sentence		
z.B. *ir* + *m-dr sdm=f*	sentence	*n-dr.t sdm=f*	sentence	Temporal	sentence
ir + *iw=f sdm*	sentence	*iw=f sdm*	sentence	(ЄЧϢΑΝϹѠΤⲘ	sentence)
		(*iw=s ḫpr iw=f sdm*	sentence)	ЄϹϢѠⲠЄ sentence	sentence
inn + First Present		*in-nȝ* + First Present	sentence	—	—
inn + Third Future	sentence	*in-nȝ* + Third Future			
inn + pret. *sdm=f*					
hn (+ *wn*) + First Present	*wn* + Third Future	*(r)hwn-nȝ* + sentence	sentence	ЄⲚЄЧϹΟΟΥⲚ	ⲚЄЧⲚΑϹѠΤⲘ
hn + prät. *sdm=f*	*iw*-clause			ЄⲚЄ + sentence	
hn + Nominalsatz		(*hmy*+*iw* + sentence	sentence)		

Observations:

"Sentence" signifies sentence conjugations (First Present; Third Future; preterite *sdm=f*; Emphatic Sentence; and Imperative and Prospective with *inn*/*in-nȝ* constructions), Nominal Sentences and clause complexes (for Late Egyptian, both First Present and *iw*-clause in NIMS-role); in Demotic and Coptic, it includes the Second Tenses. For the precise tabulations, cf. supra §§ 6.1.1(2); 6.2.1(2).

The Demotic *in-nȝ* + Third Future construction appears to be known only with nominal agents.

6.4.2 Bibliography

Johnson, *Demotic Verbal System*, 250-260; 269-270; Junge, *iw=f ḥr (tm) sdm*, 122ff

6.5 Exercises

6.5.1 An ostracon letter (oDM 303)

Short, letter-like note with a teasing complaint sent by a draughtsman of the Tomb Building Administration to his chief, the secretary Qenhikhapshaf. Transcribed and published by J.Černý, *Catalogue des ostraca hiératiques non littéraires de Deir el Médineh*, vol. 4, number 303.

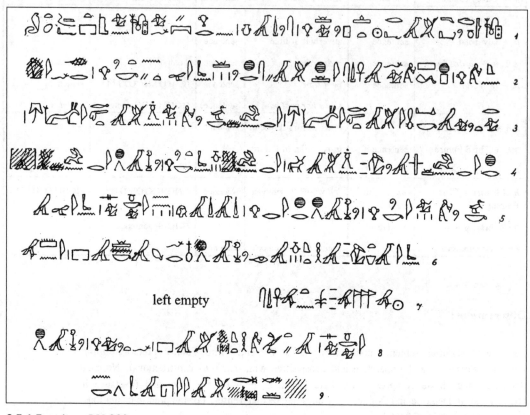

6.5.1 Exercise: oDM 303

Purpose: Example of the text of an ostracon of Dynasty XIX; *ìr*-constructions.

Notes:

line 1   cf. appendix § 7.2 for the introductory lines of letters. *zḫ3.w n s.t-m3ꜥ.t* — rarely used in hieratic — is the more official version of the title *zḫ3.w n p3 ḫr*. Note the stylistic interplay between the very formal introduction and the tone of the letter itself;

lines 2-3   *ì.r=ì* as a variant writing of the status pronominalis of *r* (here as rection of *ìrì* "to act with regard to me");

line 3   *m.dì* "with someone", cf. French *chez*; here nearly "for you";

ỉr wn(n) bȝk: sdm=f after ỉr (cf. supra § 6.1.3[3]), "if there is work" (note the absence of article); ỉn: passive sdm;

line 4   the bull-logogram should probably be read ỉḥ;

lines 4-5   ỉr wn [pȝ] bȝk, now: "but if the work is available";

line 5   ỉr ḥr-dȝdȝ-n=n: roughly: "Between us: …"; for the construction of ỉr with an adverbial phrase, cf. supra § 6.1.3(1), here not temporal;

bỉn m bỉ.t m ḥnq.t "(someone) who has bad manners with beer", "who is bad with beer";

lines 5-6   construction: ỉr + AP as protasis, a clause grouping with Nominal Sentence (tonal question) and Prohibitive as apodosis; the apodosis is a very good example illustrating the structure of such apparent conditional sentences, resulting from questionanswer relationships (cf. supra § 6.2.1[1]): "Am I a man who can't behave himself?! (If that is the case:) Then don't invite me!" > "If I am indeed a man who cannot behave himself, then you really should not invite me!" The zỉ without article is a reference to the class name (which nevertheless remains grammatically specific!);

line 6   the terminal phrase in the letter, nfr sdm=k "good reading!" (prospective sdm=f of nfr with nominal sdm=f as agent/subject, literally "may your reading be agreeable"). This is an example of the use of sdm.n=f as an allomorph of sdm=f (also with nominal sdm=f);

line 8   construction with the negative relative adjective ȝtỉ < ỉwty: "a man who does not dispose of the beer which is due to his household" (< "without beer from the one belonging to his household". Note the construct combination ḥnq.t pȝ (n) pr=f *"beer of the one of his house"; for the form of the possessive prefix, cf. supra § 2.1.2[2]);

line 9   nothing should be missing in the lacuna at the beginning of the line (wḫȝ mḥ ḫȝ.t=ỉ "to seek to fill my body"). The end is probably an abbreviated form of <m> pȝy=ỉ hȝb n=k.

6.5.2 A passage from a Late Ramessid story (Wenamun 2,26-37)

Excellently written literary text dating to the end of the New Kingdom. The text includes a date to Year 5 of the "Renaissance-Era" which is Regnal Year 24 of Ramesses XI. Political power over Upper Egypt is in the hands of Herihor, while Smendes and Tentamun rule Lower Egypt. The papyrus was found in el-Hiba and is now in the Pushkin Museum in Moscow. It was published by Gardiner, *Late Egyptian Stories*, pp. 61ff.: the passage reproduced here is pp. 69f. The following passage contains the decisive speech of Wenamun which finally convinces Tjekerba'al, the ruler of Byblos, to deliver the desired wood.

Purpose: Example for the advance of the Late Egyptian of the lower hierarchical registers into literature; clause groupings (ỉr- and ḥn-constructions).

Notes:

2,26-27   This passage is preceded by: "It was Amun-Re, the King of the Gods, who ordered Herihor, my Lord, to send me, and he had me come with this great god (Amun-of-the-Way)";

2,27   read ỉw=f mnỉ <m> tȝy=k mr, although the occasional adverbial use of locational expressions as absolute nouns should be borne in mind;

6.5.2 Exercise: Wenamun 2,26-37

iw bw rḫ=k in sw di: example of an object clause following *rḫ*, which can be understood as an indirect question: "without your knowing whether he is there" (< "although you could not know: 'is he here?'");

2,27-28   interrogative negated Adverbial Sentence (First Present) omitting preposition *m*: *in bn sw* <*m*> *pȝ nty wn=f* "Is he no longer what he was?" (a Nominal Sentence should be: **in bn mnt.f pȝ nty wn=f* or **in bn mnt.f iwnȝ pȝ nty wn=f!*); for the construction of *nty* with preterite *sdm=f* cf. § 5.1.2(3);

2,28   read *m.di* rather than *m-ḏr* (as there is a writing *m.di* for *m-ḏr*, *m-ḏr* can also be a writing of *m.di*);

2,29   *wn-di=w* (> *wn.t=w*) is a phonetic writing (with assimilated *m*) for the existential sentence *wn m.di=w NP* "NP belongs to them", "they possess NP", in which Coptic OYⲚ̄Tϩ OY is already apparent;

construction: *ir*-protasis with complex apodosis itself consisting of a *ḥn*-clause grouping: "As for this-and-that — if they had had this, they would not have had to bring that!";

2,34   restore: *'Imnw-Rᶜw* <*nzw*> *nṯr.w*;

ȝḫ.t=f: note the change in the form of the determination of *ȝḫ.t* here and in lines 2,29 and 2,30, *nȝ ȝḫ.t* "the things", but *ȝḫ.t=f* "his things" meaning "his (inalienable) possessions";

Ns-sw-Bȝ-nb-ḏd.t: sentence name: "He belongs to the Ram of Mendes", Hellenized as Smendes; *Tȝ-nt-'Imnw* is an appelative name: "She of Amun";

2,36   *mtw=w di.t in.tw pȝ nty-nb*: Conjunctive as continuation of the final prospective *sdm=f* (*hȝb=i sw*) following an imperative;

imm in.tw=f: resumption of *pȝ nty-nb*; here and in the following, the person being addressed is changed (speech within speech), and Tjekerbaᶜal is no longer addressed, but rather Smendes (although hitherto Smendes and Tentamun were always referred to in the plural); the messenger should assure Smendes that Herihor will guarantee Wenamun's expenses after his return (the assurance is effective, as the text following this passage indicates).

6.5.3 A letter concerning tax demands (pValençay I)

This letter was written by the mayor of Elephantine Maryana to the Chief Taxing Master Manmuarianakht, probably during the reign of Ramesses XI. In a very elegant fashion, the mayor attempts to deny an obligation to pay what appears to him to be an unjustified demand. Gardiner published the letter in *RAD* 72-73 and *RdÉ* 6 (1951): 115-127.

Purpose: Example of an official letter to a very high ranking official of the central administration; *ir*-constructions; use of oaths

Notes:

rt. 1   the name of the "Chief Taxing Master" *Mn-mȝᶜ.t-Rᶜw-nḫt.w* is formed with the throne name of Ramesses XI (or Sethos I). A little later he is probably, as *im.y-rȝ pr-ḥd* "Treasurer" and *im.y-rȝ šnw.ti* "Superintendent of the Granaries", the most powerful financial official in the land;

NN (ḥr) s:wḏȝ-ib: "NN greets", an abbreviated form of address which is balanced out by the very polite beginning of the letter: the initial position of the recipient of the letter — before the writer — and the letter introduction with "May Amun praise NN";

rt. 2   restore: *[tw=i ḏd] n ['Imnw-Rᶜw]-Ḥrw-ȝḫ.ty*; the request is to Amun-Re and the gods of Elephantine;

rt. 3   abbreviated writing *ȝbtw* for Elephantine;

rt. 4   *pȝ ꜥȝ n št*: the "Chief Taxing Master" is the head of the office responsible for tax assessments on the basis of the land survey. pWilbour is one of the reports of this office (cf. Gardiner, *The Wilbour Papyrus*, Vol.II: 10, 150, § 200);

rt. 6   *rꜥw-nb zp-2*: "day-in-day-out", best understood as an adverb related to the introductory *tw=ì ḏd n 'Imnw* (a reference which in other cases often does not appear to be possible, however);

     Pȝ-ṯȝw-m.dì-'Imnw, sentence name ("The Breath of Life is Amun's" < "with Amun");

     dwȝ.t-nṯr n 'Imnw: at this time the "Divine Adoratrice of Amun" (also *ḥm.t-nṯr n 'Imnw* "Divine Consort of Amun") still was a high-ranking position held by queens and princesses (liturgical representation of the goddess Mut), with its own administration (*pr*) and income;

rt. 7   *nȝ ìt r.tks=tw*: "the grain assessed"; for the grain terminology, cf. infra § 7.3.2(3);

6.5.3 Exercise: pValençay I, rt.1-vs.1

6.5.3 Exercise: pValençay I, vs. 1-11

rt. 8-9   *iw mn ḫ.wt ḥr=w*: "but there aren't (any) fields with that much" (< *"although there are no fields with them", the 100 sacks); note the writing of the status pronominalis of *ḥr* (*ḥr-r-r⸗w* > ϨⲀⲢⲞ⸗ⲞⲨ);

rt. 9-10   *ḥr wꜥ ḫ.t n ḫꜣ-(n-)tꜣ n (<m) iwn Nby.t*: "because of a leasehold of Crown Land on the ridge of Kom Ombo" (for the individual words, cf. the glossary § 9); note the writing of *ḥr*: the transliterated *n* should be read only as a meaningless stroke;

rt. 10   *i.n=w n=i*: "they said to me", change of the pronoun from sing. to pl. (the secretary of the Divine Adoratrice has a group of men with him to collect duties);

rt. 11-vs. 2   up to this point a situation has been described; with the oath, the author of the letter has now addressed himself to the recipient of the letter; for this part of the text, cf. supra § 3.3.2;

vs. 23   for the main clause (Pseudo-Cleft Sentence) of this longer sentence cf. supra § 4.3.3; note that *ḫ.t* "field (on lease); leasehold estate" is construed as a grammatical masculine;

vs. 34   *iw=w ꜥḥꜥ s:wd pꜣy⸗f nbw r pr-ḥd n Pr-ꜥꜣ*: "and they go about transferring its gold (the gold which is assessed for the leasehold) to the Treasury of Pharaoh"; for the use of *ꜥḥꜥ* as an auxiliary verb, cf. supra § 2.2.3(3);

vs. 5 *m swȝ.w n ḏbȝ*: "in the region of Edfu";

  4 stȝ.t-ȝḥ.t: "4 arouras of fields"; note the aroura-specific numeral;

vs. 5-6 construction: converted Pseudo-Cleft Sentence, which — concerning the preceding phrase — can be rendered as: "(it is not irrigated) — or rather, it is only 4 arouras of it that were irrigated";

vs. 6 *ḥtr*: here "ox team";

vs. 7 *pȝ nkt n ȝḥ.t*: "the bit of field";

vs. 8-9 *ỉw bw.pw=ỉ ḥn n wᶜ ỉp.t ỉm=f*: it is possible (but not necessary) to understand this sentence as anterior to the preceding phrase, "not having touched one oipe of it" > "without touching one oipe ...";

  for the grain measures here and in the following note, cf. infra § 7.3.1;

vs. 10 for the construction of content clauses, cf. supra § 5.3.2(2) (here with a "binding" oath which as such is not discussed in the appendix, § 7.1);

vs. 11 *wᶜ ḫȝr 0 (ỉp.t) $^{1}/_{2}$*: "(not) even one half of an oipe" (< *"a zero sack, 1/2 [oipe])";

  for the terminal formula (and other elements of the epistolary style), cf. infra, § 7.2.3.

7. Appendix

7.1. The New Kingdom oath

7.1.1 Characteristics

Oaths are of two kinds: (1) the "simple" oath and (2) the "extended" version. Both share simple and extended oaths the same formula (compare the English "I swear" or "So help me God"). The simple oath is followed by a statement of what is to be sworn. The extended oath includes the facts which are sworn to, and the following statement specifies the sanctions facing the oath-taker ("such-and-such will happen to me").

The oath itself is grammatically an independent prospective *sdm=f* form of the verbs ᶜ*nḫ* "live" (with occasional extensions with *mrỉ*, *ḥzỉ*) or *wȝḥ* "endure". One swears by the Ruler, gods (generally Re or Amun), or both. The facts asserted in the simple oath, and the sanctions specified in the extended oath, are formulated as independent sentences, generally *ỉw*-sentences, Adverbial Sentences (First Present) or sentences using second tenses.

the oath formula

On the basis of their contents a distinction can be drawn between assertory oaths facts sworn to ("this-and-that is/is not so") and promissory ones ("I will/will not do this-or-that").

7.1.2 The simple oath

(1) The earlier type: the ᶜ*nḫ*-oath

The basic pattern of the simple oath is: ᶜ*nḫ n=ỉ NN ḏd.n=ỉ m mȝᶜ.t* "As NN lives for me, I have spoken truly" (cf. Gardiner, *Grammar*, § 218). Oaths of the period extending down to the early New Kingdom follow this pattern. In the Ramessid Period, they still appear in the higher textual registers (Qadesh Poem). With extensions (which can be numerous, with many variations):

(Urk.IV 751,17-752,4)

ᶜ*nḫ n=ỉ mry wỉ Rᶜw*
ḥzỉ wỉ ỉty=ỉ ʾ*Imnw*

ḥwn fnḏ=ỉ m ꜥnḫ wꜣs
ỉw ỉrỉ.n=ỉ nn [r mꜣꜥ.t]

"As Re lives for me and loves me, and as my father Amun favours me, and my nose is rejuvenated with life and prosperity, I have truly done this." (Statement: *ỉw sḏm.n=f* sentence). Similarly

(Urk.IV 776,6-9) *ꜥnḫ n=ỉ [mry wỉ] Rꜥw ḥzỉ wỉ ỉty=ỉ ꜣImnw nn r ꜣw ḫpr r wn-[mꜣꜥ]* "As Re lives for me and loves me, and as my father Amun favours me, all of this truly is." (Statement: Adverbial Sentence with Old Perfective).

(2) The Ramessid type: the *wꜣḥ*-oath

In the Ramessid period, the formula of the oath is transformed through the use of *wꜣḥ* :

(pAnast.I 7,6-7)

wꜣḥ kꜣ n Ḏḥwtỉ (< *ḏd.w*) *ỉrỉ.n=ỉ ḥr-tp=ỉ ỉw bw ꜥš=ỉ n zḫꜣ.w r dỉ.t mtr=f* "As the Ka of Thoth endures, I have acted on my own, without calling a scribe so as to have him present." (Statement: *sḏm(.n)=f* sentence; the scribe Hori emphasizes that he himself is competent enough to write a letter).

The most common version in this period is the oath *wꜣḥ ꜣImnw wꜣḥ pꜣ ḥqꜣ* "As Amun endures and the Ruler endures":

(oDM 58) *ꜥnḫ n nb ꜥ.w.s. ỉr.n A wꜣḥ ꜣImnw wꜣḥ pꜣ ḥqꜣ ỉ.dỉ=ỉ ḫpr r-šꜥ 10 ỉw dỉ=[ỉ] pꜣy wrs n B* "Oath of the Lord sworn by A: 'As Amun and the Ruler endure, I will let no more than 10 days pass until I shall have given this head-rest to B" (statement: Second Tense with adverbial *sḏm=f*).

7.1.3 The extended oath

(1) The detailed version

In the Ramessid Period, the oath generally consisted of three parts: (1) the fixed oath formula *wꜣḥ ꜣImnw wꜣḥ pꜣ ḥqꜣ*; (2) the formulation of what is sworn (in the form of the Conjunctive); and (3) the statement of the sanctions to which one will be subjected in case of non-compliance (in the form of an independent sentence, frequently the old *ỉw*-sentence!):

(oGardiner 104,2-4)

(1) *wꜣḥ ꜣImnw wꜣḥ pꜣ ḥqꜣ*

(2) *mtw=ỉ mdw m pȝy ꜥȝ.t*

(3) *ỉw=f ḥr 100 n sḫ.t*

"As Amun and the Ruler endure, and I bring up the matter of this donkey, [I] shall be subjected to 100 blows".

Observation:

The regular change from the 1st pers. sing. to the 3rd pers. sing. betrays that the oath was Egyptian indirect speech (to which such pronominal change belongs): "and the speaker will be subjected to 100 blows".

(2) The abbreviated version

A common variant is the abbreviation of the oath by omitting the introductory formula (1). Such oaths thus seem to begin with an apparently independent Conjunctive:

(pBM 10403, 2, 4-5)

mȝꜥ.t m pȝ ḏd=ỉ nb

(1) —

(2) *mtw=tw gm.t=ỉ ỉw ḏd=ỉ ꜥḏȝ*

(3) *ỉw=f dd.t tp ḫt*

"What I have said is truth. Should I be found to have spoken falsehood, then [I] should be impaled."

7.1.4 Bibliography

John A. Wilson, The Oath in Ancient Egypt, in: *JNES* 7, 1948, 129-156; Frandsen, *Outline*, § 81 (2), 127-140

7.2 The disposition of letters

7.2.1 Letters as a genre of text

As a typical means of communication in complex societies, a great many letters (*šꜥ.t*; or *hȝb* "sending") of the New Kingdom have been preserved, both official and private. Although usually written on papyrus, many informal letters are preserved on ostraca. Couriers and messengers will have taken official letters, while private letters were usually entrusted to retainers, servants, or people who happened to be travelling to the required destination. Papyrus letters were dispatched after being cut off the roll, folded in half,

tied and sealed (cf. supra § 0.3.2). The names of recipient and writer were written on
the outside of the resulting packet (cf. Bakir, *Epistolography*, pp. 24-29).

conventions of
letters

    Like letters everywhere, Egyptian letters reveal culturally specific conventions which
at the same time reflect social stratification and the individual's virtuosity in manipulating
the conventions. Although these are very clear, we should not assume that they were very
strictly observed, however, precisely because they leave room for personal idiosyncrasies, and can even be completely ignored on occasion. They change over the years,
but are also included in instructions (one of the letter writer's guides, pSallier I — *LEM*
79-88 — has the heading *ḥ3.t-ᶜ m sb3y.t šᶜ.wt* "Beginning of Epistolary Instruction").
Within the conventional framework of letters, the language is rather colloquial, and they
are representative of the linguistic norms of ordinary communication, so that their
expressions have played a very important role in grasping the linguistic forms of the new
Kingdom.

7.2.2 Structure of a letter

A Dynasty XX letter can be structured as follows (text in imitation of *LRL*, 27-28):

letterhead

(1) *zẖ3.w* Thutmosis *n zẖ3.w* Amenophis

Letterhead: "The secretary Thutmosis to the secretary Amenophis";

salutation

(2) *m ᶜnḫ wḏ3 snb*

    m ḥs.t ʾImnw-Rᶜw nzw-nṭr.w Mwt Ḫnsw nṭr.w nbw n w3s.t

Salutation: "(Be) in life, prosperity and health; in the favour of Amun-Re, king of the
gods, of Mut and Khons, and all the gods of Thebes";

introductory
address

(3) *tw=ỉ ḏd n ʾImnw-Rᶜw-ḥrw-3ḫ.ty* (+ additional epithets; additional gods)

ỉmm n=k ᶜnḫ wḏ3 snb ᶜḥᶜ.w k3 ỉ3w.t ᶜ3 nfr

ỉmm n=f ḥzỉ m b3ḥ ʾImnw (+ epithets)

mtw ʾImnw ỉn.t=k

mtw=n mḥ qnỉ=n ỉm=k rᶜ-nb

Introductory adddress, requesting blessings: "I ask Amun-Re-Harakhte .... that [he] give
you life, prosperity, health, a long life, and good old age, and that [he] grant [you] favour
in the presence of Amun; and that Amun [of the Thrones of the Two Lands] may return
you safely, so that we may embrace you daily";

subject matter

(4) *ḥnᶜ ḏd r.nty:*

sdm=ỉ md.t nb ỉ.h3b=k n=ỉ ḥr=w

p3 h3b ỉ.ỉr=k ... st m sš

...

Subject matter: "and I now say: ..."

   Typical introductory formulae: "I have taken note of everything that you wrote to me about. Concerning what you wrote (whether so-and-so are well): they are well";

...

(5) *nfr snb=k*   closing line

Closing line: "May you be in good health" < "May your health be good";

(6) *ky ḏd n zḫ3.w NN n p3 ḫr ...*   postscriptum

Postscript: "Another communication for Secretary NN of the Tomb Building Administration".

7.2.3 Summary of conventions used in letters

(1) Letterhead

The Dynasty XX letterhead names the writer (W) and the recipient (R) as: W *n* R "W to R", where the preposition *n* need not be understood as more than a mere separator. Where the intention is to honour the recipient, his name comes first. This letterhead is an abbreviation of the earlier and more formal type (which appears frequently in the model letters of the miscellanies), with three principal variations. (1) A formula honouring the recipient, W *(ḥr) s:wḏ3-íb n (nb=f)* R, "W addresses himself to his Lord R" (< "W gladdens the heart of his Lord R") — or likewise placing the recipient first: R W *(ḥr) s:wḏ3-íb (n nb=f)*. (2) The more familiar form W *ḥr nḏ-ḫr.t (n)* R "W inquires after the state of R". (3) The businesslike abbreviated form: W *ḏd n* R "W informs R", or else *ḏd(.n)* W (*n* R).

(2) Salutation

The recipient is initially greeted with *m ꜥnḫ wḏ3 snb m ḥz.t* god NN: may he be "in life, prosperity, health and in the favor of god NN"; in tenor, these formulae correspond to our own greetings (like wishing someone "good morning", but are closer to those in use some time ago, such as "God bless you"). Grammatically, these are relics that follow the principle governing the construction of Middle Egyptian requests and wishes, which could be marked by the omission of the NP (of the recipient) in the adverbial clause (cf. Junge, *Syntax*, § 8.4.1). The salutation is comprehensively extended in the addresses to gods which usually follow.

   Where the writer has a very high status, or where the letter is particularly businesslike, the writer begins without any of the usual greetings, blessings, or small-talk, and goes straight to the point.

(3) Address with requests for blessings

The writer makes it clear that it is his concern to get the gods to bless the recipient. These pleas are mostly formulated as *tw=i ḏd n* god NN *imm snb=k*. This can be translated in two ways: either as "I pray to god NN that [he] give you (recipient) health", or "I pray to god NN: Let [him] (recipient) be healthy". In either case, the pronominal references have to be adjusted, and it is impossible to reproduce the Egyptian construction in translation. This necessity of adjusting the pronouns is a characteristic of indirect speech (cf. supra § 5.3.2[3]).

individual
variations

    The contents of the requests can show personal variations, such as "(I pray to Ptah and the gods) *imm ptr=i tw snb.ti mtw=i mḥ qni im=k* that [they] let me see you again in health, and let me embrace you". They can also establish that the recipient is a very highly placed individual, with forms like "I pray to Amun: *s:snb R* 'keep R healthy'".

(4) Subject matter

The actual subject of the message is introduced with *ḥnc ḏd* with or without *r.nty* — or occasionally with only *r.nty*. This can confirm the receipt of a letter, assuring that everything has been understood, and certain things can be emphasized by topicalization constructions (e.g., with an initial *pꜣ hꜣb i.ir=k/ir pꜣ hꜣb i.ir=k* with a quotation from the letter in question, "as for what you mentioned, saying that ..." The following main clause can be much shorter than the protasis, e.g., in the form of a First Present *sw m šs*, "he is well", etc.).

questions
about health

    Questions about the correspondent's health and remarks about one's own are common: *tw=tn mi iḫ* "How are you?", *iḫ hꜣb=k n=i ḥr c=k* "Please let me know about the state of your health", or else *mk tw=i m šs* "I am well", or *tw=i m šs m pꜣ hrww dwꜣw ḥr c.wy pꜣ nṯr* "I'm well today, tomorrow is in the hands of god" (earlier versions also: *tw=i m šs m pꜣ hrww bw rḫ=i c=i n pꜣ dwꜣw* "..., but I do not know the state I shall be in tomorrow").

wishes and
instructions

    Wishes and instructions can be introduced with the formula *wnn tꜣy=i šc.t spr r=k* (earlier version: *ḫft spr tꜣy=i šc.t r=k*) "When my letter reaches you", and be expressed by *iw=f ḥr sdm* forms. Other wishes and further advice can follow in the Conjunctive. In letters to servants or letters from high-ranking individuals, the Imperative is common, continued with a Conjunctive. Many of these letters thus contain a very high proportion of Conjunctive formulations.

    Other topics can be introduced — even after the closing line, as in the example, supra § 7.2.2(6) — with *ky ḏd* "another message".

(5) Ending the letter

The closing formula is brief and expresses the wish that the recipient may enjoy good health, *nfr snb=k* "May your health be good!" (compare "Farewell", earlier "Fare thee well!"). What was probably an earlier variation is *nfr sdm=k* "May your reading be enjoyable!" (< *"may your hearing be pleasant"). This closing line can occasionally be followed by *iw=i h3b r di.t ʿm=k* or something similar: "I have written to inform you/let you know". Very businesslike letters are terminated with the formula: *iḫ rḫ=k sw* "Please note this".

7.2.4 Bibliography

Bakir, *Epistolography*; Černý, *LRL*; Wente, *LRL*; Wente, *Letters*; Caminos, *LÄ* I s.v. Brief; Sweeney, *Correspondence*

7.3 Measures and indications of value

7.3.1 Measures of capacity and weight

Amounts of metals (silver or copper, rarely gold) are in the New Kingdom measured in [deben (*dbn*)]
terms of ingots weighing one *dbn* (91 grammes), fractions being measured in *qd.t*

(kite, Coptic **KITE**) being $1/10$ of a *dbn*. During Dyn. XIX, 1 *dbn* of silver was worth 100 *dbn* of copper, while during Dyn. XX, 1 *dbn* of silver was worth 60 *dbn* of copper.

Grain was mostly measured in "sacks" (*ḫ3r*; 76.88 ["sack" (*ḫ3r*) and "oipe" (*ip.t*)]
litres) and fractions thereof: a quarter sack was termed an

ip.t (oipe, Coptic **OIⲚⲈ**; 19.22 litres), which in turn consisted of four *ḥq3.t*. The fractions of the oipe or "quadruple *ḥq3.t*" were written with signs previously used for the simple *ḥq3.t*, using the elements of the "Eye of Horus", as shown in the diagram.

It is important to note how the measure signs were used: the usual hieratic writing for [writing and use of fraction signs]
ip.t is a dot (or a small circle like Gardiner's sign N33); the sign for $1/2$ ◁ is reversed in hieratic, ▷ , and is thus identical to the sign for $1/16$, ≻ ; the sign ⌢ for $1/8$ is written ⌣ . Units of measure are generally preceded by the "sack" sign, and where this is not immediately followed by a digit, it means "zero sacks", and the following fractions are to be understood as oipe-measures, which are generally rendered in terms of quantities of sacks in translation (and must thus be multiplied by $1/4$). Examples:

$ꜣ$||₁|●▷ _ḫȝr 5, (ỉp.t) 2 $^1/_2$_ "5 sacks, 2 $^1/_2$ oipe" means "5 $^5/_8$ sacks" ($< 5 + 2 * ^1/_4 + ^1/_2 * ^1/_4 = 5 + ^1/_2 + ^1/_8 = 5 + ^4/_8 + ^1/_8$);

$ꜣ$●●○⟍ _ḫȝr 0, (ỉp.t) 3 $^1/_4$ $^1/_8$_ "0 sack, 3 $^1/_4$ $^1/_8$ oipe" means "$^{27}/_{32}$ sacks" ($< ^3/_4 + ^1/_{16} + ^1/_{32}$).

7.3.2 Units of value

(1) Calculation of value

In all relatively complex economies a value must be specified for goods and services if these are to be exchanged. This requires abstract units of value, permitting the value of different things to be calculated and compared. Even without minted coins, such units of value approach those of a "monetary economy". In the New Kingdom, these units of value take the form of grain and metal. Their "monetary" value can be presented in tabular form thus (_dbn_ of copper):

šnꜥ.t/(znỉw)	ḫȝr	dbn	ỉp.t	double ḥqȝ.t	ḥqȝ.t	hnw	
1	2	4	8	(16)	32	320	
$^1/_2$	1	2	4	(8)	16	160	= 76.88 l
$^1/_4$	$^1/_2$	1	2	(4)	8	80	=91g copper
$^1/_8$	$^1/_4$	$^1/_2$	1	(2)	4	40	=1 artabe
($^1/_{16}$)	($^1/_8$)	($^1/_4$)	($^1/_2$)	(1)	(2)		
$^1/_{32}$	$^1/_{16}$	$^1/_8$	$^1/_4$	($^1/_2$)	1	10	
$^1/_{320}$	$^1/_{160}$	$^1/_{80}$	$^1/_{40}$	($^1/_{20}$)	$^1/_{10}$	1	
					$^1/_{320}$	$^1/_{32}$	= 1 rȝ

Observations:

šnꜥ.t/(znỉw)   The reading _znỉw_ is Janssen's in _Commodity Prices_; the unit goes out of use during the reign of Ramesses III;

dbn/ỉp.t   as a rule, lower prices are indicated in grain, higher ones in deben;

ḥqȝ.t   an earlier unit which drops out of use in the New Kingdom. It is presented here in order to convey the relationship of the various values. This is even more true of the "double ḥqȝ.t".

(2) Comparison

To understand the Egyptian value system, it seems necessary to compare it with our own value systems, but this is not easy. It may help to give some indication of income and the cost of living to get an overall impression of the economic background in which the value system functions:[1]

The ordinary members of the Gang of the Tomb Building Administration (*rmṯ-ỉz.t n*   wages *p3 ḥr*) who lived at Deir el-Medina had a monthly wage of four sacks of emmer (*bd.t*) and 1 $^1/_2$ sacks of barley (*ỉt*), which (at the rate of 5 kg of bread a day) was quite sufficient for a large family, apart from its value as a means of exchange. Beyond that, they received regular deliveries (*ḥtr*) of vegetables, fish, oil, pottery, firewood, and water. These were occasionally supplemented with wine, meat, cakes, beer, clothing and sandals. Altogether it amounted to an income of about 25-30 deben a month. The foreman (*ꜥ3 n ỉz.t*) received 5 $^1/_2$ sacks of emmer and 2 sacks of barley.

A goat could be purchased for 1-3 deben, a donkey for 25-40, a head of cattle for   prices 20-50 or 100-120; sandals cost about 2 deben a pair; a bed 12-25; a coffin 20-40. The value of the loot from a tomb could amount to 150, 222, 1100 or 1200 deben (pBM 10383).

(3) Graphemes and terms in the grain measure

The grain mentioned in accounts and similar documents is mostly ♦🏛 *bd.t* (Coptic ⲂⲰⲦⲈ) "emmer; spelt", and 🏛 *ỉt* (Coptic ⲈⲒⲰⲦ) "barley". Both together are *šs* (< *šsr*) "grain". As 🏛 has very often already taken on the meaning of *ỉt* "grain" (e.g., *m n3 ỉt n NL* "of the grain of [the] town NL), "barley" is then called 🏛🏛 *ỉt-m-ỉt*, "'grain' in the form of barley". When the scribes used both red and black ink, from Dynasty XVIII on red was used for *bd.t* "emmer" and black for *ỉt(-m-ỉt)* "barley".

7.3.3 Bibliography

W.-F. Reineke, Der Zusammenhang der altägyptischen Hohl- und Längenmaße, in: *MIO* 8, 1963, 154ff; Janssen, *Commodity Prices*, especially pp. 510ff; Gardiner, *Grammar*, § 266; A.H. Gardiner, *The Wilbour Papyrus*. Vol.II, 59ff; W. Helck, *LÄ* III s.v. Maße und Gewichte

---

1   Cf. Janssen, *Commodity Prices*, and id., Kha'emtore, a well-to-do workman, in: *OMRO* 58, 1977, pp. 221ff.

7.4 Titles, offices and functions in Deir el-Medina

7.4.1 The Tomb Building Administration

p3 ḥr

As with the construction of pyramids in earlier times, in the New Kingdom, too, the construction of the royal tomb involved a large organization, under the supervision of the office of the *t3.ty* ("Prime Minister" or "Vizier"), and later of the High Priest of Amun (the *pr-ʾImnw* was the main administrative authority on the west bank). Financially, the *ỉm.y-r3 pr-ḥḏ n Pr-ʿ3* ("Superintendent of the Treasury") was responsible for it. The organization took its name, *p3 ḥr*, "The Tomb", from the tomb of the reigning king, which would be the one under construction at the time (abbreviation of *p3 ḥr ʿ3 šps n ḥḥw m rnp.wt n Pr-ʿ3 ʿ.w.s. ḥr ỉmnt.t W3s.t* "the Great and Noble Tomb of Millions of Years of Pharaoh in the West of Thebes"). In this book, *p3 ḥr* is mostly rendered "Tomb Building Administration".

t3 ỉz.t n p3 ḥr

The workmen of the *ḥr*, the Tomb Building Administration, were organized into a team or Gang (literally "crew", *ỉz.t*). Although in general the number of workers averaged out at somewhere between 40 and 70, the number of members of the Gang fluctuated substantially even during individual reigns, so that, e.g., Ramesses IV and Ramesses V increased its strength to 120. The members of the Gang lived together with their families in a common settlement, called *p3 dmỉ* "the village" — today called Deir el-Medina, "the monastery of the city" — in a small wadi (*t3 ỉn.t*) in the western mountains, with access to the plain and, across a mountain ridge, to the Valley of the Kings (*sḫ.t ʿ3.t*).

ḥwtyw n p3 ḥr

The Gang was directed by a collective body (*ḥwtyw n p3 ḥr*). They were supported by "auxiliary workers from outside" the settlement (*smd.t bnr*). The Tomb Building Administration was assigned a detachment of police, which generally consisted of two officers (*ḥr.y-md3y n p3 ḥr*) each with three policemen (*md3y*).

7.4.2 The organization

(1) The Gang

"The Gang of The Tomb" (*t3 ỉz.t n p3 ḥr*) is a collective appellation for the body of craftsmen and workers of the Tomb Building Administration, their officials, and superiors. Regardless of their specific responsibilities, the men are all termed "the men of the 'Gang'" (*n3 rmṯ ỉz.t*), or "workmen"; in hieroglyphic inscriptions this title is rendered as *sḏm-ʿš n s.t m3ʿ.t* "servant of the place of truth". They are also occasionally called *rmṯ ḥmww* "craftsmen" or, figuratively, *wʿw* "soldiers". Their women bear the title *ʿnḫ.t n nw.t n p3 ḥr* "citizeness of The Tomb".

The members of the Gang were also distinguished according to specialization: as *specialization*
ḥmww "carpenter", or *ḥmww ḫȝ* "excavator" ("chiseller"), *ḥr.tyw-(nṯr)* "stonemason",
ṯȝy mdȝ.t "(relief) sculptor", or *q-ḏ-y* "stucco worker", "plasterer". Among them, the
zḫȝ.w-qdw.t "draughtsmen" or "painters" ranked higher: they were "scribes" who were
not employed in administration, but created the decoration, being literate (occasionally
they helped with administrative tasks). When the title is abbreviated to *zḫȝ.w*, the
difference between their position and that of the real administrative secretaries is not
always clear. The draughtsmen were headed by a "chief" (*ḥr.i zḫȝ.w-qdw.t*), who
belonged to the managerial body of the Tomb Building Administration.

The apprentices were either appointed (being then termed *mnḥ.w*, "youths" or *apprentices*
"striplings" in the older literature), or recruited from the families of the members of the
Gang (*ms.w ḥr* *"children of The Tomb").

The craftsmen and workmen were divided into two sections, "the right side" (*tȝ ry.t* *the two*
imnt.t) and "the left side" (*tȝ ry.t smḥ.t*). These sections were primarily work-units, who *sections*
worked together in different parts of the tomb under construction, but the designations
are also used for the social reference groups of their members.

(2) The managerial body

The two "sides" were each headed by a "foreman" or "chief-workman", the *ꜥȝ n iz.t n* *ꜥȝ n iz.t*
pȝ ḥr (usually abbreviated to *ꜥȝ n iz.t* in hieratic, *ḥr.y iz.t* in hieroglyphs). The foremen
were nominated by the Vizier, and they directed the work, and represented the Gang in
its relations with the outside world and with its administrative superiors. Their pay was
higher than that received by the other workmen (cf. supra § 7.3.2[2]).

The foremen were supported by a *zḫȝ.w n pȝ ḥr* "scribe of The Tomb", "Secretary of *zḫȝ.w n pȝ ḥr*
the Tomb Building Administration". From the reign of Ramesses III on there were
probably two, one for each side. Two others headed the support staff (*smd.t bnr*).
Although the foremen and many of the members of the Gang were literate, it was generally
these secretaries who kept the records, recorded attendance and events, kept the accounts,
and generally managed all written communications with their superiors and other
departments of the administration. These notes and records make up a high proportion
of the documents preserved from Deir el-Medina. The secretaries were responsible for
organizing supplies for the Gang — and quite often went to collect the relevant dues in
the name of the state — and for distributing the equipment used in tomb construction.

The longest-serving secretary of the "right side" was called simply *the* Secretary of *ḥwtyw n pȝ ḥr*
the Tomb Building Administration. Together with the two chief-workmen, and the chief
draughtsman of the "left side", they formed the body in control, the group known as
"the captains" (or "chiefs") "of The Tomb" (*ḥwtyw n pȝ ḥr*).

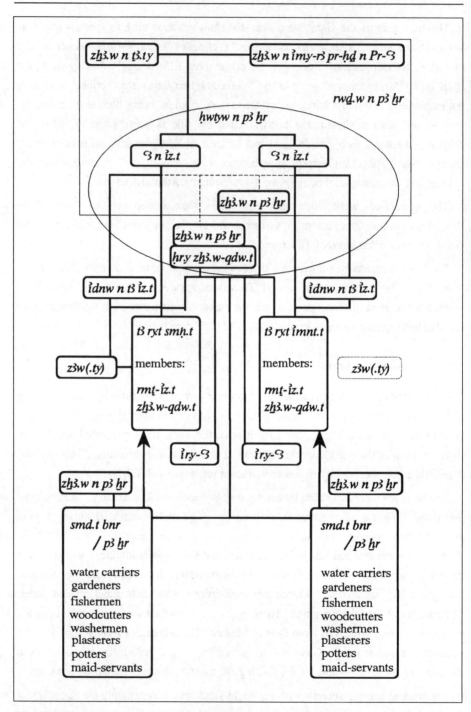

7.4:"Organigram" of the Tomb Building Administration

The top level of the administrative hierarchy was termed the *rwḏ.w n pȝ ḫr*, the   *rwḏ.w n pȝ ḫr*
"administrators" or "controllers of The Tomb". This group consisted of the on-site
"captains", i.e., the foremen and the longest-serving secretary, together with the
secretaries of the central administration (distinguished as the *rwḏ.w n bnr*): the "secretary
to the Prime Minister/Vizier" (*zḫȝ.w n ṯȝ.ty*) and the "secretary to the Superintendent of
the Treasury of Pharaoh" (*zḫȝ.w n ỉm.y-rȝ pr-ḥḏ n Pr-ˁȝ*).

(3) Minor officials

One member of the Gang on each side was the "deputy" (*ỉdnw*, abbreviated from *ỉdnw*   *ỉdnw n pȝ ḫr*
n pȝ ḫr) of the foreman. The deputies were frequently the sons of the foremen. They were
not numbered among the "officers", and were only assigned specific tasks (receiving
supplies, accepting messages, and serving on the adhoc local courts and investigative
committees).

Two "door-keepers" or "porters" (*ỉr.y-ˁȝ*) were assigned to the secretaries. They were   *ỉr.y-ˁȝ/zȝw.ty*
specifically responsible for the supplies of food, and also served as messengers or ushers,
particularly for tax collecting and courts. A porter could be promoted to "guardian"
(*zȝw/zȝw.ty*), an office which appears not to have been twinned. The guardian was
responsible for looking after the tools (particularly the valuable copper ones) and other
accessories (oils, fat, work clothing, raw materials for pigments).

7.4.3 The support staff

Given its location and the peculiar professional situation of its inhabitants, Deir el-Medina   *smd.t bnr*
had to be provisioned from outside. The residents traded the specialized items they
manufactured with one another and their neighbours in the region, but they were unable
to provide for their own sustenance. Both sections thus had to be supplied with a constant
flow of provisions — including water — from outside. This represented a part of their
income over and above the regular monthly grain deliveries of their wages. They also
benefited from numerous services. The personnel providing these services were called
the "serfs" or "support staff from outside" (*smd.t bnr*) or the "support staff of The
Tomb" (*smd.t pȝ ḫr*), and were generally accountable to a secretary of the Tomb Building
Administration. The support staff included five water carriers (*ỉn-mw*) with a leader (*ḥr.y
ỉn-mw*), three vegetable gardeners (*kȝry*) with their journeymen (*ḥr.y-ˁ*), three fishermen
(*wḥˁ*) with their leader (*ḥr.y wḥˁ*), three woodcutters (*šˁd ḫt*), a plasterer (*nty ḥr ỉr qd*,
later on *qdy*), washermen (*rḫty*), potters (*qd*) and five maid-servants (*ḥm.t*), who moved
from house to house, and occasionally a coppersmith (*ḥmtỉ.y[?]*), boatsmen (*nfw*), or a
physician (*zwnw*).

7.4.4 Bibliography

Černý, *Community*; McDowell, *Jurisdiction*; Valbelle, *Ouvriers*; Ventura, *City of the Dead*; J. J. Janssen, *Village Varia: Ten Studies on the history and administration of Deir el-Medina*, Leiden 1997; Andrea McDowell, *Village Life in Ancient Egypt: Laundry Lists and Love Songs*, Oxford 1999

L.M.J. Zonhoven, A Systematic Bibliography on Deir el-Medina, in: R.J. Demarée/J.J. Janssen (eds.), *Gleanings from Deir el-Medina*, Leiden 1982, 245ff; B. Haring, A Systematic Bibliography on Deir el-Medina 1980-1990, in: Demarée/Egberts, *Village Voices*, 111ff; website address http://www.leidenuniv.nl/nino/dmd/dmd.html

8. Bibliography

8.1 Sigla and abbreviations

It is rather difficult to be consistent when using abbreviations and text symbols. Thus, abbreviations will be found which are common or have been common in the secondary literature, alongside those which are used only here. They are, whenever possible, linked via cross-references. Papyri and ostraca are marked by initial "p" or "o" in the cross-references, otherwise by a following "P" or "O" in parentheses. Generally speaking, papyri cited here will also be found in the *Lexikon der Ägyptologie* under "Papyrus/Papyri" (*LÄ* IV: 672-750). Texts published by K.A. KITCHEN, *Ramesside Inscriptions*, are indicated as such by a parenthetical note including volume and page number (e.g. *KRI* VI 57ff).

2nd Libyan War	inscription in Medinet Habu; report of the war against the Libyans in year 11 of Ramesses III, publ. in: *The Epigraphic Survey. Medinet Habu* Vol. II, *Oriental Institute Publications* 9, Chicago 1930 (*KRI* V 57ff)
Abb	pAbbott, q.v.
Abbott (P.)	(report of the inquiry into the tomb robberies from year 16 of Ramesses IX; *KRI* VI 468-481) publ. in: G. MÖLLER, *Hieratische Lesestücke,* 3rd Fasc., Berlin 1961 (16); T.E. PEET, *The Great Tomb Robberies of the Twentieth Egyptian Dynasty*, Oxford 1930
Adoption (P.)	("Adoption extraordinary"), publ. in: A.H. GARDINER, *JEA* 26, 1941, 23ff; treatment: *HOP* 258ff (grammatical analysis by S. GROLL, A short grammar of the Spermeru dialect, in: *Studien zu Sprache und Religion Ägyptens — Fs. Westendorf*, Göttingen 1984, 41ff) (*KRI* VI 237-240)

Amarna (O.)	ostraca from Amarna, publ. in: H. FRANKFORT/J.D.S. PENDLE-BURY, *The North Suburb and the Desert Altars 1926-32. The City of Akhenaten* II, Egypt Exploration Fund Memoir 40, London 1933, pl. 57; J.D.S. PENDLEBURY, *The Central City and the Official Quarters 1926/27 and 1931/36. The City of Akhenaten* III, Egypt Exploration Fund Memoir 44, London 1951, pl. 84ff; D. SILVERMAN, Texts from the Amarna period and their position in the development of Ancient Egyptian, in: *LingAeg* 1, 1991, 301-314
Amiens (P.)	(reign of Ramesses III) publ. in: *RAD*
Amherst (P.)	papyri in the Pierpont Morgan Library, New York, cf. LeAm, cf. Astarte
Anast. I (P.)	literary letter (reign of Ramesses II), publ. in: A.H. GARDINER, *Egyptian Hieratic Texts. Series I: Literary Texts of the New Kingdom.* Part I, Leipzig 1911; HANS-WERNER FISCHER-ELFERT, *Die Satirische Streitschrift des Papyrus Anastasi I. Textzusammenstellung, Kleine Ägyptische Texte*, Wiesbaden 1983; id., *Die Satirische Streitschrift des Papyrus Anastasi I. Übersetzung und Kommentar, Ägyptologische Abhandlungen* 44, Wiesbaden 1986
Anast. II-VI (P.)	papyri in the British Museum, London (cf. also sub BM), publ. in: *LEM*
Anast. VIII (P.)	papyrus in the British Museum (reign of Ramesses II), London, publ. in: BAKIR, *Epistolography*, pl. 28-32 (*KRI* III 499-504); transl.: WENTE, *Letters*, 120ff
Anast. IX (P.)	papyrus in the British Museum (reign of Ramesses II), London, publ. in: BAKIR, *Epistolography*, pl. 32-33 (*KRI* III 504-508); transl.: WENTE, *Letters*, 122f
Apophis (and Seknenre)	("The Quarrel of Apophis and Seknenre") publ. in: *LES*
Ashmol.1945.95 (P.)	(papyrus in the Ashmolean Museum, Oxford) cf. pAdoption
Ashmol.1945.97 (P.)	(papyrus in the Ashmolean Museum, Oxford) cf. pNaunakhte
Astarte	"The Legend of Astarte", pAmherst IX, publ. in: *LES*; treatment: A.H. GARDINER, in: *Studies Presented to Francis Llewellyn Griffith*, London 1932, 74ff; P. COLLOMBERT/L. COULON, *Les dieux contre la mer. Le début du "papyrus d'Astarte"*, in: *BIFAO* 100, 2000, 193-242
Banishment-Stela	(Stela Louvre C 256), publ. in: J. VON BECKERATH, *RdE* 20, 1968, 7ff
Beatty (P.)	cf. pChester Beatty

Beatty Love Songs (P.)	(the love songs of papyrus Chester Beatty I vs.; reign of Ramesses V), publ. in: ALAN H. GARDINER, *The Library of A.Chester Beatty. Description of a Hieratic Text with a Mythological Story, Love-songs, and other miscellaneous Texts*, London 1931; transl. by LICHTHEIM, *Literature*, 182-189
Berlin 3043 (P.)	pKoller, q.v.
Berlin 8523 (P.)	("Eine zurückgezogene Pachtkündigung") publ. in: W. SPIEGEL-BERG, *ZÄS* 53, 1917, 107ff; *HOP* 274ff, pl. 76f
Berlin 10460 (P.)	publ. in: *HOP* 275f, pls. 78-79 (*KRI* VI 863f)
Berlin 10487-10489 (P.)	(letters of late dynasty XX) publ. in: *LRL*
Berlin 10494 (P.)	(letter of late dynasty XX) publ. in: *LRL*
Berlin 10496 (P.)	publ. in: *HOP* 277ff, pl. 80-83 (*KRI* V 476-478)
Berlin 10627 (O.)	(letter to the scribe Nekhemmut; reign of Ramesses IV) publ. in: *Hieratische Papyrus aus den königlichen Museen zu Berlin* III, Leipzig 1911, pl. 33; cf. A. ERMAN, in: *ZÄS* 42, 1905, 100ff (*KRI* VI 155f)
Berlin 10628-10630 (O.)	(reign of Ramesses III) publ. in: *Hieratische Papyrus aus den königlichen Museen zu Berlin* III, Leipzig 1911, pls. 37; 39; *HOP* 27 (*KRI* V 564f; 574)
Berlin 11239 (O.)	(reign of Ramesses II) publ. in: *Hieratische Papyrus aus den königlichen Museen zu Berlin* III, Leipzig 1911, pl. 38 (reign of Ramesses II; *KRI* III 545)
Berlin 11241 (O.)	publ. in: *HOP* 34, pls. 8-9 (*KRI* IV 406)
Berlin 12630 (O.)	publ. in: *HOP* 35, pls. 10-11 (*KRI* V 594f)
Berlin 12654 (O.)	(reign of Ramesses VI) publ. in: *HOP* 35ff, pls. 12-15 (*KRI* VI 344f)
Berlin 14214 (O.)	publ. in: *HOP* 38f, pls. 16-19 (*KRI* V 576f)
Bibl.Nat.196-199 (P.)	(18 letters of late dynasty XX) publ. in: *LRL*; transl. of pBibl.Nat. 196 III by VITTMANN, *Hieratic Texts*, 68ff
Blinding of Truth	the story of "The Blinding of Truth by Falsehood" of pChester Beatty II, London (pBM 10682; dynasty XIX), publ. in: *LES*; transl. in: LICHTHEIM, *Literature* 211-214
BM 5624-5625 (O.)	(reign of Ramesses III/V) publ. in: *JEA* 12, 1926, 176f, pls. 34-36; treatment: *HOP* 43ff (*KRI* V 475f; VI 252f)
BM 5627 (O.)	publ. in: *HO*; transl.: WENTE, *Letters*, 126
BM 5631 (O.)	publ. in: *HO*
BM 5634 (O.)	publ. in: *HO* (*KRI* III 515-525)
BM 5637 (O.)	publ. in: *JEA* 12, 1926, 176f, pl. 37 (*KRI* V 577)

BM 50722 (O.)	publ. in: *HO* (*KRI* VI 364)
BM 50734 (O.)	publ. in: *HO* (*KRI* V 563f)
BM 10052 (P.)	Tomb Robbery Trials, q.v. (year 1 of Ramesses XI; *KRI* VI 767-803)
BM 10053 (P.)	Tomb Robbery Trials, q.v. (rt.: year 17 of Ramesses IX; *KRI* VI 506-514; vs.: year 9 of Ramesses XI; *KRI* VI 755-763)
BM 10054 (P.)	Tomb Robbery Trials, q.v. (rt., vs. 5-6,3: year 16 and 18 of Ramesses IX; *KRI* VI 489-497; vs. 2-4,14: year 12 of Ramesses XI; *KRI* VI 743-746)
BM 10055 (P.)	pSalt 124, q.v. (reign of Siptah; *KRI* IV 408-414)
BM 10060 (P.)	Doomed Prince/Taking of Joppa, q.v. (reign of Seti I/Ramesses II)
BM 10068 (P.)	Tomb Robbery Trials, q.v. (rt.: year 17 of Ramesses IX; *KRI* VI 497-505; vs.: year 12 of Ramesses XI; *KRI* VI 747-755)
BM 10100 (P.)	(letter of late dynasty XX) publ. in: *LRL*
BM 10102 (P.)	("The Letters of Aahmose Peniati") publ. in: S.R.K. GLAN-VILLE, *JEA* 14, 1928, 294ff
BM 10181 (P.)	pSallier III, q.v. (reign of Ramesses II)
BM 10184 (P.)	pSallier IV vs., q.v. (reign of Merenptah)
BM 10185 (P.)	pSallier I, q.v. (reign of Merenptah)
BM 10221 (P.)	rt.: pAbbott, q.v. (year 16 of Ramesses IX; *KRI* VI 468-481)
BM 10243 (P.)	pAnast. II, q.v. (reign of Merenptah)
BM 10244 (P.)	pAnast. V, q.v. (reign of Seti II)
BM 10245 (P.)	pAnast. VI, q.v. (reign of Seti II)
BM 10246 (P.)	pAnast. III, q.v. (reign of Merenptah)
BM 10249 (P.)	pAnast. IV, q.v. (reign of Seti II)
BM 10284 (P.)	(letter of late dynasty XX) publ. in: *LRL*
BM 10300 (P.)	(letter of late dynasty XX) publ. in: *LRL*
BM 10326 (P.)	(letter of late dynasty XX) publ. in: *LRL*
BM 10335 (P.)	(oracle papyrus in the British Museum), publ. in: A.M. BLACKMANN/W.R. DAWSON, *JEA* 11, 1925, 247ff (*KRI* VII 416-418)
BM 10375 (P.)	(letter of late dynasty XX) publ. in: *LRL*
BM 10403 (P.)	Tomb Robbery Trials, q.v. (year 2 of renaissance era of Ramesses XI; *KRI* VI 828-833)
BM 10412 (P.)	(letter of late dynasty XX) publ. in: *LRL*
BM 10417 (P.)	(letter of late dynasty XX) publ. in: *LRL*

BM 10430 (P.)	(letter of late dynasty XX) publ. in: *LRL*
BM 10433 (P.)	(letter of late dynasty XX) publ. in: *LRL*
BM 10447 (P.)	(delivery of grain in year 55 of Ramesses II) publ. in: *RAD*
BM 10682 (P.)	Blinding of Truth, q.v.
Bol.	pBologna, q.v.
Bologna 1086 (P.)	papyrus in the museum of Bologna (reign of Merenptah), publ. in: GEORG MÖLLER, *Hieratische Lesestücke für den akademischen Gebrauch*, 3rd Fasc. (Musterbriefe und Geschäftliche Texte des Neuen Reiches), Berlin 1961, 9-11; WOLF, *Papyrus Bologna 1086. Ein Beitrag zur Kulturgeschichte des Neuen Reiches, ZÄS* 65, 1930, 89ff (*KRI* IV 78-81); transl.: WENTE, *Letters*, 124ff
Bologna 1094 (P.)	papyrus in the museum of Bologna (reign of Merenptah), publ. in: *LEM*
Boulaq 10 (P.)	(pCairo 58092) publ. by J.J. JANSSEN/P.W. PESTMAN, Burial and Inheritance in the Community of the Necropolis Workmen at Thebes, in: *Journal of the Economic and Social History of the Orient* 11, Leiden 1968, 137ff; *HOP* 289ff, pls. 88-91 (*KRI* V 449-451)
Boundary stelae, of Amarna (the later B. st.)	publ. in: MAJ SANDMAN, *Texts from the Time of Akhenaten, Bibliotheca Aegyptiaca* VIII, Brussels 1938, 119ff, transl. LICHTHEIM, *Literature*, 48ff; text, translation and commentary: WILLIAM J. MURNANE/ CHARLES C. VAN SICLEN III, *The Boundary Stelae of Akhenaten*, London-New York 1993, 84ff; WILLIAM J. MURNANE, *Texts from the Amarna Period in Egypt*, SBL Writings from the Ancient World Series 5, Atlanta 1995
BritMus	cf. BM
Cairo 25001-25385 (O.)	Egyptian Museum Cairo, *Catalogue Général*: GEORGES DARESSY, *Ostraca*, Cairo 1901 (cf. *KRI* Index VIII 34-35)
Cairo 25227 (O.)	treated in: *HOP* 55f, pl. 28 (*KRI* IV 231f)
Cairo 25235 (O.)	publ. in: *HOP* pl. 29 (*KRI* VI 159)
Cairo 25255 (O.)	publ. in: *HOP* pl. 29
Cairo 25264 (O.)	publ. in: *HOP* pl. 30
Cairo 25501-25832 (O.)	(ostraca in the Egyptian Museum Cairo, *Catalogue Général*) publ. in: JAROSLAV ČERNÝ, *Ostraca hiératiques*, 2 vol., Cairo 1935 (some of them treated in *HOP*; cf. *KRI* Index VIII 35-38)
Cairo 58034 (P.)	pNeschons, q.v.
Cairo 58053-58056 (P.)	(letters from the reign of Seti I and Ramesses II in the Egyptian Museum Cairo, *Catalogue Général*) publ. in: BAKIR, *Epistolography*; transl.: WENTE, *Letters*, 114ff; 117 (*KRI* I 322-325; III 254f)

Cairo 58057 (P.)   (letter from the reign of Ramesses I) publ. in: *HOP* 287f, pl. 86: transl.: WENTE, *Letters*, 112 (*KRI* I 238)

Cairo 58058-58060 (P.)   (letters of Dynasty XIX in the Egyptian Museum Cairo, *Catalogue Général*) publ. in: BAKIR, *Epistolography*; transl.: WENTE, *Letters*, 113; 118 (*KRI* III 251f)

Cairo 58061 (P.)   (letter of late dynasty XX) publ. in: *LRL*

Cairo 58092 (P.)   pBoulaq 10, q.v.

CarnarvTabl   Carnarvon Tablet I, publ. in: A.H. GARDINER, *JEA* 3, 1916, 95ff

CG(C)   *Catalogue Général* of the Egyptian Museum Cairo, cf. Cairo

Chester Beatty I (P.)   (rt.: HorSeth, q.v.; vs.: Love songs Beatty, q.v.; a hymn, a eulogy of Ramesses V; purchase documents) publ. in: ALAN H. GARDINER, *The Library of A.Chester Beatty. Description of a Hieratic Text with a Mythological Story, Love-songs, and other miscellaneous Texts,* London 1931

Chester Beatty III-V (P.)   publ. in: ALAN H. GARDINER, *Hieratic Papyri in the British Museum*. Third Series. Chester Beatty Gift, London 1935

Chester Beatty IX (P.)   publ. in: ALAN H. GARDINER, *Hieratic Papyri in the British Museum*. Third Series. Chester Beatty Gift, London 1935

D'Orb (P.)   papyrus D'Orbiney ("The Tale of the Two Brothers"; reign of Seti II), BM 10183, publ. in: *LES*

DeM (O.)   ostraca from Deir el-Medina, cf. oDM

DeM (P.)   papyri from Deir el-Medina, cf. pDM

DM 1-38 (P.)   JAROSLAV ČERNÝ, *Papyrus hiératiques de Deir el-Médineh* Vol.1-2, *Documents de fouilles de l'Institut français d'archéologie orientale du Caire* 8, 22, Cairo 1978; 1986; treatment: pDM 26-27, *HOP* 295ff, pls. 92-99 (*KRI* V 461-466; 578f; VI 134f; 259-269; 671-673; VII 383f)

DM 1-456 (O.)   JAROSLAV ČERNÝ, *Catalogue des ostraca hiératiques non-litteraires de Deir el-Médineh, Documents de fouilles de l'Institut français d'archéologie orientale du Caire* 3-7, Cairo 1935-1951 (a large number treated in *HOP*; cf. *KRI* Index VIII 38-42)

DM 550-623 (O.)   SERGE SAUNERON, *Catalogue des ostraca hiératiques non-litteraires de Deir el-Médineh, Documents de fouilles de l'Institut français d'archéologie orientale du Caire* 13, Cairo 1959 (some of them treated in *HOP*, a large number translated in WENTE, *Letters*, 133ff; cf. *KRI* Index VIII 42)

DM 624-705 (O.)   JAROSLAV ČERNÝ, *Catalogue des ostraca hiératiques non-litteraires de Deir el-Médineh, Documents de fouilles de l'Institut français d'archéologie orientale du Caire* 14, Cairo 1970 (some of them treated in *HOP*, a large number translated in WENTE, *Letters*, 133ff; cf. *KRI* Index VIII 42-43)

DM 1001-1675 (O.)   GEORGE POSENER, *Catalogue des ostraca hiératiques litteraires de Deir el-Médineh, Documents de fouilles de l'Institut français d'archéologie orientale du Caire* 1, 18, 20, Cairo 1932-82 (cf. *KRI* Index VIII 43)

Doomed Prince   ("The Tale of the Doomed Prince"; reign of Seti I/Ramesses II) papyrus BM 10060/pHarris 500 rt. of the British Museum, London, publ. in: *LES*

el Hibe letters   publ. in: W. SPIEGELBERG, *ZÄS* 53, 1917, 1ff; pStrassburg 39: *HOP* 307ff, pls. 104f

Elephantine scandal   Turin 1887, papyrus in the Museo Egizio, publ. in: *RAD*; transl. by VITTMANN, *Hieratic Texts*, 45ff

Gardiner (O.)   publ. in: *HO* (some publ. and a large number treated in *HOP*; cf. *KRI* Index VIII 43-45)

Gardiner 104 (O.)   publ. in: *HO* pl. 47,3 (*KRI* V 555)

Genf D 187 (P.)   (letter of late dynasty XX) publ. in: *LRL*

Genf D 191-192 (P.)   (letters of late dynasty XX) publ. in: *LRL* (D 191, also *HOP* 303ff, pls. 100f)

Genf D 407 (P.)   (letter of late dynasty XX) publ. in: *LRL*

Great hymn, of Amarna   publ. in: MAJ SANDMAN, *Texts from the Time of Akhenaten, Bibliotheca Aegyptiaca* VIII, Brussels 1938, 93ff; transl. JAN ASSMANN, *Ägyptische Hymnen und Gebete, Die Bibliothek der Alten Welt*, Zurich and Munich 1975, 215ff (92)

Griffith (P.)   (letter of late dynasty XX) publ. in: *LRL*

GTR   ("Great Tomb Robberies") Tomb Robbery Trials, q.v.

Gurob (P.)   (papyri from the Harim administration of "Mi-wer"/Kom Medinat Ghurab; reign of Ramesses II) publ. in: *RAD*

Harim Conspiracy   a number of trial records of a conspiracy in the harim of Ramesses III (pJud.Turin; pLee; pRollin; pRifaud, q.v.), publ. in: *KRI* V 350-366 (reign of Ramesses IV)

Harr.   pHarris I, q.v.

Harris 500 (P.)   Doomed Prince/Taking of Joppa/Harris Love Songs , q.v. (reign of Seti I/Ramesses II)

Harris I (P.)   ("The great Harris papyrus"), publ. in: WOLJA ERICHSEN, *Papyrus Harris I*, Bibliotheca Aegyptiaca V, Brussels 1933; PIERRE GRANDET, *Le papyrus Harris I*, 2 vols., *Bibliothèque d'Étude* 109, Cairo 1994

Harris Love Songs (P.)   (the love songs of pHarris 500), papyrus BM 10060/pHarris 500 rt. of the British Museum, London, publ. in: MAX MÜLLER, *Die Liebespoesie der alten Ägypter*, Leipzig 1899

Hittite-Treaty   (peace treaty of Ramesses II with the Hittites), publ. in: *KRI* II
                        225-232

HO   JAROSLAV ČERNÝ/ALAN H. GARDINER, *Hieratic Ostraca*
                        Volume I, Oxford 1957

HorSeth   ("The Contendings of Horus and Seth"; reign of Ramesses V.)
                        publ. in: *LES*

H.S.   HorSeth, q.v.

Israel Stele   (victory inscription of Merenptah, CG 34025 vs.), publ. in: *KRI*
                        IV 12-19

Jud.Turin (P.)   papyrus in the Museo Egizio, Turin, of the so-called "Harim
                        conspiracy", publ. in: THÉODULE DEVÉRIA, *Le papyrus
                        judiciaire de Turin, et les Papyrus Lee et Rollin, Bibliothèque
                        Égyptologique. Tome cinquième*, Paris 1897 (*KRI* V 350-360)

Jur.Turin (P.)   pJud.Turin, q.v.

Khensemhab   ("Khensemhab and the Spirit") publ. in: *LES*

Koller (P.)   papyrus in Berlin (cf. here "Berlin"), publ. in: *LEM*

KRI   KENNETH A. KITCHEN, *Ramesside Inscriptions. Historical and
                        Biographical*, 8 vols., Oxford 1975-1991

Lansing (P.)   papyrus BM 9994 (Model letter from Dynasty XX), publ. in: *LEM*

LeAm (P.)   papyri Leopold II/Amherst VII (reports of the Tomb Robbery
                        Trials, year 16 of Ramesses IX; *KRI* VI 481-489), publ. in: A.H.
                        GARDINER/J. CAPART/B. VAN DE WALLE, *JEA* 22, 1936, 169ff

Leb   pBerlin 3024 ("Gespräch eines Lebensmüden mit seiner Seele",
                        "The Dialogue of a Man and his Soul"), publ. in: R.O.
                        FAULKNER, *JEA* 42, 1956; transl. R. B. PARKINSON, *The Tale
                        of Sinuhe and Other Ancient Egyptian Poems 1940-1640*, Oxford
                        1997

Lee (P.)   papyrus Lee (= pAmherst V; reports of the Harim conspiracy,
                        probably against Ramesses III; reign of Ramesses IV) publ. in:
                        H. GOEDICKE, *JEA* 49, 1963, 71-92 (*KRI* V 360-363)

Leiden I 350 (P.)   (a collection of literary hymns to Amun and his city), publ. in: J.
                        ZANDEE, *Hymnen aan Amon van Pap. Leiden I 350,
                        Oudheidkundige Mededelingen uit het Rijksmuseum van Oudhe-
                        den te Leiden* 28, 1947; selectively transl. by ASSMANN, *Hymnen
                        und Gebete*, 312ff

Leiden I 360-368   (letters of Dynasty XIX) publ. in: J.J. JANSSEN, *Nine Letters from
(P.)   the time of Ramesses II, Oudheidkundige Mededelingen uit het
                        Rijksmuseum van Oudheden te Leiden* 41

Leiden I 369-370   (letters of late dynasty XX) publ. in: *LRL*
(P.)

LEM	(quoted by page and line in:) ALAN H. GARDINER, *Late-Egyptian Miscellanies, Bibliotheca Aegyptiaca* VII, Brussels 1937; translation and commentary: RICARDO A. CAMINOS, *Late-Egyptian Miscellanies, Brown Egyptological Studies* I, Oxford 1954
Leopold II (P.)	pLeAm, q.v.
Leop-Am	pLeAm, q.v.
LES	(quoted by page and line in:) ALAN H. GARDINER, *Late-Egyptian Stories, Bibliotheca Aegyptiaca* I, Brussels 1932
Libyan War	(inscription in the temple of Karnak: report of the war of Merenptah against the Libyans), publ. in: *KRI* IV 2-12
Literary letter Moscow	(from el Hibe, in the Pushkin Museum), publ. in: RICARDO A. CAMINOS, *A Tale of Woe*, Oxford 1977
Louvre E 4889 (P.)	so-called papyrus "Raifé", q.v.
LRL	(quoted by page and line in:) JAROSLAV ČERNÝ, *Late Ramesside Letters, Bibliotheca Aegyptiaca* IX, Brussels 1939; transl.: EDWARD F. WENTE, *Late Ramesside Letters, SAOC* 33, Chicago 1967; WENTE, *Letters*, 171-204
Mallet III-VI (P.)	(letters from reign of Ramesses IV) publ. in: BAKIR, *Epistolography*; transl.: WENTE, *Letters*, 127ff
Man and Soul	("The Dialogue of a Man and his Soul") pBerlin 3024, cf., e.g., publication and treatment by W. BARTA, *Das Gespräch eines Mannes mit seinem Ba, MÄS* 18, Berlin 1969; H. GOEDICKE, *The Report about the Dispute of a Man with his Ba*, Baltimore 1970
Mayer A and B (P.)	(reports of the Tomb Robbery Trials; reign of Ramesses IX), publ. in: THOMAS E. PEET, *The Mayer Papyri A and B. Nos. M.11162 and M.11186 of the Free Public Museum Liverpool*, London 1920; new readings: PEET, *Tomb Robberies*, pl. 24 (*KRI* VI 803-828; 515-516)
MedHab	*The Epigraphic Survey. Medinet Habu, Oriental Institute Publications* 8-9; 23; 51; 83-84; 93-94, Chicago 1930-1970
Michaelides (O.)	HANS GOEDICKE/EDWARD F. WENTE, *Ostraka Michaelides*, Wiesbaden 1962 (some of them treated in *HOP*; cf. *KRI* Index VIII 45f)
Nash 1-6 (O.)	publ. in: *HO*; treatment: *HOP* 214ff (*KRI* IV 229; 315-319; V 471f)
Nash 1 (O.)	(report of a theft trial from the reign of Seti II) publ. in: *HO* pl. 46; treated *HOP* 214-216 (*KRI* IV 315-317)
Naunakhte (P.)	("The Will of Naunakhte and the related documents"), publ. in: J. ČERNÝ, *JEA* 31, 1945, 29ff (year 3/4 of Ramesses V; *KRI* VI 236-243); treatment: *HOP* 268f; 295ff (pDM 2 A + B)

Neschons (P.)   CGC 58034, papyrus in the Egyptian Museum, Cairo (divine decree for the princess Nes-Chons, reign of Pinodjem), publ. in: B. GUNN, *JEA* 41, 1955, 83ff (with an appendix by I.E.S. EDWARDS)

Nevill (P.)   ("The Nevill Papyrus: A Late Ramesside Letter to an Oracle") publ. in: J. BARNS, *JEA* 35, 1949, 69ff

ODM   cf. oDM

Orb   cf. pD'Orb ("The Tale of the Two Brothers")

Petrie (O.)   publ. in: *HO* (some of them treated in *HOP*; cf. *KRI* Index VIII 46f)

Peasant   the "Eloquent Peasant", cited after R.B. PARKINSON, *The Tale of the Eloquent Peasant*, Oxford 1991

Petrie 18 (O.)   publ. in: *HO* pl. 70,1 (year 7 of Ramesses VII; *KRI* VI 430f)

Qadesh-Bulletin   short version of the description of the battle of Qadesh, year 5 of Ramesses II, publ. in: *KRI* II 102-124

Qadesh-Poem   long version of the description of the battle of Qadesh, year 5 of Ramesses II, publ. in: *KRI* II 2-101; cf. also pSallier III

RAD   ALAN H. GARDINER, *Ramesside Administrative Documents*, Oxford 1948 (partly translated and commented on by id., *JEA* 27, 1941, 19ff)

Raifé (P.)   papyrus E 4889 in the Louvre, Paris (part of a description of the battle of Qadesh of Ramesses II, continued by pSallier III, q.v.), publ. in: *KRI* II 14-24, §§ 34-65

Rifaud (P.)   "Papyrus Rifaud", today lost (report on the Harim conspiracy, probably against Ramesses III; reign of Ramesses IV), treated in S. SAUNERON/J. YOYOTTE, *BIFAO* 50, 1952, 107ff (*KRI* V 363-366)

Rollin (P.)   papyrus Rollin (report on the Harim conspiracy, probably against Ramesses III; reign of Ramesses IV) publ. in: H. GOEDICKE, *JEA* 49, 1963, 71-92 (*KRI* V 360-361)

Sallier I (P.)   papyrus 10185 in the British Museum, London, publ. in: *LEM*

Sallier III (P.)   papyrus 10181 in the British Museum, London (with a version of the description of the battle of Qadesh of Ramesses II), publ. in: *KRI* II 24-101, §§ 65-343

Sallier IV vs. (P.)   papyrus 10184 in the British Museum, London, publ. in: *LEM*

Salt 124 (P.)   papyrus Salt 124 in the British Museum (pBM 10055) with the bill of indictment against the foreman Paneb (early Dynasty XX/reign of Ramesses III), publ. in: J. ČERNÝ/T.E. PEET, *JEA* 15, 1929, 243ff; *HOP* 320ff, pl. 112ff (*KRI* IV 408-414)

Sinuhe   quoted after AYLWARD M. BLACKMAN, *Middle-Egyptian Stories* I, *Bibliotheca Aegyptiaca*, Brussels 1932

Strike Papyrus	Turin 1880, papyrus in the Museo Egizio, Turin ("The Turin Strike Papyrus"; from year 29 of Ramesses III), publ. in: *RAD*; treatment: *HOP* 310ff; P.J. FRANDSEN, Editing Reality: The Turin Strike Papyrus, in: *Fs-Lichtheim*, 166ff
Taking of Joppa	("The Taking of Joppa"), together with Doomed Prince on the papyrus BM 10060/pHarris 500 rt. of the British Museum, London, publ. in: *LES*
Tomb Robbery Trials	publ. in: THOMAS E. PEET, *The Great Tomb Robberies of the Twentieth Egyptian Dynasty*, Oxford 1930; cf. also pAbbott (reign of Rames IX.); pMayer A and B; pLeAm
Turin 57001-57568 (O.)	publ. in: JESÚS LÓPEZ, *Ostraca Ieratici. N. 57001-57568*, Milan 1978-1984 (cf. *KRI* Index VIII 47-49)
Turin 1875 (P.)	pJud.Turin, q.v.
Turin 1880 (P.)	strike papyrus, q.v.
Turin 1881 (P.)	publ. in: *KRI* VI 609-619 (cols. VIII-IX cf. also *HOP* 313ff, pls. 108-110)
Turin 1882 (P.)	pTurin A, q.v. (rt. *KRI* VI 70-76)
Turin 1887 (P.)	Elephantine scandal, q.v.
Turin 1895 (P.)	part of the "Turin Taxation Papyrus", q.v.
Turin 1896 (P.)	(letter of Ramesses XI) publ. in: GEORG MÖLLER, *Hieratische Lesestücke*, 3rd Fasc., Berlin 1961 (6); BAKIR, *Epistolography* (transliteration pl. 24) (*KRI* VI 734f)
Turin 1971-1975 (P.)	(letters of late dynasty XX) publ. in: *LRL*
Turin 1977 (P.)	(letter of Dynasty XIX) publ. in: BAKIR, *Epistolography* (transliteration pl. 26); treatment: *HOP* 318f
Turin 1979 (P.)	(letter of late dynasty XX) publ. in: *LRL*
Turin 2006 (P.)	part of the "Turin Taxation Papyrus", q.v.
Turin 2021 rt. (P.)	("A marriage settlement of the twentieth dynasty"), publ. in: J. ČERNÝ, *JEA* 13, 1927, 30ff
Turin 2021 vs. (P.)	(letter of late dynasty XX) publ. in: *LRL* (*KRI* VI 738-742)
Turin 2026 (P.)	(letter of late dynasty XX) publ. in: *LRL*
Turin 2069 (P.)	(letter of late dynasty XX) publ. in: *LRL*
Turin 5656 (O.)	= oTurin 57033 (*KRI* V 496f)
Turin 9611 (O.)	= oTurin 57381 (*KRI* VII 286f)
Turin 9754 (O.)	= oTurin 57458
Turin A (P.)	Turin 1882, papyrus in the Museo Egizio, Turin (late Dynasty XIX), publ. in: *LEM*; vs.1,5 - 2,2 + vs. 4,1 - 5,11, publ. in: RICARDO A. CAMINOS, *Late-Egyptian Miscellanies, Brown Egyptological Studies* I, Oxford 1954, Appendices I-II

Turin Taxation Papyrus	the papyri Nr. 1894, 1895 and 2006 of the Museo Egizio, Turin (field taxation from year 12 of Ramesses XI), publ. in: *RAD* (transl. and commentary: A.H. GARDINER, *JEA* 27, 1941, 19ff); NB: GARDINER, *RAD*, S.XIII, names pTurin 1896 (for this, however, q.v.)
Turin Indictment Papyrus	Elephantine Scandal, q.v.
Two Brothers	pD'Orb., q.v. (reign of Seti II)
Urk IV	KURT SETHE, *Urkunden der 18. Dynastie*, Reprint of the 2nd. edition: Berlin and Graz 1961; WOLFGANG HELCK, *Urkunden der 18. Dynastie*, Berlin 1955-61
Valençay I (P.)	(letter from the reign of Ramesses XI) publ. in: *RAD*; transl.: WENTE, *Letters*, 130f; VITTMANN, *Hieratic Texts*, 57ff
War with Sea Peoples	inscription in Medinet Habu; report of the war against the so-called sea peoples from year 8 of Ramesses III, publ. in: *KRI* V 37ff
Wen.	Wenamun, q.v.
Wenamun	the report of the travels of Wenamun ("The misfortunes of Wenamun"), publ. in: *LES*
Westcar (P.)	("Die Märchen des Papyrus Westcar") quoted after AYLWARD M. BLACKMAN, *The Story of King Kheops and the Magicians*, London 1988
Wilbour (P.)	ALAN H. GARDINER, *The Wilbour Papyrus*, Vol.I *Plates*, Oxford 1941; Vol.II *Commentary*, Vol.III *Translation*, Oxford 1948

8.2 Literature cited in abbreviated form

(NB: This is not a full bibliography of the titles cited but only of those abbreviated. For more see the bibliographies at the end of chapters and subchapters)

Allam, *Hieratische Ostraka*	cf. *HOP*
Assmann, *Hymnen und Gebete*	JAN ASSMANN, *Ägyptische Hymnen und Gebete*, Die Bibliothek der Alten Welt, Zurich and Munich 1975 (excellent collection of translations for a large number of religious texts)

Bakir, *Epistolography*	ABD EL-MOHSEN BAKIR, *Egyptian Epistolography from the Eighteenth to the Twenty-First Dynasty, Bibliothèque d'Étude* 48, Cairo 1970 (an examination of the phraseology and the formulation of Egyptian letters that deals with very small units of text; transliteration of a number of letters of Dynasties XIX-XXI)
Caminos, *LEM*	RICARDO A. CAMINOS, *Late-Egyptian Miscellanies, Brown Egyptological Studies* I, Oxford 1954
Cassonnet, *Les Temps Seconds*	PATRICIA CASSONNET, *Études de néo-égyptien. Les Temps Seconds i-sḏm.f et i.iri.f sḏm entre syntaxe et sémantique*, Paris 2000 (exhaustive treatment of the Emphatic Sentence)
Černý, *Community*	JAROSLAV ČERNÝ, *A Community of Workmen at Thebes in the Ramesside Period, Bibliothèque d'Étude* 50, Cairo 1973
Černý, *LRL*	JAROSLAV ČERNÝ, *Late Ramesside Letters, Bibliotheca Aegyptiaca* IX, Brussels 1939 (a collection of letters by some Secretaries of the Tomb Building Administration of Deir el-Medineh of late Ramessid times)
Černý, *Valley*	JAROSLAV ČERNÝ, *The Valley of the Kings. Fragments d'un manuscrit inachevé, Bibliothèque d'Étude* 61, Cairo 1973
Černý/Groll, *Late Egyptian Grammar*	JAROSLAV ČERNÝ/SARAH I. GROLL, *A Late Egyptian Grammar, Studia Pohl: Series Major*, Rom 1975 (Modern grammar with a focus on morphology and syntax)
Crossroad	GERTIE ENGLUND/PAUL J. FRANDSEN (ed.), *Crossroad. Chaos or the Beginning of a new paradigm*, The Carsten Niebuhr Institute of Ancient Near Eastern Studies, Copenhagen 1986
Depuydt, *Conjunction*	LEO DEPUYDT, *Conjunction, Contiguity, Contingency. On Relationships between Events in the Egyptian and Coptic Verbal System*, Oxford - New York 1993
Demarée/Egberts, *Village Voices*	ROBERT J. DEMARÉE/ARNE EGBERTS (ed.), *Village Voices. Proceedings of the Symposium "Texts from Deir el-Medina and their Interpretation". Leiden, May 31-June 1, 1991, Centre of Non-Western Studies Publications* 13, Leiden 1992
Edel, *Ortsnamen*	ELMAR EDEL, *Die Ortsnamenlisten aus dem Totentempel Amenophis III, Bonner Biblische Beiträge*, Bonn 1966
Erman, *Neuägyptische Grammatik*	ADOLF ERMAN, *Neuägyptische Grammatik*, [2]Leipzig 1933 (a bit old-fashioned in structure and syntax, but still an essential reference grammar, especially concerning morphology and graphemics)

Erman,
Schülerhandschriften

ADOLF ERMAN, *Die ägyptischen Schülerhandschriften, Abhandlungen der Preussischen Akademie der Wissenschaften*, Berlin 1925 (a concise treatment of the texts assembled in *LEM*)

Fischer-Elfert, *Lit. Ostraka*   HANS-WERNER FISCHER-ELFERT, *Literarische Ostraka der Ramessidenzeit in Übersetzung, Kleine ägyptische Texte*, Wiesbaden 1986

Frandsen, *Outline*

PAUL J. FRANDSEN, *An Outline of the Late Egyptian Verbal System*, Copenhagen 1974 (the fundamental treatment in more recent times of the Late Egyptian verbal system and of all types of verbal clauses and sentences; useful index of quotations)

Franke, *Verwandtschaftsbezeichnungen*

DETLEF FRANKE, *Altägyptische Verwandschaftsbezeichnungen im Mittleren Reich*, Hamburg 1983

Fs-Lichtheim

SARAH I. GROLL (ed.), *Studies in Egyptology Presented to Miriam Lichtheim*, 2 vols., Jerusalem 1990

Gardiner, *Grammar*

ALAN H. GARDINER, *Egyptian Grammar. Being an Introduction to the Study of Hieroglyphs*, [3]London 1957

Gardiner, *The Wilbour Papyrus*

ALAN H. GARDINER, *The Wilbour Papyrus*, Vol.I *Plates*, Oxford 1941; Vol.II *Commentary*, Vol.III *Translation*, Oxford 1948

Groll, *Negative Verbal System*

SARAH I. GROLL, *The Negative Verbal System of Late Egyptian*, London 1970 (a systematic treatment and classification of the forms and methods of negation)

Groll, *Non-Verbal Sentence Patterns*

SARAH I. GROLL, *Non-Verbal Sentence Patterns in Late Egyptian*, London 1967

Hannig, *Handwörterbuch*

RAINER HANNIG, *Großes Handwörterbuch Ägyptisch-Deutsch (2800 - 950 v.Chr.)*, Mainz 1995 (not a substitute for the large dictionary of ERMAN/GRAPOW, but very useful; the introduction includes an introduction into the basic principles of the transliteration of Egyptian by FRANK KAMMERZELL; the appendices include a sign list arranged in several ways, lists of the gods, the kings and the most important toponyms)

Hintze, *Neuägyptische Erzählungen*

FRITZ HINTZE, *Untersuchungen zu Stil und Sprache neuägyptischer Erzählungen*, Berlin 1950/52

HOP

SCHAFIK ALLAM, *Hieratische Ostraka und Papyri aus der Ramessidenzeit*, Tübingen 1973

Janssen, *Commodity Prices*

JACOBUS J. JANSSEN, *Commodity Prices from the Ramessid Period*, Leiden 1975

Junge, *Syntax*

FRIEDRICH JUNGE, *Syntax der mittelägyptischen Literatursprache*, Mainz 1978

Junge, *jw=f ḥr (tm) sḏm* — FRIEDRICH JUNGE, *Das sogenannte narrativ/kontinuative jw=f ḥr (tm) sḏm*, in: *JEA* 72, 1986, 113ff

Junge, *Sprache* — FRIEDRICH JUNGE, *LÄ* s.v. "Sprache"

Junge, *Sprachstufen* — FRIEDRICH JUNGE, *Sprachstufen und Sprachgeschichte*, *ZDMG Supplement* VI, Stuttgart 1985 (description of the linguistic development of Egyptian with an attempt to explain it)

Johnson, *Demotic Verbal System* — JANET H. JOHNSON, *The Demotic Verbal System, SAOC* 38, Chicago 1976 (the most important description of the Demotic verbal system; the treatment of the forms is accompanied by detailed discussion of their historical development)

Kitchen, *Ramesside Inscriptions* — cf. *KRI*

Korostovtsev, *Grammaire* — MICHAIL KOROSTOVTSEV, *Grammaire du Néo-Égyptien*, Moskau 1973 (a structuralist grammar covering a lot of material, which provides some good ideas particularly on phonology, but in principle remains tied to ERMAN's grammar)

KRI — KENNETH A. KITCHEN, *Ramesside Inscriptions. Historical and Biographical*, 8 vols., Oxford 1975-1991 (comprehensive publication of the historical and biographical texts from the reign of Seti I to that of Ramesses XI)

Kroeber, *Neuägyptizismen* — BURCKHARDT KROEBER, *Die Neuägyptizismen vor der Amarnazeit*, Tübingen diss. 1970

LÄ — WOLFGANG HELCK/WOLFHART WESTENDORF (ed.), *Lexikon der Ägyptologie*, 7 vols., Wiesbaden 1975-92

Lambdin, *Sahidic Coptic* — THOMAS O. LAMBDIN, *Introduction to Sahidic Coptic*, Macon 1983

LEM — ALAN H. GARDINER, *Late-Egyptian Miscellanies, Bibliotheca Aegyptiaca* VII, Brussels 1937 (essential publication of the so-called school texts); translation of the whole volume by RICARDO A. CAMINOS, *Late-Egyptian Miscellanies, Brown Egyptolocical Studies* I, Oxford 1954

LES — ALAN H. GARDINER, *Late-Egyptian Stories, Bibliotheca Aegyptiaca* I, Brussels 1932 (essential publication of the literary texts)

Lesko, *Dictionary* — LEONARD H. LESKO et al., *A Dictionary of Late Egyptian*, 5 vols, Berkeley and Providence 1982-90 (gives only the basic meaning, but is useful for finding the sources)

Lichtheim, *Literature*   MIRIAM LICHTHEIM, *Ancient Egyptian Literature. Volume II: The New Kingdom*, Berkeley/Los Angeles/London 1976 (a collection of translations of important New Kingdom texts)

Loprieno, *Ancient Egyptian*   ANTONIO LOPRIENO, *Ancient Egyptian. A linguistic introduction*, Cambridge 1995

McDowell, *Jurisdiction*   ANDREA G. MCDOWELL, *Jurisdiction in the Workmen's Community of Deir el-Medîna*, Egyptologische Uitgaven V, Leiden 1990

Möller, *Hieratische Lesestücke* II/III   GEORG MÖLLER, *Hieratische Lesestücke für den akademischen Gebrauch*, 2nd Fasc. (New Kingdom literary texts); 3rd Fasc. (model letters and business texts from the New Kingdom), Berlin 1961

Neveu, *La langue des Ramsès*   FRANÇOIS NEVEU, *La langue des Ramsès. Grammaire du néo-égyptien*, Paris 1996

Neveu, *La particule ḥr*   FRANÇOIS NEVEU, *La particule ḥr en néo-égyptien. Étude synchronique*, Paris 2001

Osing, *Nominalbildung*   JÜRGEN OSING, *Die Nominalbildung des Ägyptischen*, Mainz 1976

Peet, *Tomb Robberies*   THOMAS E. PEET, *The Great Tomb Robberies of the Twentieth Egyptian Dynasty*, Oxford 1930 (essential publication of the late New Kingdom tomb robbery trials)

Polotsky, *Coptic Conjugation System*   HANS J. POLOTSKY, The Coptic Conjugation System, in: *Orientalia* 29, 1960, 392ff (also: id., *Collected Papers*, Jerusalem 1971, 238ff; a reorganization of Coptic syntax which also extensively influenced the grammatical description of Late Egyptian)

Polotsky, *Grundlagen des koptischen Satzbaus*   HANS J. POLOTSKY, *Die Grundlagen des koptischen Satzbaus*, Vol.I,, *American Studies in Papyrology* 28, Decatur 1987; Vol.II, *American Studies in Papyrology* 29, Atlanta 1990 (development and elaboration of id., *Coptic Conjugation System*)

Polotsky, *Nominalsatz und Cleft Sentence*   HANS J. POLOTSKY, Nominalsatz und Cleft Sentence in the Koptischen, in: *Orientalia* 31, 1962, 413ff (also: id., *Collected Papers*, Jerusalem 1971, 418ff)

Polotsky-Studies   DWIGHT W. YOUNG (ed.), *Studies Presented to Hans Jakob Polotsky*, Beacon Hill 1981

Sandman, *Akhenaten*   MAJ SANDMAN, *Texts from the Time of Akhenaten*, Bibliotheca Aegyptiaca VIII, Brussels 1938

Satzinger, *Neuägyptische Studien*   HELMUT SATZINGER, *Neuägyptische Studien. Die Partikel jr. Das Tempussystem*, Vienna 1976

Schenkel, *Sprachwissenschaft* WOLFGANG SCHENKEL, *Einführung in die altägyptische Sprachwissenschaft (Orientalistische Einführungen)*, Darmstadt 1990

Sethe, *Geschichte der ägyptischen Sprache* KURT SETHE, Das Verhältnis zwischen Demotisch und Koptisch und seine Lehren für die Geschichte der ägyptischen Sprache, in: *Zeitschrift der Deutschen Morgenländischen Gesellschaft* 79, 1925, 290ff

Sethe, *Verbum* I KURT SETHE, *Das aegyptische Verbum im Altaegyptischen, Neuaegyptischen und Koptischen I. Laut- und Stammeslehre*, Leipzig 1899 (large, but in parts very outdated collection of material)

Simpson, *Demotic Grammar* ROBERT S. SIMPSON, *Demotic Grammar in the Ptolemaic Sacerdotal Decrees*, Oxford 1996 (most recent Demotic Grammar, a profound modern description based on a specific corpus of texts)

Spiegelberg, *Demotische Grammatik* WILHELM SPIEGELBERG, *Demotische Grammatik*, Heidelberg 1925 (still useful reference grammar for Demotic, especially for the area outside the verbal system; for the latter see Johnson, *Demotic Verbal System*)

Stricker, *Indeeling* BRUNO H. STRICKER, *De Indeeling der egyptische taalgeschiedenis, Oudheidkundige Mededelingen uit het Rijksmuseum van Oudheden te Leiden* 25, Leiden 1944

Sweeney, *Correspondence* DEBORAH SWEENEY, *Correspondence and Dialogue: Pragmatic Factors in Late Ramesside Letter-Writing, Ägypten und Altes Testament* 49, Wiesbaden 2001

Till, *Koptische Grammatik* WALTER C. TILL, *Koptische Grammatik*, [2]Leipzig 1961

Valbelle, *Ouvriers* DOMINIQUE VALBELLE, *Les ouvriers de la Tombe. Deir el-Médineh à l'Époque ramesside, Bibliothèque d'Étude* 96, Cairo 1985

Ventura, *City of the Dead* RAPHAEL VENTURA, *Living in a City of the Dead. A Selection of Topographical and Administrative Terms in the Documents of the Theban Necropolis, Orbis Biblicus et Orientalis (OBO)* 69, Göttingen 1986

Vernus, *Future* PASCAL VERNUS, *Future at Issue. Tense, Mood and Aspect in Middle Egyptian: Studies in Syntax and Semantics, Yale Egyptological Studies* 4, New Haven 1990

Vittmann, *Hieratic Texts* GÜNTER VITTMANN, *Hieratic Texts*, in: BEZALEL PORTEN (Ed.), *The Elephantine Papyri in English. Three Millenia of Cross-Cultural Continuity and Change*, Orientis antiqui 22, Leiden-New York-Köln 1996

Wente, *Letters* EDWARD F. WENTE, *Letters from Ancient Egypt*, Atlanta 1990

Wente, *LRL*

EDWARD F. WENTE, *Late Ramesside Letters, Studies in Ancient Oriental Civilization* 33, Chicago 1967 (a translation which made the Late Ramesside letters accessible for the first time; still indispensable for philological and historical research using the letters)

Wente, *Verbs of Motion*

EDWARD F. WENTE, *The Syntax of Verbs of Motion in Egyptian*, Diss. Chicago 1959

Westendorf, *Handwörterbuch*

WOLFHART WESTENDORF, *Koptisches Handwörterbuch*, Heidelberg 1965-1977 (contains a large number of important derivations of Coptic vocabulary from earlier Egyptian)

Winand, *Études*

JEAN WINAND, *Études de néo-égyptien, 1. La morphologie verbale*, *Aegyptiaca Leodiensia* 2, Liège 1992 (the essential and most recent inquiry into the morphology and graphemics of the Late Egyptian verb)

9. Glossary

The purpose of this glossary is to aid in understanding the examples and translating the exercises so that those words appearing in the examples and exercises are included. Words which were generally transcribed according to their writing in the main text — such as *sdm, ir, di* — appear in their traditional forms here: *sḏm, iri, rḏi*. Similarly, the 3ae inf verbs appear with *-i*, although this was not consistently used in the text, where they may appear without ending or with a *-y*. References of a type such as "Gardiner A1" refer to the sign-list in Gardiner's *Egyptian Grammar*. *z* and *s* are distinguished to facilitate search in the Erman/Grapow *Wörterbuch*, but are arranged as a single sign.

ꜣ.t	see *iꜣ.t* back, backbone
ꜣ.t	noun: time, period; moment, instant; *m km n ꜣ.t* in an instant ("in the completion of a moment"); *m ꜣ.t=f* in a moment favourable to him
ꜣꜥ	noun (fem. *ꜣꜥ.t*): vessel, container; cf. supra § 1.1.1
ꜣb	verb **intrans.**: to stop; take a break; **trans.**: cease, desist, stop doing something (with infinitive as object); part from someone
ꜣbi	verb **trans.**: to wish, long for, covet, desire something; with infinitive as object (also with preposition *n/r* + infinitive): to wish to do; to enjoy (with preposition *m*: be happy about something); *n-ꜣby* for the sake of; with infinitive: in order to do something ("because of the desire to do")
ꜣbd	noun: ✶ month; *ꜣbd n hrw* "an entire month", "a whole month" (*"a month of days"), in group writing ✶ 𓅭 𓇋𓇋𓏤𓇳 ; semogram transfer from *dwꜣ.w*, q.v. and supra § 1.2.1(2)
ꜣbḏw	toponym (also abbreviated *ꜣbtw*): Abydos
ꜣpd	noun: bird, fowl (goose, duck)
ꜣḥ.t	noun (fem., also masc.): field, land, soil; also: cultivated fields, arable land, agricultural land, fertile land; **specifically**: holding, leased land, tenancy, tenanted parcel, plot (*ꜣḥ.t ḫꜣ-tꜣ n Pr-ꜥꜣ* "leased crown land")
ꜣḫ	see *iḫ*
ꜣḫ	adjective verb: to be useful, beneficial; to be transfigured, to exist in a state of blessedness, be fit for the world of the divine; thus: to be sacred, holy, splendid
ꜣḫ.t	noun: "Inundation" = first season of the Egyptian calendar (according to the agricultural lunisolar calendar it began at the end of June; during the Late Ramessid period it began roughly a month earlier)

ꜣḫ.t   noun: horizon, either in the human or in the divine world (primarily: the places where the sun rises and sets); figuratively: tomb, temple

ꜣḫ.t   noun (with semogram 𓏛 , etc.): possessions, property; see *ỉḫ.t*

ꜣḫꜣḫ   verb **intrans.**: to be or become green: to bloom, be verdant; to prosper, flourish, grow; **trans.**: make green; improve one's self

ꜣs   verb **intrans.**: hurry; as an adverb: quickly, hurriedly, in a hurry, in haste; right away

ꜣtỉ   (with following noun) writing of the negative relative adjective *ỉwty* (> Coptic ⲁⲧ-), q.v.

ꜣtỉ   verb: writing of *ꜣd* to lack, be short of, q.v.

ꜣtỉ   verb (< *ꜣṯ*): assure that; attend to, pay attention to, be heedful of (with preposition *n*)

ꜣtp   verb **trans.** (< *ꜣṯp*): to load someone or something; to carry, bear (with preposition *m/ḥr*: with something)

ꜣtw   title, see *ꜣṯw*

ꜣṯw   noun: administrator, district officer; quartermaster; "inspector", investigatory official (cf. McDowell, *Jurisdiction*, pp. 55ff.; Ventura, *City of the Dead*, p. 183)

ꜣd   see also *ꜣtỉ*

ỉ   see *ỉ.n*

ỉ   (𓇋𓏥) as an allograph for *r* and *ỉw*; see supra § 1.1.3(2)

ỉꜣ   𓇋𓄿𓀁 particle, interjection: truly, indeed! (or the like), Coptic ⲉⲓⲉ; cf. Černý/Groll, *Late Egyptian Grammar*, § 9.4; see *ỉḥ*

ỉꜣ.t   noun: backbone, back; also metaphorically

ỉꜣwỉ   verb **intrans.**: to age; to grow, be or become old or aged; **nominal derivatives**: *ỉꜣwỉ/ỉꜣw.t* age; *ỉꜣw/ỉꜣw.t* aged ones; old man; old woman; elderly; *ỉrỉ ỉꜣwỉ* to spend one's old age; *rdỉ ỉꜣwỉ* assign, determine age

ỉꜣw.t   noun: rank, dignity; office, profession, job; *ỉrỉ ỉꜣw.t* exercise, perform, fill (the functions of) an office

ỉꜣw.t   noun, collective: herds, flocks, cattle; game; animals, domesticated or wild

ỉꜣb   see also sub *ꜣb*

ỉꜣb.ty   adjective: eastern; left; **nominal derivatives**: *ỉꜣbt.t* (< *ỉꜣb.ty.t*) East; left side, left-hand side

ỉꜣd   (*ꜣtỉ*) verb **intrans.**: be miserable, wretched; be lacking, suffer shortages (with preposition *ḥr*: of something); **trans.**: to cause misery, injure, torture or injure someone; lack; **nominal derivatives**: *ỉꜣd* the wretched, miserable, poor one; evil-doer; *ỉꜣd.t/ꜣtỉ* need, lack; desperation, despair, misery, woes, calamity, dire affliction; mischief; wishes, requirements

ỉꜣd.t   noun: see *ꜣ.t* time, moment

ỉỉ   verb: to come (see *ỉwỉ*)

ỉỉꜣ   see *ỉꜣ*

ỉ.yꜣ   see *ỉꜣ*

ỉ ͨr   verb **intrans.**: ascend (with preposition *n/r* to someone, somewhere); reach someone, something (with preposition *n/m/ḥr*); to get away *ỉwỉ/ỉỉ* verb **intrans.**: come; with preposition *r*: to a place, a person; for the sake of something; with preposition *m*: from a place; into a place; as someone; with preposition *ḥr*: from a country; on a path; because of something; with preposition *ḫr*: to god, in his presence; **specifically**: to come along, arrive, return; "occur in the future"; be delivered; cf. supra §§ 1.1.1 (for writing); 2.1.4(5); 2.1.7(3); 2.2.3(3)

ỉw () circumstantial converter; cf. supra § 5.1.1

ỉw () as allograph of *r* and *ỉ* (); cf. supra § 1.1.3(2)

ỉw noun: island (in a river or sea); **specifically**: "island" in the sense of Arabic *gezira* "ridge of land" (land with a height between the high-water and the low-water marks which is not normally covered by the waters of the inundation except at their highest; cf. *ỉw ḥr.y-ỉb* "island-in-the-middle" (designating bits of land between canals and Nile branches in the Delta)

ỉw noun: a kind of dog

ỉwꜣ noun: cattle, cow; ox; also as sacrificial animal; in association with *wnḏ.w*-cattle ("short-horned cattle") perhaps "long-horned cattle"

ỉwꜥ see also *ỉwꜥy.t*

ỉwꜥy.t noun: garrison; *rḏỉ B ỉwꜥy.t* "assign B to garrison" (cause to serve in the military abroad)

ỉwnw-šmꜥy toponym: "Upper Egyptian Heliopolis", Thebes; occasionally also used for *ỉwny* Hermonthis/Armant

ỉwny.t toponym: Esna

ỉwr verb **trans.**: to conceive or be with child; **intrans.**: to conceive, to be pregnant (with preposition *m*: with child)

ỉwty "who is not ...", "who is without ..." (Coptic ⲁⲧ-); with following noun and suffix (*"someone who does not have his ..."): *ỉw.ty sn.nw=f* who has no one like him, unique; *ỉw.ty-ỉb=f* (Coptic ⲁⲧ-ϩⲏⲧ) "foolish" (< "(someone) who is out of his mind")

ỉwtn noun: ground, earth, land; dust, soil

ỉwd verb **trans.**: to separate from, to distinguish something from something (with object and preposition *r*); as element in compound prepositions: *r-ỉwd A r B* between A and B; particularly *r-ỉwd=s* to lie between; to be between observer and object, "covering it"; to be entrusted, charged with

ỉwdn see *ỉwtn*

ỉb noun: heart; intelligence, mind, sense; thought, reflections; passion; **specifically**: as subject noun with suffix in Adverbial Sentence (*ỉb=ỉ r* ...; also omitting preposition *r*): "my heart is directed towards something" > I am inclined to(wards), I desire ("my thinking strives after something"); *rḏỉ ỉb m-sꜣ* "to set one's heart after something" > to be concerned about, attend to; *ḥr-ỉb* in the midst of

ỉp verb **trans.**: count, examine, inspect, reckon, review; size up, assess (person correctly), recognize (someone as something, with preposition *m*); **nominal derivative**: *ỉp.t* count, account, (particular) number; see supra § 2.1.4(2); **specifically**: to be capable of judging (with preposition *m*: in or with something); clever, intelligent, perceptive (frequently of Thoth); cf. supra § 1.3.3

ỉp.t noun: something that closes or is closed; **specifically**: (1) clasps, trimming, inlaid or overlaid appliqué elements (metal, on furniture, vessels, carrying staves); (2) closed parts of buildings (magazines, "cellar"); (3) Harem

ỉp.t noun (Coptic ⲟⲓⲡⲉ): "oipe", a measure of capacity (cf. Appendix, supra § 7.3.1; 7.3.2[1])

ỉpw.t noun: message, report; mission; business, work, service, assignment, commission; *ỉrỉ ỉpw.t* to deliver a message; perform an assignment; attend to business; *hꜣb ỉpw.t* to send a message; *hꜣb r ỉpw.t* to send to work *ỉpt*   (with bird semogram) see *ỉbd*

ỉmy-rȝ   noun: title of the heads of administrative departments, "director", "manager", commander, keeper, superintendent (usually rendered as "overseer"); **specifically**: *ỉmy-rȝ pr wr* "High Steward", "Lord Chamberlain" ("Comptroller of the Royal Household", manager of the royal properties); *ỉmy-rȝ pr ḥḏ* "Superintendent of the treasury" (minister or manager of finance, depending on which treasury)

ỉmw   see also *ỉmȝw*

ỉmw   noun: bark, vessel, ship (mostly a river transport vessel)

ỉmȝw   noun: tent (bedouin; military); also: hut, booth, pavilion, house; *ỉmȝw n pšš.t* "mat tent" (traveling tent made of mats)

ỉmȝmw   see *ỉmȝw*

ỉmn.t   noun: right side; west (as cardinal direction and figuratively for the realm of the dead); **derivatives**: *ỉmn.ty* western, west side (specifically: west wind, westerners); *ỉmn.t.t* (nominalized nisbe, same meaning as *ỉmn.t*) the west, west side; *ỉmn.t/ỉmn.t.t wȝs.t* (oder *nw.t*) "the west of Thebes/the City" used for the Theban west bank

(j)n   form of the interrogative particle (also *n; nn; nȝ*); cf. pp. 90f; 186; 205

ỉ.n   verb: with suffix: "said so-and-so" as postposed speech indicator (cf. supra § 3.5.1[1] and pp. 89; 161; 260; 306)

ỉn/m   conjunction introducing the Cleft Sentence (cf. supra §§ 2.2.4[2]; 4.3.2)

ỉn   preposition. by

ỉnỉ   verb **trans.**: to bring, carry, fetch, bring back, return, obtain, remove; *ỉnỉ A r swn.t* "to buy A" (< to purchase something for a price); **nominal derivatives**: *ỉn-mw* "water-carrier", "water-bearer" in the service of the Tomb Building Administration; *ỉnw* (also sing.) deliveries, tribute, goods, trade goods (< "what is brought")

ỉn.t   noun: wadi; **specifically**: *tȝ ỉn.t* "the Wadi" used for the wadi of Deir el-Medina and *rȝ tȝ ỉn.t* as its northern approach (cf. Ventura, *City of the Dead*, p. 168)

ỉnb.t   noun: wall, fortification, fort; figuratively: watch-post, guard-post

ỉnn   particle preceding clause complexes: if (cf. supra §§ 2.2.4[1]; 6.2.1[2])

ỉnr   noun: stone, mineral

ỉr   abbreviated writing of *ỉrỉ* to do, to act, q.v.

ỉr   particle of topicalization (see Index 10.4)

ỉr.y   (fem. *ỉr.t*) noun: associate ("someone belonging to"), comrade, companion, mate, accomplice, partner, relative, friend; "fellow human being"; in titles: *ỉr.y-ʿȝ* door-keeper (cf. pp. 78; 320)

ỉr.t   noun (also grammatically masc. in Late Egyptian): eye; figuratively: sight, ability to see

ỉrỉ   verb **intrans.**: to act; with preposition *r*: act against someone (and preposition *ḥr*: because of something); with preposition *ḥr-tp*: act independently (< "I act for myself, according to my head"); **trans.**: to do something, to perform something; with object and preposition *m*: to make something out of something, to make something into something; with object and preposition *n*: to make something for someone, because of someone; to prepare something for someone; with object of an office or profession: to exercise, perform, execute a function/an office; to be something (*ỉrỉ nzw* perform kingship, be king); with object of time: to spend days, years; **specifically**: *ỉry=ỉ* "Yes" (< "I will act!"); *ỉrỉ.w n A* "it amounts to A"/"it makes A" (in calculation and indications of value); *ỉrỉ m-ḥȝ.t* to meet someone; *ỉrỉ wʿ ỉrm NN* "to get together with NN" (< "to make union with NN"; with preposition *ḥr*: because of something); for the use in the periphrastic verbal constructions, cf. supra §§ 2.3.0; 2.3.1)

ỉrw   see *ỉtrw*

ỉrp   noun: wine

ỉrm   preposition: (together) with, along with, and (cf. supra § 2.2.4[3]; for writing cf. § 1.2.2[3])

ỉhy   (see also *ỉhhy*) noun: joy, joyous mood; enthusiasm, applause, acclaim, exaltation, jubilation, rejoicing

ỉhw   (also in group writing *ỉ-h-y*) noun: camp; corral, stall, stable

ỉhhy   noun: acclamation, enthusiasm, applause, acclaim, rejoicing; *ỉhhy n B* "acclaim B"; *m ỉhhy* (adverbial) with applause, feeling; (to do something) with joy, enthusiasm, feeling; (to be) jubilant, enthusiastic

ỉḥ   (fem.; Coptic ЄϨЄ) cow, ox

ỉḥwn   youth, child (see *ḥwn*)

ỉẖ   particle (cf. Index 10.4)

ỉẖ   nominal interrogative pronoun (cf. Erman , *Neuägyptische Grammatik*, §§ 740-742): please, may what?, what means?, what?, with prepositions *m/ḥr/r ỉẖ*: because of what?, why?, for what?; *mỉ ỉẖ* how?; with nominalized attribute (genitive): which? ("what on this and that?"); as element in nominal sentence with *ỉꜢ* in the (indignant) question: "what is this about?", "what is this!?"

ỉẖ.t   noun: affair, matter, thing, someone's concern; goods, wealth, things, property, possessions, products (of a country)

ỉs   particle (see *ỉstw*)

ỉz   (*ỉzy*) tomb; **specifically**: tomb chamber, tomb shaft, tomb robber's pit (cf. Baer, in: *Orientalia* 34, 1965, 428ff.)

ỉz.t   noun: troop, crew, company, team (of soldiers, workers, sailors); **specifically**: the Gang of the Tomb Building Administration (*ḥr*, q.v.), (see Černý, *Community*, pp. 99ff.); titles: *ꜥꜢ n ỉz.t* foreman, chief-workman (of the "left" or "right side"; in hieroglyphic also *ḥr.y-ỉz.t*); *rm ṯ-ỉz.t* workman, worker; *nꜢ rm ṯ-ỉz.t* "the workmen" (of the Tomb Building Administration)

ỉsb.t   noun: chair, throne; folding stool; **specifically**: socle for statues or stele; also used for the huts on the ridge between Deir el-Medina and the Valley of the Kings

ỉsbr   (< *ỉs-b-r*) noun: whip

ỉstw   particle (earlier *ỉsṯ*; similar to *ỉs*): now, while; used initially introducing independent sentences, marking parenthetical notes or tonal questions (see supra § 2.2.4.[1])

ỉqr   adjective verb: to be excellent; clever, knowledgeable, educated; worthy, precious; as adverb (also with preposition *r*): very; properly, correctly, excellently

ỉkm   noun: shield (either as defensive weapon or metaphorically)

ỉt   noun: (six-row) barley; also grain or corn in general, thus *ỉt-m-ỉt* barley; see supra § 7.3.2(3)

ỉtỉ   noun: father; in plural: forefathers, ancestors

ỉtn   noun: sun-disk, the solar disk; **specifically**: the sun as a heavenly body, and also deified as such: Aten, the god of Akhenaten/Amenophis IV

ỉtrw   noun: river, Nile (for the writing cf. supra §§ 1.1.1; 1.1.2; 1.1.3.[3])

ỉtḥ   verb trans.: to pull, draw, drag, haul something; to pull someone up; **specifically**: to bend a bow; to pull a net; to let in air; to tie up

ỉṯỉ   verb trans.: to take, take away, to carry off; to plunder, grasp, acquire or take possession of something; to seize someone, take someone prisoner (with preposition *r*: to take someone somewhere; with preposition *n*: to take someone to someone); to surpass, excel; intrans.: to rob, conquer

ỉṯȝ   verb **trans.**: to take or bring something or someone (with preposition *n*: to someone; with preposition *r*: to a place, e.g. a court), to take something away from; to deprive, carry off, steal, capture, confiscate, seize something; guide animals; with adverb *r-bnr*: to relieve (workers of their positions), to remove; **nominal derivative**: *ỉṯȝ* the thief. **Observation**: *ỉṯȝ* is in principle a Late Egyptian variant writing of *ỉṯỉ*

ỉdnw   noun, title: deputy; lieutenant, adjutant; deputy director of an organization; *ỉdnw n pȝ ẖr* "Deputy of the Tomb Building Administration" (cf. supra Appendix § 7.4.2[4])

yȝ   see *ȝ* (interjection)

ym   ⟨hieroglyphs⟩ noun: the sea (see West Semitic *yam*, cf. supra § 1.2.2[2])

ꜥ   noun: state, condition (of a person)

ꜥ.t   noun: chamber, room; then the usual term for "house, dwelling house" (> ⲠⲎ the house); **specifically**: *ꜥ.t-(n)-sbȝ* "school" (Coptic ⲀⲚⲌⲎⲂⲈ); title: *ȝ-n-ꜥ.t* "chamberlain"

ꜥȝ   adjective verb: to be great, large, big, long; plentiful; old; to grow up, be elated; adverb: very; *ꜥȝ-ỉb* "great-hearted", arrogant; **nominal derivatives**: *ꜥȝ* great one, old man, grand one, town councillor, chief; *ꜥȝ/ꜥȝ.w* greatness, power; **specifically**: *ꜥȝ* foreman, chairman (see under *ỉz.t* "troop")

ꜥȝ   noun (semogram ⟨sign⟩): leaf of a door; door; in titles: *ỉr.y-ꜥȝ* door-keeper, porter (cf. supra appendix § 7.4.2[4]); also abbreviated (*ỉr.y-)ꜥȝ* (written ⟨sign⟩)

ꜥȝ   noun (Coptic ⲈⲒⲰ): donkey, ass; *ꜥȝ.t* she-ass; load of a donkey

ꜥȝb.t   ⟨hieroglyphs⟩ noun: libation, sacrifice; *dỉ.t-mȝꜥ ꜥȝb.t* to sacrifice

ꜥb   noun: horn (of cattle and sheep, also as decorative elements of crowns and head-gear, e.g. *Ḥrw ẖnty ꜥb.w* "Horus of the Horned Crown") (< **ꜥꜥ"Horus, who has horns in front"; so-called reversed *nisbe*)

ꜥmȝm   see *ꜥm*

ꜥm   verb **intrans.**: to know, be knowledgeable, certain; **trans.**: to understand, know, comprehend, perceive, find out, take cognizance of, hear about, learn something (with object or preposition *m* of the thing perceived); with preposition *m* also: to learn about something

ꜥn   verb (with semogram ⟨sign⟩) **intrans./reflexive**: turn, turn round, turn away; return, turn back, come back, retreat (with preposition *ḥr* from); **trans.**: give someone something, devote something to someone; **specifically**: *ꜥn wšb* to give an answer, reply; call someone to account for something; **as adverb**: again, once more, all over again; already; (bring or go) back; further; **with negation**: never again; not again

ꜥn   adjective verb: to be beautiful; beautiful to behold; friendly, amusing (with preposition *n/ḥr*: to); pleasant for someone (with preposition *n*)

ꜥnḫ   verb **intrans.**: to live, be alive (with preposition *m*: live on something, e.g., food, Maat); in the initial line of oaths, *ꜥnḫ n=ỉ NN* "As NN lives for me" (cf. supra appendix § 7.1); **nominal derivatives**: *ꜥnḫ* life; *ꜥnḫ/ꜥnḫ.t* living person; **specifically**: as title *ꜥnḫ/ꜥnḫ.t n nw.t* citizen/citizeness (title of independent free town dwellers — cf. Černý, in: *JEA* 31: 44 with n.2 — perhaps specifically for "residents of Thebes")

ꜥnḫ   noun: oath (< the initial formula of the oath: *ꜥnḫ n=ỉ NN* "As NN lives for me"); **specifically**: *ꜥnḫ n nb* oath of the lord; *ỉrỉ ꜥnḫ, dd ꜥnḫ* take an oath; *dd.w ꜥnḫ n A* "A was put on oath"

ꜥr   see *ỉꜥr* verb: ascend, to get away

ꜥr.t   noun: roll of papyrus or leather; scroll, list; see supra § 0.3.2

ꜥfꜥr   verb **trans.**: to carry out, to execute, effect (a task); provide, produce, supply, employ (people)

ꜥrq   (Coptic ⲱⲣ̄ⲕ) verb **intrans.**: to swear (with preposition *m/n*: in the name of someone); abjure, forswear, renounce something, someone (with preposition *ḥr*); **trans.**: swear to something, swear by someone; **specifically**: (with reflexive object) bind oneself by oath (with preposition *r*: concerning; with preposition *n*: by god); also: by an oath (*m ꜥnḫ*); cf. McDowell, *Jurisdiction*, pp. 33ff..

ꜥḥꜣ   verb **trans.**: to combat, fight (with preposition *r*: against someone; with preposition *ḥr*: on something, or at a place; with preposition *ḥnꜥ*: with someone); with preposition *m.dỉ*: to argue, dispute, have a lawsuit with someone, reprimand

ꜥḥꜣ   adjective: disagreeable, bad; fiery, flaming

ꜥḥꜥ   verb **intrans.**: to stand, stand around; stand up, get up (with preposition *n/r-ḥꜣ.t*: in front of someone); with preposition *r*: stand up against someone, approach someone; come to rest at a place; with preposition *r-ḥꜣ.t*: to await someone; stand one's ground against someone, resist someone; **specifically**: someone, something is missing, lacking, to be short of something; to await someone, something (with preposition *ḥr/n*); also as auxiliary verb (with preposition *ḥr* + infinitive or Old Perfective, cf. supra § 2.2.3[3]): to be engaged in doing something

ꜥḥꜥ.w   noun: lifetime, life span; time, time span, period

ꜥḥꜥ   (*ꜥḥꜥ.t*) noun (fem.); see *m:ꜥḥꜥ.t* tomb

ꜥḥwty   noun: (1) cultivator, field worker; (2) tenant-farmer

ꜥḫm   (in group writing also   , see § 1.2.2; Coptic ⲱϭⲙ̄) verb **trans.**: quench fire, thirst; calm wind; dry up; put down revolt; **intrans.**: to dry up (of water)

ꜥš   verb **intrans.**: to call; **trans.** or with preposition *n*: call someone, call to, call up; *ꜥš sgb* cry, call loudly, scream

ꜥš   noun: kind of conifer, probably fir (Cilician fir, *Abies cilicica*; cf. Germer, *Flora des Alten Ägypten*, Mainz 1985, pp.7-8)

ꜥšꜣ   adjective verb: to be many, numerous, rich; to abound (with preposition *m*: in); also *ꜥšꜣ m A* to have A in abundance

ꜥq   verb **trans.**: to enter, go in; to penetrate; with preposition *m* (or object of location: to enter something, someplace): into a place; to push one's way into the crowd; with preposition *n*: to enter someone's presence (also: something enters into someone); with preposition *r*: to come to a place or a person; **specifically**: "enter" meaning join in, share in, participate in a business, "enter into" inheritance, marriage, charge; with preposition *ḥr*: to have (right of) entrance to someone, something

ꜥqꜣ   verb **intrans.**: to be accurate, correct, right; **trans.**: to be apt for; to do something correctly; **nominal derivatives**: *ꜥqꜣ* the right thing, correctness; used absolutely as adverb: (1) *ꜥqꜣ* precisely; just so; exactly as it should be; (2) across from, opposite; as noun in prepositional phrases: (1) *r ꜥqꜣ* correctly, precisely, exactly; (2) *m/r ꜥqꜣ=f* across from him,, from something

ꜥqw   (Coptic ⲟⲉⲓⲕ) noun: income (of temples, officials, funerary endowments); also **specifically**: bread; food; *irỉ ꜥqw* provide income; prepare food

ꜥḏꜣ   noun: wrong, injustice (antonym *mꜣꜥ.t*); lie, crime, evil, falsehood, guilt; error; independently or absolutely for: "wrong!", "false!"; after prepositions: *m ꜥḏꜣ.w* criminally, deceitfully, deceptively, falsely, wrongly; *n ꜥḏꜣ* unrightful; **nominal derivative**: *ꜥḏꜣ* the doer of injustice; criminal, guilty one, wicked

ꜥḏd   noun: young man; also: orderly, servant of someone; *ꜥḏd šrỉ* small boy; small child; *ꜥḏd ꜥꜣ* "page" *wȝi*   verb **intrans.**: to be far, away, distant from (with preposition *r*); adverbially: far, distant; from a distance; from far away; from a long way off; also: for a long time

wȝ.t   noun: way, route, path, road, street; side (*wȝ.t bnr* outside); as object of verbs: *iri wȝ.t* to make, pave, open a way; *rdi wȝ.t* show the way; give way

wȝḥ   verb **intrans.**: to endure, last, stand (the test of time); **trans.**: (1) to lay down, set down, place, put something; to install; (2) sacrifice, offer, dedicate something; (3) to leave something/someone, leave behind, relieve; to omit; leave someone to himself; **specifically**: *i.wȝḥ* "leave off!'", "make an end!"; also "add in!"; with prepositions: *wȝḥ dr.t ḥr B* "to lay a hand on B" > to show, point out or explain to B; *wȝḥ dr.t=f ḥr dr.t=i* "lay his hand on mine" > be tender, helpful; in expressions of divine service and oracles: *wȝḥ NN m-bȝḥ* god "to present NN to god" > "to leave NN to god" (or else, to present a written petition naming someone to god, and receive an answer); *wȝḥ mdȝ.t m-bȝḥ* god "to present a papyrus to god"; in the introduction of oaths, see § 7.1

wȝs   adjective verb: to be happy, in control of one's own destiny or fate; **nominal derivative**: *wȝs* self-determination, fortune, luck, happiness; power, rule

wȝd   (in group writing 𓏏𓄿𓇋𓇋𓂋) noun: greenery, vegetables, greens (for the writing, cf. supra § 1.2.1[2])

wiȝ   as an adverb or component of a preposition (derived from verb *wiȝ* "to reject something"?): *r-wiȝ.tw* aside from, apart from, not to say, not to speak of, regardless of; cf. Černý/Groll, *Late Egyptian Grammar*, p. 124 (with note)

wiȝwiȝ   adjective verb: to be helpless, powerless, feeble, unsuccessful

wʿi   indefinite article, sing.: a (fem.: *wʿ.t*)

wʿi   adjective verb: to be only one; to be alone, solitary, a single one

wʿ.ty   adjective/*nisbe* (Coptic ΟΥⲰΤ) : alone, solitary, unique, singular, single, only one (around, left, there)

wʿȝ   verb **intrans.**: to have evil intentions

wʿw   noun: soldier, infantryman, sailor; figuratively: *wʿw n iz.t m s.t-Mȝʿ.t* "soldier of the Gang of the 'Place of Truth'" (instead of *rmṯ-iz.t n pȝ ḫr*)

wʿb   verb **trans.**: to purify, clean, wash something (with preposition *m*: with something); also reflexive: purify oneself; **intrans.**: to be, become pure, innocent; to be neat, clean; **nominal derivative**: *wʿb* purification, purity, the pure one; the dedicated, devoted one; **specifically**: *wʿb* as general title of part-time priests ("consecration priests"; ordained priests) as opposed to the *ḥm-nṯr* as the title of professional priests (those occupying formal priestly offices)

wʿr   verb **intrans.**: to flee, desert, run off, escape

wʿr.t   noun: desert, desert plateau; used for specific parts of the necropolises, "necropolis district", "tomb district"

wʿr.t   (title) see *ȝṯw*

wbȝ   noun: attendant, cup-bearer; butler (cf. Gardiner, *Ancient Egyptian Onomastica* I *43-*44; frequently rendered as "steward", see also *wdp.w*); member of the court cabinet or staff of the king, frequently his special envoy, "(Royal) Legate"

wbn   verb **intrans.**: to rise, appear; radiate, brighten, shine (with preposition *m*: from, in a place); **nominal derivative**: *wbn* sunrise, dawn; the rising (of the sun) = the east, "orient"

wbn   noun: open wound, puncture; laceration (also as a form of corporal punishment)

wbḫ   verb **intrans.**: to be light, bright, radiant; **specifically**: (of eye) to be clear sighted; to shine

wpỉ verb **trans.**: to distinguish; to separate (judicially, with dual or plural objects!); judge a person (with singular object!); decide between A and B (with object A and preposition *ḥnᶜ* + B); to separate something from something (with preposition *r*); to explain, reveal, open, disclose something; mediate in conflict; **intrans.** and with preposition *ḥnᶜ*: to have a lawsuit with someone; **specifically:** (in accounts and records) specify something, provide details ($\overset{\times}{\underset{\smile}{}}$); **nominal derivative** *wp* details, specification

wpw.t see *ỉpw.t*

wn to be, to exist; see *wnn*

wn preterital converter, see supra §§ 3.6; 6.2.1(2)

wn verb **trans.**: to uncover, open something; **intrans.**: to (be) open (of doors, etc.); with preposition *n*: open for someone; *wn-ᶜȝ* opening of a door; opener of door > "porter" (df. de Meulenaere, in: *CdÉ* 61, 1956, 299); see however also *ᶜȝ*

wnỉ verb **intrans.**: to hurry; **trans.**: to pass someone, something over; not to worry about someone, something; to pay no attention to someone, something, neglect, disregard

wnw.t noun: (1) hour; figurative (with specification — "genitive" — of thing): hour, moment of an event; (specification with person) someone's hour, time suitable for person; *ỉrỉ wnw.t* to spend an hour (with Old Perfective: doing something); *m wnw.t* in an instant; *m tȝ wnw.t* in this hour, now; (2) hourly service (duty) of teams: phyles, part-time priests; watchmen; *ỉrỉ wnw.t* do, perform service

wnf verb **intrans.**: to rejoice; to be content, joyful; to be happy about (with preposition *ḥr/n*)

wnm verb **trans.**: to eat or consume something; to devour; **intrans.** with preposition *m*: to eat (some) of something; **nominal derivative:** *wnm* food (for people); appetite, hunger; *wnm(.t)* animal fodder, but also human food; for the writing, see supra § 1.2.1(2)

wnmy adjective/*nisbe* and noun: right, right side; at the right of, right hand side

wnn form of verb *wn*, used in Closed Complexes, see supra § 6.2.2

wnḏw noun: short-horned cattle, calves, or cattle deprived of horns, cf. W. Ghoneim, *Die ökonomische Bedeutung des Rindes* (Bonn, 1977), p. 80; Franke, *Verwandtschaftsbezeichnungen*, p. 294

wr adjective verb: to be great, large, mighty, significant, important

wr noun: chief, elder, magnate, magistrate, the Great One, leader; (non-Egyptian) prince, (non-Egyptian) king (also for Akkadian *šarru* "king"); *wr ᶜȝ* Great Chief, Grand King (see Coptic ΟΥΡΟ)

wr interrogative pronoun: "how many?", "how long?" (Coptic ΟΥΗΡ)

wrrj.t noun: chariot (ceremonial or military)

wrs noun: headrest

wrš verb **intrans.**: to spend the day, all day, doing something; for use as auxiliary verb, see supra § 2.2.3[3]

wḥ.t ( ) noun: settlement, village, town

wḥᶜ verb **trans.**: to release; stop (doing), leave off, quit; finish; return home (with preposition *r*: to a place)

wḥᶜ (Coptic ΟΥШ2Є) noun: catcher, fisherman or fowler, occasionally specified: *wḥᶜ rmw, wḥᶜ ȝpdw*

wḥm (also *wḥm-ᶜ*) verb **intrans.**: repeat, do again, repeatedly; **nominal derivatives:** *wḥm* repetition; *wḥm.w* spokesman, "repeater", "speaker" (of a ruler, superior; "mediator"), herald; also of a god: the Apis bull is *wḥm.w* of Ptah; as priestly title: "oracle priest"; *m wḥm* again, once more, anew *wḫ*   see also *wḫȝ*

wḫ   (semogram Gardiner N2 and/or ☉) noun: the dark, evening, darkness, night (also of the "darkening" of the moon, new moon, see supra § 1.3.2)

wḫ   (semogram ⌣ or ▭) noun: column; pillar, pole, support (of wood or stone)

wḫȝ   see also *wḫ*

wḫȝ   noun: dispatch, (official) communication in writing; edict, decree (an ordinary letter is *šꜥ.t*)

wḫȝ   verb **trans.**: to seek or fetch something, someone; to seek to find, reach a person; to claim something; to desire, look for, search for, require, demand something; to wish someone's appearance; to want to do something; to be concerned about, interested in attaining, reaching something (with infinitive as object)

wḫȝḫ   see *wḫȝ*

wḫȝ.t   🐦🖐️🔺 noun (fem.): cake (*WB* under *wḫȝ* type of baked food)

wzf   verb **intrans.**: to be absent; to be inactive, not to work; to be or become lazy, slothful, idle; to be negligent; to hesitate (< *wdf*); **trans.**: not to do something; to neglect something, to ignore something; to bring to naught, nullify; passive: to be left unworked, untilled, fallow, unfinished; in writing frequently abbreviated to "bad" bird, Gardiner G37

ws   see also *wzf*

wsy   Late Egyptian admirative particle "how (beautiful) ... is!" (derived from the use of -.*wy* with enclitic pronoun in Adjectival Sentence — *nfr.wy sỉ* "how beautiful she is!"; see Erman, *Neuägyptische Grammatik*, § 684)

wsr   (Coptic ⲞⲨⲞϹⲠ̄) noun: oar, steering oar, rudder

wsḫ.t   noun: hall (for ceremonies); court, broad hall, courtyard (in temples and palaces, with columns or pillars)

wstn   verb **intrans.**: to go, move about, move freely, stride (for the writing, see supra § 1.1.1)

wšwš   (in group writing *w-šȝ-w-šȝ*) verb **trans.**: to smash, batter, break up; to beat something or someone severely, to bits (also hyperbolically: to be "dead-beat", exhausted); to break open a building

wšb   verb **intrans.**: to reply, answer (with preposition *n*: someone, to something); **trans.**: to answer something, respond to; with preposition *ḥr*: answer for someone; to intercede for someone

wt   verb **trans.**: to enclose, wrap up (also in embalming); to dress, bandage; **nominal derivative**: *wt* the mummy wrappings; bandage

wt   noun: (anthropomorphic) inner coffin

wṯz   verb **trans.**: to raise someone, something up; to carry; to express, voice something; to announce someone; to praise someone

wdp.w   noun: attendant, servant ("cupbearer"; see also *wbȝ*)

wdf   verb **intrans.**: to hesitate, be slow; **trans.**: to delay, cause a delay (for the writing, see supra § 1.1.3[4])

wdn   verb **intrans.**: to offer, sacrifice, immolate (with preposition *n*: for someone); **trans.**: to present something, offer, sacrifice (with preposition *n*: for someone); **nominal derivative**: *wdn* sacrifice, offering

wḏ   verb **trans.**: to command, decree, ordain, order; with preposition *n*: someone; also (passive, in Old Perfective): to be recommended, assigned to someone (with preposition *ḥr*, see supra § 2.2.6[1]); **nominal derivative**: *wḏ* stela, inscription, decree, regulation, command

wḏi   verb **trans.**: to dispatch, send someone, something; **intrans.**: to go off, depart, leave (with preposition *m*: from somewhere; with preposition *r*: for somewhere; with preposition *ḥr*: travel from) *wḏy*   see *wḏ* command (stela)

wḏꜣ   adjective verb: be safe, secure, sound, unharmed, uninjured, intact, prosperous; **nominal derivative:** *wḏꜣ* prosperity

wḏꜣ   (semogram ☐) noun: storeroom, magazine, warehouse, storehouse

wḏꜥ   verb **trans.**: to decide something or about something; to arbitrate, determine, pass judgment, judge someone, judge over someone; *wḏꜥ-ry.t* (also written *wḏꜥ-rꜣ*) to judge in the last instance; make, reach the final judgment, make the final decision; **nominal derivative:** *wḏꜥ* decision, judgment, verdict

wḏf   see *wdf* hesitate, delay

bꜣ   noun: "ba", concept for the faculty of god and divine beings to become manifest in this world, and the reverse: divine power behind phenomena (the sun is the "ba" of Re, or conversely, Re is the "ba" of the sun); used also for the "soul" of humans (in the earlier philosophical sense: psyche, the divine spark which manifests itself in matter as a human being, and returns to his "ka" — *kꜣ*, q.v. — at death)

bꜣ.w   noun: "power demonstrations" (forms in which "ba" appears; thus **specifically:** fame, awe, respect; power, might, strength; will, fate, destiny; wrath, fury, anger; illness, disease

bꜣ-j-r   see *br*

bꜣḥ   noun in compound prepositions: *m-bꜣḥ* in the presence of; before, in front of, facing

bꜣk   verb **intrans.**: work, serve (with prep. *n*: for someone; with prep. *m*: work at something); **trans.**: to work something; with prep. *m*: to cover something with something; **nominal derivatives:** (1) *bꜣk* servant, subordinate of someone (also used of oneself to express subservience); subject; (2) work (also: the thing worked on), product, delivery, tax, rent, fee; (3) *pꜣ bꜣk* "the work", "project", naming a construction site (with preposition *n* + royal name: the tomb of the reigning king under construction; cf. Černý, *Community*, pp. 81-84); also *pꜣ rꜣ-ꜥ bꜣk* "what is under construction", "continuing work"; *pꜣ rꜣ-ꜥ bꜣkw ꜥꜣ n Pr-ꜥꜣ* "the great work of Pharaoh" (for the tomb under construction) — note: *bꜣkw=f* "his work", "his dues", not *pꜣy=f bꜣkw*

bꜣ.t   noun: character; behaviour, conduct, way of acting; temper, mood; education, upbringing, refinement

bꜣꜣ.t   see *bꜣ.t* character

bꜣꜣ.t   noun: miracle, marvel, wonder; miraculous deed; thing which is miraculous, amazing, wonderful, precious

bin   (Coptic ⲃⲱⲱⲛ) adjective verb: to be bad, evil, wicked, ugly, dreadful, ill, naughty, dangerous; **nominal derivative:** *bin* evil (said or done); displeasure

bw   negative particle, used in preterital negations, Negative Aorist, see supra §§ 2.3.2(3); 3.5.1(2)

bw   (Coptic ⲙⲁ) noun: place; *m bw wꜥ* at one place; together; collectively; *bw nb* everywhere, everyone

bn   negative particle, used in First Present, Prospective and Third Future, see supra §§ 3.1.1(4); 3.1.3; 3.2.1(2); 3.4.1

bnꜣ   variant writing of *bin* evil, q.v.

bnjꜣ.t   variant writing for *bꜣ.t* character, behaviour, q.v.

bnr/bl   noun: outside, exterior; adverbial: *r-bnr/bl* outside, away (Coptic ⲉⲃⲟⲗ); see supra §§ 2.2.4(4); 1.1.2(3) (for the writing)

br   noun (fem.; Coptic ⲃⲁⲁⲣⲉ): sea-faring vessel for transport of passengers and freight, scow, freighter, galley, ship, coaster

bḫn   noun: villa, manor, fortress; also figuratively: princely residence

bt3   noun: crime, evil deed; sin, wrong, fault; offense, harm, damage, charge; accident, catastrophe, damage; *bt3 ḥr* a crime such that ...; *iri bt3* to commit a crime, do injustice; *s:ʿḥʿ bt3 r* to accuse someone of a crime, charge someone with an injury; *bt3 ʿ3 n mwt* capital crime

bty   see *bd.t*

bd.t   noun: cereal with few seeds, "spelt", "emmer" (*Triticum dicoccum*, two-row emmer); see supra appendix §§ 7.3.2(2); 7.3.2.(3)

bḏ.ty noun: (?) metal worker, smith (see also *ḥmty*)

bḏn   (in group writing *b-ḏ-n*) noun: club, cudgel, bastinado (as an instrument of torture and corporal punishment); *qnqn m bḏn* to beat with stick

p3   (*p3; p3y*) article, demonstrative pronoun (see § 2.1.2[2])

p3   verb **intrans.**: fly, fly up; also: leap, jump; flee, escape; rush off

p3-wn conjunction with sentence conjugation (First Present, Emphatic Sentence): because, since, for

p3d   (*pd/pt*; Coptic ΠⲰⲦ) verb **intrans.**: kneel, run (with preposition *n*: to someone); run after someone, pursue someone (with preposition *m-s3*); to flee, keep away from someone (with preposition *r-ḥ3.t*)

pwy   see *p3* fly, jump

pnʿ   verb **trans.**: to overturn, upset, overthrow something; to turn something round, upside down, over; to upend, reverse, disfigure, pervert something; take something back, go back on something; to dispute something, throw something into doubt (legally); reflexive: to turn (a)round (with preposition *n*: to turn oneself to someone)

pr   noun: house, household, estate, home; the entirety of structural and administrative elements of a holding or organization; domain, demesne; *pr-ḥḏ*: "Treasury", financial administration, department of finance; *pr-ḫnr* "office of the Harem", property administration of the Harem; *pr* of a god: temple properties, administration, temple area (temple building with temenos, administration and properties)

pri   verb **intrans.**: to go out, go or come forth, get out, emerge, leave, proceed (with preposition *m*: from; with preposition *r*: to); to go up (with preposition *r*: to); to go out (with adverb *r-bnr*); also: parade (in procession), march (to battle, with preposition *r*: against someone), to go abroad (with preposition *r* of place); **specifically**: *pri m* to originate from someone, to be a descendent of, to be born of; **nominal derivatives**: *pr.t* Festival ("coming forth", procession, epiphany of god); *pr.t* winter (q.v.); *pri-ʿ* ("the arm goes forth" >) to be courageous, valiant; to be violent; *pr-ʿ* "hero"

pr.t   noun: the seed of a plant; **specifically**: fruits of the field, grain, seed-corn; figuratively: seed, descendants, children, offspring

pr.t   noun: "Winter" (season), sowing time (when the earth "comes forth" from the inundation; or when the newly sown plants "come forth" from the earth) = Second Season of Egyptian calendar (in the agricultural year, begins at end of October; by the end of the Ramessid Period it began at the beginning of October in the official calendar)

pḥ   verb **trans.**: to reach, attain, approach, assail, penetrate, get to a place, a person; to meet someone; to turn to someone; to assault or attack someone; **intrans**: with preposition *r*: to reach a place, extend as far as a place; to reach a person; with preposition *m*: *pḥ m ḥd* "to reach the north, arrive in the north"

pḥ.ty noun (fem.): strength, power, might, force, virility

pḥpḥ   verb **intrans.**: circle about (of poison in the members), to run in circles

psỉ   verb **trans.**: (1) boil (in a vessel); (2) cook or bake (prepare, soften, also used for inedible things); see generally U. Verhoeven, *Grillen, Kochen, Backen*, Rites Égyptiens IV, Brüssel 1984, pp. 85ff.; *ps-s:nṯr* "incense preparer, fumigator"

psš   verb **trans.**: to divide, apportion, distribute, assign something (with preposition *m*: in shares, lots, portions; with preposition *n*: among people); to share something with someone (with preposition *ḥnꜥ/n/ỉrm*); to participate in, to share in (with preposition *m*)

psš.t   (semogram ⤫) noun: share, portion, lot, apportionment, division, distribution, half (with preposition *m*: of something)

psš.t   (semogram ⋔) noun: mat

psd   see *psḏ*

psḏ   noun: back (for writing, see supra § 1.2.1)

psḏ.t   noun: all the gods: divine assembly, "council of gods" ("ennead")

pš   (with semogram ⤫) noun, fem., see *psš.t*

pš   (Coptic ⲠⲰⲰϢ) verb: to divide, see *psš*

pd   see *pȝd* run

pt   see *pȝd* run

ptpt   verb **trans.**: tread, step on; tread something down, trample enemies into the dust

ptr   verb **trans.**: to see, perceive visually, look at (with object or preposition *m*); to learn something, get to know someone; with dependent clause: see that; *ptr*, particle, "look!, now!, see here!" as substitute of Middle Egyptian *mk*

pḏ.t   noun: bow; *pḏ.t 9* "the nine bows" (metaphorically for the non-Egyptian lands, "the other peoples"); military unit "archers", military formation "host"; in title: *ḥr.y pḏ.t* "captain of archers", "commander of the host"

fȝỉ   verb **trans.**: to lift, pick up something; to raise something up; to bear, carry, transport; bring, present, deliver goods; weigh something; with reflexive object: to raise oneself, get up; with *r* + infinitive: to set about doing something; **nominal derivative**: *fȝỉ* ( ) "weight"; *fȝỉ ṯȝw* "set sail, sail"

fy   see *ft* "have had enough"

fnḏ   noun: nose, nostrils

fqȝ   noun: reward, gift, present

ft   verb **intrans**: to be tired, weary, discouraged, disgusted; to have had enough of, be sick of (with preposition *m/r*: of something or someone); *ft ỉb/ḥȝ.ty* the heart, the mind has had enough, is disgusted, is sick of something; be sick and tired

m   preposition: from, out of, in, at, with, etc.; graphically used interchangeably with preposition *n*, see supra § 1.1.3(2)

m   particle; graphic variation of *ỉn* in Cleft Sentences; see *ỉn*

m'w.t   noun: see *mw.t* mother

mȝȝ   verb **trans.**: to see, behold, observe, regard, look at, learn; also: to imagine something ("put it before one's eyes")

mȝỉ   noun: lion

m3ͨ verb **intrans**.: to be correct, straight, true, right, real, genuine; **trans**.: to guide, lead, direct (with preposition *m*, at a place); figuratively: to present, offer, sacrifice, donate, give; *m3ͨ-hrw* blessed (justified, acceptable to god, even during lifetime), vindicated; *rdỉ m3ͨ* (with object) to justify someone before someone (with preposition *r*); *rdỉ-m3ͨ* (with object) offer, donate; also in concrete sense: to "sacrifice" something for offerings or sacrifice; **nominal derivative**: *m3ͨ* what is correct, right, true, just; justice, truth

m3ͨ.t noun: order of the state, world, universe, its divine personification (goddess Ma'at) and its phenomena: law and order, justice, law, truth

m3ͨ.ty adjective: innocent, virtuous, truthful, just, blessed; **nominalized**: a just one; someone found innocent

m3w.t noun: what is new; novelty, innovation; *m/n m3w.t* anew

m3nw toponym: designation used for the Western Mountain; also figuratively: the place where sun and moon set; the realm of the dead; the west

mỉ preposition: like, according to, as, even as, etc.

mỉ imperative of *ỉy/ỉwỉ* "come!"

mỉ.t noun: way, route, path, road, street

mỉ.t.t noun: the same; adverbially: *(m-)mỉt.t* likewise, similarly, also; as preposition (like *mỉ*): as; as co-ordinating particle (with nominal phrases and clauses): and, and likewise (cf. Erman, *Neuägyptische Grammatik*, § 591)

mỉ.n3 adverb (Coptic ⲘⲚⲀⲒ): "here"; also literally "like this", and as graphic variant of *mỉn* "today", "now"

my particle for strengthening the imperative, cf. § 2.2.2(2)

my (with semogram ⟿) noun: semen, human seed; metonymically: son

m-ͨ compound preposition: through someone; in someone's possession; see *m.dỉ*

mͨy noun: see *my* semen

mͨn see *m-n*

mͨnn see *m-n*

m:ͨhͨ.t noun: tomb, sepulchre (of non-royal persons); mausoleum; also: cenotaph

mw noun: water, body of water, liquid; **specifically**: *p3(y) mw* flood, inundation

mw.t *(m'w.t)* noun: mother

mwt verb **intrans**.: to die, be dead (with preposition *n/hr*: through, because of something; also reflexive: by one's own hand); **nominal derivative**: *mwt* death, dying; dead man, the deceased; *mwt.t* dead woman

m-n (Coptic ⲘⲚ̄-) verb negating existence: "there is no, it is not, there is not"

m-n ⟨semogram⟩ verb **trans**.: to wind, turn, twist something; **nominal derivative**: *mnn* "wrist screw" (as instrument of torture)

mn (Coptic ⲘⲞⲨⲚ) verb **intrans**.: to stay, remain, endure; to continue to exist; to be firmly in place; *mn-ỉb* firm of heart, reliable, standfast

mn (semogram/abbreviation ⟨⟩) noun: remainder, balance, final line of accounts

mn (Coptic ⲘⲀⲚ) noun: "certain", "so-and-so", "NN", to indicate unknown or unnamed persons; **specifically**: *mn n ỉh.t* an unspecifiable number of things, "so many things"

mn.t (Coptic ⲘⲒⲚⲈ) : fashion, manner, kind; roughly; *m t3y mn.t* of this kind, the like *mn.t*   in adverbial *m mn.t* daily, every day (> Coptic ⲘⲘⲎⲚⲈ)

mnw   noun: monument; also in concrete sense: statue; *iri̯ mnw* erect a monument

mni̯   (semogram ⌐ and/or ⮫) verb **intrans.**: to land (with preposition *r/m/n/ḥr*: at); moor, dock; metaphorically: die; **trans.**: to land someone or something, to bring to land, to steer; to lead a country well

mnn   (group writing *mꜥ-ni̯-ni̯*) see *m-n*

Mn-nfr   toponym: Memphis

mnḫ   noun: youth of marriageable age (the female equivalent is *nfr.t*); **specifically**: *mnḫ* apprentice of the craftsmen at Deir el-Medina, youth employed in field work (usually rendered "stripling")

mr   in titles: see *imy-rꜣ*

mr   (semogram ‿‿) : canal, branch of a body of water, pool, lake, channel, water-borne communication route; also *tꜣ mr* for *mri̯.t* harbor, port, q.v.

mr   noun: pyramid; also in general: royal tomb (with or without pyramid)

mr   adjective verb: to be ill; to suffer, be pained (also with preposition *m*, from something); **nominal derivative**: *mr* pain, sorrow, woe

mri̯   verb **trans.**: to love, cherish, adore, covet, demand someone or something; to wish or want something; to wish, want, desire something for one's self (with preposition *n* and reflexive pronouns); desire, choose

mrw.t   noun: love (*mrw.t=f* his love, which he feels, or the love of him, which he receives), wish, desire; choice, selection (in the sense of loving hierarchically from "above"), Late Egyptian *tꜣ mrw.t*

mr.t   noun, collective (fem.): workers, ensemble of servants, personnel; lower classes (frequently rendered "serfs"); **specifically**: weavers

mri̯.t   (fem., *tꜣ mr*) noun: bank or shore (of river or sea); quay, mooring place, harbour, port; market, market-place

mrkbt   ⟨hieroglyphs⟩ noun: chariot (ceremonial or military); see Akkadian *marakabtu*, West Semitic *narakabtu*, Hebrew *merkava*

mḥ   (Coptic ⲘⲞⲨϨ) verb **trans.**: to make full, fill up (with preposition *m*: with something), accomplish, inlay, grip, begin; **as Old Perfective**: be full, complete (with preposition *m*: with something); with preposition *r* + infinitive (*mḥ r*): to be busy, engaged in (doing) something (continuously do something, be industriously engaged in [doing] something); **specifically**: *r mḥ* + number "whereby a number is made complete" (< to make a number complete); then: construction of ordinal numbers (*hrw mḥ 3* "the third day"); *mḥ qni̯ m* ("to fill the embrace with") to put one's arms around someone, embrace someone; *mḥ-ib* confident, trusting

mḥ   verb **trans.**: to seize, grip, grasp, grab, hold, capture, catch, take possession; with preposition *m* (*mḥ m B* "to grab B"): to take command of something; to hold a person; arrest; to seize, take, conquer a city; *ini̯ m mḥ* take someone prisoner

mḥ   noun: measure: cubit (= 52.5 cm)

mḥi̯   verb **intrans.**: to be in water, float, swim, navigate; to be flooded, inundated, full of water; flow copiously

mḥi̯   see *mḥꜥ.w* flax

mḥy   noun: epithet of the god Thoth ("the filler", "the one who fills [the moon]"; or "the provider")

m-ḥ-y   noun: burial chamber; tomb

mḥ.t(j)   noun: north; adjective: north, northern

mḥꜥ.w   (Coptic ⲘⲀϨ), in group writing also ⟨hieroglyphs⟩ flax

mẖnỉ   see *mẖn.t*

mẖn.t   noun: ferry, ferryboat; **derivative**: *mẖn.ty* ferryman, boatman

mẖr   noun: granary, silo, grain silo (also of private houses)

mz   verb **trans.**: to bring something (with preposition *n*: to someone), offer, present; **intrans**. or with reflexive object and preposition *r*: to take oneself to someone, present oneself; step before someone, come into someone's presence

mzḥ   noun: crocodile

msỉ   verb **trans.**: to bear, give birth; also beget (from divine father); to bring something forth, to form, mould, fashion, create (with preposition *m*: out of a material)

msw.t   noun: bearing, birth; **specifically**: *wḥm msw.t* be born anew, "repeating of births", "Renewal of the Creation" as designation of the "Renaissance" Era beginning with regnal year 19 of Ramesses XI

mstỉ   noun: carrying basket (also used as measure of capacity); leather container

msḏr   (also *msḏr.t*) noun: ear; figuratively: hearing, sense of hearing

mšꜥ   noun: group, crowd, people; squad; **specifically**: *mšꜥ* army, infantry; expedition; *pꜣ mšꜥ* army, division; *nꜣ mšꜥ* troops, soldiers; *ỉm.y-rꜣ mšꜥ* general; *ỉm.y-rꜣ mšꜥ wr* "generalissimo" (Commander in Chief of the Army, title of Crown Princes); *ỉdnw n mšꜥ* lieutenant (in the older sense of the word as deputy of the commander)

mšꜥỉ   verb **intrans.**: to march, journey, travel (for the writing, see supra §§ 1.1.1; 1.1.3[3]); **nominal derivative**: *mšꜥ* march, journey, trip

mqḥꜣ   see *mkḥꜣ*

mk   particle: look!; surely, indeed, now; used as initial particle of independent clause (see also § 2.2.2[3] Observation)

mkḥꜣ   verb **trans**: to neglect, ignore (for issue of phonetic change, see supra § 1.1.2[3])

mgꜣ   noun: young warrior, combatant

mt   see *mtr*

mt   verb: to die, see *mwt*

mtr   verb **intrans.**: to be present; to be a witness (with preposition *ḥr*: for someone); also **trans.**: to witness; to attest, testify to something; to provide evidence for, proof of something; to account for something; to be a witness for someone; **nominal derivatives**: *mtr.w* witness (see also *mtr.t* testimony); *mtr* presence, proximity, nearness; **specifically**: *m-tꜣ-mtr n* in the midst of something

mtr   adjective verb: to be correct, right, legal, precise, exact, reliable; *mtr ỉb* sincere, open minded; *tp mtr* correctness, rectitude, right; *mtr mꜣꜥ* truly reliable

mtr.t   (see *mtr* be present) noun: testimony, instruction, precept, advice, admonition; *ỉnỉ mtr.t* to produce evidence, provide, supply proof

mtr.t   (semogram ☉) noun: midday, noon

m.dỉ   compound preposition, wide usage: with, at, by someone; in the company of; in the charge of; in the employ of; to fight with someone; to consult with someone; to find something in someone's possession; (indication of possession:) something is "with someone", in his possession; (indication of source:) something is acquired from or through someone (from *m-ꜥ*); cf. French *chez*; cf. supra § 2.2.4(3)

md.t   see *mdw*

mdw   verb **intrans.**: to speak, talk, converse, contest, quarrel, disagree; with prepositions: *mdw ḥnꜤ/m.dἰ/ἰrm* to talk with someone, agree with him; to dispute before the law (**specifically**: *mdw m.dἰ* to speak with someone disagreeably, to come into conflict, to reflect on; conflict, argue, pursue a civil suit with someone; to have a disturbing effect on someone); with *n/ ḥr/ḥft*: to speak to someone; with *ḥr*: talk about someone or something; with preposition *m*: to speak derogatively about someone, against someone or something; **nominal derivative**: *tꜣ mdw/md.t* (either written or spoken) word, speech, statement, discourse, meaning, message; also thing, affair, matter, method

mdt   see *mdw*

mdꜣἰ   noun: designation for the nomads of the Nubian mountains, then for the soldiers recruited from them; **specifically**: policeman (of the Theban Necropolis)

mdꜣ.t   ⌒ ◯ 𝈍   noun: chisel of hardened copper, particularly used by relief sculptors (the "large chisel" was valuable state property issued to the Gang working in the tomb)

n   preposition: of, to, for, by, on behalf of, against (people), near, belonging to, etc.; graphically used interchangeably with preposition *m*, see supra § 1.1.3(2)

nꜣ   definite article (pl.)

nꜣy   demonstrative: this (independently used as a noun, followed by the particle of attribution *n* — "genitive" —also as plural article); writing of the possessive prefix *nꜣ n* (see § 2.1.2[2]); **specifically** as adverb: "here", "from here"

nꜣhꜣ   see *nhy*

nἰwy   noun: spear, lance

nἰm   interrogative pronoun: who; see supra §§ 4.3.2 Observation; 1.2.3 (for writing)

nꜤἰ   (semograms ⊿ and/or ⟨⟩) verb **intrans.**: to go, go off, travel, proceed, walk; **trans.**: to navigate a body of water, to enter a place; *m nꜤy r* to be on the way to a place

nw   verb **intrans.**: to see; to look, gaze, regard, watch for; with preposition *r*: to see, view, glimpse something (Coptic ΝΑΥ Є-); to look, gaze, regard, watch for; to look at someone or something

nw   (semogram ☉) noun: time, moment, a propitious moment, the right time for someone (with suffix); time as duration (during which something takes place, with genitive); adverbial: *r nw* timely

nw.t   toponym: city; **specifically**: *the* City, meaning Thebes (here transcribed *Nw.t*)

nwy   verb (3ae inf.) **intrans./trans.**: to care, be concerned about, pay attention to (with object **or** preposition *r*); to collect, gather, assemble something (occasionally also in Old Perfective/passive: something is gathered or collected)

nb-nty   writing for *nty nb* everything; *pꜣ nty nb* entirety, the whole thing

nb   demonstrative ("adjective"): all, every, each

nb   noun: lord; owner, proprietor of something; *nb wꜤ* the sole lord; *nb-r-ḏr* All Lord ("Pantocrator")

nbw   noun: gold (as precious metal, but also used figuratively for the goddess Hathor)

nbd   verb **trans.**: to weave, twist, braid, plait something (reflexive: to braid oneself, i.e., one's own hair); **nominal derivatives**: *nbd* (masc.) hairstyle; *nbd* (fem.) wickerwork, woven work; **specifically**: tressplait, braid (of hair)

nfἰ   demonstrative: for earlier *nfꜣ*

nfἰ   (Coptic ΝΙϤЄ) verb **intrans.**: blow, exhale, breathe

nfw   (Coptic ΝЄЄϤ) noun: boatman (as proprietor of boat or sailor); boatswain (as official responsible for vessels of the administration) *nfr*   adjective verb: to be good, beautiful, perfect, well-meaning, kind, happy; **specifically**: *nfr n=f* "it is good for him"; *r-nfr-n=f* "for his sake"; **nominal derivatives**: *nfr* (what is) good, being good, well being, benefactions, goodness, good thing; *nꜣ nfr.w* (completely spelled) good things, good deeds; *nfr.w* (with semogram stroke or papyrus roll) beauty, goodness

nfr.t   noun: the beautiful one; **specifically**: maiden, young woman, girl of marriageable age (female equivalent to male *mnḫ*)

nmḥ.w   noun: poor, poverty-stricken, powerless; orphan; **specifically**: commoner, free subject (fem. *nmḥy.t*) of a city, of the land of Pharaoh (person without a title, as opposed to civil servants; frequently understood as "private person" or "citizen"); see supra § 4.3.3; D. Warburton: "low and mid-level civil servants, state employees with land grants"

nn   particle of negation (Late Egyptian *bn*); way of writing the question marker *ỉn*

nnỉ   verb **intrans.**: to be weary, tired, idle, slack, negligent (with preposition *m/n* and infinitive: in an activity)

nrw   noun: fear, dread, terror, awe, respect; *rḏỉ nrw* to spread panic, terror (with preposition *m*: among people, at a place, in a country, etc.)

nh.t   (Coptic ΝΟΥϨΕ) noun: sycomore

nhy   some, a few; **then**: plural indefinite article (see supra § 2.1.2[2])

nhm   verb **intrans.**: to be enthusiastic, triumphant, joyous; with preposition *n/ḥr*: to exult someone; with preposition *m*: enthusiastic about something something; **nominal derivative**: *nhm* jubilation, shouting, rejoicing

nḥm   verb **trans.**: to steal, rob, take something, someone; to deprive, commandeer, confiscate; to rescue, deliver someone, to protect someone (with preposition *m-ꜥ*, rarely *m/r*: from)

nḥm   (< *nḥm.t*) lotus bud

nḥḥ   noun: eternity, infinity ("eternal recurrence")

nḫt   (Coptic ΝϢΟΤ) adjective verb: to be victorious, strong, powerful, firm; **nominal derivative**: *nḫt/nḫt.w* (article *nꜣ* or *pꜣ*) power, strength, victory, victories, magnificence, splendour; *qn.t nḫt* (in, with) victory and power, courage and splendour; *s:mn nḫt.w* record victories (< make them last, "immortalize" them)

ns   noun: tongue, speech

nzw   reading of the title of the Egyptian King preferred here (< *n.j-sw.t*)

nkt   noun masc.: matter, affair; (any)thing; something of; someone's concern, property; **specifically**: small matter, detail

nty   relative adjective or relative converter (transforms clauses into attributes); see supra §§ 2.1.4(5); 4.3.1; 5.1.2

nḏ   noun: flour (derived from *nḏỉ* rub, press, grind, crush > Coptic ΝΟΕΙΤ)

nḏ   verb **trans.**: to inquire, to ask something, to seek advice (with preposition *m-ꜥ*: of, from someone); consult with someone (with preposition *ḥnꜥ*); *nḏ-ḥr.t* inquire about someone's condition (as form of greeting and in the introduction of letters); also "greet" (with preposition *m*: with a word; as king)

nḏm   adjective verb: to be sweet, pleasant, delightful; *nḏm ỉb/ḥꜣ.ty* to be joyful, happy, to enjoy (with preposition *m, n, ḥr, ḫr*: to be happy about something); **nominal derivative**: *nḏm-ỉb* happiness, joy, pleasure, well-being

n-ḏ-r   noun: ostracon (see W. C. Hayes, *Ostraka and Name Stones from the Tomb of Sen-Mut [Nr.71] at Thebes*, New York 1942, p. 37) *rȝ*   noun: mouth; figuratively ("mouth of something"): entrance, opening, entry, door; saying, utterance, spell (said, read, known, written); statement; **specifically**: *rȝ n tȝ ỉn.t* designation for the northern entry into the wadi of Deir el-Medina (cf. Ventura, *City of the Dead*, p. 168)

rȝ-ꜥ   (Coptic ⲢⲀ-) word and word-forming element used widely with many functions: (1) noun: end of something; *ỉnỉ rȝ-ꜥ* to reach the end of something; *r (mn) rȝ-ꜥ* as far as (spatially and temporally); (2) noun: position; *r rȝ-ꜥ=f* in his position; (3) prefix used to form words with nouns and infinitives: state, etc.; *rȝ-ꜥ zḥȝ.w* writing equipment; *rȝ-ꜥ mwt* state of death; *rȝ-ꜥ bȝk* continuing work, work process, procedure; work plan, undertaking

rȝ-ꜥ   (Coptic ⲢⲰ) nominal particle: *m-rȝ-ꜥ* also, likewise, again, as well; see supra § 2.2.4(1)

rȝ-wy   see *rwhȝ*

rȝ-pw   nominal particle: or, or else; see supra § 2.2.4(1)

rỉ.t   [glyphs] noun: side of something; **specifically**: unit, *tȝ rỉ.t ỉmn.t.t (n.t ỉz.t)* "the right 'side' (of the Gang)" of the Tomb Building Administration

rꜥw-nb   noun used adverbially: every day, daily, always; also with preposition *m/r*; *nty rꜥw-nb* (adjectival, as form of the nominal attribute) daily

rwỉȝ   see *rwỉ*

rwỉ   (Coptic ⲖⲞ) verb **intrans.**: to go away, avoid, escape, retreat, yield, give in; with preposition *n*: to make a move for someone; to hurry to someone; to flee before someone; with preposition *r*: to move or go to a place; to distance one's self, to go away from (because of something); with preposition *m*: yield, avoid, go around a person, a place; to stop; cease to exist as somebody, something; cease, desist, decline, give up, surrender, leave, stop (performing an office, etc.); with preposition *ḥr* + infinitive/Old Perfective: cease to do something; **trans.**: to leave, abandon (a place, an office, etc.), with preposition *m*: dismiss, relieve someone (of office); banish, turn away, drive off, cause to stop; to remove something from (with prepositions *ḥr/r-ḥȝ.t*); with reflexive pronoun and *ḥr* + infinitive "to prevent oneself from doing something" (> cease, stop doing)

r-wjȝ   see *wỉȝ* aside from

rwhȝ   (actually *r-h*) noun: evening

rwšȝy   see *r-š-ỉ* noun: summit

rwḏ   adjective verb: to be firm, stable, enduring, sturdy, steadfast; to remain firm; to persevere; to be competant, able; to feel good, to prosper, flourish; to be lucky (with preposition *m*: with something); to show dedication, interest, enthusiasm (with preposition *m*: in doing something)

rwḏ   [glyphs] noun: commissioner, representative (of the king or vizier); delegate, inspector, agent (charged with the administration of a city, necropolis, stores); **specifically**: the "controller" of the Tomb Building Administration (*ḥr*, q.v.), i.e. officials of the central administration along with the scribe and the two foremen; *rwḏ.w n bnr* officials of the central administration (see Černý, *Community*, pp. 255ff.; McDowell, *Jurisdiction*, pp. 59ff.)

r-b-r-n   toponym: Lebanon

rmỉ   verb **intrans.**: wail, weep, cry; also: shed tears in shame (with preposition *n*: because of, or for someone); graphic variant: *ṯm*

rmw   noun: fish

rmṯ   noun: human being, mortal, person, people, personnel; **specifically** (in opposition to woman): man; common in bound expressions with attributes (Coptic ⲢⲘ-, ⲢⲘⲚ-), as designation for members of groups: *rmṯ-zȝw* prisoner; *rmṯ-ꜥȝ* wealthy, influential, important person (Coptic ⲢⲘⲘⲀⲞ); also in titles, e.g., *rmṯ-ỉz.t* "(work)man of the Gang" (see *ỉz.t*); see supra §§ 1.1.2(3); 1.1.3(3) (for the phonetic change)

rn   noun: name; for *rn.w* or *rn zp-2* see *rnrn*

rnp.t   noun: year

rnpꞽ   verb **intrans.**: to flourish; to be rejuvenated, become youthful; adjectival: youthful, youthfully vigourous, (endowed with the) the strength or vigour of youth; **trans.**: to rejuvenate someone, something (with preposition *m*: by or through something)

rnpw.t   noun: fresh greens, plants, vegetables

rrn   (*rn zp-2*, auch ⌒🏛⏉) noun: list of names, register, roll call

r.nty   (< *r-nt.t*) conjunction: thus, so, quote, as follows; see supra § 2.2.4(2)

rr   (< *pḥr*) noun: hoop, circular band, bracelet, necklace; also as fittings (> Demotic *ll*, Coptic ⲖⲎⲖ)

rrm   see *rmꞽ*

r.ḥnꜥ   preposition: with; graphic variation of *ḥnꜥ*, see supra §§ 1.2.2(3), 2.2.4(3)

rḫ   verb **trans.**: to know someone, something; to take note, be acquainted with, attest; to find out, learn something; to make someone's acquaintance; to know something; with object clause: to know that; with infinitive as object: to know how to do something, be able, skilled at, capable of doing something; **specifically**: get to know, learn; imperative: *rḫ B* "find (out) A!", "take note of A!"; *r-rdꞽ.t-rḫ.tw* list (noun; cf. under *rdꞽ*)

rḫty   noun: washerman, launderer

rs   verb **intrans.**: to awaken, to be wakeful, vigilant; to keep watch; **trans.**: guard, protect

rs.y   adjective: southern; combinations: e.g., *rs.y ꞽmn.ty* south-western

r-š-y   noun: summit, top (see Arabic, Hebrew *r's*)

ršw   (Coptic ⲢⲀ(Ⲩ)Ⲉ) verb **intrans.**: to be happy, glad, joyful, joyous; to rejoice (with preposition *n/m*: about; with preposition *m* also: to have feelings of triumph over); infinitive: *ršw.t* rejoicing, joy, delight, pleasure

rd   verb **intrans.**: to flourish, grow, grow up (with preposition *m*: to something); also as graphic variant of *rwḏ*, be firm, q.v.

rdꞽ   see *rdꞽ*

rdꞽ   (see also *dꞽ*) verb **trans.**: to give someone something (with preposition *n*); to give, offer, present, pass on, turn over, bequeath; to lay down, place, put, set (with all prepositions: on, at, in, below, around, by, near, beside); with preposition *r*: to deliver something to someone, hand over something to an administration; **specifically**: (with object): to raise one's voice, to give light, declare laws, sell something for its price; cause something to happen, to effect that; with preposition *m*: appoint, nominate someone to something; make someone to something (e.g. prisoner); with preposition *n*: to leave someone to someone, to turn someone over, to turn someone loose on someone; *rdꞽ m-ḥr* to give someone an assignment; **intrans.**: (with presposition *n*): to award someone, include, bribe (with preposition *m*: in something, with something); also: consider someone, include (in will or testatment); *r-rdꞽ.t-rḫ.tw* list (< "to cause to know"); *rdꞽ ꞽb/h3.ty m-s3* ("to put one's heart behind > into something") to worry about, think about, be concerned about

h   (⌷\\Ɪ⏉) see *h3w*

h3ꞽ   verb **intrans.**: to descend, go down, embark, come down, fall (for writings, see supra § 1.2.1[2])

h3(y)   (semogram 🏛) interjection oh!, oh that!, cry of joy or sorrow (common in prayers and statements addressed to the gods)

h3y   ⌷🏛𓏏 noun: male spouse, husband

h3w   noun: environment (temporal, spatial, social): (1) age, era (semogram ☉); (2) region, area, neighbourhood; *m/r h3w n* in the vicinity of someone or something; (3) relations, kin (semogram 👥); (4) affair, property (semogram ⎯), specifically also: use, costs, expenses (writing also ⎯); *dỉ.w r h3w n A* "given to A for expenses"; *ỉrỉ h3w* (with suffix or "genitive" or preposition *m*) to take possession of something; to be concerned with someone, to hold someone

h3w.t   see *hrww*

h3w3   (group writing *h-w*) see *h3w* age, region

h3b   verb **trans.**: send someone (with preposition *n*: to someone; with *r*: to a place; with *r* + infinitive: to do something); to write something; convey a message; in the epistolary formula *h3b n=ỉ ꜥ=k* "write to me about how you are"; **intrans.**: send (with prepositions *n* and *ḥr*: to send to someone with something); write, prepare a message (with preposition *n*: for someone; with preposition *ḥr*: about something; with *ḥr* + infinitive: write about something to be done); *h3b r-ḏd* "convey a message concerning", "to write the following"; **nominal derivative**: *h3b* (the "thing sent"), writing, message, letter, epistle, note

h3n(3)   see *hn, hnn*

hy   see *h3y*

hw.t   see *hrww*

hp   noun: law, decree, statue, guideline, order, regulation

hn   interjection and initial particle of "unreal" ("contrary to fact") conditional clauses: "oh, if only …"; see §§ 2.2.4[1]; 6.2.1[2]

hnw   (Coptic 2NAAΥ; 2NO) vessel for liquids or grain; cooking pot of stone, clay or metal

hnn   verb **trans.**: to incline, bend, bow, bend back (also with preposition *m*: under something heavy); to lean one's back on someone (with preposition *n*); to incline to someone's words (= to listen); to bow to something (= to concede, admit something); reflexive: to rely on someone or something (with preposition *n/ḥr*); **intrans.**: to be inclined to do something (with preposition *r*), agree, consent, allow, concur with someone, approve (with preposition *n/ḥr*); to nod approvingly, in agreement (in oracles)

hrw   verb (3ae inf.) **intrans.**: to be content, pleasing, satisfied, happy, soothing; **trans.**: with something or someone; with preposition *ḥr*: about, with

hrww   noun: day; *m p3 hrww* today; for phonetic change, see supra § 1.1.2(2)

ḥ.t   see *ḥw.t*

ḥ3   (*ḥnr/ḥl*) particle expressing wish: would that!

ḥ3   noun ("what is behind") in compound prepositions: *m-ḥ3* behind something or someone; *r-ḥ3* behind someone; as adverb: beyond, outside (to go); backwards (turned); *n-ḥ3* (stand) behind someone or something; (look) behind oneself

ḫ3w   noun: growth, increase, excess, addition; *rḏỉ ḫ3w n* + infinitive: to do something in abundance (*ỉmm ḫ3w* "do even more"; "do a bit more")

ḥȝ.t   noun: front, beginning, lead, start (of a thing, a text, a place, a period); the best; **specifically**: vanguard of military units; in compound prepositions:
r-ḥȝ.t as unbound preposition: (to be or to go) before someone or something; "to be before someone" > be under someone's command; also: because of someone or something; as rection of verbs: something lies before someone, awaits him; to make a stand before, to flee from someone; as adverb: towards, forwards, first, earlier, before;
ḥr-ḥȝ.t first, earlier; what-was-before, the earlier situation; before someone or something as adverb, noun, and preposition;
m-ḥȝ.t as preposition: before someone; to be at the very front, frontmost, foremost; as rection of verbs: to go or to move towards someone or something; to be afraid of; to be concealed, hidden from; as adverb: in front, at the front, first, in the beginning;
preposition ḥȝ.t (Coptic ϩΗΤ ⸗) before (spatially/temporally, < r-ḥȝ.t);
ỉrỉ m-ḥȝ.t (*"to do before someone") to meet someone; ꜥḥꜥ r-ḥȝ.t to wait for someone; to resist someone

ḥȝ.t-ꜥ   noun: as heading in anthologies: beginning, start, commencement; with preposition m: of something

ḥȝ.ty-ꜥ   noun: in the New Kingdom, title of head administrators of the large cities: mayor, city-governor

ḥȝ.ty   noun: heart (as member of body, but also as the location of thought and feeling: sense, consciousness, courage); dỉ.t ḥȝ.ty m-sȝ to worry, be concerned about someone (< "to put the heart behind something")

ḥȝwty   𓀀 ꜥ╲╲ noun: first, foremost; adjectivally: earlier, ancient (kings)

ḥȝp   verb **trans.**: to conceal, hide, keep secret, cover, envelop, shroud something; to be silent about something, keep it secret (with preposition r: from someone); to keep something locked away; be silent (with preposition ḥr: about, concerning something)

ḥȝq   verb **trans.**: to capture, plunder, seize, destroy

ḥy   noun (fem.): investigatory commission, inspectorate; examination, testimonial document; (masc.): inspector, supervisor

ḥꜥ   noun: body, flesh; person; with suffix: self (intensive: r ḥꜥ⸗f him himself; n ḥꜥ⸗ỉ my own)

ḥwỉ   𓂝𓏤 verb **trans.**: to hit, strike, smite, beat; **specifically**: to push, shove (of cattle); thresh (and other forms of harvest activity); subdue, defeat, repress, overthrow; enter a place; partial group writing also: 𓊪𓄿𓂝𓂜𓏲

ḥw.t   noun: house (meaning the actual building as opposed to the property of the entire household, domain or estate: pr); **specifically**: ḥw.t chapter, stanza; tȝ-ḥw.t the temple of Medinet Habu; Ḥw.t-kȝ-Ptḥ Memphis

ḥwn   verb **intrans.**: to become young, youthful; **trans**: to make someone young; **nominal derivative**: ḥwn childhood, youth, youthfulness, rejuvenation; ḥwn m ꜥnḫ wȝs to be full of life (of the nose); ỉrỉ ḥwn/ỉḥwn to be rejuvenated

ḥwntỉw   (ḥ-n-ty) see ḥwtyw

ḥwtỉw   (ḥ-ty) noun: chief, boss, commander, head; **specifically**: ḥwtyw n pȝ ḫr the chiefs of the Tomb Building Administration

ḥbs   verb **trans.**: to clothe, wrap, cover; **nominal derivatives**: ḥbs clothing, garment, wrapping, cloth; ḥbs.wt clothing, clothes, wrappings, coverings, attire, things

ḥpt   noun: arm, an armful of something (also as a unit of measure: fathom = 4 cubits); group writing also: 𓂝𓈖𓏥𓏤𓏤 (HorSeth 8,12)

ḥpt   verb **trans.**: to embrace someone; to hold, encircle, encompass with the arms (also with preposition m)

ḥfꜣ.w noun: serpent, snake

ḥm noun: "majesty" in address or reference to king, related to the following word "servant" (really meaning not the "majestic" but the human manifestation of the ruler; cf. Prussian King as "first servant of the state" or the pope as "servus servorum Dei")

ḥm noun (fem. *ḥm.t*): servant, domestic: the meaning varies from prisoners of war without rights to "trusted household servant" (who could even have been born into the household), subject or acolyte (of a god); the rendering "slave" is socially misleading, for the "purchase" of a "servant" must be understood more as an indemnification of a previous master/employer (or the soldier-master, in the case of prisoners of war) than a purchase in the narrow sense

ḥm-nṯr noun: used for the professional priest (derived from *ḥm*, as "servant of god"), as opposed to the part-time priest (*wꜥb*); *ḥm-nṯr tpy* High Priest (First Priest in a hierarchy limited to the first three or four office holders)

ḥm.t noun: female spouse, wife; woman; *ḥm.t-nzw* queen

ḥmww noun: craftsman, artist, artisan, carpenter, handworker; *ḥmww ḫꜣ* chiseller, stonemason (see *ḥnr,, ḫꜣ*, q.v.)

ḥmn noun: variation of *mn/mn.t* (q.v.): fashion, way, manner; so-and-so, such-and-such; *ḥmn n* so many, such-and-such a number

ḥmsỉ verb intrans. to sit, sit down, take a seat; stay, live, reside; reflexive: be seated, to seat oneself; *ḥmsỉ ỉrm* to live with someone; common as auxiliary verb (with *ḥr* + infinitive or Old Perfective, see supra § 2.2.3[3]): to be engaged in doing

ḥmty noun: copper, metal ore; **nominal derivative**: *ḥmty.y* (?), smith, coppersmith, metal worker

ḥn verb trans.: to organize, command, regulate, control, put in order, equip, provide, supply (with preposition *m*: with something); to command, order something (with preposition *n*: someone; with *r* + infinitive: to do something); to assign, appoint, entrust, order something to someone (with preposition *n*); **nominal derivative**: *ḥn.t* task (see following entry)

ḥn.t noun: orders, task, job, profession, business, professional activity, service (official or commercial affairs; religious ceremonies; legal affairs, lawsuit, civil suit); **specifically**: someone's concerns, affairs

ḥn (with semogram *Ꝃ*) verb intrans.: hurry, go, journey, reach, hasten to (with preposition *r*: go to place; with preposition *n*: go to someone; with preposition *m*: to come from a place; with preposition *ỉrm/ḥnꜥ*: go together with; also with preposition *r* + infinitive: go to do); trans.: to enter, pass through a place; for writing, see supra § 1.1.3(4)

ḥnꜥ preposition: (together) with, and (see supra § 2.2.4[4])

ḥnw see also *ḥn.t*

ḥnw noun: (1) vessel (for liquids, grain, cooking; of clay, stone or metal); (2) things, chattels, household goods, furniture, furnishings (in the sense of movable property, as opposed to *ỉḫ.t*, immovables), see also *ḥn.t*

ḥnw.t noun: mistress, lady, ruler of something, someone; also the most noble, distinguished among others ("a princess among women")

ḥnr see *ḫꜣ*

ḥnq.t noun: beer (for the writing, see supra § 1.1.3[3])

ḥr noun: face (of people and animals; figuratively of things); *r-ḥr* before someone, on something; as adverb: forwards; *rḏỉ ḥr r/m/ḥr* to pay attention, turn the face to, something; turn to someone; take up a matter; *rḏỉ m-ḥr* to set someone a task (draw to someone's attention); *rḏỉ ḥr r* + infinitive: to begin to, to be about to do something

ḥr (writing also with the group with the Gardiner Z5 stroke and apparent *n*) preposition: on, at, with; due to, because of, on account of, concerning, and, from, about, upon, by, toward (for the phonematic preservation, see supra § 1.1.2[2]; for the status forms, supra § 2.2.4[3]; for use and preservation, supra § 3.1.1[3]); in compound prepositions with *tp*, q.v.

ḥr.y prepositional *nisbe*: above, over, on, physically above; *ḥr.y-tꜣ* "someone living on earth", living, survivors

ḥr.y noun: the superior; common in titles: master, chief, boss, captain, overseer, director or manager of a department, group or division, e.g., *ḥr.y-iḥ* stable master; *ḥr.y-iz.t* foreman (in hieroglyphic, corresponds to hieratic *ꜥ n iz.t*); as military rank also: colonel, commander

ḥrì verb **intrans.**: to be distant, far off, far away, away, gone; to go off, away; to keep a distance, stay away (with preposition *r*: from someone, something); **trans.**: to remove someone or something

ḥrw (with or without the preposition *ḥr/r*) adverb: apart from, except

ḥrr noun: flower (in group writing, see § 1.2.2[3])

ḥḥ noun: million; great number (of persons, years); with article or demonstrative: *pꜣy ḥḥ n rnp.wt* ("this million of years") era, eon, epoch

ḥzì verb **trans.**: to praise or favour someone, show favours; (officially) recognize someone (with preposition *ḥr*: because of something); to approve (of) something; **nominal derivatives**: *ḥzy* the one who is praised, favoured, respected, appreciated, treasured; the favorite; *ḥzw.t* (also written without *-t*), kindness, favor (either expected or received), proof of favor (appreciation, etc.); praise (either spoken or received); *rḍi ḥzw.t/ḥzì* to do a favor

ḥsì verb **intrans.**: sing; **nominal derivatives**: *ḥs.w* male singer; *ḥs.t* female singer; in titles: *ḥs.t n 'Imnw*, Chantress of Amun

ḥsb verb **trans.**: count, reckon; see Arabic *ḥasaba*; in titles *zḥꜣ ḥsb šsr*, grain accountant

ḥsbwpt see *ḥsp* vineyard

ḥsp noun: vineyard; garden bed (also written in partial group writing ⸗⸗ , HorSeth 11,9)

ḥqꜣ noun: ruler

ḥqꜣ.t noun: earlier unit of capacity (see appendix supra §§ 7.3.1; 7.3.2[1])

ḥqr (Coptic ⳢⲔⲞ) verb **intrans.**: to be hungry; also: to have an appetite for, be greedy for (with preposition *r*); **nominal derivative**: *ḥqr* hunger; *n ḥqr* (to die, etc.) because of hunger, out of hunger

ḥkꜣ noun: divine or other-worldly power to exercise influence on earth ("magic")

ḥtp verb **intrans.**: to be satisfied, content, pleased (with preposition *ḥr/m*: with someone or something); to be merciful, generous (with preposition *n*: to someone); to be peaceful, to stay, reside, rest (with preposition *ḥr/m*: in or on something); to set (of heavenly bodies); **trans.**: *ḥtp A* "to satisfy A", "to make A content"; **nominal derivatives**: *(pꜣ) ḥtp* the setting, (sun-)set; peace; *ḥtp(.t)* offerings (specifically: *ḥtp-nṯr* divine offerings; temple property; administration of offerings)

ḥtp.w noun: flowers, flower offerings

ḥtr noun: team, yoke, span (of horses, oxen); the team of horses; also (pl.): horses, cavalry, charioteers

ḥtr (semogram ⸗) noun: levy, assessment, income, revenue; supplies, rations, contributions; **specifically**: the extra rations (as opposed to *di.w*) of fish, beer, vegetables, etc., for the workmen of Deir el-Medina (Warburton, *State and Economy in Ancient Egypt*, Freiburg 1997, pp. 263ff.)

ḥḏ   noun: silver (as material, as means of payment — in the form of rings — and abstract means of assessing value, "money"); also as concept for a totality of valuable things: *pȝ ḥḏ* wealth, capital, treasure; *pr-ḥḏ* see under *pr*

ḥḏ.t   noun: white crown of Upper Egypt

ḥḏỉ   verb **trans.**: to damage, injure someone; to slander someone; to mar, disturb, destroy something; **intrans.**: to be reduced, minimized; to be missing, unaccounted for

ḥḏn   verb **intrans.**: to be vexed, unwilling, opposed to something

ḫ.t   noun: fire; *rḏỉ ḫ.t* to light, set on fire (with preposition *m/r*: something); *ḫ.t-s:nṯr* incense flame; title: (*ḫ.ty-s:nṯr*): incense burner

ḫȝ   noun: pick, spike (see *ḫnr*)

ḫȝ-tȝ   noun: a unit of 10 *sṯȝ.t* "arouras" = 10 * (100 * 100) cubits = 1000 * 100 cubits ("Thousand of Land"); **specifically**: piece of land, parcel, plot; *ḫȝ-tȝ n Pr-ʕȝ* Crown Land, tenanted Crown Land (surveyed land subject to the king, who can lease it, even if it belongs to other institutions, see Gardiner, *The Wilbour Papyrus*, Vol. II, p. 166)

ḫȝy.t   noun: illness, disease; suffering, pain, hurt; complaints

ḫȝʕ   verb **trans.**: to throw, let loose, reject, disregard something; lay something down (with preposition *ḥr/r*: at or on a place; on the ground, into water); to leave, abandon, quit someone or something (with compound preposition *r-ḫȝ.t* because of something or someone); to leave someone alone; omit, neglect, leave off something; **specifically**: *ḫȝʕ ḏr.t m A* "leave off A" (< "to leave the hand off A"): with adverbials: *ḫȝʕ r-bnr/bl* dispatch, send someone off (also meaning "divorce"), dismiss, relieve, sack, fire someone; kick someone out (with preposition *m*: from a place); send them off or out; *ḫȝʕ ḥr wȝ.t* not to finish something; leave something unfinished, incomplete; **intrans.**: to be abandoned.

ḫȝr.t   see *ḫȝr.t* widow

ḫȝs.t   noun: foreign land, hill-country, mountain, desert; sometimes in general: abroad

ḫʕỉ   verb (3ae inf.) **intrans.**: to rise, go up, appear, reveal oneself; with prepositions *m*: to appear as, in (a place); *ḥr* in a chariot, specifically: *ḥr ssm.t ḥr wrrj.t* with horse and carriage (the second *ḥr* is co-ordinating and not rection!) **specifically**: to go out in a procession, parade, with *m*: from a place; with *r*: to a place

ḫʕw   noun: the "splendid appearance", manifestation (of heavenly bodies, divinities in festivals, kings at accession to the throne, kings at appearances); **specifically**: the crowns; *nb ḫʕw* "lord of crowns" (royal epithet)

ḫʕm   (with semogram 𓏤) see *ẖʕm*

ḫʕw   noun: place of fire, "purgatory" (see supra § 3.1.5[2])

ḫỉ   interjection before nouns ("oh how!", etc.); also interrogative particle (*ḫỉ ʕ* "How is the state, condition?" > "How are you?")

ḫw   noun: fan (also as standard of military unit or symbol of dignity)

ḫpr   verb **intrans.**: to become, emerge, appear, come into existence, develop, transform (with preposition *m*: to develop out of something; to become something); to begin; to happen, occur, arrive (with prepositions *m/m-ʕ/m.dỉ*: with or through someone); something happens to someone (with preposition *r*); to be, to exist (with preposition *m.dỉ*: with someone); **specifically**: with preposition *mỉ*: to behave, to become like, to be like someone or something; for writings, see supra §§ 1.1.2(2); 1.1.3(3)

ḫpr.w   noun: being, form, appearance, "transformation", manifestation; *ỉrỉ ḫpr.w* to assume a form; to transform oneself, be transformed (with preposition *m*: as, in, into) *ḫpš*   noun: sword, falchion (scimitar)

ḫm   (semogram ⏗) verb **trans.**: to fail to recognize someone; not to know someone or something; to forget someone or something; not to consider, not to have regard for; (with object; from Dynasty XIX on, also with preposition *r*); **intrans.**: to be ignorant, not to know; without someone's knowing, to be unknown; as infinitive after *m*: *m ḫm(=f)* unknowingly, unwittingly; without someone's approval, permission, agreement, knowledge

ḫmnw   toponym: Hermopolis (Hermupolis magna), capital of the 15th Upper Egyptian Nome with a Thoth temple (Coptic ⲱⲘⲞⲨⲚ, modern el-Ashmunein)

ḫmt   (with semogram ⏗) see *ḫm*

ḫn   noun: speech, statement, expression; affair, matter

ḫnr   noun: the so-called "harem" and its members (actually the institution responsible for the provisioning and accommodation of the women and children of the royal court); *pr-ḫnr* "office of the Harem"; property and property management/administration of the Harem

ḫnr   (*ḫ3/ḫl*) noun: copper pick, chisel, spike, pickaxe (occasionally called "large pick", as a tool used by a group which is state property and issued only for specific purposes)

ḫnt   preposition: in front of, on top of something, in, among; adjectival derivative (*nisbe*) *ḫnt.y* (to be) in front of, to the fore of something; *A ḫnt.y B*: A, who is in front of B/A, in front of whom is B

ḫntỉ   verb (4ae inf. with *t*-infinitive) **intrans.**: to sail, go upstream (southwards); sail

ḫntš   verb **intrans.**: to be delighted, rejoice, enjoy something, to be happy about something (with prepositions *m/n/ḫr*);

ḫnd   verb **(in)trans.**: to enter, walk; to step on something (with object or preposition *ḥr*)

ḫ-r   toponym: Syria (Khuri, Land of Khuri, Land of the Hurrians)

ḫr   (1) preposition: with someone or something; from someone; through someone; as verbal rection: speak, come, bring to someone; do something under the majesty of; (2) conjunction of "contingency": then, thus, and so, but, rather, and also, still more; see § 2.2.4(1)

ḫr   variant writing of interjection, interrogative *ḫỉ* ("how?", "oh how!"), q.v.

ḫr   speech marker, following or inserted (with suffix or nominal subject): *ḫr=tw* "one says/said"; *ḫr=f* "he says/said"

ḫr   noun: the tomb, **specifically** the tomb of the reigning king (completely: *p3 ḫr ˁ3 šps n ḥḥ m rnp.wt n Pr-ˁ3 ˁ.w.s. ḥr jmnt.t w3s.t* "the great and noble tomb of millions of years of Pharaoh in the West of Thebes"), its location (the area of the Valley of the Kings), and its structure with administration and personnel (cf. Černý, *Community*, pp. 1ff.; Ventura, *City of the Dead*, pp. 1ff.), thus: the Tomb Building Administration; official designation in hieroglyphic inscriptions: *s.t-M3ˁ.t* "Place of Maˁat" (usually rendered "Place of Truth")

ḫrw   noun: voice, sound, noise; **specifically**: (sound of) thunder; screeching, howling (of wind), etc.; *rdỉ ḫrw* to raise the voice, have one's say (see supra § 1.3.2)

ḫrwyw   noun: conflict, war, combat, hostilities, revolt, rebellion, disturbance (derived from *ḫrw* noise); *irỉ ḫrwyw* start fight, act aggressively, conduct military operation, wage war, revolt

ḫsbd   (*ḫsbd.t*) noun: lapis lazuli (semi-precious blue stone) or artificial blue glass (*ḫsbd iry.t*)

ḫšb   verb **trans.**: to mutilate someone (cut off nose, ears; as judicial punishment); to mutilate oneself

ḫt   (semogram ⟋) see *ḫdỉ*

ḫt   noun: wood, tree, log, staff, stick; *ḫt-t3w* "mast" of a boat; **specifically**: pole, post, stake (as instrument of death sentences, *rdỉ tp ḫt* put on the stake > "impale") *ḫt* in *m-ḫt* (initial *ı̓r m-ḫt*): (1) compound preposition (with noun): behind someone or something (spatial); following, after someone or something (temporal); after an activity (with infinitive); (2) conjunction (with *sdm=f*): after, when; (3) adverb: after; (4) nominal: the future, what is after

ḫtꝫ toponym: Hatti, Hittite Empire

ḫtı̓ verb **trans.**: inscribe, engrave, carve something (with preposition *ḥr*: on something); to describe something (with preposition *m*: with something); **nominal derivative:** *ḫt* seal

ḫtm verb **trans.**: to seal; close, lock (with preposition *ḥr*: behind someone; with prepositions *n*: for someone; preposition *r*: because of, against someone; with compound preposition *r-ḥꝫ.t*: before someone); **nominal derivatives:** *ḫtm* (masc.) seal, seal ring; *ḫtm* (masc.) lock, closed area, enclosure, protected domain (rooms and areas which can be closed or cut off); **specifically:** *pꝫ ḫtm n pꝫ ḫr* the administrative and storage area of Deir el-Medina (cf. also McDowell, *Jurisdiction*, pp. 93ff.)

ḫdı̓ verb **intrans.**: to sail downstream, go north; to be northbound; but also: *m ḫd* "in the north"; for the writing, see supra § 1.1.2(3)

ḥ.t see *ḥꝫ.t* body

ḥꝫ.t noun: body, belly; **specifically**: womb

ḥꝫr (𓏘) noun: measure of capacity, "sack" (see appendix supra § 7.3)

ḥꝫr.t noun: widow

ḥ ͨm verb **trans.**: to approach someone, come up to someone, to meet up with someone; to come too close to someone, injure someone (with preposition *n*)

ḥn verb **(in)trans.**: to approach, come close, up to someone (with preposition *m/n*); to approach a place (with prepositions *m/n/r*); to touch (with object or preposition *n*)

ḥnw noun: interior, home, court, residence; compound preposition: *m-ḥnw*, sometimes still precisely "inside, in the interior of", but mostly "in"

ḥr preposition: under, beneath, with; **specifically** (with verbs): (come) with something; bearing, carrying, holding something; **adverbially:** *ḥr-ḥꝫ.t* before, previously, earlier

ḥr.y see *ḥr.ty*

ḥr.y-ͨ noun: apprentice, assistant

ḥr.t-ͨ noun: wooden container for writing instruments and files

ḥr.t-ntr noun: cemetery, necropolis; realm of the dead

ḥr.ty (< *ḥr.ty-ntr* "member of the necropolis") noun: stonemason, quarryman, stone cutter (in quarries or tombs); **specifically:** those who worked underground in the tunnels, cutting away the stone, or excavated the rock tombs (see Černý, *Community*, pp. 251f.)

ḥry see *ḥrw*

ḥrw noun: underside, bottom, base; adverbial: *r-ḥrw* (Coptic ⲉⲥⲣⲁⲓ) below, downwards

ḥrd noun: child, offspring (all ages, mostly male: unborn, baby, child, youth, lad, boy); also: someone's child (including daughter)

ḥd see *ḥdb* kill

ḥdb verb **trans.**: to slay, kill

zı̓ noun: man, person (**specifically**: male person); someone; *zı̓ ͨꝫ* adult

z.t   noun: woman, female person; **specifically**: adult woman (in contrast to girl); z.t-ḥm.t female person, wife (Coptic C2IMЄ)

s.t   noun: place, place of residence, residence, location (of someone or something); **specifically**: s.t landed property (in wills and documents of inheritance); s.t ꜥ3.t "august place", used for the royal tombs (cf. Černý, Community, pp. 69f.); m/r-s.t=f at someone's appropriate place; appropriate, suitable for someone (according to his quality); as component of abstract concepts: s.t-qrs "burial place"; s.t-ỉb "affection", "wish"; s.t-r3 "linguistic capacity"; ḥr s.t-r3=f under his direction, because of someone, for someone; toponyms: s.t-Pr-ꜥ3 as term for the Valley of the Kings, or the tomb of the ruling king; s.t-M3ꜥ.t "Place of Ma'at" (the goddess of the order of the universe, justice, law and truth, and thus frequently translated "Place of Truth"), term for the necropolises or sacred places; **specifically**: designation for the Theban Necropolis and the official religious and administrative term (for p3 ḥr, q.v.) for the Theban Tomb Building Administration (cf. Černý, Community, pp. 27ff.)

z3/z3.t noun: son/daughter; z3.t-nzw royal daughter, princess; z3-nzw n k3š Viceroy of Cush

s3   noun: the back; also figuratively: "ridge" (of mountains, countries, etc.); in compound prepositions: m-s3 behind someone or something; follow someone (pursuing, seeking, after someone; watching, observing someone); (to come) because of a person or a thing; temporally: after; **specifically**: someone is m-s3 nꜣy=f j3w.t with his herds (< after his cattle); (ḥr-)s3 (Coptic CA-) behind, after (spatially and temporally); adverb: afterwards, later

z3w   verb **trans.**: to guard, watch someone; to preserve, protect something; to protect oneself before someone or something (object); to restrain, withstand, ward off; followed by clause or infinitive: prevent from/that; **nominal derivatives**: z3w/z3w.ty guard, guardian, observer, archivist, record keeper; rmṯ-z3w prisoner

z3w   (semogram ⌣̽) verb **trans.**: to break, split, shatter, demolish something

s3ḥ   verb **intrans.**: to approach, to come close, to come along; **nominal derivative**: m s3ḥ.w/s3ḥ.t in the vicinity, neighbourhood of; s3ḥ/ s3ḥ-t3 neighbours, friends

s3-kt see sk

sỉ3   verb **trans.**: to recognize, notice, perceive someone or something; to understand; to have knowledge, profound understanding of something (of life, of plans); with prepositions: sỉ3 A m B "to recognize A as B"; sỉ3 A r B "to distinguish, differentiate A from B"

sỉm   see sm

s:ỉn   verb **intrans.**: to wait (with preposition n: for someone)

syf   see sfỉ

s:ꜥḥꜥ   verb **trans.**: to raise, erect, cause to stand, set something or someone up(right); **specifically**: to accuse, testify against, bring evidence against someone

s:ꜥq   verb **trans.**: to cause someone or something to enter; to enter, drive in, deliver; to gain entry for, lead in (with prepositions r/m: into something or somewhere); **specifically**: to drive animals to a place; to bring in grain ("pour it into" the silo, granary)

sw   (logogram ☉ ; Coptic COY): "day" in dates

s:w3   verb **intrans.**: to pass (with preposition ḥr: by); to elapse, dwindle, wither away, go off (with preposition ḥr: because of); **trans.**: to pass someone

sw3.w noun: district, region, area, environment, neighbourhood

s:w3ḏ verb **trans.**: to make green, fresh; renew; cause to prosper, flourish

s:w3ḏ see s:wḏ

zwỉ   see zwr

s:wn   verb **trans.**: to open a way, to identify a way (> swn "to know", Coptic COOYṄ) *s:wn*   (semogram 𓏏) see *s:wnwn*

swn   verb (with *t*-infinitive) **intrans.**: to trade, sell, buy; **nominal derivative**: *swn.t* trade, price; |*n*| *X r swn.t* "to buy X" (< to purchase something for its price); *rḍi swn.t* give, name, establish, the price

zwnw   noun: physician, doctor

s:wnwn   verb **trans.**: to show respect, awe, admiration (with object or preposition *n*: to someone); also: to flatter someone; to coax, cajole; **nominal derivative**: *s:wn/s:wnwn* reverence, awe, adulation, flattery; *iri s:wn* to show reverence for someone (with preposition *n*)

zwr   (*zwi*) verb **(in)trans.**: drink (for writing see supra § 1.1.3[3])

swḥ.t   noun: egg; figuratively: "egg" as designation for (1) offspring, child; (2) innermost coffin; (3) "mask" of the mummy wrappings out of cartonnage; (4) shroud; (5) shrine

swgꜣ   (actually *sg*, Coptic **ϭⲟϭ**) verb **intrans.**: to be silly, foolish

swt   enclitic particle with adversative effect: "but", "yet"; frequently with *iw* (*iw swt*) and following the initial particles of clauses (*ir*; *ḥr*)

swtwt   verb **intrans.**: to stroll, promenade, walk about, stride (with prepositions *m/r/ḥr*: in or to a place; with preposition *ḥnꜥ*: with someone; voyage, travel

s:wḏ   verb **trans.**: to pass something on to someone; to refer someone on, to assign someone or something to someone or something, to recommend someone to someone; to pass on, convey, bequeath (in wills and testaments, "to will" something to someone); with object and preposition *n* with persons, preposition *r* for institutions

s:wḏꜣ   verb **trans.**: to invigorate, make prosperous; to keep safe; to cause someone or something to be in good condition; *s:wḏꜣ ib n NN* to wish to make someone's heart rejoice > the formula in the initial passages of letters to superiors: *NN ḥr s:wḏꜣ ib n nb=f* "NN lets the heart of his lord rejoice", turns to his superior, writes a message or letter

sbꜣ   verb **(in)trans.**: instruct, educate, raise, tend (with object: someone; with preposition *m*: concerning, about something; with preposition *r* + infinitive: to do something); **nominal derivatives**: *sbꜣ* pupil, student; *sbꜣ.w* teacher, instructor, master; *sbꜣ.w* instruction, education, teaching; *sbꜣy.t* teaching, instruction, lore; punishment, penalty, sentence; *iri sbꜣy.t n A* to execute a punishment, carry out a sentence, on A.

sbꜣ   (Coptic **ⲥⲃⲉ**) noun: door, gate (also in wider sense: gateways, gate buildings, door frames, and door leaves)

zbi   see *zbṯ*

zbṯ   verb **intrans.**: to laugh; with preposition *m/n*: to ridicule someone, to laugh at someone's expense, to laugh someone out; to joke about someone (Coptic **ⲥⲱⲃⲉ ⲘⲚ̄**)

zp   noun: matter, case, instance; with *n* + infinitive or abstract noun: *zp n rḫ* "erudition"; *zp n ꜣḫ.t* "good works, deeds"; *iri zp n grg* "to commit an evil deed"

spr   verb **(in)trans.**: to reach a place or person, arrive at a place (with preposition *r* or object!); to come to, reach, attain a place or person (with preposition *r* or object! occasionally also with preposition *n* or *m*); with *r* + infinitive: to succeed in doing something, to manage something, to do something

s:pḥr   verb **trans.**: to write, copy, enroll, inscribe something (with preposition *ḥr*: on something); to draw, paint (with preposition *ḥr*: on something); write upon something, colour something (with preposition *m*: with something); **specifically**: to register, record (grain, harvest yields)

spt   see *ḥsp* vineyard, plant bed

spd   adjective verb: to be sharp, pointed; to be clever; *spd-ꜥb.w* "pointed of horn" (of a bull)

sfi   noun: child, young man, boy, lad, youth; offspring (of gods and kings) *zf.t*   (Coptic ⳤⲎϤⲈ) noun (fem.): knife, sword; (for the writing, see supra § 1.1.3[4])

sm   noun: greens, herbage, herbs, plants, vegetables; fodder, grass; (for the writing, see supra § 1.2.1[2])

smỉ   verb **trans.**: to report, complain, accuse, charge someone, something (with preposition *n*: to someone; with preposition *ḥr*: about someone); **nominal derivative**: *smỉ* report; see also *sḫ3*; *dd smỉ* to make a report; with "genitive"/suffix after *smỉ*: report something, about something; to accuse someone, to indict someone; with preposition *ḥr*: to report from someone; with preposition *m*: to report officially about something; also: to denounce

sm3   verb **trans.**: to kill, slay or slaughter persons or animals; to amputate, cut off (members)

zm3y   noun: woodwork, carving

zm3-t3   (with semogram ⵁ) verb **trans.**: to bury, to be buried (< to be united with the earth)

s:mn   verb (*t*-infinitive) **trans.**: to cause to remain, to make firm, make lasting (with preposition *ḥr*: with the aid of); to fasten; to found, establish, fix, erect, build, construct (buildings, monuments, etc.); with preposition *m*: out of (stone, etc.); to confirm, record deeds, accomplishments, edicts (to make them last by writing them down < "immortalize"); **intrans.**: to stay, remain standing; stand around; endure

smḥy   adjective: left; noun: left; left side

s:mḫ   verb **trans.**: to forget, neglect someone or something; to be thoughtless; not to think about; to be negligent; (antonym: *sḫ3* to recall, remember, bear in mind)

s:mtỉ   see *s:mtr*

s:mtr   verb **trans.**: to examine, investigate someone or something; to conduct a judicial or criminal investigation; to interrogate (with torture); **nominal derivative**: (*p3*) *s:mtr* interrogation, investigation, examination; *ỉrỉ s:mtr=f* interrogate him (with torture); *t3 s.t s:mtr* the investigatory commission, court

smd.t   noun (fem.): auxiliary workers, reserve workers; personnel, staff, subordinates; **specifically**: *smd.t bnr* "support staff" (as a designation for personnel providing for the Gang of the Tomb Building Administration; also *smd.t p3 ḫr*; frequently rendered as "serfs", "dependents")

sn   noun: brother; but also the whole set of collateral male relations, and relations through marriage (thus also used for married spouses), brethren, siblings; and thus also figuratively for "friend", "lover"; see Franke, *Verwandschaftsbezeichnungen*, pp. 61ff.

sn   (with semogram ⌇) verb **trans.**: to smell something; to kiss someone

znỉ   (semogram ⌐) verb **(in)trans.**: to surpass, outstrip, pass by; with object or preposition *ḥr* or *r*: to go by something, to pass it (figuratively: to traverse, cross, surpass something; to go beyond the acceptable, the known, to go too far); **specifically**: "to strike", "to stop working", "to down tools", shortened from *znỉ/zš t3 5 ỉnb.t* "to pass the five watch-posts (of the *md3y*-police at Deir el-Medina)"

znỉw   noun: measure of value, see *šnˁ.t*

snb   verb **intrans.**: to be well, cured, become healthy; **nominal derivative**: *snb* health, well-being

znny   (with semogram ⌐) see *zn/znỉ*

znny   (with semogram ⌇) see *sn*

znnty   see *sn-t3*; see *sntỉ/snt*

snty   see *sntỉ*

sn-t3   (also) verbal expression: to kiss the earth (as a gesture of respect, allegiance; with preposition *n*: to the one who is respected)

snṯỉ   verb **trans.**: to found, establish (with object and preposition *m*: something as something); make, create; **nominal derivative**: *snṯ* (*znty/znnty*; also *tȝ znty* < *snṯ.t*) foundation wall, foundation, plan, blueprint; also *snṯ-tȝ* foundation

s:nṯr   noun: incense (congealed green-white resin of Boswellia bush or tree, from Sudan, Eritrea, Somalia or South Arabia; see R. Germer, *Untersuchungen über Arzneimittelpflanzen im Alten Ägypten*, Hamburg 1979, pp. 69ff.)

sr   (*sñw*; Coptic **CIOYⲢ**) noun: official, magistrate, councillor, advisor, notable, grandee; designation for high officials and members of judicial and advisory councils (*qnb.t*) in the provinces and in the Residence (*qnb.t ˁȝ.t*); see also McDowell, *Jurisdiction*, pp. 65ff.

sr   verb **trans.**: to predict, foresee, foretell; to see in advance; to promise, declare expectation, anticipate (victories, etc.); to proclaim, make known, announce

zḥ   noun: council hall, official hall

sḥn   verb **trans.**: to order, assign, command, authorize, organize (with preposition *r* + infinitive: to do something); equip, provide, supply; **nominal derivatives**: *sḥn* order, command, task, work, commission, business, duties, assignment; *sḥnw* equipment

s:ḥtpỉ   noun: censer (instrument for burning incense in cult)

zḫ   verb **trans.**: to strike, beat, hit; **nominal derivative**: *zḫ.t* strike, hit, blow; idiomatically: *ḫr š(n)t n zḫ.t* (***"to be under 100 blows" >) to receive 100 blows, lashes, strokes

sḫ.t   noun: field, fields; arable fields, cultivable lands; meadows, pasture; countryside, rural area (as opposed to urban, house, residential area); **specifically**: *sḫ.t ˁȝ.t* the great field (= Valley of the Kings, Biban el-Muluk)

sḫȝ   verb **trans.** (or **intrans.** with preposition *m*): to recall, recount, mention, remember something or someone; to consider someone's affair, to think about a matter; **nominal derivatives**: *zḫȝ* thought, memory; *sḫȝ n* notice, memorandum concerning

sḫȝ   🏛 *sḫȝ r* accusation concerning; charge, complaint lodged about, because, on account of, concerning (derived from *sḫȝ* thought, memory); see McDowell, *Jurisdiction*, pp. 16-18

s:ḫpr   verb **trans.**: to foster, bring up, rear, fashion; to cause something to emerge, appear, become; to create; to raise someone, to promote someone (with preposition *r*: to entrust with a task, to promote to an office)

sḫr   noun: thought, idea, plan, advice, counsel, means; nature, fashion, manner, habit, way (preposition *n* with infinitive: to do something, of doing something); affair, matter; *m pȝy=f sḫr* in his way, how someone usually does something (also *m pȝy=f sḫr nty rˁw-nb* in his habitual way, fashion); *irỉ sḫr* to form, compose plans, distribute instructions, assign tasks; with suffix/"genitive" or other indication following *sḫr*: to care for, attend to, take care of someone; carry out someone's plans, instructions, tasks, assignments; **derivative**: *sḫr.y* counsellor, advisor

sḫry   noun: counsellor, advisor (see *sḫr*)

zḫȝ   noun: writing, written matter, text; picture; books, documents, records; **specifically**: *zḫȝ n rn.w* "Name-text" for an official writing of the king; **derivative**: *zḫȝ.w* "scribe", q.v.

zḫȝ.w   ("scribe") (1) administrative title of indiscriminate rank (according to office and position): secretary of a particular department, e.g., *zḫȝ.w n pȝ ḫr* Secretary of the Tomb Building Administration; *zḫȝ.w n pr-ḥḏ* Secretary of the Treasury; (2) "status title" for a specific education (e.g., abbreviation for *zḫȝ.w qd.wt* "outline writer" > painter, draughtsman)

ssm.t   noun: horse, team of horses; also specifically: to go out *ḥr ssm.t ḥr wrry.t* ("with horse and chariot"), in a chariot

s:snb   verb **trans.**: to make or keep someone healthy; used in the initial paragraphs of letters for very high ranking recipients ("I bid Amun *s:snb NN*, keep NN healthy")

zš   see *zḫȝ*, *zḫȝ.w*

zš (with semogram ◿) see *znỉ*

sšd (Coptic ϢΟΥϢΤ) noun: window

s:qꜣ verb **trans.**: to raise, lift someone or something; to hold them high; to raise someone, distinguish them; to exalt; **specifically**: divine, "exalted" power

sqnn see *sgnn* anoint

sk noun (masc. or fem.; Coptic ϭΗϬ): foal of donkey, ass

skỉ verb **trans.**: to cause someone or something to perish; to destroy, utterly eliminate, expunge, wipe out; **nominal derivative**: *sk.w* battle, fight, contest, combat

skꜣ verb **trans.**: to plough, till (object: fields, etc.); cultivate, plant, grow (object: wheat, barley, etc.); with preposition *m*: with something (tool, animal); at a place

s:km verb **trans.**: to make something complete; to finish, complete, end; to bring to an end; to cause to stop; **specifically**: to spend a period of time

sgꜣnn see *sgnn*

sgn see *sgnn*

sgnn verb **trans.**: to anoint, oil, salve someone, something, oneself; **nominal derivative**: *sgnn* salve, ointment, oil, fat (for the writing, see supra § 1.12[3])

stỉ see *sṯỉ* smell, odour, fragrance

stỉm see *sm* greens

stw.t noun: rays of the sun (and thus figuratively of bright, radiant objects)

stš (*stḫ/stḫ*) god "Seth"

s:tꜣḫ verb **trans.**: to confuse, trouble, disturb (pChester Beatty vs. C1,8; an otherwise unknown verb, causative of *tꜣḫ* sink, be dipped > Coptic ΤⲰϨ confuse)

stp verb **trans.**: to choose, pick, select someone (with preposition *m*: from, among; with preposition *r*: for a specific purpose; with preposition *n*: for someone); also as adjective: elect, chosen; choicest; see also supra § 1.3.3 Notes line 4

stm see *sm*

sṯ.tw noun: the inhabitants of the lands to the north-east of Egypt, "Asiatics"

sṯỉ noun: smell, scent, odour, fragrance, perfume

sṯꜣ verb **trans.**: to draw, drag, tow someone or something; to bring someone; to conduct, usher someone in; to bring them along; introduce them; *pr (n) sṯꜣ* mortuary furnishings, funerary equipment ("towed property")

sṯꜣ.t noun: "aroura", a unit of measure of 100 * 100 cubits (10,000 square cubits, *mḥ-tꜣ*; 2756.5 m²); as measure for fields, also *sṯꜣ.t-ꜣḥ.t* (Coptic ϭⲉΤⲉΙⲰϨⲉ) "field aroura"

s:ḏfꜣ verb **trans.**: to feed someone; to provide, equip, supply, endow, furnish someone (with preposition *m*, with); *s:ḏfꜣ-try.t* the official oath of officials and functionaries (oath "to assure that one will take care of what is respected", see K. Baer, *JEA* 50 [1964]: 179f.); see also McDowell, *Jurisdiction*, pp. 202ff.

sdm see *sḏm*

sḏ verb **trans.**: to break, fragment, shatter, smash, beat, hew, pierce; break into pieces; break open (also metaphorically); **intrans.**: to go forth, to break out, to break through *sḏm*   verb **intrans.**: to hear; to be able to hear, capable of hearing; to listen; to understand, comprehend; to acknowledge, obey, hearken; be obedient; to conduct an interrogation, interrogate; with preposition *n*: listen to someone or something; obey someone; with preposition *ḥr*: conduct interrogation, interrogate because of; **trans.**: to hear something; to recognize, accept something; to listen to someone, interrogate someone; to pay attention to someone; to learn, read something; with preposition *m.dì*: to hear something from someone; figuratively: receive (letter, meaning "heard from")

sḏm   noun: servant (< "the one who listens", independently or as a title); **specifically**: *sḏm-ʿš* (< "the one who listens to the call", with additional elements), official title of the members of the Gang of the Tomb Building Administration and the male residents of Deir el-Medina (*sḏm-ʿš n s.t Mꜣʿ.t*, in hieroglyphic inscriptions)

sḏr   verb **intrans.**: to spend the night, sleep; to lie, lie around, to go to bed (antonym: *ʿḥʿ*); with preposition *ḥr*: lie on something (stomach, floor); common as auxiliary verb (with *ḥr* + infinitive or Old Perfective, see supra § 2.2.3[3]): to be doing something; *s.t-sḏr* stretcher, bier

s:ḏd   verb **trans.**: relate, explain, tell; talk about something (with object); **intrans.**: speak (with preposition *m*: about something); **nominal derivative**: *s:ḏd* words, tale, talk, story, recital, conversation; manner of speech; *m sḫr n s:ḏd* in the course of conversation

šꜣ   verb **trans.**: to ordain, assign, determine, identify a fate; to destine; to decide, arrange, order that something will happen (with preposition *ḥr/m-ḥr*: to order someone something); to reach a conclusion, decision concerning (with preposition *ḥr*); with infinitive or following clause; to arrange or order that something be done; determine that something will be done

šꜣʿ   verb **trans.**: to begin, start, commence something (with object or infinitive: begin to do something); *šꜣʿ ḫpr* to begin existence, being; exist first, be the first

šꜣʿ   preposition: until, as far as, up to, since; in various combinations with simple prepositions: *(r/m) šꜣʿ m* from ... to; *(r) šꜣʿ r* from ... as far as, until, to; *r šꜣʿ* until (spatially and temporally)

šꜣšꜣ   verb **trans.**: to twist (cords, strings, ropes); to be "twisted", foolish, silly, a fool, mad, crazy; to be unreliable

šʿ   see *šm.t*

šʿ.t   noun: letter, epistle, message, dispatch (< what is cut off); generally: piece of writing

šʿd   verb **trans.**: to fell; to cut something off, down, up; to work on, cut into shape; fell trees; **specifically**: *šʿd ìnr* break stones, work in quarry (for the writing, see supra § 1.2.1)

šʿt   see *šʿd* cut (off)

šw   noun: light, sunlight (also figuratively for king), sun

šw.t   noun: side (as part of human body: hips); *šw.t-mr.w* pyramid area (< "the side of the pyramids", see D. Wildung, *Die Rolle ägyptischer Könige im Bewusstsein ihrer Nachwelt*, [Berlin: MäS 17, 1969], pp. 162f.)

šwy   noun: merchant, trader (also *šwy.ty*); *ìrì šwy(.ty)* to trade, pursue trade, make a deal, be a merchant; *ìrì šwy n A m.dì B* to negotiate with B about A

šp   receive, see *šzp*

šps   adjective verb: to be splendid, noble, august, venerable, magnificent, costly, rich, precious *šm* verb **intrans.**: to go; to go along; to depart, set off, go off, return; with prepositions: *šm m* go in/to a place; *n*: to someone; to pursue a thing, matter (specifically: *šm n=f* to depart, — see Coptic (ⲀϤ)ϢⲈ ⲚⲀϤ); *šm r* to go to, in the direction of a place; proceed against someone; *šm ḥr* to go to someone in order to stay with them; *šm m-sʒ* to go after someone or something, follow them; tend (cattle); *šm ḥft* to go before someone, step up to them; **trans.**: to cross through or over something, enter something; **nominal derivatives**: *šm.w/šm.t* going; way of business; task, business, concern (for the writing, see supra § 1.1.3[3])

šmꜥy.t noun: singer, "chantress" (of a divinity) as title of female incumbents of temple offices, of priestesses

šmw noun: Summer, Harvest-season (Coptic ϢⲎⳘ; its field of meaning associates it with both *šm.t/šm.w* "heat" and *šmw* "harvest") = Third Season of the Egyptian calendar (in the agricultural calendar it began at end of February; by the end of the Ramesside Period it began near the beginning of February); **specifically**: tax, impost (usually rendered "harvest-tax")

šmsꜣ verb **trans.**: to follow, accompany someone; serve someone; bring someone, something along; **nominal derivative**: *šmsw*, q.v.

šmsw noun: follower, "vassal" — member of an entourage, companion; also: person who has voluntarily entered the service of another person, or institution ("employee"); **specifically**: messenger, envoy, emissary (of an authority, office, officer, official); (for the writing, see supra § 1.2.1[2])

šn net (WB IV: 493,11); group writing also 𓏴𓊵𓏺𓀀𓊮𓏤 *šn-nu*, cf. supra § 1.2.3

šnꜣ (Coptic ϢⲰⲚⲈ) verb **intrans.**: to feel pain; suffer; to grieve; to be vexed, troubled; **trans.**: to suffer something (with direct object as cause or source of pain)

šnꜣ (Coptic ϢⲒⲚⲈ) verb **trans.**: to inquire, question, to ask or say something; to investigate officially (with preposition *r*: to make an investigation concerning something); **specifically**: to think about something, to strive for, aspire to something (with direct object); to feel something

šnꜣ verb **trans.**: to conjure (with preposition *m*: with magic); to repeat or recite spells; **intrans.** and **specifically**: *šnꜣ m ḥkʒ* reciting, exercising power in the world by speech (practicing magic, conjuring)

šnꜣ noun: hair (on the head and body of humans and animals; even plants); **specifically**: *šnꜣ-tʒ* "hair of the earth", metaphorical for plants

šnꜥ.t (*šnꜥ.ty/šnꜥ/šꜥt/šꜥty*) noun: measure of weight or value, used exclusively for silver, see appendix supra § 7.3.2(1)

šnw.t (Coptic ϢⲈⲨⲚⲈ) noun: granary, barn, grain silo, warehouse, storehouse, workhouse; **specifically** in titles: *zḥʒ.w n šnw.t* secretary of the granaries, *ꜣm.y-rʒ šnw.ty* director of grain storage (usually rendered as "Overseer of the Double Granary") of the Two Lands, of the Estate of Amun, etc.

šnty see *šnꜣ*

šrr (> *šrꜣ, šr*) verb **intrans.**: to be small, little, young; **nominal derivative**: *šrꜣ*

šrꜣ (Coptic ϢⲎⲢⲈ) noun: child, boy, lad, young man, son; *šrꜣ.t* (Coptic ϢⲈⲈⲢⲈ) maiden, daughter; *šrꜣ* the small one, the little one, the younger (for the writing, see supra § 1.1.1)

šzp verb **trans.**: to receive, take, grasp, attain, secure something (*m-ꜥ/m-ḏr.t* from, through someone); assume, take over, accept something (*ḥr-tp* because of); to take receipt of (deliveries, tribute, payments, presents; *m-ḏr.t* from, by someone; *m* from a place); *šzp fqʒ* to accept gifts, presents; also with preposition *m* indicating what is delivered (prepositional object), *šzp m nʒ ꜣt n B* "receive the grain from B"; **specifically**: begin, commence, start something, *šzp wʒ.t/šzp tp wʒ.t* "to get on the way", "to begin to get underway"; *šzp ḥs.wt ḥr-tp ꜥnḥ wḏʒ snb* to be favoured with prosperity and health; *šzp n-ḥʒ.t n B* "to take in B", "to take responsibility for B"; also to take someone into custody, arrest; (for the writing, see supra § 1.1.2[4])

šsꜣ	verb **intrans.**: to be experienced, knowledgeable, knowing, skilled, clever, versed (with preposition *m*: in something); *šsꜣ-ḥr* cleverness, competence ("knowing faced")
šs	noun: valuables, good thing; as a noun in prepositional phrases with preposition *m*: in good shape; *sw m šs* "it is okay, in order" (negated: not fair, not nice, not in order)
šs	(*šsr*) grain; see appendix, supra § 7.3.2(2)
št	noun: estimate, assessment; assessment of obligatory payments, tax payments; **specifically**: *tꜣ št* "rate-payers" ("the assessed") or "gatherers" ("the assessors"); in title: *ꜥꜣ n št* chief assessor (usually rendered "Chief Taxing Master")
šdỉ	verb **trans.**: to withdraw, take, take away, pull, levy, collect, extract (with preposition *m.dỉ*: from someone; also **specifically**: to exact, collect deliveries, tax payments from someone); to take something out, remove (with preposition *m*: from a silo, treasury, mould)
šdỉ	(meaning variation of *šdỉ*, take) verb **trans.**: to rescue, save, protect, preserve, keep something safe, secure (with preposition *m-ḏr.t*: from someone's hands, with preposition *m*: out of something)
qꜣỉ	see *qrỉ* "arrive"
qꜣ-rꜣ-ḏỉ-nꜣ	see *qrḏn*
qꜣb	(written without *ꜣ*; Coptic Ⲕⲱⲃ) verb **trans.**: to double, increase, multiply (with preposition *m*: with a something; with preposition *r*: beyond something); to increase someone in (preposition *m*) his property, to increase his wealth; **specifically**: to double; *m qꜣb* double, twice over
qꜣ-ḏꜣ	see *q-ḏ*
qꜥḥ.t	noun: sheet of papyrus (see supra § 0.3.2)
qb	see *qꜣb* multiply
qbḥ	verb **intrans.**: to be cool, to be refreshing; **nominal derivatives**: *qbḥ.w* cool water; water offerings, libations (as offering and in liturgy); *qbḥ.w* lake district, swamp or marsh-land; watery, cool land; humid or moist areas; areas defined by water (of the cataracts, of the water fowl); also the heavenly bodies of water
qn	verb **intrans.**: to be at an end, to cease, stop; to be completely equipped (with preposition *m*: with something); **trans.**: to finish, complete something, to end it; make an end of it; to finish off, bring to an end, terminate; to put and end to it; with following infinitive: to stop doing something, cease, desist; to have finished an activity
qn.w	adjective: many, plentiful, numerous, abundant
qnỉ	verb **trans.**: to embrace; **nominal derivative**: embrace, lap
qnỉ	adjective verb: to be strong, courageous, bold, mighty, valiant; **nominal derivatives**: *qn* the strong one, hero; *qn.t* power, courage, valor, victory (*rḏỉ qn.t* to give strength; to offer, assure victory
qnb.t	noun: court, tribunal, judicial, advisory council in temples, provincial metropolises and districts (city council, court of magistrates, court) and in the residence (*qnb.t ꜥꜣ.t* court of appeal; also used for court of one's peers (in Deir el-Medina; see McDowell, *Jurisdiction*, pp. 143ff.); **derivative**: *qnb.tj* councillor (of a district)
qnqn	verb **trans.**: to hit, strike, assault, beat; crush, grind; *m qnqn* (copper) as scrap, beaten (copper)
qrỉ	verb **intrans.**: to near, reach, to draw nigh; to associate with someone (with preposition *n/r*); in compound preposition: *r-qrỉ-n*, *ỉ.qrỉ-n*, *qrỉ-n* (also *qꜣỉ*) "with someone"; with following verbs, also "to someone"

qrs   verb **trans.**: embalm; bury, inter; **nominal derivatives**: *qrs/qrs.t* funeral, burial, interment;
            qrs.w sarcophagus, coffin

qrḏn   (*qrḏ/qḏr/qḏn*) noun: hoe

qṯn   noun: variant of *kḏn* charioteer, q.v.

qd   verb **trans.**: to build, erect, build something up; to build on something (with object and preposition
            m: with something); form, mould, fashion, make, create something; **nominal derivative**: *qd*,
            q.v.

qd   noun: nature, being, character, kind, condition, type, form, figure; **specifically**: *iri qd* to make
            something according to its kind — to do something in exemplary fashion; compound prepositions:
            mi-qd after the kind of, like; also with suffix: entirely, through and through, thoroughly; in its
            entirety; completely; for the writing, see supra § 1.1.1

qd.t   noun: a unit for measuring value, used exclusively for silver and gold, see appendix supra § 7.3.1

qdy   toponym: Cilicia (south-eastern region of Asia Minor on the Mediterranean coast, bordering on
            northern Syria)

qdw.t   noun: picture, image, drawing; *zḫ3.w qdw.t* (literate) painter, draughtsman

q-ḏ   noun: gypsum, plaster; derivative: *qḏy* stucco-worker, plasterer (as distinguished from the plaster
            preparer, *nty ḥr ir(i.t) qḏ*); later used to designate the plaster preparer as well

k3   noun: the human personality (the divine archetype of the human being, to which its "soul" returns
            at death — cf. also *b3*); *n k3 n NN/n k3=f* as a solemn or respectful address

k3   (with semogram ⸻) noun: food, nourishment, sustenance, provisions (also plural)

k3   (with bull semogram/ideogram) noun: bull

k3   (with semogram 𓀢) particle: used before independent prospective *sdm=f* (request, wish; wished
            for future events): "then"

k3.t   noun: the female sex organ; vagina, vulva; also metonymic, as contemptuous term for a woman

k3mn   verb **intrans.**: to be blind, dark; **trans.**: to blind someone, to make someone blind

k3ry   noun: gardener (for vegetables and flowers); vintner

k3š   toponym: Cush (in the new Kingdom, a designation for the entire province from Aswan to Gebel
            Barkal — "Nubia" — and also the specific term for the administrative unit beginning south of
            Semna and the Second Cataract, "Upper Nubia")

ky   noun: (fem. *k.t*; pl. *ky.wy*) other, others; another, next, second; the group *k.t-iḫ.t* "other things"
            becomes one word *ktḫ*, which as a plural precedes its noun of reference: *ktḫ rmṯ* other people;
            n3 ktḫ rmṯ the other people (for writing, see supra § 1.2.2[3])

kfi   (semogram 𓈖) verb **trans.**: to reveal, bare, lay bare, unveil, uncover; to take something away,
            to remove (with preposition *ḥr*: from); to plunder, rob someone

kn-   see *k-n-n-r* lyre
in.iw-r

k-n-n-r   (*kn-nu-r*) lyre, stringed musical instrument (see Greek κιννυρα, Hebrew *kinnor*)

k-n-i-š   toponym: Knossos; (for the writing, see supra § 1.2.3)

k-r   𓊔𓃀 noun (masc.): ship, transport vessel (with considerable cargo capacity); also
            specifically: fishing boat

k-r-y   𓎡𓂋𓇌 in *kry šri* young man (see Westendorf, *Handwörterbuch*, p. 453) *k-s-k-s*   noun: crookedness, bentness (after Lichtheim, *Literature*; derived from *ksỉ* to bow), but perhaps alternatively from *ksks* dance, play (*"shakiness", *"totteringness" > fragility, feebleness)

kš   see *k3š*

kty   see *ky*

k-t-n   see *kḏn*

ktẖ   see *ky*

ktkt   verb **intrans.**: to shudder, quiver, tremble, totter, shake, move, shift; be moved; twist; **trans.**: to take something away, to steal; to shake, hit, stir, cause something to shudder

kḏn   ⊔ | 𓀀𓀁𓀂𓀃   noun: charioteer, chariot warrior (also *kṯn*); equerry, groom

g3y   (Coptic ϬⲀⲓ) noun: bowl, jar (of clay or bronze) for liquids, fruit, flowers, meat, bread; *g3y n mw* "bowl of water"

g3b(.t)   see also *gbỉ*; *g3b.t*

g3b.t   (Coptic ϬⲰⲰⲂⲈ) noun (fem.): leaf (of plant), blade (of grass)

g3š   see *gš*

gbỉ   (Coptic ϬⲂⲂⲈ; qualitative ϬⲞⲞⲂ) verb **intrans.**: to be weak, poor, lame, deprived, deficient (with preposition *m*: from something); **trans.**: (with preposition *m*) to injure someone in something, to rob a person of something; **nominal derivatives**: *gb* injury, damage, need, affliction, deficiency; misbehaviour, injury, guilt, compensation, indemnity; also specifically: expenses; *ỉnỉ gb* to pay expenses

gb3   see *gbỉ*

gmỉ   verb **trans.**: to find (seek and find); to find a way; to find something or someone; discover; to pick, out; to verify, prove, judge; to encounter, meet someone (unexpectedly, accidentally); to recognize someone or something; to establish something (officially, medicinally): confirm, diagnose; **specifically**: *gmỉ A r ỉr.t B* "to find A useful or suited to do B"

gmḥ   verb **trans.**: to see; to espy, glimpse someone; to look at, catch sight of; to behold, observe, watch, stare at; see, how something is (with object and Old Perfective); **intrans.**: to be sighted (antonym: to be blind); to keep an eye on, to follow with the eyes, to keep in view, to not lose sight of (with preposition *n/r*)

gnn   verb **intrans.**: to be weak, soft, tender, comfortable, yielding, indulgent, slothful, slow; to yield to someone, to succumb to someone (with preposition *n*)

gr   particle: used after a clause or word (common after independent pronouns) to resume or emphasize: again, also, likewise

grḥ   noun: night; *m grḥ* at night; *m p3 grḥ* tonight

grg   verb **trans.**: to found, establish something; to prepare, provide, organize, arrange, furnish, make ready; to equip (with preposition *m/ḥr*: with something); to settle at a place (with preposition *m*: with people); to settle people; also: to settle (one's self; with preposition *m/ḥr*: at a place); to prepare one's self; **intrans.**: to be prepared, ready

grg   noun: lie, deceit, untruth, injustice, wrong, falsehood; *ỉrỉ grg* to commit injustice, to do wrong

gs   noun: side of something; half; *r-gs* at the side of, beside, by, alongside, with someone or something; *m-gs* partly, halfway, half; specifically: *ỉw=f m gs* it is halfway done, almost ready

gš   noun: migratory birds

t   noun: bread, offering bread, loaf

$t\beta$ noun: land, country, earth, world; $t\beta$-$mr\hat{\imath}$ Egypt (etymologically: "lovingly chosen land"); **specifically**: land chosen by god, then also "homeland", "fatherland"; $p\beta\ t\beta\ n\ Pr$-$\mathcal{C}$ the realm of Pharaoh; kingdom, empire

$t\beta\check{s}$ noun: border, boundary, frontier; frontier districts or regions

tw see $twt\hat{\imath}$

tw-k-$s\beta$ see tks

$twt\hat{\imath}$ (Coptic ⲦⲞⲞⲨⲦⲈ) verb **trans.**: to collect something, someone; to gather, bring together (with preposition r: for something, for a purpose); **intrans.**: to be assembled ($twt\hat{\imath}$=sn they are assembled, they are together)

tp noun: head (of humans and animals); figuratively "head" of object: top, tip, summit (also tip-top quality, best of something); in abstractions: beginning, model, ideal plan = way to do something; "head" (of group, chief); **specifically**: tp-$w\beta.t$ beginning of the way; tp-$hw.t$ roof; compound preposition: hr-tp (1) on, above, on top of something, someone; also specifically: on someone's head; to be at the very front; (2) for the benefit of someone (see also $\hat{\imath}r\hat{\imath}\ hr$-$tp$)

$tf\hat{\imath}$ verb **trans.**: to remove someone, something by force (with preposition hr: from his/its position, place); to push, dislodge someone; to drive someone off; **specifically**: to uproot trees; to remove people from work; **intrans.**: to be pressed, to perceive oneself as pressed; with r + infinitive: to press that something be done

tm verb of negation, see supra § 2.2.3(4)

$tnw/tn\hat{\imath}$ see $\underline{t}nw/\underline{t}n\hat{\imath}$

$tnh\beta$ (tn-h) see dhn appoint, name

tr noun: time; season; (for the writing, see supra § 1.1.2[2])

$th\hat{\imath}$ verb **intrans.**: to do wrong, to act wrongly, to sin (with preposition r: against someone or something; injure someone, damage something, do evil against; with preposition hr: to depart from, take wrong path); **trans.**: to transgress, violate, damage, mislead, disobey (a rule), go against (the rules), fail to observe (the rules); to give in, do evil against, to someone; to trespass against someone; damage something

thb verb **trans.**: to dip, soak something in something, to moisten with something (with preposition m/hr); to make something wet; to irrigate (land); passive: to be steeped in, immersed, irrigated

tzm noun: small boat (courier skiff)

tks (Coptic ⲦⲰⲔⲤ) verb trans.: to penetrate, pierce; fix, settle, establish, fortify (< "hammer in"); thus **specifically**: to assess (for rate payments, tax)

$\underline{t}.t$ noun (fem.): lumber, building wood for boats; woodwork; dining table of ruler or god

$\underline{t}\beta.ty$ noun: title of the highest official in the central administration (prime minister, vizier); during the late New Kingdom there were mostly two $\underline{t}\beta.ty$, one being responsible for the north and another for the south

$\underline{t}\beta\hat{\imath}$ (Coptic Ϫⲓ) verb (3ae inf.) **trans.**: to seize, grasp, acquire, lay hold of, take something; to take something away; to steal something; to rob someone (for $\underline{t}\beta w$); **specifically**: $\underline{t}\beta\hat{\imath}\ m\ md\beta.t$ chisel, engrave with a burin; **nominal derivative**: $\underline{t}\beta\hat{\imath}$ bearer (of something; in titles: $\underline{t}\beta\hat{\imath}\ hw$ fan-bearer; $\underline{t}\beta\hat{\imath}\ md\beta.t$ sculptor)

$\underline{t}\beta\hat{\imath}$ ($\underline{t}\beta y$) verb **trans.**: to find fault with, reproach, criticize (with preposition n: someone; with object and preposition r: criticize someone about something, punish someone for something); $\underline{t}\beta y\ A\ r\ B$ "to criticize A about B", "punish B for A"; $d\hat{\imath}.t\ \underline{t}\beta y\ n$=$f\ NN$ "cause that NN criticize him"; **nominal derivative**: $\underline{t}\beta y$ criticism, damage, injury

ṯ3w   (Coptic ϪΙΟΥΕ) verb trans.: to steal something, steal something from someone; *m ṯ3w* (1) thievishly; (2) by stealth; stealthily; **nominal derivative**: *ṯ3(y)* thief, robber

ṯ3w   noun: air, wind, breeze, breath

ṯ3b   noun: vessel, beaker, bowl (of metal, stone, clay, in form of narrow-mouthed bucket: with lip, low centre of gravity and round bottom, "situla") as container for foodstuffs, liquids; also used as a unit of measure

ṯ3ḥw   (*ṯḥw*) see *ṯḥḥw.t*

ṯwfy   (Coptic ϪΟΟΥϤ) noun: papyrus, papyrus thickets; reed swamps

ṯbw   see *ṯ3b*

ṯm   see *rmỉ* to cry; for variant writings, see *LES* 45a n. b

ṯnỉ   (Coptic ΤΩΝ) interrogative pronoun: where?, where from? where to?; also used adverbially as an absolute noun, e.g.: *ỉy=k ṯnỉ* "Where did you come from?"

ṯnw   noun: numeral, number (for the writing, see supra § 1.1.2[3])

ṯnw   (noun, followed by noun) each, every, every time that, whenever); adverbial: *r-ṯnw hrw* every day

ṯ-n-r   adjective verb: to be strong, powerful, mighty, successful (see Accadian *dananu* "to be strong", Görg, *GM* 68 [1983]: 53f.)

ṯḥw   see *ṯḥḥw.t*

ṯḥn   verb (in)trans.: to meet, encounter, engage with, grapple with someone (with object or preposition *n/r*); *ṯḥn ḥnꜥ* to meet someone (in battle), clash with

ṯḥḥw.t   noun: joy, applause, acclaim, exultation, delight (in group writing also *ṯ-ḥ-w*, *ṯ3-ḥw*)

ṯz   noun: spell, words, speech, statement, saying, expression; sentence

ṯzỉ   verb trans.: to raise, lift, exalt; **intrans**: to mount, ascend, climb, go up

ṯzm   noun: hound, dog

ṯṯt   verb intrans.: to argue, quarrel, dispute (with preposition *ỉrm, m.dỉ*: with someone); **nominal derivative**: *ṯṯt* argument, dispute, conflict

dỉ   adverb: here, there (Late Egyptian for Middle Egyptian *ꜥ3*); see supra § 2.2.4(4)

dỉ   abbreviated writing for *rdỉ*, q.v.

dỉ.w   noun: income, wages (for employees and workers)

dw3   verb trans.: to praise, revere, respect, worship, adore someone; **nominal derivatives**: *dw3.w* paean, hymn; *dw3.t nṯr* Divine Adoratrice (parallel to *ḥm.t nṯr* Divine Consort) as title of queens and princesses serving in liturgical functions (*dw3.t nṯr n 'Imnw* as human representative of the goddess Mut)

dw3.w   noun: morning, dawn, early morning; in adverbial use: in the morning, mornings; *m dw3.w* in the morning; *(ḥr-)s3 dw3.w* after tomorrow; also: *m dw3.w s3 dw3.w* in the future

dwn   verb trans.: to stretch something out, extend; reflexive: to raise oneself, get up, stand up

db.t   see *ḏb.t*

dbn   noun: unit of weight, unit of value; see appendix supra § 7.3.1; 7.3.2[1]

dmỉ   (Coptic ΤΩΩΜΕ) verb (3-rad.!) trans.: to touch someone or something; to lay, join, stick (with preposition *n*: on, to someone); **intrans**.: to touch around something, feel (with preposition *n/r*); something fits itself to something, touches something; sticks, affixes itself to something (with preposition *r/m/ḥr*); to join someone (with preposition *n/r*) *dmỉ*   noun (occasionally also fem., *tȝ dmỉ*): town, locality, place (also figuratively: home); landing place, harbour, port; city; *nȝy.w tȝ dmỉ.t*, urban dwellers, city people; **specifically:** "the village" = Deir el-Medina

dmḏ   verb **trans.**: to unite, assemble, collect, put things together, fix together, combine, unite, join; to join something with something (preposition *n/ḥnꜥ*); to be united, joined, together (as Old Perfective); **nominal derivative:** *dmḏ* totality; total; sum; also as expression for the sums in calculations, etc. (also abbreviated ⸗): sum; together; altogether

dns   verb **intrans.**: to be burdensome, weighty, heavy (for writing, see supra § 1.2.1[2])

dr   verb **trans.**: to subdue, deter, repel, expel, overwhelm, remove, drive off; **specifically:** to keep enemies down; destroy, eliminate, defeat, beat them, cast down

dhn   (also partly in group writing *tn-h*) verb **trans.**: to name, appoint, assign, promote (with preposition *r*: to an office)

dḥ   verb **trans.**: to defeat, subdue, beat someone; reflexive: to surrender, yield oneself up, concede defeat

dqr   noun: fruit, fruits (general expression for edible fruits)

dgȝ   see *dqr*

dd   form of *rḏỉ*, q.v.

ḏ.t   noun: eternity

ḏȝ.t   noun: remainder, balance or deficit in accounts

ḏȝỉ   verb **intrans.**: to ferry across, cross, traverse, ferry over (for writing, see supra § 1.1.3[3])

ḏȝy.t   noun: transgression, violence, evil

ḏȝhy   toponym: name of the Phoenician and Palestinian coastal region (later "Land of the Philistines", Palestine)

ḏȝḏȝ   noun: head, summit; in compound prepositions: *ḥr-ḏȝḏȝ-n* on, over, at, by, for, through, from (> Coptic ⲀⲨⲚ-, ⲀⲨⲰ⸗; see Westendorf, *Handwörterbuch*, pp. 443; 408)

ḏȝḏȝ.w   noun (fem.): jar, vessel, pot (as container for honey, as a drinking vessel)

ḏꜥb(.t)   noun: charcoal, black pigment; derivatives: *ḏꜥb.t* (coal-)soot; *ḏꜥb* verb **trans.**: to blacken (with soot)

ḏꜥm   noun: white gold, electrum (a gold-silver alloy), common for gold foil fittings

ḏw   (< *ḏw.t*) noun: bad, evil; **specifically** (in negative superlatives): *mrỉ r ḏw ꜥȝ n wr* "to love in the worst, most desparate fashion"

ḏw   noun: mountain, hill

ḏb.t   (*db.t*) brick; for writing see § 1.1.2[3]

ḏbȝ   (*ḏby*) name of the modern city of Edfu

ḏbȝ   (Coptic ⲦⲰⲰⲂⲈ) verb **trans.**: to replace, substitute for something; to reimburse, provide compensation for something, perform substitute service; to make up for, to repay, to pay for, to pay back (with preposition *m*: with, through something; with preposition *n*: to someone); to clothe someone, equip, provide (with preposition *m*: with something); **nominal derivative:** *ḏbȝ.w* substitute, replacement, payment; in compound preposition: *r-ḏbȝ.w* (> Coptic ⲈⲦⲂⲈ, ⲈⲦⲂⲎⲎⲦ⸗; also in abbreviated writing *ḏbȝ*) instead of something; in place of, in lieu of, as substitute for; because, for something; for someone

ḏbȝ.w   noun: leaf

ḏbꜥ   noun: finger, toe

ḏfꜣ   noun: food, nourishment, sustenance, provisions, victuals, reserves, stores (also plural)

ḏnn   (group writing ḏꜣ-nꜣ-zp2-zp2 > ḏ-n-nn) see ḏnr

ḏnr   (Coptic ϪⲀⲖ) noun: branch, twig; baton, bat, rod (as instrument of torture)

ḏr   preposition: since (temporal); from, where, from there (spatially); with infinitive: since, when; as conjunction with sḏm=f: since, when, while, because; ḏr-ntt because, since; m-ḏr (with noun) because of something (see pD'Orb 8,1; Wenamun 2,67)

ḏr.t   noun (Late Egyptian frequently masc. also): hand; many combinations with prepositions: m-ḏr.t (to do something) with the hand; in (someone's) hand(s); to be (someone's) responsibility, in (someone's) property; through someone; (to send something) through someone; (to receive something) through or from someone; ḥr-ḏr.t to be under someone's direction, in his care

ḏrì   (with semogram) adjective verb: to be firm, strong; to be excellent (as synonym of mnḫ); to be difficult, harsh, tough, painful, severe; adverb: (investigate, tend) suitably; entirely, very

ḏs   noun: self (independent or appositional noun); with suffix: so-and-so himself

ḏd   verb **trans.**: to speak, talk, say, relate, converse (with preposition n/ḥnꜥ: to, with someone); to name someone (passive: be named; with preposition n/r: "called, named"

ḏd.w   toponym: Busiris; the modern Abusir Banna, south of Samannud

10. Indexes

(Abbreviations in the indexes: AP = adverbial phrase; NP = noun phrase; bib. = Bibliography; PP = prepositional phrase; emph. = emphatic; nom. = nominal; prosp. = prospective; pret. = preterite; M.E. = Middle Egyptian; L.E. = Late Egyptian; imp. = imperative; inf. = infinitive; prep. = preposition; pres. = present; fut. = future; neg. = negative/negated; m. = marginal note)

10.1 Concepts explained

10.2 Sources cited

pAbbott
    5,1 ....143; 228
    5,4 61
    5,5-6 153
    5,7-8.............90
    6,13-14...........147
    7,8-9.............55, 63
    7,12..............83
    7,13-14..........218

pAdoption
    rt. 16-17 156
    rt. 23-24 ....126; 210; 268

pAnast. I
    7,6-7.............290
    10,5-6 264
    28,2-3 170

pAnast. II
    1,1-2,5 119-121
    6,5-7.............121-122

pAnast. III
    4,4-11 150-151
    5,5-6.............141
    vs. 3,2...........62; 114

pAnast. IV
    5,1 168

pAnast V
    10,6-7 ....250f
    21,6-7 ....230f

pAnast. VI
    33-34 ....104; 230

pAnast IX, 1-2 154

10.3 Coptic words, morphemes and conjugations

(conjugations are listed separately at the end)

ⲀⲘⲞⲨ; f. ⲀⲘⲎ (<*mi̯*) "come!" 78

ⲀⲚⲄ ⲞⲨⲀⲄⲀⲐⲞⲤ "I am good" 182

ⲀⲚⲞⲔ ⲞⲨⲰⲰⲤ "I am a shepherd" 182

ⲀⲢⲒ- (<*i̯.ir*) "do (it)!" 78

ⲀⲦ-ϨⲎⲦ (<*iwty-ib=f*) "foolish" 94

ⲀⲨⲰ/ ⲞⲨⲞϨ "and" (<*i̯.wȝḥ* "add!") 78

ⲀϨⲢⲈⲨ (<*hrw*) "days" 35

ⲀⲒⲬⲒ ⲘⲘⲞⲤ ⲚⲀⲒ ⲚϹϨⲒⲘⲈ "I took her to wife" 58

ⲀⲬⲒ- (<*i̯.ḏd*) "speak!" 78

ⲂⲈⲢⲈϬⲰⲨⲦ (<*mrkbt*) "chariot" 43

ⲂⲰⲦⲈ (<*bd.t*) "emmer" 35; 297

Ⲉ- (<*iw*; circumstantial converter) 241

Ⲉ-/ⲈⲢⲈ- (<*iw/iri̯*; Third Future) 96; 128; 129

Ⲉ-(<*i̯.ir*)/ⲈⲦⲈ-/ⲚⲦ- plus sentence conjugation (second tense converter) 132; 240; 241

Ⲉ- (<*r*; prep.) 144 (Ⲉ- + inf.); status pronominalis ⲈⲢⲞ=Ⲛ (<*r=n*) 255; ⲈⲢⲰ=ⲦⲚ (<*r=tn*) 146; 277; ⲈⲢⲞ=ⲞⲨ (<*r=w*) 89

ⲈⲂⲞⲖ (<*r-bnr*) "outside" 44; 91

ⲈⲦ(Ⲉ) (<*nty*; relative converter) 67; 200

ⲈϨⲞⲨⲚ (<*r-ḫnw*) "into, inside" 91

ⲈⲒⲞⲘ (<*ym*) "(the) sea" 43

ⲈⲒⲞⲞⲢ (<*itrw*) "river" 35

ⲈⲒⲰⲦ (<*it*) "barley" 297

Ⲕ- (First Present pronoun 2nd masc. sing.) 112; 211

ⲔⲈ-; ϬⲈ/ⲔⲈ, ⲔⲈⲦ, f. ⲔⲈⲦⲈ, pl. ⲔⲞⲞⲨⲈ (<*ky/kt/ky.wy*) "others" 44; 61

ⲔⲒⲦⲈ (<*qd.t*) 295

ⲖⲎⲖ (<*rr*) "ribbons" 185

ⲘⲘⲀⲨ (<*im*) "there" 91

ⲘⲘⲎⲚⲈ (<*m-mn.t*) "daily" 91

ⲘⲚ-, ⲚⲘⲘⲀ= (<*irm*; prep.) 89; 118

ⲘⲚⲦ-ⲢⲰⲘⲈ (<*md.t-rmṯ) "man-kind" 61

ⲘⲚⲦⲈ-/ⲘⲚⲦⲀ= (<mn m.dỉ) 172

ⲘⲚ- (<nn wn) "there aren't…" 118

ⲘⲠⲞⲞⲨ (<m-pȝ-hrww) "today" 91

ⲘⲠⲢ̄- (<m-ỉr; Prohibitive) 79

ⲘⲒⲤⲈ (<ms.t) "bear"; forms of verbal state ⲘⲈⲤ-/ⲘⲀⲤⲦ= (<ms.t=ỉ "to bear me") 52; 81

ⲘⲈⲤⲞⲢⲎ (<msw.t-Rᶜw; name of month) 48

ⲘⲈⲰⲀⲔ (<bw rḫ=k) 100

ⲘⲞⲞⲰⲈ (<mšᶜỉ) "march, travel" 39

Ⲛ̄- (<m; prep.); status pronominalis Ⲙ̄ⲘⲞ=ϥ (<n.ỉm=f) 89; 186; Ⲙ̄ⲘⲰ=ⲦⲚ̄ (<n.ỉm=tn) 118

Ⲛ̄- (<bw/n; negation) 100

Ⲛ̄- (<bn; First Present negation) 113

Ⲛ̄ … ⲀⲚ (<n … ỉwnȝ/ỉn) 113

Ⲛ- (article) 53

ⲚⲀ- (possessive prefix) 53

ⲚⲀⲒ/ⲚⲈ (demonstratives) 53

ⲚⲈϥ- (possessive article) 53

ⲚⲈ-/Ⲉ-ⲚⲈ- (relative converter) 161

ⲚⲈ-, ⲚⲈⲢⲈ- (imperfect converter)/ ⲚⲈϥⲤⲰⲦⲘ̄ (imperfect) 161

-ⲚⲞϥⲢⲈ/-ⲚⲞⲨϥⲈ "beautiful" 66

Ⲛ̄ⲦⲀ-/Ⲛ̄ϥⲤⲰⲦⲘ̄/Ⲛ̄ⲦⲈϥⲤⲰⲦⲈⲘ (<mtw=f sdm; conjunctive) 104

ⲚⲒⲘ (<nỉm) "who?" 44; ⲚⲒⲘ ⲠⲈⲦ-ⲈϥⲈⲤⲰⲦⲈⲘ (<nm pȝ nty ỉw=f sdm) "who is it who will listen?" 182

Ⲛ̄Ⲧ- (<m-dr) (89); 227

Ⲛ̄ⲦⲈ-/Ⲛ̄ⲦⲀ= (<m.dỉ) 90

Ⲛ̄ⲦⲈⲢⲈ- (Temporal prefix) 89; (227); Ⲛ̄ⲦⲈⲢⲈϥⲤⲰⲦⲘ (<m-dr jr=f sdm <m-dr sdm=f; Temporal) 226; 241

ⲚⲞⲈⲒⲦ (<nḏ) "flour" 37

Ⲛ̄ⲦⲞϥ (<ntf) personal pronoun 38

Ⲛ̄ⲀⲞⲨⲚ (<m-ḥnw) "within" 91

ⲞⲒⲠⲈ (<ỉp.t; unit of measure) 76; 295

Ⲡ- (<pȝ) definite article 34; 53; Ⲡ-ⲚⲞⲨⲦⲈ Ⲡ-ⲈⲦ-ⲤⲞⲞⲨⲚ (< pȝ ntr pȝ nty swn) "it is God who knows" 177

ⲠⲀ- (possessive prefix) 53; 54

ⲠⲀⲒ/ⲠⲈ, ⲦⲈ, ⲚⲈ (<pȝy, tȝy, nȝy; demonstrative pronoun) 53; 173; 183

ⲠⲈϥ- (possessive article) 53

Ⲣ̄ϥⲘⲞⲞⲨⲦ "the deceased" 202

ⲢⲰⲘⲈ (<rmṯ) "people" 36; 38

ⲢⲀⲚ, ⲢⲒⲚ=ϥ "name, his name" (status pronominalis) 59

ⲢⲰ (<rȝ-ᶜ) "but, even, at all" 87

ⲠⲰⲰ (<pšš) "separate" 37

Ⲥ- (First Present pronoun 3rd fem. sing.) 112

ⲤⲈ- (First Present pronoun 3rd pl.) 112

ⲤⲞⲞⲨ (<srsw/sỉsw) "six" 94

ⲤⲞϬⲚ (<sgnn) "unguent" 36

Ⲧ-causatives 240

Ⲧ- (article) 53

ⲦⲀ- (possessive prefix) 53

ⲦⲀⲒ/ⲦⲈ (demonstratives) 53

ⲦⲀⲒ/ⲦⲎ (<dỉ) "here" 91

ⲦⲈ- (First Present pronoun 2nd fem. sing.) 112

ⲦⲈϥ- (possessive article) 53

ⲦⲚ̄- (First Present pronoun 1st pl.) 112

ⲦⲰⲚ (<tnw) "where?" 91

ⲦⲀⲚⲌⲞ⸗Ϥ "to keep him alive" (belonging to ⲰⲚⲌ "live"; from *dỉ.t ꜥnḫ꞊f* "cause that he live") 147

ⲦⲰⲢⲈ, ⲦⲞⲞⲦ⸗Ϥ "hand, his hand" (status pronominalis) 59

ⲦⲈⲦⲚ̄- (First Present pronoun 2nd pl.) 112

-ⲦⲎⲨⲦⲚ̄ (suffix pronoun 2nd pl.) 52

ⲦⲰⲌ "confuse" 94

ⲞⲨ- (indefinite article) 53

ⲞⲨⲘⲈ ⲦⲈ†ⲪⲰ Ⲙ̄ⲘⲞⲤ "it is the truth that I say" 183; ⲞⲨⲘⲈ ⲡⲈ ⲡⲉ†ⲪⲰ ⲘⲘⲞϤ "what I say is true" 183

ⲞⲨⲚ̄ⲦⲈ-/ⲞⲨⲚ̄ⲦⲀ⸗ (*<wn m.dỉ*) "have" 172; ⲞⲨⲚ̄Ⲧ⸗ⲞⲨ 285

ⲞⲨⲰⲰⲤ ⲡⲈ "he is a herdsman" 182

ⲬⲞⲒⲀⲔ (*<k꜄-ḥr-k꜄*; name of month) 75

ⲰⲈ (*<šm.t*) "go" 39

ⲰⲰⲡ (*<šzp*) "receive" 37

ⲰⲰⲡⲈ (*<ḫpr*) "become, be" 36

ⲰⲎⲢⲈ, ⲰⲈⲈⲢⲈ: ⲡⲰⲎⲢⲈ (*<p꜄ šrỉ*) "the boy" 34; ⲦⲰⲈⲈⲢⲈ (*<ß šrỉ*) "the girl" 34

Ϥ- (First Present pronoun 3rd masc. sing.) 112

ⲌⲒ (*<*prep. *ḥr* followed by nouns; "status pronominalis") 35

ⲌⲀⲘⲞⲒ (*<ḥn-my*) "if only" 88

ⲌⲈⲚ- (article) 53

ⲌⲞⲞⲨ (*<hrww*) "day" 35; 59; ⲌⲞⲞⲨ-ⲘⲒⲤⲈ "birthday" 59

ⲌⲀⲢⲞ⸗ⲞⲨ (prep.; status nominalis) 287

ⲌⲒⲪⲚ-, ⲌⲒⲪⲰ⸗ (*<ḥr-ḏ꜄ḏ꜄-n*) 246

ⲬⲈ (*<r-ḏd*; as conjunction or to introduce direct speech) 81; 142; 240

ϬⲈ cf. ⲔⲈ-

ϬⲈ (*<gr*; adverbial particle) 88

ϬⲰⲰⲂⲈ "leaf" 61

ϬⲂ̄-ⲪⲞⲈⲒⲦ "olive leaf" 61

ⲬⲀⲗ (*<ḏ-n-nn*) "rod" 185

ⲬⲞⲨⲰⲦ number "20" 34

†- (First Present pronoun 1st sing. c.) 112

Conjugations

ⲀϤⲤⲰⲦⲘ̄ (*<ỉr꞊f sḏm*) 97; 155

ⲈϤⲤⲰⲦⲘ̄ (*<ỉw꞊f sḏm*; Circumstantial First Present) 115; 241

ⲈϤⲈⲤⲞⲦⲘ̄ (*<ỉw꞊f (r) sḏm*; Third Future) 128

ⲈϤⲰⲀⲚⲤⲰⲦⲘ̄ (Conditional) 281

ⲈⲚⲈϤⲤⲞⲞⲨⲚ̄ ("Irrealis") 281

ⲈⲚϤⲤⲰⲦⲘ̄ ⲀⲚ (Neg. First Present) 241

ⲈⲤⲰⲰⲡⲈ plus sentence (Conditional) 281

ⲈⲦⲈ Ⲛ̄†ⲤⲰⲦⲘ̄ (Neg. Relative First Present) 241

ⲈⲦⲢⲈϤⲤⲰⲦⲘ̄ (*<r dỉ.t sḏm꞊f/r dỉ.t ỉr꞊f sḏm*; Causative Infintive) 148

Ⲉ†ⲤⲰⲦⲘ̄ (Relative First Present) 241

ϤⲚⲀⲤⲰⲦⲘ̄ (First Future) 127

ⲘⲈϤⲤⲰⲦⲘ̄ (*<bw ỉr꞊f-sḏm*; Neg. Aorist) 100

Ⲙ̄ⲡⲀⲦϤⲤⲰⲦⲘ̄ (*<bw ỉr.t꞊f-sḏm*; "not yet") 101; 155

Ⲙ̄ⲡⲢ̄ⲦⲢⲈϤⲤⲰⲦⲘ̄ (*<m-ỉr dỉ.t ỉr꞊f-sḏm*; Neg. Causative Imp.) 80; 146; 148

Ⲙ̄ⲡⲈϤⲤⲰⲦⲘ̄ (*<bn.p꞊f-sḏm*; Neg. Perfect) 155

10.4 Egyptian morphemes, phrases and syntagmas

(for terms and concepts cf. 10.5 General Index)

10.5 General Index